bases of the United Nations, which involve the general character and nature of the Organization, and the scope and qualifications of its Members. Part Three deals with the proposals relating to the powers and functions of the United Nations for maintaining peace and security, which involve the peaceful settlement of disputes, the taking of collective security action, and the regulation of armaments.

Part Four examines the proposals relating to the powers and functions of the United Nations for promoting the general welfare, which involve international co-operation in the solution of economic, social, and human rights problems, and in the advancement of dependent peoples. Part Five covers proposals relating to the general organizational structure and administration of the United Nations—membership and voting in the Security Council; representation and voting in the General Assembly; the jurisdiction of the International Court of Justice; the functions, organization and status of the Secretariat; and budgetary and financial problems.

The volume concludes in Part Six with a brief summary of some of the general problems involved in effecting future changes in the United Nations. Consideration is given to the advantages and disadvantages of the alternative methods that might be used.

Francis O. Wilcox and Carl M. Marcy were, at the time they prepared this volume, Chief-of-Staff and Consultant, respectively, for the Committee on Foreign Relations, United States Senate. Because of their extensive experience in matters concerning the United Nations, they are highly qualified to deal with the complex subject of proposed changes in the Organization.

PROPOSALS FOR CHANGES IN THE UNITED NATIONS

THE BROOKINGS INSTITUTION

The Brookings Institution is an independent organization engaged in research and education in the social sciences. Its principal purposes are to aid in the development of sound public policies and to provide advanced training for students in the social sciences.

The Institution was founded December 8, 1927 as a consolidation of three antecedent organizations: the Institute for Government Research, 1916; the Institute of Economics, 1922; and the Robert Brookings Graduate School of Economics and Government, 1924.

The general administration of the Institution is the responsibility of a self-perpetuating Board of Trustees. In addition to this general responsibility the By-Laws provide that, "It is the function of the Trustees to make possible the conduct of scientific research and publication, under the most favorable conditions, and to safeguard the independence of the research staff in the pursuit of their studies and in the publication of the results of such studies. It is not a part of their function to determine, control, or influence the conduct of particular investigations or the conclusions reached." The immediate direction of the policies, program, and staff of the Institution is vested in the President, who is assisted by an advisory council, chosen from the professional staff of the Institution.

In publishing a study, the Institution presents it as a competent treatment of a subject worthy of public consideration. The interpretations and conclusions in such publications are those of the author or authors and do not necessarily reflect the views of other members of the Brookings staff or of the administrative officers of the Institution.

Proposals for Changes in the United Nations

By
FRANCIS O. WILCOX
and
CARL M. MARCY

THE BROOKINGS INSTITUTION
WASHINGTON, D.C.

© 1955 BY

THE BROOKINGS INSTITUTION

Set up and printed
Published November 1955

Library of Congress Catalogue Card Number 55-11379

Printed in the United States of America
George Banta Publishing Company
Menasha, Wisconsin

Preface

I N the summer of 1951, the Brookings Institution began
a series of studies on the United Nations. The series was initiated
by the late Dr. Leo Pasvolsky who, until his untimely death on
May 5, 1953, was Director of the International Studies Group at
the Institution. The general plan for the research was formulated in
the winter of 1949-50 when many proposals for changes in the
United Nations system were being widely discussed in the United
States. Much of the public discussion indicated the need for a sys-
tematic analysis of the issues arising from the experience with the
United Nations system and for a careful evaluation of the immediate and ultimate implications of the various courses of action
being proposed. To assist in meeting this need, became, therefore,
the central purpose of the Brookings studies.

While this research has been under way, new developments have
further affected the attitude of many Americans toward the United
Nations. Paramount among these have been the difficulties encountered in dealing with aggression in Korea and in trying to
achieve a settlement of the situation there, within the broader
context of the whole Far Eastern situation. Some American pressures for changes in the United Nations system have been increasing, and the General Assembly is expected to consider at its tenth
session the question whether a General Conference for the purpose
of reviewing, and possibly revising, the Charter, should be called.
In these circumstances, it is hoped that the Brookings studies will
be of special value in contributing to better public understanding
of the problems that will be involved.

The studies are being published in seven volumes, of which
this is the second to appear. Although these volumes form a related series, each of them constitutes a separate study of a major
feature of the United Nations system. The order given below is not
the actual order of publication, but it represents the logical arrangement of the series.

One volume is entitled *A History of the United Nations Charter*.
It will present, from the American point of view, the evolution
and negotiation of the Charter as part of the developing United

Nations system during the period from 1940 to 1945. A major purpose of the volume will be to show the principal ideas and proposals considered by the United States Government in reaching its final position on the specific provisions of the Charter.

Three volumes will analyze and appraise the principal activities and organizational problems of the United Nations and its related agencies since January 1946 when the Organization came into being.

One of these, entitled *The Organization and Procedures of the United Nations,* will cover the general organizational development of the United Nations. It will be concerned both with particular organizational problems in each of the principal organs—the General Assembly, the Security Council, the Economic and Social Council, the Trusteeship Council, the International Court of Justice, and the Secretariat—and with some of the general problems encountered, such as the interpretation of the Charter, the definition of domestic jurisdiction, and the admission of new Members.

The second of these, which has already been published and is entitled *The United Nations and the Maintenance of International Peace and Security,* deals with methods and processes for maintaining peace and security through the United Nations. It covers the procedures that have been developed under the Charter for the peaceful settlement or adjustment of disputes and situations, the use of collective measures in threats to or breaches of the peace, and the regulation of armaments, and seeks to evaluate these methods and processes in light of the conditions in which the United Nations has had to function.

The third, entitled *The United Nations and Promotion of the General Welfare,* will cover the major activities undertaken by the United Nations in response to the insistent pressures that, during the postwar period, have brought to the fore issues in the field of general welfare. The work of the Organization and its related agencies in dealing with problems of international co-operation in economic and social affairs, in the promotion of human rights, and in the advancement of dependent peoples will be analyzed, and the efforts made to harmonize conflicting national views in solving these problems will be appraised.

Another volume in the series will deal with *Regional Security and the United Nations.* It will analyze and appraise the history and activities of the principal regional security, collective defense, and similar arrangements that have developed within the framework of the United Nations Charter. The volume will describe how and why the arrangements came into existence and the manner in which they have functioned, and will analyze some of the problems raised by their establishment and operation, both within the scope of the individual groupings and in relation to the broader United Nations system.

A sixth volume, which is the present one, entitled *Proposals for Changes in the United Nations,* presents a description and analysis of the principal proposals advanced by governments and by private groups and individuals for changes in the United Nations system. The analysis includes a review of the major arguments advanced both for and against particular proposals, the impact of the proposals on the United Nations, and their implications for United States policy.

The final volume, entitled *The United States and the Future of the United Nations,* will attempt an over-all appraisal of the United Nations system from the American point of view. This volume, which will be based primarily on the studies in the other six volumes, will present general conclusions and recommendations regarding such changes as may appear to be desirable in the United Nations Charter or in the organization and functioning of the system.

A special word should be said about the scope of the present volume. Although the analysis seeks to cover both the favorable and unfavorable implications of the proposals that are examined, it does not reach conclusions or make recommendations regarding the official attitude the United States should take with respect to them. Such conclusions and recommendations are reserved for the volume on *The United States and the Future of the United Nations.* Furthermore, authors of the individual volumes in the series are free to express their opinions on those features of the United Nations system that they are studying. Therefore, the analyses and appraisals in this volume may not coincide with those in the other volumes in the series that deal with the record of the United Nations system from other special points of view.

Francis O. Wilcox and Carl M. Marcy collaborated in the preparation of this volume. At the time of their collaboration, they were chief of staff and consultant, respectively, for the Committee on Foreign Relations, United States Senate. The views and opinions expressed are, of course, the personal ones of the authors and are not intended to reflect those of the Committee. The authors acknowledge with gratitude the assistance of Marion Montague, who aided generally in preparing materials for this volume; of Willard N. Hogan, State University Teachers College, New Paltz, New York, who prepared a special study on proposals for supranational government which provided some of the background for several chapters; of A. Evelyn Breck, who with the aid of Medora Richardson edited the final manuscript; and of Inez Gardner, who prepared the index.

The authors and the Institution also acknowledge with gratitude the many thoughtful comments and constructive suggestions made by a number of present and former officials in both government and international organizations who responded to inquiries or read drafts of various sections of the manuscript. Their courtesy and willingness in making their expert knowledge and experience available have aided in clarifying many difficult points and issues. Although custom precludes the citing of these persons by name, the Institution greatly appreciates the individual assistance of each of them.

The studies on which this volume is based were planned by Dr. Pasvolsky. After his death, Robert W. Hartley was given the responsibility for bringing the entire research project to completion, and the manuscript for the present volume was prepared under his direction. We have had the benefit of continuing consultation with Ernest A. Gross, James N. Hyde, Joseph E. Johnson, C. Easton Rothwell, and Willard L. Thorp, who comprise an informal group, organized during the summer of 1953, to advise on the direction of the project, and to whom the Institution is heavily indebted for many helpful suggestions.

Finally, on behalf of the Institution, I wish to express grateful appreciation to the A. W. Mellon Educational and Charitable Trust of Pittsburgh for the generous grants that have made possible this series of studies on the United Nations system. The conclusions and recommendations of these studies have been reached, however, wholly independently of the Mellon Trust, which is not to be understood as approving or disapproving the views expressed in this and the other volumes in the series.

ROBERT D. CALKINS
President

Contents

ix

PART SIX: CONCLUSION

CHAPTER XV

APPENDIXES

Introduction •

THE Charter of the United Nations, as it emerged from the San Francisco Conference in 1945, represented a series of compromises among states with diverse interests, varying political, economic, and cultural backgrounds, and wide disparities in national power. It was hoped that most of these compromises would endure, but it was anticipated that some of them might not last. Accordingly, many powers and functions of the Organization were stated in general terms with the expectation that they would be interpreted in the light of future, specific situations, and provision was made in Articles 108 and 109 of the Charter for its amendment and review.[1] The founders of the United Nations recognized at the time that the Charter was "a human rather than a perfect instrument. It has within it ample flexibility for growth and development, for dynamic adaptation to changing conditions."[2]

The appearance of the atomic bomb only a few weeks after the San Francisco Conference, however, inspired doubt in some quarters whether the United Nations had been endowed with sufficient powers to cope with situations in which the threatened use of new weapons of mass destruction would be ever present. Consequently, interest revived in suggestions made during the planning of the United Nations for a world government or some other kind of supranational authority to maintain world peace. Furthermore, interest generally increased in proposals for changes in the United Nations when, soon after the Organization came into being, it became apparent that it was not going to operate as effectively as many had hoped.

During the ten years of its existence, the United Nations has become quite a different organization from the one envisaged by the Charter. Primarily because of the attitude of the Soviet Union, it has been necessary to adapt the functioning of the Organization in the peace and security field to the constant threat of a Soviet veto

[1] To facilitate reference to the articles of the Charter and of the Statute of the International Court of Justice, the complete texts of both these documents are given in Appendixes A and B, respectively.

[2] Statement by former Secretary of State Cordell Hull, June 26, 1945, on the occasion of the signing of the Charter. U. S. Department of State *Bulletin*, Vol. 13 (July 1, 1945), p. 13.

in the Security Council. The nations of the free world have sought to supplement the operations of the Organization by establishing regional security and collective defense arrangements. Similarly, the functioning of the Organization in promoting the general welfare has had to be adapted to postwar conditions, many of which were not foreseen when the Charter was drafted. The fact that the destruction caused by the war was greater than had been expected retarded reconstruction and economic recovery. Also, the insistent demands of dependent peoples for self-government and of underdeveloped nations for assistance in achieving higher standards of living required more rapid action than had been anticipated.

Such adaptation as has been possible of the United Nations to the changing world conditions since 1945 has not been easy. Nearly every change has provoked disagreements, some protracted and acrimonious. With rare exceptions, none of the changes has fully satisfied all Member states. As a result, numerous proposals continue to be made. It can be expected that the number will increase if the General Assembly, at its tenth session, should decide that it would be desirable to hold a General Conference for the purpose of reviewing the Charter.

None of the changes made to date, however, has been accomplished through the amending process provided by the Charter. To some extent this has been due to the difficulties inherent in the process, especially to the fact that any one of the five permanent members of the Security Council could veto a proposed amendment. Inasmuch as most of the important amendments that the majority of the Member states might approve would not be ratified by the Soviet Union—and possibly other permanent members—the prospect of effecting changes by amendment of the Charter has not appeared promising.

The changes made thus far have been brought about in other ways. When certain provisions of the Charter have proved to be inapplicable or could not be implemented, substitute arrangements have been improvised. Other provisions have been reinterpreted in light of developments since the San Francisco Conference. The conclusion of supplementary treaties or agreements also has made it possible to effect further changes. And last, but not least important, the organs and procedures of the United Nations have undergone an evolutionary growth through the process of trial and error.

The United States has taken the lead in encouraging the adoption of many of the changes made. Furthermore, as one of the leading supporters of the United Nations system, the United States inevitably must be prepared to take a position on any proposal for revising the system. Even a decision to take no position at all will exert an influence because of the important role the United States plays in United Nations affairs. The possibility that a conference for reviewing the Charter might be convoked serves, therefore, to focus American attention on the whole range of proposals for further changes in the United Nations system. This range encompasses suggestions to transform the United Nations into some form of world government, or to reduce substantially its present powers and functions; to make it exclusively an anti-Communist alliance by seeking to get the Soviet Union and its satellites out of the Organization, or to withdraw United States participation. These proposals, as well as less drastic changes, need careful study.

Accordingly, it is the purpose of this volume to analyze and appraise the principal proposals for further changes in the United Nations in order to determine their impact on the Organization and their implications for United States policy with respect to the United Nations. Such a study will contribute, it is hoped, to a better understanding of the issues involved, and thus provide a better basis for decisions regarding the attitude the United States Government should take toward the proposed changes.

This study covers primarily the proposals and ideas advanced by private persons and agencies in the United States and by the executive and legislative branches of the United States Government, because the pressures of public opinion that may be generated by such proposals will be important in determining the official position the United States will take regarding them. But that position will also be influenced by the attitudes of other Member states, and the proposals they may advance. The scope of this study, consequently, includes the principal proposals for changes made by Member states and some of those made by private persons and agencies in foreign countries. The proposals examined are not limited, however, to those that could be given effect only by amendment of the Charter. The more important ones that could be effected by other means are also analyzed.

As a general background for the main body of analysis, Part One of this volume describes the kinds of changes that have taken place in the United Nations system and analyzes the provisions of the Charter that relate to the amending process. It also describes the movement for revision of the United Nations system that began ten years ago and is now approaching a climax with the growing public debate on the question whether a General Conference for review of the Charter should be called.

The next four parts of the volume are devoted to the analysis and appraisal of the principal proposals for further change. The approach taken in these parts is essentially that of a comparative analysis of the various proposals in relation to the principal powers and functions of the United Nations system.

Thus, Part Two covers proposals relating to the bases of the system, which involve the general character and nature of the Organization and the scope and qualifications of its membership. Part Three deals with the proposals relating to the powers and functions of the United Nations for maintaining peace and security, which involve the peaceful settlement of disputes, the taking of collective security action, and the regulation of armaments. Part Four examines the proposals relating to the powers and functions of the United Nations for promoting the general welfare, which involve international co-operation in the solution of economic, social, and human rights problems and in the advancement of dependent peoples. Part Five covers proposals relating to the general organizational structure and administration of the United Nations—membership and voting in the Security Council; representation and voting in the General Assembly; the jurisdiction of the International Court of Justice; the functions, organization, and status of the Secretariat; and budgetary and financial problems.

In order to make the analysis and appraisal as meaningful as possible, it has been necessary to provide the setting of the problems that have given rise to particular proposals. For most such problems this has required a brief review of the relevant provisions of the Charter and of the experience with them since the United Nations came into being. As a result, there is some unavoidable overlapping between this volume and the other volumes in this Brookings series.

There is also some overlapping among the main parts of the present volume because of the method of analysis used. Certain of the proposals, especially those that would change the United Nations into some form of supranational authority, are of such a comprehensive nature that they would affect nearly every power and function of the United Nations. Although these comprehensive plans are treated generally in Part Two of the volume, references to some of their detailed aspects are made in later parts where consideration is given to specific problems with which they deal.

This volume concludes, in Part Six, with a brief summary of some of the major problems involved in attempts to effect changes in the United Nations. Consideration especially is given to the various advantages and disadvantages of the alternative means that can be used and their implications for United States policy.

Three difficulties have been frequently encountered in preparing this study. First, it has not always been possible to ensure that the person or organization cited as the author of a particular proposal is, in fact, the one who originated the idea. Therefore, if credit for the authorship of a proposal is incorrectly given in this volume, the error has been unintentional. Second, although efforts have been made to state proposals in the exact words of their authors, it has often been necessary for the purpose of the analysis to summarize or paraphrase them. The result may be that in some instances the author of a particular proposal may think that justice has not been done to his idea. If so, this has been an unintentional error. Third, informal suggestions have been received from a number of individuals and have been treated as proposals without indicating their source. Furthermore, ideas have emerged that may not have appeared elsewhere and for which no source can be cited.

In the preparation of this volume, a conscientious effort has been made to present the suggestions and ideas for changes in the United Nations in as objective a manner as possible. This task is made more difficult by the divisions of American opinion that exist regarding the United Nations. There are some Americans who are generally satisfied with the way the Organization has grown and consequently, are reluctant to disturb its roots. Others, however, would not hesitate to uproot it either in order to plant a new species of organization or to get the United States out of the United Nations. It is not, however, within the scope of the present study to make a final judgment on which of these or any other of the general approaches that might be taken to the problem is the correct one.

PART ONE

BACKGROUND

CHAPTER I

Available Methods for Effecting Changes in the United Nations[1]

WHEN the President of the United States submitted the Charter of the United Nations to the Senate in 1945 for its consent to ratification, he made the following observation: "Improvements will come in the future as the United Nations gain experience with the machinery and methods which they have set up. For this is not a static treaty. It can be improved—and, as the years go by, it will be—just as our own Constitution has been improved."[2] Thus, the Charter, like the Constitution, was designed to lay a broad base for an institution that might develop to meet changing needs. And the Charter, like the Constitution, has proven flexible enough to be adapted to many new situations without the need for formal amendment.

It is important to keep this fact in mind when the problem of revising the Charter is under consideration. During the nearly ten years that the United Nations has been in existence, no proposed amendment has reached the final voting stage in the General Assembly. Even so, many far-reaching changes have taken place within the United Nations system. Some important articles of the Charter have already fallen into disuse. Others have been applied in a way that those who participated in the San Francisco Conference did not contemplate. It follows that the Charter of 1955 as it has been amplified by custom and usage, resolutions of the various United Nations organs, and supplementary or supporting treaties, is by no means the Charter that was drafted in 1945. For this reason, it may

[1] The materials in this chapter have been based on *How the United Nations Charter Has Developed,* Staff Study No. 2, written by Francis O. Wilcox for the Subcommittee on the United Nations Charter, Senate Committee on Foreign Relations, 83 Cong. 2 sess. (May 18, 1954).

[2] *Address by the President of the United States delivered before the Senate on July 2, 1945 presenting the Charter of the United Nations, with the Statute of the International Court of Justice Annexed Thereto,* S. Exec. F, 79 Cong. 1 sess. (July 2, 1945), p. 4.

prove helpful to examine briefly the methods by which changes can be made in the United Nations. First the methods employed since 1945 will be surveyed. Then the provisions of the Charter relating to the formal amending process will be examined.[3]

Methods Used to Date

It is likely that when the formal amending procedures set forth in a charter or a constitution of an organization are too rigid to allow necessary changes, or when political circumstances are not conducive to their use, other ways and means will be found to achieve the desired ends. The Charter has been subjected to changes in a variety of ways: (1) by not implementing or not applying certain provisions of the Charter; (2) through the interpretation of the Charter by various organs and Members of the United Nations; (3) through the conclusion of supplementary or supporting treaties or agreements; and (4) through the creation of special organs and agencies. These changes substantially affect the provisions of the Charter although they leave its text intact.[4]

[3] On the question of the growth and the amendment of the Charter see the following: Leland M. Goodrich and Edvard Hambro, *Charter of the United Nations: Commentary and Documents* (1949), Chap. 18; Hans Kelsen, *The Law of the United Nations* (1951), pp. 816-24; Amry Vandenbosch and Willard N. Hogan, *The United Nations: Background, Organization, Functions, Activities* (1952), Chap. 20; Salo Engle, "The Changing Charter of the United Nations," *Yearbook of World Affairs*, Vol. 7 (1953), pp. 71-101; Eugene P. Chase, "The Future of the United Nations," *The United Nations in Action* (1950), pp. 377-94; Ernest A. Gross, "Revising the Charter: Is It Possible? Is It Wise?," *Foreign Affairs*, Vol. 32 (January 1954), pp. 203-16. See also Subcommittee on the United Nations Charter, Senate Committee on Foreign Relations, *Review of the United Nations Charter: A Collection of Documents*, S. Doc. 87, 83 Cong. 2 sess. (Jan. 7, 1954); U. S. Department of State, *Charter of the United Nations: Report to the President on the Results of the San Francisco Conference by the Chairman of the United States Delegation, The Secretary of State*, Publication 2349 (June 26, 1945), Chap. 18; Norman L. Hill, *International Organization* (1952), Chap. 17; Salo Engle, "*De facto* Revision of the Charter of the United Nations," *Journal of Politics*, Vol. 14 (February 1952), pp. 132-44; Hartley Shawcross, "The Constitutional Structure of the United Nations," *Nebraska Law Review*, Vol. 30 (November 1950), pp. 11-20; Abraham H. Feller, *United Nations and World Community* (1952); Hans J. Morgenthau, "The United Nations and the Revision of the Charter," *The Review of Politics*, Vol. 16 (January 1954), pp. 3-21; John Foster Dulles, *War or Peace* (1950); Clark M. Eichelberger, *U.N.: The First Ten Years* (1955), especially Chaps. IX and X; and Philip E. Jacob (ed.), "The Future of the United Nations: Issues of Charter Revision," *Annals of the American Academy of Political and Social Science*, Vol. 296 (November 1954), pp. 1-162.

[4] See especially the articles by Engle, *loc. cit.* See also Feller, *op. cit.*

A detailed examination cannot be made here of the growth of the Charter since 1945. But it seems desirable to look at the process in general terms, for, without a knowledge of what has been happening during the past decade, serious study of the broader problem of further change cannot be undertaken.

Failure to Apply Certain Provisions

In a number of instances, organs or Members of the United Nations have disregarded or have failed to implement certain provisions of the Charter. As a result, several articles, which the framers believed were highly important in making the United Nations an effective instrument for maintaining world peace, have already fallen into disuse. Perhaps the best example is Article 43. This article, which was to be the central core of the collective security system provided for in the Charter, was designed to put teeth into collective security action under the United Nations system. Under its terms, Members were to conclude agreements to make available to the Security Council the armed forces, assistance, and the facilities necessary for maintaining international peace and security. But after years of fruitless negotiations, the great powers remain deadlocked over such questions as the numbers and types of forces each country should make available, their locations, and their degree of readiness. Consequently, the agreements referred to in Article 43 have never come into existence, and these provisions of the Charter remain a dead letter.[5] Much the same situation exists with respect to Articles 44, 45, 46, 48, and most of Article 47, which relate to the use of armed forces by the Security Council and which are largely contingent on the entry into force of Article 43. Taken together, they constitute the heart of the collective security system of the United Nations as it was envisaged at the San Francisco Conference by the framers of the Charter.

Article 106 offers still another striking example. Briefly, this article provides that prior to the time the Security Council is ready to begin its peace-keeping functions under Articles 42 and 43, the five permanent members should consult with one another with a view to such joint action as might be necessary to maintain world peace. The great powers, in other words, were given the joint responsi-

[5] See below, Chap. VI.

bility for maintaining peace, on a transitional basis, until the Organization was properly equipped to perform its functions in an effective manner. The split between the Communist and non-Communist worlds has not only hamstrung the Council, but it has also prevented giving effect to the transitional arrangement that was supposed to hold the line until the Organization could swing into action.

Mention should also be made of Article 23(1), which specifically provides that the General Assembly, in electing the six non-permanent members of the Security Council, shall pay special regard, in the first instance, to the contribution of Members of the United Nations to the maintenance of peace and security and to the other purposes of the Organization, and also to equitable geographical distribution. In practice the Assembly has paid relatively little attention to the first of these criteria, placing most of its emphasis on equitable geographical distribution. Normally two members have been elected from Latin America, one from Western Europe, one from the British Commonwealth, one from the Middle East, and, during the first few years at least, one from the Soviet satellite bloc. The Asian countries as such have never been represented.

Of course it can be argued that these criteria are in no way legally binding on the Assembly. Certainly, if they are disregarded, there is no method provided for appealing the action of the Assembly. But when these guideposts are ignored it means that, in effect, an important part of Article 23(1) has been dropped, at least temporarily, from the Charter.[6]

New Interpretations

The only provision in the Charter relating to its interpretation is the one implied in Article 96, under which the General Assembly or the Security Council may request the International Court of Justice to give an advisory opinion "on any legal question." Such opinions, however, have no binding legal effect. In practice, and in line with the general understanding reached at the San Francisco Conference, the organs and Members of the United Nations have felt free to interpret the various articles of the Charter as they have seen fit. Consequently, any interpretation that a provision of the Charter might reasonably have, in the opinion of a majority of the Members, can prevail in any particular instance.

[6] See below, Chap. X.

This flexibility in the Charter has led to a number of interesting developments, of which the most significant relates to the all-important question of voting in the Council. The language of Article 27(3) seems quite clear. It provides specifically that for other than procedural matters, decisions of the Council are to be made "by an affirmative vote of seven members including the concurring votes of the permanent members." Does this mean that action cannot be taken by the Council unless it is concurred in by *all five* of the great powers? Does it mean that when a permanent member abstains or is absent at the time the vote is taken no decision can be reached? Certainly, a strict construction of the Charter might lead to that conclusion.

Early in its history the Council took the position that an abstention or an absence of a permanent member did not constitute a negative vote.[7] It was this liberal interpretation of the Charter, together with the absence of the Soviet representative from the meetings at the time, that paved the way for a swift decision by the Council when the Republic of Korea was attacked in June 1950. With only four permanent members present, the Council brushed aside some fairly important legal problems and approved three resolutions that made possible decisions and action by the United Nations against the aggressor in a way hardly contemplated by the signatories of the Charter in 1945.[8]

It might be well to point out also that Article 27, perhaps more than any other article, illustrates how differently the Charter may be interpreted by certain Members on the one hand and by an organ of the United Nations on the other. At the San Francisco Conference, the great powers agreed on a narrow interpretation of "procedural" questions, which—for the most part—were those involved in the organizational matters referred to in Articles 28 to 32 of the Charter: the adoption of the rules of procedure of the Council; the selection of the President of the Council; the time and place of meetings; the establishment of subsidiary organs, etc. Beyond this point, argued the five major powers in their statement of June 7, 1945, decisions of the Security Council might have "major

---

[7] *Ibid.*

[8] For a detailed discussion of the practice of abstention, see Subcommittee on the United Nations Charter, Senate Committee on Foreign Relations, *The Problem of the Veto in the United Nations Security Council*, Staff Study No. 1, 83 Cong. 2 sess. (Feb. 19, 1954). See also N. J. Padelford, "The Use of the Veto," *International Organization* (June 1948).

political consequences," and, accordingly, would require the unanimous vote of the permanent members.[9]

Since that time the General Assembly—in an attempt to narrow the area within which the veto should apply—has been inclined to define procedural questions very broadly. In April 1949, the Assembly recommended to the Council that some thirty-one decisions should be made by an affirmative vote of any seven members, and that the Council should conduct its business accordingly. Included in the list were a number of decisions that previously had been considered as substantive in character, such as those relating to the peaceful settlement of disputes and the admission of new Members to the United Nations.[10] The difference between the narrow interpretation of the sponsoring governments at the San Francisco Conference and the liberal interpretation urged on the Council by the Assembly is substantial. As the Charter itself does not spell out the distinctions between procedural and substantive questions, either of these interpretations could apply. Clearly, there is great elasticity in this part of the Charter if the Members wish to use it.

There has also proved to be considerable elasticity in those provisions of the Charter relating to the role of the Secretary-General in the United Nations. The articles in Chapter XV of the Charter might leave the impression that his political functions were to be quite limited in scope. As chief administrative officer of the United Nations (Article 97) with authority to appoint his staff (Article 101) and submit an annual report to the General Assembly on the work of the United Nations (Article 98), the post naturally carries with it a certain amount of prestige and influence. But in Article 99, under which he is authorized to bring to the attention of the Security Council matters that in his opinion might threaten world peace, there is a real grant of political initiative.[11]

In practice, however, the influence exercised by the Secretary-General has been one of the significant developments within the United Nations. Both the General Assembly and the Security Council—and still more important the Secretary-General himself—have taken a broad view of his functions. He has made statements be-

[9] U.N. Information Organizations and U. S. Library of Congress, *Documents of the United Nations Conference on International Organization*, Vol. 11 (1945), pp. 711-14. Also see below, Chap. X.

[10] Res. 267(III), Apr. 14, 1949.

[11] See below, Chap. XIII.

fore both bodies on a variety of questions, and he has undisputed authority to place any item he considers necessary on the provisional agenda of the Assembly. It is necessary only to recall his vigorous role in the Korean crisis, which the Soviet Union bitterly resented, his proposal for a United Nations guard force, his attempts to bring about a *rapprochement* between the Soviet bloc and the free world, and more recently his mission to Peiping to negotiate for the release of the eleven American airmen, to understand the expanding nature of his political activities.

Still another demonstration of what custom and usage can do is reflected in the interpretation by the Assembly of Article 73(e) regarding non-self-governing territories. According to the provisions of this article, the Member states are obligated to submit to the Secretary-General "for information purposes," data of a technical nature relating to the economic, social, and educational conditions in the non-self-governing territories for which they are responsible. Strictly interpreted, this does not grant to any United Nations organ the express authority to deal with the information furnished or to make recommendations regarding it. The Assembly, however, despite opposition from the colonial powers, has gone considerably beyond the express provisions of Article 73(e). In 1949, it created a special committee to examine the information transmitted and to submit reports thereon to the Assembly "with such procedural recommendations as it may deem fit, and with such substantive recommendations as it may deem desirable relating to functional fields generally but not with respect to individual territories."[12]

With this as a starting point, the General Assembly has gradually expanded its activities and its influence in this field. It has approved a standardized form for governments to use in submitting information. It has requested additional information from Member states. It has debated at considerable length the reports submitted to it on the information received. If the present trend continues, the time may come when practice may harden into precedent, and world opinion will expect the colonial powers to be fully accountable to the United Nations for the administration of their non-self-governing territories.

Finally, perhaps the most significant change in the Charter has

[12] Res. 332(IV), Dec. 2, 1949. This resolution established the special committee for a three-year period. It was first established on an annual basis in 1946. Also see below, Chap. IX.

resulted from the sharp shift in the roles of the Security Council and the General Assembly. During the past five years, the Council, meeting less and less frequently, has faded into the background. The Assembly, on the other hand, has played a much different and probably a much more important role than was foreseen by those who framed the Charter.[13]

At the San Francisco Conference, much emphasis was placed on the primary responsibility of the Council for the maintenance of world peace. It was to be so organized as to be able to function continuously. Armed forces were to be placed at its disposal. It could make decisions binding on all Member states. It was to be a small organ capable of acting with vigor and dispatch in order to keep the peace. The Assembly, on the other hand, was designed to be a much less powerful organ. It was scheduled to meet in regular annual sessions. It was to have no armed forces at its disposal. It could not make decisions binding on Members—only recommendations. Its main weapons were discussion and debate and control of the United Nations purse strings.

As the Council has fallen into disuse, largely because of dissension among the great powers, the Assembly has become a stronger and more vigorous organ. By various devices, including the creation in 1947 of the Interim Committee, ways and means have been found to keep the Assembly in virtually continuous session if necessary. Moreover, the "Uniting for Peace" resolution, which was approved in 1950 after the attack in Korea, geared the Assembly to take action against an aggressor in the event the Council failed to exercise its responsibility for the maintenance of peace.[14]

Today, the Assembly may be convened in an emergency session within 24 hours. It may make appropriate recommendations to the Members for collective measures, including the use of armed forces. It has created two important subsidiary organs: a Collective Measures Committee of fourteen members to report on methods that might be used to strengthen international peace and security; and a Peace Observation Commission, also made up of fourteen members, to observe and report on any situation that might endanger international peace and security. Member states have been asked to earmark certain of their armed forces so organized, trained, and

[13] See below, Chaps. X and XI.
[14] Res. 377(V), Nov. 3, 1950.

equipped that they could be made available promptly for service as United Nations units.

In filling this new role, the Assembly has already demonstrated that it can make far-reaching recommendations. Thus, in early February 1951, it approved a resolution finding that Communist China had engaged in aggression in Korea.[15] This was followed in May by a second resolution calling for an embargo on the shipment of war materials to Communist China and North Korea.[16] It can be argued, of course, that resolutions of this kind are only recommendations to the Member states, and as such have no binding effect. But the embargo on strategic materials was put into operation by some forty-five countries and has considerably limited strategic trade with aggressor nations.

Conclusion of Supplementary or Supporting Agreements

The character of the Charter has also been changed as a result of numerous treaties and agreements that have been entered into by various Member states. These agreements, which must be accepted by the Members in accordance with their constitutional processes, define in greater detail the general provisions of the Charter. They usually spell out in more specific form the rights and duties of Member states and the powers and functions of the United Nations organs. In some instances they lay down obligations and commitments that go beyond those contained in the Charter. A few examples may be helpful to show the nature of this development.

The Charter sets forth in only the broadest terms the basic principles relating to the legal capacity of the Organization and the privileges and immunities to be enjoyed by representatives of the Member states and by United Nations officials (Articles 104 and 105). At the San Francisco Conference, it was assumed these were matters that could be worked out more satisfactorily at a later date. Indeed, Article 105(3) specifically calls upon the Assembly to make recommendations with a view to determining the details of the application of the principles regarding privileges and immunities or to propose conventions to the Members for this purpose.

[15] Res. 498(V), Feb. 1, 1951.
[16] Res. 500(V), May 18, 1951.

Under the Convention on the Privileges and Immunities of the United Nations concluded in February 1946, what were once two short articles of the Charter—some nine lines—have been elaborated into thirty-six sections, setting forth in considerable detail the juridical personality of the United Nations, the immunity of United Nations property, funds, and assets, the right of the United Nations to use communication facilities, the privileges and immunities of officials accredited to the United Nations, etc.[17] As of October 1953, forty-two Member states—the United States not among them—had ratified the convention.

In the same category is the Headquarters Agreement between the United States and the United Nations signed on June 26, 1947. This agreement defines the headquarters district in New York and clarifies the rights and duties of the United Nations and of the Member states with respect to postal and radio facilities, the use of an airport, the inviolability of the headquarters, police protection, and related matters.[18] Like the Convention on Privileges and Immunities, it gives substance to the general provisions of the Charter.

Of a somewhat different character are the declarations forty-four states have made voluntarily accepting the compulsory jurisdiction of the International Court of Justice. It is true, of course, that all Members of the United Nations are obligated to settle their disputes by only peaceful means. But the Charter does not impose any particular method of solution on the parties to a dispute. Consequently, when Member states accede to the so-called optional clause of the Statute (Article 36) and agree in advance to accept the jurisdiction of the Court with respect to legal disputes in which they may become involved, they not only enlarge the competence of that organ but they enter into obligations over and above those already embodied in the Charter.[19]

Even more important, from the point of view of the future development of the United Nations, are the changes that have taken place as a result of the conclusion of such agreements as the Brussels Pact, the Inter-American (Rio) Treaty of Reciprocal Assistance, the North Atlantic Treaty, and the Southeast Asia Collective De-

[17] U.N. General Assembly, First Session, *Convention on the Privileges and Immunities of the United Nations,* Doc. A/43 (Feb. 13, 1946), Annex 1, pp. 687 ff.
[18] *United Nations Treaty Series,* Vol. 11, No. 147 (1947), pp. 11-41.
[19] See below, Chap. XII.

fense Treaty. The Charter of the United Nations was designed to approach the problem of collective security on a world-wide basis and vested primary responsibility for the maintenance of international peace and security in the Security Council. That approach soon proved unworkable. As a consequence, Member states that feared the growing threat of aggression in the world were compelled to continue their quest for security in other directions. In such agreements as the Rio Treaty and the North Atlantic Treaty, they shifted their emphasis from universal collective security to security based on regional pacts and the idea of collective self-defense as expressed in Article 51.[20]

There are, to be sure, some critics who still argue that the North Atlantic Treaty is not a regional arrangement and that it violates the spirit if not the letter of the Charter. Whether the treaty is based on Chapter VIII of the Charter, or whether it derives its justification from Article 51, is beside the point. The real point is that these agreements, in developing as they do different techniques for joint action against armed attack, give changed emphasis to all these articles of the Charter. The conclusion of bilateral mutual defense treaties by many countries and the suggestions made in various quarters that comprehensive security pacts be developed for both the Middle East and the Far East, also serve to emphasize that in existing world conditions the Charter must remain fairly flexible.

Creation of Subsidiary Organs

Somewhat akin to the development of supplementary or supporting agreements has been the creation of special organs within the United Nations system. Although both of these devices were envisaged by the Charter, they have helped to round out the system in a way that was not foreseen clearly a decade ago. The accompanying Chart shows the principal organs of the United Nations and subsidiary bodies.

The Charter provides in Articles 22 and 29 that the General Assembly and the Security Council, respectively, may establish such subsidiary organs as are deemed necessary for the performance of their respective functions. Many standing committees have been set up under the rules of procedure of the two bodies. Among these are the six main committees of the Assembly; its Advisory Committee

[20] See below, Chap. VI.

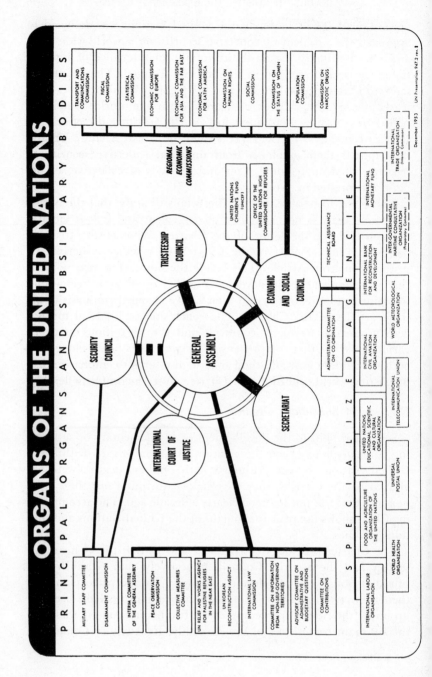

ORGANS OF THE UNITED NATIONS

PRINCIPAL ORGANS AND SUBSIDIARY BODIES

SECURITY COUNCIL
- MILITARY STAFF COMMITTEE
- DISARMAMENT COMMISSION

GENERAL ASSEMBLY
- INTERIM COMMITTEE OF THE GENERAL ASSEMBLY
- PEACE OBSERVATION COMMISSION
- COLLECTIVE MEASURES COMMITTEE
- UN RELIEF AND WORKS AGENCY FOR PALESTINE REFUGEES IN THE NEAR EAST
- UN KOREAN RECONSTRUCTION AGENCY
- INTERNATIONAL LAW COMMISSION
- COMMITTEE ON INFORMATION FROM NON-SELF-GOVERNING TERRITORIES
- ADVISORY COMMITTEE ON ADMINISTRATIVE AND BUDGETARY QUESTIONS
- COMMITTEE ON CONTRIBUTIONS

TRUSTEESHIP COUNCIL

INTERNATIONAL COURT OF JUSTICE

SECRETARIAT

ECONOMIC AND SOCIAL COUNCIL
- ADMINISTRATIVE COMMITTEE ON CO-ORDINATION
- UNITED NATIONS CHILDREN'S FUND (UNICEF)
- OFFICE OF THE UNITED NATIONS HIGH COMMISSIONER FOR REFUGEES
- TECHNICAL ASSISTANCE BOARD

REGIONAL ECONOMIC COMMISSIONS
- TRANSPORT AND COMMUNICATIONS COMMISSION
- FISCAL COMMISSION
- STATISTICAL COMMISSION
- ECONOMIC COMMISSION FOR EUROPE
- ECONOMIC COMMISSION FOR ASIA AND THE FAR EAST
- ECONOMIC COMMISSION FOR LATIN AMERICA
- COMMISSION ON HUMAN RIGHTS
- SOCIAL COMMISSION
- COMMISSION ON THE STATUS OF WOMEN
- POPULATION COMMISSION
- COMMISSION ON NARCOTIC DRUGS

SPECIALIZED AGENCIES
- INTERNATIONAL LABOUR ORGANISATION
- WORLD HEALTH ORGANIZATION
- FOOD AND AGRICULTURE ORGANIZATION OF THE UNITED NATIONS
- UNIVERSAL POSTAL UNION
- UNITED NATIONS EDUCATIONAL, SCIENTIFIC AND CULTURAL ORGANIZATION
- INTERNATIONAL TELECOMMUNICATION UNION
- INTERNATIONAL CIVIL AVIATION ORGANIZATION
- WORLD METEOROLOGICAL ORGANIZATION
- INTERNATIONAL BANK FOR RECONSTRUCTION AND DEVELOPMENT
- INTER-GOVERNMENTAL MARITIME CONSULTATIVE ORGANIZATION (Preparatory Commission)
- INTERNATIONAL MONETARY FUND
- INTERNATIONAL TRADE ORGANIZATION (Interim Commission)

December 1953

UN Presentation 947.2 rev. 1

on Administrative and Budgetary Questions, and the Committee on Contributions of the General Assembly; and in the Security Council the Committee on Admission of New Members. These standing committees are largely designed to facilitate the proceedings of the two most important organs of the United Nations.

In addition, a large number of committees and commissions have been established by resolutions of the two parent organs to perform certain specific functions. Some of these are of a relatively permanent nature, such as the Interim Committee of the General Assembly, the International Law Commission, and the Disarmament Commission. Still others are *ad hoc* organs such as the Commission for India and Pakistan, the Special Committee on the Balkans, the Palestine Conciliation Commission, the Commission for the Unification and Rehabilitation of Korea, and the Committee on the Question of Defining Aggression. The titles of these organs give some indication of their diversity. Recently, there were at least thirty-two subsidiary organs of the General Assembly and three of the Security Council.[21]

The Interim Committee is one of the best examples of this type of development. It was established by a resolution of the General Assembly in 1947 for one year, continued in 1948 for another year, and re-established indefinitely by a resolution of the Assembly in November 1949.[22] Because it was created to strengthen the Assembly and thus to help make up for the inability of the Security Council to take action in certain cases, it was given broad competence to deal with questions within the jurisdiction of the Assembly when the latter was not in session. Its jurisdiction includes matters referred to it by the Assembly; important disputes or situations proposed for inclusion in the agenda of the Assembly or referred to the Assembly by the Security Council; and methods of implementing Article 11(1) and Article 13 (1(a)) of the Charter, which deal with the political functions of the Assembly. For the proper exercise of these functions, the Interim Committee was given authority on behalf of the General Assembly to conduct investigations, to appoint commissions of inquiry, to adopt additional rules of procedure not inconsistent with those of the Assembly, and to advise on the calling of special sessions of the Assembly.

[21] U.N. Department of Public Information, Research Section, *Structure of the United Nations* (Sixth Revision), Doc. ST/DPI/7 (March 1953).
[22] Res. 295(IV), Nov. 21, 1949. See below, Chap. V.

The resolution creating the Interim Committee underlined its character as a subsidiary organ of the Assembly in accordance with the terms of Article 22. Nevertheless, the Soviet Union and its satellites challenged the legality of the committee. They charged that it was designed to circumvent and weaken the Security Council, which had primary responsibility for the maintenance of peace and security under the Charter. They insisted, too, that the committee possessed such broad powers that it was equal in rank with the Assembly and consequently did not constitute a "subsidiary organ" within the meaning of Article 22.

The General Assembly did not accept these arguments, but at the same time the terms of reference of the Interim Committee were narrowed somewhat as a result of the criticisms launched against it. Its authority to conduct investigations was circumscribed, and its power to advise on the calling of special sessions of the Assembly was limited to questions actually under discussion by the committee. In addition, it was made clear that the committee was not to trespass on the sphere of activity of any other organ of the United Nations. Despite these assurances, the Soviet Union and its satellite states have continued to regard the Interim Committee as illegal and have refused to participate in its work. The committee has met only twice since 1950 (primarily for the purpose of electing its officers), largely because the General Assembly has been able to function more effectively than formerly thus obviating the need for this particular type of interim machinery.

The Soviet Union has vigorously opposed on legal grounds the creation of a number of other subsidiary organs. It has attacked the Commission for the Unification and Rehabilitation of Korea, insisting that the commission constituted intervention in a civil war and interference in the internal affairs of another state. Similarly, the Soviet Union held that the terms of reference of the Special Committee on the Balkans were incompatible with the Charter and the principle of the sovereign equality of Member states. But these organs were established and discharged their responsibilities.

Out of experience of the United Nations with subsidiary organs, the following general principles emerge:

1. The authority of the General Assembly and the Security Council to establish subsidiary organs to perform a wide variety of functions has been established. Without this kind of assistance,

they could not effectively discharge their responsibilities under the Charter.

2. The authority that these agencies exercise cannot go beyond the authority possessed by the parent organ under the Charter.

3. Most of the subsidiary organs exercise their mandates within a definite time period, the length of which depends on the nature of the task to be performed.

4. The subsidiary organs are strictly accountable to the General Assembly or the Security Council and must submit reports on their activities at regular intervals.

The subsidiary organs do not have a free rein; they are carefully hedged about by restrictions and limitations. The establishment of such organs does not amend the Charter in any substantive way, but it does constitute an important feature of the developing United Nations system under the Charter.

Provisions for Formal Amendment

At the San Francisco Conference, the formal amending process, which was inextricably bound up with the problem of the veto, became the subject of prolonged and heated debate. The question before the Conference may be simply stated: Was it possible to inject sufficient flexibility into the Charter in order to provide room for adaptation, without at the same time making it too easy for groups of Member states to upset, through the amendment procedure, the delicate balance of power that had been so carefully worked out between the large and the small states?

Those who favored a rigid Charter presented convincing arguments to support their case. Many of the provisions of the Charter—especially those relating to the privileged position of the great powers—were the result of uneasy compromises and had been agreed to only after long and painful negotiations. Any premature tinkering with the Charter, it was argued, would therefore only re-open a Pandora's box of difficult issues and hamper the functioning of the new Organization. Moreover, from the point of view of the five major powers that were to be the permanent members of the Security Council, no amendment procedure was either logical or acceptable unless it incorporated the principle of the veto. For what protection would the veto offer them if it could later be removed from the Charter by an amendment that might be adopted without their unanimous consent?

On the other hand, some of the nations that bitterly opposed the veto, agreed to ease their opposition if they could obtain some kind of assurance that the amending process might be liberalized. They objected to any arrangement that would freeze the *status quo* and permit any great power, through the exercise of the veto, to prevent needed changes in the Charter. The veto in itself was bad enough they felt, but the veto irrevocably imbedded in a rigid Charter was doubly bad.

The Normal Amending Process: Article 108

As a result of this debate, two different methods of amending the Charter were finally agreed upon. The ordinary procedure is set forth in Article 108, which outlines two distinct steps that are to be followed in the normal amending process: adoption of the proposal by a two-thirds vote of the General Assembly; and ratification by two thirds of the Members of the United Nations, including the permanent members of the Security Council. Four important points should be noted in connection with these steps.

First, proposed amendments may be adopted by the General Assembly without any concurring action by the Security Council. In the initial stages, at least, the will of a majority of two thirds of the Members prevails. No single Member state or small group of Member states can prevent an amendment from being approved and sent to the other Members for further consideration and possible ratification. On the other hand, Article 108 expressly provides that amendments must be approved by a vote of two thirds of the members of the Assembly. This requirement has the effect of discouraging frivolous attempts at revision of the Charter. At the same time, it guarantees that only those proposals that have strong enough support in the United Nations to make ratification by two thirds of the Members probable will be forwarded to the Member states for final action.

Second, Article 108 reiterates the predominant position of the great powers in the United Nations. The requirement that amendments must be ratified by two thirds of the Member states, including the five permanent members of the Security Council, means that no amendment can become effective if it is opposed by any of the permanent members. By failing to take positive action on an amendment adopted by the General Assembly, any one of the major powers can prevent the entry into force of the amendment even though it may be ratified by all other Members of the United Nations.

Third, once an amendment receives the required number of ratifications, including those of the five permanent members of the Security Council, it becomes effective with respect to all Members, even those that voted against it or failed to ratify it. This is an interesting example of the impact of the Charter on the traditional concept of state sovereignty, because, except for the permanent members, the entire membership of the United Nations is committed in advance to accept any new obligations that amendments to the Charter might impose. If, however, a Member state vigorously opposes an amendment and does not wish to be bound by its provisions after its entry into force, that state has the option of withdrawing from the United Nations. Although the Charter itself contains no express provision for withdrawal, the following declaration of interpretation adopted by the San Francisco Conference leaves no doubt on this point: "Nor would a Member be bound to remain in the Organization if its rights and obligations as such were changed by Charter amendment in which it has not concurred and which it finds itself unable to accept, or if an amendment duly accepted by the necessary majority in the Assembly or in a general conference fails to secure the ratifications necessary to bring such amendment into effect."[23] An avenue of withdrawal is thus left open to dissatisfied states, but presumably the right would not be exercised except in very rare instances. Such a step would be a serious one, and any state, about to lose the benefits that accrue to it from membership in the United Nations, probably would hesitate a long time before taking it.

Fourth, no reference is made in Article 108 to any time period within which amendments proposed by the General Assembly must be ratified. This could give rise to some interesting consequences. Member states might consider it a legitimate reason for withdrawal from the United Nations if an amendment approved by the Assembly failed to obtain the requisite number of ratifications to

[23] U. S. Department of State, *Charter of the United Nations: Report to the President on the Results of the San Francisco Conference*, pp. 48-49.

bring it into effect. Without a specific dateline, however, a question can be raised regarding when a Member would be justified in assuming that an amendment had failed to obtain the necessary number of ratifications. It should also be noted that amendments must be ratified by Member states "in accordance with their respective constitutional processes." There is no doubt that under this provision the President of the United States would follow the regular treaty procedure outlined in the Constitution and obtain the advice and consent of the Senate before ratifying a proposed amendment because any other course would seem to be contrary to the treaty-making process. Certainly, it would be an illogical arrangement if the President, after obtaining a two-thirds vote of the Senate approving the ratification of the original Charter, could proceed to alter drastically the nature of United States commitments in the United Nations by accepting important amendments without referring them to the Senate for approval.

In one sense, even with the veto accorded to the five major powers, the amending process set forth in the Charter is a comparatively flexible one. Many multilateral treaties cannot be amended without the consent of all the signatories. The North Atlantic Treaty is a good case in point. No change, however slight, in the text of the treaty can be accomplished without the specific approval of each one of the fourteen parties to it. Theoretically, at least, the Charter is much more flexible. If forty Member states, including the five major powers, should agree, it would be possible to bring about far-reaching changes in the Charter even against the opposition of as many as twenty other Member states.

In this connection, it is interesting to recall the experience of the League of Nations. Article 26 of the Covenant provided that amendments would take effect when ratified by *all* the Member states represented on the Council and by a majority of those represented in the Assembly. Thus not only the great powers but every other member of the Council possessed a veto. This unanimity requirement proved to be an almost insuperable hurdle because the membership of the Council changed from time to time. For example, in 1923 the ratifications of only two states represented on the Council—Uruguay and Spain—were necessary to bring an amendment relating to Article 26 of the Covenant into force. These ratifications were obtained in 1924 and 1930, respectively. Meanwhile, however, the composition of the Council changed from year to year so that by 1935 the ratifications of Argentina, Germany, Mexico, the Soviet Union, and Turkey still had to be obtained before the amendment could come into effect.[24] In practice, this "transitory" veto exercised by the non-permanent members of the Council of the League proved almost as exasperating—and certainly far more bewildering—than the veto power of each of the permanent members of the Security Council of the United Nations.

General Conference to Review the Charter: Article 109

The normal amending procedure outlined in Article 108 was not enough, as has been noted above, to satisfy the demands of many delegations at the San Francisco Conference. Some argued that they would be unable to obtain ratification of the Charter unless assurances could be given that, within a reasonable period of time, there would be an opportunity to review the Charter and to strengthen its provisions. For this reason, Article 109 was developed. It is the result of an attempt to set up a second method of amending the Charter different from and easier than that found in Article 108. The attempt fell short of its mark. Although Article 109 establishes a somewhat different procedure, as the following text shows, it is certainly no easier than that envisaged in Article 108.

1. A General Conference of the Members of the United Nations for the purpose of reviewing the present Charter may be held at a date and place to be fixed by a two-thirds vote of the members of the General Assembly and by a vote of any seven members of the Security Council. Each Member of the United Nations shall have one vote in the conference.

2. Any alteration of the present Charter recommended by a two-thirds vote of the conference shall take effect when ratified in accordance with their respective constitutional processes by two thirds of the Members of the United Nations including all the permanent members of the Security Council.

3. If such a conference has not been held before the tenth annual session of the General Assembly following the coming into force of the present Charter, the proposal to call such a conference shall be placed on the agenda of that session of the General Assembly, and the conference shall be held if so decided by a majority vote of the members of the General Assembly and by a vote of any seven members of the Security Council.

[24] See Francis O. Wilcox, *The Ratification of International Conventions* (1935), pp. 249-57.

It may be useful to recall the history of this article. Even before the San Francisco Conference convened, the United States delegation agreed that the opportunity offered by Article 108 for the piecemeal amendment of the Charter would not suffice. The Charter was formulated during the war, and it seemed desirable to provide an opportunity to look at the entire Organization at some future date. The United States delegation was opposed, however, to any provision that would make the United Nations seem temporary or transitory in character. At the same time, it recognized the value of creating procedures for a more general review of the Charter than would be possible under the system of having the Assembly consider isolated amendments from time to time.[25]

On the opening day of the San Francisco Conference, the United States delegation agreed on the text of an article to be inserted in the Charter. This new article provided that a General Conference to review the Charter might be called whenever three-quarters of the General Assembly and any seven members of the Security Council so voted. It also provided that any amendments recommended by a two-thirds vote of such a conference would take effect when ratified by two thirds of the Members of the Organization, including the five permanent members of the Security Council. These are essentially the provisions of paragraphs 1 and 2 of Article 109, as they were accepted by the Conference.

But some delegations at San Francisco wished to go even farther. Specifically, they argued that the convening of the General Conference should be made easier, and a date for the conference should be indicated. Some insisted that a fixed date be set, preferably five or seven years after the establishment of the new organization. Others, following the lead of Brazil and Canada, suggested that the conference might be made mandatory at some undesignated time within a period of five to ten years.

The first of these propositions was agreed to, and the language of Article 109 was liberalized so as to make possible the calling of a conference for review of the Charter by a two-thirds (instead of a three-fourths) vote of the General Assembly. The second, however, met with considerable opposition. Who could say in advance when

---

[25] See U. S. Department of State, *Charter of the United Nations: Report to the President on the Results of the San Francisco Conference.* See also Goodrich and Hambro, *op. cit.,* pp. 482 ff., and Kelsen, *op. cit.,* pp. 816-23.

it would be wise to hold such a conference? Suppose the date selected should by chance fall during a period of world crisis, thus
making such an enterprise inadvisable? Would it not be more
logical to await events and permit the Members of the Organization
to determine whether such a conference might serve a useful
purpose?

These conflicting issues were straddled in the compromise incorporated in paragraph 3 of Article 109. Although the final compromise is based on a time limit of a kind, it does not guarantee that
a General Conference will be convened on any fixed date. The
only guaranty involved is that the question of calling the conference
will be placed on the agenda of the General Assembly after ten
years have elapsed. This in itself is not a concession of any great
moment because under the Rules of Procedure of the Assembly,
any Member has the right to request that an item be placed on
the agenda, and the Assembly approves its agenda by a simple
majority vote.

One significant point, however, should be noted. If ten years
elapse, and the question of calling a General Conference is automatically placed on the agenda of the Assembly, the decision to
call the conference may be taken by a majority vote of its members
instead of the two-thirds vote required under paragraph 1 of
Article 109. This decision must be concurred in by an affirmative
vote of any seven members of the Security Council. A permanent
member cannot, by its negative vote, prevent the convening of a
General Conference. Under the terms of paragraph 2 of Article 109,
however, a permanent member can prevent an amendment to the
Charter from coming into force by failing to ratify it.

So far as revision of the Charter is concerned, there is little difference between Articles 108 and 109. Actually, the General Conference contemplated in Article 109 has the same composition as the
General Assembly referred to in Article 108. In both cases each
Member of the United Nations would be represented and would
have one vote. Furthermore, any amendment approved by either
the General Assembly or the General Conference would require a
two-thirds vote of the entire membership of the United Nations.
Moreover, whether "alterations" or "amendments" to the Charter
are contemplated, they would come into force under exactly the
same procedures—namely, through ratification, in accordance with

their constitutional processes, by two thirds of the Members of the United Nations including the five permanent members of the Security Council.[26]

Thus Article 109, as it was finally adopted, provides no easier process, from a legal point of view, for changing the Charter than does Article 108. The process of amendment is just as long and just as difficult under one article as under the other. And there is no reason to suppose that a fundamental change in the Charter that has been rejected by the General Assembly would muster any more support in a General Conference called under Article 109.

In some respects, however, it might prove simpler to obtain action through the General Assembly because it is an established organ of the United Nations and meets at least once every year. The Assembly is regularly available, and no special diplomatic effort, no positive vote, is required to bring it into being as is the case with the General Conference. Moreover, a broad review of the Charter could be undertaken either in a regular or special session of the Assembly. On the other hand, there are practical difficulties involved in attempting to divert the attention of the Assembly to such a controversial matter as the amending process. Confronted in each regular session by an overflowing agenda, most Member states have been inclined to postpone any serious discussion of amendments to the Charter pending the convening of a General Conference under Article 109.

The atmosphere in a General Conference, or indeed, in a special session of the General Assembly called for reviewing the Charter, should be much more conducive to a balanced appraisal of the various arguments relating to review and revision. That would be the task of such a conference or special session. It would be convened for that specific purpose. Delegations would be briefed on the issues involved and would have instructions from their governments.

There is one important further difference between Articles 108 and 109 that should be noted. Article 109 envisages a "review" of the Charter, which might be something quite different from the revision or amendment contemplated in Article 108. It is possible, for example, that a conference might be called solely for the pur-

[26] *Ibid.*, pp. 817-18.

pose of reviewing the first ten years of the United Nations without any attempt to amend the Charter. Alternatively, such a conference might be convened to consider and act on formal amendments put forth by various Member states.[27]

The Problem Ahead

As the time approaches for a possible review of the Charter, those who are interested in determining whether the United Nations can become a more effective instrumentality for world peace will want to examine carefully the available alternatives. Should an effort be made to bring the Charter up to date through the formal amending process? Or would it be more prudent to wait on the normal development of the Charter through informal adaptation and change? These are fundamental questions that must be faced before a General Conference is convened.

In his book entitled *War or Peace,* published in 1950, Secretary of State John Foster Dulles commented as follows:

I have never seen any proposal made for collective security with "teeth" in it, or for "world government" or for "world federation," which could not be carried out either by the United Nations or under the United Nations Charter.

If the principal members of the United Nations, including the Soviet Union, are willing to take part in a proposed new world organization, then the United Nations itself could quickly be made into that organization.

If, as is the fact, the Soviet Union and others would not take part in the projected organization, then those who want to go ahead without them can form a collective security association under Article 51.[28]

This suggestion, that there is still a great deal of room for the development of the United Nations system within the framework of the Charter, reflects the experience of the Organization to date. As the examples outlined above illustrate, Members of the United Nations have inclined toward a liberal rather than a strict or narrow interpretation of the Charter. Many of the imperfections in the United Nations system could be remedied without the change of a word in the Charter. Certainly the impact of the veto could be softened quietly and quickly if the permanent members would

[27] For a further discussion, see below, Chap. XV.
[28] Dulles, *op. cit.,* p. 204.

informally agree to refrain from using it. Moreover, many nations now awaiting admission to the United Nations could be admitted without any formal change in the Charter.

Although the Charter is gradually being developed by methods apart from formal amendment, it should be kept in mind that there are important differences in the results produced by such methods and by amendments. For one thing, the methods used to date generally produce changes that are much less permanent in character, while a formal amendment is firmly embedded in the Charter for years to come. On the other hand, the methods used so far have produced changes that can be relatively easily modified or abrogated, or more important still, they may be much more limited because they apply only to those states that are directly involved. A particular interpretation of the Charter, for example, agreed to by the five great powers has no legal validity beyond this limited group. But a formal amendment, once in effect, is binding on all the Members of the United Nations whether they voted for it or not.

Some may question the legality or the constitutionality of many of the changes so far made in the United Nations system. In practice, however, there is no satisfactory way in which the legality of some of the changes can be effectively challenged. The International Court of Justice may hand down advisory opinions, but such opinions have no binding effect either on the Members or on the organs of the United Nations. There is no broad power of judicial review within the United Nations system, and Member states and the various organs of the United Nations alone are competent to pass on the legality of their actions. Hence, changes brought about to date through the processes discussed above must be considered legal so long as the Member states involved remain within their general obligations under the Charter.

Growth of the Charter through interpretation can only proceed, however, within well-defined legal limits. The United Nations is not a superstate. It is based on the principle of the sovereign equality of all its Members, and it must function within the specific limitations laid down in the Charter. However broad an interpretation placed on the Charter, the United Nations—by reason of Article 2(7)—is not authorized to intervene in matters essentially within the domestic jurisdiction of any state. Nor can the authority of the General Assembly be increased beyond a certain point, for under the express provisions of the Charter, it can only recommend;

in general it cannot make decisions binding on Members of the United Nations.

Many changes in the United Nations have been brought about by methods and agreements made outside, but at the same time collateral to, the Charter. Some changes that have been proposed, however, could become effective only through formal amendment. Thus, a change in the permanent membership of the Security Council, a modification of the formal amending process, or a grant of authority to enable the General Assembly to make firm decisions instead of recommendations, would undoubtedly require formal amendment before any of them could be made effective. In fact, it has been argued by the Soviet Union that some of the changes that already have come about, many of which were developed as the result of American leadership, are of the type that should have been submitted for approval under the formal amending procedures provided in the Charter.

Today those who advocate revision of the Charter are confronted by the hard fact that any amendment, no matter how widely accepted, will require the consent of the Soviet Union and the other permanent members of the Security Council. Although the Soviet Union may be counted on to do more than its share of objecting, it would be erroneous to assume that it and its satellites are the only obstacles in the way of revising the Charter. The small states, for example, would bitterly resent any proposal to change the system of voting in the General Assembly in such a way as radically to alter their position of equality with the great powers. Great Britain, France, and other countries with colonial possessions no doubt would oppose amendments conferring on the United Nations greater authority with respect to non-self-governing territories. And certainly the United States would vigorously object to any change in the Charter that would empower the United Nations to use United States troops for enforcement action without the consent of the United States.

Since its inception, the Charter has been demonstrated to be a remarkably flexible instrument adaptable to changing needs and circumstances. This flexibility may provide the way in which the United Nations can be made more effective in protecting the interests of the United States and in preserving peace without recourse to formal changes in the Charter.[29]

[29] For further discussion, see below, Chap. XV.

CHAPTER II

The Movement for Revision of the Charter

SECRETARY OF STATE John Foster Dulles on August 12, 1953, gave the first public indication of the attitude of the Eisenhower administration on the question of review of the Charter when he wrote Senator Alexander Wiley, then chairman of the Senate Committee on Foreign Relations, that "the Department will favor the calling of the review conference when the question is put to the 1955 session of the United Nations General Assembly." He also expressed the belief that the conference provided "a great opportunity" but that final United States policy on the matter "must await full public discussion of the issues as well as consultations with members of Congress."[1]

Some two weeks later the Secretary of State repeated this statement in a speech delivered before the American Bar Association in Boston. He also pointed out that: "This Administration has a vision of something better than bare survival in the face of danger. We have faith that it is possible to end the menace under which humanity has existed for so long. It was hoped that the United Nations would achieve this, and I still believe that it can. But to realize this hope will require that the Charter be altered in some important respects."[2]

This speech brought into focus some of the principal issues the United States Government and the American people must face in this connection. Should the United States take the lead in convening a conference for the purpose of reviewing the Charter? If so, what, if any, specific proposals should it put forth in the way of formal amendments to the Charter?[3] Since the fall of 1953, con-

[1] U. S. Department of State *Bulletin,* Vol. 29 (Sept. 7, 1953), pp. 310-11.
[2] *Ibid.,* pp. 309-10.
[3] On the problems raised in this chapter see Ernest A. Gross, "Revising the Charter: Is it Possible? Is it Wise?," *Foreign Affairs,* Vol. 32 (January 1954), pp. 203-16; Trygve Lie, *In the Cause of Peace* (1954), Chap. 23; Philip E. Jacob (ed.), "The Future of the United Nations: Issues of Charter Revision," *Annals of the American Academy of Political and Social Science,* Vol. 296 (November 1954), pp. 1-162; Subcommittee on the United Nations Charter, Senate Committee on Foreign Relations, *Review of the United Nations Charter: A Collection of*

siderable controversy has arisen in the United States over both these questions. For example, the American Assembly, made up of some fifty leading Americans meeting at Arden House under the auspices of Columbia University in August 1954, said:

Many of our American Assembly participants feel that a Charter review conference might arouse extravagant hopes, the disappointment of which might lead to disillusionment and a weakening of public support for the United Nations. Some of the participants, however, feel that the United States should support the calling of a review conference and in any case should prepare for it.[4]

Origin and Scope of the Movement

Actually, the movement for revision of the Charter began to gather momentum even before the document was signed. At the San Francisco Conference many of the smaller states, although convinced they had done as well as they could expect to do in the circumstances, were disgruntled at certain results of the Conference. First and foremost, they bitterly protested the inclusion of the provision for the veto in the Charter, and they resented the position of dominance the five great powers had in the new organization. They complained that the General Assembly was not granted sufficient authority in the political field; they objected that the Security Council was too small adequately to represent their interests; they opposed the provision of the Charter providing for the selection of the Secretary-General; they were disappointed because the great powers would not agree to grant the International Court of Justice compulsory jurisdiction over legal disputes arising among the Members; and they protested that the amending process was far too rigid. In the end the small states yielded; but only after assurances had been given them, through the addition of Article 109, that after ten years, a conference might be convened by a majority vote of the Members for the purpose of reviewing the Charter in the light of experience.[5]

Documents, S. Doc. 87, 83 Cong. 2 sess. (Jan. 7, 1954); Jacob Robinson, "The General Review Conference," *International Organization,* Vol. 8 (August 1954), pp. 316-30; *Review of the United Nations Charter,* Hearings before a Subcommittee of the Senate Committee on Foreign Relations, 83 Cong. 2 sess., Pts. 1-7 and *ibid.,* 84 Cong. 1 sess., Pts. 8-12; Yuen-Li Liang, "Preparatory Work for a Possible Revision of the United Nations Charter," *American Journal of International Law,* Vol. 48 (January 1954), pp. 83-97.

[4] The American Assembly, *The U. S. Stake in the U.N.* (1954), p. 132.

[5] See above, Chap. I.

Attitude in the United Nations

Even though all the small states represented at the San Francisco Conference signed the Charter, some of them did not stop pressing their point of view in favor of revision. In 1946, 1947, and again in 1948, during the sessions of the General Assembly, the delegations of Cuba and Argentina put forth formal proposals either to convene a special conference under Article 109 in order to abolish the veto, or to call a conference for the purpose of reviewing the Charter.[6] In the circumstances then prevailing, these suggestions did not command much support in the Assembly. Many Members expressed the conviction that proposals for revising the Charter were at that time premature; that such a movement, however well conceived, might place in serious jeopardy the constructive work being done by the new organization. The United States delegate stated in 1946 that his government did "not favor a hasty attempt to amend the Charter," but thought it was preferable "to build slowly and to test potentialities for growth by letting experience be a guide to a better understanding of that instrument."[7]

No comparable proposals have been put before the General Assembly since 1948. Nor have any attempts been made to amend the Charter under the procedures outlined in Article 108.[8] Indeed, between 1948 and 1953, when a general debate on review of the Charter took place during the course of the eighth session of the Assembly, the United Nations paid relatively little attention to the problem of amending the Charter.

Attitude in the United States

In the United States prior to 1953, the movement for revision

[6] See U.N. General Assembly, First Session, *Convocation of General Conference of Members of the United Nations Under Article 109 of the Charter,* Doc. A/75 (Sept. 17, 1946); U.N. General Assembly, First Session, *General Conference of Members of the United Nations for the Purpose of Reviewing the Present Charter,* Doc. A/102 (Oct. 10, 1946); U.N. General Assembly, First Session, First Committee, *Letter from the President of the Cuban Delegation to the Secretary-General Forwarding a Proposal for the Convening of a General Conference of the United Nations,* Doc. A/C.1/49/Rev. 1 (Nov. 14, 1946); U.N. General Assembly, Second Session, Interim Committee, *Draft Resolution Submitted by Argentina: Convocation of a General Conference Under Article 109 of the Charter to Abolish the Privilege of the Veto,* Doc. A/AC.18/12 (Jan. 13, 1948).

[7] U.N. General Assembly, First Session, Second Part, First Committee, *Official Records,* 20th Meeting (Nov. 15, 1946), p. 93.

[8] See above, Chap. I.

of the Charter went through two distinct phases. During each of these phases, considerable concern was expressed over the structural weaknesses of the United Nations, and considerable popular sentiment was mobilized in favor of strengthening the Organization. But in each instance, the movement fell short of its goal of obtaining revisions in the Charter.

The first phase, which was inspired by the advent of the atomic bomb and the obvious inability or unwillingness of the great powers to work together in behalf of world peace, culminated in the passage of the Vandenberg resolution in June 1948. This was an interesting demonstration of the leavening force of an aroused public opinion at work in a democracy.

In the spring of 1948, the Senate Committee on Foreign Relations had before it eight resolutions aimed at revising the Charter or at charting a course for American foreign policy through the United Nations. A somewhat similar situation existed in the House of Representatives. Clearly something needed to be done.

The result was a compromise, conceived after careful deliberation by the Committee on Foreign Relations and based on frequent consultation between the legislative and executive branches of the government. The Vandenberg resolution, which won the overwhelming approval of the Senate by a vote of 64 to 4, proposed that the United Nations be strengthened in two specific ways: (1) that every effort be made to obtain agreement on restricting the use of the veto, on furnishing the Security Council with armed forces as provided in the Charter, and on the regulation and reduction of armaments; and (2) that steps be taken to develop regional and other arrangements for individual and collective self-defense. Finally, the resolution recommended that, "if necessary, after adequate effort toward strengthening the United Nations, a General Conference be called under Article 109 at an appropriate time," for the purpose of reviewing the Charter.[9]

It is interesting to note the reaction of the committee to this latter recommendation. After reviewing the world situation, the committee concluded in its report that it would be "unwise to insist at the present time on the revision of the Charter" inasmuch as such insistence would entail "serious risk of breaking up the United Nations. . . . Peace and security could be undermined just as much by impatient attempts to make fundamental alterations

[9] S. Res. 239, 80 Cong. 2 sess. Also see below, Chap. VI.

of the United Nations as by failure to make firm and determined efforts to strengthen the United Nations where improvement is needed."[10]

But the passage of the Vandenberg resolution and the subsequent conclusion of the North Atlantic Treaty only temporarily retarded the movement for revision of the Charter. The second phase came some two years later. At that time, notwithstanding the positive effects on the collective strength of the free world of the Marshall Plan, the North Atlantic Treaty, and the Mutual Defense Assistance Program, tensions between the Soviet Union and the Western powers were still increasing, and the Congress was confronted by another demonstration of public concern. Over one hundred members of the House of Representatives and over forty Senators sponsored various resolutions urging the creation of international machinery strong enough to keep the peace and to relieve tensions among the great powers. Moreover, there was continuous pressure on the Congress and the Executive Branch to consider these proposals, a number of which moved into the realm of world government.

Once again the United States Government decided not to press for formal alteration of the Charter. After extensive hearings in both the House and the Senate, the Senate Committee on Foreign Relations submitted a lengthy report on the revision of the Charter, but agreed not to make any recommendations to the Senate with respect to either the strengthening of the United Nations machinery or the establishment of any institutions resembling a world government. There were a number of reasons for this reluctance to take more positive action, chief among them being the serious constitutional questions involved, the anxiety of the United States not to jeopardize the gains already made by the United Nations, and the outbreak of hostilities in Korea. In its conclusions, the committee made one comment in particular that bears repeating at this point. "The fundamental issue of the day," said the committee, "is the east-west conflict, not the question of the nature and extent of international organization."[11]

---

[10] See Senate Committee on Foreign Relations, *Reaffirming the Policy of the United States to Achieve International Peace and Security Through the United Nations and Indicating Certain Objectives to be Pursued,* S. Rept. 1361, 80 Cong. 2 sess. (May 19, 1948), p. 8.

[11] Senate Committee on Foreign Relations, *Revision of the United Nations Charter,* S. Rept. 2501, 81 Cong. 2 sess. (Sept. 1, 1950), p. 54.

It is, of course, impossible to estimate with any degree of precision the impact on the United Nations of the first two phases of the movement for revising the Charter. It seems safe to say, however, that the net result of the first phase was the conclusion of the North Atlantic Treaty. It is probable, too, that the second phase was instrumental in the passage of the "Uniting for Peace" resolution, which was approved by the General Assembly in 1950. Although neither the treaty nor the resolution amended the Charter, each had a significant impact on the United Nations system.[12] Since 1950, the situation has changed markedly. The advocates of world government, who sparked the first two phases of the movement, appear, for a variety of reasons, to have lost some of their former vitality. What effect that development will have on the third phase remains to be seen.

Debate in the Eighth Session of the Assembly

In the past one of the most effective arguments that has been used in opposition to suggestions that the Charter should be amended has been that it would be more logical to wait until 1955 when Article 109 would automatically come into effect. Then, instead of taking a piecemeal approach, there would be ample time to consider carefully the whole problem of reviewing and revising the Charter. As the date for decision draws near, there is obviously a considerable amount of cautious interest in the question of review. But a fairly large number of Member states remain reluctant to commit themselves either with respect to the desirability of convening a conference or of supporting any particular amendments to the Charter.

This attitude of watchful waiting was well demonstrated by the debate that took place during the eighth session of the General Assembly.[13] Three items were placed on the agenda of the Assembly relating to review of the Charter. Argentina proposed that the Assembly entrust the Secretary-General with the task of preparing a study of the interpretation of the Charter by various Members of the United Nations and other basic documentation.

[12] See above, Chap. I.

[13] See U.N. General Assembly, Eighth Session, Plenary, *Official Records,* 458th Meeting (Nov. 27, 1953), pp. 296-301; see also Yuen-Li Liang, *loc. cit.*

The Netherlands suggested that Member states be invited to submit their preliminary views on the amendments they planned to offer. And Egypt proposed the creation of a special technical committee charged with responsibility for undertaking certain necessary preparatory work.

Vigorous opposition to these ideas was voiced by several Member states, including especially those in the Soviet bloc, which insisted that any preparatory steps at so early a stage would be premature, harmful to the United Nations, and illegal under the Charter. Some Members argued, too, that the proposals under consideration were part of an organized campaign designed to prove in advance that the Charter is seriously defective and badly in need of revision. In addition, the debate reflected the general reluctance of many Members to become involved too deeply in the substance of review questions or to become committed at that time to any fixed policy positions. The proposals that Member states be invited to submit their preliminary views on these matters was defeated by a vote of 24 to 23. Likewise, the suggestion that the Secretary-General be requested to undertake the preparation of a comprehensive legislative history of the Charter was rejected.

The resolution finally approved by the General Assembly, by a vote of 48 to 5, cited the need for preparatory work in connection with review of the Charter and called on the Secretary-General to prepare certain documentation for use by the members prior to the convening of the Assembly in 1955. This included (1) a compilation of the unpublished documents of the San Francisco Conference; (2) a complete index of the documents of that conference; and (3) a repertory of the practice of various United Nations organs. It is significant that a number of Member states, including Israel, the Netherlands, New Zealand, and the United Kingdom, pointed out that the decision to undertake preparatory work should not be interpreted as favoring a General Conference but rather as a step designed to help the tenth session of the Assembly decide the question in a logical manner.

To those who have been arguing that thorough-going preparatory work is essential for an intelligent reappraisal of the United Nations system, the action of the Assembly may appear somewhat disappointing. Certainly it would be unwise for the United Nations to convoke a General Conference without taking the necessary steps to make available to Member states the right kind of basic data to enable them to subject the issues to careful analysis and appraisal. On the other hand, there is some merit in the argument that it would also be unwise if Members were urged to formulate their views too far in advance, for premature pronouncements of this character might tend to freeze their positions and deprive the conference of the flexibility necessary for success.

Preparatory Work in the United States

An integral part of the ground work being laid in the United States for review of the Charter is the activity of the Senate Committee on Foreign Relations. On July 28, 1953, even before the Executive Branch of the Government had expressed an opinion on the desirability of convening a conference, the Senate approved a resolution, introduced by Senator Gillette of Iowa, providing for the creation of a special Subcommittee on the United Nations Charter. The subcommittee has a bipartisan membership, initially consisting of six members chosen from the Committee on Foreign Relations and two members from the Senate at large. Under the terms of the resolution, the subcommittee was "empowered and directed to make a full and complete study of proposals to amend, revise or otherwise modify or change existing international peace and security organizations, for the purpose of guiding the Senate in the fulfillment of its responsibility . . . to advise the President with respect to the foreign policy of the United States."[14]

The committee has pursued this objective on two fronts. At the outset the staff of the subcommittee, with the assistance of the Legislative Reference Service of the Library of Congress, embarked on a series of studies that were designed to present in an objective way, an analysis of the main problems encountered by the United Nations and the various proposals to change the United Nations system. These studies have dealt with such varied problem areas as the veto, peaceful settlement of disputes, membership in the Organization, financial and budgetary matters, the development of the Charter, voting in the General Assembly, and enforcement action.

Concurrently, the subcommittee undertook the important task of seeking the assistance of the American people by conducting hearings in a number of cities throughout the United States. These

---

[14] S. Res. 126, 83 Cong. 1 sess., as amended by S. Res. 193, 83 Cong. 2 sess. and S. Res. 36, 84 Cong. 1 sess. The latter resolution provided for the appointment of two additional members from the Senate Committee on Foreign Relations.

hearings, which represented the first attempt on the part of a congressional committee to take a major issue of foreign policy to the people of the country for discussion and consideration, have done much to stimulate public interest in the problem.[15]

The subcommittee has emphasized the fact that the hearings were not designed to serve as a public opinion poll on the popularity of the United Nations. They have, however, provided a fairly good cross section of public reaction to the United Nations, and the information gathered will no doubt be helpful in the formulation of the recommendations of the subcommittee to the Senate on the question of review of the Charter.

Of considerable value, too, in developing an informed public opinion is the work of the foundations and the private organizations. The Carnegie Endowment for International Peace and the Commission to Study the Organization of Peace, for example, are in the process of preparing detailed studies about the United Nations and various aspects of the problem of reviewing and revising the Charter. Similarly, many of the nongovernmental organizations such as the veterans groups, the bar associations, the farm, labor, religious, civic, and educational organizations, as well as many private individuals, are doing important work in encouraging a thorough public discussion of the matter.

It would be difficult to overemphasize the significance of this activity. The contribution of the United States to a conference for review of the Charter will depend, in part at least, on the measured consideration that the American people give to the subject during the months before a conference might convene. It would be dangerous for the United States to participate in such a conference armed with only vague notions about the kind of United Nations the American people would be willing to support. In such circumstances the role of the United States, of necessity, would be somewhat negative in character.

Not much publicity has been given to the preparatory work being done in the Department of State. It is clear, however, from statements made by officials of the department, that a considerable amount of effort has been devoted to the preparation of background papers that will eventually form the basis for the policy decisions

[15] See Alexander Wiley, "The Senate and the Review of the United Nations Charter," *Annals of the American Academy of Political and Social Science,* Vol. 296 (November 1954), pp. 156-62.

of the United States concerning review. This is a large and time-consuming task, for each paper must take into account not only the position of the various departments of the Executive Branch, the Congress, and the American people, but also the practice of the United Nations as it has developed over the years and the attitudes of other countries.[16] It is the expectation of the Department of State that these preliminaries, including the hearings of the Senate Committee on Foreign Relations, will be completed by the fall of 1955, so that the Government of the United States will be in a position to consult in some detail with other Members of the United Nations. This time schedule must be met if the United States is to assume a role of leadership with respect to the issues involved.

In this connection, officials of the United States Government repeatedly point out that review of the Charter is basically a political matter and that what can be achieved will depend on the circumstances that prevail at a given time. There are probably many experts in the world who could retire to their studies and emerge with a more perfect Charter, from a technical point of view, than the one the United Nations now has. But government officials are compelled to think in more practical terms. A Charter that might be considered technically perfect by some would no doubt prove impracticable or unworkable for political reasons. The whole problem of review must be examined, therefore, not only in terms of the national interest of the United States, but also in terms of its practical impact on the United Nations system generally and on the relations of the United States with the rest of the world.

Preparatory Work Abroad

Although no special study has been made of the preparatory work undertaken in other Member states, on the surface there appears to be considerably less interest abroad in review of the Charter than has been manifest in the United States. It is true that, by the spring of 1955, some governments had created *ad hoc* machinery to deal with the problem. In Canada, for example, a working group had been set up in the Department of External Affairs, and in Belgium and the Netherlands, the foreign affairs ministries had

---

[16] See especially the speeches of David Wainhouse, Deputy Assistant Secretary of State for International Organization Affairs, U. S. Department of State *Bulletin*, Vol. 30 (Apr. 26, 1954), pp. 642-45; *ibid.*, Vol. 31 (Aug. 30, 1954), pp. 296-99; and *ibid.* (Nov. 15, 1954), pp. 737-42.

created special committees made up of members of Parliament, government officials, and qualified citizens to advise with their governments on the question. In a somewhat similar vein, the Yugoslav Ministry for Foreign Affairs had encouraged universities, scientific institutions, and law associations to devote some attention to problems of review. But such steps, taken by a few governments, appeared to be the exception rather than the rule.

In addition to the preparatory work being done by governments there has been a limited amount of activity abroad during the past few years among various international nongovernmental organizations. A number of proposals emerged from the conferences of the World Association of Parliamentarians for World Government held in London in 1951 and 1952, and from the Conference of the Young World Federalists, held in Amsterdam in 1953. Similarly, extensive recommendations for review of the Charter were approved in Copenhagen in 1953 by the Joint Conference of the World Movement for World Federal Government and the World Association of Parliamentarians for World Government. A few other organizations such as the World Federation of United Nations Associations and the International Law Association have encouraged a discussion of the issues or have made reports on them. In so far as these organizations have made recommendations or suggestions relating to revision of the Charter, they are referred to later in this volume.

Special mention should be made of the studies being carried on in twenty-four Member states under the auspices of the Carnegie Endowment for International Peace. These studies, which are being conducted by local committees of qualified citizens, deal with the participation of the particular states in the United Nations and the evolution of opinion relating to that participation as it is reflected in the press, scholarly publications, and other local media of communication. Inasmuch as these studies, a number of which will be printed, will contain recommendations for increasing the effectiveness of the United Nations, they should prove valuable sources of information for any review of the Charter.

Official Attitude of Various Member States

Only fragmentary and inconclusive information is currently available on the official attitudes of various Member states with respect to either the convocation of a General Conference or the amendment of the Charter. Moreover, the Members that went on record during the general debate at the eighth session of the General Assembly still consider it their sovereign privilege to change their positions before the final vote is taken. Nevertheless, from the various public statements that have been made thus far, and from the traditional roles that have been played by certain states in the United Nations, some tentative conclusions may be drawn.

The opposition of the five Member states in the Soviet bloc to a General Conference has been persistent and unmistakable. At the San Francisco Conference, the Soviet Union pointedly announced that it "was opposed to facilitating the convocation of such a conference for which there might be no need in the future."[17] That the Soviet Union has not receded from its position was demonstrated eight years later when the proposals to undertake preparatory work prior to the convening of the conference were being debated in the General Assembly. As noted earlier, the Soviet Union and its satellites not only voted against the proposals but also against even placing the matter on the agenda of the Assembly.

Soviet opposition to any amendment of the Charter has been even more persistent and even more unmistakable. Those who urge the revision of the Charter, the Soviet Union argues, are bent on weakening the Security Council and destroying the fundamental principle on which the United Nations is based—the unanimity of the five permanent members of the Council. Soviet representative Vyshinsky reiterated this charge in September 1953, when he attacked the suggestion by Secretary of State Dulles that a conference for review of the Charter can be of major importance. Said Vyshinsky: "There is every indication that the campaign for the revision of the Charter is to be turned into a cold-war campaign in order to arouse reactionary sentiments and thereby to increase international tension."[18]

This attitude, which has been openly reflected by each of the satellite countries, is in harmony with what seems to be the desire of the Soviet Union to do what it can to prevent the United Nations from becoming a more effective agency for world peace. A strong

[17] U.N. Information Organizations and the U. S. Library of Congress, *Documents of the United Nations Conference on International Organization,* Vol. 7 (1945), p. 250. Also see below, Chap. XV.
[18] U.N. General Assembly, Eighth Session, Plenary, *Official Records,* 438th Meeting (Sept. 21, 1953), p. 54.

United Nations, they apparently believe, would run counter to the proclaimed grand design of international communism for eventual world domination. Many people feel that it would be unwise to expect any substantial change in this approach toward the United Nations unless, of course, the attitude of the Kremlin toward world affairs undergoes a marked transformation. Sudden reversals of position have been known to take place before, however, on other important questions and the "summit" meeting in Geneva in July 1955, would indicate that increased flexibility in the Soviet position is by no means impossible. Consequently, the nations of the free world cannot afford to be caught unprepared for such a contingency.

On the other side of the question, the Latin American states have been almost as consistent as the Soviet bloc although somewhat less vocal. Traditionally, the Latin American Members have taken a juridical approach to the Charter. From the very beginning, they have maintained that the idea of a conference for review of the Charter was a condition precedent to their approval of the Charter and that the great powers are honor bound to co-operate in reviewing the work of the Organization after the first decade of experience. At least half the Latin American Members have gone on record since 1953 in favor of such a conference. In so far as they have indicated their positions, the Arab-Asian states must be placed in the same category.[19]

In the final analysis, the attitude of the great powers will be the key to the situation. So far the United States is the only one of them that is publicly committed to support the calling of a conference. Nationalist China, already in a difficult position in the United Nations, because of the repeated attempts of certain Members to replace its delegation with that of Communist China, is certainly not anxious to compound its troubles by encouraging a movement for revision of the Charter. Great Britain and France, it is true, have not been openly hostile to the idea, but they have remained noncommittal. In 1953, for example, when the Swedish representative spoke in a negative way about review of the Charter, the British representative advised the General Assembly to "ponder very carefully indeed the wise words" of the Swedish representative. This cautious approach has characterized a majority of the Members of the Organization.

[19] During the eighth and ninth sessions of the General Assembly, Egypt, Lebanon, Pakistan, the Philippines, and Syria spoke in favor of a conference.

During the ninth session of the Assembly in 1954 there appears to have been some decrease in interest among the Member states regarding the idea of a conference. In the eighth session of the Assembly, twenty-five members referred to the problem during the general debate with a substantial majority of them in favor of convening such a conference. During the ninth session of the Assembly, only ten speakers touched on the matter and only two dwelt on it at any length. This led the Ecuadoran delegate to remark: "It would seem that the enthusiasm of many delegates for a possible amendment has declined, doubtless owing to the fear that, instead of benefiting us all, what we have achieved would be destroyed and we should be left in a lawless world."[20] The noticeable lack of interest was possibly due, in part, to the fact that the problem was not on the agenda of the Assembly as it had been a year earlier. It may also be due to a growing apprehension among the Members lest the convening of a conference might stir up needless controversy in the United Nations that, in the end, would prove harmful to the Organization.

Attitudes are subject to change, however, and many Member states that are now uncertain regarding the wisdom of holding a conference might vote for it if international tensions decrease and the political climate should seem more favorable in the autumn of 1955. Another uncertain but important factor will be the vigor of American leadership in behalf of a conference. That, too, will depend in part, at least, on the political climate when the Assembly convenes in the autumn of 1955.

It follows that the United States Government has a two-fold task in the event a conference is to be convened. Initially, it must find out what is the common denominator of agreement among the American people. Where possible, differences of opinion must be reconciled, and an acceptable line of policy developed through public debate and discussion. If the American people are badly split, a conference to review the Charter might tend to widen internal schisms, and in such circumstances some people believe it could even have an adverse impact on American support for the United Nations. On the other hand, if there is substantial agreement on basic principles, the United States might be able to move into such a conference with the possibility of achieving positive results. Con-

---

[20] U.N. General Assembly, Ninth Session, Plenary, *Official Records*, 485th Meeting (Oct. 1, 1954), pp. 145-46.

currently, the United States Government must consult with other Member states in order to determine how much agreement there is among the free world. If it finds an encouraging display of unity, that is one thing. But if it finds that its friends and allies are unwilling to stand with it, or are uncertain, or are lukewarm in their support, the best diplomatic efforts may not be sufficient to make certain that a conference for review of the Charter would result in a net gain for the United States, the United Nations, and the cause of world peace.[21]

[21] See below, Chap. XV.

PART TWO

PROPOSALS RELATING TO THE BASES OF THE UNITED NATIONS SYSTEM

CHAPTER III

General Character and Nature of the Organization

THE purposes for which nations join together are almost as varied as the activities of mankind. They have, for example, co-operated to establish communications systems, promote commerce, control traffic in narcotic drugs, care for refugees, or defend themselves from attack. But the most pervasive concern of man in banding together, whether at the tribal level, the national level, or the international level, has been to help him survive. In recent years, this has meant his concentration on the maintenance of international peace and security. Man seeks an answer to the question how he, either individually or as a member of an organized group, can create a situation in which his survival will not be threatened by war.

In modern times there has been a procession of attempts to create international organizations able to prevent war.[1] It was not until after the First World War, however, that it was possible to develop a world-wide organization dedicated to this great purpose. The twentieth century has seen two major efforts in this direction—the League of Nations and the United Nations. The primary purpose in creating the United Nations was to establish an organization for maintaining international peace and security. Its purpose was generally the same as that of the League of Nations, which was established "to promote international co-operation and to achieve international peace and security."

Although there are few who would quarrel with this basic purpose, there are many who believe that no international organization created on the principles and assumptions that underlie the United Nations can successfully keep the peace. Furthermore, the ink was scarcely dry on the Charter before movements were underway to change it. Proposals to alter the United Nations system

[1] See J. Eugene Harley, *Documentary Textbook on the United Nations* (1947), for peace documents from 264 B.C. to 1947.

range from those the purpose of which could be attained by the changing of occasional words in the Charter, to suggestions to "rewrite" the Charter "so drastically . . . that nothing of the document will remain except the two opening words: 'Chapter one.' "[2]

Fundamental Principles

The attempt at the San Francisco Conference to build an organization able to keep the peace was based on the judgment of the governments represented there regarding the type of international organization that was feasible and that was thought to be practical in the reasonably near future. That judgment was conditioned by history, by the experience of the League of Nations, by the nature and extent of wartime co-operation, by estimates of future developments, and, most important, by opinions on the acceptability of the final document to the parliaments of many potential Members.

When the San Francisco conferees concluded their work in the spring of 1945, the Charter of the United Nations to which they had agreed was an instrument that created an international organization with stated purposes which was based on certain fundamental principles and assumptions. The purposes and principles of the Organization were set forth in the Charter. The fundamental assumptions, however, were largely implicit in the nature of the total organization and were not stated in precise terms in the Charter.

The more important principles of the Charter had been enunciated in public statements prior to the San Francisco Conference. The Moscow Conference in 1943 produced a Declaration of Four Nations on General Security, commonly referred to as the Moscow Declaration of 1943, which stated that the signatories "recognize the necessity of establishing at the earliest practicable date a *general international* organization, based on the principle of the *sovereign equality* of all peace-loving *states,* and open to membership by *all* such states, large and small, for the maintenance of international peace and security."[3] The Connally resolution approved by the United States Senate on November 5, 1943, five days after the Moscow Declaration, repeated these principles word for word.[4]

[2] Emery Reves, *The Anatomy of Peace* (1945), p. 243.
[3] Italics supplied. For full text of the Declaration see U. S. Department of State *Bulletin,* Vol. 9 (Nov. 6, 1943), pp. 308-09.
[4] S. Res. 192, 78 Cong. 1 sess.

Thus, the general character and nature of the United Nations Organization were laid down at the very outset. The United Nations as it was envisaged and finally established is a voluntary association of states based on the principle of sovereign equality. It is an organization of states, not of individuals. Membership is voluntary, but at the same time, it is to be as nearly universal as possible, consistent with the proposition that no state can be compelled to apply for membership and that those accepted as Members must be peace-loving and able and willing to carry out their obligations under the Charter. Member states are to retain their sovereignty and are legally equal.

Membership and Scope

Such authority as the United Nations possesses is exercised on states, and only incidentally on individuals. In drafting the Charter, it was not contemplated that the new organization would be radically different from earlier international organizations that were based on the theory that the primary unit of organized international co-operation should be the national state. Although the Preamble of the Charter speaks of "We the peoples of the United Nations" and some have drawn the inference from these words that peoples are subjects of the United Nations, the Preamble concludes with appropriate reference to "our respective Governments." Article 3 provides that "the original Members of the United Nations shall be . . . states" and Article 4 makes it clear that "membership . . . is open to all other peace-loving states."

No individual can be called before any organ of the United Nations and held accountable for his acts, except, of course, as he may be accountable through his own state. Serious consideration was not given at the San Francisco Conference, or earlier, to creating an organization with authority to act directly on individuals. Indeed, in the very earliest planning for the Charter in the United States Department of State during late 1942, the view was taken that "states should be members of the international organization. The vitality of the national state was regarded from the outset as of primary importance in the postwar world."[5]

Distinct from, but related to, the question whether an interna-

[5] U. S. Department of State, *Postwar Foreign Policy Preparation: 1939-1945.* Publication 3580 (February 1950), p. 113.

tional organization shall have direct authority over states or persons are two other questions: whether the organization should be universal in character; and whether, even though world-wide, it should be based on regional organizations.

With respect to the first question, the Charter set up three criteria for membership. Applicants must be (1) "peace-loving states," (2) willing to "accept the obligations contained in the present Charter," and (3) "in the judgment of the Organization, . . . able and willing to carry out these obligations."[6] Some delegations at the San Francisco Conference proposed that the Organization should be universal and "that all communities should be members . . . and . . . their participation . . . obligatory. . . ." Other delegations, however, indicated their belief in the principle of universality as "an ideal toward which it was proper to aim" but that it was "not practicable to realize at once."[7]

The second question, whether the world organization should be based on decentralized, regional organizations or should be a centralized, global organization, was resolved in favor of creating a single world-wide organization. Former Secretary of State Cordell Hull has stated that as early as 1943, even though Prime Minister Churchill and President Roosevelt had doubts about creating a world-wide organization, the officers in the Department of State working on this matter were "fully agreed on the necessity of a universal international organization, as opposed to regional organizations, although regional associations of the Pan American type should of course continue and be brought into a proper relationship with the world organization."[8] The United Nations Charter thus established a world-wide organization not responsible to, or deriving power from, regional organizations.

Sovereign Equality of Members

Article 2(1) of the Charter states that the Organization is "based on the principle of the sovereign equality of all its Members." The concept of state sovereignty is also embodied in the provisions of Article 2(7), which state: "Nothing contained in the present Charter shall authorize the United Nations to intervene in matters

---

[6] Art. 4.

[7] U.N. Information Organizations and U. S. Library of Congress, *Documents of the United Nations Conference on International Organization*, Vol. 7 (1945), pp. 325-26.

[8] *The Memoirs of Cordell Hull*, Vol. 2 (1948), p. 1643.

which are essentially within the domestic jurisdiction of any state or shall require the Members to submit such matters to settlement under the present Charter. . . ."

Up to the present time, no international organization to maintain peace and security, including the United Nations, has been given any substantial amount of power of the type that states normally exercise over their own citizens. States are able to punish individuals under their jurisdiction for breaches of the peace, to levy taxes, to take property, to compel military service, and, in general, exercise powers of life or death over the citizen. Except in a few unusual cases, no international organization has been able to prevent a state within its borders, or in its relations with other states, from conducting its domestic affairs or its relations with other governments much as it pleases.

With respect to the United Nations, Senator Vandenberg during his speech in July 1945 supporting ratification of the Charter stated:

. . . There is no "superstate," even remotely or by the widest indirection, in this Charter. . . . The United States retains every basic attribute of its sovereignty. . . . We can effectively co-operate for peace without the loss of these things. To co-operate is not to lose our sovereignty. It is to use our sovereignty in quest of the dearest boon which the prayers of humankind pursue.[9]

Fundamental Assumptions

Distinct from what have been referred to as fundamental principles underlying the United Nations system, are what might be described as the fundamental assumptions. These assumptions had nearly as much effect on the type of organization created at the San Francisco Conference as the principles on which the Organization was founded.

One of the most important assumptions was that wartime cooperation of the great powers would continue into the reasonably foreseeable future. The Moscow Declaration of 1943 referred to the fact that the united action in the prosecution of the war "will be continued for the organization and maintenance of peace and security."[10] This assumption was not seriously questioned at the

[9] *Congressional Record,* Vol. 91, Pt. 6, 79 Cong. 1 sess., pp. 7956-57.

[10] It might be debated whether the assumption was that the major powers would necessarily continue to co-operate, or rather that it was merely assumed that co-operation would need to continue if peace were to be preserved.

Conference partly because of the realization that if any one of the great powers in the future should become an aggressor, peace could not be maintained because the use of force needed to put down such an aggressor would most likely result in another world war. The only hope for the success of the United Nations in maintaining peace and security therefore was to be found in the unanimous agreement of the major powers, at least on vital issues.

A second important assumption was that the peace treaties would be concluded outside the United Nations structure within the reasonably near future, and therefore no provision relative to those treaties was necessary in the Charter. It was the job of the United Nations to *maintain* peace, not to *create* the peace.

A third assumption was that reasonably prompt solutions for the critical postwar problems in the political and economic fields would be forthcoming. From this it followed that the United Nations would need to concern itself primarily with the longer-range problems so that over a reasonably long period of peace, nations could learn to live together in the international community.

A fourth assumption was that future wars would imperil the world no more than past wars. The Charter was drafted without general knowledge of the destructive power of atomic weapons. Hence, disarmament in the Charter was treated as a grave problem, but with no sense of urgency and dire peril that might have led to the formulation of more specific commitments that might have been less easy to ignore.

The history of the past ten years has shown that the hopes of the drafters of the Charter were not fulfilled. Every one of these assumptions has been demonstrated to be partially or wholly erroneous. Had it been assumed that the great power victors would soon be quarreling among themselves, that they would find it impossible to agree on peace treaties with Germany and Japan, that economic reconstruction and recovery, both in Europe and the Far East, would require sustained and large-scale international cooperation for a long period rather than emergency action for a short period, and that nuclear weapons within seven years would be uncontrolled in the hands of at least three of the five major powers, the United Nations Charter might well have been a very different instrument than it is. Greater emphasis might have been given to the development of regional groupings of states, the United Nations might have been given authority in connection with the conclusion of the peace treaties, the Economic and Social Council might have been given different terms of reference, or an atomic energy authority unhampered by the veto might have been created. In fact, if those who drafted the Charter at the San Francisco Conference had foreseen these developments, they might have tried to base the United Nations on different principles than those underlying the present system. On the other hand, it can be argued that if the drafters had sought to proceed on different assumptions or to base the United Nations on different principles, there might have been no United Nations at all.

Regardless of the validity of the fundamental principles of the Charter or the assumptions that guided those who drafted it, the United Nations Charter did not "collapse like a house of cards within 2 years after its adoption," as predicted by one critic.[11] Neither has it proved to be the effective instrument to prevent aggression and to maintain peace that many had hoped. But now that these fundamental assumptions have been found for the most part to have been unwarranted and overly optimistic, the question arises: What, if any, changes should be made in the United Nations system?

The Movement for Supranational Government

At the time of the San Francisco Conference, and for many years before, some students of international organization believed that it would be impossible to establish an organization capable of preserving peace and security on the principle of the sovereign equality of states. That principle, they felt, had been discredited by history. Some who questioned the principle would substitute therefor the principle of supranationality. Instead of creating an organization geared to the idea that member states are legally equal and sovereign, and thus could not be compelled as states to take, or to refrain from taking, any particular action against their will, proponents of the supranational principle would build the peace-maintaining organism on the idea that there must be an authority superior to that of any national state. In a governmental system, authority to compel action, whether imposed on an individual or a state, implies legal power, and hence it is that many of the proponents of

---

[11] Statement by Ely Culbertson, *The Charter of the United Nations,* Hearings before the Senate Committee on Foreign Relations, 79 Cong. 1 sess., p. 416.

supranational proposals speak of creating an organization with authority to enact, interpret, and enforce world law.[12]

The long history of supranational proposals cannot be chronicled here. Suffice it to point out that the signature of the Charter and its ratification did not deter many people and organizations from commencing work immediately to seek changes in the United Nations system that would alter the fundamental principles on which it was built.[13] Only one advocate of a supranational proposal, however, appeared before the Senate Committee on Foreign Relations in 1945 to oppose ratification of the Charter. Proponents of other supranational plans seemed to accept the United Nations, at the time of the hearings on the Charter, as a step in the right direction provided additional steps were taken quickly.

Before the Charter came into effect, greater urgency was given the issue of supranationality in the minds of many by the atomic destruction of Hiroshima. The fear that man was developing the potentiality of self-destruction faster and more efficiently than had been anticipated at the San Francisco Conference seemed to mobilize support for those who believed that the United Nations should have been cast in a different mold. In addition, it soon became apparent to many who had hoped for a long period of postwar collaboration among the great powers, that such collaboration was not long to continue.

These factors led to a resurgence of proposals to strengthen the United Nations by giving it some of the attributes of a superstate. In 1949 the House Committee on Foreign Affairs held hearings on a number of pending resolutions advocating a strengthened United Nations. The campaign to create a supranational organization, led by the United World Federalists, reached a peak in 1950, when a subcommittee of the Senate Committee on Foreign Relations held lengthy hearings to consider proposals to revise the United Nations Charter.

[12] To distinguish between an international and a supranational organization the term "supranational" is used in this study to describe proposed world-wide or regional arrangements with one or more of the following characteristics: (a) authority to enact and interpret law; (b) authority to enforce law; (c) authority to control the use of military force. This definition is one suggested by Willard N. Hogan.

[13] As early as October 1945, a Conference on World Government sponsored by proponents of world federation held at Dublin, New Hampshire, resolved that the United Nations should be replaced by a World Federal Government. See the Dublin Conference Committee, *Proposals for Amendment of the United Nations Charter* (February 1946).

As pointed out earlier, some 140 members of Congress had sponsored resolutions calling for the development of international machinery strong enough to maintain peace.[14] Many state legislatures had adopted resolutions approving in principle the concept of a world federation. The Senate subcommittee found that, largely as the result of the conflict between the Communist and non-Communist worlds, the United Nations was being thwarted in its efforts to keep the peace. Excessive use of the veto, stalemates on atomic energy, disarmament, the provision of armed forces for the United Nations, and the admission of new Members were all contributing to a growing lack of confidence in the United Nations.

The subcommittee considered a variety of proposals, four of which were based on the supranational principle in some form. These plans provided for (1) a federal world government with broad powers; (2) a federal world government of limited powers; (3) a revision of the Charter to eliminate the veto in matters of aggression, control of atomic and other armaments, and to establish an international police force; and (4) a federal union of the North Atlantic democracies. It also considered a proposal for a supplementary pact under Article 51 of the Charter to enable the United Nations to take more expeditious action against aggression.[15]

The subcommittee concluded as the result of its studies, and the full Committee on Foreign Relations agreed, that the issues presented by these supranational proposals "go to the heart of the foreign policy of the United States. They raise in varying degrees an issue as fundamental as that which faced the American people in 1789 for all of them involve some degree of restriction on the freedom of the people of the United States." Inasmuch as the resolutions before it "involved serious constitutional questions," the subcommittee did not believe there was a sufficient consensus among the American people to warrant a "position on propositions as fundamental as proposals for world federation or a more limited federation which would involve extensive amendments to the United States Constitution until the issues have been debated, discussed, and understood."[16]

The supranational suggestions studied by the Senate subcom-

[14] See above, Chap. II.

[15] This proposal is considered below in Chap. VI.

[16] Senate Committee on Foreign Relations, *Revision of the United Nations Charter*, S. Rept. 2501, 81 Cong. 2 sess. (Sept. 1, 1950), pp. 51, 53. See also Carl Marcy and Francis O. Wilcox, "Congress and the United Nations," *Foreign Policy Reports*, Vol. 27 (May 15, 1951).

mittee in 1950 have not changed substantially since then. However, they have been subjected to the debate and discussion that the
committee suggested, with the result that considerable opposition to
them has developed. Most of the state legislatures that adopted
"world federalist" resolutions in 1949 and 1950 subsequently reconsidered them and either repealed or reworded them. In contrast to
the earlier period, practically no resolutions looking toward supranationality have been introduced in the Congress since 1954.

Many of the supporters of the Bricker Amendment relative to the
treaty power forcefully made the point that any strengthening of
the United Nations Charter along supranational lines would, as
the Committee on Foreign Relations pointed out in 1950, involve
such limits on the sovereignty of the United States as probably to
require constitutional amendment. Senator Bricker during a speech
before the Senate on August 5, 1954 declared:

. . . The treatymaking ambitions of the United Nations and its agencies
continue to reflect a zeal to regulate the political, economic, and social
rights and duties of people everywhere. Those who seek to make the
United States a mendicant province in some U.N.-operated world government are determined to destroy the concept of national sovereignty.
This they hope to accomplish at the U.N. Charter Revision Conference
in 1956. . . .

. . . The current debate on the subject of United Nations Charter
revision has revealed a determined effort on the part of influential persons
and organizations to scuttle the sovereignty of the United States at the
proposed U.N. Charter Revision Conference in 1956 in favor of some form
of limited or full world government. In hearings before the Wiley subcommittee on U.N. Charter revision, many world government enthusiasts
have made it clear that they seek to transform the United Nations from
an organization of sovereign states into a superstate either by treaty or
by executive agreement, or if that is not feasible, by the even more
dangerous process of informal charter amendment, that is, by far-fetched
interpretation or by unwarranted usurpation of power.[17]

Some of the opposition that has developed to supranational proposals has probably been reflected in the opposition that has developed to the United Nations. Some believe that there is an element of supranationality in the United Nations. However, Ambassador Lodge, the United States Representative to the United
Nations, has remarked: "Those who fear that there is any danger of
a super-government in the United Nations are in error. . . . That

---

[17] *Congressional Record,* Vol. 100, Pt. 10, 83 Cong. 2 sess., pp. 13457-58.

suspicion is sheer fantasy and there is nothing to justify it in the theory or the practice of the United Nations."[18]

The proposals that are analyzed below have been advanced in good faith by individuals and organizations that believe international organization must move toward supranationality if peace is to be preserved and the calamity of a third world war averted. Although many people would reject these ideas as visionary and impractical, they cannot be disposed of merely by alleging that they would impair or destroy the concept of national sovereignty. They must be considered on their merits as well as from the point of view whether there is any reasonable chance of their acceptance. But it must be kept in mind that such plans would, in the case of the United States, require not only their approval by a treaty, but also an amendment of the Constitution. Some nations, however—but not the United States—have constitutional provisions that would permit them to join a supranational state.[19]

Proposals for World Federation

Proposals for world federation, if adopted, would have the immediate effect of virtually eliminating the nation-state system or the concept of state sovereignty on a world-wide basis. Such proposals upset the basic United Nations principle of sovereign equality. Three of the principal groups urging world federal government are the United World Federalists, the World Association of Parliamentarians for World Government, and the Committee to Frame a World Constitution.[20]

[18] Highlights of remarks of Henry Cabot Lodge, Jr., Annual Banquet of the Chamber of Commerce of Metropolitan St. Louis, Mo., Feb. 16, 1955. Mimeo.

[19] The 1946 Constitution of France states that, "On condition of reciprocity, France accepts the limitations of sovereignty necessary to the organization and defense of peace." Amos J. Peaslee, *Constitutions of Nations*, Vol. 2 (1950), p. 9. Italy, in its Constitution effective January 1948, provided that "Italy . . . on conditions of equality with the other states, agrees to the limitation of her sovereignty necessary to an organization which will assure peace and justice among nations. . . ." *Ibid.*, p. 280. The Bonn Constitution of Western Germany permits the transfer by legislation of sovereign power to international institutions. *Ibid.*, p. 29. The lower house of The Netherlands Parliament approved, on Dec. 2, 1952, constitutional amendments which would grant power to the Government to entrust legislative, administrative, and judicial authority to international organizations. *New York Times* (Dec. 3, 1952).

[20] For similar proposals, see Grenville Clark and Louis B. Sohn, *Peace Through Disarmament and Charter Revision* (Preliminary Print, July 1953). For discussion

Summary of Proposals

World federation plans are based on the general proposition that peace cannot be maintained so long as the world is organized as a group of sovereign, independent states. One policy statement, for example, notes that: "World peace can be created and maintained only under world law, universal and strong enough to prevent armed conflict between nations."[21] Another statement makes the point that:

The fundamental problem of regulating the relations between great powers without the permanent danger of major wars cannot be solved so long as absolute sovereign power continues to reside in the nation-states. Unless their sovereign institutions are integrated into higher institutions expressing directly the sovereignty of the community, unless the relations of their peoples are regulated by law, violent conflicts between national units are inevitable. . . .[22]

States must, therefore, so world federal groups argue, delegate to a world-wide supranational government sufficient authority to enact law and to enforce that law on constituent states and individual citizens of the world community.

Proposals for world federation have many common character-istics. They seek to create a world government based on a federal system, *i.e.,* that states delegate specific powers to a central world government but retain non-delegated, or residual, powers for them-selves. They are designed to be universal in appeal and membership. They propose world citizenship with the citizen subject directly to the authority of the federal government in those fields where it has power. They envisage a break with the historic system of inter-national organization—the system based on the concept of sovereign equality of nation-states. And, in general, they propose that the move toward world federation be started by amending the United Nations Charter.

Impact on United Nations

The amount of authority to be delegated to the world govern-ment would vary considerably depending on the plan under con-

---

of all such proposals, see "World Government," *Annals of the American Academy of Political and Social Science,* Vol. 264 (July 1949), pp. 1-114; and Edith Wynner, *World Federal Government* (1954).

[21] World Government House, "Policy Statement" (undated).

[22] Reves, *op. cit.,* p. 184.

sideration. The minimum delegation would give the federal government authority only in relation to the control, reduction, or elimination of armed force in relations between states. According to one authority:

The minimum structural requirements of World Government are plain enough. A World Government must have a monopoly of arms. It must be a federal government, so as to preserve the cultural values that now exist in the states and regions of the world. It must be a government which acts directly on the individual, wherever he may be; for otherwise it is merely a league of sovereign, and hence warlike states. But those are minimum structural requirements. . . .[23]

Or, as others put it: "If war is to be prevented in the modern age, *all* countries and *all* individuals must at *all* times be bound by world law against the use of violence between nations."[24]

The maximum delegation of power would be that which would in effect create a unitary type of world state. The Committee to Frame a World Constitution, for example, rejected the idea that world government could be limited in its powers to those related to the maintenance of security on the grounds that "peace and *justice* stand or fall together."[25] The committee argued that there can be no peace unless world government has power to manage those large segments of the world economy that affect the welfare of the inhabitants of the earth. The superstate must have power to change domestic institutions in individual states if it needs to do so in order to promote justice.

Between these extremes are the proposals of the United World Federalists, one of whose spokesmen has stated: "We do not advocate the creation of a world superstate with vast power to change the domestic institutions of the various nations and stamp out the differences between peoples and impose a common form of economic and social structure of the world."[26]

Another suggestion in the direction of a world state is that of the World Association of Parliamentarians for World Government.

[23] Extracts from a lecture by Robert M. Hutchins at the University of Denver, Oct. 13, 1947, "Constitutional Foundations of World Order," reprinted in *Congressional Digest* (August-September 1948), p. 204.

[24] Clark and Sohn, *op. cit.*, p. iii.

[25] Italics supplied. "Preliminary Draft of a World Constitution," *Common Cause* (July 1947).

[26] Cord Meyer, Jr., "A Plea for World Government," *Annals of the American Academy of Political and Social Science*, Vol. 264 (July 1949), p. 9.

According to reports, this group will seek to have the United Kingdom make a formal proposal at the tenth session of the General Assembly to give the United Nations control of the high seas and the sea bed and subsoil under the high seas. It is also proposed that the disputed Antarctic areas be declared United Nations territory. The group sees this proposal as "a way toward making the United Nations more effective. By leasing mineral rights below the bed (especially for oil) the United Nations would gain a substantial independent income of its own. In order to police its seas it would need a small naval force."[27]

There are practical problems that would have to be solved in order to give effect to this suggestion. It would be necessary to obtain the agreement of states on the limits of their territorial claims and to placing these potential resources under the control of the United Nations. The United States, for example, has claimed the mineral rights on the continental shelf that runs seaward about 100 miles; and Peru has claimed territorial jurisdiction 200 miles to sea. Steps taken in the direction suggested would give the United Nations some of the attributes of a state.

Proponents of world federation generally agree, however, that even a minimum world government must have reliable sources of revenue. They suggest therefore that the organization be given power to levy taxes as distinguished from the authority merely to make requisitions on the constituent states.[28] Also there is general agreement, and this is a characteristic of most of the proposals, that the central government should have direct authority over individuals with respect to those matters that have been delegated to the central government. Although proposals for world federation differ with regard to the extent of the power that would be so delegated, there is no doubt that, if any of them were to become effective, the world of the nation-state as we know it today would cease to exist.

The proponents of world federation insist that if their plans are to be successful, membership must be virtually universal. Indeed, if

[27] *Manchester Guardian Weekly* (Mar. 31, 1955), p. 9.

[28] See, for example, the statement of Alan Cranston, President of the United World Federalists in 1950: "No government can exist without the power to raise sufficient funds to sustain its functions, for it cannot survive on the basis of voluntary hand-outs from its members." *Revision of the United Nations Charter,* Hearings before a Subcommittee of the Senate Committee on Foreign Relations, 81 Cong. 2 sess., p. 524. Also see below Chap. XIV.

all states did not become members, the grand design of federation to eliminate war might fail because states outside it might continue to equip themselves with armaments and resort to aggressive tactics. Moreover, failure of all states to become parties to the federation might give it the appearance of being a coalition of states federating for the purpose of destroying the independence of the remaining nations. Several of the plans consequently advocate compulsory membership on the part of *all* states and prohibit secession from the federation. A former official of the United World Federalists stated: "If any nation were allowed to secede the world would again face an arms race."[29]

If the assumption is granted that most of the rest of the world would be willing to join a world federation, the question has been raised whether the Soviet Union would also join. If it should refuse to join, the Communists would undoubtedly view world federation as an instrument directed against them. If the Soviet Union should join, the struggle for the hearts and minds of men might simply be transferred from the nation-state level to the world government level. Proponents of world federation generally take the view that failure to obtain Soviet agreement on disarmament, on supplying forces to the United Nations, and similar matters within the United Nations framework does not necessarily mean that it would be impossible to arrive at agreement within some new framework. Furthermore, it is argued, if the Soviet Union were to see the world organizing as a federation without Communist participation, the Soviet Union would be compelled to join the organization in its own interest.

Most of the plans for world federation accept the United Nations as a first step toward world government. Some proponents, for example, advocate a series of specific amendments to the Charter, although they recognize that, if the proposed amendments were accepted, the result would be a "complete revision of the Charter and a complete change in the character of the United Nations. Under the revision the United Nations, instead of being essentially a league of independent states retaining their respective sovereignties almost unmodified, would become a true federation."[30] The United World Federalists would accomplish their objective by

[29] See statement of Alan Cranston, *Revision of the United Nations Charter,* Senate Hearings, p. 521; see also Clark and Sohn, *op. cit.,* p. 13.
[30] *Ibid.,* p. 141.

"making use of the amendment processes of the United Nations to transform it into such a world federal government."[31] The proposals of the Committee to Frame a World Constitution go so far toward the creation of a unitary type of world state, however, that it might be difficult as a practical matter to achieve the aims through any process of amending the Charter. But the proponents of world federation generally insist that nothing should be done that would destroy or impair the effectiveness of the United Nations at least until something better can be established to take its place.

Implications of Proposals

Those who support world federation urge that mankind has no other course if the world is to survive atomic war. But many who question the feasibility of federation proposals do so on the ground that it is impossible to have world government and world law unless and until there is a world community. One commentator has observed:

The creation of any world state is more likely to be the result of an evolutionary development. In any particular stage of development law must have roots in these social and political realities or be reduced to the fatuity of a Kellogg Pact. . . .

. . . In fine, any belief that by setting up a world state, making its laws directly applicable to individuals, passing laws to solve problems which have baffled the efforts of men since the beginning of time, and devising automatic sanctions for their enforcement, any such belief rests upon the greatest assumption of all, namely, that human nature and the world upon which the world state emerges will already have changed so as to ease the tasks of world government.[32]

Another critic has suggested that there are still those who propose a quick total solution by total organization of the world. He believes they rely on the federal form because of a misunderstanding of the federal system of the United States, which is based on the power of the central authority to guarantee the republican form of government in all the states. There is no such authority in the world community, and the elements of a federal state or a constituency at the world

[31] United World Federalists, Beliefs, Purposes and Policies (November 1947), p. 1.
[32] Herbert W. Briggs, "The Problem of World Government," American Journal of International Law, Vol. 41 (January 1947), pp. 109, 111.

level do not exist.[33] Thus, while proponents of world federation believe a world government is possible because necessity leaves no other course, skeptics urge that "what is manifestly impossible . . . is a waste of time to regard as necessary."[34] In a similar vein, the Senate Committee on Foreign Relations has observed: "There would be no assurance that in a true world federation Communist and Fascist parties would not, even though representing a minority of the people in the world, be able to obtain control of the world government."[35]

If the ideological conflict between democracy and communism is at the basis of the cold war and poses the danger of a hot war, is there any assurance that the conflict could be decided by a worldwide plebiscite or by the parliament of a world government in the same way the American people decide between presidential candidates, the minority being willing to abide by the decision of the electorate? At the moment, even if Americans were willing to acquiesce in such decisions, it is doubtful whether the Soviet Union would peacefully accept the principle of majority rule.[36]

The participation of the United States in a world federation unquestionably would require amendment of the United States Constitution with respect to such matters as the authority of Congress to provide for the common defense and general welfare, to declare war, and to raise and support armies. Other amendments would be required to delimit the authority of the Executive Branch and the

[33] C. B. Marshall, unpublished lecture delivered at Hollins College (Oct. 10, 1953).

[34] Bernard Brodie, "The Atomic Dilemma," *Annals of the American Academy of Political and Social Science,* Vol. 249 (January 1947), p. 35.

[35] S. Rept. 2501, 81 Cong. 2 sess., p. 30. It must be remembered that communism envisages a universal state but of a different kind. As one observer points out: "If those who are suspicious of Russia's policy interpret correctly the plans of the Soviet government and the role assigned in these plans to the Communist parties of the various states outside Russia, then there exists a political movement having as its goal the establishment of a type of world government which by many adherents of the world-state idea . . . is regarded as undesirable even if it should produce universal peace. . . ." Walter Schiffer, *The Legal Community of Mankind: A Critical Analysis of the Modern Concept of World Organization* (1954), p. 295.

[36] See, for example, "In Defense of the Basic Principles of the United Nations," *News,* A [Soviet] Review of World Events (Oct. 1, 1953), p. 5, as translated from *Trud,* Moscow: "Those forces in America who would convert the United Nations into a sure-fire weapon of American policy, into an instrument for imposing that policy on other nations, have repeatedly attacked the Charter, and especially the principle of unanimity. . . ."

Judiciary. There may even be some question whether the United States could, by constitutional amendment, relinquish authority reserved to the states and to the people by the Tenth Amendment and turn that authority over to a world organization.[37]

It has been suggested that it cannot be known whether plans for world federation are possible or practical until they have been tried. Two points need to be kept in mind in this connection. First, if there should be an attempt on the part of governments to work out a plan for world federation, they would be justified in doing so only if assured that there was substantial world-wide support by states and individuals, for their effort. Second, if progress should be made to the point where some type of world federation were to come into existence, it might be virtually impossible for states to reconsider their action. One of the first steps to be tried, for example, might be to reduce, and perhaps to eliminate, national armed forces. But if this step were taken, and it then turned out that the world federal government sought to curtail individual liberty in the interest of the world state, as might be the case in the event of dictatorial control of the instruments of government, it would be too late for constituent states to take effective action in defense of individual liberty.

The idea of world federation does not seem to have the degree of support in the United States that it had several years ago. Such proposals had their greatest appeal in the United States during those years immediately after the war when the United Nations was found to be incapable of resolving fundamental disagreements among the great powers and while the hope was still alive that many of the issues among those powers were capable of solution, provided proper procedures or an instrumentality for that purpose could be devised.

One of the most important cornerstones of the United Nations, however, the assumption of the unanimity of the major powers, has proved fallacious. And as it has not been possible to obtain such unanimity with respect to holding free elections in Korea, the control of armaments, or the making of armed forces available to the Security Council, the question arises: How is it possible to expect unanimity in an organization with far greater power than that possessed by the United Nations?

[37] For brief discussion see "Proposals for Now Revising the United Nations into a Federal World Government," *Congressional Digest*, Vol. 27 (August-September 1948), p. 197.

It has been suggested that the larger the organization, the lower the common denominator in terms of governmental authority; the more universal a world organization is in concept, the greater the difficulty in reaching agreement to give the organization power. Proponents of world federation seek to do two difficult things simultaneously. They propose a universal organization, and at the same time they propose to give that organization greater power than has ever before been wielded by even a regional organization, let alone a world organization.

As one observer has pointed out:

If the inhabitants of Mars or another planet suddenly descended upon the earth and threatened to conquer, all the nations of our small world would immediately get together. . . . Are we certain that the unleashing and national use of atomic energy, the apocalypse of an atomic world war, is not an equal threat to our civilization and to mankind, imperatively requiring us to rise above our outdated international conflicts and to organize human society politically so that an atomic world war could be checked?[38]

Another observer, however, has written that:

Virtually all arguments for world government rest upon the simple presupposition that the desirability of world order proves the attainability of world government. Our precarious situation is unfortunately no proof, either of the moral ability of mankind to create a world government by an act of the will, nor of the political ability of such a government to integrate a world community in advance of a more gradual growth of the "social tissue" which every community requires more than government.[39]

There is thus doubt whether a substantial number of people throughout the world have yet accepted the proposition that the precarious situation requires the surrender of national sovereignty to some form of supranational organization.

The "ABC" Plan

The so-called "ABC Plan," sponsored by the Citizens Committee for United Nations Reform, might be considered by some as a proposal for a type of world federal government. Its emphasis is not on the application of world law to world citizens, but rather it is almost exclusively on creating a situation in which internationally controlled force could be directed against an aggressor. Neverthe-

---

[38] Reves, *op. cit.*, p. 247.
[39] Reinhold Niebuhr, *Christian Realism and Political Problems* (1953), p. 25.

less, the creation of force subject to international control, as distinguished from national control, is in derogation of one of the most important elements of national sovereignty.

Summary of Plan

Proponents of the ABC Plan suggest amendments to the United Nations Charter that would (1) eliminate the great power veto; (2) limit the manufacture of weapons by quantity and type so that they could not be used for aggressive purposes; and (3) create a United Nations police force, backed by national contingents, capable by joint action of preventing aggression. In the event amendments designed to accomplish these purposes could not be adopted by the United Nations because of the refusal of the Soviet Union to participate, the plan contemplates that steps should be taken immediately to create, under Article 51 of the Charter, a world-wide pact along the lines of the North Atlantic Treaty. It would thus be possible for states desiring to do so to build overwhelming power based on the principle of enforceable law against aggression.

Specific amendments of the Charter would abolish the veto with respect to matters concerning aggression and preparation for aggression. Membership and voting procedures of the Security Council would be changed to maintain the voting advantages of the great powers, but their right of veto would be restricted. There would also be created an "impartial" World Court to interpret the revised United Nations Charter—thus giving the Court a power it does not now have. The result of these changes would be to establish two world laws, one a law against aggression and the other a law against preparation for aggression. These two fundamental laws, interpreted by the Court, would then be enforced against states and individuals. The Security Council, without the veto in these matters, would be the instrument to decide on methods of enforcement.

Supporters of the ABC Plan believe that unless firm, quick action is taken now to give the United Nations, or such of the international community as may be willing to accept the proposal, power to prevent war, those whose "avowed purpose is a Communist world-state and who have proclaimed the United States their Enemy Number One" will bring on the third world war.[40]

[40] Ely Culbertson, *Revision of the United Nations Charter*, Senate Hearings, pp. 190-226.

It is suggested therefore that, if the Soviet Union does not accept these amendments and continues to build atomic weapons, the remaining members of the Security Council might "declare Russia a threat to the peace of the world and an aggressor. Russia then will be given an ultimatum: either to stop atomic armament by submitting to the reasonable international control and inspection prevailing for all other states, or to evacuate her industrial centers in expectation of immediate atomic coercion. At the same time, the door will be left wide open for Russia to rejoin the [revised] U.N. as a permanent member."[41]

The ABC Plan differs from world federation proposals in several important respects. Proponents do not suggest such substantial changes in the nation-state system as do supporters of world federation. Except with respect to the maintenance of armed forces, control of the production of military equipment, and the surrender of the veto power relating to matters involving aggression, the Member states would continue to exercise the powers they now have. Supporters of the plan claim they do not advocate world citizenship, with the citizen directly responsible to the world government, except in connection with acts of aggression. Although the proposal is couched in terms inviting universal membership, there is a clear alternative provided in case the Soviet Union should seek to stay outside the Organization—an element missing from most world federation suggestions.

The proponents of the ABC Plan believe that peace can be assured by eliminating the veto with respect to matters of aggression and giving the Security Council power to control the use of force in the relations of states. They do not advocate going beyond these important, but narrow, limits. They are not especially concerned with removing the causes of tension, or with promoting justice on a world-wide scale. Emphasis is on the planned use of international force as a deterrent to aggression. Most proponents of world government, on the other hand, think in terms of other types of power to be exercised by the world state, ranging from the power to tax for limited purposes to the power to compel individuals to comply with a lengthy bill of rights.

[41] Ely Culbertson, "The ABC Plan for World Peace," *Readers' Digest* (June 1948), p. 85. One of the unique elements of the ABC proposal is the so-called quota force plan, designed to permit the great powers to have enough armed force to protect themselves from attack by any other great power and yet not enough force to undertake aggression successfully. That plan is described in detail later in this volume. See below, Chap. VI.

Impact on the United Nations

In terms of the principle of sovereign equality, the ABC proposals would limit only those elements related to the size of military forces that could be retained by Member states. If the Soviet Union should not accept the plan, however, there would presumably be no limit on the forces of members until the Soviet "threat to the peace" had been eliminated. References in the ABC Plan to elimination of the veto seem to be predicated on the proposition that the only state that would have occasion to use the veto would be the Soviet Union—a proposition that is not even acceptable today so far as the United States is concerned.

So far as loss of sovereignty by the United States under this proposal is concerned, the armed forces of the United States might conceivably be committed to international action against its wishes. This is not too clear, however, as "national contingents" would remain under national control—subject to "constitutional processes,"—despite the abolition of the veto.

With respect to membership in the United Nations, it would continue as it now is. But there seems to be a strong presumption that the Soviet Union would not accept the ABC Plan and that the Organization might need to go ahead without the membership of the Soviet Union. It is suggested, however, that if the revised organization should obtain its collective defense organization operating under a Council without the veto, "Russia will soon realize that it is to her best interests to join the family of nations in banishing war from the face of the earth."[42]

Implications of the Plan

Of all the proposals discussed here, the ABC Plan seems most clearly to challenge the Soviet Union. It would risk war on the theory that if the risk is not taken now, war will surely come later. It does so at a time when even democratic nations with a common heritage have not been willing to share important atomic secrets among themselves. A first step to indicate that the ABC Plan may be practical would be the exchange of important atomic military information between one or two of the great powers—a step that the United States has not yet taken.

[42] Citizens Committee for United Nations Reform, *The Case for United Nations Revision and Progress Report* (1949), pp. 12-13.

The part of the ABC Plan that contemplates a world-wide pact under the terms of Article 51 of the Charter in the event the fundamentals of the plan are not accepted, is similar in some procedural respects to the Article 51 pact considered later in this study. Such a world-wide pact, however, would presumably become an instrument for a "showdown with Soviet Russia." The Senate resolution advancing this concept calls for creating "a united world front of all cooperating nations, in possession of overwhelming atomic and military power," so that it "shall avert, by firm action now, the Third World War later. . . ."[43] If the world-wide pact is to become an instrument of a showdown, it is vastly different from the Article 51 pact, which is designed as a method of eliminating the veto with respect to the enforcement provisions of the Charter.

The ABC Plan needs to be scrutinized most carefully to see whether it may not in fact advocate a "preventive war" in order to avoid another world war. The Senate Committee on Foreign Relations in its report of 1950 noted that the proposals "might lead to the inference that war is to be prevented by threatening to start one."[44] It seems doubtful whether this plan would find wide acceptance among Members of the United Nations. Those Members that believe war may be avoided in the future only within a context of peaceful coexistence are not likely to subscribe to planned amendments to the Charter that would be imposed on reluctant Members by force if necessary.

Proposal for Federal Union

A movement to establish a federal union of the United States and other leading democracies originated in 1939 based largely on a proposal of Clarence K. Streit. Groups of supporters formed committees that led to the organization in 1940 of Federal Union, Inc. The organization survived the war and the peace that created the United Nations. It has a continuity of membership unrivaled by other organizations proposing supranational plans for government.[45]

[43] S. Res. 133, 81 Cong. 1 sess. See below, Chap. VI.

[44] S. Rept. 2501, 81 Cong. 2 sess., p. 32.

[45] Although Federal Union was organized in 1940 for the purpose of education in the principles of federal union, subsequently, in 1949, the Atlantic Union Committee was organized to engage in political action looking toward holding a convention to explore the possibilities of applying the principles of federal union to the Atlantic area.

Summary of Proposal

Federal Unionists urge that the United Nations system be strengthened by creating, totally independent of the Charter, a federal union comprising initially the United States, Canada, Great Britain, France, The Netherlands, Belgium, and Luxembourg. These countries would meet together in a federal convention to draft a constitution delegating to the new union authority with respect to the creation of a defense force, the control of foreign policy, the creation of a free market, and the establishment of monetary, postal, and tax systems.[46] This plan would create a new type of state somewhat along the lines of the United States. It would have generally less power than was given by the original thirteen states to the federal government, but would encompass a vastly larger land area and population.

The general framework of the Atlantic Union plan is found in Senate Concurrent Resolution 57 of the Eighty-first Congress. That resolution outlined the experience of the United States in developing a federal state and requested the President to "invite the democracies which sponsored the North Atlantic Treaty" to send delegates to a "federal convention to explore how far their peoples and the peoples of such other democracies as the convention may invite to send delegates, can apply among them, and within the framework of the United Nations, the principles of free federal union."[47] Supporters of this proposal have prepared sample draft constitutions for purposes of study and comment. They recognize, however, that within this broad framework, the details would need to be filled in by a convention to draft a constitution.

It is probable that many of the advocates of Atlantic Union would support the more far-reaching objectives of the Federal Union move-

[46] See Clarence K. Streit, *Union Now* (postwar ed., 1949); S. Con. Res. 57, 81 Cong. 2 sess.; *Revision of the United Nations Charter,* Senate Hearings, pp. 227-315.

[47] For latest version see S. Con. Res. 12, 84 Cong. 1 sess., favoring the calling of an Atlantic Exploratory Convention. This resolution introduced by Senator Kefauver for himself and 14 other senators places more emphasis on the "exploratory" nature of the proposed convention, relates it to the North Atlantic Treaty instead of to the federal convention of 1787, and calls on the delegates (to be named by governments but to vote as individuals) "to report to what extent their peoples might further unite within the framework of the United Nations, and agree to form, federally or otherwise, a defense, economic, and political union." For description of differences between this resolution and earlier ones see *Freedom & Union,* Vol. 10 (February 1955), pp. 1-3.

ment. Some would not be willing to go that far, at least until an exploratory conference is convened in order to determine the extent to which the principles of federal union might be practicable among the democratic countries of the North Atlantic area. This prime objective of the Atlantic Union movement—the holding of an exploratory conference—appears to be acceptable to the Federal Union group as the first essential step in their longer-range program.

Considerable emphasis is placed on the practicability of the proposal on the grounds that it seeks initially to bring together peoples with a common heritage and belief in democracy. As the union would be based on a substantial community of interests, it is suggested that it would be feasible to give the proposed central government a degree of authority that people might be far more reluctant to grant to a supranational government not based on such common interests. In the words of one of the principal proponents of Federal Union, it would be designed:

(a) To provide effective common government in our democratic world in those fields where such common government will clearly serve man's freedom better than separate governments, (b) to maintain independent national governments in all other fields where such government will best serve man's freedom, and (c) to create by its constitution a nucleus world government capable of growing into universal world government peacefully and as rapidly as such growth will best serve man's freedom.[48]

Although this idea does not involve amendment of the Charter, the creation of a federal union including the membership suggested would have a tremendous impact on the United Nations system. Supporters of the proposal contend that the United Nations is valuable to the world as a town meeting device, but is not able to preserve peace. Peace can be achieved, they claim, only by building a preponderance of power, and a safe preponderance of power can be built only by uniting the democracies. They envisage the union as a nucleus that might grow much as the United States did and that might eventually become a world government. But until it becomes a world government, it would be a Member of the United Nations.[49] Those who support the proposal maintain that "None of the countries who formed NATO abandoned the United Nations; nor would they do so if that alliance were transformed into a Fed-

[48] Streit, *Union Now*, p. 4.
[49] *Freedom & Union*, Vol. 7 (March 1952), p. 9.

eral Union. Unlike NATO, however, the Union would itself be a member of the United Nations—its strongest member."[50] It is assumed that the present voting power now enjoyed by the several prospective members of the Union would still be retained following the precedent established by the three votes of the Soviet Union. Proponents note that the Soviet Union could not veto the formation of the union. It could presumably, however, veto the admission of the union as such into the United Nations. In that event, the separate states belonging to the union would continue their present membership in the United Nations and vote with the unanimity that is evidenced among members of the Soviet bloc.

Precedent for federal union is allegedly found in the formation of the United States of America. The success of the Swiss, Australians, and the Canadians in forming federal unions is also cited as reason for believing that a similar project might be undertaken on a larger scale. It is pointed out further that the North Atlantic Treaty has already involved some of the potential members of a federal union in commitments to strengthen their free institutions and to encourage economic collaboration.[51]

Impact on the United Nations

The fundamental principle underlying the proposal for federal union is basically different from that underlying the United Nations Charter. Federal union would not be an organization of nation-states based on the principle of sovereign equality as is the United Nations. Instead, it would be a supranational government of limited powers exercising its authority directly on the citizens of the constituent countries. Sovereignty, in the concept of the supporters of the plan, would reside in the people.

Although proponents contemplate that the federal union would leave member states free to exercise many powers themselves, and mention is made of "independent national governments" in limited fields, the proposed union would go far beyond any existing international organization in establishing a new type of superstate. At

[50] Clarence K. Streit, *Freedom Against Itself* (1954), pp. 215-16.

[51] See suggestion by 169 prominent citizens from eight North Atlantic countries that the North Atlantic Treaty Organization be developed "as a central agency to coordinate the political, trade and defense policies of the member nations," and recommending the "creation of an advisory Atlantic Assembly, representative of the legislatures of the member nations, which would meet periodically to discuss matters of concern." *New York Times* (Oct. 4, 1954).

its inception, such a federal union would not upset the existing nation-state system except for those states that would be charter members of the union. They would merge their national entities into a larger unit, but, if and as the federal union grew, it would eliminate national states, substituting for them a world federal state. In such circumstances, it is argued, the time would come when there would be no need for the United Nations, and presumably it would cease to exist.

This proposal, by placing emphasis on a union of the democratic countries, geographic contiguity, and substantial delegations of power to a central government, contemplates an organization with a limited membership. The concept of universal membership would necessarily remain far in the future, and could not be realized until the ideas of democracy are widely accepted.

The criteria for admission to federal union are far more severe than those prescribed by the Charter for admission to the United Nations. To be a "peace-loving" state is not enough. A candidate state must be willing not merely to accept the relatively mild provisions of the Charter that preserve the individuality and the power of the nation-state, but, to be invited to participate in federal union, the state must be democratic, must border on the Atlantic, and must be willing to surrender substantial portions of its national identity and power. The price of membership is high, the contemplated rewards are great.

It would seem that only in a situation in which likeminded, relatively contiguous, states find compelling reasons to merge certain governmental powers in their mutual interest would it be possible, by peaceful means, to propose, with any chance of success, the delegation to a central authority of powers as broad as those contemplated in the proposal for a federal union. The formation of any government that has power of life or death over individuals requires a mutuality of interest and confidence that does not exist among any substantial group of nation-states today—perhaps not even among the North Atlantic states that proponents suggest might form the nucleus of an Atlantic Union.

Implications of Proposal

The idea of a federal union of democracies patterned along the lines of the American experience has intrigued many people, who point out that the United States is far stronger as a nation today than it would have been had there been no union. But in measuring the practicability of the proposal for a federal union, several considerations must be kept in mind. Although the proposal has strong appeal to those who believe the United Nations is incapable of preserving peace, it is possible that creation of such a union might raise as many problems as it seeks to solve.

An initial question to be raised is whether the trend in the world today as between states is centrifugal or centripetal. Among colonial areas the drive of nationalism is centrifugal in its impact. But it may be that among the older nation-states, the trend is toward unity. Recent experience with the Council of Europe and the European Defense Community, however, has not been encouraging for those who would promote a supranational concept on a limited scale. Even a limited union of the United States and Canada in the first instance does not seem to be a possibility at present. Furthermore, so far as the United States is concerned, it could not join a federal union without amending the Constitution. Although this is not an impossible impediment, it is clear that federal union would need a much wider basis of public support than it now has among the American people.

It must be recognized, however, that people have a strong tendency to draw together in order to defend themselves from what they believe is common danger. And that danger may exist today in atomic and hydrogen weapons. A sudden public realization that survival depends on the close unity of free peoples conceivably could have the effect of mustering great and quick support for proposals along the lines of federal union. The North Atlantic Treaty Organization is in some respects a move in the direction of establishing an Atlantic Union. Although military collaboration under an international command has been accepted during war, the North Atlantic Treaty Organization is the first international institution establishing an elaborate pattern for such collaboration in time of peace. It may well be a significant step toward a broader organization with political and economic aspects.

On the other hand, free trade within the area to be encompassed by the proposed federal union could be expected at the outset to cause widespread business dislocation. The extent of government control over, or actual participation in, business enterprise would be a difficult problem to settle in the light of present differences between socialist governments and the United States. Moreover, the relationship of colonial areas to constituent states or to the federal government would pose difficult questions for a federal union as it has in the United Nations, and problems relating to the free movement of persons between constituent states would raise many difficult questions, as would matters relating to taxation, the monetary system, and foreign policy.

It has been suggested in some quarters that creation of a federal union would widen the breach between the Communist and the non-Communist nations whereas the hope for peace must rest on bridging that gap. Certainly one of the fundamental questions currently is whether during the next decades it will be possible for democracy and communism to live side by side or whether one or the other must prevail by force of arms or of ideas. Some would argue that in either eventuality, freedom would be more likely to survive if it were organized into a federal union. It should be noted, however, that a vigorous attempt to create now a powerful federal union might be construed by the Communist states as the beginning of an attempt to create a "world empire," and the Communist nations might feel compelled to organize their defenses against such a creation.

The supranational proposals considered above are blueprints for extensive overhauling of the United Nations system. They do not recommend small or faltering steps toward world government nor do they seek simple modernization of the United Nations structure. They propose to erect a new building on a new foundation. The principle of sovereign equality of states, they urge, is not an adequate foundation for a peaceful world.

These proposals have been conceived because of the belief of their proponents that the United Nations is incapable, as presently organized, of maintaining the peace, or, if war should come, of ensuring victory for the forces of freedom. War, they believe, is inevitable unless the international community is organized in such a way as to make it possible for all nations to disarm or, on the other hand, for overwhelming force to be applied against an aggressor. They agree that the freedom of nation-states to use force as an instrument of national policy must be abridged to some extent and that power to use force must be transferred from the individual nation-state to a combination of states.

They are not in agreement, however, on the amount of power or authority that must be delegated to the supranational government. They are not agreed on the way in which power is to be transferred to a world government—whether it is to be transferred by the negotiation of a multilateral treaty, by amendment of the Charter, or by the calling of a conference of representatives of peoples throughout the world. They are not agreed whether states or individuals are to be brought into the organization by persuasion or coercion or whether the organization should be universal or regional, based on a common ideology or geographic contiguity or both.

In assessing these proposals to determine which, if any, might help maintain peace and ensure the freedom of man, several considerations need to be kept in mind. A close examination must be made of the basic assumption of the supranationalists that nation-states must give up power to a supranational organization if peace is to be preserved. Also, it must be questioned whether it is true that sovereign states dealing on a basis of legal equality cannot agree voluntarily to abstain from war, or cannot agree to a reduction of armaments with effective instrumentalities for inspection. Belligerents did not use gas in the last war because of fear of retaliation or because they did not believe it was in their national interest to do so. Furthermore, the prospects of another war in which nuclear weapons would be used may be so terrifying as to make states unwilling to risk it. As Sir Winston Churchill has recently suggested, the world may have a "peace of mutual terror."

It may be questioned whether world government proposals are practical in the sense that the majority of the people of the United States, for example, would be willing to accept them. Citizens may be able to control to some extent their destiny in time of war by sacrifices to help their government wage war. But it is uncertain whether they could control a supranational organization in possession of world-wide instrumentalities of government, including armed forces, especially if these instrumentalities should fall into the hands of representatives of a minority or a tyrant. There is no assurance that these supranational proposals, if adopted, would lead to democratic government.

In this connection, what seem to be contradictory trends in the concept of world government may be noted. In some parts of the world, as in Asia and Africa, colonial empires are disintegrating, and the emphasis is on an increasing number of sovereign independent states. In other areas, such as Western Europe, states are in the process of surrendering elements of their national sovereignty to supranational organizations for economic or collective defense purposes. But it is uncertain at present whether the future will bring more emphasis on national sovereignty or on world government, or perhaps on some combination of these seemingly contradictory trends.

CHAPTER IV

Scope and Qualifications of Membership

T HE problem of membership has been an irritating one for the United Nations since 1946 when the Soviet Union vetoed the admission of Jordan, Portugal, and Ireland even though these states met the criteria of the Charter for admission as interpreted by the vast majority of Member states. Today the problem has reached serious proportions. The effectiveness of the United Nations will be impaired so long as many countries, including such great states as Italy, Japan, and Germany, remain outside the Organization.

Over a nine-year period, thirty applications for membership have been received. Of these only nine have been approved. Five applications, those of Albania, Bulgaria, Hungary, Rumania, and the Mongolian People's Republic, failed to receive even the majority of seven votes required for approval by the Security Council. The Council has refused to give serious consideration to applications for membership submitted by Viet Minh and North Korea. The rest, fourteen in all, have been rejected by a series of Soviet vetoes. The roll call of vetoed states is impressive: Austria, Ceylon, Cambodia, Finland, Ireland, Italy, Japan, Jordan, Laos, Libya, Portugal, Republic of Korea, Nepal, and Viet-Nam. The significant thing is that these applicants have been judged qualified for membership by the great majority of the Members of the United Nations. Only the Soviet veto stands in the way of their admission.[1]

Former Secretary of State James F. Byrnes, while a member of the United States Delegation to the General Assembly in 1953, noted that: "Our Organization will never speak with full authority until it speaks for ALL peace-loving nations."[2] A few months later,

[1] For a more detailed discussion of membership see the volume in this Brookings series, *The Organization and Procedures of the United Nations*. For a list of the current Members of the United Nations, see App. C. of the present volume.

[2] Statement by James F. Byrnes, U. S. Delegation to the General Assembly, Press Release 1766 (Oct. 5, 1953); reprinted in Subcommittee on the United Nations Charter, Senate Committee on Foreign Relations, *Review of the United Nations Charter: A Collection of Documents*, S. Doc 87, 83 Cong. 2 sess. (Jan. 7, 1954), pp. 415-16.

Secretary of State Dulles told a Senate subcommittee: "It is useful that there be an organization which is, generally speaking, universal and whose processes run throughout the world. Otherwise the association takes on the character merely of an alliance. . . . Doubtless, at the Charter Review Conference, consideration will be given to these problems of universality or limited membership. It will perhaps be considered whether Article 4 . . . expresses the desirable standards for membership."[3]

Provisions of the Charter

Article 4 of the Charter provides that membership in the United Nations is open to "all" peace-loving states that accept the obligations of the Charter and, "in the judgment of the Organization, are able and willing to carry out these obligations"; and that admission to membership "will be effected by a decision of the General Assembly upon the recommendation of the Security Council."

This article has given rise to problems of interpreting both qualifications and procedures. In regard to qualifications for membership, it was agreed at the San Francisco Conference that the article not only requires an applicant to declare itself a "peace-loving" state, but before admission "it is also necessary to prove two things: that a nation is ready to accept and fulfill the obligations of the Charter and that it is able to accept and fulfill them."[4] In regard to procedures for admission, one problem concerns the interpretation of the provision that the "decision of the General Assembly" on the matter of membership is to be "upon the recommendation of the Security Council." From a mere reading of the Charter, it is not clear whether the Assembly can act only when the Council makes an affirmative recommendation, or whether the Assembly can act on the basis of a negative recommendation by the Council. It is also not clear whether the negative vote of one of the five permanent members of the Council is sufficient to prevent the Council from submitting a recommendation on membership to the Assembly.[5]

[3] *Review of the United Nations Charter,* Hearings before a Subcommittee of the Senate Committee on Foreign Relations, 83 Cong. 2 sess., Pt. 1, p. 6.

[4] U.N. General Assembly, Seventh Session, Second Part, *Drafting of the Provisions of Article 4 of the Charter (Admission of New Members),* Doc. A/AC.64/L.1 (Apr. 22, 1953).

[5] See Hans Kelsen, *The Law of the United Nations* (1951), pp. 57 ff.

The application of the provisions of Article 4 has not been an easy task. Legitimate questions have been raised about the interpretation of the *qualifications* for membership as well as about the interpretation of the *procedures* for admission. Most of the arguments of the past years, however, have reflected disagreements motivated to some extent by political considerations fundamentally unrelated to the meaning of the words in Article 4. The approval or disapproval of the applications of certain states for membership has been directly related to the cold war.

The only way a "peace-loving" state "able and willing to carry out" the obligations of the Charter can be admitted to the Organization is for it to obtain seven affirmative votes in the Security Council including the affirmative votes of all permanent members, plus the votes of two thirds of the members of the General Assembly. The adverse vote of one member of the Council with the veto power is sufficient to exclude any applicant. The negative votes of any five members of the Council can also prevent it from making an affirmative recommendation of membership to the Assembly and thus prevent that body from acting on an application.

Despite the statement in Article 4 that membership is open to "all" peace-loving states, the other requirements for membership, and the year-to-year practices of the United Nations have resulted in the creation of an organization that has many of the elements of an exclusive club. Election is not dependent on whether a state is "peace-loving" and able to carry out the obligations of the Charter, but rather on the society it keeps and the nature of its associations with either the Soviet Union or the Western powers. For as surely as a state has been sponsored for membership by the Western powers, its admission has been vetoed by the Soviet Union. And as surely as a state has been sponsored for membership by the Soviet Union, it has been confronted by at least seven votes against its admission by other members of the Security Council. With some twenty-one applicants unable to qualify for membership under the practice of the day, it cannot be said that the United Nations has many of the characteristics of a "universal" organization.[6]

---

[6] "The United Nations clearly falls into the category of associations selecting their members . . . in spite of the language . . . in Article 4 . . . proclaiming that 'Membership . . . is open. . . .'" Alexander W. Rudzinski, "Admission of New Members: The United Nations and the League of Nations," *International Conciliation* (April 1952), p. 144.

It is apparent that there are no generally accepted criteria of selectivity, except that the applicant must not be unacceptable to the Soviet Union on the one hand or to the free world on the other. The United Nations as an organization is thus neither universal nor selective. It has among its Members states that, if required to reapply for admission today, would be rejected by veto, or by adverse vote of the Council as unqualified. Membership has become one of the issues in the cold war. The impact of the cold war on applications for membership has left its indelible effect on the practice of the United Nations in the admission of new Members. Moreover, proposals to change the United Nations system with respect to membership have often been designed with considerations of the current conflict between the major powers uppermost in mind.

The deadlock on the admission of new Members has some serious consequences for the United Nations. Italy and Japan, although former enemy countries, are assuming a position of prime importance in the postwar world. Free Germany is on its way toward becoming an essential contributor to the defenses of Western Europe. And in the Far East and Middle East, the Republic of Korea, Cambodia, Laos, Viet-Nam, and Ceylon are states the counsel of which might contribute strength to the United Nations. The required majority of members of the General Assembly are willing to support the applications of most of the states that have applied for membership. But they have been kept out by the negative vote of the Soviet Union in the Security Council. The result of the exclusion of these states, nearly one third of the present membership if the five candidates sponsored for admission by the Soviet Union are included, is that many important matters cannot be dealt with within the United Nations framework. Their absence is one of the factors that may make it increasingly difficult for the United Nations to fulfill its role of encouraging peaceful settlement of disputes and maintaining international security.

It will be noted that many of the proposals to change the qualifications or requirements for admission to the United Nations are directed at devising methods to gain admittance for states qualified for admission in the opinion of at least two thirds of the Members of the Organization but denied admission by the Soviet veto. Much agitation for change in admission procedures or qualifications is based not so much on dissatisfaction with the existing standards and requirements of Article 4, as on misuse of the veto by the Soviet Union.

Proposals on Qualifications

Proposals to change the United Nations Charter with respect to the admission of Members fall broadly into two general types. First are those that might be described as "universalist" in tendency. They seek to make the United Nations, either in theory or in fact, into a more nearly universal organization than it now is. Included among suggestions of this type are those that, if accepted, would change the United Nations into a truly universal organization by eliminating virtually all criteria for membership and by simplifying procedures for admission. Others suggest that certain states, unable to gain admission as full-fledged Members, might be given an associate or an observer relationship to the Organization. The second general category of proposals might be described as "selective" in tendency. They seek either to restrict the United Nations to its present membership or to make it into an even more selective organization than it now is.

Admittedly, there is a degree of artificiality in dividing proposals into these broad types. The dividing line between those tending toward universality on the one hand, or toward selectivity on the other, must be drawn arbitrarily. For purposes of this study, the dividing line is fixed on the basis of the Organization as it now exists. Thus, if plans would tend to increase the number of Members in the Organization, they will be treated as universalist in principle. If they tend to decrease or limit the number of Members in the Organization, they will be treated as based on the principle of selectivity.

Universality

"Universality of membership" or the "principle of universality" as it applies to membership in an international organization has been a loosely used concept. Studies of the subject refer frequently to "the principle of universality" that underlies the United Nations Charter.[7] Although that principle may underlie the Charter, the

---

[7] See, for example, reference in draft resolution submitted by Peru referring to "the principle of universality which underlay the Charter." U.N. General Assembly, Eighth Session, *Report of the Special Committee on Admission of New Members*, Doc. A/2400 with Annexes (June 25, 1953), p. 2. This report contains frequent reference to the importance attached to the "principle of universality" and the repeated desire of Member states to make the United Nations as universal as possible.

United Nations is in fact far from a universal organization. Those who drafted the Charter at the San Francisco Conference did not endorse the proposal put forth by Uruguay and supported by several other Latin American states that "all communities should be members of the Organization and . . . their participation is obligatory."[8] Hence the Charter seems to reject universality as a basis of organization. In recent years, however, proponents of universality have been encouraged to put forth their proposals with renewed vigor because the Organization has been frustrated in its attempts to admit new Members.

When a child is born he automatically becomes a member of an organized community. The child of his own volition cannot reject membership. Duties are imposed and rights are acquired that cannot be denied. By analogy, it has been argued that all states, by being states, should automatically become members of any world-wide organization, and should not be permitted to withdraw from the organization. A truly universal international organization, then, would be a faithful reproduction, a mirror of the world of states as it exists at any given moment of history.

Among those who suggest that the United Nations should become a truly universal international organization are proponents of world federation or world government. Some, for example, believe that "a genuine system of world law, strong enough to guarantee peace, can be realized in no other way . . . every nation, without exception, shall, irrespective of its wishes, be subject to world law."[9] The Committee to Frame a World Constitution refers in its draft proposals to "the universal government of justice" that is to include everyone. It specifies that delegates are to be elected "by the people of all states and nations."[10]

Although generally this approach is confined to proponents of some form of world government, a spokesman for the American Association for the United Nations took a somewhat similar posi-

---

[8] U.N. Information Organizations and U. S. Library of Congress, *Documents of the United Nations Conference on International Organization*, Vol. 7 (1945), p. 325. (Hereinafter cited as *UNCIO Documents*.) See also S. Doc. 87, 83 Cong. 2 sess., pp. 364-72.

[9] Grenville Clark and Louis B. Sohn, *Peace Through Disarmament and Charter Revision* (Preliminary Print, July 1953), pp. 9-10. "All nations which now exist as independent states and any nation that may become an independent state in the future, shall be deemed members of the United Nations." *Ibid.*, p. 13.

[10] Robert M. Hutchins, "A Federal World Government Now?," *Congressional Digest*, Vol. 27 (1948), p. 202.

tion in 1950 when he suggested that as "each state is a member of the family of nations" it should be viewed as "a member of the United Nations." He continued: "To my thinking, automatic membership is the most important principle that must be adopted if the United Nations is to advance on the road to world government."[11]

A second group of proposals that tends strongly toward universality includes those suggesting that all states should be members of a world organization, provided they first accept the terms of the Charter or the instrument of the world organization. Membership would not be quite automatic. Proponents of this position speak in terms of "universal membership with non-secession of states" for "all States *which agree to accept the obligations* contained in the Charter."[12] The Copenhagen Declaration, proposing that the United Nations should be transformed into a world federal government, recommended, for example, that:

A. All states shall have a *right* to membership in the United Nations, *provided* they accept the terms of the Charter.
B. Once a state has been admitted into membership, it shall have no right of secession.
C. The Charter shall define what is a state.
D. The Secretary General of the United Nations shall be competent to decide whether an applicant is eligible within the terms of the Charter. His decision shall be subject to appeal to the International Court of Justice by either the aggrieved applicant or any member of the U.N.[13]

One of the plans considered by the Second London Parliamentary Conference on World Government, which recommended that membership should be "open to all states of the world, and all must be urged to join," rejected the "idea of compulsory initial adherence, since this might well involve war." This recommendation describes its approach as one of "voluntary universality of membership."[14] A second plan considered by the London group—a plan designed to

[11] Clark Eichelberger, National Director of the American Association for the United Nations, *Revision of the United Nations Charter,* Hearings before a Subcommittee of the Senate Committee on Foreign Relations, 81 Cong. 2 sess., p. 355.
[12] See "Copenhagen Proposals on UN Reform," *Catholic Association for International Peace,* Vol. 15 (October 1953), p. 5.
[13] See "World Congress Report: The Copenhagen Declaration," *The Federalist,* Vol. 3 (October 1953), p. 10. (Italics supplied.) See also "Copenhagen Shows the Way," Report on the World Congress on U.N. Charter Reform and the Fifth Annual Conference of the World Movement for World Federal Government, *Federal News* (September/October 1953), pp. 3-5, 16.
[14] See World Association of Parliamentarians for World Government, *Report of the Second London Parliamentary Conference on World Government* (Sept. 25, 1952), p. 100.

be politically feasible—proposed that Article 4 of the Charter should be amended to make membership "open to all States which accept the obligations contained in the Charter." There was to be no provision for withdrawal and, by inference, no requirement that applicants be voted into membership. The recommendation also proposed that Article 4 should define a "state" and that the interpretation of that clause should be left to the International Court of Justice and not to political decision.[15]

It is much easier to draft a plan to create a universal world organization than it is to make specific, practical proposals acceptable to states. Even though at the present time a number of states that want to join are excluded, it is doubtful that true universality could be achieved by any amendment of the United Nations Charter short of making the Organization into a supranational organization, able to force recalcitrant states into membership. It follows that a condition precedent to the existence of a truly universal organization would be the existence of sufficient power to compel recalcitrant states to accept the duties and responsibilities of membership inasmuch as it is conceivable that some sovereign entities might decide that they would prefer to live outside such a universal group rather than within it. The concept of true universality would seem to be realistic only within the framework of a supranational organization, supplemented by some device for determining when a political entity has the essential characteristics of a state. Theoretically, admission cannot be automatic no matter how limited the qualifications or simple the procedure so long as there is the question of determining whether the applicant is, or is not, a state. And the problem is not simplified materially by defining what is meant by the word "state," for the definition itself must be interpreted.

Those who propose universality are concerned with fitting the Soviet Union into the system. One such proposal, for example, notes that "this concept of universal membership presupposes a general East-West settlement."[16] A spokesman for the United World Federalists took the position in 1950 that the Soviet Union might "reject an honest attempt to give real legal authority and power to the United Nations," but at least, he felt, an effort should be made to bring it into the system.[17]

[15] *Ibid.*, p. 108.
[16] Clark and Sohn, *op. cit.*, p. 10.
[17] Statement by Cord Meyer, Jr., *Revision of the United Nations Charter*, Senate Hearings, 81 Cong. 2 sess., p. 130.

This, of course, poses probably the biggest problem to those who suggest that the United Nations should not only have more power, but should also be universal. Even if the free world were willing to grant the United Nations power to enact law and to compel obedience to law, it is most unlikely that the states in the Communist world would willingly come into an organization to which they would need to surrender control over their military establishment and at the same time be heavily outvoted. As noted above, the Second London Parliamentary Conference on World Government rejected the concept of compulsory membership on the grounds that it might involve war.

One final observation should be made with respect to the concept of universality in international organizations. If the United Nations were to become truly universal, with anything like compulsory membership, it would tend to be either supranational in character with power to compel all states to maintain the peace, or, it would be a loose association of states without much power. If states retain sovereign equality, it would seem to follow that their obligations as among themselves and with respect to the Organization would tend to decrease as membership increases, although as a practical matter the difference between a membership of sixty or eighty states would probably not be significant. On the other hand, the smaller the Organization, the more likely would be the existence of mutual confidence based on mutuality of interests. If this be true, the more universal an organization is that does not have its own force to preserve peace or prevent aggression, the more likely it is that it will have a membership requiring that serious defense planning be carried on outside the organization. As one commentator has suggested:

> Under modern technological conditions of warfare the effectiveness of any collective enforcement action depends substantially on advance planning and preparation. . . . Once the attack is launched in full force it may well be too late to counteract. . . . It would seem to follow that some advance planning and preparation must be done by a body which does not include the suspected country, once the first symptoms of a threat to the peace appear.[18]

Thus nations do not feel it is safe to rely on a universal organization to formulate plans and to protect them against a breach of the peace when the potential aggressor is a member of the organization.

[18] Rudzinski, *loc. cit.*, p. 102.

So it is that within the United Nations, cold-war suspicions have made it impossible to build a reliable general security mechanism with the result that many states look to Article 51 as authority for the organization of their collective defenses.

Simplification of Qualifications

Qualifications for membership under the Charter are simple. As has been noted above, the applicant must be a state, must be "peace-loving," must "accept the obligations" of the Charter, and must, in the judgment of the Organization, be "able and willing" to carry out its obligations under the Charter. Proposals to simplify these qualifications, however, encounter difficulty.

If the requirement that an applicant be a "state" is eliminated, the fundamental nature of the Organization might well be changed. It could no longer be an organization based on the principle of sovereign equality of states. Elimination of the criteria of statehood for membership would seem in effect to be a decision to create a supranational government with authority to bring its power directly to bear on individuals, not on states.

It might, of course, be possible to define the term "state" as something different from that which has normally been accepted by international law—a definition usually based on the concept that a sovereign state must satisfy certain minimum requirements such as control over a land area and having responsibility for the conduct of its foreign relations. The definition of the term was, for political reasons, stretched at the San Francisco Conference when the Ukrainian and Byelorussian Soviet Socialist Republics were accepted as original Members of the United Nations. But as all land areas, with the possible exception of the Antarctica, are already under the political dominion of some recognized, existing state, the possibility of redefining the term "state" in order to give it a special meaning with respect to membership in the United Nations is fraught with controversy.[19]

As it is now, the question whether an applicant is a "state" is, in effect, decided by the recommendation of the Security Council

[19] At the Second London Parliamentary Conference on World Government, M. Toussant (Belgium) moved to strike out the word "states" in the recommendations on membership, and insert in lieu thereof the word "peoples." This motion was rejected. *Report of the Second London Parliamentary Conference on World Government*, p. 128.

and the decision of two thirds of the General Assembly. Simplification of the procedures of admission by elimination of the veto or by reducing the size of the vote required in the Assembly might have as a collateral effect the admission of applicants that normally would not be viewed as states under current, accepted definitions of the term. There are other devices available that might have a similar effect. It might be provided, for example, that any applicant that had been recognized by twenty-five states (or some other appropriate number) as being a state, would automatically be a qualified applicant so far as the meaning of the word "state" in the Charter is concerned. Power might be delegated to some agency or individual outside the political influence of the Organization itself to determine whether a particular applicant was a "state," with the additional provision that such a decision might be appealed to the International Court of Justice.[20]

Provisions of this type would no doubt promote considerable controversy. A dependent area, for example, that believed it should be independent of its metropole might apply for membership in the United Nations over the objections of the metropole. A decision that such an applicant was a "state" within the meaning of Article 4 would have the effect of conferring on the United Nations authority to determine the self-governing status of all colonial territories.

If the constituent Soviet republics were to make unilateral declarations that they were ready, able, and willing to accept the obligations of the Charter, or if certain colonial areas were to declare their acceptance of the Charter, it is likely that many Members would believe that such action would be carrying the principle of universality too far. In the present climate of world affairs, any vote in a body such as the General Assembly, even on the narrow question whether an applicant meets the requirements of statehood, would be a political vote—conditioned not as much by the words of a definition as by the political consequences of admission or nonadmission of the applicant.[21]

---

[20] The Copenhagen Declaration calls for the Charter to "define what is a state" and for giving the Secretary-General competence to "decide whether an applicant is eligible." See *The Federalist* (October 1953), p. 10.

[21] For discussion of the effect of recognition of states by an international organization, see Hans Aufricht, "Principles and Practices of Recognition by International Organizations," *American Journal of International Law,* Vol. 43 (October 1949), pp. 679-704.

It has been suggested that, if the United Nations were to become a more universal type organization, the requirement that the applicant be "peace-loving" might be eliminated from Article 4.[22] But elimination of this qualification is of relatively little positive importance if applicants are still required to "accept the obligations" of the Charter. Article 2(3), for example, requires that: "All Members shall settle their international disputes by peaceful means in such a manner that international peace and security, and justice, are not endangered." And Article 2(4) requires that Members "shall refrain in their international relations from the threat or use of force against the territorial integrity or political independence of any state."

If elimination of the qualification "peace-loving" is to mean anything, it would appear necessary to qualify the requirement that applicants must accept the obligations of the Charter. It would also be necessary to eliminate the requirement that the Organization pass judgment on whether the applicant is "able and willing" to carry out the obligations of the Charter. There would be no basis on which to make a judgment as the obligations themselves would not have been accepted. If these qualifications were eliminated, the proposition logically would have to be accepted that a state is fully qualified for membership by making a simple, unilateral declaration that it will adhere to the Charter.[23] This, in effect, would amount to universality, except for the fact that states would presumably still be free to decide whether they wished to apply for membership in the Organization, and Member states would still need to approve such applications.

It seems doubtful whether, as a practical matter, the United Nations could be transformed into a more nearly universal organization by changing the qualifications for membership as set forth in Article 4(1), unless a decision is first reached that the fundamental nature of the Organization is to be changed by making it into a supranational organization with power to compel universality. Short of such a decision, any watering down of the qualifications for membership would raise more problems than it would solve. Furthermore, it would be strange indeed to drop the qualification of "peace-loving" so long as the main purpose of the Organization

---

[22] See Phillip C. Jessup, *A Modern Law of Nations* (1948), p. 49.
[23] See Kelsen, *op. cit.*, pp. 64-75.

is the maintenance of peace. Relinquishment of the right of Member states to judge whether applicants are able and willing to carry out the obligations of the Charter would leave the door open to such aggressor states as might, by their own free will, desire to join the Organization for their own purposes.

Proposals to Simplify Procedures for Admission

The ambiguities of Article 4(2) and questions regarding the applicability of the veto to membership applications leave wide room for interpretation. Despite the fact that these ambiguities have been resolved by practice, and practice has hardened into precedent, there have been continuous efforts to change the precedents.[24]

A number of proposals have been considered by the United Nations designed to open the door to applicants excluded from membership either by exercise of the veto or by inability to obtain the seven votes necessary to constitute an affirmative recommendation by the Security Council on which the General Assembly might act. After several successive meetings of the Assembly in which the membership question was extensively debated, a special committee of the Assembly was instructed in 1952 to make a study of "proposals and suggestions which had been made in the General Assembly" and elsewhere. The committee considered two groups of proposals, those aimed at a political solution of the impasse and those that "envisaged a solution . . . along the lines of interpretation of the Charter based on the view that the voting procedure of Article 27, paragraph 3, of the Charter did not apply to the admission of new Members and that under Article 4, paragraph 2, it was for the Council to make recommendations but for the General Assembly to decide."[25]

Restricting the Use of the Veto

One of the proposals pushed most vigorously, which would have the effect of admitting more Members to the United Nations, suggests that the veto should not be applicable with respect to recommendations of the Security Council on applications for membership. It has been argued by a group of Latin American Member

---

[24] For examples see *ibid.*, pp. 61 ff. See also the variety of proposals considered in U. N. General Assembly, *Report of the Special Committee on Admission of New Members.*

[25] *Ibid.*, p. 16. See also Res. 620 (VII), Dec. 21, 1952.

states that the application of the unanimity rule to the admission of new Members was not contemplated at the San Francisco Conference. They have contended that the United Nations is based on the "principle of universality" and that a more liberal interpretation of Article 27 is needed.

A resolution proposed by Peru during the seventh session of the General Assembly provided that the Assembly should consider, in connection with other proposals relative to admission, that, "in the matter of admission of new Members . . . the final decision lay with the Assembly, and . . . accordingly the Council's recommendation, though necessary, was a previous step or a procedural stage which did not require the application of the unanimity rule."[26] The problem confronting the proponents of this suggestion is to devise a workable method of changing the prevailing interpretation. The United States, supported by some other members of the Security Council, believes that there is a right to veto applications for membership but that the right should be waived. All of the permanent members except the Soviet Union believe that this right to use the veto has been abused by the Soviet Union to deny admission to qualified applicants. Nevertheless they agree that the admission of new Members is a substantive question, not procedural, and therefore that an applicant can receive the affirmative recommendation of the Council *only* if it has the support of seven members of the Council, including all of the permanent members.

There are devices that might be used in attempts to liberalize this interpretation of Article 27. It has been suggested, for example, that despite consistent precedents to the contrary, the President of the Security Council might be prevailed on at some point to rule that the negative vote of a permanent member against the admission of an applicant did not constitute a veto because he would deem the question procedural in character. Inasmuch as the President's ruling could be challenged, it is likely that a vote on such a ruling would not win the required support of the five permanent members. Moreover, the Council and the Assembly have consistently proceeded on the understanding that the right of veto does exist in such cases.

Although the permanent members of the Security Council have been unwilling to go along with suggestions that admission is a

[26] U. N. General Assembly, *Report of the Special Committee on Admission of New Members,* pp. 2-3.

procedural matter, the United States, supported by China and the United Kingdom, has indicated its willingness to agree with the other permanent members that the veto should not be used in connection with "decisions with respect to admission of States to membership in the United Nations, pursuant to Article 4, paragraph 2."[27] This position was supported by a resolution of the Assembly in April 1949, recommending that votes of the Council on admission be viewed as procedural and be considered as having been adopted if approved by *any* seven members of the Council.[28] This is consistent with the proposal contained in the Vandenberg Resolution that one of the objectives of the United States should be to seek "voluntary agreement to remove the veto from all questions involving . . . the admission of new members."[29]

The Special Committee of the General Assembly concluded as a result of its study that "such an approach was not generally acceptable, principally on the grounds that the unanimity rule in the Security Council applied to the admission of new Members and that the provisions of Article 4 did not allow the General Assembly to admit new Members in the absence of a favourable recommendation by the Council."[30]

Delegating Full Authority to General Assembly

Closely related to, but different from, plans to eliminate the veto in membership cases, has been the suggestion that the provisions in Article 4(2) to the effect that admission is to be effected "by a decision of the General Assembly upon the recommendation of the Security Council," can be interpreted to mean that the General Assembly is the only body that can make a decision on membership. The argument is made that the Charter contemplated that the Assembly should decide who should be admitted to the Organization regardless whether the Council submitted an affirmative or a

[27] U.N. General Assembly, Second Session, *United States Proposals on the Veto Question*, Doc. A/AC.18/41 (Mar. 10, 1948).

[28] Res. 267 (III), Apr. 14, 1949.

[29] S.Res. 239, 80 Cong. 2 sess.

[30] U. N. General Assembly, *Report of the Special Committee on Admission of New Members*, p. 17. For a summary of proposals regarding membership see Stuart Chevalier, "Goals of the United Nations," speech delivered at the 31st Assembly of the Institute of World Affairs, Riverside, Calif., Dec. 13, 1954. Printed in *Vital Speeches of the Day* (Feb. 15, 1955), pp. 1043 ff.

negative recommendation in a specific case.[31] Substantially the same proposal was presented to the Assembly by the Argentine delegation in the fall of 1949. It was argued that the Assembly was entitled to interpret the provisions of the Charter dealing with its own powers, just as had other organs of the United Nations. Nevertheless, the Argentine delegation proposed that the International Court of Justice be asked to rule on the competence of the Assembly in the matter of admissions.[32] The Court, however, in its advisory opinion, by a vote of 12 to 2, stated that it:

> . . . is of opinion that the admission of a State to membership in the United Nations, pursuant to paragraph 2 of Article 4 of the Charter, cannot be effected by a decision of the General Assembly when the Security Council has made no recommendation for admission, by reason of the candidate failing to obtain the requisite majority or of the negative vote of a permanent Member upon a resolution so to recommend.[33]

Although this opinion has no legal force, it does have compelling moral force, and that force, combined with the position taken by the permanent members of the Security Council that an affirmative resolution of the Council is a condition precedent to action by the Assembly on a membership application, makes it most unlikely that a voluntary reinterpretation of Article 4(2) could succeed in broadening membership in the United Nations, unless the permanent members change their policy.

An amendment of the Charter could, of course, make it clear that any designated number of votes in the General Assembly would suffice to admit an applicant to membership. Former Secretary of State Byrnes when serving on the United States delegation to the General Assembly in 1953, observed that if by the time a conference for review of the Charter is held, "a solution of the membership problem has not been found, there will be proposals to deal with it by amendment of the Charter."[34]

[31] It is interesting to note that in one of the initial drafts of the Charter, prepared in August 1943 in the Department of State, it was recommended that admission should be determined by a three-fourths vote of the General Assembly with no participation by the Council. *Post-War Foreign Policy Preparation, 1939-1945*, Publication 3580 (February 1950), p. 526.

[32] U. N. General Assembly, Fourth Session, *Ad Hoc* Political Committee, *Admission of New Members: Argentina: Draft Resolution* Doc. A/AC.31/L.18 (Oct. 31, 1949).

[33] See International Court of Justice, *Reports of Judgments, Advisory Opinions and Orders* (1950), pp. 4-11.

[34] U. S. Delegation to the General Assembly, Press Release 1766 (Oct. 5, 1953).

Package Deals

From time to time it has been proposed that applicants be admitted on some type of group basis, with free world members waiving their objections to Soviet-sponsored candidates and *vice versa*. These are the so-called package deals. Thus, the Secretary-General suggested in 1950 that the United Nations should proceed "as rapidly as possible toward universality of membership." To that end, he proposed that the fourteen states then awaiting admission "should all be admitted, as well as other countries which will attain their independence in the future."[35]

As early as 1946, it had become apparent that the Soviet Union was at odds with other Members of the United Nations in the matter of admitting new states. In that year, the Security Council considered eight applications for membership. Only three states were admitted. The others were rejected either by a Soviet veto, or, as in the case of Albania and Outer Mongolia, by their failure to obtain the necessary seven affirmative votes in the Council. In 1947 the majority of the Members of the United Nations realized that the Soviet Union would be willing to forego the use of the veto on applications for membership if a deal could be arranged so that candidates sponsored by the Soviet Union might be admitted even though most Members could not honestly consider those states as peace-loving or able and willing to carry out the Charter obligations.

As a result, the General Assembly asked the International Court of Justice whether a Member of the United Nations (the Soviet Union by implication) could "make its consent to the admission [of a new Member] dependent on conditions" other than those specified in Article 4. The question was asked whether it would be legitimate for a member to insist "that other states be admitted to membership" as a *quid pro quo* for the admission of a state vetoed for admission. The Court answered in the negative.[36] Nevertheless, the Soviet Union has continued to offer its package proposals. At the eighth session of the Assembly in 1953, the Soviet Union proposed

---

[35] See Trygve Lie, "The Secretary-General's Formula for 'A Fresh Start Toward Peace,'" including a "Memorandum by the Secretary-General on Points for Consideration in the Development of a Twenty-Year Program for Achieving Peace Through the United Nations," *United Nations Bulletin*, Vol. 8 (June 15, 1950), pp. 510-13, 540.

[36] Res. 113 (III), Nov. 17, 1947; I.C.J., *Advisory Opinion*, May 28, 1948.

that fourteen applicants be admitted to membership *en bloc*. It indicated that it would vote for admission of some nine states previously vetoed by the Soviet Union, provided the five candidates sponsored by the Soviet Union were also accepted.

Despite the fact that the United States in 1946 had indicated that it would waive certain reservations that it had regarding the qualifications of Albania and the Mongolian People's Republic, in recent years it has taken a leading position in opposition to all such package proposals. The United States representative explained the position of the United States to the Assembly in 1953 as follows:

> We cannot engage in bargaining where the question is one of principle. Heretofore, we have objected to the admission of these five [Soviet-sponsored] applicants on the ground that they are not peace-loving, as required by the Charter. If under any package deal we now agree to admit them, by implication we are saying that they have become "peace-loving" States. We cannot say that. . . . The United States Government is unwilling to do that.[37]

Two political solutions that represented modified versions of the package proposal were offered to the Special Committee. Argentina suggested that the Security Council should re-examine each application for admission and make a specific recommendation on each of them to the General Assembly, either favorable or unfavorable. It would then be up to two thirds of the Assembly to decide which of the applicants should be admitted. Egypt and the Philippines suggested that the Council should consider the fourteen applicants simultaneously and recommend their *en bloc* admission to the United Nations. This recommendation of the Council would then be considered by the Assembly, which would have power "to reject the Council's joint recommendation as a whole or adopt certain parts of it and to reject others."[38]

After lengthy debate of these political proposals, during which opposition to them was expressed by China, the United States, France, and the United Kingdom, the Special Committee was unable to find a basis for a recommendation to the Assembly. The committee concluded that:

> Although the importance of the political aspects of the problem was recognized, the specific methods suggested did not secure general accept-

[37] U. S. Delegation to the General Assembly, Press Release 1766 (Oct. 5, 1953).
[38] U. N. General Assembly, *Report of the Special Committee on Admission of New Members*, pp. 13-14.

ance. If was felt that the courses proposed either would not be in strict accordance with Article 4, or, if they were, were no more likely to lead to practical results than earlier recommendations for reconsideration by the Security Council.[39]

The plethora of proposals designed to widen the membership of the United Nations indicates general approval of the idea that the Organization should be more universal than it is under present practice. A prevailing view is indicated by the report on the United Nations transmitted to Congress by the President for the year 1949, which noted that:

> The United States position has been the same: that the United Nations ought progressively—and as soon as possible—to become a universal organization. President Truman stated in his address at the ceremonies in which the cornerstone of the United Nations building in New York was laid this year that ". . . We hope that eventually every nation on earth will be a fully qualified and loyal member of this organization."[40]

This is a prevailing view. It is incapable of fulfillment at the moment, because the question of admission to the United Nations has become a political issue between the free world and the Communist states. In these circumstances, any change in qualifications or procedures would be viewed either as a victory or a defeat for a position taken by one or more of the great powers.

Special Membership Status

Changes in the procedures for admission, such as the elimination of the veto in the Security Council, decreasing the size of the vote required in the General Assembly, and delegating full authority to the Assembly for decision in admission cases, have potentialities for increasing the membership in the United Nations without altering its fundamental character. Some of these proposals, such as limiting the use of the veto, could be put into effect by simple agreement among the great powers not to exercise their veto power. Others would require the adoption of new rules of procedure or amendment of the Charter. The choice of the method depends largely on the political climate in which changes might be considered. Given a recognition on the part of the five permanent

---

[39] *Ibid.,* p. 17.

[40] U. S. Department of State, *United States Participation in the United Nations: Report by the President to the Congress for the Year 1949,* Publication 3765 (May 1950), p. 89.

members of the Council of a prolonged period of peace, it is not impossible to envisage agreement that might result in a larger membership than the United Nations now has.

Another possible partial settlement of the membership issue looks in the direction of a larger working membership. It has been suggested that states that have not been admitted to the United Nations might be given a general "observer" role, or an "associate membership," with permission being granted to them to sit on all committees of the United Nations and with the right to indicate how they would vote on given issues, had they the right to vote. There is precedent for this suggestion in the United States Congress where delegates from territories have the rights and privileges of members, but do not vote. In this connection, it was reported that Senator Fulbright of the United States delegation, during the ninth session of the Assembly, sounded out other delegations on the acceptability of a plan to permit some states not Members of the Organization to participate in debate in the Assembly without a vote. Apparently the plan was not well received by certain other delegations, which questioned its legality as well as the fact that it would have by-passed the Security Council.[41]

A similar approach was suggested by the United States representative in a statement before the *Ad Hoc* Political Committee in November 1954. He noted that the United States "has been giving serious study . . . to the possibility of arrangements whereby qualified applicants might participate in the work of the General Assembly to the maximum extent possible even though they have not formally been admitted to membership." He also called specific attention to the fact that if by the time a General Conference is held, "a solution of the membership problem has not been found, there are likely to be proposals for amending the Charter."[42]

A further possibility might be to provide for membership on a provisional basis.

. . . Thus, a potential new member would be invited on a trial membership basis for a determined period of years . . ., and, if it demonstrated that it was qualified for permanent membership by demonstrating that it is a "peace-loving state," it could then be so accepted, by majority—or perhaps three-fourths—vote of the General Assembly, as a permanent member at the end of the trial period. . . . This system might encourage po-

[41] See *New York Times* (Oct. 10, 1954).
[42] U. S. Department of State *Bulletin*, Vol. 31 (Nov. 22, 1954), p. 788.

tential new members who do not currently demonstrate characteristics of "peace-loving states" to mend their ways, in order to be admitted to the international forum.[43]

A variation of these suggestions is that an association of states not Members of the Organization might be formed and that representatives of it might be given authority to make known its views to the United Nations. These suggestions have not received much support. There is little inclination on the part of states not Members of the United Nations to participate with other sovereign states on a basis of nonequality. Such states can and do participate in regional security organizations, which give them a chance to bring their influence to bear on the United Nations system in an indirect but influential way. Furthermore, some supporters of the United Nations hesitate to encourage the creation of an association outside the United Nations because such a step would be moving away from the universality they hope the Organization will achieve.

Proposals for Greater Selectivity

Proposals that, if adopted, would increase the number of Members in the United Nations, would not, except for the supranational proposals, alter the fundamental nature of the United Nations. This is not true with respect to proposals to decrease the number of Members. Any suggestion having the effect of decreasing the number of Members, especially if it were applied to any of the five permanent members, would radically affect the very nature of the Organization. Membership could be reduced by (1) expulsion, (2) withdrawal, or (3) complete reorganization of the United Nations. The tightening of qualifications for admission would not decrease the existing number of Members although it might curtail admissions even more than has been the case under existing conditions.

At the San Francisco Conference some consideration was given to inserting in the Charter tighter requirements for applicants for admission. An interpretation of the Charter that was approved by the Conference set up a qualification for admission that was selective in nature. Having in mind the Franco regime in Spain, the Conference

[43] Testimony of David R. Toll, Chairman, International Relations Committee, Denver Junior Chamber of Commerce, *Review of the United Nations Charter*, Hearings before a Subcommittee of the Senate Committee on Foreign Relations, 84 Cong. 1 sess., Pt. 11, p. 1570.

expressed the understanding that admission could not be accorded to states whose regimes had been set up with the help of military forces belonging to the countries that had waged war against the United Nations, so long as those regimes remained in power. No other restriction on admission, except those set forth in Article 4, was adopted. Consideration was given, however, to proposals that there be inserted in the Charter "specific conditions which new Members should be required to fulfill especially in matters concerning the character and policies of governments." It was concluded that "the difficulties which would arise in evaluating the political institutions of states" would be of such a nature as to be a "breach of the principle of nonintervention."[44]

It is possible, of course, that plans rejected at the San Francisco Conference that would have spelled out qualifications based on the character and policies of applicants might be revived. It seems likely, however, that they would receive less support today than they received at the Conference. The years since 1945, for example, have shown that the phrase "democratic government" means one thing to the Soviet Union, and something entirely different to the free world. Even the unanimity with which the conferees at San Francisco rejected the admissibility of Spain to the Organization is missing in the United Nations today.

Proposals to reduce membership in the United Nations go to two extremes. On the one hand are those who suggest that the Communist nations should be removed from the Organization by expulsion, forced withdrawal, or, if necessary, the reorganization of the United Nations. On the other hand are those who propose that the United States withdraw from the Organization. Both proposals relate to the subject of membership, but those who suggest the idea of Soviet exclusion believe that the United Nations can become an effective instrument of collective security only if the Soviet Union is put out of the United Nations. The suggestion that the United States withdraw is related to the problem of collective security in a negative way, as it is based on the belief that the United Nations as presently constituted cannot provide collective security and may in fact be an opiate to the making of effective de-

[44] *UNCIO Documents*, Vol. 7, pp. 289-90. The Charter contains no specific provision that would preclude the admission of former enemy states, but it is interesting to note that no such state has been admitted, although Austria, Finland, Italy, and Japan have sought membership.

fense plans by the United States. It is therefore suggested that the United States should withdraw and look to its own defenses.

The Charter in Article 6 provides a method by which the United Nations may have a more exclusive membership than it now has. Under that article a Member state that has "persistently violated the Principles" in the Charter may be expelled from the Organization by the General Assembly on the recommendation of the Security Council. Because such a recommendation by the Council would not be a procedural matter under the terms of Article 27, it would require the affirmative vote of seven members of the Council, including the votes of the five permanent members. In this respect, therefore, the Soviet Union is in control of its own destiny as a Member. Presumably, it would veto any recommendation by the Council for its own expulsion, or for the expulsion of any of its satellites. The Soviet Union could take the initiative, of course, and withdraw if it desired to leave the Organization. But the effect of Article 6 read in connection with Article 27(3) is to make it impossible to expel any Member from the United Nations except with the consent of all five permanent members of the Council. This means that proposals to get the Soviet Union out of the United Nations and to reorganize the United Nations into an anti-Soviet coalition could only be given effect by creating a new international organization, or by inducing the Communist states to withdraw.

It is conceivable that there might be situations in the future when the five permanent members of the Security Council would agree to recommend the expulsion of some Member of the United Nations, and thus reduce the size of the Organization. Isolated cases of this type, however, would not affect the nature of the Organization. But any move to get rid of one of the permanent members of the Council or to remove a group of states because of their political belief or form of government, would radically alter the United Nations and might have a profound effect on its collective security functions. As the Secretary-General of the United Nations has commented: "If we turn the United Nations into a club of like-minded, we would push outside this body those very conflicts which we hope to solve by such negotiation procedures as are provided for in the United Nations."[45]

[45] U.N. Press Release SG/379 (Apr. 15, 1954). See also *New York Times* (Apr. 15, 1954).

Reorganization of the United Nations
Without the Soviet Union

There is no provision in the Charter for reorganizing the United Nations. Those who suggest this method of forcing Communist nations out of the United Nations envisage the creation of a new international organization not open to Communist states. If such a step were taken, it would tend to make the United Nations into a more selective type organization than it now is, although still envisaging it as a world-wide, as distinguished from a regional type, organization.

Suggestions that the Communist states be expelled from the United Nations over the protest of the Soviet Union could be given effect only by inducing them to withdraw or as a result of revisions made in the Charter by a General Conference that would not view itself as bound by the terms of Articles 108 and 109 regarding the adoption of amendments to the Charter. There is some evidence that the Soviet Union fears the latter possibility. Soviet representative Vyshinsky, in connection with the preliminary debate on a review conference, has suggested that "those who want to revise the Charter would like to turn the United Nations Organization not into an effective instrument for the defense of peace . . . but into an instrument of an aggressive policy which, in itself constitutes a threat to the peace."[46]

Many prominent Americans, however, have suggested that the United Nations be reorganized without the Soviet Union. Former President Herbert Hoover, for example, speaking in 1950 before a dinner of the American Newspaper Publishers Association said: "I have a proposal to make. I suggest that the United Nations should be reorganized without the Communist nations in it. If that is impractical, then a definite New United Front should be organized of those peoples who disavow communism, who stand for morals and religion, and who love freedom." The argument made in support of this proposal was that the Charter has been violated time after time by the Soviet Union, that the Charter was designed for a "one world" community but in fact there are two worlds, one believing in God and the other "atheistic and without compassion," and that "what the world needs today is a definite, concrete mobilization of the nations who believe in God against

[46] See U.N. General Assembly, Eighth Session, Plenary, *Official Records,* 439th Meeting (Sept. 21, 1953), pp. 13-16.

the hideous ideas of the police state and human misery." Such a reorganization of the international structure would make it clear who stands with the United States, and the "phalanx of free nations" thus created "could come far nearer to making a workable relation with the other half of the two worlds than the United States can ever do alone."[47]

More recently, Gen. Mark W. Clark (U.S.A. Ret.), testified, in answer to a question whether he favored United States withdrawal from the United Nations, that he believed "to permit the Soviet Union to have its large number of spies and saboteurs over here spawning in our country [was] wrong . . . and the thing ought to be organized as a United Nations against the Soviet Union."[48]

Somewhat the same point has been made by James Burnham who has asked: "Is it not obvious that it is the *presence,* not the absence, of the Communist representatives that paralyzes the United Nations?" The United Nations, he argued, was powerless to act against the threat of war because of the veto. The veto, therefore, must be limited "even at the risk of withdrawal (or expulsion) of the Soviet Union and its satellite nations." He concludes that Soviet withdrawal is not something to be afraid of because "even if the Communist governments withdrew, the United Nations would still represent the overwhelming bulk of mankind. . . ."[49] A similar position was taken in a resolution adopted by the Wisconsin State Federation of Labor in 1950 when it called for a conference for review of the Charter "for the purpose of building the United Nations into a true federation of nations." But "should Russia abstain, our Nation should proceed to unite with other like-minded nations in a partial world federation, thus taking a realistic step toward realizing man's dream of a united world and, at the same time, giving to the democratic nations a strength through unity so great as to deter further Russian armed aggression."[50]

[47] Address by former President Hoover before American Newspaper Publishers Association, New York, Apr. 27, 1950, *The Commercial and Financial Chronicle,* Vol. 171 (May 4, 1950), p. 17.

[48] *Interlocking Subversion in Government Departments,* Hearings before the Subcommittee to Investigate the Administration of the Internal Security Act and Other Internal Security Laws of the Senate Committee on the Judiciary, 83 Cong. 2 sess., Pt. 21, p. 1708.

[49] James Burnham, "How the United Nations Can Be Made to Work," *Reader's Digest* (January 1948), pp. 81-86.

[50] Resolution passed by the Fifty-eighth Annual Convention of the Wisconsin State Federation of Labor. *Congressional Record,* Vol. 96, Pt. 17, 81 Cong. 2 sess., p. A-6386.

There is, however, a body of opinion opposed to any action to expel the Soviet Union. John Foster Dulles, for example, wrote in 1950:

. . . Some persons would like to throw out Soviet Russia because we disagree with their representatives and they with us. A world organization without Soviet Communists would be a much more pleasant organization. But they have power in the world, and if the United Nations gets away from that reality it becomes artificial and exerts less influence. The United Nations should mirror more accurately, not less accurately, the reality of what is. . . .

Events may lead to a separation of the Soviet Union and its satellites from world organization. That, however, would be a grim event. . . .

A scrapping of the United Nations to eliminate the Soviet Union is something that the United States ought to oppose if we want peace. It gives us no possibilities we do not now have, and would get us nowhere but backwards in our search for peace.[51]

Former President Hoover in the spring of 1955 recalled his earlier suggestion that the United Nations should be reorganized without the Soviet Union, but stated that such a policy would not be "acceptable" now. He added that the United States will need "to go on and worry with the Russians" in the Organization in the hope that in time the situation may improve.[52] The former editor of *American Mercury* has also taken a position in opposition to creating a world organization without the Soviet Union. In answering the question why we should not force the "Communist agitators" out of the United Nations, he suggested that "for the present it may be wise strategy to leave them in the U.N. and try to damage them there politically with superior diplomatic maneuver."[53]

Those who propose that the United Nations be reorganized to exclude the Soviet Union from the Organization contemplate that by such action the United Nations would become either an anti-Soviet coalition or an organization of the free nations, so strong that it would promote disintegrative tendencies within the Soviet states. They apparently assume that most of the states in the free world would be willing to continue their membership in the United Nations —an assumption that may be questionable in the case of some states

[51] John Foster Dulles, *War or Peace* (1950), pp. 188, 204-05.
[52] *Review of the United Nations Charter*, Senate Hearings, 84 Cong. 1 sess., Pt. 12, p. 1745.
[53] William Bradford Huie, "Seven Ways to Save the UN," *American Mercury Magazine* (December 1952), p. 33.

such as India. They assume furthermore that there is no purpose in maintaining the United Nations as a bridge between the East and the West and that it cannot become effective as an instrument for preserving the peace by trying to build a world in which communism and freedom may live side by side. It is also assumed by most proponents of this position that the only way to ensure a peaceful world in the future is by the creation of overwhelming military and economic strength in a world organization dedicated to freedom and opposed to communism.

United States Withdrawal

In marked contrast to proposals that the United Nations could be strengthened by reorganizing it to exclude the Soviet Union, are suggestions for withdrawal of the United States. Should the United Nations be reorganized without the United States, there is little doubt that a very fundamental change in the United Nations system of collective security would take place. Indeed, many students of world affairs believe that withdrawal of the United States at this time would greatly weaken the United Nations and in all probability destroy it.

In the period from 1946 to 1951, as has been noted earlier, there was a strong movement toward increasing the power of the Organization. At one point the legislatures of twenty-three states approved resolutions calling on the United States Government to take the lead in organizing the United Nations into a world federation. Many members of the Congress introduced resolutions calling for strengthening the United Nations by converting it into some form of world government. By 1953, however, strong reaction had set in. Congressman Gross announced in the House of Representatives that of the original twenty-three state legislatures that had approved world government proposals, all but four had changed their positions.[54] Earlier some members of Congress had introduced resolutions calling for United States withdrawal from the United Nations. House Resolutions 5080 and 5081, introduced in 1951, proposed that "from and after the effective date of this act, the ratification by the Senate of the United States on July 28, 1945, of the United Nations Charter, making the United States a member of the United Nations, be, and said ratification hereby is, rescinded, revoked, and held for naught; and all acts and parts of acts designed and intended to perfect and carry out

[54] *Congressional Record*, Vol. 99, Pt. 3, 83 Cong. 1 sess., p. 3393.

such membership of the United States in the United Nations are hereby repealed."[55]

Another resolution introduced in 1951 provided that "(1) membership of the United States in the United Nations shall be held and considered to be terminated."[56] Another resolved that Senate approval of the Charter "is hereby vacated and set aside as void under the Constitution of the United States."[57] In 1953, House Concurrent Resolution 79, introduced in the Eighty-third Congress, called for a "new sixty-nation conference" to consider, among other things, "whether or not in fact, as alleged, said body has utterly failed in its endeavors to create peace while its actions and machinations have brought war and have increased rather than diminished the areas of the world ruled by totalitarianism, and thus caused distrust and fear of its actual future and that said body has proven to be the most expensive and disappointing alliance the United States has ever embraced." During the same period a number of private organizations adopted resolutions urging the United States to withdraw from the United Nations.[58]

While not going so far as to propose United States withdrawal, Senator John Bricker of Ohio commented in 1952, that "the United Nations seems destined for an early demise . . . it is suffering from a disease which affects every bureaucracy, an insatiable lust for power."[59] In 1955, however, Senator Bricker stated that: "The United Nations does have . . . a very important role to play. It serves as a world forum for the airing and possible settlement of international disputes. However, the United Nations cannot act simultaneously as an effective mediator and as the world's policeman."[60]

[55] *Ibid.*, Vol. 97, Pt. 7, 82 Cong. 1 sess., p. 9574; text, *ibid.*, Vol. 98, Pt. 8, 82 Cong. 2 sess., p. A-258. See also H.R. 105, 83 Cong. (Jan. 3, 1953).

[56] H. J. Res. 125, 82 Cong. (Feb. 8, 1951); *Congressional Record*, Vol. 97, Pt. 11, 82 Cong. 1 sess., p. A-696.

[57] H. Con. Res. 166, 82 Cong. (Oct. 3, 1951). See also H. Con. Res. 3, 83 Cong. (Jan. 3, 1953).

[58] See, for example, resolution adopted by the California State Society of the Daughters of the American Revolution (Mar. 17, 1953), *Congressional Record*, Vol. 98, Pt. 2, 82 Cong. 2 sess., p. 2348; resolution adopted by the United States Flag Committee of New York State in support of H.R. 5080 (82 Cong.), which urges United States withdrawal from the United Nations (Feb. 7, 1952), *ibid.*, Pt. 8, p. A-749; a resolution of Christian Citizens of Oklahoma in support of H.R. 5080 (Jan. 28, 1952), *ibid.*, p. A-422.

[59] *New York Times* (May 18, 1952).

[60] *Review of the United Nations Charter*, Senate Hearings, 84 Cong. 1 sess., Pt. 12, p. 1651.

Although there are some who think that the best way of ensuring security for the United States is to withdraw from the United Nations, not all people who are critical of the United Nations believe that the United States should withdraw. Some of those who oppose withdrawal of the United States do so principally because they believe that such an act would turn the United Nations over to the Soviet Union. They believe that nothing would please the Soviet Communists more than to be able to operate within the United Nations framework unhampered by the leadership of the free world that the United States is able to exercise as a Member of the Organization. They feel that withdrawal of the United States would isolate it from the world and would hurt the United States more than it would hurt the Soviet Union. They also urge that the United Nations should mirror the world as it exists and that peaceful settlement of the differences between the free world and the Communist states is more likely to be worked out within the framework of the United Nations than by withdrawal of the United States, which would tend to "bipolarize" the world even more than is now the case.

No matter what reasons are advanced for such action, the arguments against withdrawal seem to be much the same. The former editor of *American Mercury,* for example, points out that the suggestion that the United States withdraw from the United Nations is

. . . the most unrealistic suggestion of all. The United States shouldn't desert any more arenas of conflict with communism. We should use the U.N. to damage the cause of communism, and if anyone is to be driven out it should be the Communists. But at present the enemy is within the U.N.; and since the U.N. is housed in New York, the enemy is within our own national gates. And this means risk. But the risk can be minimized if we understand what we are doing. . . .[61]

And Ambassador Henry Cabot Lodge, Jr., when asked what he thought of the suggestions that the United States withdraw from the United Nations, declared:

I think it would be the utmost folly. I don't know what would happen to the United Nations; I do know what it would mean to the United States. I think it would be a very bad thing to do, from our own viewpoint. In all these questions, the one question you must always ask yourself is:

[61] Huie, *loc. cit.,* p. 33.

"Is it good for America?" And if it wasn't good for America to belong to the United Nations, we ought not to belong to it.

I think it is good for America. It is very advantageous for us to belong. I think if we were to pull out and leave the Russians there, it would be a fantastic thing to do—very dangerous, very imprudent.[62]

The late Senator Taft took a similar position when he urged in 1952 that the United States remain in the United Nations, doing its best to amend the Charter so that its action could be based on international law and the impartial adjudication of an international tribunal.[63] President Eisenhower in his State of the Union Message of January 7, 1954, also supported continued membership of the United States in the United Nations. He said:

In the world as a whole, the United Nations, admittedly still in a state of evolution, means much to the United States. It has given uniquely valuable services in many places where violence threatened. It is the only real world forum where we have the opportunity for international presentation and rebuttal. It is a place where the nations of the world can, if they have the will, take collective action for peace and justice. It is a place where the guilt can be squarely assigned to those who fail to take all necessary steps to keep the peace. The United Nations deserves our continued firm support.[64]

There is much in common among those who take the opposite positions that the United Nations should be reorganized without the Soviet Union or the United States should withdraw from the United Nations. They believe, for example, that the participation of the Soviet Union in the United Nations is motivated by the desire of the Soviet Union to destroy free governments. They see it using the United Nations as a forum for "propaganda, agitation and organization,"[65] and as a device to penetrate free countries, to destroy their freedom, to propagandize the masses. Although they are likely to be in basic agreement on the proposition that the Soviet Union uses the United Nations to further world revolutionary aspirations of the communists, they disagree on the best course of action for the free world to take. Both of these groups regard the split between the free world and the Communist world as unbridgeable. They view as hopeless any attempt to bridge the gap.

[62] *Review of the United Nations Charter*, Senate Hearings, 83 Cong. 2 sess., Pt. 1, p. 42.
[63] *New York Times* (June 2, 1952).
[64] U. S. Department of State *Bulletin*, Vol. 30 (Jan. 18, 1954), p. 76.
[65] See Burnham, *loc. cit.*, pp. 81-86.

The Problem of
Chinese Representation

It appears that the issue whether the United States should withdraw from the United Nations is most likely to arise in its sharpest form in connection with the increasing support for the admission of Communist China, which includes the idea that Communist China might sometime be recognized as being entitled to the seat now occupied by Nationalist China. The United States Government takes the position that this is a question of which government *represents* China, and should be considered apart from the problem of admitting a new state to the United Nations. It thus sharply distinguishes between the question of *admission* of states to the United Nations and the question of *representation* of states now Members. Ambassador Lodge, for example, has stated that "there is one change that it seems everyone should support, and that is the change which would eliminate the use of the veto on the admission of new members." But this matter, in Ambassador Lodge's view, "has nothing to do with Red China. China is already a member and what the Chinese Reds have been trying to do is to get China's seat in the United Nations, which is rightfully held by the Nationalist Government."[66]

From the point of view of the United States, the issue poses special problems. Senator Knowland, for example, in the summer of 1954 suggested that:

> On the day when Communist China is voted into membership into the United Nations, I shall resign my majority leadership in the Senate, so that without embarrassment to any of my colleagues or to the administration I can devote my full efforts in the Senate and throughout the country to terminating United States membership in that organization and our financial support to it. My conscience would not permit me to remain silent or inactive if this last grand appeasement takes place.[67]

And although Senator Smith of New Jersey has not gone so far as to propose that the United States withdraw in the event Communist China is admitted to the United Nations, he has declared that such an act would mean the "death knell" of the Organization. He observed that there might still be "many reasons why we should try

[66] Highlights of remarks of Henry Cabot Lodge, Jr., Annual Banquet of the Chamber of Commerce of Metropolitan St. Louis, Mo., Feb. 16, 1955. Mimeo.

[67] *Congressional Record*, Vol. 100, Pt. 7, 83 Cong. 2 sess., p. 9426.

to stay in and at least attend the obsequies and send flowers to the burial."[68]

The Congress also has suggested that the seating of Communist China would raise serious questions about United States membership in the Organization. The Mutual Security Act of 1954, for example, reiterates congressional "opposition to the seating in the United Nations of the Communist China regime," and requests the President in such event to "inform the Congress . . . of the implications of this action upon the foreign policy of the United States and our foreign relationships, *including that created by membership in the United Nations,* together with any recommendations which he may have with respect to the matter."[69] Both the House of Representatives and the Senate have voted unanimously that "the Communist Chinese Government should not be admitted to membership in the United Nations as the representative of China."[70] This language is broad enough to encompass not only the matter of admission, but the matter of representation as well.

Congressman Richards of South Carolina, Chairman of the House Committee on Foreign Affairs, however, has admitted that the seating of Communist China might gain the necessary support "within a reasonable number of years" to permit the participation of that regime in the work of the United Nations. But, in that event, he thinks it would be "folly" for the United States to play into the hands of the Communists by "withdrawing from the United Nations and thus destroying it."[71]

In the final analysis, of course, the decision of the United States should be made on the basis of what is best in the national interest. In making such a decision, the American people must balance the advantages and disadvantages of membership in the United Nations with its Communist Members against the advantages and disadvantages of operating outside the framework of the United Nations.

In considering the practicability of proposals that would have the effect of broadening or narrowing membership in the United Nations, it must be remembered that the qualifications for membership and the procedures to be followed for admission are di-

[68] *New York Herald Tribune* (July 19, 1954).
[69] 68 Stat. 833. Italics supplied.
[70] 67 Stat. 372, Sec. 111.
[71] *New York Herald Tribune* (July 19, 1954).

rectly related to the purpose for which the Organization has been created. There is little doubt, however, that many more states could be admitted to the United Nations as presently constituted and some few states could be expelled without altering its fundamental purpose or character. Indeed, most of the suggestions relating to simplified procedures for admission and the package proposals that have been given serious attention by the General Assembly have been based on the assumption that the membership of the United Nations could and should be enlarged without altering its fundamental character.

But sooner or later, as the Organization moves toward universality or toward greater selectivity, a point is reached where decisions on membership may affect the fundamental purposes of the Organization.

Should the United Nations move in the direction of world government or confine its activities merely to seeking the peaceful settlement of disputes, true universality of membership might become a feasible proposition. Should the Organization move in the direction of developing the concept of collective security on a global basis by implementing Article 43, it might be expected that there would be vigorous efforts to exclude potential aggressors from the councils of the United Nations.

Proposals affecting qualifications and procedures for membership cannot be considered, however, outside the context of the mutual suspicion that underlies the cold war. So long as suggestions are put forward that the United Nations might be organized into an anti-Communist coalition, the Soviet Union is unlikely to accept suggestions that there be no use of the veto in membership matters. On the other hand, so long as the Soviet Union does not give evidence of respect for the principles and purposes of the Charter, there is little inclination on the part of the majority of the Members of the United Nations to accept into membership Soviet-sponsored states that would be likely to view obligations under the Charter in the same cavalier fashion as has the Soviet Union.

PART THREE

PROPOSALS RELATING TO THE
MAINTENANCE OF PEACE
AND SECURITY

CHAPTER V

Peaceful Settlement of Disputes

IN June 1950, when the forces of North Korea launched an armed attack against the lawfully established Government of the Republic of Korea, the Security Council, in a series of resolutions adopted while the Soviet Union was boycotting the Council, took the initiative in organizing forces of Member states to oppose the aggression. It called on Members to furnish assistance to the Republic of Korea to help repel the aggression, asked the United States to exercise a unified command over those forces, and authorized the use of the United Nations flag during the course of operations against North Korea.[1] Six months later, the General Assembly adopted a resolution asking the President of the Assembly, with two other persons, to determine a basis for a "satisfactory cease-fire in Korea" to the end that steps might then "be taken for a peaceful settlement of existing issues in accordance with the Purposes and Principles of the United Nations."[2]

By these actions the United Nations was exercising its two principal functions, as set forth in Article 1: first, the taking of "effective collective measures for the prevention and removal of threats to the peace, and for the suppression of acts of aggression"; and, second, seeking "to bring about by peaceful means . . . adjustment or settlement of international disputes or situations." The procedures by which the United Nations is to act in these two capacities are set forth in Chapter VII of the Charter, concerning "action with respect to threats to the peace, breaches of the peace, and acts of aggression," and in Chapter VI, which deals with the pacific settlement of disputes.

The question has been raised whether the United Nations can discharge both the function of peaceful settlement and that of enforcement. The British representative, Sir Gladwyn Jebb, for exam-

[1] U.N. Security Council, Fifth Year, *Resolutions Concerning the Complaint of Aggression Upon the Republic of Korea,* Docs. S/1501 (June 25, 1950); S/1511 (June 27, 1950); and S/1588 (July 7, 1950).
[2] Res. 384(V), Dec. 14, 1950.

ple, has suggested that the United Nations should serve principally as a meeting place where disputes can be settled by peaceful procedures. The task of maintaining peace and security as distinguished from the peaceful settlement of disputes is, in his opinion, one that can best be handled by regional defense arrangements.[3] Senator John Bricker has voiced a similar position: "It is on this network of mutual defense alliances and not on the United Nations that the United States must rely for collective security."[4]

As these statements indicate, there are some who question the necessity of a close relationship between the Charter functions of peaceful settlement and collective security. Although there are those who believe that the United Nations should concentrate its energies on peaceful settlement, there are others who place primary emphasis on the enforcement role of the United Nations, believing that peace can only be preserved if the Organization is able to provide reasonably adequate collective security on a world-wide basis. Some proponents of this latter point of view have suggested that the United Nations cannot police the world with potential aggressors on the police force. Consequently, they advocate reorganization of the United Nations into an anti-Soviet coalition.

There is undoubtedly a close relationship between the functions of peaceful settlement under Chapter VI of the Charter and enforcement action under Chapter VII, because failure to settle a dispute peacefully may lead to a breach of the peace and hence the need for enforcement action. Inasmuch as the principal burden in the event of enforcement action would fall on the great powers, they argued at the San Francisco Conference that, if they were to have authority to veto enforcement action, it was logical for them to have authority to veto recommendations for pacific settlement of disputes that might lead to a breach of the peace in which enforcement action would be required. Otherwise they might find themselves committed to take military action because of the failure of recommended procedures for peaceful settlement with which they had not agreed.

Attention here will be focused primarily on proposals relating to the pacific settlement operations of the United Nations. Later in this study proposals relating to enforcement action will be considered.

[3] Sir Gladwyn Jebb, "The Free World and the United Nations," *Foreign Affairs,* Vol. 31 (April 1953), pp. 383-91.
[4] *Review of the United Nations Charter,* Hearings before a Subcommittee of the Senate Committee on Foreign Relations, 84 Cong. 1 sess., Pt. 12, p. 1651.

Provisions of the Charter

The Charter recognizes that disputes arising between states, if not settled at an early stage, might endanger the peace. The methods available to the United Nations in dealing with such disputes have been described in detail elsewhere.[5] It is sufficient to note here the general characteristics of the system of peaceful settlement under the Charter and the effectiveness of that system.

Article 33 of the Charter obligates parties to disputes that might "endanger the maintenance of international peace and security" to seek a solution of their difficulties by all peaceful means including among others negotiation, mediation, conciliation, and arbitration, as well as by other methods "of their own choice." If the parties fail to settle the dispute, "they shall refer it to the Security Council" (Article 37(1)). Provision is also made for any Member to bring any dispute that might lead to international friction to the attention of the Security Council or the General Assembly at any time.

When the Council is seized of a dispute or situation, it is empowered by Article 34 to make investigations for the purpose of determining whether continuance of the dispute or situation is likely to endanger the maintenance of international peace and security. If, on the basis of its investigation, the Council finds that the dispute is likely to endanger the peace, it may call upon the parties to seek settlement by means of their own choice, recommend procedures for adjusting the dispute, or recommend other terms of settlement that might be appropriate. The Council has authority only to make recommendations—it cannot compel the peaceful settlement of disputes.

The procedures for handling disputes brought to the attention of the General Assembly are more flexible than those outlined for the Security Council. Operating under the general mandate of Article 10, and the particular mandate of Article 14, the Assembly is authorized to recommend measures for "the peaceful adjustment of any situation" with which the Security Council is not seized, "regardless of origin, which it deems likely to impair . . . friendly relations among nations."

[5] See the volumes in this Brookings series, *The United Nations and the Maintenance of International Peace and Security*, Chaps. IX-XIII, and *A History of the United Nations Charter*. See also Leland M. Goodrich, "Pacific Settlement of Disputes," *American Political Science Review*, Vol. 39 (October 1945), pp. 956-70.

Several aspects of the pacific settlement provisions of the Charter need to be noted:

1. The authority of the Security Council to make recommendations in this field extends only to disputes "likely to endanger the maintenance of international peace and security." Thus its authority does not technically include disputes *not* likely to endanger international peace. Article 38 provides, however, that *any* dispute may be considered by the Council if *all* the parties so request. A dispute regarding the extent of the immunities to be extended to diplomatic representatives, for example, probably would not be a dispute likely to endanger the peace, whereas a dispute over an international boundary might, in certain circumstances, be likely to do so. As a practical matter, however, the Council has not required that a dispute be of the kind that would endanger the peace before it takes cognizance of it.

2. Furthermore, *international* peace must be endangered in order to make the provisions of the Charter applicable. The use within a state of force that would not endanger international peace would presumably not be within the purview of the authority given the Council under the provisions of Chapter VI. Here again, however, the Council has intervened, as it did in the Indonesian case, in disputes or situations that one of the parties has believed were internal or domestic in nature.

3. Action taken to settle disputes likely to endanger peace is confined to the making of recommendations. Neither the Council nor the Assembly could, under the provisions of Chapter VI, call upon Members to use force to compel a settlement of the dispute, although the Assembly might recommend that the Council take such action under Chapter VII. But it is only when, according to Article 39, there is a "threat to the peace, breach of the peace, or act of aggression" that force may be used.

4. Recommendations of the Security Council under Chapter VI relating to the pacific settlement of disputes are not subject to an unqualified veto. Article 27(3) provides that "a party to a dispute shall abstain from voting." Thus, no permanent member of the Council could, by its negative vote, defeat a resolution relating to a dispute to which it was a party. It is possible, however, for a permanent member to veto a resolution, perhaps because of its interest in the dispute, when it is not a party.

It is most difficult to draw valid conclusions on how well the pacific settlement procedures of the Charter have worked. Ambassador Lodge has recently described some of the United Nations accomplishments as follows:

The threat of war in Iran in 1946, due to pressure of Russian troops, was moderated and gradually extinguished.

The initiative was taken, with substantial American backing, to prevent Communist encroachment on Greece in 1947.

Open warfare over Kashmir between India and Pakistan was stopped.

The advent of Israel into the family of nations was determined and an end put to a bloody war in the Holy Land, although of course the situation is still dangerous.

It is a place where—

Working with the Netherlands and the Indonesians, full independence was given to the 76 million people inhabiting Indonesia.

Part of the free world was organized to repel the bloody aggression in Korea, which threatened the whole free world—and not only in Asia.[6]

The effectiveness of the United Nations in the field of pacific settlement, as in the case of border attacks on Greece, has been hampered by frequent use, and threat of use, of the veto by the Soviet Union. Despite the difficulty of evaluating the existing procedures for peaceful settlement in the Charter, there is certainly some truth in the observation that at the present time the function of peaceful settlement is more important from a practical point of view than the function of collective defense. Sir Gladwyn Jebb has suggested that planning for collective resistance to Soviet aggression is most difficult within the confines of the United Nations, but that the United Nations might be most useful over a long period of time in working out "negotiated settlements between the West and the Stalinist world."[7] A number of proposals have been put forth designed to improve the United Nations machinery in this field and to increase the likelihood that the Organization will be more effective in the future.

Proposals of the Interim Committee

It was contemplated at the San Francisco Conference that the principal United Nations organ for promoting the peaceful settlement of disputes was to be the Security Council. In recent years, however, the General Assembly has become the most important organ operating in this field. So many postwar disputes have been

[6] *Hon. Henry Cabot Lodge, Jr.,* Hearing before the Senate Committee on Foreign Relations, 83 Cong. 1 sess., p. 4.

[7] Jebb, *loc. cit.,* p. 387.

associated with the cold war that it has been virtually impossible
for the five permanent members of the Council to agree on recommendations for their settlement. Failure to reach agreed recommendations in the Council has caused disputants to turn to the
Assembly under Article 14 to seek recommendations concerning
"measures for the peaceful adjustment of any situation, regardless
of origin, which it deems likely to impair the general welfare or
friendly relations among nations." In accordance with Article 35
and the precedents now established, Member states can at their discretion, decide whether to seek assistance through the Council or
through the Assembly. In those disputes in which it is not likely
that the Council will be able to make a recommendation, states
are inclined to take them to the Assembly.

It was largely as a result of this trend that Secretary of State
Marshall in September 1947 proposed that the Assembly create a
standing committee that "might consider situations and disputes
impairing friendly relations brought to its attention by member
states or by the Security Council pursuant to Articles 11 and 14
of the Charter." This committee was to be an organ on which all
United Nations Members were to have seats. Its creation would
"strengthen the machinery for peaceful settlement and place the
responsibility for such settlement broadly upon all the Members of
the United Nations."[8]

The resolution that grew out of this proposal (adopted by the
General Assembly on November 13, 1947 by a vote of 41 to 6, with
6 abstentions) established the Interim Committee.[9] The creation of
the committe was important in the operations of the United Nations, not only in the field of peaceful settlement, but in the field of
enforcement action as well. The existence of this body, able to meet
while the General Assembly was not in session and with an authorized membership of all Member states, provided a forum for
adopting resolutions of recommendation even though a recommendation by the Security Council might have been vetoed.

The Interim Committee met twenty-nine times in 1948—its first
year. Much of its time was devoted to a study of methods to give

[8] "A Program for a More Effective United Nations," Address by George C.
Marshall before the General Assembly of the United Nations, Sept. 17, 1947.
U. S. Department of State *Bulletin,* Vol. 17 (Sept. 28, 1947), p. 622.
[9] Res. 111 (II), Nov. 13, 1947. See above, Chap. II.

effect to the provision of Article 11 of the Charter that grants the Assembly authority to consider "the general principles of co-operation in the maintenance of international peace and security" and to that part of Article 13 dealing with the promotion of international co-operation in the political field. In August 1948 the Interim Committee reported to the Assembly the results of its study of proposals submitted to the committee concerning the pacific settlement of international disputes.[10] Some delegations felt there were advantages to be gained by a long-range study of the entire system of pacific settlement of disputes as such study might lead to the discovery of inadequacies in procedures and techniques. Others suggested immediate measures that might be taken to improve existing procedures. The proposals that follow are those the Interim Committee recommended to the Assembly for its consideration.

Reactivation of General Act for Pacific Settlement

Belgium proposed that action be taken by the General Assembly to revise and revive a multilateral treaty of 1928, known as the General Act for the Pacific Settlement of International Disputes, to which the United States is not a party. That act required disputants to use devices of conciliation, arbitration, and judicial settlement in seeking peaceful settlement of their disputes. The Assembly at its spring session in 1949 adopted a resolution restoring the General Act to its original efficacy and amending it to enable organs of the United Nations to undertake functions that the League of Nations had formerly been authorized to perform.[11] Nineteen states had been parties to the convention originally, and it was adhered to later by several more countries.[12] The General Act, if fully accepted by adherents, makes resort to procedures of pacific settlement compulsory in the case of disputes arising among the

[10] U.N. General Assembly, Second Session, *Report of the Interim Committee to the General Assembly on a Study of Methods for the Promotion of International Co-operation in the Political Field,* Doc. A/605 (Aug. 13, 1948).

[11] Res. 268 (III)A, Apr. 28, 1949.

[12] By Nov. 21, 1931, Australia, Belgium, Canada, Denmark, Estonia, Finland, France, Great Britain, Greece, India, Irish Free State, Italy, Luxemburg, the Netherlands, New Zealand, Norway, Peru, Spain, and Sweden had adhered to all or part of the General Act.

signatories and thus imposes a stricter regime of pacific settlement than does the Charter.

Adherence to the act is voluntary. Only states that are unequivocally resolved that any dispute in which they might become involved must be settled by peaceful means are likely to become parties to the General Act. Even then, it could be argued, that adherence to such an act would not prevent a sovereign state from resorting to force in the settlement of a dispute if it believed that it was acting in self-defense.

Some proponents of peaceful procedures believe that the General Act is a step in the right direction in that it constitutes one more device to encourage states to accept as obligatory the peaceful settlement of their controversies. On the other hand, states that are most likely to become involved in international disputes because of the aggressive nature of their national policies simply do not adhere to the act and thus are not obligated to accept peaceful settlement of their disputes. In view of the lack of interest that has been demonstrated in the General Act so far, its effectiveness in the future will probably be limited to the less serious types of disputes that are likely to arise among genuinely peace-loving nations.

Appointment of Rapporteur

The United Kingdom proposed to the Interim Committee that the Security Council, as a general practice in the case of disputes before it, should appoint a conciliator or *rapporteur* to attempt to conciliate the disputants—a practice that was followed by the League of Nations. It was suggested that, during a reasonable time while such efforts were underway, the Council should suspend consideration of the matter. A resolution embodying this proposal was adopted by the General Assembly in the spring of 1949.[13] In early 1950, the Council agreed in appropriate cases to bear the proposal in mind. Thus far it has not used the recommended procedure.

The strength of this suggestion lies in the fact that it would provide an opportunity for negotiations behind the scenes that might make it possible for disputants to agree on some rational settlement of their dispute. Public discussion of disputes sometimes serves to exacerbate feelings and arouse emotions whereas a *rapporteur* might be able to keep the dispute from being publicized

---

[13] Res. 268 (III)B, Apr. 28, 1949.

while the underlying facts are being determined and analyzed. Moreover, the report of a competent *rapporteur* might be helpful in giving guidance to states that might be called on later to pass judgment as between the disputants. The appointment of a *rapporteur* also allows a cooling-off period, which could be most beneficial when tensions are high.

It must be remembered, however, that in some instances time may operate in favor of one of the disputants, and thus the appointment of a *rapporteur* might serve to promote the interests of that disputant. There may also be instances in which the main reason for bringing a matter to the attention of the Security Council would be to focus attention on the dispute so that world public opinion may wield an influence in its settlement.

The circumstances in which a dispute might arise are so varied and so unpredictable that it is at least doubtful whether there should be a hard and fast rule calling for the appointment of a *rapporteur* by the Security Council in all instances. Certainly it is advantageous, in the peaceful settlement of disputes, to employ procedures sufficiently flexible so that the unique factors that apply to each individual case can be evaluated and dealt with in an effective manner.

Establishment of a Panel for Enquiry and Conciliation

A joint United States-Chinese proposal was made to the Interim Committee that a panel of qualified individuals be established to be available to perform tasks of enquiry or conciliation in connection with disputes between states. This proposal was accepted by the General Assembly in 1949.[14] The panel of persons nominated by Member states is now available at the United Nations, but it has not been used.[15]

The theory underlying this proposal was that it would be helpful to have readily available a panel of qualified persons to conciliate

[14] Res. 268 (III)D, Apr. 28, 1949.

[15] Although the Panel for Enquiry and Conciliation has not been used technically for that purpose, it has provided a list of individuals available for special United Nations assignments. Thus Holger Anderson was on the list at the time of his selection as Director of the Refugee Office under the Palestine Conciliation Commission and Dr. Frank Graham was on the list when he was nominated for the post of United Nations Representative for Kashmir. See United States Mission to the United Nations, Press Release 1179 (Apr. 30, 1951).

disputes, and that its existence would increase the probability that states involved in disputes would turn to it for assistance. The suggestion was opposed by the Soviet Union, as were the other suggestions put forward by the Interim Committee, on the grounds that the committee itself was illegal and that it was attempting to set up conciliation procedures outside the control of the Security Council.

The difficulty with the suggestion for the creation of the panel of conciliators is that it also places the emphasis on the procedural rather than the substantive aspects of international disputes. It provides a useful mechanism or a means for peaceful settlement, but it does not provide states with the incentive they need to resolve their differences by peaceful procedures. It suggests a method for settlement but does not encourage resort to the procedure.

Permanent Commission of Good Offices

In 1949, Lebanon submitted to the Interim Committee a proposal for the creation of a permanent committee of conciliation to be a subsidiary organ of the General Assembly. It was hoped by the creation of such a committee that states involved in disputes would have readily available an agency that in time might build up a tradition of equity and justice applicable in the conciliation of disputes. The Interim Committee did not recommend this proposal to the Assembly. Neither did it recommend proposals submitted by Belgium, concerning submission of disputes to the Security Council for arbitration; by Canada, relating to minor amendments of the rules of procedure of the Security Council; and by Ecuador, concerning attempts by parties to disputes to take refuge in the domestic jurisdiction clause of the Charter. These proposals were kept before the Interim Committee for additional study.

In 1950, however, Yugoslavia proposed the inclusion of an item on the agenda of the Assembly for the establishment of a permanent commission of good offices. As the result of consideration by the Assembly of the Yugoslav proposal, a resolution proposed jointly by Lebanon and Uruguay was adopted referring the matter to the Interim Committee to be considered along with other similar proposals. The proposal has not been revived.

The record of the Interim Committee during its first year of existence was satisfactory. Three of its recommendations were accepted by the Assembly. As a practical matter, however, it must be noted that none of the recommendations have in fact created instruments of peaceful settlement that have been used. After the first year of operations, moreover, the Interim Committee lapsed into a period of relative inactivity. The mere existence of the committee may serve a pacific settlement purpose, however, although it appears that, if a dispute is important enough to be brought to the United Nations, there is a tendency for the Assembly itself to continue in session. Since its establishment, the Interim Committee has "never on its own initiative considered any situation or dispute or created a commission of inquiry."[16] Having failed to do this in its first seven years of existence, it seems unlikely that the committee offers much hope for future improvement of the pacific settlement procedures of the United Nations.[17]

Other Proposals

A number of proposals that might make the United Nations more effective in the field of peaceful settlement are considered elsewhere in this study because their emphasis is not primarily on the peaceful settlement procedures but on some other aspect of the Charter. Thus the suggestion that the veto power not be exercised in cases arising under Chapter VI of the Charter and other proposals that have been suggested with respect to the voting formula in the Security Council or the composition of that organ might tend to increase the effectiveness of the Council in the peaceful settlement of disputes, but these proposals are not primarily concerned with procedures for peaceful settlement, and therefore are considered later in this study.[18] Proposals designed to increase the effectiveness of the United Nations in the field of collective security action, for example, also might be expected to increase the effectiveness of the

[16] H. Field Haviland, Jr., *The Political Role of the General Assembly* (1951), p. 155.

[17] The existence of the Collective Measures Committee, which may serve to organize the collective use of force in enforcement cases, may also have the effect of encouraging disputing parties to settle their disagreements before they deteriorate into situations subject to enforcement action.

One suggestion has been made that the Assembly might create a committee similar to the Collective Measures Committee to consider methods of developing the work of the United Nations in the field of peaceful settlement. This proposal was made by Luis Padilla Nervo of Mexico in September 1952 at the time he turned over the presidency of the Assembly to his successor.

[18] See below, Chap. X.

United Nations in the field of peaceful settlement, but these are treated later.[19]

Most of the proposals to change the United Nations system with respect to procedures for peaceful settlement have been received and considered by the Interim Committee. There have, however, been other suggestions that might increase the effectiveness of the United Nations in this field.

Greater Use of the International Court

It has been suggested that the United Nations might be strengthened in the field of pacific settlement if the Security Council or the General Assembly would adopt the practice of refusing to consider legal disputes and of recommending to the parties that such disputes be taken to the International Court of Justice.[20] Indeed, one of the earliest criticisms of the Charter was voiced by those who were disappointed that more adequate provision was not made to expand the jurisdiction of the International Court with respect to legal disputes.[21]

Some current proposals suggest that the General Assembly or the Security Council, in cases involving legal questions so serious as to endanger international peace and security, might direct that the legal questions be submitted to the International Court of Justice for decision to be enforced by a reconstituted Assembly.[22] They suggest further that in disputes or situations endangering peace that may involve questions that "should be considered from the standpoint of what is reasonable, just and fair, rather than upon strictly legal principles, the General Assembly or the Executive Council may refer the dispute or situation to the World Equity Tribunal" for study and for recommendations. The recommendations would be submitted to the Assembly for approval.[23]

Although it might have been possible to strengthen the procedures for peaceful settlement by referring legal aspects of disputes to the Court, there is little evidence to indicate a disposition on the

[19] See below, Chap. VI.

[20] Clyde Eagleton, "Proposals for Strengthening the United Nations," *Foreign Policy Reports*, Vol. 25 (Sept. 15, 1949), p. 110.

[21] See Goodrich, *loc. cit.*, p. 969.

[22] Grenvilie Clark and Louis B. Sohn, *Peace Through Disarmament and Charter Revision* (Preliminary Print, July 1953), p. 69.

[23] *Ibid.*, p. 70.

part of Members to ascertain whether there are legal aspects of disputes that might be subject to judicial interpretation. Too often there has been resort to the Court only after a dispute has reached a political impasse, and the organ considering it has been at a loss for some place to turn. Judicial consideration ordinarily has not preceded political consideration of disputes. This is probably due in part to the fact that, by the time a dispute is before a United Nations organ, it has such overwhelming political overtones, and the disputants are so committed to their positions, that discernible legal aspects of the issue tend to be viewed as periphery.

Many disputes have legal aspects, but settlement of justiciable issues is not necessarily a major step toward the settlement of vital political issues that may be at stake. For example, the question whether approval of a resolution by the Assembly in a particular case might be inconsistent with the provisions in Article 2(7) of the Charter regarding domestic jurisdiction might be a legal matter for decision by the International Court of Justice. But even if the Court should decide that such an issue is a matter of domestic jurisdiction, the opinion would be only advisory in character, and the Assembly would be free to ignore that advice. In a case such as that concerning the treatment of Indians in South Africa, the Assembly has voted itself competent to deal with the matter despite the fact that it was argued that the domestic jurisdiction question should first have been referred to the Court for an advisory opinion.[24]

The Council and the Assembly have shown little tendency to cite authority of the Charter for the adoption of resolutions concerning peaceful settlement. Technical legal arguments have often been submitted in debate, but United Nations organs have not permitted legalisms of the Charter to hamper their recommendations. The Interim Committee in its 1950 report stated that: "The essentially political character of the General Assembly inclines it to decide its competence for itself or more often to assume competence without an express decision."[25] One commentator has observed that: "Each organ, and each Member State, has reserved the right to interpret the Charter as it pleases, and has not been willing to refer the matter to the Court. The decision in each case has been a political one;

[24] Res. 684(VII), Nov. 6, 1952.
[25] U.N. General Assembly, Fifth Session, *Official Records,* Supplement No. 14, p. 26.

if enough votes were available, the Charter was disregarded."[26] If these statements picture the true situation, it might well be questioned whether any amendments requiring the legal aspects of disputes to be referred to the Court would improve the pacific settlement functions of the United Nations.

The main stumbling block to acceptance of the suggestion that the United Nations refer legal aspects of disputes to the International Court is to be found not in restrictions of the Charter, but in the attitudes and practices of the states themselves. To the extent that states are willing to have the legal aspects of disputes threatening peace referred to the Court for settlement, the authority to invoke a recommendation for the adoption of such a procedure is already available. What is needed is more encouragement to states to do this, and the cultivation of attitudes of greater respect for the judicial function and specifically for the Court as a major organ of the United Nations.

Closely related to the general suggestion that the United Nations could be strengthened by more frequent reference of legal aspects of disputes to the International Court is the proposal made by Ecuador. It has suggested that if one party to a dispute refused to use the pacific settlement methods prescribed in Article 33 on the ground that the subject matter of the dispute is domestic in nature, then the issue whether the question is one of domestic jurisdiction should be referred to the Court for decision.

Experience has shown a tendency on the part of disputants to take refuge in the domestic jurisdiction clause of the Charter, which provides that the United Nations is not competent "to intervene in matters which are essentially within the domestic jurisdiction of any state."[27] Ecuador has suggested that if the organ of the United Nations considering the dispute, or the agent of such organ, should not be able to get the parties to agree to submit the aspect of the question regarding domestic jurisdiction to the Court, the General Assembly or the Security Council should request an advisory opinion on the matter. It was also suggested that the principle of referring the question of domestic jurisdiction to the Court should be incorporated in future agreements and that the International Law Commission should study the desirability of defining matters generally

---

[26] Eagleton, *loc. cit.*, p. 104.
[27] Art. 2(7).

accepted by international law as being within the domestic jurisdiction of a state.[28]

The proposal to refer questions regarding domestic jurisdiction to the Court was the subject of much debate in the Interim Committee. It was pointed out that those who drafted the Charter at the San Francisco Conference had considered giving the Court authority to decide the question of domestic jurisdiction but that, after lengthy discussion, it had been agreed that this issue should be left for determination by the United Nations organs concerned and to the individual states. The Ecuadoran proposal was closely related to decisions made at the San Francisco Conference relating to the Statute of the Court, particularly Article 36(2), regarding compulsory jurisdiction. Some Member states that were members of the Interim Committee felt that when they accepted the compulsory jurisdiction of the Court, the existence of the domestic jurisdiction clause had the effect of excluding from the jurisdiction of the Court disputes regarding matters essentially within domestic jurisdiction as determined by the Member state itself.[29] As the Ecuadoran proposal was highly controversial, the Interim Committee simply recommended that it be one of the matters that the Assembly might wish to recommend for further study by the committee. The instructions of the Assembly to the committee have continued to include reference to the study of recommendations such as the Ecuadoran proposal.

Periodic Meetings of Security Council Attended by Foreign Ministers

In 1950, when Secretary-General Lie proposed a twenty-year program for achieving peace through the United Nations, the first point in his memorandum suggested the "inauguration of periodic meetings of the Security Council, attended by Foreign Ministers or heads or other members of governments . . . together with further development and use of other United Nations machinery for ne-

[28] For summary see U.N. General Assembly, *Report . . . on a Study of Methods for the Promotion of International Co-operation in the Political Field,* p. 17.

[29] See, for example, S. Res. 196, 79 Cong., by which the United States accepted the compulsory jurisdiction of the Court, but stated that the declaration of acceptance "shall not apply to '. . . disputes with regard to matters which are essentially within the domestic jurisdiction of the United States as determined by the United States.' "

gotiation, mediation and conciliation of international disputes."[30] It was the Secretary-General's thought that semiannual meetings of this type at various places in the world would provide occasions for informal exchanges of views on outstanding problems and provide an opportunity not only to avert potential misunderstadings but also to iron out existing differences. He also suggested that the practice of using the President of the Security Council as a *rapporteur* for mediation and conciliation of disputes should be encouraged. Debate of the proposal in the Assembly quickly revealed Soviet opposition to the suggestion unless it were related to the admission of Communist China to the United Nations.

Over Soviet objections, the Assembly referred this recommendation to the Security Council for its consideration.[31] A year later, the Council had not considered the matter, and the Secretary-General reported: "I still believe that direct contact between the top policy makers of the great powers together with the non-permanent members of the Security Council around a conference table would be one of the best means to help reduce tensions and to promote a peaceful settlement of the conflicts that divide the world."[32] Consequently, the General Assembly resolved that the "appropriate organs of the United Nations . . . continue to give consideration to those portions of the memorandum of the Secretary-General with which they are particularly concerned."[33] No further action, however, was taken by the Council.

Although the proposal might be revived at any time, the idea of holding regular meetings of the heads of state or the foreign ministers of the five major powers under the auspices of the Security Council is now so related to political considerations that it probably would not be accepted unless a general relaxation of tensions takes place even though the problem of Chinese representation might be settled. Moreover, it is doubtful whether regular meetings of this type would by themselves improve the procedures in

[30] U.N. General Assembly, Fifth Session, Plenary, *Official Records*, 308th Meeting (Nov. 17, 1950), pp. 437-41.

[31] Res. 494(V), Nov. 20, 1950.

[32] U.N. General Assembly, Sixth Session, *Official Records*, Supplement No. 15, p. 1. John Foster Dulles in his book *War or Peace* (1950), makes the point in referring to the General Assembly, as distinguished from the Security Council, that "attendance by the foreign ministers of the great powers is particularly important." P. 197.

[33] Res. 608(VI), Jan. 31, 1951.

the Charter for peaceful settlement. The present Charter permits such meetings, and in fact Article 28(2) refers to periodic meetings of the Council "at which each of its members may . . . be represented by a member of the government or by some other specially designated representative." Meetings of the foreign ministers or the heads of state of the five major powers might not be an issue today if such informal consultations of these powers as those held at the San Francisco Conference had continued, or if the Charter had *required* such meetings at periodic intervals.

Quiet Diplomacy

The Secretary-General in proposing regular meetings of the heads of state suggested that they should be held "not primarily for public debate but for consultation—much of it informal—to gain ground towards an agreement to clear up misunderstandings."[34] It has been suggested from many other quarters that the United Nations has become too much a town meeting of the world—too much a propaganda forum. As one observer has pointed out:

> . . . to allow the debate [in the Council or the Assembly] to go on to the passage of a resolution frequently results . . . in a hardening of positions and an exacerbation of the conflict.
> It has been suggested, therefore, that the Security Council and possibly even the General Assembly should experiment with a plan under which, in certain cases, it would terminate debate following the principal statements on the part of all interested parties and at that point turn the negotiation over to a more private treatment.[35]

Public debate and discussion can have two principal effects. They can on the one hand be devices to bring out facts and ideas and to focus world attention and opinion on particular issues. On the other hand, they can also often lead to strained relations and bad feelings. The view has been expressed that "live issues, that might have been settled in the ordinary course of political negotiation, enter the doors of the United Nations to have their blood drawn (by frustrating wrangles which might have been solved easily by traditional diplomatic negotiation) and to be laid away on

[34] U.N. Department of Public Information, *Yearbook of the United Nations, 1950*, p. 215.
[35] Elmore Jackson, "Developing the Peaceful Settlement Functions of the United Nations," *Annals of the American Academy of Political and Social Science,* Vol. 296 (November 1954), p. 33.

slabs."[36] The concept of the Charter prevalent at the San Francisco Conference, however, was that it was an instrument under which there would be complete freedom "for the discussion of problems relating to peace and security . . . [and that] no state or group of states can prevent any nation from bringing a dispute before the Security Council and obtaining a hearing."[37]

It is undoubtedly true that the United Nations has provided a forum for public debate of many disputes that in the past might have been handled through diplomatic channels. Disputants have taken public positions from which it is hard, if not impossible, for them to withdraw without domestic political consequences they have been unwilling to face. There is some evidence to indicate that discussion in the United Nations of the dispute between India and South Africa regarding the treatment of Indians in South Africa has discouraged, rather than encouraged, settlement of the dispute.

At the same time, it must be remembered that the United Nations provides a meeting place where the representatives of sixty states gather daily in an atmosphere in which off-the-record discussions are easily possible. It might be noted in this connection that the proposal of the Interim Committee for the appointment of a *rapporteur* for situations or disputes brought to the attention of the Security Council makes the point that in the event such a *rapporteur* is appointed, "it would be desirable for the Security Council to abstain from further action on the case for a reasonable interval during which actual efforts at conciliation are in progress."[38] The final success of the United Nations Acting Mediator in the Palestine case may be attributed in no small measure to the fact that he persisted, in spite of many obstacles, in bringing representatives of the various principals together for quiet, confidential talks in which alternatives might be canvassed and flexibility maintained. Certainly, there seems to be fairly clear realization that in some cases the pacific settlement of disputes is more likely to be encouraged by what Secretary-General Hammerskjold has recently called "quiet diplomacy" than by public debate.

[36] James Burnham, "How the United Nations Can Be Made to Work," *Reader's Digest* (January 1948), p. 82.

[37] Francis O. Wilcox, "The Yalta Voting Formula," *American Political Science Review*, Vol. 39 (October 1945), p. 943.

[38] Res. 268 (III)B, Apr. 28, 1949. See U.N. Department of Public Information, *Yearbook of the United Nations, 1948-49*, p. 416.

*Increased Use of Authority
to Recommend Settlements*

Article 37(2) of the Charter gives the Security Council authority to "recommend such terms of settlement as it may consider appropriate" in disputes the continuance of which is likely to endanger the maintenance of peace. One writer has observed, however, that states parties to a dispute might be reluctant to have their disputes classified as likely to endanger peace, and frequently, "it is not politic or conducive to a prompt settlement" so to classify them. He suggests, therefore, that it might be wise "at some time when other Charter revisions are being made, for Article 37 to be redrafted" to eliminate the requirement that disputes subject to recommendation of the Council must be those likely to endanger peace. He notes that any dispute of sufficient importance to be put on the agenda of the Council or the Assembly is important enough for those bodies to be able to recommend terms of settlement without limiting that authority only to those cases likely to endanger peace.[39] There have been few cases in which the Council has recommended specific terms of settlement because such recomendations might be subject to a veto and would tend to freeze a situation that might later on be found possible of settlement on terms other than those recommended. There seems to be some fear, also, that the Council might lose prestige should it recommend terms of settlement only to have those recommendations ignored.

It has been proposed that the Council nevertheless should be less reluctant in attempting to spell out possible terms of settlement even though they might be vetoed. More specifically, pacific settlement of disputes might be improved if both the Assembly and the Council were to make use of subsidiary negotiating organs to settle international disputes and in appropriate cases "to make recommendations for settlement, and to release these recommendations if they felt that public consideration of them might promote settlement." It is urged that "if the negotiating organs had the power to publicize recommendations, the disputing parties might take these recommendations more seriously in the preceding private negotiations."[40]

Although this practice might in some instances encourage settle-

[39] Jackson, *loc. cit.*, p. 34.
[40] *Ibid.*

ment of disputes, the question would arise whether the Council or the Assembly, as the case might be, would approve the terms of settlement recommended by the subsidiary body. If the veto in the case of the Council, or a reluctant majority in the case of the Assembly, were to make it impossible to endorse terms of settlement recommended by subsidiary negotiating bodies, it would seem doubtful whether much advantage would be gained by this device. It is possible, of course, that terms of settlement recommended by subsidiary bodies might be so fair and reasonable as to command sufficient support and respect to encourage settlement along the lines recommended.

The suggestion that recommendations of subsidiary bodies be made public is not inconsistent with the proposal considered above that private, confidential negotiations may encourage the settlement of some disputes. It would be only in the event that a settlement had not been achieved by negotiations that consideration would be given to publication of recommendations for settlement. Publication of recommendations would presumably be for the purpose of using public opinion, in a mild way, to encourage disputant states to reach a settlement.

Responsibility for Disputed Areas

The suggestion has been made that one way in which the United Nations might make itself more effective in encouraging the peaceful settlement of some disputes would be to develop the practice of placing disputed or troubled areas, or areas of strategic importance, under the direct administration of the United Nations. As one analyst has suggested, "A precedent has been established in the case of Trieste. Such a procedure might have proved useful in the Palestine situation . . .; it might . . . serve to alleviate disputes over the Antarctic regions, or maintain order in troubled areas until a settlement had been reached."[41]

In the case of Trieste, which was finally settled outside the United Nations, the question whether the United Nations possessed authority to accept responsibility for supervision and guaranteeing the territorial integrity of Trieste was resolved by agreement of the major powers that the Security Council had such authority. An extension of the Trieste precedent to other disputed areas such

[41] Eagleton, *loc. cit.*, p. 110.

as Kashmir, Jerusalem, or the islands off the mainland of Communist China, however, would surely raise many serious questions.[42] Should the occasion demand, interested United Nations organs would probably find they have the necessary authority especially if the major powers should agree to such a course of action as they did in the case of Trieste.

A clear distinction must be maintained between the case of Trieste, which was a disputed area, and the idea that the United Nations might in some type of situations become the "administering authority" for a trust territory. Although there would seem to be no question that the United Nations under Article 81 might be such an "administering authority," Article 77 of the Charter limits trust territories to (1) territories formerly under mandate, (2) territories detached from former enemy states, and (3) territories voluntarily placed under the trusteeship system by states responsible for their administration. It has been suggested in some quarters, however, that Formosa might be found to be a territory "detached from" a former enemy state "as a result of the Second World War" and therefore be proper territory for which the United Nations might act as administering authority.

The availability of the United Nations to act as a third party in a situation involving either a disputed area or a trusteeship is an important factor to be taken into account in the peaceful settlement of disputes. The possibility of further development along these lines cannot be ignored. On the other hand, the United Nations has become a forum in which political rivalries meet and clash. So long as the United Nations is viewed primarily as a political body, it is not to be expected that it will serve as an impartial administrator. In those cases, however, in which the major powers do not find themselves at issue, it may be possible for the United Nations to develop the technique of international administration of disputed territory.

Peaceful settlement of disputes requires that the parties to the dispute be brought together to accept some *modus operandi* for the future. It requires that disputes be neither aggravated nor enlarged. Devices are available under the Charter for peaceful settlement

---

[42] Professor Louis B. Sohn has suggested that Quemoy and Matsu might be neutralized and demilitarized under supervision of the United Nations, finding precedent for such action in the case of guarantees of the League of Nations in the Aaland Islands. See letter to *New York Times* (Feb. 4, 1955), p. 20.

when the parties are desirous of resolving their disputes by peaceful means. The procedures do not need elaboration or improvement as much as they need to be used. There is danger that concentration on proposals to improve the procedures of the Charter may cause Member states to forget the fundamental principle that disputes can always be settled peacefully if there is an honest desire for such settlement.

The existence of the United Nations as a forum with world-wide press coverage is in some cases an open invitation to a disputant to bring his case to the attention of the public. The United Nations is also available for use by states that may be interested in promoting disputes instead of settling them. On the other hand, because of the existence of the United Nations, states cannot enter into disputes as lightly as they might have done in the past, in view of the fact that a dispute may now attract the attention of more states than those directly involved. In practice the United Nations has shown that it is interested in all international disputes brought to its attention even though they may not be controversies likely to endanger the peace.

Some of the proposals considered above might, if given effect, help strengthen the United Nations in inducing the peaceful settlement of disputes. The possibility that the General Assembly could expand the scope of the operations of the Interim Committee, in which the Soviet Union does not participate, might discourage excessive use of the veto under Chapter VI of the Charter simply because the Soviet Union might desire to keep the Security Council as an active participant in attempts to settle disputes. The suggestion of the United States and other countries that the veto power not be used in peaceful settlement may have some tendency to discourage its use in the future, especially in cases in which the five permanent members are not involved.

The suggestion has been made that the United Nations could be most effective as an instrumentality for the maintenance of international peace if it were to concentrate its energies on developing means for the peaceful settlement of disputes, leaving the main job of providing for collective security to regional organizations. Until the United Nations action in Korea, this was the direction in which the Organization appeared to be moving. But in Korea the United Nations became deeply involved as both policeman and judge.

Although it succeeded in stopping the aggression, it has not yet solved the political problems arising from it.

Serious question may be raised, however, whether peaceful settlement functions can effectively be divorced from collective security. If a dispute is not settled by peaceful means, it either continues as a point of conflict or it leads to hostilities. Once armed force is used by parties to a dispute, there is always a chance that hostilities may spread with the likelihood that more and more states will feel that their security is endangered, and they will demand that collective action be taken.

The fact is that the conflict—the so-called cold war—between the major powers is the situation most likely to endanger the maintenance of international peace. This situation cannot be manipulated out of existence by changes in the provisions of the Charter for peaceful settlement. Indeed, excessive concentration on and discussion of ways to improve provisions and techniques for peaceful settlement might create the dangerous illusion that peace can be maintained if only the proper procedures can be worked out. The result might be that false hopes would be raised only to be dashed when states showed they had no intention of following the procedures available.

CHAPTER VI

Collective Security Action

THE Charter of the United Nations distinguishes between action that may be taken by the Security Council in situations or disputes likely to endanger peace and security, and action in cases when there may exist threats to the peace, breaches of the peace, or acts of aggression. In the event of a situation or dispute likely to endanger the peace, suggestions in the form of recommendations may be prescribed to encourage settlement. But when the Council finds that peace is actually threatened, or has been breached, or that an act of aggression has taken place, it may take steps that might ultimately lead to the use of force to preserve or restore peace or to repel aggression. The Council may take such steps, however, only when the five permanent members and two nonpermanent members of the Council so agree. The effectiveness of these provisions to maintain peace is thus dependent on the unity and the collective determination of the great powers. But the necessary unanimity of the five permanent members of the Council has not existed since the Organization has been in being. In fact, the United Nations as an instrument attempting to preserve peace in a divided world is quite different from the organization envisaged at the San Francisco Conference.

Proposals to change the United Nations system with respect to its enforcement or collective security functions have included the creation of devices external to operations of the United Nations that proponents believe would have the effect of improving the United Nations system of collective security. They have also included suggestions for changes in the operations and procedures of the United Nations itself. For example, the wide acceptance of the proposition that the Security Council is not now and is not likely in the near future to be able to discharge its collective security responsibilities, has given rise to a number of suggestions on ways in which it might be reorganized to become a more effective organ for the United Nations. Although none of the great powers has advocated the abolition of the veto with respect to enforcement action as a way to improve the functioning of the Council, the United States and China have taken the lead in proposing limitation on the veto in other areas. Proposals to abolish the veto in enforcement action have been numerous, however, and ingenious devices have been suggested to change the voting formula in the Security Council. Suggestions have also been made that the Council should be reconstituted in various ways. It has been proposed that India be substituted for China as a permanent member, that the size of the Council be increased, that permanent membership be abolished, and that provision be made for Germany, Italy, and Japan to participate in some way in the work of the Council.[1]

Another result of the failure of the Council to become an effective instrumentality in the use of international force to preserve the peace is an increasingly important role for the General Assembly in this field. If there were a serious breach of the peace tomorrow, it is probable that the Members of the United Nations would resort to the Assembly rather than the Council as the organ best able to mobilize international force to restore peace or repel aggression.

The authority of the Council has not been effective primarily because the permanent members have been unable to agree on action when specific cases have been before the Council, and secondarily because they have been unable to agree on plans to make armed forces available at the call of the Council as contemplated by Article 43. The Council was able to act promptly in the Korean case because of the absence of the Soviet Union, but it was unable to act after the representative of the Soviet Union resumed his place at the Council table. Hence, although Chapter VII of the Charter gives the Security Council primary responsibility for the maintenance of peace and security, it would seem to be somewhat unwise at the present time to place much reliance on these provisions.[2]

[1] Matters regarding the veto and the organization of the Security Council are discussed below in Chap. X.

[2] See the volume in this Brookings series, *The United Nations and the Maintenance of International Peace and Security*. See also Leland M. Goodrich, "Regionalism and the United Nations," *Columbia Journal of International Affairs*, Vol. 3 (Spring 1949), p. 19: ". . . It must be recognized that when conditions have deteriorated to the point that they have reached within the United Nations, when the world security organization has, for all practical purposes ceased to exist as the result of the disintegration, or perhaps better the absence of great power unity, it is obviously unrealisic and dangerous to rely on non-existent guarantees for peace and security. Substitutes have to be found."

"Uniting for Peace" Resolution

In recognition of the fact that there is no promising future for the Security Council in the field of enforcement action so long as there is danger of a permanent member breaching the peace and the veto is exercised without restraint, the General Assembly on November 3, 1950, adopted the "Uniting for Peace" resolution. In the preamble, the Assembly noted that it was conscious of the failure of the Security Council to discharge its responsibilities especially with respect to "its primary responsibility for the maintenance of international peace and security."[3] This resolution, which changed the rules of procedure to make it possible to call the Assembly on twenty-four hours notice, in combination with that establishing the Interim Committee, has had the effect of making the Assembly, instead of the Council, the principal United Nations organ able to take action not only with respect to peaceful settlement activities but also with respect to enforcement functions. It has also had the effect of by-passing the veto as a device to forestall collective security measures in those cases in which two thirds of the members of the Assembly may be ready and willing to act.

Some view the experience of the United Nations in the Korean action as having the effect of practically eliminating the "great-power veto in the operation of collective security and collective self-defense, thus modifying the original conception of the Charter, that collective security could not function against a great power or any other state which such power wished to defend."[4] Others, however, view the "Uniting for Peace" resolution as having created a dangerous illusion—an illusion that the United Nations can be effective as a collective security instrument even when not backed up by the great powers; that a recommendation by the Assembly is as effective as a legal obligation imposed by the Security Council; and that forces need not be committed to the United Nations to make it effective in enforcement action. Whichever view is correct, the fact is that in the years since the beginning of the Korean conflict the United Nations has sought to increase the effectiveness of the General Assembly in the field of enforcement action.

[3] Res. 377(V), Nov. 3, 1950.
[4] Commission to Study the Organization of Peace, *Regional Arrangements for Security and the United Nations,* Eighth Report and Papers Presented to the Commission (June 1953), p. 17.

As a part of the program to strengthen the General Assembly, the "Uniting for Peace" resolution created the Collective Measures Committee. That committee of fourteen members was instructed to study and report on methods "which might be used to maintain and strengthen international peace and security in accordance with the Purposes and Principles of the Charter, taking account of collective self-defense and regional arrangements." A year later (January 12, 1952), after consideration of its first report, the Assembly directed the committee to continue its work and to pursue such further studies as it deemed advisable. The life of the committee has now been extended indefinitely on a stand-by basis.

The committee did not "attempt to anticipate any specific situation."[5] It concentrated instead on collective measures that might be taken by the United Nations or related agencies within the scope of *existing* international agreements. Its recommendations fell into four general categories: (1) preparatory action that Members might take to enable them to participate promptly and effectively in any future collective action, involving such steps as "ear marking" of units of national forces for possible United Nations service, and national legislation to permit them to provide assistance and facilities to United Nations forces engaged in collective military action; (2) collective political measures that might be taken to promote peace and security, ranging from simple appeals that disputes be settled by peaceful means, to collective agreement that changes brought about by force would not be recognized; (3) collective economic and financial measures, including the preparation of lists of arms, ammunitions, implements of war and other strategic items that might be subject to embargo in the event of future collective action, the suggestion that machinery be created to help see that burdens resulting from enforcement action might be equitably shared, and the use of specialized agencies in their particular fields of competence to assist in putting pressure on any state subjected to collective measures; and (4) military measures including recommendations that in the event of aggression the United Nations should immediately designate a state or group of states to act as an "executive military authority" on behalf of the United Nations, and recommendations designed to increase contributions of Members to military action by the creation of

[5] U.N. General Assembly, Seventh Session, *Official Records,* "Report of the Collective Measures Committee," Supplement No. 17 (1952), p. 2. (Hereinafter cited as "Second Report of the Collective Measures Committee.")

a "negotiating committee." In 1954 the Assembly approved a resolution endorsing certain principles of collective action recommended
by the committee, including one to the effect that, in the event of future United Nations action to repel aggression, logistic support
should be given to states willing to contribute man power but unable to train or supply their own contingents.[6]

The creation, and the continued existence, of the Collective
Measures Committee itself is one of the most important changes
that has taken place in the United Nations system since its inception. Furthermore, the establishment by the "Uniting for Peace"
resolution of the Peace Observation Commission of fourteen members, which "could observe and report on the situation in any area
where there exists international tension," provided both the Council
and the Assembly with a mechanism that might be useful both in
reducing threats to the peace and if enforcement decisions were to
become necessary. The full potentialities of the "Uniting for Peace"
resolution, and of the suggestions from the Collective Measures Committee, have not been tested.[7] An act of aggression would be necessary to determine whether the proposals of the committee have the
essential element of reality to make them effective. The committee
has itself recognized this fact. "Above all," it has noted, "the success
of any collective security effort depends upon the will and determination of individual States, which taken together constitute the organized strength of the international community of nations."[8]

In addition to the increasing role of the Assembly in the maintenance of international peace and security, there has been a cease-
less search for other methods to protect states from military aggression. The Charter itself suggested two complementary methods for
developing a collective defense system. The Vandenberg resolution
focused attention on (1) the possibility of the "progressive development of regional and other collective arrangements for individual
and collective self-defense in accordance with the purposes, princi-

---

[6] Res. 809 (IX), Nov. 4, 1954. See also U.N. Doc. A/2713 (Aug. 30, 1954); and
Chap. XIII below.

[7] One proposal with respect to future operations was put forth in these
words: "For purposes of collective security, might it be possible to associate
them [Germany, Italy, and Japan] with the work of the Peace Observation Commission established under the 'Uniting for Peace' Resolution? The Resolution
invites the cooperation of all governments with the Commission, and explicitly
authorizes the Commission to appoint sub-Commissions without saying whether
or not the members of these must be representatives of member states. . . ."
Hamilton Fish Armstrong, "The World Is Round," Foreign Affairs, Vol. 31 (January 1953), p. 198.

[8] "Second Report of the Collective Measures Committee," p. 2.

ples, and provisions of the Charter" (Articles 51 and 52 of the Charter) and (2) the possibility of contributing to peace by making clear the determination of the United States "to exercise the right of individual or collective self-defense under Article 51 should any armed attack occur affecting its national security."[9] Either course, or the two in combination, might serve to strengthen the collective defenses of peace-loving states that felt their security impaired by the ineffectiveness of the Security Council under cold-war conditions. The two possibilities have been explored by the development of regional security and collective defense pacts on the one hand and by a proposal to create a virtually world-wide defense arrangement under the terms of Article 51.

Regional Security and Collective Defense Pacts

A most important group of proposals that would change the United Nations system in the field of collective security action would involve either the substitution of regional security and collective defense arrangements for the world-wide collective security system envisaged by the Charter, or the use of such arrangements to augment the collective security system of the United Nations.[10]

The provisions of Chapter VIII of the Charter recognize that establishment of the United Nations did not preclude the "existence of regional arrangements or agencies for dealing with such matters relating to the maintenance of international peace and security as are appropriate for regional action." Article 51 under Chapter VII provides that "nothing in the present Charter shall impair the inherent right of individual or collective self-defense if an armed attack occurs against a Member of the United Nations." It has

[9] S. Res. 239, 80 Cong. 2 sess.

[10] For discussion of regionalism see "Regional Organizations: Their Role in the World Community," *Columbia Journal of International Affairs,* Vol. 3 (Spring 1949). Discussion here is principally of regional pacts that relate primarily to security, although most such arrangements do have economic aspects. The issue of "regionalism *v.* globalism" is not new—the convinced regionalist being one who would give regional organizations many functions other than defense. Sir Winston Churchill, who in 1943 proposed a regional approach toward a postwar organization, recently remarked in the House of Commons that if he had had the power, "I should not have made the United Nations organization in its present shape or form. On the contrary, I always said that it ought to be based on regional organizations which should aim at drawing the largest and most important minds from large groups of nations and bringing them to a sort of super-assembly at the summit." Great Britain, *Parliamentary Debates,* 524 H. C. Deb., Col. 204. See also N. J. Padelford, "Regional Organization and the United Nations," *International Organization* (May 1954), pp. 203-16.

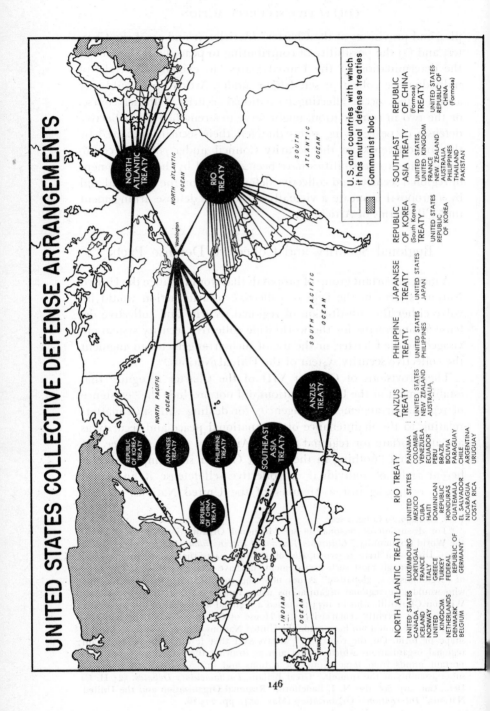

UNITED STATES COLLECTIVE DEFENSE ARRANGEMENTS

NORTH
ATLANTIC
TREATY

RIO
TREATY

Washington

REPUBLIC OF KOREA TREATY

JAPANESE TREATY

PHILIPPINE TREATY

REPUBLIC OF CHINA TREATY

SOUTHEAST ASIA TREATY

ANZUS TREATY

☐ U. S. and countries with which it has mutual defense treaties
▨ Communist bloc

NORTH ATLANTIC
OCEAN

SOUTH
ATLANTIC
OCEAN

SOUTH PACIFIC
OCEAN

NORTH PACIFIC
OCEAN

INDIAN
OCEAN

FRANCE

NORTH ATLANTIC TREATY

UNITED STATES
CANADA
ICELAND
NORWAY
UNITED KINGDOM
NETHERLANDS
DENMARK
BELGIUM

LUXEMBOURG
PORTUGAL
FRANCE
ITALY
GREECE
TURKEY
FEDERAL REPUBLIC OF GERMANY

RIO TREATY

UNITED STATES
MEXICO
CUBA
HAITI
DOMINICAN REPUBLIC
HONDURAS
GUATEMALA
EL SALVADOR
NICARAGUA
COSTA RICA

PANAMA
COLOMBIA
VENEZUELA
ECUADOR
PERU
BRAZIL
BOLIVIA
PARAGUAY
CHILE
ARGENTINA
URUGUAY

ANZUS TREATY

UNITED STATES
NEW ZEALAND
AUSTRALIA

PHILIPPINE TREATY

UNITED STATES
PHILIPPINES

JAPANESE TREATY

UNITED STATES
JAPAN

REPUBLIC OF KOREA (South Korea) TREATY

UNITED STATES
REPUBLIC OF KOREA

SOUTHEAST ASIA TREATY

UNITED STATES
UNITED KINGDOM
FRANCE
NEW ZEALAND
AUSTRALIA
PHILIPPINES
THAILAND
PAKISTAN

REPUBLIC OF CHINA (Formosa) TREATY

UNITED STATES
REPUBLIC OF CHINA (Formosa)

146

been established that this provision does not prevent collective defensive preparations in advance of attack.[11]

Postwar Development

Prior to the Korean action, the realization grew that "largely because of Soviet obstruction and abuse of the veto, the United Nations [had] not yet become so fully effective in achieving collective security as had been hoped."[12] As a result, attention was turned to regional security and collective-defense arrangements as a device to provide collective security that states were not finding in the United Nations.

The Inter-American Treaty of Reciprocal Assistance (1947), the Brussels Pact (1948), as amended (1954), the North Atlantic Treaty (1949), the Security Treaty Between the United States, Australia, and New Zealand (1951), similar treaties with Japan, the Philippines, Korea, and the Republic of China, as well as the South East Asia Collective Defense Treaty (1954), were based on the inherent right of self-defense, which is recognized in Article 51 of the Charter, although the Pacific treaties do not make specific mention of Article 51.[13] The network of regional, as well as bilateral, defense arrangements to which the United States is a party is indicated on the accompanying map.

During this same period, the Soviet Union was developing its own system of alliances. Although this system differs "both in form and substance, from [the] 'regional arrangements' [of the free world], in the textual, formal sense of the term, the Soviet treaties . . . fit within the provisions of Articles 51 and 107, and of Chapter VIII of the United Nations Charter."[14] A student of political and military agreements in the Far East and the Pacific, after a review

[11] See Senate Committee on Foreign Relations, *North Atlantic Treaty*, S. Exec. Rept. 8, 81 Cong. 1 sess. (June 6, 1949), p. 22.

[12] U. S. Department of State, *The North Atlantic Pact: Collective Defense and the Preservation of Peace, Security, and Freedom in the North Atlantic Community*, Publication 3462 (March 1949), esp. pp. 9-11.

[13] For analysis of regional security, collective defense, and similar arrangements see the volume in this Brookings series, *Regional Security and the United Nations*.

[14] Harry N. Howard, "The Soviet Alliance System and the Charter of the United Nations," in Commission to Study the Organization of Peace, *Regional Arrangements for Security and the United Nations*, p. 79. See, however, W. W. Kulska, "The Soviet System of Collective Security Compared with the Western System," *American Journal of International Law*, Vol. 44 (July 1950).

of the agreements concluded among the free nations as well as between the Soviet Union and China, comments that these treaties "in motivation as well as character . . . do not supplement but rather express distrust in the peace machinery of the United Nations. This, of course, does not necessarily prevent them from contributing to peace and security. But they are doing so not in the Charter's spirit of cooperative, collective effort toward mutual restraint but instead by the precarious balancing of mutually opposed groupings."[15] More recently, the Soviet Union, in proposing a European security arrangement, has advocated utilizing the provisions of Article 51 of the Charter and has contended that such an arrangement would be in support of the purposes of the United Nations.

The crucial question in considering suggestions that more emphasis should be placed on creating regional security and collective defense arrangements, is whether such arrangements will help to preserve international peace. In 1952 John Foster Dulles said that "we must reverse" the trend toward regional arrangements, which has "undermined the United Nations to a certain extent."[16] But in the spring of 1953 as Secretary of State, he expressed the view that "the feeling has grown that security may have to be achieved primarily through regional organizations which are authorized by the United Nations Charter, but which to some extent function outside of the scope of the United Nations' direct authority." Although the establishment of such organizations may involve a departure from the principles and hopes of the Charter, after they are all made and put together, the end result may be just about what is contemplated by the Charter. These regional associations are "actually a demonstration of the basic principle of the United Nations, and a realization of that principle in the ways which perhaps are at the moment the most practical, having regard to the exercise of the veto power by the Soviet Union."[17]

Similar views were expressed by Secretary of State Dulles in August 1953, to the American Bar Association at Boston. At that time he

[15] Werner Levi, "Political and Military Agreements in the Far East and Pacific," in Commission to Study the Organization of Peace, *Regional Arrangements for Security and the United Nations,* p. 124.

[16] *New York Times* (July 16, 1952).

[17] "An Expression of Faith in the United Nations," Remarks of Secretary Dulles, Mar. 1, 1953, U. S. Department of State *Bulletin,* Vol. 28 (Mar. 16, 1953), pp. 403-04.

said: "Because the United Nations itself does not provide adequate security, the United States has, by bipartisan action, entered into a series of treaties with other nations for the purpose of furthering collective self-defense. This is authorized by the U.N. Charter."[18]

The position taken by Secretary Dulles that regional and other collective defense pacts strengthen, rather than weaken, the United Nations is consistent with the position taken by the previous administration when it negotiated the North Atlantic Treaty. That treaty was "designed . . . to fit precisely into the framework of the United Nations and to assure practical efforts for maintaining peace and security in harmony with the Charter." Its purpose was "to help bring about world conditions which will permit the United Nations to function as contemplated at the San Francisco Conference."[19]

Somewhat in contrast to this view is that taken by the Commission to Study the Organization of Peace, the research affiliate of the American Association for the United Nations. The commission has been concerned that such arrangements might "encourage aggression and . . . stimulate the creation of a rival arrangement . . . [as] political competition . . . [may tend] to draw states into a bi-polarized world of great instability."[20] Consideration of the arguments for and against the establishment of any additional arrangements leads the commission to the conclusion that "stability would probably be promoted if there were a larger number of more nearly equal regional and collective self-defense arrangements in the world. In such circumstances, the United Nations could be strengthened as a force in the world equilibrium and as the agency for collecting national and regional forces against aggression."[21] The commission recommended therefore that the United Nations be strengthened "so that no regional or collective defense arrangement can be more powerful [than the United Nations] in any situation." It felt, however, that action needs to be taken "to stop a trend toward a bipolarized world by fostering various [regional] centers of power and of committing each to United Nations responsibilities."[22]

---

[18] *Ibid.*, Vol. 29 (Sept. 7, 1953), p. 307.

[19] U. S. Department of State, *The North Atlantic Pact: Collective Defense . . . in the North Atlantic Community*, see pp. 5-8.

[20] Commission to Study the Organization of Peace, *Regional Arrangements for Security and the United Nations*, p. 28.

[21] *Ibid.*, p. 34.

[22] *Ibid.*, p. 10.

Hamilton Fish Armstrong, Editor of *Foreign Affairs,* is also concerned about any moves to strengthen regional organizations at the expense of the United Nations, especially by the suggestion that the United Nations should concentrate on the function of peaceful settlement, leaving to regional and other collective defense arrangements responsibility for resisting aggression. He believes that "playing down the role of the United Nations as a security organization and extolling it as a forum for discussion" is dangerous because in that process the United Nations will "little by little be turned into an agency of appeasement." He points out that so many United States interests "are not covered by the Atlantic organization that our choice must necessarily be the larger grouping and the strategy which it makes possible."[23]

Secretary-General Hammarskjold has also cautioned against any tendency to by-pass the machinery of the United Nations. In his report of 1953-54 he wrote:

. . . developments outside the organizational framework of the United Nations, but inside its sphere of interest, do give rise to certain problems which require serious consideration. In the short view, other approaches than those provided by the United Nations machinery may seem more expedient and convenient, but in the long view they may yet be inadvisable. To fail to use the United Nations machinery on those matters for which Governments have given to the Organization a special or primary responsibility under the Charter, or to improvise other arrangements without overriding practical and political reasons—to act thus may tend to weaken the position of the Organization and to reduce its influence and effectiveness, even when the ultimate purpose which it is intended to serve is a United Nations purpose.

The balance to be struck here must be struck with care.[24]

On the matter of security the "regionalists" and the "globalists" undoubtedly have a different fundamental approach. The United Nations was founded on the assumption that it was in the interest of all states to attempt to achieve universal security by the creation of a nearly universal international organization. When the Charter

[23] Armstrong, *loc. cit.,* pp. 196-97. In the same vein, the former United States representative to the United Nations, Ernest A. Gross, has asked: "Might it not be argued that much of the talk about regional guarantees and security pacts is debasing the value of the underlying guarantee of the Charter, which has been called 'the most solemn peace pact of history'?" "United Nations Charter Review," *Social Action* (December 1954), p. 11.

[24] U.N. General Assembly, Ninth Session, *Official Records,* "Annual Report of the Secretary General on the Work of the Organization, 1 July 1953–30 June 1954," Supplement No. 1 (1954), p. xi.

referred to the taking of "collective measures" to maintain peace, the reference was to all Members of the United Nations, not to regional groupings of states. But is it true that the security of a particular state is best ensured by the United Nations? Might it not be that a regional organization would be more effective in organizing collective defense for an area and putting that defense to use in the event of need?

It would seem to be easier to comprehend a threat to the security of a state if aggression is directed at its neighbor than if it is aimed at a nation half a world away. It was Winston Churchill's view in 1943 that the postwar international organization should be based on the regional principle because "it was only the countries whose interests were directly affected by a dispute that could be expected to apply themselves with sufficient vigor to secure a settlement."[25] It is also safer for nations to plan defense against possible aggression when the potential aggressor does not sit in on the council charged with the responsibility for making that plan. An additional consideration is that when aggression is threatening a group of nations in a given area of the world, there is no choice but to resort to regional and other collective defense arrangements when efforts of the world organization can in fact be stymied by the aggressor, or its ally, through use of the veto and other delaying tactics. If the issue is one of survival and halting aggression already in motion the choice is clear, as it was in the formation of the North Atlantic Treaty Organization and the South East Asia Collective Defense Treaty Organization.

Co-ordination with the United Nations

The principal concern of supporters of the United Nations who have viewed the development of regional organizations with some alarm is that such organizations may tend to weaken the United Nations. The late Senator Taft wrote: "The very adoption of the Atlantic Pact seems to me to constitute recognition of the impotence of the United Nations."[26]

Proposals to integrate regional security and collective defense arrangements more closely with the United Nations find their principal support among those who have been most closely associated

[25] *The Memoirs of Cordell Hull*, Vol. 2 (1948), p. 1642.
[26] Robert A. Taft, *A Foreign Policy for Americans* (1951), p. 44.

with the United Nations. A number of such suggestions are found in the reports of the Collective Measures Committee. Some of those recommendations have been elaborated by the Commission to Study the Organization of Peace. The commission points out that two "gigantic" regional systems (the North Atlantic Treaty Organization and the Soviet alliance system) have functioned relatively independently of the United Nations, and their rivalry and mutual fears have resulted in an arms race that has tended to draw states to one side or the other, to weaken the United Nations as an agency of collective security, and to threaten a new world war. According to the commission, "Regional arrangements which become very large and powerful tend to withdraw the interest of their members from the United Nations, to reduce the confidence of others in the United Nations, to escape the control of the United Nations, to be looked upon by neighboring non-members as dangerous, to divide the world into hostile poles of power, and thus to reduce international security and prospects of peace generally."[27]

To reduce this threat to the United Nations and to try to limit the tendency toward "bipolarization," the commission has made a number of recommendations concerning the relationship between collective defense or regional arrangements and the United Nations. The commission recommends that forces created pursuant to the terms of regional arrangements should, "like national contingents, be made available to the United Nations in case of aggression anywhere and preparations should be made for the effective use of such forces by the United Nations as suggested in the first report of the UN Collective Measures Committee."[28] The Collective Measures Committee, it should be pointed out, had suggested that:

. . . If a breach of the peace or act of aggression involving the application . . . of the provisions of one of these collective self-defense or regional arrangements occurred, and if, to meet that situation, the United Nations resolved to undertake collective military measures for the restoration of international peace and security, there should be a mutually supporting relationship between the activities of such arrangements or agencies and the collective measures taken by the United Nations. . . . Also, the Security Council or the General Assembly might consider whether some or all of the States parties to such an arrangement in the area where the situation

[27] Commission to Study the Organization of Peace, *Regional Arrangements for Security and the United Nations*, pp. 9, 33.

[28] *Ibid.*, p. 10. National contingents, of course, have not been made available to the United Nations as contemplated by Article 43.

arose might, in certain cases, be invited to act jointly, within the limits of such arrangements, on behalf of the United Nations.[29]

Although collective defense arrangements might incorporate provisions authorizing the detail of their forces to the United Nations, consideration might also be given to amending Articles 43-47 of the Charter in order to make it clear that the United Nations would have authority to call on regional military units for assistance.[30] In view of the fact that, at the present time, the only sizable forces under an international command are the contingents of the states members of the North Atlantic Treaty Organization, such an amendment would make it possible for the United Nations to seek military assistance from forces in being if the need should arise.

Intimately related to the proposal for the detail of contingents to the United Nations is the suggestion that if regional organizations are required to act in self-defense, "they should discontinue any defensive action undertaken when so directed by the General Assembly."[31] The Collective Measures Committee proposed that in the event "of the failure of the State or group of States designated as the executive military authority to carry out their responsibilities to the satisfaction of the United Nations, the appropriate United Nations body should determine whether the mandate should be continued or brought to an end."[32] In the opinion of the Commission to Study the Organization of Peace, members should agree to modify any provision of the regional arrangement "found by a vote of any seven members of the Security Council or by a two-thirds vote of the General Assembly to be inconsistent with the purposes and principles of the United Nations." Furthermore, regional organizations should respect "recommendations for the utilization of regional arrangements by the United Nations in enforcement measures" when such recommendations are made by "a vote of any seven members of the Security Council or by a two-

[29] U.N. General Assembly, Sixth Session, *Official Records*, "Report of the Collective Measures Committee," Supplement No. 13 (1951), pp. 23-24. (Hereinafter cited as "First Report of the Collective Measures Committee.")

[30] Article 43(3) authorizes the conclusion of agreements between the Security Council and "groups of Members" to be ratified by signatory states in accordance with their constitutional processes. This language might be broad enough to encompass the purposes suggested.

[31] Commission to Study the Organization of Peace, *Regional Arrangements for Security and the United Nations*, p. 10.

[32] "First Report of the Collective Measures Committee," p. 25.

thirds vote of the General Assembly."[33] The commission also recommended that reports required by Articles 51 and 54 of the Charter
respecting collective self-defense arrangements and regional arrangements should be sent to the General Assembly as well as to the
Security Council.[34]

The total effect of this series of proposals, if adopted, can be
better appreciated if they are restated as a group: (1) If the United
Nations does not like any provision of a regional arrangement,
members of the regional organization should modify that provision
to satisfy the United Nations. (2) If a regional organization takes
action that it believes is required to ensure the defense of its members, but the United Nations finds differently and directs the regional group to cease its action, it should do so. (3) If the United
Nations recommends that a regional organization should be utilized
for United Nations purposes, the particular organization should
comply, but if at any time the United Nations changes its position
and is not satisfied with the action of the regional organization
undertaken at the request of the United Nations, the United Nations should be able to call a halt to such action.

If these proposals were accepted by regional and other collective defense arrangements, the United Nations would have substantially more control than it now has over these arrangements
even though such control was not contemplated by the Charter.
Supporters of these ideas believe, however, that their acceptance
would tend to put the United Nations back into its "rightful" position on the world scene—the principal organization responsible for
the maintenance of international peace and security. According to
the Commission to Study the Organization of Peace, "regional arrangements should be so controlled by the United Nations as to assure that they will be used for collective security purposes. . . . Political action by such arrangements should be subject to ultimate review,
judgment and control by some organ of the United Nations."[35]

The United States Government has strongly supported the conclusion of certain regional security and collective defense pacts. It
has also been the leading proponent of the "Uniting for Peace" resolution and the proposals made by the Collective Measures Commit-

---

[33] Commission to Study the Organization of Peace, *Regional Arrangements for
Security and the United Nations*, pp. 10-11.

[34] *Ibid.*, p. 11.

[35] *Ibid.*, p. 33.

tee. It follows that, officially speaking, there is no inconsistency between support of the creation of regional groupings and at the same time taking other types of action to streamline United Nations machinery in the field of collective security.

Indeed, it may be argued that it is a good idea for a state, as a matter of insurance, to participate in two collective defense arrangements—one on a world-wide basis and the other on a regional basis. The United States is now a key member in four such arrangements on a regional basis. There are some who believe, however, that the danger always exists that preoccupation with the development of such arrangements on a regional basis may draw attention away from the often reiterated proposition that the United Nations is the "cornerstone" of United States foreign policy. Moreover, despite the best of intentions, there is likely to be an area of competition between a regional organization and the United Nations when both are concentrating on collective security. If a nation, for example, has committed military forces to the North Atlantic Treaty Organization, will it be as ready and able to commit forces to the United Nations for use in areas other than the Atlantic area? If it contributes funds to the regional secretariat, are there sufficient funds left for the United Nations?

The concept of a world organization to preserve peace rests on the assumption that a breach of the peace anywhere is of concern to the organization. Official preoccupation with establishing regional and other collective defense arrangements however, would seem to indicate some lack of confidence in the United Nations as being able to provide adequate collective defense forces. It also suggests that there are still some who believe that peace may be divisible or that small wars may be fought and controlled without erupting into world wars.

It will be recalled that the North Atlantic Treaty was concluded because there was general recognition that the United Nations was not developing as an effective instrument to prevent aggression. But when the one big postwar aggression in Korea confronted the world, the United Nations was instrumental in stopping it. Probably one of the greatest deterrents to aggression is knowledge on the part of a potential aggressor that it will meet quick, unified, well co-ordinated, and carefully planned reaction to attack. One of the best ways of deciding on the desirability of particular proposals to change the United Nations system with respect to the maintenance of peace is to determine whether such proposals actually make peace-loving states better able to plan and effect a strong defense in the case of attack.

World-Wide Pact Under Article 51

Although the arrangements discussed above are devices to give effect on a regional basis to the "inherent right of individual or collective self-defense" recognized by Article 51 of the Charter, it has been suggested that this article might also serve as the basis for the conclusion of defense arrangements on a world-wide scale. A universal collective defense system might be devised that would be within the terms of Article 51, and at the same time would avoid the pitfall of the veto and the problem resulting from the inability of the great powers to reach agreement to supply armed forces to the Security Council.

Such a proposal was embodied in a resolution introduced in the Eighty-first Congress by the late Senator Thomas of Utah and Senator Douglas of Illinois. Senate Concurrent Resolution 52 pledged the support of Congress to a "supplementary agreement under Article 51 of the Charter open to all members of the United Nations, by which the signatories [would] agree, if the Security Council is prevented from fulfilling its duties, to come to the aid of the victim of attack if requested to do so by a two-thirds vote of the General Assembly, including three of the permanent members of the Security Council." Senator Douglas, testifying before the Senate Committee on Foreign Relations in support of the resolution, stated that if such a convention to be proposed by the United States were adopted, it would mean that the signatories would "agree to use force against any nation which is adjudged to be an aggressor by a two-thirds vote of the General Assembly of the United Nations, including three of the so-called Big Five Powers." In addition, the proposed convention would bind the signatory powers "to name in advance the specific military, naval, and air components which they [would] maintain and furnish to an international police force."[36]

---

[36] For resolution and full argument in support, see *Revision of the United Nations Charter,* Hearings before a Subcommittee of the Senate Committee on Foreign Relations, 81 Cong. 2 sess., pp. 3 ff. For draft supplementary treaty along the line suggested, see Commission to Study the Organization of Peace, *Collective Defense under the United Nations,* Sixth Report (May 1948).

The way in which such a pact would operate can be indicated by referring to the Korean situation, and assuming for purposes of illustration, that the Soviet Union, instead of being absent when the Security Council called on Members of the United Nations to assist the Republic of Korea to repel aggression, had been present and had vetoed the resolutions designed to deal with the aggression. In such circumstances, the Security Council would have been unable to act. Had the proposed Article 51 pact been in effect, however, the Council by a simple procedural vote not subject to a veto could have referred the matter to the General Assembly. If the Assembly had by a two-thirds vote, including the votes of three of the five major powers, called on states that had ratified the pact to come to the aid of South Korea, they would have been obligated by treaty to do so. Moreover, the pact would have specified the forces that each of its signatories agreed to maintain for immediate use by the United Nations.

Although the Article 51 pact proposal would not involve formal amendment of the Charter, it would have profound implications for the United Nations system. It would be a device to bring a substantial number of Members of the Organization, including at least three of the five major powers, to the aid of a victim of aggression in those cases in which the exercise of the veto might prevent the United Nations from taking action.[37] It would provide a method to by-pass the requirement of the Charter that decisions of the Security Council relating to breaches of the peace or aggression could only be taken with the concurring votes of the five permanent members. Moreover, as the proposal calls for a treaty to be concluded outside the Charter, it would by-pass the amending provisions of the Charter, which, before becoming effective, require the approval of all the permanent members of the Council.

Another effect of the proposal would be to put the five major powers more nearly on a par with other Members of the United Nations with respect to accepting decisions of the Security Council on action in the event of aggression. Article 25 of the Charter requires Members to accept and carry out certain decisions of the Security Council. That article, however, does not apply to the

[37] For full discussion see Hamilton Fish Armstrong, "Coalition for Peace," *Foreign Affairs*, Vol. 27 (October 1948), pp. 1-16; Paul H. Douglas, "United to Enforce Peace," *ibid.*, Vol. 30 (October 1951), pp. 1-16; Commission to Study the Organization of Peace, *The Security of the United States of Western Europe* (January 1949).

permanent members of the Council as they could veto any substantive decision that might apply to them. The Article 51 pact would, in a limited class of cases, make it possible for a number of Members of the United Nations, acting on the basis of a decision by the Assembly, to take action against as many as two of the five major powers simultaneously, provided the other three permanent members of the Council agreed—a situation that might easily provoke a general war.

Those who support the Thomas-Douglas resolution believe that a world or regional federation is not feasible under existing conditions and that regional defense arrangements would detract from the United Nations. They believe that amendments to the Charter are neither a solution for the real problem of international peace and security, nor practicable as an immediate policy. They urge that by the proposed pact the United Nations could be strengthened in such a way that aggression might be effectively deterred.[38]

Proponents of the Article 51 pact likewise point out that there is ample precedent for their proposal. They argue that the Inter-American Treaty of Reciprocal Assistance (the Rio Treaty) and the North Atlantic Treaty are instances in which certain Members of the United Nations exercised their "inherent right" to self-defense by banding together outside the United Nations. Such action is authorized by Article 51 of the Charter. The principal difference between the Thomas-Douglas proposal and these other self-defense arrangements, according to proponents, is that the Thomas-Douglas proposal would merely enlarge the area covered (an open-ended North Atlantic Treaty, so to speak) so that a larger number of states would agree among themselves that in certain contingencies they would take specific defense action. It is also pointed out that this proposal is consistent with the primary purpose of the United Nations—the maintenance of international peace and security—in the same way that the Rio and North Atlantic treaties promote that purpose.[39]

It is not necessary, of course, to tie a supplementary pact of this character so closely to the United Nations as to bring it into effect only when two thirds of the General Assembly believe an armed

---

[38] For principal arguments in support of resolution, see Senate Committee on Foreign Relations, *Revision of the United Nations Charter*, S. Rept. 2501, 81 Cong. 2 sess. (Sept. 1, 1950), p. 26.

[39] See S. Exec. Rept. 8, 81 Cong. 1 sess., p. 1.

attack has occurred. The general formula can be varied. Lord Cecil, Viscount Cecil of Chelwood, for example, has proposed a supplementary treaty to come into effect when approved by at least three permanent members of the Security Council and not less than twenty other Members of the United Nations. Action in the case of aggression or a threat of aggression would be determined by a vote of two thirds of the parties to the treaty present and voting—not by vote of the Assembly as in the case of the Thomas-Douglas proposal. "Aggressive war" (which would bring this pact into effect) is defined as "an armed attack by any State on any of the High Contracting Parties likely to impair its political independence or territorial integrity in order to compel such High Contracting Party to comply with the demands of the aggressor." This proposal has the serious practical shortcoming of making it possible to authorize military enforcement action even though it might be opposed by the states possessing substantial military forces.[40]

If the proposed Article 51 pact were to go as far as its proponents suggest, and if the United States were to become a party to the pact, it would thereby pledge itself in advance to go to the aid of a state that is attacked if requested to do so by two thirds of the General Assembly, including three of the permanent members of the Security Council. In other words, even though the United States might be one of the permanent members of the Security Council opposed to the proposed action, if the requisite two-thirds vote were obtained, and if three other permanent members agreed, the United States would be legally committed "to come to the aid of the victim." It might be argued that "aid" does not mean that this country would be committed to use force, but as the proposed agreement contemplates the earmarking of specific military forces to be available on call, it must be assumed that a situation might arise in which American military forces might be committed, even if the United States were opposed.

Senator Arthur Vandenberg, in describing the commitments of the Charter to his colleagues in the Senate during July 1945, remarked that the United States "cannot be called to participate in any sort of sanctions, military or otherwise, without our own free and untrammeled consent."[41] Under the proposed Article 51 pact, if

[40] For text of proposed pact and discussion see Alan de Rusett, *Strengthening the Framework of Peace* (1950), pp. 1-15.

[41] *Congressional Record*, Vol. 91, Pt. 6, 79 Cong. 1 sess., p. 7956.

approved by the Senate, however, the United States would consent in advance to commit armed forces to possible military action at some future time, in unknown circumstances, and on decision of two thirds of the members of the General Assembly, including three of the five major powers. This would be a more substantial international commitment than the United States has ever before taken. It would abridge the concept of sovereignty to a substantial degree and would raise the question whether the United States could enter into an agreement of this nature without amending the Constitution.

Neither the North Atlantic Treaty nor the Rio Treaty carries such far-reaching obligations. The commitment in the North Atlantic Treaty is, in the event of attack on any of the parties, to take forthwith such action as "the Party deems necessary, including the use of armed force." (Article 5.) The Rio Treaty provides that in case of an armed attack on any party, the parties shall "assist in meeting the attack." (Article 3.) Although decisions of the "Organ of Consultation" created by the Rio Treaty are to be taken by a two-thirds vote, decisions that require the use of armed force are qualified by the "sole exception that no State shall be required to use armed force without its consent." (Article 20.) Thus in each of these cases the United States could, without violation of the terms of the treaties, refuse to commit its armed forces on the grounds that such action was not deemed "necessary" in the case of the North Atlantic Treaty, or because it would not "consent," in the case of the Rio Treaty.[42]

In observing what effect the Article 51 pact would have on the principle of sovereign equality, it must be noted that, technically at least, it has no effect on the United Nations Charter. The doctrine of sovereign equality in Article 2 would remain unimpaired. As a practical matter, however, those permanent members of the Security Council that might become parties to such a pact would in fact sacrifice part of their control over their own armed forces—not through the United Nations, but through the terms of the proposed agreement.

The proposed Article 51 pact would be much broader in geographic scope and membership than either the Rio or the North

[42] For text of Rio Treaty see *United Nations Treaty Series*, Vol. 21, No. 324 (1947), pp. 78-185. For text of North Atlantic Treaty see *ibid.*, Vol. 34, No. 541 (1949), pp. 244-55.

Atlantic treaty, although not so broad in scope as the United Nations. In order to become effective, the pact would need to be ratified by a majority of the Members of the United Nations, including three of the permanent members of the Security Council. Thus its membership would include at least thirty-one states, bound together by a pledge to take action in the case of aggression. States that might join the pact would not need to be geographically contiguous, have any ideological community of interest, or even be Members of the United Nations.

Theoretically, there would be no limit on the number of participating states. Proponents do not expect, however, that there would be any enthusiasm on the part of the Soviet bloc to join a pact that would in effect abolish the veto and pledge joint international action against aggression. In fact, if the Soviet Union were willing to join in an agreement to refrain from the use of the veto in cases in which Soviet interests might be involved, there would be no real need for the pact.

So far as the United States is concerned the acceptability of this proposal must, as a practical matter, turn largely on the question whether the American people and the Congress are willing to forego this attribute of sovereignty at this time. The Department of State has indicated that it is not in favor of proposing that the United States give up its veto power. There would certainly be a serious question whether a treaty embodying such a proposal could receive the necessary advice and consent to ratification of two thirds of the Senate. Furthermore, a major question arises with respect to its effect on the constitutional provision giving Congress power to declare war. In the light of recent public concern with the scope of the treaty power, it seems likely that there would be vigorous objection to United States ratification of any such agreement unless and until the constitutional question had been resolved.

Even if it were assumed that the United States might be willing to join in a proposal of this type, one effect might be to extend the potential military commitments of the United States beyond its capabilities. If every nation except those in the Soviet bloc were to become a party to such a convention, in effect the United States would be undertaking to come to the military assistance of virtually every country in the world. If the United States were prepared to undertake such a commitment, some people have suggested that it might be simpler to enunciate a Monroe-type doctrine for the world—a statement to the effect that the United States would be willing to oppose aggression whenever and wherever it might occur and to give assistance if so requested by the victim. It should be noted, however, that the Article 51 pact would assure the United States of some allies with commitments to take collective action whereas a world-wide Monroe doctrine would be a unilateral pronouncement.

It has been suggested that the United Nations at present has the capacity for achieving the same type of result as that sought by the proposed pact.[43] The action of the Security Council (with the Soviet Union absent) and of the General Assembly in the Korean case indicates that means may be found within the existing framework of the Charter to bring at least token organized strength of the community of nations to bear against an aggressor if there is a desire on the part of the members to do so. The "Uniting for Peace" resolution makes it possible for the Assembly to meet within 24 hours and, theoretically, to make "recommendations to Members for collective measures, including in the case of breach of the peace or act of aggression the use of armed force when necessary." This resolution provides a method for *recommending* that Members use force for collective defense purposes as distinct from a *legal obligation* to use force as suggested by the proposed Article 51 pact.[44]

Proposed Definition of Aggression

The Article 51 pact proposal is concerned with developing a method of organizing states to meet a potential aggressor. It has been suggested in some quarters, however, that a widely accepted definition of aggression would be helpful in giving effect not only to the Article 51 proposal, but also in strengthening the present enforcement machinery of the United Nations itself.

Thus it has been proposed that the Charter be amended to define aggression, that the Security Council itself agree in advance

[43] Assistant Secretary of State Hickerson testified in 1950 that "if there is the will on the part of its members . . . to take action, they can take that action . . . under Article 51 without this formal procedure." *Revision of the United Nations Charter,* Senate Hearings, 81 Cong. 1 sess., p. 417.

[44] For a discussion of the resolution see Joseph E. Johnson, "The Uniting for Peace Resolution," *Annual Review of United Nations Affairs* (1952), pp. 239 ff. Also see the volume in this Brookings series, *The United Nations and the Maintenance of International Peace and Security.*

what type of act would constitute aggression, or that the General Assembly adopt a resolution defining aggression. It is urged that if there could be agreement on a definition of what constitutes aggression, the international community would then have a yard-stick to determine which state would be subject to international disciplinary or punitive action in the event of a breach of the peace. If it could be agreed, for example, that crossing a frontier by armed force is aggression *per se,* it would be clear against whom the Security Council would be expected to take action under Article 41 or 42. It has been suggested that such a definition would be a useful supplement to the United Nations system of collective se-curity and would make it difficult for a great power to exercise a veto in cases clearly falling within the definition. Although pro-ponents of the attempt to define aggression generally recognize that it would be difficult to work out such a definition, they believe that an imperfect definition is better than no definition at all.

The proposal that aggression be defined in the Charter was considered at the San Francisco Conference, but was rejected.[45] Since then it has been the subject of protracted consideration in the General Assembly, the Sixth Committee of the Assembly, and the International Law Commission, and has been considered by a Special Committee that reported on its studies to the ninth session of the Assembly.[46]

In this connection, it is important to keep in mind the relationship of various types of indirect aggression to world peace. Many people are inclined to look upon the Charter in a very limited way, thinking primarily of its application to direct aggression or open, armed attack. It is clear today, however, that in certain areas of the world, the real threat to world peace lies not so much in direct aggression as in more indirect forms such as political intrigue and subversion and the fomenting of revolutionary movements.

The United States has proposed that the Assembly discontinue its efforts to define aggression "as no satisfactory [definition] could

[45] For a complete study of the question see U.N. General Assembly, Seventh Session, *Official Records,* "Annual Report of the Secretary-General on the Work of the Organization, 1 July 1951–30 June 1952," Supplement No. 1A (1952), which dis-cusses attempts to define aggression in the League of Nations and in the United Nations and summarizes the arguments for and against defining aggression.

[46] U.N. General Assembly, Ninth Session, *Official Records,* "Report of the Special Committee on the Question of Defining Aggression, 24 August–21 September 1953," Supplement No. 11 (1954). Also see the volume in this Brookings series, *The United Nations and the Maintenance of International Peace and Security.*

be found. A definition which enumerated all possible acts of aggression would necessarily be incomplete and could thus be harmful; conversely, an abstract and general formula would be too vague to prove useful." The United States, and a number of delegations have, therefore, "considered it preferable to leave the United Nations organs, which are responsible for determining an aggressor, full discretion to consider all circumstances of each case."[47] One former government official has observed that if aggression had been defined as crossing a border with armed forces at the time Czechoslovakia succumbed to the Nazis in 1938, Czechoslovakia would have been the aggressor. He commented that aggression might possibly be defined by listing what it is *not* rather than what it is.[48]

The suggestion has also been made that attempts to define more precisely United Nations obligations would merely strengthen the hand of the objector by offering him more points on which to object. It might be added that even if it were possible to define aggression in terms acceptable to most states, facts have a tendency to become confused in the presence of violence. And even if a generally accepted definition could be agreed upon, a definition in itself would not prevent aggression.

Aggression will be prevented by the likelihood that it will be quickly recognized as such by the organized community and punitive action taken. At best, a definition of aggression might be of collateral assistance to the United Nations in taking action to preserve or restore peace; at worst, it might serve as a shield to an aggressor capable of cleverly camouflaging aggression so that it would not fall within the terms of the definition.

International Police Force

Another approach to the problem of strengthening the enforcement machinery of the United Nations is by the creation of an international police force. Whether to give an international organization its own military forces, on the theory that war between sovereign states can be prevented only if there exists a central force capable of compelling nations to settle disputes by peaceful means,

---

[47] U. S. Department of State, *United States Participation in the United Nations: Report by the President to the Congress for the Year 1951,* Publication 4583 (July 1952), p. 253. See also "The Problem of Defining Aggression," U. S. Department of State *Bulletin,* Vol. 31 (Dec. 6, 1954), pp. 871-76.

[48] Johnson, *loc. cit.,* p. 249.

has been one of the principal problems that has vexed man in his search for peace.[49]

A number of suggestions for the creation of an international police force have been made. At Dumbarton Oaks, for example, the Soviet delegation tentatively suggested the development of an international air force, but the proposal was later withdrawn.[50] A participant at the San Francisco Conference observed in connection with proposals to give the United Nations its own military forces that "government officials realized that such a force would presuppose the existence of a federated world state whose creation would involve a far more drastic pooling of national sovereignties than most of the members would be willing to contemplate." Moreover, he noted, an organization based on the principle of sovereign equality "would not be compatible with a powerful international police force." For these and other reasons, "the search for a satisfactory means of coercion [at San Francisco] was conducted in an area between the extremes of the League system of recommendation and a logically attractive but technically and politically impracticable international police force."[51]

The result of the deliberations at the San Francisco Conference was embodied in Article 43 of the Charter, which provides that the Security Council is to conclude agreements whereby Members undertake to make available to the Security Council, on its call, armed forces, assistance, and facilities necessary for maintaining international peace and security. Paragraph 3 of this article permits the Security Council to conclude such agreements either with Members or with "groups of Members," thus presumably making possible

[49] For a brief analysis of alternative approaches to the problem of creating an international police force, see Commission to Study the Organization of Peace, "Fourth Report," in *International Conciliation*, Vol. 396 (January 1944), esp. pp. 50-61. The suggestion is made that there are four general methods of creating an international police force: (1) a system based on *co-ordinating* national contingents; (2) an *integrated* international force possible only in a centralized world state; (3) a *quota* international force based on national states limiting the size of their military forces in such a way as to leave the controlling force in the hands of the international organization; and (4) a *specialized* international force based on giving certain types of effective armament to the international organization. See also William Buchanan, Herbert E. Krugman, and R. W. Van Wagenen, "An International Police Force and Public Opinion," Publication No. 3 of the Center for Research on World Political Institutions, Princeton University (1954),

[50] See the volume in this Brookings series, *A History of the United Nations Charter*.

[51] Grayson Kirk, "The Enforcement of Security," *Yale Law Journal*, Vol. 55 (August 1946), p. 1083.

the conclusion of such agreements with regional organizations. The Charter does not authorize the creation of an international force with international loyalties and subject to United Nations control. Instead, it provides for the detail of *national* contingents for international use.

Article 43, mild as it is in the opinion of most proponents of world government, has remained a dead letter. Representatives of the major powers have not been able to agree on such matters as the size of the forces to be furnished the United Nations, the ratio of ground forces to air and naval forces, and the exercise of supreme command.[52] In 1948, the Military Staff Committee, established by Article 47 of the Charter to advise and assist the Security Council on questions related to military requirements for the maintenance of peace, reported that "owing to the divergencies of view" it had not been possible to "achieve further progress . . . towards the conclusion of the special agreements required by Article 43 of the Charter."[53]

Despite the fact that the great powers have been unable to agree on the terms by which they might make national military forces available to the Security Council, there have been numerous plans to give the United Nations forces that would be subject to its control. Some plans envisage the virtual elimination of military forces controlled by any single Member state and the creation of an international force subject to international control. At the other extreme, are plans that involve the establishment of only a small, unarmed United Nations guard. Those that would create substantial military forces subject to direct control by the United Nations would involve either amendment of the Charter or the conclusion of special agreements under Article 43. Proposals for limited guard forces might be given effect by a resolution of the General Assembly.

United Nations "Peace Force"

An example of a proposal for a supranational government type of police force is the one that was advanced by Clark and Sohn. In their proposals for the revision of the Charter, they suggest the creation of an international military force to be known as the

---

[52] For detail on areas of disagreement, see U.N. Security Council, *Report of the Military Staff Committee on General Principles Governing the Organization of Armed Forces*, Doc. S/336 (Apr. 30, 1947). Also see the volume in this Brookings series, *The United Nations and the Maintenance of International Peace and Security*.

[53] U.N. Doc. S/956 (Aug. 9, 1948).

"United Nations Peace Force." Creation of this force would be an integral part of an over-all plan and therefore would not stand by itself. It is illustrative, however, of the thinking of some who believe that peace can only be ensured if predominant force is under the control of an international organization.

Under this proposal, steps would be taken during a twelve-year period that would lead to the "complete abolition of national military forces" and the creation of "a standing United Nations military force of not less than 300,000 or more than 700,000 men, the strength from year to year to be determined by the General Assembly."[54] The force would be composed of well-paid volunteers coming, for the most part, from the smaller countries. Volunteers would swear allegiance to the United Nations, be provided with "excellent quarters for themselves and their families" and would participate in a "generous retirement system." The force would be equipped with atomic weapons. It would be backed up by a "United Nations Reserve" to be composed of national contingents that could be called into service when the General Assembly "determines that the situation is of so serious a character that it cannot be dealt with by the United Nations Peace Force alone."

Elaborate controls are suggested to make the proposed peace force "tyranny proof." The general control of the force would be in a proposed executive council, subject, however, to the broader guidance and authority of the General Assembly, thus ensuring civilian control. Moreover, the strictly military command "would be assigned not to any single individual but to a Military Staff Committee appointed by the Executive Council, subject to confirmation by the General Assembly. Further safeguards would include provisions that (1) no member of the Staff Committee could be a national of any of the six nations having the largest representation in the General Assembly; (2) no two members could be nationals of the same member Nation; (3) terms of appointment to the Staff Committee would be limited to four years; and (4) every commander of a separate main element must be a national of a different country and not a national of any country already having one of its nationals on the Staff Committee."[55] Provision is made for the geographical distribution of the peace force so that not more than 10 per cent of the force would be concentrated in one region,

---

[54] For full description see Grenville Clark and Louis B. Sohn, *Peace Through Disarmament and Charter Revision* (Preliminary Print, July 1953), esp. pp. 28-29.
[55] *Ibid.*, p. 30.

except in the event of enforcement action. The force would be supplied with weapons by the United Nations "through the exclusive control and operation . . . of its own ordnance plants, including plants for the production of atomic weapons."[56]

Even a cursory examination of this suggestion indicates that its acceptability is dependent on whether sovereign states, including the United States, are ready and willing to entrust their security to an international organization and to make the consequent sacrifices of national sovereignty. Whether states are ready to take that step depends on the factors considered earlier in this study in connection with the analysis of proposals for world government.[57]

The Clark-Sohn proposals, however, spell out in more detail than most the type of military organization contemplated. Similar, but more general, suggestions are numerous. The Legislature of the Commonwealth of Massachusetts, for example, resolved in 1947 that American delegates to a conference to review the United Nations Charter should advocate "world inspection police and military forces . . . necessary to enforce world law and to provide world security" and that they should seek "gradually and progressively to eliminate national armaments (other than those necessary for internal policing)."[58] The Legislature of the State of Washington petitioned the President and Congress in 1949 to "take all possible steps to strengthen the present form of the United Nations so that it shall possess the means and legal authority to preserve world peace. . . ." The resolution called for a "progressive disarmament," the establishment of a United Nations Inspection Force, and a "United Nations Police Force to enforce decisions of the United Nations courts and of the United Nations Legislature."[59] And the State of Connecticut in 1949 by resolution brought to the attention of the Congress the expression of "the youths of the State of Connecticut" that "an international police force (should) be established with powers to enforce decisions of the Security Council of the United Nations."[60]

Another plan similar in some respects to the plan for a United

---

[56] *Ibid.*, p. 31.

[57] See above, Chap. III.

[58] Resolution of the Legislature of the Commonwealth of Massachusetts, presented to the U. S. House of Representatives, Apr. 24, 1947. *Congressional Record*, Vol. 93, Pt. 3, 80 Cong. 1 sess., p. 3896.

[59] A joint resolution of the Legislature of the State of Washington (House Joint Memorial 13) presented to the President and to Congress, Mar. 25, 1949. *Ibid.*, Vol. 95, Pt. 3, 81 Cong. 1 sess., p. 3149.

[60] *Ibid.*, Pt. 1, 81 Cong. 1 sess., p. 1321.

Nations Peace Force has been proposed by an organization in London called the New Commonwealth. This organization proposed an "International Peace Force," but it envisages not a new or revised Charter, but the creation of an international force without amendment of the Charter.[61] The plan calls for the conclusion of a treaty outside the framework of the United Nations, but authorized by Article 51, by which participating states would begin creating the international force by contributing troops to a nucleus force, wearing distinct uniforms, trained outside their own countries and recruited voluntarily. A supranational oath would be required of all recruits. After this nucleus force had built up its strength, it would eventually develop into a force of "volunteers, owing no allegiance to any individual national government, dedicated by profession and oath to the suppression of aggression." The theory is that aggression could be so clearly defined that the "standing orders" of the force would bring it automatically into action against any aggressor. The force would be twice as strong as any national force, equipped with the best weapons, including atomic weapons, and have its initial base in North Africa. The link between the force and states contributing to its support would be a Board of Control composed of competent individuals relieved of national allegiance.

According to its authors, "The permanence and stability of such a system of security will depend in the last resort not so much upon the pooled military force as upon the willingness of the co-operating states to base their relationship and behaviour on morality, equity, and justice. They must be prepared to replace war by the rule of law."[62]

Quota Force Plan

Another plan to give military force to the United Nations sufficient to preserve peace is the "quota force" plan proposed by the Citizens Committee for United Nations Reform. In the creation of an international police force, two principal aims are sought, first, a force "strong enough to suppress aggression by any state," and, second, a force "so designed that it cannot become an instrument of world tyranny."[63]

[61] New Commonwealth, *A World Security Force* (1949), as described in Alan de Rusett, op. cit., pp. 26-34.
[62] New Commonwealth, *The Atlantic Pact—The Next Step* (1949).
[63] Citizens Committee for United Nations Reform, *The Case for United Nations Revision* [*together with*] *Progress Report* (1949), pp. 5-8. For political aspects of proposal, see above Chap. III.

There would be an "international contingent, under direct control of the Security Council" or of an "autonomous United Nations police authority."[64] Its allegiance would be "solely to the United Nations."[65] It would consist of "a volunteer, paid, professional, balanced land, sea, and air force, operating on a full-time basis. . . ." The force would be recruited from "volunteers who are not citizens of the five permanent member states of the Security Council," and it would include volunteers from citizens of states such as Germany and Japan not Members of the United Nations.

The national armed forces of the five major states would constitute a reserve for the international contingent. They would remain under the full control of their respective governments, pledged, however, to be made available "as reserves to the international contingent upon majority decision of the revised Security Council."[66] The plan as originally submitted contemplated that the strength of the national contingents would be linked to a limitation of military production so that the *international* contingent would have 20 per cent of the military strength of the world, the United States, the British Commonwealth, and the Soviet Union would have 20 per cent each, and France and China, 10 per cent each.[67] A force thus constituted would be designed to give each of the great powers strength enough to protect itself from aggression, but not enough strength to commit aggression. Moreover, any state subject to an aggressive attack would, in co-operation with the international contingent, have enough force to repel the aggression.

It should be noted, however, that resolutions introduced in Congress in 1950 did not place as much emphasis on the "quota-force" aspects of these proposals as the original plan contemplated. Instead, increasing emphasis was placed on the creation of an international contingent powerful enough to enforce peace without the assistance of national contingents,[68] and on the control of that contingent by "an autonomous United Nations Police Authority" which was to be established either on recommendation of the General Assembly

[64] S. Con. Res. 50, 80 Cong. 2 sess. (Apr. 12, 1948). *Congressional Record,* Vol. 94, Pt. 4, 80 Cong. 2 sess., p. 4299.

[65] H. Con. Res. 253-61, 81 Cong. 2 sess. (Aug. 25, 1950). *Congressional Record,* Vol. 96, Pt. 10, 81 Cong. 2 sess., p. 13529.

[66] S. Con. Res. 50, 80 Cong. 2 sess.

[67] *Ibid.* See also Citizens Committee for United Nations Reform, *The Case for United Nations Revision,* pp. 5-8.

[68] See H. Con. Res. 253-61, 81 Cong. 2 sess.

or pursuant to Article 51 of the Charter. Although the way was left open for the Soviet Union to participate in the plan, it was not contemplated that it would be an original participant.

A variation to these proposals was contained in a resolution introduced in Congress in 1949 with the suggestion that the international contingent be established first on a regional basis by the creation of the "Atlantic international contingent, to operate in defense against armed attack as auxiliary to the national armed forces of participating member states."[69] This Atlantic contingent was to be recruited, as in the case of the world-wide plan, from "volunteers who are citizens of smaller sovereign states only. . . ." The force, "owing its allegiance to the Atlantic Council," would be well paid and highly trained. The contingent would be financed with funds appropriated by the United States in implementation of the terms of Article 3 of the North Atlantic Treaty. Command of the Atlantic contingent would be vested in the special defense committee authorized by Article 9 of the North Atlantic Treaty.[70]

Examination of the police force proposals shows that they contain elements of supranationality. Thus the suggestion that members of the international (or the Atlantic) contingent owe allegiance to an international body would seem to require an abridgment of the concept of national citizenship and substitution therefor of a type of international citizenship. Moreover, those aspects of the proposals that limit the size of the military forces that Member states could maintain would clearly abridge the elements of sovereignty they now retain under the United Nations Charter. They would also require acceptance of the proposition that national military forces would be subject to international control without the consent of national states.

It will be noted that there are a number of similarities between the Clark-Sohn proposals and those of the Citizens Committee for United Nations Reform. The essential difference between these two international police proposals, however, is found not in the detail of the military establishment and its ultimate control by political bodies, but rather in the fundamental assumptions on

[69] S. Res. 133, 81 Cong. 1 sess. (July 8, 1949). *Congressional Record*, Vol. 95, Pt. 7, 81 Cong. 1 sess., p. 9119.

[70] For description of plan, see *Revision of the United Nations Charter*, Senate Hearings, 81 Cong. 2 sess., pp. 172-226.

which the proposals are based. Those of Clark and Sohn contemplate that the organization to control the proposed "United Nations Peace Force" would be universal. "All nations . . . shall be deemed members of the United Nations." Moreover, for their plan to become fully effective, they presuppose "a general East-West settlement." The proposals of the Citizens Committee for United Nations Reform are based on a contrary assumption. They assume the likelihood that the Soviet Union would not choose to accept the proposed plan. In that event the Soviet Union would "be given an ultimatum: either to stop atomic armament . . . or to evacuate her industrial centers in expectation of immediate atomic coercion."[71]

International Air Force

In the search for an international military force capable of maintaining peace, the Commission to Study the Organization of Peace, from time to time, has proposed the creation of an international air force, a proposal similar on the surface, at least, to one put forth by the Soviet Union at Dumbarton Oaks.[72]

The idea first submitted by the commission in 1943 noted that the airplane "is as perfect an instrument as could be devised" to serve as the basis of "a small international police force, not to fight wars but to warn against them and to remind intending violators of international peace that the crime of aggressive war could no longer be indulged in without bringing down upon the law-breaker the full penalty of suppression by the cooperative action of the United Nations."[73] The commission suggested that at the conclusion of the Second World War "the international air force might get its start by assembling squadrons ceded to it by the principal United Nations." Such members of the force initially would "wear the United Nations uniform." After the organization got started, however, the force would be recruited from volunteers "ready to swear allegiance to the world organization." The commission did

[71] See Clark and Sohn, *op. cit.*, pp. 10, 13; and Ely Culbertson, "The ABC Plan for World Peace," *Reader's Digest* (June 1948), p. 85.

[72] See Commission to Study the Organization of Peace, *Security and Disarmament Under the United Nations*, Fifth Report (June 1947). Article 45 of the Charter calls for members to "hold immediately available national air-force contingents for combined international enforcement action." Implementation of this section depends on the conclusion of military agreements contemplated by Article 43.

[73] See Commission to Study the Organization of Peace, "Fourth Report," *loc. cit.*, p. 14.

not estimate the size of the proposed force, but suggested that the number of volunteers needed would not be great inasmuch as it was based on the assumption that the big powers would largely disband their own military forces. The international air force would have "bomber and fighter planes" as basic equipment, supplemented by "its own large cargo planes for freight and troop carriers." Planes would be manufactured in Member states to specifications prepared by the general staff serving the international organization. "The cession of air bases for use of the international air force would greatly contribute to its effectiveness."[74] The commission recognized that "an international air force would not operate in a vacuum" and that its successful operation depended on "a sufficient sense of world solidarity . . . to enable such institutions to perform their functions."[75]

Despite the fact that this "sense of world solidarity" had not been achieved by the creation of the United Nations, the commission in 1947 reiterated a modified version of its previous recommendation, calling for a " 'relatively small international air force' directly under the United Nations for the purpose of reconnaissance and pre-liminary warning against overt acts on the part of any nation." The commission noted that "a similar proposal was made by the Soviet Union at Dumbarton Oaks in September 1944" and that "estab-lishment of such an air police force could be accomplished by agreements between the Security Council and the Members, or by action of the Security Council and the General Assembly. It would not require amendment of the Charter." The commission also recommended that: "For instant action in case of a threat to the peace, there should also be plans for making immediately available to the Security Council national air force contingents as provided in Article 45." Such contingents should be maintained at designated bases, which under certain circumstances might "be temporarily administered directly by the United Nations."[76] As late as 1949, the commission favorably referred to its earlier recommendations regard-ing the establishment of an international air force.[77]

Proposals for an international air force are similar to other

[74] *Ibid.*, pp. 56-58.
[75] *Ibid.*, p. 61.
[76] Commission to Study the Organization of Peace, *Security and Disarmament Under the United Nations*, p. 20.
[77] Commission to Study the Organization of Peace, *United Nations Guards and Technical Field Services* (September 1949), p. 20.

proposals for the creation of an international police force. They involve the surrender of control by a Member over certain areas of government normally regarded as essential to the security of a nation. They also are based on the expectation that the great powers will materially reduce, if not eliminate, their own national armaments.

The inability of the permanent members of the Security Council to reach even preliminary agreement on the size and composition of armed forces to be made available to the Council, rights of passage, base facilities, and similar matters indicates the tremendous difficulties that would be involved in creating an international police or air force. The creation of such forces as these would involve surrender of far more sovereignty than would be involved in giving effect to Article 43.

United Nations Guard Force

A more modest series of proposals for an international force than those considered above are those suggesting the establishment of an armed unit, not designed to deter aggression, but rather to act as a guard for United Nations property and personnel. The Commission to Study the Organization of Peace suggested in 1947 that "the United Nations should have certain police forces of its own. They should be composed of volunteers wearing a United Nations uniform. They should be used to police United Nations headquarters and other areas to be placed under United Nations or international administration." Although such units would not be "designed to be used against an aggressor, they might in an emergency serve as protection for United Nations services, provide a warning against aggression, and thus help to prevent the outbreak or lessen the extent of violence."[78]

A year later, after the assassination of Count Bernadotte, United Nations Mediator for Palestine, the Secretary-General of the United Nations publicly proposed a small guard force to be recruited by him and placed at the disposal of the Security Council. He proposed to the General Assembly the voluntary recruitment of a United Nations Guard to consist of from one to several thousand men, to wear United Nations uniforms, and to subscribe to the pro-

[78] Commission to Study the Organization of Peace, *Security and Disarmament Under the United Nations*, p. 20.

visions of Article 100 of the Charter, by which they would agree not to seek or receive instructions from any external authority, and to respect the exclusively international character of their responsibilities. He estimated that such a force would cost about $4 million annually. The guard was to be equipped with "limited emergency personal defense weapons, to include either revolvers, light automatic weapons . . . but *not* tanks, artillery or aircraft and vessels."[79] The report of the Secretary-General noted that:

> The Secretary-General clearly recognizes that both on practical and legal grounds such a Guard could not be used for enforcement purposes as envisaged under the Charter, nor for the purpose of maintaining law and order in an area. It is, however, his view that the provision of a Guard such as he proposes would immeasurably strengthen the hands of United Nations Missions which are established for the express purpose of assuring pacific settlements without recourse to the use of force and would assist them to expedite peaceful settlements.[80]

The Commision to Study the Organization of Peace supported this proposal and urged the immediate establishment of such a force. Secretary of State Marshall gave the proposal a qualified endorsement, advocating its "sympathetic consideration" and pointing out that the "guards would be entirely distinct from the armed forces envisaged under Article 43 and would not carry out military operations."[81]

In general, however, reception of the Secretary-General's proposal was cool. The Communist countries opposed it as a violation of the Charter. Nevertheless, the Assembly set up a special committee in April 1949 to study the matter. That committee, on the basis of debate in the Assembly, considered a modified plan submitted by the Secretary-General. It limited the proposal to the establishment of a "United Nations Field Service" of three hundred men, to be backed up by a field reserve panel, subsequently called the United Nations Panel of Field Observers. In November, the General Assembly, over the objections of the Soviet Union and its satellite states, adopted a resolution recognizing that the Secretary-General "has authority to establish the United Nations Field Service, subject to budgetary limitations and the normal administrative controls of the General Assembly." It also requested the Secretary-

[79] See U.N. General Assembly, Third Session, *Report of the Secretary-General on the Need for a United Nations Guard*, Doc. A/656 (Sept. 28, 1948).
[80] *Ibid.*, pp. 26-27.
[81] U. S. Department of State *Bulletin*, Vol. 19 (Oct. 3, 1948), pp. 434-35.

General to maintain a list of persons "qualified to assist United Nations missions in the functions of observation and supervision" to be known as "the United Nations Panel of Field Observers."[82]

Although it may be maintained that the original proposal of the Secretary-General for the creation of a United Nations Guard did not envisage the creation of an international police force that would be capable of taking enforcement action, some observers saw in such a step a start in a small way to give the United Nations forces of its own. One, for example, in referring to these proposals, noted that the establishment of a United Nations corps of armed guards "will be incidentally helpful in enforcement action. . . . It would further be possible—although this is not intended within present proposals—to enlarge the corps of guards and call on them for police action, perhaps as an advance body to hold until other forces arrived." He also observed that "there is nothing in the Charter that forbids the establishment of an independent police force. The General Assembly has authority to appropriate money for, and to establish such a force, although it would presumably be under the direction of the Security Council once it was in being."[83]

United Nations Legion

Despite the watering down of the Secretary-General's proposal for the creation of a United Nations Guard, the idea of establishing some kind of an international police force stronger than a guard force has persisted. One of the matters considered by the Collective Measures Committee was the proposal of the Secretary-General for the creation of a "United Nations Legion." In its first report in 1951, the Collective Measures Committee recommended that an analysis be made of the Secretary-General's suggestion for such a United Nations Legion.[84] Its second report in 1952 included a summary of the Secretary-General's plan, but after noting that it was impractical at the present time, and commenting that the plan might better be described as a "United Nations Volunteer Reserve," the committee recommended that further consideration be given the matter.[85]

It should be recalled in considering this proposal that when the

---

[82] Res. 297 (IV) A and B, Nov. 22, 1949.

[83] Clyde Eagleston, "Proposals for Strengthening the United Nations," *Foreign Policy Reports,* Vol. 25 (Sept. 15, 1949), p. 110.

[84] "First Report of the Collective Measures Committee," pp. 4-5.

[85] See "Second Report of the Collective Measures Committee," pp. 12-13.

United Nations responded to the attack on South Korea in 1950, thousands of individuals over the world sought to enlist with the United Nations in defense of South Korea. No facilities were available to make it possible to use these volunteers. Moreover, a number of countries with small contingents available did not have the means of sending their forces to Korea.

Secretary-General Lie's plan recognized that, when the United Nations takes action to resist aggression, as a practical matter "primary reliance must be placed upon national forces . . . and no international or supra-national forces . . . could, under present circumstances, substitute for a United Nations force composed of . . . elements contributed from national forces."[86] He suggested, however, that consideration be given to two ways in which additional military strength might be made available to a "United Nations Executive Military Authority" created to deal with a specific aggression. First, states not able to contribute "self-contained combat or ancillary units" might consult on the possibility of organizing in advance "combatant or auxiliary units (such as labour or transport units) of a nature adequate for effective integration into a United Nations force charged with resisting an act of aggression."

The second proposal called for examination of the possibility of "enlisting the services of individual volunteers who would wish to serve within a United Nations Volunteer Reserve in support of United Nations principles to resist aggression and who would, in advance, undertake to be trained and held in reserve to this end." The Secretary-General estimated that from fifty to sixty thousand volunteers could be recruited by the national military establishments "on behalf of the United Nations." They would be trained as special units, the costs of training, recruiting, and equipping them to be borne by the respective national military establishments.

These proposals were put forth in a most tentative way by the Secretary-General. They were undoubtedly motivated by recognition of the fact that there are thousands of young men throughout

[86] *Ibid.*
Secretary-General Lie tells of making a proposal during Korean hostilities to augment the forces of the Unified Command by organizing a brigade of volunteers. ". . . such a brigade would bear the United Nations name and wear United Nations uniforms and be enlisted for a term of two to three years. I anticipated that the number of volunteers would be large, but felt that the only practical way of organizing the brigade was to entrust the responsibility—and the expense—to the United States." Lie noted that the reaction of American representatives was "mixed." Trygvie Lie, *In the Cause of Peace* (1954), p. 339.

the world who for idealistic and other reasons would avail themselves of an opportunity to volunteer for such a force. The third report of the Collective Measures Committee noted that it had been advised that the "Secretary-General did not wish for the time being, to proceed with the proposals." In those circumstances the committee had undertaken no further study of the matter.[87]

The proposals described above do not exhaust all, but are illustrative of, the ideas to give the United Nations some type of military force. Some of the proposals would call for amendments of the United Nations Charter so substantial that the result would be not an organization based on the principle of sovereign equality, but rather an organization having limited elements of supranational government. Others could be given effect under the terms of the existing Charter. Despite the range of these suggestions, despite the interest in giving the United Nations forces of its own, the General Assembly, when faced with even the simplest of plans, the creation of a limited, unarmed, United Nations Guard Force, has had great difficulty in reaching any substantial unanimity of views. The United States, for example, has never indicated more than a reserved interest in these suggestions, and the attitude of the Soviet Union and its satellites has remained one of constant objection to all such recommendations. Even proposals that the majority of the Members have agreed might be given effect within the present terms of the Charter have been objected to by the Soviet Union as illegal under the Charter. They profess to see these moves as calculated attempts to get around the veto, to create United Nations forces without adherence to the provisions of Article 43, and to give the Secretary-General, instead of the Security Council, military units for his use.

The Security Council can only be effective in taking collective measures in case of a breach of the peace if the permanent members unanimously can "decide what measures" to take, including "such action by air, sea, or land forces as may be necessary to maintain or restore international peace and security." In the absence of unanimity, the Council is virtually incapable of taking action that would have the effect of applying collective measures to any state.

The failure of the Security Council to conclude the military agreements under Article 43 by which Members were to make military

[87] U.N. General Assembly, Eighth Session, *Official Records*, "Report of the Collective Measures Committee," Supplement No. 17 (1953), p. 4.

forces available to the Security Council and the recognition that the use of the veto would, even in the event such forces were available, make it difficult if not impossible to use them under United Nations auspices, have resulted in careful examination of alternative methods of providing some degree of collective security. Regional and collective defense agreements are one method of attaining some measure of collective security. The "Uniting for Peace" resolution, by giving the General Assembly, with its authority to make recommendations, responsibility in the field of collective security action, has given states another method of acting together against aggression. But the search still goes on for other devices of providing for collective security. Plans to create some type of international peace force tend in that direction as do proposals for a world-wide Article 51 pact discussed above.

The practicability of proposals to create United Nations forces can only be measured in terms of the likelihood of their acceptance by Members of the United Nations, especially the five major powers. There is little evidence in the current state of world tension to indicate that the great powers would be able to agree on making armed forces available to the United Nations.

Two methods to improve the enforcement or collective security functions of the United Nations are being tried. Regional security and collective defense arrangements of a limited nature have been entered into, and the General Assembly has assumed an increasing amount of responsibility for action if the Security Council should be unable to act. In the years immediately ahead there would seem to be two main lines of development that might take place.

First, there is the possibility that Soviet tactics might encourage the development of additional regional and other collecive defense pacts, with the further possibility of linking them together, thereby creating a world-wide interrelated defense system having at least a nominal relationship to the United Nations.

Second, there is the possibility that the enforcement functions of the United Nations envisaged in Chapter VII of the Charter might be viewed as too difficult of achievement in a world-wide organization and that the United Nations should instead confine its operations mostly to the field of pacific settlement.

The experience of the past decade has not disproved the premise of the San Francisco Conference that if the five major powers were in agreement on the application of enforcement measures, peace could be maintained. It has become apparent, however, that if the great powers are badly split over fundamental economic or political principles, world peace is threatened. This would seem to indicate that in the event a General Conference to review the Charter is held, principal attention might well be focused not on the problem of preventing little wars by the combined exercise of great power force, but on the problem of preventing a big war resulting from a conflict between the great powers.

CHAPTER VII

Regulation of Armaments

ONE of the most important problems that has confronted the United Nations since its inception has been the regulation of armaments. The lack of progress in the control of atomic and other weapons suggests that the provisions of the Charter dealing with this question should be carefully examined to determine whether they are adequate and realistic. Grave doubt has been expressed that they are, and consequently it has been claimed that in this respect, the Charter is a "pre-atomic-age Charter."[1]

Article 11 provides that the "General Assembly may consider the general principles of cooperation in the maintenance of international peace and security, including the principles governing disarmament and the regulation of armaments, and may make recommendations with regard to such principles to the Members or to the Security Council or to both." Article 26 states that: "In order to promote the establishment and maintenance of international peace and security with the least diversion for armaments of the world's human and economic resources, the Security Council shall be responsible for formulating, with the assistance of the Military Staff Committee referred to in Article 47, plans to be submitted to the Members of the United Nations for the establishment of a system for the regulation of armaments." Article 47, which provides for the establishment of the Military Staff Committee, stipulates that one of its duties is "to advise and assist the Security Council on all questions relating to . . . the regulation of armaments, and possible disarmament."

Except for the reference in Article 26 to the relationship between armaments and resources available for human and economic needs, the Charter does not mention disarmament as a desirable goal for

---

[1] Address by Secretary Dulles before the American Bar Association at Boston, Aug. 26, 1953, U. S. Department of State *Bulletin*, Vol. 29 (Sept. 7, 1953), p. 310; see also his statement of Jan. 18, 1954, *Review of the United Nations Charter*, Hearings before a Subcommittee of the Senate Committee on Foreign Relations, 83 Cong. 2 sess., Pt. 1, pp. 4-9.

the world community. Nor does the Charter provide any plan for disarmament or the regulation of armaments. In recommending United States ratification of the Charter, the Senate Committee on Foreign Relations pointed out that the Security Council can submit "only recommendations to the governments—and every country, including our own, will be free to accept or reject them according to its conception of its national interest."[2]

Background of United Nations Effort

Inasmuch as all the United Nations can do is to propose plans for the regulation of armaments, any study of the activities of the Organization in this field is necessarily an examination of proposals that have been considered by it. Although some disarmament proposals have been put forth by private groups and individuals, by far the largest number of suggestions are those that have been considered by United Nations organs within the framework of the Charter.

It may be argued that the United Nations can do nothing in the field of disarmament because it has no compulsory power. On the other hand, as the Organization has authority only to formulate and make plans for submission to Members, there would seem to be no limitation on the scope of the proposals that might be considered. The United Nations is, therefore, a comparatively free agent in the field of disarmament—free in the sense that it can submit proposals to Members for any system of regulating armaments that it deems appropriate for consideration—but not free in the sense that it could impose any plan on any Member state or group of such states.

Although the point is made here that the Charter does not authorize the imposition of disarmament proposals on any Member, it is conceivable, as suggested by one authority, that if a Member should refuse to accept an approved plan for disarmament or control of atomic weapons, the Security Council acting under Article 39 might find such refusal to constitute a threat to the peace and hence invoke enforcement action against the recalcitrant state.[3] It

---

[2] Senate Committee on Foreign Relations, *The Charter of the United Nations,* S. Exec. Rept. 8, 79 Cong. 2 sess. (July 16, 1945), p. 11.

[3] For discussion see Hans Kelsen, *The Law of the United Nations* (1951), p. 105.

might also be possible to conclude a treaty under Article 51 calling for military action, in the event a disarmament plan formulated by the Security Council were rejected by any one Member, or to take some kind of economic action, such as a blockade, to compel acceptance of disarmament proposals. None of these courses of action as a method of forcing disarmament on the world would be likely to succeed, however, for the reason that in all likelihood it could not be given effect without the possibility of precipitating the war that disarmament proposals seek to avoid.

There are several reasons the Charter did not include more emphatic and realistic provisions on the regulation of armaments. In the first place, the world was still at war when the San Francisco Conference was held, and many states were heavily armed. In those circumstances it would have seemed somewhat unrealistic to seek precision in disarmament provisions in the Charter. In the second place, the matter of arms reduction was intimately related to the system of collective security under the Charter. Any general arms regulation agreement, it was held, would need to be co-ordinated with the development of the security system under the Charter if it were to make sense. Thus under Article 43, it might have been necessary for some states to manufacture armaments in order to meet their commitments to the United Nations, and at the same time they might have found it necessary to reduce armaments not maintained for purposes specified in Article 43. Moreover, it was apparent to some of the conferees at San Francisco that the problem of working out a system for the control of armaments was so complicated and difficult that it would have been virtually impossible to negotiate a workable agreement within the time limits set for the Conference.

In view of the fact that it has not been possible in ten years to reach any agreement on the regulation of armaments, including agreement on the control of atomic energy, there might be some justification for the conclusion that the provisions of the Charter in this respect are not realistic. Before reaching such a conclusion, however, the proposals for disarmament and the control of atomic energy that have been considered under the auspices of the United Nations should be examined in order to determine whether any provisions of the Charter have prevented progress in these fields.[4]

---

[4] For full discussion see the volume in this Brookings series, *The United Nations and the Maintenance of International Peace and Security* (1955), Chap. XXI.

At the meeting of the Foreign Ministers in Moscow in December 1945, agreement was reached to "recommend, for the consideration of the General Assembly of the United Nations, the establishment by the United Nations of a commission to consider problems arising from the discovery of atomic energy and related matters."[5] Based on the recommendation of this meeting, the General Assembly in January 1946, as one of the first acts of its session in London, unanimously adopted a resolution to create a Commission on Atomic Energy. The resolution, which was jointly sponsored by Canada, China, France, the United Kingdom, the United States, and the Soviet Union, instructed the commission to make specific proposals:

(a) For extending between all nations the exchange of basic scientific information for peaceful ends;
(b) For control of atomic energy to the extent necessary to ensure its use only for peaceful purposes;
(c) For the elimination from national armaments of atomic weapons and of all other major weapons adaptable to mass destruction;
(d) For effective safeguards by way of inspection and other means to protect complying States against the hazards of violations and evasions.[6]

Two years later, after more than 200 meetings, the Commission on Atomic Energy reported that it had reached an impasse, and four years later, in January 1952, the General Assembly dissolved the commission.[7]

In addition to the Commission on Atomic Energy, the United Nations had in operation the Commission for Conventional Armaments, which was established by the Security Council in February 1947. This commission was instructed to prepare and submit to the Council proposals "for the general regulation and reduction of armaments and armed forces" and "for practical and effective safeguards in connection with the general regulation and reduction of armaments."[8] In establishing the Commission for Conventional Armaments, the Security Council was guided by a resolution of the General Assembly, which, acting under the authority of Article 11

---

[5] "Soviet-Anglo-American Communiqué, December 27, 1945," U. S. Department of State *Bulletin*, Vol. 13 (Dec. 30, 1945), pp. 1031-32.
[6] Res. 1(I), Jan. 24, 1946.
[7] U. S. Department of State, *Third Report of the United Nations Atomic Energy Commission to the Security Council*, Publication 3179 (July 1948), p. 1; and Res. 502 (VI), Jan. 11, 1952.
[8] U.N. Doc. S/268/Rev. 1 (Feb. 13, 1947).

of the Charter, had recommended that the Council "give prompt consideration to formulating the practical measures . . . essential to provide for the general regulation and reduction of armaments and armed forces" and that Members undertake a "general progressive and balanced reduction of national armed forces."[9]

Thus the United Nations had two commissions operating in the field of armament control, one concerned with so-called conventional armaments functioning under the Security Council, and the other concerned with atomic and other weapons of mass destruction, created by a resolution of the General Assembly but reporting to the Security Council. The two commissions operated separately until January 1952, when they were combined in the Disarmament Commission, established by the General Assembly to function under the Security Council.[10] This commission was instructed to carry on work not only in the field of atomic weapons but in the field of conventional armaments as well.[11] It was thus recognized that proposals for the regulation of conventional armaments and those dealing with control of atomic energy are closely related. Inasmuch as the subjects were dealt with separately by the United Nations over a period of some six years, however, the proposals will be considered separately in this study.

Control of Atomic Energy

When the United Nations Atomic Energy Commission held its first meetings in New York in the spring of 1946, United States representative, Bernard M. Baruch, presented a plan for the creation of an International Atomic Development Authority. This plan followed closely the recommendations of the so-called Acheson-Lilienthal report setting forth the fundamental considerations de-

---

[9] Res. 41(I), Dec. 14, 1946.

[10] Res. 502(VI), Jan. 11, 1952. Although reports of the Disarmament Commission have been submitted to both the Security Council and the General Assembly, the Assembly in recent years has carried principal responsibility for disarmament matters.

[11] For summary of early United Nations action on atomic energy and conventional armaments see James M. Ludlow, "The Establishment of the Commission for Conventional Armaments," U. S. Department of State *Bulletin*, Vol. 16 (Apr. 27, 1947), pp. 731-40; see also Marion W. Boggs, "Regulation and Reduction of Armaments: Action of the General Assembly," *ibid.* (Feb. 23, 1947), pp. 311-20, 333.

termining American policy and suggesting proposals that the United States might make to the United Nations.[12]

United States Plan

The United States plan proposed the creation of an International Atomic Development Authority to be entrusted with all phases of the development and use of atomic energy, including:

1. Managerial control or ownership of all atomic-energy activities potentially dangerous to world security.
2. Power to control, inspect and license all other atomic activities.
3. The duty of fostering the beneficial uses of atomic energy.
4. Research and development responsibilities of an affirmative character intended to put the Authority in the forefront of atomic knowledge and thus to enable it to comprehend, and therefore to detect, misuse of atomic energy. To be effective, the Authority must itself be the world's leader in the field of atomic knowledge and development and thus supplement its legal authority with the great power inherent in possession of leadership in knowledge.

The plan called for an adequate system for control of atomic energy and renunciation of the use of the atomic bomb. When these essentials have "been agreed upon and put into effective operation and condign punishments set up for violations of the rules of control which are to be stigmatized as international crimes," the United States proposed that:

1. Manufacture of atomic bombs shall stop;
2. Existing bombs shall be disposed of pursuant to the terms of the treaty, and
3. The Authority shall be in possession of full information as to the know-how for the production of atomic energy.

With respect to violations, the United States suggested that serious, immediate, and positive penalties should be fixed for:

1. Illegal possession or use of an atomic bomb;
2. Illegal possession, or separation, of atomic material suitable for use in an atomic bomb;
3. Seizure of any plant or other property belonging to or licensed by the Authority;
4. Wilful interference with the activities of the Authority;
5. Creation or operation of dangerous projects in a manner contrary to, or in the absence of, a license granted by the international control body.

[12] See U. S. Department of State, *A Report on the International Control of Atomic Energy*, Publication 2498 (Mar. 16, 1946).

United States Representative Baruch concluded his presentation of the plan as follows:

It would be a deception, to which I am unwilling to lend myself, were I not to say to you and to our peoples, that the matter of punishment lies at the very heart of our present security system. It might as well be admitted, here and now, that the subject goes straight to the veto power contained in the Charter of the United Nations so far as it relates to the field of atomic energy. The Charter permits penalization only by concurrence of each of the five great powers—Union of Soviet Socialist Republics, the United Kingdom, China, France and the United States.

I want to make very plain that I am concerned here with the veto power only as it affects this particular problem. There must be no veto to protect those who violate their solemn agreements not to develop or use atomic energy for destructive purposes.

The bomb does not wait upon debate. To delay may be to die.[13]

Soviet Proposal

At the second meeting of the Atomic Energy Commission Soviet Representative Gromyko, without referring to the United States plan, submitted the proposal of the Soviet Union:

As one of the primary measures for the fulfilment of the resolution of the General Assembly of 24 January 1946, the Soviet delegation proposes that consideration be given to the question of concluding an international convention prohibiting the production and employment of weapons based on the use of atomic energy for the purpose of mass destruction. The object of such a convention should be the prohibition of the production and employment of atomic weapons, the destruction of existing stocks of atomic weapons and the condemnation of all activities undertaken in violation of this convention. . . . This act should be followed by other measures aiming at the establishment of methods to ensure the strict observance of the terms and obligations contained in the above mentioned convention, the establishment of a system of control over the observance of the convention and the taking of decisions regarding the sanctions to be applied against the unlawful use of atomic energy.[14]

One fundamental difference between the approach of the Soviet Union to the control of atomic energy and the approach suggested by the United States relates to the control and inspection of the production of atomic energy. The United States took the position

[13] Statement to the U.N. Atomic Energy Commission, June 14, 1946. For full text of plan, see U. S. Department of State, *International Control of Atomic Energy: Growth of a Policy,* Publication 2702 (1946), pp. 138-47.

[14] Statement to the U.N. Atomic Energy Commission, June 19, 1946. For text see *ibid.,* pp. 209-16.

that the first step toward control was the creation of an international authority able to control all atomic production potentially dangerous to world security. If such an authority were eventually to prohibit manufacture of atomic weapons, it was essential that it have first-hand information through on-the-spot inspection of the production of all fissionable materials. If such materials were produced in violation of imposed controls, then it was essential that there be a reliable method of punishment available to the international community—punishment that could not be avoided by the exercise of a veto. Only after an adequate inspection system had been created could the second step be taken—the destruction of existing supplies of weapons.

The Soviet Union, on the other hand, took the position that the first step in control of atomic weapons should be the destruction of existing stocks of weapons and the conclusion of a convention to prohibit the production and employment of atomic weapons. *After* the destruction of existing weapons, measures might be taken to establish a system of control of *national* production of atomic materials, and provision might also be made for a system of *periodic* inspection. The Soviet proposals were also tied to the proposition that any waiver of the veto in the field of atomic energy would be an attack on the basic structure of the United Nations and the principle of unanimity, thus implying that the veto would continue to apply to any fundamental decision-making power that might be delegated to an international atomic agency.

The difference in the approach of the United States and the Soviet Union to the problem of control of atomic weapons is understandable when consideration is given to their respective security situations. The United States had a supply of atomic weapons and presumably a temporary monopoly on atomic know-how. It had reduced the size of its conventional military establishment immediately after the war and was therefore dependent on its atomic stockpile for its main defensive strength. The Soviet Union at that time presumably had no atomic weapons but did retain a large conventional military establishment. If the Soviet Union could induce the United States to destroy its atomic stockpile, the comparative military strength of the Soviet Union in contrast to the United States would have been greatly improved.

The Soviet and the American proposals clashed. Although it could be argued that the interests of each nation might best be protected by "peaceful coexistence," the situation in the late 1940's, as well as past experience with totalitarian governments, made it unsafe for the free world to accept a promise of the Soviet Union that it would abide by a convention prohibiting the production and employment of atomic weapons *unless* an air-tight system could be devised that would make sure no atomic weapons were being secretly manufactured. The failure of the Soviet Government to alter its position in any important respect during the years of negotiation indicates that in turn it has felt that its interests would best be served by refusal to accept at face value proposals of the Western powers for the development and control of atomic energy.

In the light of prolonged discussion by the commission of these two proposals, it became clear that a second fundamental difference revolved around the question whether control of atomic energy should be within the fundamental concepts of the United Nations Charter. As noted above, the United States representative said: "There must be no veto to protect those who violate their solemn agreements not to develop or use atomic energy for destructive purposes."[15] This would seem to constitute recognition that in the control of atomic energy, any plan, in the opinion of the United States, would have to go beyond the provisions of the Charter in so far as the veto might apply to action to prevent violation of an atomic control agreement.

The Soviet representative, however, made clear during the frequent debates on the subject the view of his government that the United States proposals were in violation of the Charter. He noted that: "The proposals submitted for consideration of the Commission by the representative of the United States of America in their most important parts are in conformity neither with the resolution of the General Assembly [setting up the Commission] nor with the United Nations Charter."[16] United States Ambassador Austin, commenting on the Soviet representative's remarks, stated that the Soviet representative had raised a question of law: "that is, whether effective and enforceable safeguards against the use of atomic energy for destructive purposes can be established within the four corners of the . . . Charter of the United Nations, and without depending solely

---

[15] *Ibid.*, p. 142.

[16] See "The United Nations Atomic Energy Commission," *International Conciliation* (April 1947), p. 273. This issue contains a summary of the first year of work of the Commission.

on the Security Council for enforcement."[17] He might have added that the comment by the Soviet representative was in reality a *non sequitur* as any agreement embodying the United States proposal would have required approval by all participating governments in accordance with their constitutional processes.

"Majority Plan"

The Third Report of the United Nations Atomic Energy Commission to the Security Council in May 1948 noted that "after twenty-two months of work, the commission finds itself confronted by virtually the same deadlock that stultified its initial discussions." The difficulties had become apparent early in the work of the commission, which had proceeded along the general lines suggested by the United States. But this approach was rejected by the Soviet Union "on the ground that such a plan constituted an unwarranted infringement of national sovereignty." The Soviet Union insisted that "a convention outlawing atomic weapons and providing for the destruction of existing weapons must precede any control convention"—an approach unacceptable to the majority of the members of the commission.[18]

Despite the opposition of the Soviet Union, the General Assembly in November 1948 adopted by a vote of 40 to 6, with 4 abstentions, a resolution that approved the recommendations made by the Atomic Energy Commission in its first report and the specific proposals made by the commission in its second report. In short, the recommendations in the first report called for a strong and comprehensive international system of control and inspection to be established by treaty among Members and states not Members of the United Nations; suggested the creation of an international control agency not subject to the rule of unanimity (the veto) with powers of inspection; pointed out that violation of the proposed treaty might give rise to the inherent right of self-defense recognized by Article 51; and noted that the entire program of control and inspection should proceed step by step.[19] The second report of the commission

---

[17] *Ibid.*, pp. 169-70.

[18] U. S. Department of State, *Third Report of the United Nations Atomic Energy Commission to the Security Council,* Publication 3179 (July 1948), pp. 2, 46-48.

[19] See U. S. Department of State, *First Report of the United Nations Atomic Energy Commission to the Security Council,* Publication 2737 (December 1946).

of September 11, 1947, presented detailed and specific proposals regarding the operational and developmental functions of the proposed international control agency.

A year later, the General Assembly recommended, again over Soviet objections, that "all nations, in the use of their rights of sovereignty, join in mutual agreement to limit the individual exercise of those rights in the control of atomic energy to the extent required . . . for the promotion of world security and peace." The vote was 49 to 5, with 3 abstentions.[20] By this action, forty-nine nations, including the United States, gave qualified approval to a limited surrender of national sovereignty in connection with proposals for control over the use of atomic energy for destructive purposes. They agree in effect with the original United States proposal that there must be "no veto to protect those who violate their solemn agreements." It must be recalled, however, that the action of the General Assembly in this case, as in all others, constituted merely a recommendation that Member states were free to accept or to reject. So far as the United States was concerned, American acceptance of a treaty whereby the United States might surrender its veto power with respect to control over the use of atomic materials for destructive purposes would require approval by the Congress or by a two-thirds vote of the Senate in the case of a treaty.[21]

McMahon Proposal

Although the United Nations Atomic Energy Commission had reached an impasse in efforts to develop a plan for the international control of atomic energy, suggestions from sources outside the commission were forthcoming.

The late Senator Brien McMahon of Connecticut repeated in a speech in 1951 a proposition first put forth by him in 1950 and supported by President Truman in his speech to the General Assembly in 1950. Senator McMahon proposed that at such time as an "effective and enforceable system of world-wide disarmament and control takes effect—a substantial portion of all money saved for a

[20] Res. 299(IV), Nov. 23, 1949.

[21] The McMahon Act provides that "any provision of the act or any action of the Commission to the extent that it conflicts with the provisions of any international arrangement made after August 1, 1946, shall be deemed to be of no further force or effect." The term "international arrangement" is defined to mean "any treaty approved by the Senate or international agreement approved after August 1, 1946, by the Congress." 60 Stat. 765, Sec. 6.

period of five years" should be expended by the United Nations for the peaceful development of "atomic energy, technical-assistance programs to underdeveloped areas, and general economic aid and assistance to all war-ravaged countries."[22] The Senator referred to his earlier proposal as follows: "The example which I cited at the time was that of spending fifty billion American dollars over a 5-year period, not for bombs but for bread, always on condition that other countries, and Russia in particular, do exactly what we propose to do."[23]

The McMahon proposal for the diversion of armament funds to peaceful pursuits was directed at national expenditures for "conventional armaments, biological and chemical agents, and atomic and hydrogen bombs." He tied his proposition to the requirement that there must be "an effective and enforceable system of world-wide disarmament and control." Until such an effective plan of disarmament could be devised and accepted, however, he believed it was essential that the United States increase its production of atomic weapons. "Massive atomic deterring power can win us years of grace, years in which to wrench history from its present course and direct it toward the enshrinement of human brotherhood."[24]

No action was taken in the United States Senate on Senator McMahon's proposal. The idea was recognizable, however, in President Eisenhower's speech delivered on April 16, 1953. After calling for the international control of atomic energy and limitations "by absolute numbers or by an agreed international ratio, of the sizes of the military and security forces of all nations," the President stated that "This Government is ready to ask its people to join with all nations in devoting a substantial percentage of the savings achieved by disarmament to a fund for world aid and reconstruction." He suggested further that all nations "set an agreed limit upon that portion of total production of certain strategic materials to be devoted to military purposes."[25]

The McMahon resolution, sponsored by Senator Jackson of Washington and a number of other Senators, was reintroduced into the Senate shortly after the President's speech. It was passed in an

---

[22] S. Con. Res. 47, 82 Cong. 1 sess.

[23] *Congressional Record*, Vol. 97, Pt. 9, pp. 11498-99.

[24] *Ibid.*, pp. 11498, 11501.

[25] Foreign Policy Address of the President of the United States delivered before the American Society of Newspaper Editors, Apr. 16, 1953. U. S. Department of State *Bulletin*, Vol. 28 (Apr. 27, 1953), p. 602.

amended form, repeating the statements made by the President that continued efforts must be made to limit armaments and control the destructive power of atomic energy.[26] The Senate Committee on Foreign Relations noted that the purpose of reliable control of armaments was to enable free men to "put their backs to the job of building a peaceful world devoted to the well-being of mankind."[27]

During the period of the stalemate on atomic energy in the United Nations, an interim control plan was suggested that was to be based on the absolute prohibition of the manufacture of all fissionable materials as well as on the absolute prohibition of the manufacture of atomic weapons until such time as a permanent control system could be developed and agreed upon. This proposal would, of course, still have required inspection of the type unacceptable to the Soviet Union as it would be essential to be sure that all states were abiding by the prohibition.[28]

Eisenhower Proposals—Atoms for Peace

On December 8, 1953, President Eisenhower sought to break the seven-year atomic energy deadlock when he went before the United Nations General Assembly to make the following proposals:

The Governments principally involved, to the extent permitted by elementary prudence, to begin now and continue to make joint contributions from their stockpiles of normal uranium and fissionable materials to an International Atomic Energy Agency. We would expect that such an agency would be set up under the aegis of the United Nations.

The ratios of contributions, the procedures and other details would properly be within the scope of the "private conversations" I have referred to earlier.

The United States is prepared to undertake these explorations in good

[26] S. Res. 150, 83 Cong. 1 sess.
[27] Senate Committee on Foreign Relations, *Resolution to Seek a Durable Peace*, S. Rept. 620, 83 Cong. 1 sess. (July 24, 1953), p. 4.
[28] For discussion of this proposal see Robert W. Frase, "International Control of Nuclear Weapons," *Annals of the American Academy of Political and Social Science*, Vol. 290 (November 1953), esp. pp. 24-26. At various times others have suggested plans for limited production of atomic materials. See *Bulletin of Atomic Scientists* (December 1947), p. 352; (June 1946); (April-May 1947); (October 1947). For discussion of possible ways of reconciling position of the non-Communist and Communist states, see *The New Republic* (Apr. 17, 1950), pp. 5 ff., which suggests that the "most obvious solvent to these mutual fears, the way to overcome Russia's resistance to adequate inspection and the U. S.' resistance to modifying certain of the provisions of the Majority Plan, is to achieve a general disarmament agreement. . . . If the deadlock is to be broken, only a bold strike along this broad front offers the possibility of success."

faith. Any partner of the United States acting in the same good faith will find the United States a not unreasonable or ungenerous associate.

Undoubtedly initial and early contributions to this plan would be small in quantity. However, the proposal has the great virtue that it can be undertaken without the irritations and mutual suspicions incident to any attempt to set up a completely acceptable system of world-wide inspection and control.

The Atomic Energy Agency could be made responsible for the impounding, storage, and protection of the contributed fissionable and other materials. The ingenuity of our scientists will provide special safe conditions under which such a bank of fissionable material can be made essentially immune to surprise seizure.

The more important responsibility of this Atomic Energy Agency would be to devise methods whereby this fissionable material would be allocated to serve the peaceful pursuits of mankind. Experts would be mobilized to apply atomic energy to the needs of agriculture, medicine, and other peaceful activities. A special purpose would be to provide abundant electrical energy in the power-starved areas of the world. Thus the contributing powers would be dedicating some of their strength to serve the needs rather than the fears of mankind.

The United States would be more than willing—it would be proud to take up with others "principally involved" the development of plans whereby such peaceful use of atomic energy would be expedited.

Of those "principally involved" the Soviet Union must, of course, be one.

I would be prepared to submit to the Congress of the United States, and with every expectation of approval, any such plan that would:

First—encourage world-wide investigation into the most effective peacetime uses of fissionable material, and with the certainty that they had all the material needed for the conduct of all experiments that were appropriate;

Second—begin to diminish the potential destructive power of the world's atomic stockpiles;

Third—allow all peoples of all nations to see that, in this enlightened age, the great powers of the earth, both of the East and of the West, are interested in human aspirations first, rather than in building up the armaments of war;

Fourth—open up a new channel for peaceful discussion, and initiate at least a new approach to the many difficult problems that must be solved in both private and public conversations, if the world is to shake off the inertia imposed by fear, and is to make positive progress toward peace.[29]

Despite the fact that these proposals are directed primarily toward the peaceful use of atomic energy, it seems possible they will have an important impact on the control of atomic weapons. The proposals represent the first significantly fresh approach toward

[29] "Atomic Power for Peace," Address by the President, Dec. 8, 1953, U. S. Department of State *Bulletin*, Vol. 29 (Dec. 21, 1953), pp. 850-51.

control of atomic energy since those put forth by the United States in 1946. The President mentioned some of the events that had taken place since 1946 that indicated the desirability of a new attempt to break the atomic stalemate:

In size and variety, the development of atomic weapons has been . . . re-markable. . . .

But the dread secret, and the fearful engines of atomic might, are not ours alone.

. . . the secret is possessed by our friends and allies, Great Britain and Canada, whose scientific genius made a tremendous contribution to our original discoveries, and the designs of atomic bombs.

The secret is also known by the Soviet Union.

The Soviet Union has informed us that, over recent years, it has devoted extensive resources to atomic weapons. During this period, the Soviet Union has exploded a series of atomic devices, including at least one in-volving thermo-nuclear reactions. . . .

But let no one think that the expenditure of vast sums for weapons and systems of defense can guarantee absolute safety for the cities and citizens of any nation. . . .

The United States, heeding the suggestion of the General Assembly of the United Nations, is instantly prepared to meet privately with such other countries as may be "principally involved," to seek "an acceptable solution" to the atomic armaments race, which overshadows not only the peace, but the very life, of the world.[30]

The Eisenhower proposals were couched partially in terms of an answer to a resolution of the General Assembly of November 28, 1953, suggesting that "the Disarmament Commission study the de-sirability of establishing a sub-committee consisting of representa-tives of the Powers principally involved, which should seek in pri-vate an acceptable solution."[31] President Eisenhower suggested that an International Atomic Energy Agency should be "set up under the aegis of the United Nations," but that certain details might be worked out in "private conversations" with those principally in-volved. The first conversations designed to explore the proposals were held in secret in the spring of 1954 between the Soviet Am-bassador and the Secretary of State.[32]

As the United States proposals were not designed to control the

[30] *Ibid.*, pp. 848, 850.
[31] Res. 715(VIII), Nov. 28, 1953. As noted below, the "private" conversations concerned with disarmament, not the peaceful use of atomic energy, took place in London in the spring of 1954.
[32] "Correspondence with Soviet Union on Atomic Pool Proposal," U. S. De-partment of State *Bulletin,* Vol. 31 (Oct. 4, 1954), pp. 478-89.

development of atomic weapons, it has been possible to eliminate from discussion at this stage consideration of the principal points in the past that have been an issue between the United States and the Soviet Union, namely, whether inspection and control should come before or after prohibition and destruction of existing stocks, and whether the veto would apply to the operations of any international control agency that might be established. One commentator observed with respect to the Eisenhower proposals:

It is healthy to give up the pretense that we think the Soviet Union would, or that we ourselves would, agree to international control and inspection of the top-most secret military operation. It was embarrassing to be involved in the pretense that Congress would ratify or that the people would support a system of what would be denounced as licensed international espionage.[33]

Another editorial comment was:

This differs from the outmoded Baruch plan principally in that it would start from a much more modest base and would avoid much of the cumbersome and now unworkable machinery which that plan called for. It would replace an all-or-nothing approach with a gradual, stage-by-stage basis of cooperation. . . . This approach has the great virtue of beginning with the easiest, rather than the hardest, part of the problem.[34]

Initial Soviet reaction to the proposals indicated readiness to take part in private discussions but criticized the President's plan on the ground that it would not remove the threat of atomic weapons and that the first step should be "to undertake solemn and unconditional pledges not to use atomic, hydrogen or other weapons of mass extermination." The second step should be the establishment of a strict international control that would "insure the fulfillment of the agreement on the ban of the use of atomic energy for military ends."[35] Thus, initially, the Soviet Union continued to take the same position that it had taken earlier.

That the President's proposals were not designed to control the use of atomic weapons is underlined by the fact that the Secretary of State on January 12, 1954, about a month after the atomic proposals were put forth, defined the "new strategy" of the Eisenhower administration as one of dependence primarily upon a great capacity "to respond vigorously at places and with means of its own choosing,"

---

[33] Walter Lippmann, in *New York Herald Tribune* (Dec. 10, 1953).
[34] *Washington Post* (Dec. 9, 1953).
[35] *New York Times* (Dec. 22, 1953).

a strategy interpreted generally as reference to the use of atomic weapons whenever and wherever the strategic interests of the United States might seem to require.[36] At nearly the same time, however, the Secretary of State testified before the Senate Special Subcommittee on the United Nations Charter that the problem of armament "carries so hideous a threat to the hopes of the peoples expressed in the preamble to the Charter" that "perhaps consideration should now be given to the creation of a special organ of the United Nations comparable to the Economic and Social Council." He added: "I think there is a real question as to whether or not it would not be desirable to have another subsidiary organ of the United Nations which could deal constantly and fully with this problem, and which would not be subject to the veto."[37]

During the 1954 session of the General Assembly, unanimous approval was given a resolution introduced by the United States and seven other states by which the Assembly endorsed negotiations for the establishment of an "International Atomic Energy Agency to facilitate the use by the entire world of atomic energy for peaceful purposes," and approved the calling of a conference under United Nations auspices "to explore means of developing the peaceful uses of atomic energy through international cooperation."[38]

Ambassador Lodge described the steps taken by the United States to help disseminate information about the peaceful uses of atomic energy and made known the willingness of the United States to allocate 100 kilograms of fissionable material for use in connection with the atoms for peace proposal.[39] Debate on the resolution was thorough and, at times, confused. At one point the Soviet representative announced that the Soviet Union, referring to disarmament instead of peaceful use of atomic energy, would no longer make its agreement to an atomic disarmament plan contingent on prior agreement to prohibit nuclear weapons. Subsequently, however, he demanded that the proposed new agency report to the Security

---

[36] "The Evolution of Foreign Policy," Address by Secretary Dulles, Jan. 12, 1954, U. S. Department of State *Bulletin,* Vol. 30 (Jan. 25, 1954), p. 108. For comment on the Eisenhower plan see David E. Lilienthal, "The Eisenhower Atomic Peace Plan," *Foreign Policy Bulletin* (Feb. 1, 1954).

[37] *Review of the United Nations Charter,* Senate Hearings, 83 Cong. 2 sess., Pt. 1, pp. 7, 33-34.

[38] Res. 810(IX), Dec. 4, 1954.

[39] U. S. Department of State *Bulletin,* Vol. 31 (Nov. 29, 1954), pp. 828 ff; also *ibid.* (Dec. 13, 1954), pp. 918 ff.

Council as well as to the General Assembly, suggesting thereby that the veto would control its operations. Despite defeat of Soviet amendments that would have made the agency responsible to the Assembly and the Security Council, the Soviet Union voted for the resolution on final passage.

An important question not solved by the resolution as adopted was whether negotiations could be successfully concluded to establish an International Atomic Energy Agency. And in these negotiations a further important, but perhaps not decisive, question will be whether the Soviet Union will participate and, if so, on what basis.

In a statement made to the First Committee of the Assembly during its session in 1954, Ambassador Lodge adverted to the relationship that the proposed new agency might have to the Security Council and the General Assembly. He indicated that such relationship might be defined in an agreement between the new agency and the United Nations, adding, "We may perhaps be forgiven for hoping and for expecting that it will not be a relationship in which the Security Council veto paralyzes the agency." Subsequently, he expressed the view that the agency should be under the "aegis of the United Nations" but that it would "not be practical to spell out the possible relationships at this time until we know better just what the agency will look like when it comes into being." Although the proposed new agency was to be concerned with peaceful uses of atomic energy, it was hoped that, "this experiment" in international co-operation would make it easier to make "genuine progress" in reaching agreement on disarmament.[40]

The proposed new agency is not as broad in concept as the suggestion of the Secretary of State that the Charter might be revised to create a permanent subsidiary organ along the lines of the Economic and Social Council to deal with the total problem of armament without being subject to the veto. Regardless whether progress is made during 1955 with negotiations to set up an International Atomic Energy Agency to deal with peaceful uses of atomic energy, a movement might still develop, in the event a General Conference to review the Charter is held, to establish an agency along the lines suggested by the Secretary of State.

Only time will tell whether this resolution, which constitutes an endorsement of President Eisenhower's proposal, and which indicates the flexibility of the Charter, will prove productive. It is

[40] *Ibid.* (Nov. 29, 1954), pp. 828, 833, 834.

not clear that the atomic stalemate has been broken. If progess in effecting the formation of such an agency is made during the years ahead, it seems likely that it will be attributable to a general relaxation of tensions and not to an improved technique of the United Nations in handling the problems posed by the development of atomic energy.

The Regulation and Reduction of Conventional Armaments

Proposals for the limitation of conventional armaments have been blocked by many of the same factors that have prevented the conclusion of acceptable agreements for the control of the destructive forces of atomic energy. Suggestions first put forth in high hope were eventually found unacceptable by either the free world or the Communist nations. Subsequently, proposals were presented not with any real expectation that they would become the basis of agreement, but because the appearance needed to be maintained that something was being done, else the hopes of mankind for a peaceful world might be changed to a desperate acceptance of the inevitability of future war.

Many people equate peace with disarmament. Hence, in considering disarmament proposals, the cynic may believe that they have been advanced not in the expectation of acceptance, but rather because nations that are not active in putting forth such propositions may be criticized as not being peace-loving states. To put it more bluntly, there is a danger that disarmament proposals emanating from states active in the cold war may have been put forth for propaganda reasons rather than in the expectation that the proposals were likely to be accepted. This is not to say that states submitting plans for control of armaments may not hope that they will be taken seriously and would not be pleased if their ideas were accepted—at least as a basis of serious negotiations that might lead to reduction in armaments. It is important, however, that those who study proposals put forth during these years of the cold war, be thoroughly aware of the fact that some of them have propaganda overtones that cannot be ignored.

Aside from supranational types of proposals for the regulation and reduction of armaments discussed later, most plans for action in this field have been considered by the United Nations Commission for Conventional Armaments. The resolution creating that commission called on it to prepare and to submit to the Security Council within the space of not more than three months, proposals: "(a) for general regulation and reduction of armaments and armed forces, and (b) for practical and effective safeguards in connection with the general regulation and reduction of armaments."[41]

Soviet Proposal for a One-third Reduction

One of the earliest proposals for reduction of conventional armaments advanced in the United Nations was presented by the Soviet Union. At the third session of the General Assembly in 1948, the Soviet Union proposed a resolution recommending that as a first step toward the reduction of armaments and armed forces, permanent members of the Security Council should within one year reduce their existing land, naval, and air forces by one third. Tied to this proposal was the proposition that atomic weapons should be prohibited.[42] During subsequent discussion of this plan, the Soviet representative emphasized that the problem of control of atomic weapons and the reduction of conventional armaments were so closely related that in the Soviet view they could not be considered separately.

The Soviet theme throughout subsequent discussions of plans for the limitation of armaments was based on two principal points: (1) a flat percentage reduction of existing armament and armed forces, and (2) the prohibition of atomic weapons. The Soviet delegation took the position that the Atomic Energy Commission and the Commission on Conventional Armaments should be guided in their work by the principle that the prohibition of atomic weapons and the establishment of control over atomic energy must be an integral part of the general plan for the reduction by one third of the armaments of the permanent members.[43] The Soviet plan, with variations, has been put forth a number of times. Its main features have just as persistently been rejected by other Members of the United Nations.

[41] U.N. Doc. S/268/Rev. 1 (Feb. 13, 1947).

[42] U.N. General Assembly, Third Session, Part I, Plenary, *Official Records,* 147th Meeting (Sept. 28, 1948), pp. 265-66; and U.N. General Assembly, Third Session, First Committee, *Official Records,* 143rd Meeting (Sept. 29, 1948), pp. 2-9.

[43] U.N. Doc. S/1246/Rev. 1 (Feb. 9, 1949).

In February 1949, a Soviet resolution proposed in the Security Council calling for a one-third reduction in armaments was unacceptable to a majority, and in October 1949, a Soviet resolution calling for the submission of information on conventional armaments *and* atomic weapons was rejected.[44] In September 1950, a Soviet resolution in the General Assembly calling again for a one-third reduction of existing armed forces during 1950-51 was voted down. In the fall of 1951, Soviet amendments to the resolution establishing the Disarmament Commission, proposing a one-third reduction of existing armaments and armed forces, were defeated.[45] Again in 1953, the Soviet Union recommended a one-third reduction in armed forces within one year, "a concept" according to the United States representative "repeatedly turned down by the General Assembly because of its obvious unfairness to those who, like the United States, materially reduced their armaments at the end of World War II."[46]

General opposition to the Soviet proposal has been based on the knowledge that reduction in armed forces and armaments of the five major powers by a fixed fraction would preserve the unfavorable balance between Soviet forces and forces of the other permanent members of the Security Council that has existed since shortly after the Second World War. Moreover, Soviet insistence that such reductions be tied to prohibition of the manufacture or use of atomic weapons meant, if accepted, that in the case of the United States, it could not build up its conventional armaments and armed forces, which had been greatly reduced after the war. At the same time, the United States would be bound not to use the one weapon in which it had clear superiority. States that opposed the Soviet one-third reduction plan felt that, if it were accepted, the result would be to destroy any real possibility of defense by the free world against aggression.

At various times during discussion of the Soviet proposal, it was suggested that reduction of armaments might be achieved by some proportionate method of reduction based on the forces in being as of 1945, or based on balanced curtailment of forces to a level adequate for defense, but not for aggression.[47] None of these sugges-

---

[44] U.N. Doc. S/1405/Rev. 1 (Oct. 13, 1949).
[45] U.N. Doc. A/C.1/698 (Jan. 12, 1952).
[46] U. S. Department of State *Bulletin,* Vol. 29 (Dec. 14, 1953), p. 836.
[47] For summary of views, see U.N. Department of Public Information, *Yearbook of the United Nations, 1948-49,* pp. 362 ff.

tions was acceptable to the Soviet Union. Moreover, so far as the other permanent members of the Security Council were concerned, they felt their national security required that some system of international control must be established and in operation before they would have the means of knowing whether other permanent members of the Council in general and the Soviet Union in particular, were abiding by commitments to reduce their armed forces and armaments. The representative of the United States indicated during debate in 1948 that it was inconceivable that Members of the United Nations could disarm unless there were positive evidence that the Soviet Union would be willing to participate in a control system.

French Proposal to
Collect Information

Much of the work of the Commission for Conventional Armaments during 1949 was devoted to a consideration of a proposal put forth by France, calling for the collection and verification of information on the size of existing armed forces and armaments. Although the French plan was not a disarmament proposal in the sense that it suggested specific reductions in arms as had the Soviet plan, nevertheless the French plan considered essential preliminaries to taking practical steps toward disarmament.

Following a resolution of the General Assembly,[48] the French representatives at a series of meetings of the Commission on Conventional Armaments, developed an approach they had first suggested a year earlier.[49] The French proposal called for a census or counting of armed forces and armaments, a verification of the census, and the creation of an International Organ of Control to administer the census and the verification. The census called for figures on the size of ground forces, naval forces, air forces, paramilitary forces, and national police forces, including figures on those in the active and reserve components of each category. The figures were to be submitted simultaneously by all states to the control authority. The census was also to include figures on conventional armaments, such as the number of automatic weapons and the tonnage of armored equipment of the ground forces, the types and classifications of naval vessels, and the number and type

[48] Res. 192 (III), Nov. 19, 1948.
[49] U.N. Doc. S/C.3/40 (July 20, 1949).

of combatant aircraft. So far as verification was concerned, the control authority was to have power to "direct investigations by international verification teams," including spot checks within each state. The International Organ of Control, in giving effect to the census and verification measures, was to operate in a role subordinate to the Security Council and in accordance with terms of the international agreement that would be required to bring it into being. It was suggested that the organ was to have authority over its own procedures and that decisions "on all matters which require voting will be adopted by a simple majority."[50]

The French proposal was opposed step by step by the Soviet Union on the ground that it ignored atomic weapons and did not get immediately at the problem of reduction of armaments. It was essential, the Soviet Union argued, that information be collected on atomic armaments as well as on conventional armaments. Moreover, the way to reduce armaments, in the Soviet view, was to reduce them, and a discussion of census, verification, and control agencies could come later. Such discussion, said the Soviet representative, was in reality an attempt to by-pass the important problem. Other members of the Council felt, however, that census, verification, and control were essential if there were to be sufficient international confidence to warrant states reducing their armed forces.

Although it was generally recognized that Soviet opposition would prevent any practical effect being given the French proposal, the General Assembly nevertheless approved it.[51] It also called for the supplying "of full information on . . . conventional armaments and armed forces and the verification thereof, as constituting the necessary basis for the implementation of "recommendations for the reduction of armaments."[52] The Security Council was asked to continue its efforts to make progress along these lines.

The French proposal foundered, as had the other proposals in the field of atomic energy and armament control, because none of the great powers could risk placing its national security in the hands of others at a time when there was evidence that some nations were

[50] U.N. Security Council, Fourth Year, *Working Paper Adopted at the 19th Meeting of the Commission for Conventional Armaments*, Doc. S/1372 (Aug. 9, 1949), pp. 7-8.
[51] The French proposal was vetoed by the Soviet Union in the Security Council, but the records of discussion were transmitted to the General Assembly.
[52] Res. 300 (IV), Dec. 5, 1949.

willing to use military means to achieve political ends. Within the year, the United Nations had great need for military force to repel aggression in Korea.

The Disarmament Commission

Subsequent to consideration by the General Assembly in 1949 of the French proposal, steps were taken to reorganize the approach of the United Nations to the problem of disarmament and the control of atomic energy. In April 1950, the Soviet Union withdrew from the work of the Commission on Conventional Armaments because the representative of Nationalist China was not excluded from the commission. For the remainder of the year the commission continued its technical studies of methods of setting up an international system of controls of armaments. In December 1950, however, the General Assembly established a Committe of Twelve to examine the possibility of co-ordinating the work of the Atomic Energy Commission and the Commission for Conventional Armaments.[53] A year later, acting on the report of the committee,[54] the General Assembly created under the Security Council the Disarmament Commission, directing it "to prepare proposals to be embodied in a draft treaty (or treaties) for the regulation, limitation and balanced reduction of all armed forces and all armaments, for the elimination of all major weapons adaptable to mass destruction, and for effective international control of atomic energy to ensure the prohibition of atomic weapons and the use of atomic energy for peaceful purposes only."[55]

Initial Proposals Considered by Commission

During 1952 the Disarmament Commission agreed on a plan of work and considered a number of proposals put forth by members.[56] Two of these deserve special attention.

[53] Res. 496 (V), Dec. 13, 1950.
[54] U.N. General Assembly, Sixth Session, *Report of the Committee of Twelve,* Doc. A/1922 (Oct. 23, 1951).
[55] Res. 502 (VI), Jan. 11, 1952.
[56] U.N. Disarmament Commission, *Official Records,* Second Report, Special Supplement No. 1 (1952), pp. 3-19.

The United States presented a paper to the commission suggesting five steps, to be taken one by one, looking toward disclosure and verification of armed forces and armaments as a first move toward practical disarmament. The stages were as follows: First, Member states would be asked to disclose in "breadth," but not in "depth," the "general contours" of their military establishments including an indication of their atomic strength. Second, Members would give more detailed information on the organization of their armed forces and the basic materials required to produce armaments, including atomic weapons. Third, detailed disclosures would be made of armaments as well as the kinds and amounts of fissionable material available. There would also be disclosure of data on the operation of installations producing armaments and fissionable material. Fourth, detailed information would be given on installaitons used to produce "novel armaments," including atomic weapons. Finally, there would be revelation of the novel armaments themselves and of atomic weapons.[57]

This proposal was rejected forthwith by the Soviet representative on the Disarmament Commission, who characterized it as an effort to develop a workable intelligence and espionage operation, unrelated to disarmament.

Later in 1952, the United Kingdom, France, and the United States submitted a working paper directed toward a numerical reduction of the man-power strength of the armed forces of the permanent members of the Security Council.[58] As a basis of discussion, this tripartite proposal suggested that equal maximum ceilings on military man power be fixed at from 1,000,000 to 1,500,000 for the United States, the Soviet Union, and China, and that maximum ceilings for the United Kingdom and France be fixed at from 700,000 to 800,000. Similar types of ceilings might be fixed for other states with substantial armed forces, possibly at something less than 1 per cent of the population of such countries. The United States representative to the Disarmament Commission pointed out that these proposals stressed one of the fundamental objectives in the disarmament field, "the prevention of war by reducing the likelihood or possibility of successful aggression."[59]

[57] *Ibid.*, pp. 22-30.
[58] *Ibid.*, pp. 99-102.
[59] *Ibid.*, p. 105.

Despite Soviet rejection of the proposals as "cynical and hypo-
critical" and allegations that they did not deal with the allocation
of armed forces as among the various services or with the prohibition of weapons of mass destruction, the three powers in August
1952 submitted a supplement to the earlier working papers suggesting procedures to achieve a balanced relationship among the reduced forces.[60] The three powers proposed a conference of the five
major powers to work out tentative agreement among themselves,
to be followed by regional conferences to be attended by other
Member states with substantial forces. It was suggested that the
tentative agreements thus developed might then be embodied in
a draft treaty bringing into balance all the essential parts of the
program. But the Soviet representative refused to accept this working paper even as a basis for discussion.

London Conference, 1954

The General Assembly at its eighth session in 1953 adopted a
resolution suggesting that the Disarmament Commission consider
setting up a subcommittee of the nations principally involved in
the disarmament question that might seek in private conversations
to make some progress.[61] Accordingly, a Subcommittee of Five
(Canada, France, United Kingdom, United States, and the Soviet
Union) was established and held nineteen secret meetings in London
in the spring of 1954, with negative results.[62] The United States representative to the meeting reported that: "The discussions gave a
clear indication of the present direction of Soviet thinking on disarmament. The Soviet Union showed no serious desire to negotiate
the subject. It confined its efforts to glib distortions to support the
propaganda slogan 'ban the bomb.' "[63]

During these London conversations two principal proposals were
put forth by the Western powers. The first was a working paper by
the United States spelling out in some detail the nature of a proposed control organ for disarmament and atomic energy matters.
The second was an Anglo-French memorandum concerning the
phasing and timing of elements of the disarmament plan.

[60] *Ibid.*, pp. 130-31.
[61] Res. 715 (VIII), Nov. 28, 1953.
[62] U. S. Department of State, *The Record on Disarmament*, Report of the
U. S. Deputy Representative to Disarmament Commission on London Meeting
of Subcommittee of Five and on Disarmament Commission Meetings, Publication
5581 (July 1954).
[63] *Ibid.*, p. 11.

The United States working paper envisaged the creation, by treaty, of a United Nations disarmament and atomic energy authority, or control organ, to be composed of members of the Security Council, plus Canada. That control organ would be given authority to control atomic energy so as to ensure that atomic and hydrogen weapons would be prohibited, to supervise programs for limitation and balanced reduction of armaments, and to control the safeguards necessary to enforce the disarmament program. It was suggested in the working paper that the authority should operate by majority rule with respect to the matters delegated to it. The authority would be given power to determine the method and details of enforcing agreed reductions of armaments; to organize and conduct necessary inspections; and to station personnel in countries accepting the agreement. In the event the agreement should be violated, the control authority would report such violations to the Security Council for appropriate action. The authority would also have power to suspend the supply of nuclear material to offending states and to close plants in offending states that might be using such materials. The Soviet Union, however, rejected the working paper, which was based on the concept of international managerial control of atomic energy, just as it had rejected the earlier American plan based on the concept of international ownership of atomic energy facilities.

It might be argued that the new United States working paper would have had the effect of eliminating the veto in the control of atomic energy and in plans to limit armaments. It must be noted, however, that the plan would not go into effect unless approved by states in accordance with their constitutional processes. Inasmuch as it is inconceivable that the Western powers would accept proposals of this kind without full agreement of the Soviet Union, the plan would be subject to veto before it could become operative. Moreover, if violations of the proposed treaty should occur, they would be reported to the Security Council and the Assembly for "appropriate action." Such "appropriate action" in the Council would presumably be subject to the veto, and appropriate action by the Assembly would necessarily be in the form merely of recommendations. It would seem, therefore, that if the general outlines of the United States working paper were adopted, it would still be necessary to consider amendments to the Charter if the United Nations were to be an effective instrument for enforcing the disarmament treaty, otherwise enforcement measures could be vetoed in the Council and subject only to recommendatory procedures in the Assembly.

The Anglo-French memorandum was for the purpose of indicating the relationship, from the point of view of timing, between prohibition of atomic weapons and reduction of armaments, on the one hand, and, on the other hand, the inauguration of safeguards to ensure observance of such prohibitions and reductions as might be agreed upon. The basic factor to be taken into account should be, in the view of the memorandum, the actual existence of ability in the control organ to ensure observance of agreements to prohibit and reduce armaments. Once there was assurance that the control organ could act in order to ensure that agreements would be observed, it would then be possible as a first step to freeze over-all military expenditures and military man power. Thereafter, scheduled prohibitions and reductions of armaments could be undertaken. The prohibition would proceed concurrently with reduction of weapons other than nuclear weapons and of armed forces.

The United States representative reported that "the Soviet Union completely rejected the British-French memorandum."[64] In the light of the action of the General Assembly at its session in 1954, however, it might be argued that the Soviet Union has made some concessions in the direction of the memorandum. The Soviet representative, in a speech of September 30, 1954, apparently dropped the earlier insistence of the Soviet Union that the use of atomic weapons must be prohibited before any other steps could be taken looking toward disarmament and agreed that a disarmament program needed to be carried out by stages—a concession to the Anglo-French view. Finally, he voted, as noted earlier, for the disarmament resolution that suggested re-convening of the Subcommittee of Five to meet in private and proposed that the whole program of disarmament be carried out in such a way that "no State would have cause to fear that its security was endangered."[65]

The final resolution jointly sponsored by the United States, the United Kingdom, France, Canada, and the Soviet Union won unanimous approval of the Assembly. In addition to the points noted, it endorsed sending to the subcommittee of the Disarmament Commission all projects for disarmament then pending in the United Nations, including an Indian proposal for a standstill agreement

[64] Ibid., p. 9.
[65] Res. 808 (IX), Nov. 4, 1954.

on the production of arms pending a disarmament convention, and a joint Australian-Philippine suggestion for the Secretariat to draft a paper setting forth the areas of agreement and disagreement on disarmament between the states in the free world and the Communist states. The subcommittee was again asked to hold its sessions in private.

It is difficult to know whether the area of agreement between the Soviet Union and the non-Communist world is more than superficial. Certainly the test whether progress can be made awaits the secret discussions of the proposals that will take place in the future meetings of the Disarmament Subcommittee. One observer has noted that:

> . . . there is still almost—though not quite—as much disagreement between the Soviet Union and the West as there was September 20 when Soviet Delegate Andrei Y. Vishinsky made a series of sensational "concessions" and the discussion began.
> These "concessions" have not stood up under the scrutiny of the Assembly . . . even Mr. Vishinsky acknowledged that "substantial divergencies persist." But he minimized them, and said the Soviet position was subject to further change. . . .[66]

Just prior to the convening of the second series of meetings held by the United Nations Disarmament Subcommittee, the deputy United States representative to the United Nations, stated that the United States "believes that secure disarmament in a world without trust requires two things above all: First it must cover not just atomic weapons but *all* armaments in a single plan—for bayonets and high explosives are still deadly in this atomic age. Second, the disarmament plan must contain safeguards so that each side actually disarms in plain sight of the other with firm certainty that all pledges are being carried out every step of the way."[67]

The action of the President in April 1955 in creating a new post of Presidential Assistant for Disarmament, to which he appointed Harold E. Stassen, emphasized the importance attached by the United States to the problem of disarmament. It also emphasized that action by the United Nations was not proving fruitful. The

[66] William R. Frye, "Climax in U.N. Arms Curb Talks," *Christian Science Monitor* (Oct. 28, 1954).

[67] Address by Ambassador James J. Wadsworth, Deputy United States Representative to the United Nations, before the Massachusetts State Federation of Women's Clubs, Boston, Mass., Feb. 17, 1955. United States Mission to the United Nations, Press Release 2117.

President observed in referring to the 1955 sessions of the Disarmament Subcommittee in London that they have "again resulted in no progress and no clear crystallization of thinking on this subject."[68]

The creation of this position cannot help but raise questions about the future of United States policy in this area. The Presidential Assistant is given responsibility for developing the "broad studies, investigations, and conclusions which, when concurred in by the National Security Council and approved by the President, will become basic policy toward the question of disarmament." According to the President, the Assistant for Disarmament "will be expected to take into account the full implications of new weapons in the possession of other nations as well as the United States, to consider future probabilities of armaments, and to weigh the views of the military, the civilians, and the officials of our Government and of other governments."[69]

So far as the United States is concerned, the creation of this post might well have an important impact on American policy. It is possible of course, that it may lead to significant redirection of policy. Certainly the development of hydrogen weapons with possibilities of potential radioactive fall-out that transcend scientific thinking of recent years has injected a new factor into the international picture. The question remains, however, whether this new factor will lead to any fundamental reassessment of national policies of the great powers that have heretofore been found irreconcilable.

It will be recalled that the United States and the other free nations have consistently rejected Soviet proposals calling for outlawing or destroying atomic weapons—the one field in which the free world presumably had superiority. The free world has been unwilling to strip itself of its most effective defenses and permit itself to stand relatively undefended before an armed Soviet Union. For reasons that seem valid to it, the Soviet Union has refused to accept proposed man-power ceilings on its military forces that, while leaving it on a numerical par with the United States, would require it to bring about a greater proportional reduction in its armed forces, leave it numerically inferior to the combined forces of the free nations, and presumably leave it behind in the number of atomic weapons at its disposal.

[68] *New York Times* (Apr. 20, 1955).
[69] *Ibid.*

The Supranational Approach

Not all of the proposals with elements of supranationality considered earlier in this study envisaged substantial disarmament as
an immediate goal. The Federal Union proposal and the ABC
Plan were predicated on the proposition that participating states
must look to their security not through disarmament, but rather
through mutual organization of defenses that would thereby give
them strength enough to provide a reasonably reliable defense
against aggression. World federation proposals, however, based on
the proposition that a supranational legislative body must have
power to enforce peace and that world organization must be virtually universal if it is to succeed, contemplate the elimination of
national military forces, except small police units, the establishment of international control of atomic energy, and the existence
of an international military force to preserve the peace. Thus the
United World Federalists state that "Enforceable disarmament can
only come under the protection of an all-inclusive world organization which can guarantee to each nation security from attack by
others."[70]

One proposal for supranational government that focuses directly
on the problem of disarmament suggests that the first guiding and
underlying principle should be that: "Disarmament is the crux of
the problem of world order. By this is meant national disarmament
that is not only universal (as to all nations) and enforceable (by
United Nations inspection and military forces) but also complete,
in all arms, right down to strictly limited and lightly armed forces
for internal order only."[71] Disarmament, according to this view,
must be universal and enforceable. Partial disarmament, or reduction, or control proposals will "almost certainly bog down in disputes over 'quotas' and the so-called 'needs' of the Powers." Disarmament must be written into the Charter itself—a Charter creating a "federation of all the nations to enforce complete national
disarmament."

The main features of this disarmament proposal would be included in the proposed revised Charter and in an annex, on the

[70] *The Federalist* (August 1953), p. 18.
[71] Grenville Clark and Louis B. Sohn, *Peace Through Disarmament and Charter
Revision* (Preliminary Print, July 1953), pp. ii-iii.

theory that these features must "be agreed upon in advance during negotiations on the revised Charter." Article 11 of the existing Charter would be completely rewritten. It would take away from the Security Council and give to the General Assembly "the primary responsibility for the maintenance of international peace and security." The Assembly would have legislative power "To enact appropriate laws to implement the provisions of Annex I of this Charter, relating to general and complete disarmament, including the control of atomic energy."

In describing the plan, its sponsors point out that it "calls for total abolition of all national military forces and weapons (including atomic weapons) within a twelve-year period by stages, with the proviso that the period for the elimination of the last thirty per cent may be extended by the General Assembly by not more than three years." The annex also provides for the control of atomic energy. "This would be done by a plan calling for (a) inspection of mining and refining of materials from which atomic energy is capable of being produced; (b) the actual lease by the United Nations of the plants where the process of converting the materials into fissionable products takes place; (c) inspection of the disposition and use of these fissionable products, all to the end that none of such products can be used for weapons."[72]

An essential part of the plan would be the creation of a strong United Nations military force of from 300,000 to 700,000 men that would be available to suppress any violation of the disarmament plan. "This Peace Force would be methodically organized during the 12-year period . . . during which the process of complete disarmament would be carried out . . . so that by the time national disarmament is completed a fully equipped United Nations military force would be in being, ready to assume the task of maintaining peace under the law of the United Nations."[73] Responsibility for seeing that disarmament steps would be carried out would be placed on a re-vamped Security Council—the Executive Council—as "upon acceptance of the revised Charter, each member Nation would be automatically bound to carry out the detailed disarmament plan; and what is required is the creation of an effective agency" with that responsibility.[74]

[72] *Ibid.*, p. 28.
[73] *Ibid.*, p. 29.
[74] *Ibid.*, p. 58.

These proposals would require that disarmament plans must be written into a revised Charter and accepted by nations as a part of a total plan for a stronger United Nations. They do not seek to give a revised United Nations unlimited authority to legislate disarmament into existence, once states have become Members of the Organization, without a blueprint in advance of what might be expected. They do not propose a simple rewriting of Charter provisions relating to the control of armament. They treat disarmament on the premise that "until the present system of national military forces is totally abolished it will be impossible to achieve genuine peace. . . . It has been repeatedly demonstrated that the existence of strong national military forces will of itself engender such mutual fears as to constitute a major influence toward ultimate conflict."[75]

The essential difference between these supranational proposals and those that have been considered under the present Charter is that the former would write into the Charter specific requirements for disarmament whereas the existing Charter, as noted earlier, simply authorizes the United Nations to make recommendations to accomplish that purpose.

A disarmament proposal similar in many respects to the proposal described above was considered by the Second London Parliamentary Conference on World Government. It called for a Charter that "should provide for complete, universal and enforceable disarmament, carried out by rapid stages" with the details of the proposal to be spelled out in an annex to the Charter. The production of atomic weapons was to be prohibited and subject to strict supervision by the United Nations. Proposals as bold as these were recognized as proposals for "world government." The conference also considered the report of a subcommission to consider revision of the Charter that would include only changes "which were judged to be politically acceptable to the governments of those states represented . . . at the conference." Interestingly, the subcommission made no recommendations with respect to disarmament.[76]

[75] *Ibid.,* p. 27.
[76] See World Association of Parliamentarians for World Government, *Report of the Second London Parliamentary Conference on World Government* (Sept. 25, 1952), pp. 100 ff. For further developments see World Association of Parliamentarians for World Government, *Report of the Third World Parliamentary Conference on World Government,* Copenhagen, Aug. 22-29, 1953 (1954).

Other Disarmament Proposals

In addition to the proposals relating to the regulation of armaments that have been discussed above, other suggestions have been made, which might have, as a collateral effect, some impact on the size of the armed forces now maintained by states. It has been suggested, for example, that if the power of the United Nations were increased by arrangements that could be made under the Charter to supply the Organization with military forces, states might be persuaded to reduce their armaments. Another proposal would limit the proportion of the resources of nations devoted to military purposes in order to increase the levels of living. Still another would strive for total universal disarmament.

Disarmament as a Result of Collective Security

If it should prove possible at some future time to create the United Nations armed forces envisaged by Article 43, and if the agreements contemplated by that article were so drafted and accepted by Member states as to place strong forces at the disposal of the United Nations, some Members might feel that the United Nations could effectively maintain international peace and security and thereby be willing to reduce their national armaments. No such agreements have been possible thus far.

It is conceivable that at some future time Member states possessing substantial military forces might agree to make them available to the United Nations, and then, acting pursuant to recommendation of the General Assembly under the terms of the "Uniting for Peace" resolution, this force might be used to persuade recalcitrant states to reduce their armaments. The Commission to Study the Organization of Peace observed in 1947 that "The problem of security from war involves both an increase in the power of the United Nations and the regulation and reduction of national armaments. The United Nations would gain in power by arrangements under the Charter (Article 43) for supplying it with military forces and facilities. . . ."[77] The likelihood of progress along such lines at the present time seems remote.

[77] Commission to Study the Organization of Peace, *Security and Disarmament Under the United Nations*, Fifth Report (June 1947), p. 18. See also discussion of "Quota Force" Plan and Article 51 pact above in Chap. VI.

"Guns or Butter"

There is a direct relationship between the proportion of the resources of a nation that can be devoted to peaceful purposes and the proportion that can be devoted to military purposes. It has been suggested many times that relief from the pressing burden of armaments would leave nations free to devote larger proportions of their resources to productive pursuits.

With this in mind, an observer proposed in early 1955 that "The United States should sponsor before the United Nations a bold new plan of economic and military disarmament which would: Limit the proportion of any nation's resources that could be devoted to 'guns'—that is, to war industries and all other direct and indirect military expenditures—as against 'butter,' meaning what goes to lifting levels of the people."[78]

This proposal was touched off by the belief that the downfall of Malenkov indicated in a dramatic way that the Soviet Union was following a "guns-over-butter" policy. The suggestion was embodied in a resolution introduced into the Senate by Senator Symington and some forty co-sponsors. The resolution, which was approved by the Senate in late July 1955, requested the President to "explore the possibilities of limiting the proportion of every nation's resources devoted to military purposes, both direct and indirect, so as to increase steadily the proportion devoted to improving the living levels of the people." It also stated that any limitation should "provide adequate means of inspection and control and be made part of any comprehensive regulation, limitation, and balanced reduction of all armed forces and armaments."[79]

Few would quarrel with the laudable purpose of the underlying premise of this suggestion—that armaments burdens should be lifted so that more resources could be devoted to peaceful uses. The main criticism of the proposal would seem to be that it is impractical as a disarmament suggestion because the Soviet Union is not likely to accept it. The probable reason for such rejection is that inasmuch as Soviet Communist resources are smaller than those of the free nations, acceptance of the plan would be viewed by the Soviet Union as one-sided. Senator Symington, indeed, remarked

[78] Samuel Lubell, "Butter Over Guns—A Peace Plan for the Free World," *Congressional Record,* 84 Cong. 1 sess. (daily ed. Mar. 2, 1955), p. 1955.

[79] S. Res. 71, 84 Cong. 1 sess. For reprints of relevant articles and statements see *Congressional Record,* 84 Cong. 1 sess. (daily ed. Mar. 2, 1955), pp. 1953 ff.

that the plan was not "put forward with any thought that such a disarmament program could serve as a substitute for our capacity for instant retaliation with nuclear weapons in case of an all-out attack."[80]

Although the "guns or butter" idea was advanced as a disarmament proposal worthy of serious consideration, it obviously contains some psychological overtones. The author wrote that this proposal might touch off a "dramatic moral offensive to make clear to the world why high living standards are a built-in reassurance of peace, and any industrial nation which deliberately depresses the living of its people to build military power is a threat to peace."[81] Its chief purpose would be "to get over in a dramatic way to the peoples of the world, including as far as possible the Russian people, the difference to them individually between the economy enjoyed by the United States and the economy suffered by the people of Russia." And it would be "fantastic . . . to have any real expectation that the Russians ever would agree to any workable disarmament program."[82]

Total Universal Disarmament

For the past thirty-five years nations have struggled with plans for the regulation of armaments with no success. One observer has stated:

. . . The history of the League of Nations is full of fruitless and tedious wrangles on qualitative disarmament, in which many efforts were made to distinguish between offensive and defensive weapons, without result. The U.N.'s history thus far is similar. As long as the nations must plan for war, they will not agree on partial disarmament, for each will say it needs more for its security than the others are willing to grant it; and what they will describe as "defensive" will unfailingly look "offensive" to their neighbors. A disarmament conference which aims only at reduction or control will wind up in exhaustion and irritation. . . . If the political will can be established to achieve disarmament at all, it will be found easier to arrive at agreement on complete disarmament than on partial disarmament.[83]

General Douglas MacArthur recently suggested a similar approach. In early 1955, in Los Angeles, he pointed out that modern war contains "the germs of double suicide." This raises the great question whether "war can be outlawed from the world!" He

---

[80] *Ibid.*, p. 1954.

[81] *Ibid.*, p. 1955.

[82] *Ibid.*, p. 1957.

[83] Statement of Charles G. Bolte, representing the American Veterans Committee, Inc. *Review of the United Nations Charter*, Senate Hearings, 84 Cong. 1 sess., Pt. 12, pp. 1898-1914.

suggested that, if war could be outlawed, it would no longer be a matter of trusting other nations not to rearm because "the self-interest of each nation outlawing war would keep it true to itself. . . . It would not necessarily require international inspection of relative armaments, the public opinion of every part of the world would be the great denominator which would ensure the issue, each nation would so profit that it could not fail eventually to comply." He added, however, that, if war were to be outlawed, it would not mean "the abandonment of all armed forces, but it would reduce them to the simpler problems of internal order and international peace." He concluded that there must be one nation to lead. "We should now proclaim our readiness to abolish war in concert with the great powers of the world. The result might be magical."[84]

Since that time writers and commentators have endorsed and elaborated on General MacArthur's suggestion. It has been argued, for example, that partial or piecemeal disarmament is unattainable for various reasons; that total and universal disarmament is the only practical and realistic way to approach the problem as it is the only kind of disarmament that carries with it a minimum amount of external control over the activities of the sovereign state. Also, if the manufacture of both conventional and unconventional weapons were prohibited, any violation of the prohibition would be known at once and appropriate steps could be taken to investigate the affair and punish the violator. According to this line of reasoning, anything short of an absolute outlawry of war and a complete prohibition of armaments would be inadequate to cope with the present world situation.

It is difficult to analyze plans as embryonic as these. They are more in the nature of expressions of aspirations than concrete proposals for disarmament. Agreements of the past such as the Kellogg-Briand Pact of 1928, which have renounced recourse to war as a means of settling international controversies, have not led to peace. Indeed, the Charter itself binds Members to settle disputes by peaceful means, and they undertake to refrain from "the threat or use of force" in any manner inconsistent with the purposes of the United Nations. Agreements to outlaw war have not had the effect in the past of encouraging nations to reduce their armaments. The situation of the world today, however, may be so much more pre-

[84] For reprint of speech, see *Congressional Record* (daily ed., Feb. 7, 1955), p. A-681.

carious in terms of survival, that a new declaration outlawing war would be more effective than in the past.

But if the United States should proclaim its readiness to abolish war in concert with the other great powers would the United States be expected forthwith to scuttle its military forces as evidence of its good faith, or would it defer disarmament until the other nations had agreed? Even should a treaty be signed, would that be a sufficient basis on which the United States should proceed on the treaty date to disarm? Or might the American people feel that their national interests would require some method of ascertaining that the other great powers were also complying with the treaty terms? If the United States were willing to take the pledges of other nations at face value, there already is available a basis for such action under existing commitments under the Charter.

On the other hand, if the United States were not willing to rely solely on the written, pledged word of the Soviet Union, as might well be the case, then it is confronted immediately by the problem of establishing an "air-tight system" of inspection to ensure that other parties to such an agreement were living up to their commitments. Moreover, should a system of inspection reveal violations of agreements to disarm, the world would immediately be confronted by the extremely difficult problem of enforcement. These are issues that have been at fruitless debate under the auspices of the United Nations for the past ten years.

The record of the United Nations in the control of conventional armaments and of atomic energy is disappointing. The positive contribution of United Nations machinery has been principally that of providing a forum for discussion. Existence of the forum has induced Member states to keep trying to control weapons for mass destruction. It has led to the development of plans for procedures and control that are available for use if and when international conditions are favorable.

International conditions since the war, however, have not been propitious for disarmament. Existing international tensions that might degenerate into military action do not create the climate of mutual confidence essential to reduction of armaments and few would argue that there is not a close relationship between increasing national armaments and rising international tension. But the relationship is not clear. The critical issue is "whether the regulation and reduction of armaments rests on conditions of international security or whether disarmament itself establishes and contributes to international security."[85]

It has been suggested that the position of the United States during much of the period under review has been that tensions should be relieved before armed forces can be reduced. In recent years, however, the attitude of the United States appears to have undergone some change. President Eisenhower in his Inaugural Address emphasized the desirability of concurrent action to reduce tension and to reduce armaments. He declared the readiness of the United States "to engage . . . in joint effort to remove the causes of mutual fear and distrust among nations and so to make possible drastic reduction of armaments."[86]

The problem of the regulation of armaments has become bogged down in a vicious cycle—more tension, more arms; more arms, more tension. The United Nations has not been able to break this cycle. The provisions of the Charter, however, have not prevented progress. As noted earlier in this study, Article 26 of the Charter merely calls for the submission to Members of plans for the regulation of armaments. States are free to accept or to reject plans that may be developed, and all proposals considered by the United Nations have contemplated the conclusion of a treaty that would be submitted to states for their approval.

As a practical matter, there would seem to be little difference in legal status between a disarmament proposal in the form of a treaty put forth by a United Nations organ, and a proposal put forth in terms of an amendment to the Charter. In either event, the proposal would need to be ratified by each of the great powers, as well as other states with military potentialities, or it would be meaningless in the case of a treaty or could not come into effect in the case of an amendment to the Charter. As has been noted, however, the only proposals relating to the control of armaments that would involve amendment of the Charter are the supranational proposals and the suggestion for the creation of a permanent, vetoless, United Nations organ to deal with armament matters. All other proposals considered could be given effect under existing provisions of the Charter.

[85] Ludlow, *loc. cit.*, p. 731.
[86] *Inaugural Address of Dwight D. Eisenhower*, S. Doc. 9, 83 Cong. 2 sess. (Jan. 20, 1953).

The hard fact seems to be that no proposed amendment of the Charter is likely to improve present chances of obtaining an effective agreement to control armaments or atomic energy. Progress in that direction is not prevented by existing provisions of the Charter relating to the control of armaments. It may be true, of course, as some have suggested, that the Charter should contain more realistic provisions on the subject. But it is not clear what these provisions should be. Moreover, at the present time, it is extremely doubtful whether any proposed amendment to the Charter could be devised that would materially increase the chances of the United Nations to develop a disarmament plan likely to be accepted by the states that have the preponderance of military power.

PART FOUR

PROPOSALS RELATING TO PROMOTION
OF THE GENERAL WELFARE

CHAPTER VIII

Economic, Social, and Humanitarian Affairs

In the performance of its functions in the fields of economic, social, and humanitarian affairs, the United Nations has been censured for undertaking programs beyond the proper scope of an international organization. It has been criticized for timidity in the conception, and slowness in the execution, of these programs. It has been reproached for overstepping the bounds of the Charter, and condemned for not fully meeting its responsibilities under the Charter. On many occasions, it has even been praised for a particular job well done.[1]

The diverse criticisms directed at the United Nations in connection with some of these activities are a reflection of the diverse points of view that are held, not only by Member states but also by important segments of opinion within those states, regarding its proper role in this field. The United Nations has therefore had to grapple with the vast difficulties inherent in international economic, social, and humanitarian problems, as well as with the difficulties resulting from the fact that some of its most prominent Members—including the United States—had difficulty in deciding how these problems should be approached.

Within the United States, for example, important individuals have become so alarmed over some of the activities of the United Nations, especially those concerning human rights, that they have proposed—and the Senate very nearly approved—a constitutional

[1] On the economic, social, and humanitarian activities of the United Nations generally see Leland M. Goodrich and Edvard Hambro, *Charter of the United Nations: Commentary and Documents* (1949), Chaps. 9-10; Daniel S. Cheever and H. Field Haviland, Jr., *Organizing for Peace: International Organization in World Affairs* (1954), Chaps. 8-9; U. S. Department of State, *Charter of the United Nations: Report to the President on the Results of the San Francisco Conference by the Chairman of the United States Delegation, The Secretary of State,* Publication 2349 (June 26, 1945); L. Larry Leonard, *International Organization* (1951), Chaps. 18-22; Herman Finer, *The United Nations Economic and Social Council* (1946); Alexander Loveday, "Suggestions for the Reform of the United Nations Economic and Social Machinery," *International Organization,* Vol. 7 (August 1953), pp. 325-41. See also Quincy Wright, "Human Rights and Charter Revision," and Raymond F. Mikesell, "Barriers to the Expansion of United Nations Economic Functions," in *Annals of the American Academy of Political and Social Science,* Vol. 296 (November 1954), pp. 46-55, 36-45.

amendment that would have altered the treaty-making process and had an important impact on the general conduct of United States foreign relations. Other individuals have been equally critical of the reluctance with which the United States has supported certain United Nations activities in this area, especially those concerning the economic development of underdeveloped countries. It is clear, therefore, that until the Member states decide precisely what they want the United Nations to be and to do, the Organization will continue to reflect the conflicts that exist both among and within its Members.

Scope of Activities

Because of the diverse and intricate problems confronting the United Nations in the fields of economic, social, and humanitarian affairs, the activities of the Organization and its related agencies in dealing with these problems have become widespread and complex.[2] These activities now involve the work of ten specialized agencies covering such matters as labor, food and agriculture, civil aviation, health, meteorology, telecommunications, postal services, education, and international monetary affairs, and of various commissions covering such fields as regional economic problems, human rights, transportation, the status of women, population problems, and freedom of information. Unforeseen emergency problems of great magnitude in connection with refugees and relief and rehabilitation work have had to be dealt with, and attempts have been made to handle such far-reaching and controversial matters as the maintenance of full employment, re-establishment of the network of international trade and financial relationships, and the promotion of economic development of underdeveloped countries. At the same time, the United Nations has undertaken such relatively noncontroversial activities as the control of narcotics, the suppression of traffic in women and children, and measures dealing with obscene publications. In all of these, however, a basic issue has been how the work was to be organized and financed and how far an international organization could go before it impinges on matters that should properly be left to the domestic jurisdiction of its Member states.

Before the establishment of the United Nations—during the days

---

[2] For an extensive analysis of these activities, see the volume in this Brookings series, *The United Nations and Promotion of the General Welfare.*

of the League of Nations—there was awareness of the importance and the necessity of international co-operation in these fields as an essential aspect of the maintenance of peace and security. During the early 1940's, a number of international declarations and agreements dealt with various facets of the problem. Among these were the Atlantic Charter, the Declaration by United Nations of January 1, 1942, various inter-American declarations, and Article VII of the Lend-Lease agreements.

Before the decision in 1943 that an international organization should be created for the maintenance of peace and security, considerable emphasis, especially on the part of the United States, had been placed on the desirability of co-operation in the economic, social, and humanitarian spheres. In fact, the American Government believed that improvement of international economic relations was an indispensable foundation for world peace. Aware of the difficulties involved in developing political and military co-operation, the United States therefore thought that it would be desirable first to reach agreement on economic and related policies and arrangements. Thus its first concrete proposals concerning international co-operation related to economic questions.

As a result, at least in part, of this early interest in the economic and social functions of a world organization and of American initiative in the matter, both the organizational structure and the substantive work in these fields were well advanced by the time the United Nations itself was created. The United Nations Relief and Rehabilitation Administration was a going concern, for example, and there had already been held the conferences that led to the establishment of the International Civil Aviation Organization, the Food and Agriculture Organization, the International Monetary Fund, and the International Bank for Reconstruction and Development. Thus in one respect the San Francisco Conference did not have the latitude in dealing with economic, social, and humanitarian affairs that it had in dealing with political questions relating to the maintenance of international peace and security. The decisions of the Conference with respect to economic and social matters were to some extent conditioned and controlled by the fact that it had already been agreed that the work of the United Nations in these areas should be decentralized. Consequently, the Charter provides for various unnamed specialized agencies in "economic, social, cultural, educational, health, and related fields" that are to be "brought into relationship with the United Nations" (Article 57) through agreements with the Economic and Social Council approved by the General Assembly (Article 63). The policies and activities of these specialized agencies are to be co-ordinated by recommendations of the United Nations (Article 58) and by the Economic and Social Council through consultation and recommendations (Article 63). The Assembly is to "consider and approve any financial and budgetary arrangements" with the agencies and is also to examine the administrative budgets of the agencies "with a view to making recommendations to the agencies concerned" (Article 17).

In addition to organizational and administrative provisions relating to the specialized agencies, the San Francisco Conference wrote into the Charter other provisions putting great emphasis on international co-operation in economic and social affairs. Thus the Charter states in Article 1(3) that one of the purposes of the United Nations is "to achieve international cooperation in solving international problems of an economic, social, cultural, or humanitarian character, and in promoting and encouraging respect for human rights and for fundamental freedoms for all without distinction as to race, sex, language, or religion." A further purpose set forth in Article 1(4) is "to be a center for harmonizing the actions of nations in the attainment of these common ends." These objectives are spelled out in more detail in Chapter IX (International Economic and Social Cooperation) and especially in Article 55, which provides that the United Nations shall promote:

a. higher standards of living, full employment, and conditions of economic and social progress and development;

b. solutions of international economic, social, health, and related problems; and international cultural and educational cooperation; and

c. universal respect for, and observance of, human rights and fundamental freedoms for all without distinction as to race, sex, language, or religion.

In Article 56, all Members "pledge themselves to take joint and separate action in cooperation with the Organization for the achievement of" these purposes. Primary responsibility in this field is given to the General Assembly and, under its authority, to the Economic and Social Council (Article 60), which is named in Article 7 as one of the principal organs of the United Nations. It is composed of eighteen Members of the United Nations elected by a two-thirds vote of the Assembly for three-year staggered terms

(Article 61). Each member of the Economic and Social Council has one vote, and decisions are made by a majority of the members present and voting (Article 67). The Council is directed to set up various economic, social, and human rights commissions "and such other commissions as may be required for the performance of its functions" (Article 68). It is also given general powers to make studies and recommendations with respect to "international economic, social, cultural, educational, health, and related matters" (Article 62). This includes the preparation of draft conventions for submission to the Assembly.

The Charter itself, therefore, permits a very wide range of activities by the United Nations. Within the discretion of the Organization, these activities can vary from a relatively small number of programs of modest proportions to elaborate and extensive programs in many fields. The Charter clearly requires the United Nations to perform certain functions, but the scope and extent of those functions are largely left to be worked out by the United Nations itself. Indeed, the Charter is so broad that it might be said that it established only general goals or objectives and left the methods of attaining those goals to future determination. Thus, many of the proposals that have been made for enlarging the economic, social, and humanitarian activities of the United Nations could be carried out under the Charter as it now stands and would not require any amendment to it. The Special United Nations Fund for Economic Development and the atoms-for-peace program, for example, would not require any amendments in order to be put into effect.

Therefore, apart from the supranational proposals that move into the realm of world government, few suggestions have been made for amending the Charter in order to expand the economic and social activities of the United Nations. In fact, there would seem to be little occasion for such suggestions. These activities could be expanded quite considerably under the Charter as it is now written. The question is not so much what the Charter permits as what the Member states are willing to agree to—and pay for. Consequently, so far as the range of United Nations activities is concerned, most of the concrete proposals for Charter amendment are restrictive in nature. Other types of proposals have to do with the organization of economic and social activities and with the domestic jurisdiction of Member states.

Proposals to Expand Activities

Most of the suggested amendments to the Charter for expanding the economic and social activities of the United Nations have been advanced as integral parts of proposals made to transform the Organization into some form of a supranational authority.

Through Increased Revenue

The most far-reaching specific proposals to enlarge on the economic and social activities have been developed by Grenville Clark and Lewis B. Sohn. Except for changes in the structure of the Economic and Social Council, however, the detailed suggestions made by them would not drastically alter Chapters IX and X of the Charter.[3] But the changes suggested in other articles, especially Articles 2(7), 11(1(c)), and 17, would result in a substantial broadening of the economic and social activities of the United Nations.

The most important of these changes is the proposed revision of Article 17(2) so as to authorize the General Assembly to "lay and collect an income and other taxes which, taken together, shall in no event exceed two per cent of the estimated world gross product for that year." The purposes of these taxes would be "to meet the expenses, to pay the debts of the United Nations, and to provide funds for the promotion of the economic and social advancement of all peoples."

The authors of the proposal comment:

> These provisions would provide a reliable means for raising a considerable, though strictly limited, amount of money for the Economic and Social Council and the specialized agencies, so that they would be able to increase their activities at least tenfold. Technical and financial assistance to underdeveloped countries would thus be put on a sound operating basis, and long-term plans might be put into effect without fear that member Nations would suddenly stop their voluntary contributions for that purpose. It can be confidently hoped that the enlarged activities of the United Nations in this field would accelerate world economic development, and that by constantly increasing the world gross product they will provide increasing funds for further improvements. With the growth of new centers of economic strength throughout the world, the burden which will initially fall on only a few nations will become better distributed, and "conditions of stability and well-being" will be brought to all corners of the earth.[4]

[3] Grenville Clark and Lewis B. Sohn, *Peace Through Disarmament and Charter Revision* (Preliminary Print, July 1953), pp. 99-104.
[4] *Ibid.*, p. 94.

A number of questions might be raised with respect to this proposal. There is serious doubt, for example, whether the sovereign states that are Members of the United Nations are yet ready to share with it the power to tax, which is one of the most important attributes of sovereignty.[5] It seems unnecessary to explore all the implications of such a step, but it should be noted that the limitation proposed is 2 per cent of the *world* gross product—not 2 per cent of the gross *national* product of each country. This might well lead to efforts to induce the wealthier countries to pay most of the bill while the poorer countries paid relatively little or nothing. On the basis of 2 per cent of the gross *national* product, the United States would pay $7.3 billion on a product of $365 billion in 1953. This compares with a total United States contribution to all United Nations activities, including the United Nations Technical Assistance Program, that amounts to something less than $100 million a year—or with a total United States appropriation for foreign economic, military, and technical assistance that reached a peak of $7.6 billion in 1951, or 2.3 per cent of the gross national product.

Wholly apart from the cost involved, and apart also from the problems raised by the principle of even limited supranational taxing authority, suggestions along these lines open up a great many other difficult questions. Should the United Nations expand its activities to this extent, even if the money were forthcoming? Could the underdeveloped countries possibly absorb the yearly sums that would be envisaged under such a scheme? Would steps in this direction eventually create a vast area of activity that might overwhelm the Organization by its sheer magnitude? Are these problems that might more properly be handled by individual nation states or by a group such as the Colombo powers rather than by a more nearly all-embracing international organization? Would such an extensive program encourage the United Nations to intervene in matters ordinarily considered within the domestic jurisdiction of its members? Would such a program further the maintenance of peace and security or would it lead to more disputes and complications and perhaps the necessity for more international organization?

It is necessary to raise such questions in order to indicate the difficulties and complexities that are inherent in proposals of this

[5] On this point see below, Chap. XIV.

character. But however questionable the proposal for a grant of taxing power to the United Nations might be, the idea of the designation of a fixed percentage of national income—or of gross national product—for international economic purposes is not new. The United Nations Relief and Rehabilitation Administration, established during the war, called on its member states to contribute 1 per cent of their national income—and it actually received such contributions from a number of states.

Both former President Truman and President Eisenhower have advanced the idea that savings resulting from disarmament would make possible increased expenditures for world economic development.[6] The amounts involved were not specified, but they could easily be a great deal more than 2 per cent of the gross national product of the United States if world tensions were reduced and practicable proposals for disarmament acceptable to the great powers could be put into effect. Under their proposals, however, the payments made would be voluntary and not compulsory as would be the case if the United Nations were granted the power to tax.

Other Proposals

The proposals for Federal Union and Plan "A" of the London conference of the World Association of Parliamentarians for World Government are based on a form of world government with executive, legislative, and judicial branches somewhat similar to the system of American Government. They do not, therefore, envisage a body comparable to the Economic and Social Council, although each of them deals to a greater or lesser extent with economic and social matters.

The proposal for Federal Union gives considerable emphasis to the anticipated economic benefits that would result from putting the proposal into effect, but the means by which these benefits are to be brought about are not worked out in detail. Plan "A" of the London conference has given more emphasis to the human rights aspects, but from the point of view of protecting individual

---

[6] See U. S. Department of State, *A New Page in History,* Address by President Truman before the U.N. General Assembly, Oct. 24, 1950, Publication 4000 (October 1950), and U. S. Department of State, *The Chance for Peace,* Address by President Eisenhower before the American Society of Newspaper Editors, Apr. 16, 1953, Publication 5042 (April 1953). See above, Chap. VII.

rights from infringement by a more powerful world organization and not from infringement by the national government of the individual. Under this plan, every person in the world would be a citizen of the United Nations as well as of his own country, and the "Charter and the laws enacted thereunder shall bind each individual." This proposal, it was explained, is designed to ensure that international law can be enforced by the organs of the United Nations against individuals, who would be precluded from sheltering behind national allegiance.[7]

Whereas most proposals relating to human rights have been designed to establish certain minimum rights that would be recognized by all governments, Plan "A" deliberately recommends against any attempt to safeguard individual rights against action by national governments. This recommendation was made because "to attempt to do otherwise would invite rejection on the ground of potential interference with the domestic affairs of the nation." Plan "A" is concerned, instead, with personal and political rights vis-à-vis the United Nations itself, and its sponsors recommend a bill of rights in an annex to the Charter with provisions that would "safeguard all persons against violation by the United Nations of certain basic liberties." The explanation for this provision was that there might be a danger of abuse of power by organs of the United Nations as reorganized under the proposal, especially by the world police. If individual rights were enshrined in a bill of rights, they would be enforced by the World Court. This in itself could be construed as a form of intervention, however, and the question would at once arise whether national or United Nations law would be superior. To bring the United Nations into direct relationship with individuals regardless of the will of states, would be opening the door to precisely what sponsors of the Bricker Amendment have feared would ultimately happen.

The authors of Plan "A," however, also include in their proposals a recommendation that minority groups should have a right of petition to the proposed World Equity Tribunal and world legislature for redress of grievances. It is pointed out that the tribunal

[7] See World Association of Parliamentarians for World Government, *Proposals for the Revision of the United Nations Charter* (1954), together with earlier reports of conferences held by the Parliamentarians. See also "Report on the World Congress on U. N. Charter Reform," *Federal News* (September-October 1953), pp. 3-5. For discussion of applicability of world law to individuals see below, Chap. XII.

would be empowered to give only advisory judgments and the world legislature would have only the right of debate on such an issue. The sponsors recognize that, even in this limited form, the recommendations could deter certain countries from joining the proposed federation.

Alternative Plan "B" of the London conference of parliamentarians does not envisage any redrafting of the Charter but merely urges the governments of Member states of the United Nations to take action to strengthen the Economic and Social Council by increasing its responsibility for the work of the specialized agencies, and by giving it wider powers and ampler means for the development of backward areas. Although this is stated in such general terms as to be not readily susceptible to precise analysis, it would seem more practical than the proposal in Plan "A." Whatever the theoretical merits of Plan "A," the realities of the cold war probably preclude any agreement of this type. Among the other difficulties is that of semantics, or reaching agreement on the meaning of basic words. The same words, especially in the field of human rights, evoke a variety of conflicting concepts, as the lengthy debates in the United Nations have so clearly revealed.

There have, of course, been other proposals made for international action in the field of human rights. These include such matters as the establishment of an International Court of Human Rights, an international writ of habeas corpus, and all the issues covered in the various proposals for an International Covenant of Human Rights.[8] But these proposals do not contemplate changes in the United Nations Charter. In some cases, their proponents argue that they could be carried out under the Charter as it now stands; in others, a separate multilateral treaty is contemplated.

Much of the energy of the Commission on Human Rights since 1947 has been devoted to the drafting of the Universal Declaration of Human Rights and the two covenants on human rights. In addition, many other organs of the United Nations have attempted to encourage respect for human rights in various ways. These have included efforts to foster equal rights for women, to advance the right of the self-determination of peoples, to outlaw the crime of genocide, to ensure freedom of information, and to protect minority groups. They have also included efforts to abolish slavery and

[8] See below, Chap. XII.

forced labor, to repatriate prisoners of war, and to deal with violations of human rights in particular countries.[9]

In many of these activities, Member states have questioned the competence of the United Nations. Indeed, in some cases, in spite of the developing role of the General Assembly as the "town meeting of the world," the competence of the Assembly even to discuss the matter has been challenged. A big question confronting the United Nations, therefore, is how to reconcile the broad objectives in regard to human rights set forth in the Charter with the domestic jurisdiction limitations imposed on the Organization in Article 2(7).

No doubt there will continue to be many pressures exerted on behalf of expanding the activity of the United Nations in this field. There are indications, however, that some Members are fearful lest the Organization defeat its purposes by moving too far and too fast in an area in which different mores and standards of conduct make international co-operation extremely difficult. In 1953, the United States announced that it did not intend to ratify the two draft covenants on human rights and called for a "fresh appraisal of methods through which we may realize the human rights goals of the United Nations."[10] To replace what it considered the unsatisfactory approach of using treaties to deal with the problem, the United States presented a new action program involving three related proposals. First, the Commission on Human Rights should institute studies of various aspects of human rights throughout the world such as freedom of religion and the right to a fair trial. At each of its sessions, a particular topic could then be selected by the commission for its consideration and general recommendations. Second, Member states would be requested to prepare annual reports on developments in the field of human rights. These reports would be considered by the commission, which would submit its comments thereon to the Economic and Social Council. Third, the United Nations and the various specialized agencies should provide technical assistance in the field of human rights comparable to that now being made available in the economic and social fields.

[9] For a summary of United Nations activity in this field see the volume in this Brookings series, *The United Nations and Promotion of the General Welfare,* Part Three.

[10] "U. S. Policy on Human Rights," U. S. Department of State *Bulletin,* Vol. 28 (Apr. 20, 1953), p. 579.

Several major objections have been advanced with respect to the proposed action program, among them the charge that the United States desires to undermine the draft covenants before they are completed. It is also argued by representatives of the Soviet bloc that the proposals violate the provisions of the Charter and impinge on the domestic jurisdiction of the Member states. Regardless whether the program is eventually accepted as the basis for United Nations activity in the future, it is probable that the tempo of the Organization in the field of human rights will be slowed down rather than accelerated, and the scope of activity contracted somewhat rather than expanded.[11]

Proposals to Contract Activities

In contrast to the proposals for a general broadening of the economic and social functions of the United Nations, are the proposals for drastically limiting these functions, if not eliminating them altogether. Articles 55 and 56 of the Charter in particular have been the target of vigorous criticism in the United States on the ground that they open the way to infringement of American sovereignty and to the destruction of constitutional relationships between the Federal Government and the various states. Through Article 56, it is argued, Congress not only has acquired the authority but has assumed the duty to legislate in regard to the objectives of Article 55, at least some of which are outside the powers delegated to Congress by the Constitution. This argument has been rejected by the President, the Secretary of State, the Attorney General, and by a preponderance of constitutional and international legal authorities. Nevertheless, the fear persists in some quarters that these articles of the Charter may open the way to the possible destruction of the American form of government if not of American sovereignty itself.

[11] In this connection the suggestion of former President Harry S. Truman made before the Senate Committee on Foreign Relations on Apr. 18, 1955, should be noted. "I would like to see a bill of rights attached to the United Nations Charter," he said. He later pointed out that what he had in mind was a bill of rights comparable to the first ten amendments of the United States Constitution. Two days later Senator Bricker agreed in principle with Truman but pointed out that "We cannot accept anything less than our Bill of Rights, and there are not many nations in the world . . . that will accept our Bill of Rights. . . . I don't see how you can get . . . in the United Nations, a universal bill of rights that would be acceptable to this country, so diverse are the mem-

Limiting the United Nations to Peace and Security Functions

During the hearings on review of the Charter, some groups have consistently indicated opposition to the activities of the United Nations Commission on Human Rights and, in fact, to all activities of the United Nations in promoting the general welfare. These activities, it has been argued, are "plainly indicative of the 'statist' concepts held by the majority of the members of the United Nations."[12] Thus it has been recommended that Articles 55, 56, and 57 of the Charter be reviewed "with a view to either their modification or rescission." This is on the ground that:

> It must be faced conclusively that the social and political concepts embraced by a majority of the nations constituting the United Nations have been repudiated by the Congress of the United States on a number of occasions. If the United States is not to be put in the position of constantly refusing to ratify treaties designed by the majority of the United Nations, and recommended by the General Assembly, it would be well to consider the question of rescission of those parts of the U. N. Charter dealing with economic and social matters.[13]

The consequences, as the author of this suggestion notes, would be to leave the United Nations "as an organ strictly for the maintenance of peace and security." Such proposals would negate some of the main purposes of the United Nations, as stated in Article 1 of the Charter. They raise directly the issue of the concept of the United Nations—whether it is to be primarily an international enforcement agency or whether it is at the same time an important means for achieving wider international co-operation. Had the San Francisco Conference adopted the concept of the United Nations "as an organ strictly for the maintenance of peace and security," some of the achievements of the Organization would have been made vastly more difficult, if not impossible.

But the dividing line between peace and security matters on the one hand and economic and social matters on the other hand is not so clear-cut as the opponents of the economic and social activities of the United Nations apparently believe. Even if the international police force concept of the United Nations is adhered to, it should

bers." *Review of the United Nations Charter,* Hearings before a Subcommittee of the Senate Committee on Foreign Relations, 84 Cong. 1 sess., Pt. 12, pp. 1630, 1656.

[12] *Ibid.,* 83 Cong. 2 sess., Pt. 4, p. 459. Statement by Voters U.S.A.

[13] *Ibid.,* p. 461.

be remembered that the problem of law enforcement in most local communities is very closely related to various economic and social activities designed to create "conditions of stability and well-being." Moreover, it cannot be overlooked that to a very large percentage of the population of the world, economic and social advancement is by far the most vital concern today. If the free nations do not help these peoples to advance—including action through the United Nations—the Communists will do so, to the peril of the free world. Even if there were no Communist threat, the disparity between standards of living in the developed and underdeveloped countries would require concerted international action.

In this connection, one of the most significant aspects of the work of the United Nations has been the evolution of economic development as a top priority question. Since the very first session of the General Assembly, the scope of the concern of the United Nations with economic development issues has steadily expanded. The Economic and Social Council has established regional economic commissions for Europe, for Latin America, and for Asia and the Far East. These commissions have provided a means for bringing together experts on various regional economic problems having to do not only with such matters as international trade and inland transportation problems but also with specific industries. The commissions for Latin America and for Asia and the Far East have focused attention on problems of economic development and have contributed substantially to a better understanding of the intricate processes and interrelationships involved in economic development. Meanwhile, the action programs of the specialized agencies and the United Nations Technical Assistance Administration have produced such concrete results as better public administration in Bolivia, better rice crops in Southeast Asia, and better health in Indonesia.

The capital needs of economic development have been met in part through the loans of the International Bank for Reconstruction and Development. Proposals are now pending to supplement these loans through such devices as the International Finance Corporation and the Special United Nations Fund for Economic Development. The use of atomic energy for peaceful purposes is beginning to take shape, but although its potentialities are vast, its precise applications have yet to be determined.

In the field of economic development, as in other areas, the

United Nations has been criticized both for doing too little and for attempting too much. But in moving to meet the insistent demand in some quarters for international action to promote economic development, the United Nations has demonstrated a flexibility of method and a firmness of purpose comparable to that shown in the field of peace and security.

In connection with the argument that the United Nations should be limited to matters of peace and security, it must be pointed out that the conclusion is perhaps less interesting than the reasoning that leads to it. This reasoning is based on the premise that a majority of the Members of the United Nations hold "statist" concepts and that these concepts are reflected in the actions of the Organization, particularly those taken by the Economic and Social Council. It is somewhat curious that the principal piece of evidence cited in this connection is the draft covenants on human rights, which neither the Economic and Social Council nor any other organ of the United Nations has ever adopted. It is perhaps even more curious that documents whose purpose is to expand human rights are attacked as subversive of human rights.

Finally, it is by no means accurate to say that Congress has repudiated the social and political concepts held by a majority of the Member states. Opposition in the United States to a few treaties such as the Genocide Convention has tended to obscure favorable action on other treaties that are essentially noncontroversial—e.g., the United Nations Charter itself, conventions relating to the control of narcotics, road traffic conventions, conventions on obscene publications, and sundry conventions concluded by the International Labour Organisation.

It is quite possible, of course, to reach substantially the same conclusion concerning the extent of the economic and social activities of the United Nations without going through this particular logic. Thus, it has been recommended that "the authority of the U.N. be limited to those matters related to world peace and security." This suggestion, however, was made on the ground that "the present charter provisions may create some unnecessary internal conflicts on questions which have little or no relation to world peace" and that therefore "the charter should be clarified so that no interference with the internal affairs of nations will result."[14]

---

[14] *Ibid.*, pp. 406, 408. Testimony by Mrs. H. B. Caldwell, director of public relations of the North Carolina State Grange.

*Loveday Proposal on
Human Rights*

Another suggestion has been made to the effect that the question of human rights be taken out of the jurisdiction of the Economic and Social Council. This proposal comes from Alexander Loveday who argues that human rights could be more appropriately handled by the General Assembly, which usually has to deal with the matter eventually in any case. He suggests the following amendments to the Charter: (1) The deletion or modification of Article 68, which provides that: "The Economic and Social Council shall set up commissions in economic and social fields and for the promotion of human rights, and such other commissions as may be required for the performance of its functions." If the article is not deleted entirely, he suggests that the imperative "shall set up" be changed to the permissive "may set up." (2) The deletion of paragraph 2 of Article 62, which provides that the Council "may make recommendations for the purpose of promoting respect for, and observance of, human rights and fundamental freedoms for all."[15]

Under these amendments the General Assembly would be free to take up the question of human rights, on the basis of more general provisions elsewhere in the Charter, or not to do so, as it might see fit.

Loveday finds it difficult to imagine that the same organ could deal effectively with economic and social questions and with human rights. He points out that:

> . . . the question of human rights is not economic or social, but directly political. If the Commission on Human Rights had been composed, as the United Kingdom and the United States governments urged it should be composed, of experts serving in their personal capacity, the proper procedure would be for a council to select its members and for it to report to its nominating body. In fact it is composed of government nominees, and there would seem to be no good reason why it should not be appointed by the Assembly and report direct to the Assembly. The Economic and Social Council would then become what its name suggests it should be.[16]

He also appears to be more concerned with organizational than with substantive problems, but his suggestion is premised on a view

---

[15] Loveday, *loc. cit.*, pp. 335-36.
[16] *Ibid.*, p. 330.

of human rights as political rather than economic or social. This in itself implies a narrowing of the concept, because there is a vast difference between basic political rights, such as freedom of religion and freedom of speech, and desirable economic or social rights, such as adequate education or medical care.

The proper role of an international organization in the field of human rights is an interesting topic but an unusually difficult one because it is often subject to emotional overtones. It is especially important, therefore, that it be examined in an objective way. The suggestion that the question is essentially political rather than social or economic is a good place to start.

There are, of course, certain minimum social and economic conditions that are necessary to make political rights meaningful. Governments may aid in the creation of these conditions; but no government has ever been able to bring them into being merely through a constitutional pronouncement that they should exist, and many people believe it is unrealistic to expect an international organization to do so. It is all very well to declare the "right" of everyone to adequate medical care or to an education, as was done in the Universal Declaration of Human Rights, but such a declaration may not be immediately helpful if a particular country does not have enough doctors, nurses, teachers, hospitals, or schools.

The important point is that social and economic rights of this character are not inherent; they can come into existence only as a consequence of the development of certain minimum conditions. These conditions, in turn, are frequently brought about through the exercise of political rights, which, unlike social and economic rights, are inherent. It is significant that, in the countries in which human rights are most highly developed, they are stated, not in terms of government guarantees to the people, but in terms of popular limitations on governments. Thus the First Amendment to the Constitution of the United States does not affirmatively guarantee freedom of the press; it prohibits Congress from passing laws abridging freedom of the press.

The distinction is an important one. Actually, in a democratic system people do not derive rights from governments; on the contrary, governments derive their powers from the people—or in the words of Jefferson, "from the consent of the governed." In one sense, it is not for governments to say which rights they allow their people to exercise. The real question should be which powers the people will allow their governments to exercise.

This is not to say that the United Nations is unable to make an important contribution toward promoting human rights. It can do a great deal through the careful study of specific aspects of the problem, through debate, and through focusing world attention on alleged violations of such rights. It is obvious, however, that the concrete action the United Nations can take to protect human rights is limited by the nature of the Organization and of the Member states.

From this, it may seem to some that the logical role of the United Nations in the field of human rights is more restricted than that which has sometimes been ascribed to it and that such a role might be played better in the political setting of the General Assembly. To those who accept this view, the creation of a human rights commission made up of technical experts directly responsible to the General Assembly would have a double advantage. In the first place, it would free the Economic and Social Council from responsibility in human rights matters and enable it to concentrate on other social and economic problems. Moreover, by underlining the essentially political nature of human rights, it would help dispel the confusion that has arisen between basic human rights and humanitarian economic and social standards. To others, this proposal might seem to be a distinction without a real difference. In practice, the General Assembly already devotes a good deal of time to human rights, and it is doubtful that any new relationship of the kind contemplated would greatly alter the situation, although admittedly it would ease the burden on the Economic and Social Council.

One student of the United Nations has reached the conclusion that an educational program developing a strong public opinion favorable to human rights is necessary "before states will be willing to undertake further legal obligations." The Charter, he contends, already provides suitable goals and opportunities for reaching agreement in this field. "But without an adequate world public opinion and suitable national policies real progress cannot be made. With them, the already existing procedures of the Charter permit continuous progress. Revision of the Charter in this field is not likely to prove possible at the present time and does not seem necessary."[17]

---

[17] Wright, *loc. cit.*, pp. 54-55.

Co-ordination of the Specialized Agencies

It would not be greatly inaccurate to say that the Economic and Social Council has spent almost as much time trying to organize its work as it has spent trying to do the work itself. The difficulty lies partly in the endless diversity of the work it is supposed to do and partly in the fact that it is both a co-ordinating and an operating body. At the heart of the problem lies the relationship of the Council to the specialized agencies.

It has already been pointed out above that the United Nations system, in the economic and social field, is made up of a number of commissions and some ten relatively autonomous specialized agencies. Each of these specialized agencies has its own headquarters, its own constitution, its own general assembly, executive council and secretariat, its own budget, and its own program. Consequently, it has not been easy to develop effective co-ordination either between the United Nations proper and the various specialized agencies or among the specialized agencies themselves. The accompanying chart shows the network of organs and specialized agencies for the promotion of the general welfare in the United Nations system.

Nature of the Problem

In practice, this lack of co-ordination has taken a variety of forms. In some instances, it has given rise to a certain amount of overlapping and duplication of effort on the part of the specialized agencies. This is only natural because such programs as health, food, and agriculture are so closely related. In other cases it has led to rather embarrassing conflicts of policy within the United Nations. This also is quite understandable, for with so many agencies in the field it has not always been possible for each of them (or for their members) to be fully aware of what the others are doing. Finally, it has encouraged a vigorous competition among the specialized agencies for larger portions of United Nations funds with various special interest groups exerting pressure on behalf of their particular agencies.[18]

Critics are inclined to point out that the provisions of the Charter

---

[18] For some of these points see *Budgetary and Financial Problems of the United Nations,* Staff Study No. 6, written by Francis O. Wilcox for the Subcommittee on the United Nations Charter, Senate Committee on Foreign Relations, 83 Cong. 2 sess. (December 1954), p. 22.

Coordination Between the United Nations And the Specialized Agencies

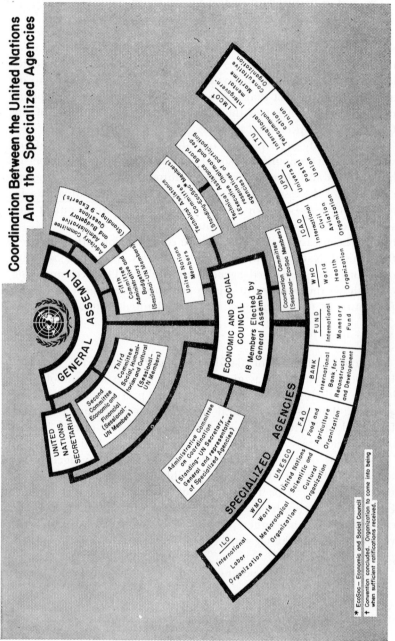

Source: U. S. Library of Congress, Legislative Reference Service, Robert L. Bostick

should have been more tightly drawn in order to prevent this lack of co-ordination. As has been noted, however, the Charter provisions are the result, at least in part, of the fact that at the time the Charter was written, there were already in existence several international organizations whose responsibilities and fields of interest were limited, but whose work was complementary to that of the Organization. Some of them, such as the Universal Postal Union and the International Telecommunication Union, had their roots in the nineteenth century; some, such as the International Labour Organisation, dated from League of Nations days; and some, such as the Food and Agriculture Organization, were established during the Second World War.

It is understandable that the framers of the United Nations Charter did not want to disturb unduly the organizational structure of old, well-established, highly technical organizations, such as the Universal Postal Union. What may not be so readily understandable to some of the more critical is that they should have invited the establishment of an unspecified number of organizations through the provision of Article 59 that the United Nations "shall, where appropriate, initiate negotiations among the states concerned for the creation of any new specialized agencies required for the accomplishment of the purposes set forth in Article 55."

In any event, the fact is that today there exist ten specialized agencies: International Labour Organisation (ILO); Food and Agriculture Organization (FAO); International Monetary Fund (Fund); International Bank for Reconstruction and Development (Bank); United Nations Educational, Scientific, and Cultural Organization (UNESCO); International Civil Aviation Organization (ICAO); Universal Postal Union (UPU); International Telecommunication Union (ITU); World Health Organization (WHO) ; World Meteorological Organization (WMO). Another, the Intergovernmental Maritime Consultative Organization (IMCO), is in the process of creation. Still another, the International Refugee Organization (IRO), has already completed its work and passed out of existence. And the International Trade Organization (ITO) was never ratified by enough states to come into being.

Between these specialized agencies and the United Nations, there exist three general types of relationships embodied in agreements entered into by the agencies and the Economic and Social Council and approved by the General Assembly.

First, and most detailed, are the agreements with the ILO, FAO, ICAO, UNESCO, and WHO. These provide for reciprocal proposal of agenda items and reciprocal representation without vote at meetings in which matters of common interest are considered. There are detailed provisions for co-operation in administrative, personnel, budgetary, and financial matters, and for the exchange of information and documents.

Second are the more general agreements with the highly technical and long-established agencies—the UPU and ITU. These agencies agree to transmit their budgets to the United Nations Organization, but, as in the case of the other specialized agencies, not necessarily to abide by recommendations of the General Assembly with respect to them.

Finally, there are the agreements with the Bank and the Fund, which are recognized as "independent" international organizations. The agencies are given full autonomy with respect to their budgets, and the United Nations Organization agrees that "it would be sound policy to refrain from making recommendations to the Bank" in connection with particular loans. Representatives of the Organization are permitted to attend meetings of the Boards of Governors on invitation.[19]

The differences among these three types of agreements are, of course, a consequence of differences in the functions of the specialized agencies and in the policy issues that confront them. In the performance of their technical regulatory work, ITU and UPU do not encounter either the number or character of the policy questions that confront the ILO, FAO, UNESCO, ICAO, and WHO and on which both the Economic and Social Council and the General Assembly frequently make recommendations. The character of the operations of the Bank and the Fund puts those agencies into a special category.

In addition to these agreements by which the specialized agencies have been "brought into relationship" with the United Nations, other helpful co-ordinating machinery exists. The Advisory Committee on Administrative and Budgetary Questions of the General Assembly every year "examines" the administrative budgets of the specialized agencies and makes recommendations about them. Thus far, however, relatively little attention has been paid these recommendations by the General Assembly. Of more practical sig-

---

[19] See *United Nations Treaty Series*, Vol. 2, Nos. 20(a), and 20(b), (1947).

nificance perhaps, is the Administrative Committee on Co-ordination, which consists of the directors of the various specialized agencies and is presided over by the Secretary-General of the United Nations.

Nevertheless, there is still some validity to the contention that the present sprawling system of independent agencies is complex and no doubt creates considerable confusion in the public mind. Perhaps its most noticeable weakness lies in the fact that it does not permit any central planning by which the members can determine in a balanced and logical way the most effective use of the total financial resources of the United Nations.

Proposals for Achieving Better Co-ordination

Recently, both Secretary of State Dulles and Ambassador Lodge have commented on the problem of relationships between the United Nations Organization and the specialized agencies. The Secretary stated:

> There is a rather curious, and I think inadequate control over those bodies, and I think they are perhaps not sufficiently integrated into the controls, budgetary and otherwise, which could be established by the United Nations itself. I believe that whole galaxy of satellites which revolves around the United Nations deserves some consideration, although those bodies are not themselves technically organs of the United Nations.[20]

Ambassador Lodge also raised the question "as to whether the present provisions of the . . . Charter are adequate for the sort of co-ordination we want, and, if not, whether the system of co-ordination should be improved, and, if so, by what changes in the charter."[21] The independence of the specialized agencies, the Ambassador said, "has been the source of many troubles." He cited delays in negotiating a separate agreement with each agency for screening its American employees, and "ill-advised" publicity from one agency—presumably UNESCO—which, he said, "had a significant and understandably irritating effect on a sizable number of Americans, with reactions which damaged the United Nations proper and which prejudiced some of the fine work actually being done by the

[20] *Review of the United Nations Charter,* Senate Hearings, 83 Cong. 2 sess., Pt. 1, p. 27.
[21] *Ibid.,* p. 39.

specialized agencies." Ambassador Lodge's suggestion to remedy this situation was to bring the agencies "somewhat more under the Secretary General."[22]

One observer thinks the difficulty stems from the fact that the Economic and Social Council has been given incompatible functions—that it is supposed to co-ordinate the specialized agencies at the same time that it also does the work of one. His remedy is to create yet another specialized agency that would serve as a sort of catch-all and take over all of the operations that remain in the Council. Establishment of such a new agency, he argues, would afford the Council "the opportunity of carrying out effectively its functions as a co-ordinating body by relieving it of all duties other than those of co-ordination, of dealing with issues that transcend the functions of any one agency, and of acting as an advisory body to the General Assembly of the United Nations and to the Trusteeship and Security Councils."[23]

This might be a helpful device, for one of the principal handicaps the Economic and Social Council labors under is its crowded agenda. The main defect in the proposal is that it does not provide adequate means by which the Council could take advantage of its new opportunity to devote itself substantially full time to co-ordinating activity. The suggestion would make for a neater organization chart, but the Council would still be left with only powers of recommendation, and so long as this is the case, it is doubtful that more efficient operations would follow in any substantial degree.

One proposal that may get closer to the root of the matter suggests the development of greater control by the General Assembly over the budget of the specialized agencies. Article 17(3) of the Charter provides that the Assembly "shall consider and approve any financial and budgetary arrangements" with the specialized agencies and shall examine their administrative budgets "with a view to making recommendations to the agencies concerned." Under the proposal the word "administrative" would be deleted, thereby extending examination of the Assembly to the total budgets of the specialized agencies. The proposal would also authorize the Assembly to allocate to the agencies "such funds as it deems necessary for meet-

[22] *Ibid.*, p. 53.
[23] Loveday, *loc. cit.*, p. 330.

ing their expenses."[24] The agencies would cease to collect funds directly from their member states, and the United Nations Organization would assume full financial control over their budgets and expenses. This would require not only revision of the United Nations Charter but also amendment of the constitutions of the specialized agencies as well as the agreements bringing them into relationship with the Organization.

To many analysts the case seems clear for some kind of strengthened control by the Assembly over the specialized agencies. As two of them put it:

At present, these agencies are fairly independent with respect to both their policies and their finances, and though the General Assembly can examine their budgets, it can make only recommendations to them with respect thereto. This power has proved to be insufficient to effect proper coordination of the activities of the specialized agencies and to prevent waste and inefficiency, and a drastic change is necessary in order to forestall even greater difficulties in the future.[25]

A similar conclusion was reached in 1951 by the Subcommittee on Relations with International Organizations of the Senate Committee on Expenditures in the Executive Departments. The subcommittee found "a general lack of effective coordination" both among the specialized agencies and between the agencies and the United Nations Organization. On this point, the subcommittee stated that:

. . . effective coordination can be achieved only if some measure of real control over the budgets and programs of the specialized agencies is given to the General Assembly. This, in turn, can be accomplished only by amendment of the constitutions of the specialized agencies, designed either to afford to the General Assembly effective control over programs and projects of the agencies, or to provide for the inclusion of the budgets of the agencies within a consolidated budget of the United Nations, to be approved by the General Assembly.[26]

If this proposal were adopted, each of the specialized agencies would approve its own budget and submit it to the United Nations for consideration. The various budgets would then be consolidated with the regular United Nations budget and would be subject to

---

[24] Clark and Sohn, *op. cit.*, p. 45.

[25] *Ibid.*

[26] See Senate Committee on Expenditures in the Executive Departments, *United States Relations with International Organizations*, S. Rept. 90, 82 Cong. 1 sess. (Feb. 12, 1951), p. 57.

the same over-all scrutiny and review as the regular budget. Alternatively, the budgets of the specialized agencies could be reviewed separately by the United Nations, instead of in a single package form. In either event the end result would be approximately the same. Member states would have an opportunity to look at the total United Nations program and would thus be in a much better position to give over-all guidance and direction to United Nations activities. Effective control over programs and projects could be established, duplication and overlapping avoided, and substantial savings brought about.

The Problem of Consolidation

These may sound like good and sufficient reasons for a consolidated budget. Why, then, has consolidation not taken place? The most obvious answer lies in the opposition of the specialized agencies, which are anxious to retain their position of autonomy within the United Nations system. They point out that budgetary control means virtually total control and that if the power of the purse were lodged in the General Assembly, the specialized agencies would lose most of their reason for existence as separate organizations of sovereign states. As a result, there are conflicting pressures at work. On the one hand, there is a desire to consolidate and co-ordinate; on the other hand, there is a desire to permit the specialized agencies to develop their own programs in their own independent way.

The tradition of autonomy is deeply ingrained in the United Nations system. At the San Francisco Conference the framers of the Charter considered the possibility of establishing a centralized, unitary system but finally rejected it. They chose instead to support the creation of a galaxy of semi-autonomous agencies.

In 1948, the Administrative Committee on Co-ordination pointed out that at least four steps were necessary before a consolidated budget could be put into effect. These were: (1) the constitutions of the various specialized agencies would have to be amended in order to transfer to the General Assembly sufficient power to handle the new combined budget; (2) state delegations to the General Assembly would have to be changed so as to include specialists equipped to discuss the budgets and programs of the specialized agencies; (3) General Assembly sessions would have to be lengthened to enable it to handle the heavy workload involved in examining carefully a greatly enlarged budget; and (4) some way would have to be found to overcome the problem resulting from the fact that some Members of the United Nations do not belong to the specialized agencies. Most of these agencies have a fairly large number of members that are not represented in the General Assembly because they do not belong to the United Nations. Because of these complications, the committee agreed that, however desirable a consolidated budget might be as a long-range goal, it did not offer a practicable solution for the problem in the immediate future. As an alternative, the committee recommended that every effort be made to put the existing machinery for co-ordination to a fair test.[27]

The problem of differing membership is especially important. It would be possible, of course, to work out some procedure by which the members of a specialized agency that are not Members of the United Nations could be given a voice in the General Assembly with respect to the budget of that particular agency. But that would complicate unduly the budget process. Moreover, some of the specialized agencies have been able to make significant progress precisely because the Communist nations have remained aloof. In the circumstances, it would not seem appropriate to permit the Soviet Union and its satellites in the General Assembly to take part in the debate on the budgets of some of the agencies to which they do not belong.

There are other potent political factors that encourage the specialized agencies to oppose further consolidation of the United Nations system. Rightly or wrongly, they strongly believe that they can make more persuasive gains in such technical fields as health, labor, and agriculture, if they are not subject to the direct control of traditional diplomatic procedures and if they are allowed to keep a safe distance from the political turmoil of the General Assembly. Also, in the event the United Nations should collapse, they would be in a better position to carry on their work as independent agencies if they were not too closely identified with the parent organization.

From the point of view of the specialized agencies, decentralization has already proved something of a blessing. Not only has it afforded the economic and social activities of the United Nations protection from the political atmosphere of the General Assembly;

[27] U.N. Economic and Social Council, Third Year, Sixth Session, *Official Records, Supplement No. 6,* Annex V.

it has also permitted the specialized agencies to develop their programs with a maximum of flexibility and the opportunity to experiment without risking the prestige of the entire United Nations
system.

Other Suggestions for Co-ordination

There is another step that has been suggested that would bring
in its wake many of the advantages of a centralized budget. The
Economic and Social Council and the General Assembly could
review the activities of the specialized agencies within the context
of the United Nations system, and then on the basis of that review,
recommend over-all budget figures for each of the specialized
agencies. These target figures would be in the nature of recommendations only; the competent organs of the specialized agencies
would still possess the authority to give final approval to the program and budget of their particular agency. In view of the fact
that the General Assembly already has ample power to make such
recommendations, no amendment of the Charter would be necessary to bring about this change.

Even though the General Assembly would still be unable to
compel the specialized agencies to do its bidding, such a procedure
could have a very salutary impact on the United Nations system.
As in the case of the centralized budget, it would make possible a
comparative analysis of various United Nations programs and
enable the Members, for the first time, to consider apportionment of
the resources of the Organization as a whole. It would also compel
each Member government to work out a coherent, unified policy
with respect to the specialized agencies so it would be able to speak
with the same voice in the Assembly as it would in each of the
agencies to which it belongs.

Meanwhile the governments concerned could help the situation
somewhat by improving the co-ordination of their own representatives to the various agencies. Decentralization has now reached the
point where a representative of a government to the Economic and
Social Council, for example, may take a position quite different
from that of a representative of the same government to the Food
and Agricultural Organization, or to the General Assembly, on the
same issue. At the same time, particular groups have developed that
publicly support some of the individual specialized agencies in dif-

ferent countries, and these groups bring pressure on the government concerned. In the United States, for example, certain farm organizations tend to support FAO as against the other specialized agencies and, indeed, some people would argue, as against the United Nations itself. This support is reflected in the difference in approach taken with respect to the problem by the Department of Agriculture and the Department of State.

A few critics advocate an extreme cure that would go far beyond mere budgetary control. They suggest that much of the present difficulty could be avoided if the specialized agencies—with the possible exception of the Bank and the Fund—were abolished as separate international entities and their experts transferred to the United Nations Organization where they could continue their constructive work with somewhat less friction and more over-all policy supervision and co-ordination. This would do away with the multiplicity of budgets and organizations, streamline United Nations machinery for economic and social affairs, and permit program planning in an integrated way.

To the supporters of the specialized agencies, this suggestion would result in a situation in which the cure might seem to be worse than the disease. It would, they fear, result in a huge bureaucracy the efficiency of which in technical fields would be greatly hampered by central regulations, by politics, and by red tape. Moreover, it would be unfortunate from a public relations point of view if the programs of such specialized agencies as FAO and WHO were submerged and lost sight of in one over-all organization. This kind of proposal, they believe, would be far worse than the idea of a centralized budget.

As another alternative, consideration might be given the establishment of the type of relationship that existed between the League of Nations and its Communications and Transit Organization. This relationship was between full autonomy and direct control. The constitution of the Communications and Transit Organization provided for membership for countries not Members of the League. The conferences of the organization could negotiate conventions that did not have to have the approval of the League; and these conferences, rather than the League Council, appointed the Advisory and Technical Committee of the organization, which conducted the day-to-day business. Yet the budget of the organization was part of the budget of the League; its secretariat was a section of the League secretariat; and its work was subject to discussion by the Assembly of the League and was in part carried out in accordance with resolutions of the Assembly and the Council.

Meanwhile, it should be noted that considerable progress has been made in recent years within the existing organizational framework toward eliminating duplication of activities, on the one hand, and the adoption of consistent policies on the other. A director general of a specialized agency recently commented that good progress is being made with the co-ordinating machinery that is already in existence and that the Secretary-General of the United Nations is providing the leadership necessary to pull the United Nations system together. This observer expressed the view that if the existing machinery is given a good trial, the demands of those who are insisting on more effective co-ordination can be satisfied. Actually, as the General Assembly and the specialized agencies have a large overlapping membership, the problem could be resolved any time the members agree on a solution—and it does not really matter whether they agree as members of the General Assembly or as members of the specialized agencies. Much of the difficulty arises from what might be called internal schizophrenia of governments; and if the governments of sovereign states insist on following conflicting policies in the United Nations and in the specialized agencies, reorganization of the United Nations will not cure them.

Reorganization of the Economic and Social Council

Several of the proposals considered above would involve some reorganization of the Economic and Social Council, or at least a new emphasis with respect to its activities. The principal organizational changes that have been suggested concern the size of the Council, whether its members should serve as representatives of states or as individual experts, and incidentally, the extent to which the Council should be burdened with operating responsibilities as well as policy functions.

Although the proposals of Clark and Sohn outlined above involve a change in the type of representation on the Council, a matter which will be dealt with later, they also recommend an increase in the over-all membership of that organ.[28] Thus, the mem-

---

[28] Clark and Sohn, op. cit., pp. 7-12.

bership of the Council would be enlarged from eighteen to twenty-four representatives—with no two from the same nation—elected by the General Assembly from the total United Nations membership. Overlapping terms of four years, instead of three years, would be provided. And the entire membership could be discharged by the Assembly on a vote of lack of confidence if it chose a new Council by the same vote. Decisions would be made by an affirmative vote of fifteen of the twenty-four members of the Council, instead of by a majority of those present and voting, as is now the case.

The net effect of such a reorganization would be to increase the power of the General Assembly over the Economic and Social Council—some would think to a degree that might tempt the Assembly to use it irresponsibly. There is also some question whether there would be any particular advantage in increasing the membership of the Council, which is already eighteen. This certainly seems ample to afford adequate representation to various geographic areas as well as to different economic and social interests. Except for the General Assembly, the Economic and Social Council is already the largest of the United Nations organs, with six more members than the Trusteeship Council and seven more members than the Security Council. Furthermore, although some countries have served on the Economic and Social Council from the beginning, there are no permanent members as such, as there are of the Security Council; nor are there any automatically designated members, as in the case of the Trusteeship Council. The entire membership of the Economic and Social Council is elected by the General Assembly.

Regardless of the size of the organ, however, representation on it might be changed in a number of ways, most of which are variants of two basic approaches. The first of these is to give different economic and social groups direct representation on the Economic and Social Council; the second is to make it a body of experts.

As things stand now, of course, the members of the Council are the governments of sovereign states. It could conceivably be argued that a government might reflect only one economic or social point of view, that it would speak for its business class, or working class, or land-owning class, leaving all the other classes in its population relatively unrepresented. An analogy could be drawn with the International Labour Organisation, which makes provision for direct representation of labor and management, as well as of governments. The Council, however, covers a vastly wider field than does the International Labour Organisation. If various economic and social groups were to be given anything like proportionate representation, the sheer numbers involved would result in a very unwieldy organ. A more fundamental objection, however, is that such class representation would emphasize class differences and make for immeasurable confusion. There are those who believe that the governments represented on the Council sometimes take too narrow a view, but most governments are in a position to take a broader view than can the representatives of special interest groups within a state.

Nor does the case for making the Council a body of experts seem very impressive to some. The Council already has at its disposal a fairly large number of experts, or it can readily acquire them. If the Council were a body of experts, its policy-determining function would have to be transferred almost entirely to the General Assembly. Much of this work is eventually done by the Assembly under the present order of things, but at least the Assembly does not have to approach it *de novo*. The objection would almost certainly be made that changing the character of the Council in this way would tend to overburden the Assembly. This has been one of the arguments used against control by the Assembly of the budgets of the specialized agencies, a task that would certainly be less time-consuming than if the Assembly were to take over the various functions of the Council. It is a sound principle that organs such as the Assembly, which is normally in session somewhat less than three months a year, should not be so overburdened with secondary functions that they cannot properly perform their primary functions. And it should be remembered, in this connection, that the Assembly is already heavily burdened because as a result of the Soviet veto, it has taken over some of the activities of the Security Council.

Indeed, it could be argued that there is a case for increasing the policy-making functions of the Economic and Social Council. Should this be done through abolishing the specialized agencies and transferring responsibility for their functions to the Council, then more extensive use could be made of bodies of experts in the subsidiary organs, such as the various commissions already in existence, and others that might be established.

Proposals Relating to Domestic Jurisdiction

The problem of interpreting and applying Article 2(7), which prohibits the intervention of the United Nations "in matters which are essentially within the domestic jurisdiction of any state," cuts across all United Nations activities, except enforcement measures undertaken by the Security Council. The article has been invoked repeatedly by various governments as an argument against almost every conceivable type of United Nations action—in connection with the Dutch-Indonesian dispute, non-self-governing territories, and the control of atomic energy, for example—but it has been especially invoked in connection with economic and social functions and with human rights.

Various organs of the United Nations have shown no enthusiasm for attempting a definitive interpretation of the article. Despite the frequency with which they have debated it, they have usually been able to avoid taking a direct stand on its interpretation.[29] In general, three main questions have arisen:

1. How should Article 2(7) and other articles of the Charter—for example, Articles 55 and 56—be interpreted in relation to each other?

2. What sort of action by the United Nations constitutes "intervention" in the internal affairs of a Member?

3. What matters are "essentially within the domestic jurisdiction" of a state?

Other Provisions of the Charter Involved

Those who take a narrow view of the functions of the United Nations argue that many of the economic and social provisions of the Charter, especially Articles 55 and 56, are contradictory of Article 2(7). But Article 2(7) exists in its present form largely because of the decision taken at the San Francisco Conference to expand the economic and social activities of the Organization. The Dumbarton Oaks proposals, which had contemplated a more limited field of United Nations activity, had provided only that the articles dealing with pacific settlement of disputes "should not apply to situations or disputes arising out of matters which by international law are solely within the domestic jurisdiction of the

---

[29] For an extensive analysis of efforts made to interpret this article, see the volume in this Brookings series, *The Organization and Procedures of the United Nations.*

state concerned." When the functions of the Organization were broadened, this provision was made applicable to the whole Charter, except the articles relating to enforcement action, and its wording was changed so that it is somewhat more restrictive on the United Nations, although somewhat more ambiguous also.

From the history of Article 2(7), it would seem that it should take precedence over Articles 55 and 56 and that these latter articles should be operative only within the limitations of Article 2(7). It should also be noted that Articles 55 and 56 refer to the United Nations promoting the goals stated and to Members co-operating with the Organization in this regard. Similarly, Article 1 refers to achieving international co-operation and to harmonizing the actions of nations to these ends. Even without Article 2(7), it is voluntary co-operation that is stressed, not coercion or compulsion. As the Organization has interpreted the matter, economic and social services are rendered only at the request of governments or with their consent. It would seem unnecessary, therefore, to amend the Charter for the sake of obtaining a greater degree of internal consistency in this respect.

Besides Articles 55 and 56, two other articles in the economic and social chapters are particularly, although less importantly, pertinent in connection with Article 2(7). The first of these is Article 62(4), which provides that the Economic and Social Council "may call, in accordance with the rules prescribed by the United Nations, international conferences on matters falling within its competence." This has been interpreted to mean either intergovernmental conferences or other conferences called with the consent of governments. Article 2(7) has been viewed as preventing the calling of international conferences of nongovernmental representatives without proceeding through governments.

The question arose in 1946 in connection with a Philippine suggestion to convene a conference of representatives of non-self-governing territories. Article 2(7) was successfully invoked against the proposal. One of the arguments advanced by the opponents was that if it were admitted that conferences might be convened over the heads of governments, there was no reason why in similar circumstances conferences of all kinds of racial or political minorities could not be called. To remove all doubts about the matter, Article 62(4) might be amended by inserting the words "of governments" after the words "international conferences."

This would preclude any conference of nongovernmental organizations under United Nations sponsorship, as well as conferences of experts such as the Conference on the Peaceful Uses of Atomic Energy held in August 1955. A less restrictive method of dealing with the problem would be to specify that the conferences could be called, "with the consent of the governments concerned" (instead of "in accordance with the rules prescribed by the United Nations").

The other article concerned with economic and social functions that bears on Article 2(7) is Article 71 dealing with consultation by the Economic and Social Council with nongovernmental organizations. This article provides that the Council may make arrangements for consultation "with international organizations and, where appropriate, with national organizations after consultation with the Member of the United Nations concerned." The Charter leaves open the question of determining when it is and when it is not appropriate to make such arrangements with national organizations and also the question whether the Council may proceed to make such arrangements after consultation with the government involved even if the government is opposed to the arrangements. One of the principles adopted by the Economic and Social Council, however, is that "national organizations should normally present their views through their respective Governments or through international nongovernmental organizations to which they belong."[30] In point of fact, the Council has from the beginning required the consent of the governments concerned, and no suggestion has ever been made to the contrary.

If it were desired to clarify the article, however, two approaches might be used. First, the article could be amended so as simply to authorize the Council to arrange for consultation with nongovernmental organizations. This would eliminate the distinction between international and national organizations and would remove the express obligation of the Council to consult with governments in the case of national organizations. Such a step would open another area for direct relations between the United Nations and private groups and might encourage a kind of lobbying at the international level that Member states could find objectionable. As a result, it would increase at least the possibility of disputes over United Nations intervention in domestic affairs.

The other way to clarify the article would be to amend it to read,

[30] U.N. Doc. E/43/Rev. 2 (June 21, 1946).

in connection with national organizations, "with the approval of the Member of the United Nations concerned," instead of "after consultation" with the Member. This would clearly require the Council to proceed through governments and would remove all possibility of a dispute over domestic interference. At the same time, however, it would just as clearly give governments a control over national organizations. Such organizations in the United States, for example, might enter vigorous objections to any such control by the Department of State.

On balance—especially in view of the fact that no serious problems have arisen under the article—the wiser course might seem to be to leave it alone.

Interpretation of Article 2(7)

The problem of interpreting Article 2(7) in relation to other articles of the Charter is not nearly so difficult as the problem of interpreting the article standing alone.

There is a considerable difference of opinion over what sort of United Nations action constitutes "intervention." At one extreme is the view, which has been cited with approval by Indian writers, that intervention means "compulsive legal processes on the part of the Organization."[31] At the other extreme has been the position that the ban on "intervention" extends even to discussion in the United Nations of such matters as South African treatment of minorities or French relations with Tunisia and Morocco. Somewhere in between is the position taken by some authorities that "while discussion does not amount to intervention, the creation of a commission of inquiry, the making of a recommendation of a procedural or substantive nature, or the taking of a binding decision constitutes intervention under the terms of the paragraph."[32]

Equally contentious has been the question of what matters are "essentially within the domestic jurisdiction" of a state. A precise definition would require determining not only the limits of "domestic jurisdiction" but also the point at which a matter comes "essentially" within those limits. The Dumbarton Oaks Proposals, which followed the language of the Covenant of the League of Nations, were considerably more precise. They referred to "a matter

[31] B. Shiva Rao, "The United Nations and Non-Self-Governing Territories," *India Quarterly* (1950), pp. 227-34.
[32] Goodrich and Hambro, *op. cit.*, p. 120.

which by international law is solely within the domestic jurisdiction" of a state. There are two important points of difference to be noted. First, the Dumbarton Oaks draft set international law as a standard for determining the extent of the domestic jurisdiction of a state. The Charter sets no standard at all unless it be the attitude of Member states at a given time. Second, the Proposals excluded matters "solely" within the domestic jurisdiction of a state. The Charter excludes only matters "essentially" within such jurisdiction. In the view of some authorities, the use of "essentially" instead of "solely" has "proved to be of no special significance."[33] But the fact is that the words mean different things. Regardless where the line may be drawn between them, there are fewer matters "solely" within the domestic jurisdiction of a state than there are "essentially" within it. In this respect, therefore, the United Nations has a somewhat narrower field of operation under the Charter than it would have had under the Dumbarton Oaks Proposals. In other respects, however, the United Nations has wider functions than it would have had under the Proposals. The change made in the language of the domestic jurisdiction clause at the San Francisco Conference was accompanied by—indeed, it was largely the result of—corresponding changes to broaden the activities of the United Nations, especially those in the economic and social fields.

It should be recalled also that the Dumbarton Oaks Proposals applied only to action by the United Nations in dealing with *international disputes*. In the Charter, it applies to *all activities* of the Organization. Although the San Francisco Conference deliberately rejected the standard of international law for determining the extent of the domestic jurisdiction of a state, the United Nations appears in fact generally to have accepted the rule of international law that, "a matter ceases to be within the domestic jurisdiction of a state if its substance is controlled by the provisions of international law, including international agreements."[34]

Despite the emotions aroused by Article 2(7), there have been few specific suggestions regarding its amendment. Implicit in the more far-reaching proposals for world government is, of course, the assumption that fewer matters would be left within the domestic jurisdiction of the individual states. On the other hand, the proposals of those who advocate that the United Nations should limit its ac-

---

[33] *Ibid.*, p. 110.
[34] *Ibid.*, p. 120.

tivities to the airing and possible settlement of international disputes, carry with them a greatly enlarged concept of domestic jurisdiction. Most, however, who are concerned with drawing a clearer line between the international authority of the United Nations and the domestic jurisdiction of the Member states would try to achieve their objectives by amending other articles of the Charter. An important exception to this observation should be noted.

Possible Changes in Article 2(7)

Senator Bricker has argued that the United Nations has circumvented the limitations imposed by Article 2(7) in three specific ways. The first method of evasion, he points out, is through the argument that there is no longer any real difference between domestic affairs and foreign affairs, thus making the article a dead letter. The second is the contention that the language of Articles 55 and 56 in effect internationalized human rights, thus lifting them from the area of domestic jurisdiction. The third is the adoption of the view that subjects are no longer to be considered matters of domestic concern when dealt with in a resolution of the General Assembly or in a United Nations treaty.

In order to remedy this situation, Senator Bricker proposed that Article 2(7) be amended "to make it clear that the United Nations has no authority to draft international agreements or resolutions on subjects that are essentially domestic in character." Such an amendment, he contended, was necessary to protect the constitutional rights of American citizens that are not appropriate subjects for United Nations treaty negotiations.[35] As the Senator pointed out, it would also be necessary to amend Articles 55 and 56 to accomplish his purpose, for these Articles confer on the United Nations and the Member states the duty to promote respect for and observance of human rights.

It is difficult to assess the possible impact of this proposal, if it were agreed to, on the United Nations system. Presumably, the Member states do not conclude treaties in the economic and social fields unless they believe there is a need for them. Presumably, too, even if they were precluded from negotiating such agreements *within* the United Nations, there is nothing to prevent them from

[35] *Review of the United Nations Charter,* Senate Hearings, 84 Cong. 1 sess., Pt. 12, pp. 1649-50.

carrying on their negotiations *outside* the Organization. One effect, therefore, might be an increasing tendency on the part of states to resort to special *ad hoc* conferences for negotiating purposes. It would seem, also, that if Article 2(7) were amended as suggested by Senator Bricker, considerable changes would necessarily follow in a number of other articles of the Charter, in addition to Articles 55 and 56. Article 62, for example, expressly authorizes the Economic and Social Council to prepare draft conventions for submission to the General Assembly. The preamble and Article 1 of the Charter also refer to international action to achieve economic and social advancement.

Basically, however, this proposal would leave unanswered the important question of precisely what matters are essentially within the domestic jurisdiction of Member states. Whether treaties could be concluded or other action taken by the United Nations would still depend on the interpretation the Members might place on the language of the Charter at any given time. Until this area is defined, it will continue to be one of the principal sources of contention, regardless how Article 2(7) may be amended in other respects.

There are, however, various ways in which the language of Article 2(7) could be amended either to afford more protection to the domestic jurisdiction of a state or to give the United Nations a wider scope of action.

First, the meaning of the word "intervention" could be spelled out in any number of ways. It could be defined, for example, as almost anything from simple discussion of problems by United Nations organs to compulsive legal process.

Second, the extent of domestic jurisdiction could be delimited more precisely, also in a variety of ways. The standard of international law might be specified. This standard was in fact proposed at the San Francisco Conference on two separate occasions, and each time it received a majority of the votes cast, but failed for lack of the necessary two-thirds.[36] The issue, therefore, might be reopened at a conference for reviewing the Charter, and, from the point of view of interpretation, it would probably be helpful to have the international law standard in the clause. However, the reluctance of the organs of the United Nations to refer questions of domestic

[36] U.N. Information Organizations and U. S. Library of Congress, *Documents of the United Nations Conference on International Organization,* Vol. 6 (1945), pp. 509-13.

jurisdiction to the International Court of Justice suggests an inclination to leave the matter alone.

The adverb "essentially" might be replaced with "solely." This
would give the United Nations somewhat greater freedom of action.
To narrow the field of action, "essentially" could be struck out, leaving the phrase "matters within the domestic jurisdiction of a state"
unmodified. The effect of such a change would be to prohibit intervention by the United Nations in matters in any degree within the
domestic jurisdiction of a state. This would, of course, narrow the
functions of the United Nations relative to Article 2(7) in its present
form.

Third, an attempt might be made to spell out "domestic jurisdiction," or at least to specify who is to determine what "domestic jurisdiction" is. This latter function might be lodged in individual governments, in the General Assembly, or in the International Court
of Justice, and could then be exercised on a case-by-case basis. It
should be remembered, however, that political organs, such as the
General Assembly, are more frequently motivated by political than
by juridical considerations and are therefore inappropriate groups
for the development of case law. On the other hand, it would also
be extremely difficult to frame a precise definition of what is within
domestic jurisdiction that would satisfy all states. The term refers to
a matter that is relative and that varies considerably with the development of states and of international relations.

Fourth, the article might be changed so as expressly to require the
United Nations to deal directly with governments and to forbid it to
"penetrate directly into the domestic life and social economy of the
member states,"—which is the phrase used by John Foster Dulles at
the San Francisco Conference to explain his interpretation of the
article.[37] But this is substantially what the Soviet Union accuses the
United Nations of seeking to do in connection with atomic energy
inspection, and, if the Dulles phraseology were to be adopted, it
might give the Kremlin a further basis for its frequent objections
that the United Nations is overstepping its proper bounds.

It is doubtful, however, whether any of the foregoing changes
would actually make Article 2(7) any clearer than it now is, and the
problem of case-by-case interpretation would remain. Although
most of the arguments over the article in the organs of the United

[37] *Ibid.*, pp. 507-08.

Nations have been couched in legal terms, the decisions with respect to it have been primarily political, and it is significant that despite repeated suggestions, the question has never yet been referred to the International Court of Justice. Furthermore, the history of Article 2(7) at the San Francisco Conference sheds little light on its precise meaning; indeed, it affords some evidence that the article was deliberately made ambiguous in recognition of the fact that it dealt with an issue so difficult of solution as to be better left unsolved.

An important difference between the Covenant of the League of Nations and the Charter of the United Nations is that the latter places much more emphasis on social and economic matters, and thus reflects the growing recognition of world interrelationships. It could be argued that these interrelationships have reached the point where almost everything is of some international concern. A crop failure in Asia may produce a foreign exchange crisis that will have its effect on the foreign policy of the United States. A strike in Pittsburgh may produce a steel shortage in South America. Who is to say that Asian land tenure customs or American labor laws—though indisputably matters of domestic jurisdiction—are not of concern to other Members of the United Nations?

Of all the functions of the United Nations, none is more essentially domestic in character than that which comes under the heading of "economic and social." The United Nations has devoted hardly more attention to the international aspects of economics—as, for example, foreign trade and balance of payments—than to what might normally be considered the domestic aspects, such as economic development and agricultural production. The resolution of the General Assembly establishing the United Nations Expanded Technical Assistance Program provides that: "The technical assistance furnished shall (i) not be a means of foreign economic and political interference in the internal affairs of the country concerned and shall not be accompanied by any considerations of a political nature; [and] (ii) be given only to or through Governments."[38] But the fact is that technical assistance, almost by definition, does amount to a kind of interference in essentially domestic affairs. True, it is interference by consent and to accomplish results that are generally considered good. But it is interference, nevertheless, although it may not meet the technical meaning of "intervention" as that term is

[38] Res. 200 (III), Dec. 4, 1948.

used in international law. Even so, no significant objection has been raised against the technical assistance program on this—or any other —score; it has been described as everybody's favorite.

It is worth repeating that, in connection with economic and social affairs, the Charter stresses co-operation, not coercion. As co-operation is inherently voluntary, the main technique available to the principal organs of the United Nations is that of setting standards and then trying to persuade Member states to meet those standards. It is difficult to see how an appeal for co-operation can be construed as intervention unless a unique interpretation is placed on the word co-operation. The Member is free to accept the appeal and to co-operate, or to reject it and not to co-operate. In limited respects, some of the specialized agencies have greater powers of persuasion, or even enforcement in certain technical fields. But the charters of these agencies are separate treaties standing on their own terms and are not covered by Article 2(7) of the United Nations Charter.

If sovereign states wish to use the United Nations as a forum for reaching international agreement for the control of opium production, or atomic energy, or the establishment of specialized agencies with special powers, there is nothing in the Charter to prevent them from doing so. They could reach the same agreement outside the Charter. It is significant that the objection of infringement on domestic jurisdiction has not been seriously raised against narcotics control, but it has been raised against atomic energy control. The cultivation of poppies is certainly as domestic as is the mining of uranium or the manufacture of atomic bombs. The difference lies not in law but in politics; one is highly controversial, the other is not.

Where the line should be drawn is primarily a political issue, rather than a legal one. Article 2(7) as it now stands has the advantage of permitting the line to be drawn at almost any point that pleases both the United Nations and the Member states concerned. Within reasonable limits, its meaning will depend on the attitude of Members as a particular situation arises. In this respect, this article is somewhat comparable to such phrases in the United States Constitution as "commerce between the states," "due process of law," and "equal protection of the laws." After 160 years of judicial interpretation, these phrases still excite legal and political controversy. To say that the founding fathers would not recognize the United States Government today is not derogatory of the changes that have taken place in it since 1789. It is, rather, a tribute to the framers of the Constitution, whose master work was flexible enough to be adaptable to changing conditions. These adaptations, it is worth emphasizing, have been mainly political and not legal.

Similarly, it could be said that Article 2(7) as now written allows the United Nations to adjust its powers and functions in accordance with the evolving attitude of its Member states. A more satisfactory method of facilitating such adjustment seems unlikely to emerge from a Charter review conference.

The organizational problems involved in the economic, social, and humanitarian activities of the United Nations and the controversy attending some of these activities, such as those concerning human rights, tend to obscure a record of solid, undramatic accomplishment. This record includes international co-operation with respect to the control of narcotics, obscene publications, traffic in women and children, and other related matters; international relief operations dealing with difficult relief and refugee problems; and much of the work done by the specialized agencies and the regional commissions of the Economic and Social Council. It includes, most notably of all, the Expanded Program of Technical Assistance, which many people believe holds very great promise for the long-term betterment of human living conditions.

The difficulties the United Nations has encountered in many of these fields are perhaps only natural, given the pioneering tasks that it has attempted in a relatively new and complicated area of human activity. Many of the difficulties were probably inherent in the work, and they have without doubt been greatly exacerbated by the cold war. Nevertheless, there may be some justification for the criticism at times advanced that in these fields the United Nations has attempted to do too much too quickly. What it has attempted has, of course, been in response to pressure from its Members, but frequently this pressure has been for all things at once. The great difficulties and the long discussions attendant on the effort to establish program priorities are testimony to the inability of the Member states to decide what they want most to accomplish. This is in part a reflection of the extraordinary urge for economic development and social improvement that characterizes significant regions of the world.

The result, perhaps inevitably, has been that, on the one hand, the United Nations has sometimes been ahead of its public support in some sectors, and on the other hand, it has sometimes disappointed its supporters in other sectors by not accomplishing enough. This is not a problem that can be easily solved by amendment of the Charter. Many would view it as a step backward, for example, to delete Article 55 and thereby to say, by implication, that the United Nations was once, but is no longer, concerned with higher standards of living, or with human rights. The remedy may lie, instead, in the more careful selection of economic and social projects by the United Nations itself, and this means by the governments that are Members of the Organization. In turning to the United Nations for more and more services, Members ought not to forget what is a cardinal principle for all of them at home—namely, that politics is the art of the possible, and that if something is impossible, it is by definition also impolitic, no matter how desirable it might be as an abstract proposition.

But even if all the economic, social, and humanitarian activities of the United Nations were noncontroversial, it apparently would still be difficult for some critics to see how they could all be carried out satisfactorily and efficiently. A simple listing of these multifarious projects makes up a formidable document of several hundred items. More real progress might be made, and some of the organizational difficulties of the United Nations might disappear, if more effort were concentrated on fewer and more carefully selected projects.

CHAPTER IX

Non-Self-Governing Territories and the Trusteeship System

THE "colonial problem" has been the subject of some of the bitterest debates and deepest divisions in the United Nations. As a cause of controversy and agitation, it ranks second only to the split between the Communist and the free nations. The root of the problem, however, lies not so much in the provisions of the Charter as in the intense feeling of nationalism that pervades large areas of the world to such an extent that it has become one of the major political phenomena of the mid-twentieth century. The conflicting emotions generated by it are not likely to be allayed by changes in the United Nations or in its Charter. They lie much deeper and, indeed, may be exacerbated by serious consideration in the Organization of any proposals for such changes.

The United Nations, however, has played an extremely useful role in dealing with the colonial problem, and can continue to do so.[1] The Organization can provide a valuable mechanism for converting the heat generated by nationalism into energy that can be used for constructive ends. Thus, to speak of a "conflict" in the United Nations between the colonial and anti-colonial forces is to oversimplify the matter and to imply an antithesis that in most cases does not exist. The differences are more those of degree—of how rapidly dependent peoples should advance toward self-government or independence, and of how far the United Nations should go in encouraging that advancement. Such differences are susceptible

[1] Daniel S. Cheever and H. Field Haviland, Jr., *Organizing for Peace: International Organization in World Affairs* (1954), Chap. 11; H. D. Hall, *Mandates, Dependencies, and Trusteeship* (1948); Leland M. Goodrich and Edvard Hambro, *Charter of the United Nations: Commentary and Documents* (1949), Chap. 12; Amry Vandenbosch and Willard N. Hogan, *The United Nations: Background, Organization, Functions, Activities* (1952), Chap. 11; Huntington Gilchrist, "The United Nations: Colonial Questions at the San Francisco Conference," *American Political Science Review*, Vol. 39 (October 1945); H. A. Wieschoff, "Trusteeship and Non-Self-Governing Territories," *Annual Review of United Nations Affairs* (1952), pp. 117-34.

to compromise and mutual accommodation, and the Organization is peculiarly well qualified to facilitate this process.

But these differences do raise the basic issue of the degree of international supervision and control that the United Nations should have with respect to dependent peoples. This issue has two aspects. First is the legal one of interpreting the present provisions of the Charter with respect to non-self-governing territories and the international trusteeship system. The second is that of determining what, if any, changes should be made in the Charter. Both of these would be involved in any General Conference that might be called for a review of the Charter.

Provisions of the Charter

Questions relating to dependent peoples arise in the United Nations under Chapter XI of the Charter, dealing with non-self-governing territories, and under Chapters XII and XIII dealing, respectively, with the international trusteeship system and with the Trusteeship Council. Moreover, when a particular territory becomes the subject of international controversy, the problem may also be discussed under the general political and security provisions of the Charter.

Chapter XI, which is a declaration regarding non-self-governing territories, provides in Article 73 that states administering such territories recognize the paramount interests of the inhabitants and accept the obligation to promote their well-being. The states agree to ensure the political, economic, social, and educational advancement of the peoples of the dependent territories; to develop self-government; to further international peace and security; to promote constructive measures of development; and to transmit to the Secretary-General "statistical and other information of a technical nature relating to economic, social, and educational conditions" in the non-self-governing territories other than trust territories. Article 74 provides that Members agree to base their policy in respect of non-self-governing territories on the general principle of good-neighborliness, taking account of the "interests and well-being of the rest of the world, in social, economic, and commercial matters."

In Chapter XII, which establishes the international trusteeship system, provision was made for placing three categories of territories under the system: those held under mandate of the League of Nations; those detached from enemy states as a result of the Second World War; and those that might be voluntarily placed under the system by states responsible for their administration. In each case, however, the specific territories to be included were left for subsequent agreement (Article 77), and territories that have become Members of the United Nations are specifically excluded (Article 78).

The terms of trusteeship in each case are to be agreed upon "by the states directly concerned" (Article 79). Each trusteeship agreement is to include the terms under which the trust territory will be administered and to designate the administering authority, which may be one or more states or the United Nations itself (Article 81). All or part of a trust territory may be designated as a "strategic area" (Article 82), in which case functions of the United Nations relating to it are to be exercised by the Security Council (Article 83). The administering authority is specifically given the duty of ensuring that the trust territory plays its part in the maintenance of international peace and security, and is authorized to use volunteer forces, facilities, and assistance from the trust territory (Article 84). The General Assembly is empowered to exercise the functions of the United Nations with regard to trusteeship agreements for all areas not designated as strategic, including approval of the terms of the agreement (Article 85).

The basic objectives of the trusteeship system as stated in Article 76 are: "to further international peace and security"; to promote the advancement of the peoples of the territories, and their development toward self-government or independence; "to encourage respect for human rights and for fundamental freedoms for all"; and "to ensure equal treatment in social, economic, and commercial matters for all Members of the United Nations and their nationals, and also equal treatment for the latter in the administration of justice."

Chapter XIII creates the Trusteeship Council, which is composed of the members administering trust territories, permanent members of the Security Council not administering trust territories, and additional members elected by the General Assembly to give administering and non-administering members equal representation (Article 86). The Trusteeship Council is to act by majority vote, with each member having one vote (Article 89). It is to make its own rules of procedure, but these must provide for holding meetings at the request of a majority of the members (Article 90).

Administering authorities are required to make annual reports to the Assembly based on a questionnaire to be formulated by the Trusteeship Council on the political, economic, social, and educational advancement of the inhabitants of the trust territories (Article 88). In conformity with the trusteeship agreements, the Assembly and the Trusteeship Council may also "accept petitions and examine them in consultation with the administering authority" and "provide for periodic visits to the respective trust territories at times agreed upon with the administering authority" (Article 87). When appropriate, the Trusteeship Council is to "avail itself of the assistance of the Economic and Social Council and of the specialized agencies in regard to matters with which they are respectively concerned" (Article 91).

Proposals Relating to the Trusteeship Council and the General Assembly

There have been remarkably few proposals for amendment of Chapters XI, XII, or XIII of the Charter. A review of the experience of the Organization under these chapters, however, suggests the possibility that a number of such proposals might be made in the event of a General Conference for review of the Charter.[2] Members of the Arab-Asian bloc and other states prominently identified with anticolonialism have generally supported interpretations that would have the effect of strengthening the control of the United Nations over the international trusteeship system and of extending that system to cover all non-self-governing territories. The traditional colonial powers of Europe and on occasion other states allied with them have supported narrower interpretations limiting the authority of the United Nations to the strict letter of the Charter. It can be expected that proposals for amendment premised on these divergent interpretations will be offered; and it can further be expected, on the basis of the record, that the anti-colonial forces will be more likely to take the initiative in pushing their views.

There can be no doubt that, as it now stands, the Charter has built into it some of the ingredients of a constitutional impasse—and one not necessarily arising from the split between traditional colonial powers and the anti-colonial states.[3] The Charter clearly places

[2] For an analysis of the experience, see the volume in this Brookings series, *The United Nations and Promotion of the General Welfare,* Part Four.

[3] *Cf.* Wieschoff, *loc. cit.,* pp. 117-34.

the Trusteeship Council under the authority of the General Assembly, but the Assembly is given no means of enforcing its authority. The Trusteeship Council is composed of sovereign governments that cannot be forced to carry out recommendations of the Assembly of which they disapprove and that, indeed, they may even have voted against in the Assembly.

In the Trusteeship Council, the administering and non-administering states are evenly balanced. In the Assembly, the anti-colonial bloc has a clear majority on most questions, although not always the two thirds that the Charter requires on trusteeship questions. This requirement, it will be recalled, was put in the Charter in an effort to preserve the balance between administering and non-administering states. Equal representation in the Trusteeship Council has been a matter of great importance to the administering states as a means of protecting their interests against what they consider to be sometimes extreme demands by non-administering states. It has, by the same token, been a source of some frustration to the non-administering states, whose representatives have reacted by trying to shift trusteeship functions from the Trusteeship Council to the General Assembly.

The conflict between the Assembly and the Trusteeship Council could, of course, be resolved by shifting the balance of power either way. It is an open question, whether such a shift would strengthen the United Nations, and it is even more doubtful whether, in the present state of affairs, either side would agree to any shift that might result in a weakening of its power or influence. Shifts of this character could be accomplished by removing or loosening the authority the Assembly has over the Trusteeship Council, or subjecting the Council to even closer control by the Assembly either by making the Council a body of experts, not representing governments, or by giving the Assembly the right of electing all members to the Council.

Two analysts have recommended tightening control over the Trusteeship Council by the Assembly and at the same time increasing somewhat the influence of non-administering states in the Council.[4] Under their plan the Council would be composed of one member from each nation administering trust territories; one member from each non-administering power among the six nations with the larg-

⁴ Grenville Clark and Louis B. Sohn, *Peace Through Disarmament and Charter Revision* (Preliminary Print, July 1953), pp. 105-20.

est population; and additional members from other nations equal to the total number of members from the administering and non-administering nations combined. Their proposal contemplates a distribution of representatives in the General Assembly according to population, with the Assembly in turn electing members of the Trusteeship Council from among its own number, so that the members of the Council would not be appointed by governments.

The essence of this proposal in so far as membership on the Trusteeship Council is concerned, however, could be put into effect regardless of the proposed change in composition of the Assembly. As the Charter now stands, the Trusteeship Council is composed of six members administering trust territories—Australia, Belgium, France, New Zealand, the United Kingdom, and the United States; two permanent members of the Security Council not administering trust territories—China and the Soviet Union; and four members elected by the General Assembly—El Salvador, Haiti, India, and Syria.

Under the suggestion referred to above, the six members administering trust territories would continue to be represented. China and the Soviet Union would continue to have seats by virtue of being among the six largest Member states not administering trust territories. India would also be assured of a seat in this category. The other three among the six largest, as reckoned by this proposal, are the United States, United Kingdom, and France, which already have seats as administering authorities.

The General Assembly would thus elect nine additional members, as against four members at present, and the administering states would be outnumbered 12 to 6. This seems to give the non-administering states more than the "slightly preponderate" representation as proposed for them by the authors of the plan.

This proposal would further increase control of the Assembly by giving it the right to discharge the Trusteeship Council as a whole by a vote of lack of confidence "provided that by the same vote a new Trusteeship Council is chosen." The proposal goes further toward control by the Assembly than did the Egyptian proposal at the San Francisco Conference that the Trusteeship Council be evenly divided between elected and non-elected states. The Egyptian proposal might have possibilities, especially if combined with other amendments to give the Trusteeship Council a larger area of independence from the General Assembly and to remove from the Trusteeship Council those permanent members of the Security Council not administering trust territories. There seems to be little reason for such permanent members to have been on the Trusteeship Council in the first place—except that the Soviet Union insisted that they be members. Nor does there seem to be any special justification for the suggestion of representation of the six largest nations simply because they are big.

The interests of the Security Council in the administration of the strategic areas in trust territories are adequately protected by Article 83 of the Charter. Furthermore, under its general powers for the maintenance of international peace and security, the Council has ample authority to concern itself with any legitimate threat to peace that may arise in a trust area not designated as strategic—and such a threat would seem to be the only legitimate concern of the Security Council with nonstrategic trust areas.

In fact, the Trusteeship Council probably would have functioned just as well without the membership of China and the Soviet Union, the two states that are there by virtue of being permanent members of the Security Council not administering trust territories. If the permanent members of the Security Council that are not administering states were dropped from the Trusteeship Council, a balance could be achieved between elected and non-elected states without destroying the balance between administering and non-administering states. The Assembly would then elect six out of twelve members of the Trusteeship Council, instead of four out of twelve, as at present. If the permanent members of the Security Council were not removed from the Trusteeship Council, a balance between elected and non-elected members would give the Assembly the right to elect eight out of sixteen. The administering powers would be outnumbered 10 to 6, which compares with the 12 to 6 ratio under the proposal referred to above.

If the Assembly were given a larger voice in selection of the membership of the Trusteeship Council, the Council at the same time could appropriately be given more independence from the Assembly. The powers of the Trusteeship Council could be most increased by giving the Council, rather than the Assembly as is now provided in Article 85, authority to exercise the functions of the United Nations with regard to trusteeship agreements for areas not designated as strategic.

A less drastic change would be to amend Article 85 so that it would read as follows: "The functions of the United Nations with regard to trusteeship agreements for all areas not designated as strategic shall be exercised by the Trusteeship Council; provided, however, that the General Assembly shall approve the terms of the trusteeship agreements and of their alteration or amendment." If any change along these lines in Article 85 were agreed to, minor amendments would follow in Articles 87 and 88.

Another alternative would be election by the Assembly of all members of the Trusteeship Council. Administering states, however, should be assured of places on the Council. There is more involved here than simply the protection of the interests of administering states. The Council also provides a forum for the exchange of information and experience among states administering trust territories with similar problems and conditions.

In any event, it would still seem desirable to some Members to increase the influence of the Assembly in choosing members of the Council. The Council needs to be made more broadly representative. The elective seats have so far been held mainly by countries that are newly independent or economically underdeveloped, or both. Many of these countries have been able to draw on their own experience to play a helpful, constructive role. But it might also be useful if seats on the Council could be found for some of the smaller states that are not colonial powers and that have a long record of independence and economic development. At the same time the elective members need longer terms so that they might make better use of the experience they acquire on the Council.

Finally, the Council could be converted into a body of experts, along the lines of the Permanent Mandates Commission of the League of Nations. This would, of course, be the final step in bringing about control by the Assembly over trusteeship problems, and would probably transfer the political debates of the Trusteeship Council to the General Assembly, without any compensating advantages.

The results of such a change would depend not only on the caliber of the experts chosen to serve on the Council but also on the conception held by the Assembly of its own role in the matter. If the Assembly attempted to administer the trusteeship system and regarded the Council as only an advisory group, or as an agency to carry out its directives, little good could come of the proposal. If, however, the Assembly should use forbearance and self-restraint in the exercise of what is virtually its plenary authority, a Trusteeship Council of experts, divorced from political turmoil, would be in a position to render significant service. The recent temper of the Assembly with respect to trusteeship matters gives little ground for belief that it would exercise such self-restraint.

Proposals Relating to Non-Self-Governing Territories

Although at the San Francisco Conference the trusteeship system was the center of attention, most of the subsequent controversy has arisen in connection with the authority of the United Nations and the obligations of administering states under Chapter XI of the Charter regarding non-self-governing territories that are not under trusteeship. In this chapter of the Charter, states administering such territories "recognize the principle that the interests of the inhabitants . . . are paramount" and accept "as a sacred trust" the obligation to promote the well-being of the inhabitants "to the utmost." The colonial powers have generally taken the view that this is a unilateral declaration on their part. The United Kingdom, for example, has argued that it is no more than a statement of the British colonial policy that was in effect before the United Nations came into being and that would continue in effect even if there were no United Nations. The anti-colonial powers, on the other hand, view this provision as a treaty, as a compact between colonial and noncolonial powers, and thus as something that is subject to international supervision and enforcement.

Difficulties have arisen not only over what this chapter of the Charter means but also over who is entitled to say what it means. Under the stimulus of anti-colonial powers, and over the protests of administering states, the General Assembly, without even asking the Court for an advisory opinion, has asserted its competence and jurisdiction in this respect. There has, as a matter of fact, been a steady growth of activity in the United Nations under Chapter XI. Some of the questions of interpretation that have arisen are discussed below.

Question of "Full Measure of Self-Government"

It was recognized at the San Francisco Conference that self-government is not necessarily synonymous with independence, although the anti-colonial states made it clear that in most instances they considered this a distinction without a difference.[5] The Assembly has followed much the same line. It has repeatedly debated the question regarding how far short of independence "a full measure of self-government" can begin.

In 1952, the Assembly established the *Ad Hoc* Committee on Factors of Self-Government to continue a study of factors bearing on the question whether a territory is or is not self-governing. Members were invited to transmit their views on factors to be included. This committee drew up a list of thirty-four factors divided into three parts: those indicative of the attainment of independence; those indicative of the attainment of other separate systems of self-government; and those indicative of the free association of a territory on an equal basis with the metropolitan or other country as an integral part of that country or in any other form.

The committee recognized that no one list of factors would be conclusive, that each case would have to be considered in the light of its individual circumstances. As a matter of fact, many of the recognized sovereign states of the world would not be self-governing when measured by all the factors on this list.[6] The list of factors was approved by the Assembly in November 1953, in a resolution asserting its competence "to consider the principles that should guide the United Nations and the Member States in the implementation of obligations arising from Chapter XI of the Charter and to make recommendations in connection with them." The resolution also recommended that the list be used as a guide so that "a decision may be taken by the General Assembly on the continuation or cessation of the transmission of information required by Chapter XI."[7]

The process of drawing up the list was accompanied by much controversy, not only over the specific factors to be included, but also over the competence of the Assembly to concern itself with the matter at all. Belgium, the Netherlands, the United Kingdom, and others argued that the determination whether a territory is or is not

---

[5] See speech of the Philippine delegate, U.N. Information Organizations and U.S. Library of Congress, *Documents of the United Nations Conference on International Organization,* Vol. X (1945), p. 562. (Hereinafter cited as *UNCIO Documents.*) See also Ernest B. Haas, "The Attempt to Terminate Colonialism: Acceptance of the United Nations Trusteeship System," *International Organization,* Vol. 7 (February 1953), pp. 1-21.

[6] Clyde Eagleton, "Excesses of Self-Determination," *Foreign Affairs,* Vol. 31 (July 1953), p. 600.

[7] Res. 742 (VIII), Nov. 27, 1953.

self-governing lies entirely with the home government in the light of its constitutional relationship with the territory. The Arab-Asian and some Latin American nations held that such a determination not only could be made but should be made by the Assembly.

It can be anticipated that the issue may come up at any General Conference to review the Charter, in the form either of spelling out the competence of the Assembly or of attempting to define more precisely, in the Charter itself, what is meant by "a full measure of self-government." Agreement on such a definition, however, would be extremely difficult to obtain. After prolonged consideration, the *Ad Hoc* Committee reported that it was "agreed that it was not possible to find a satisfactory definition of the concept of a full measure of self-government for the purposes of Chapter XI of the Charter. Even if the concept of self-government could be satisfactorily defined, such a definition would be insufficient unless completed by the definition of 'a full measure' of self-government within the framework of Chapter XI."[8]

A further difficulty could well arise if the administering states pursued the idea, which has already been advanced by both Belgium and the United States, although in different contexts, that Chapter XI applies to all non-self-governing peoples and is not limited to "colonies" in the traditional sense.[9] The argument that, for example, the Soviet Union should report on Latvia could be an interesting counter-weapon for administering states to use, although it might be interpreted as implying recognition of the Soviet annexation of that country.

Conflict Between Articles 2(7) and 73

Despite the fact that the Assembly has endorsed the view that the list of factors drawn up by the *Ad Hoc* Committee on Factors of Self-Government could only be regarded as a guide and that no single factor or combination of factors could be applicable to all

[8] U.N. General Assembly, Eighth Session, *Report of the Ad Hoc Committee on Factors Which Should Be Taken Into Account In Deciding Whether A Territory Is or Is Not A Territory Whose People Have Not Yet Attained A Full Measure of Self-Government*, Doc. A/2428 (Aug. 4, 1953), p. 2.

[9] Josef L. Kunz, "Chapter XI of the United Nations Charter in Action," *American Journal of International Law*, Vol. 48 (January 1954), pp. 103-10. See also Francis B. Sayre, "Legal Problems Arising from the United Nations Trusteeship system," *American Journal of International Law*, Vol. 42 (April 1948), pp. 263-98.

cases, a number of Members are inclined to apply the list quite rigidly.

Article 2(7) of the Charter, which is designed to protect the domestic jurisdiction of Member states, has frequently been invoked by powers administering non-self-governing territories as a bar to action by the Assembly under Chapter XI. Other powers have as frequently denied that a non-self-governing territory can be considered to be "essentially within the domestic jurisdiction" of any state.[10]

The question, when it is raised in good faith, hinges on the definition of what is essentially within the domestic jurisdiction of a state. France has perhaps been the leading exponent of a broad definition of domestic jurisdiction. It was especially insistent on the point at the San Francisco Conference, and it has since used it as an argument against Arab demands for consideration by the General Assembly of the situation in Tunisia and Morocco. India, on the other hand, has led in taking a narrow view of domestic jurisdiction. It has adopted the thesis that intervention means "compulsive legal process on the part of the Organization"—which, of course, it does not have. Indian delegates have argued from this that Article 2(7) does not prevent discussion and investigation of situations arising from complaints of violations of human rights, or recommendations on this subject.[11]

The pressure from states holding the Indian view—or something close to it—has been so persistent and so persuasive that the United Nations at times has ignored the argument that the relations of a state with its dependent territories are essentially within its domestic jurisdiction. These actions have been more political than legal. Commenting on the argument that dependent territories are within the domestic jurisdiction of a state, one observer concludes that:

> Whatever the merits of this argument in law, its futility in an essentially political context is apparent. . . . In the field of the state's relations with its dependent territories or with particular sections of its population, the claim to determine policy without outside interference or criticism is, for a variety of reasons, no longer one most states can successfully assert.[12]

[10] See above, Chap. VIII.

[11] B. Shiva Rao, "The United Nations and Non-Self-Governing Territories," *India Quarterly* (1950), pp. 227-34.

[12] Coral Bell, "The United Nations and the West," *International Affairs,* Vol. 29 (October 1953), pp. 468-69.

Transmission of Information

Under Article 73(e) of the Charter, states administering non-self-governing territories, other than trust territories, undertake "to transmit regularly to the Secretary-General for information purposes, subject to such limitation as security and constitutional considerations may require, statistical and other information of a technical nature relating to economic, social, and educational conditions in the territories for which they are respectively responsible." Several questions have arisen under this provision, leading sometimes to bitter debates. The provision, indeed, has been one of the most controversial of any of those dealing with non-self-governing or trust territories. Yet it is interesting to note that at the San Francisco Conference it was agreed to practically without dissent.

There is, in the first place, the question of which territories are covered, and this involves not only the question whether a territory is or is not self-governing but also the question of who is to make that determination. At the San Francisco Conference, Australia proposed that reports be required on territories through the voluntary action of the administering state or "by the General Assembly, after consideration of the recommendations of a conference or conferences, specially convened by the United Nations, of members responsible for the administration of dependent territories."[13] And the Philippine delegate suggested that an entity independent of the administering government should judge the degree of advancement of dependent people.[14]

The Assembly approached the question of territories on which information is required under Article 73(e) by inviting Member states to submit their own ideas. Seventy-four territories were named by Members, but within a year the transmission of information had ceased with respect to eleven of them. The question of the right of the administering state to make a determination in the matter first arose, however, in a negative way in 1948 when the Soviet Union criticized the Netherlands for continuing to report on Indonesia. But the most vigorous debate took place in 1953. The United States had notified the Secretary-General that it would no longer transmit information on Puerto Rico, which had become a self-governing commonwealth in 1952. Similarly, the Netherlands had announced it would no

---

[13] *UNCIO Documents,* Vol. 3, p. 549.
[14] *Ibid.,* Vol. 10, p. 429.

longer transmit information on Surinam and the Netherlands An-
tilles, in view of constitutional changes that had taken place in those
territories. Both the Netherlands and the United States emphasized
the constitutional impossibility of continuing to transmit information. The peoples of the territories involved, they said, had themselves requested that transmission cease; the territories felt that to
continue transmission was derogatory of their new self-governing
status.

In the end, the Assembly approved the action of the United
States and in effect disapproved that of the Netherlands. In the
resolution on Puerto Rico, the Assembly adopted language that
asserted its competence to "decide whether a non-self-governing
territory has or has not attained a full measure of self-government."[15] And in the resolution on the Netherlands, that country was
requested to continue reporting "until such time as the General
Assembly takes a decision" that reporting should be discontinued.[16]

It has also been argued that a "full measure of self-government"
is not necessary for the cessation of reporting on non-self-governing
territories, but only a full measure of local responsibility for the
specific fields mentioned in Article 73(e)—economic, social, and educational affairs. In its resolution of November 1953, however, the
Assembly adopted the view that a territory could not be considered
self-governing in these matters unless it had, in fact, "a full measure
of self-government."[17]

Another question that has arisen under Article 73(e) is what is to
be done with the information once it has been received. The Charter
merely says it is to be transmitted "to the Secretary-General for
information purposes." But obviously this is only the first step,
which could conceivably lead to various types of action by the
United Nations. The Assembly in 1946 established the *Ad Hoc* Committee on Information from Non-Self-Governing Territories to examine the Secretary-General's summary and analysis of this information "with a view to making recommendations to the General Assembly regarding the procedures to be followed in the future and the
means of insuring that the advice, expert knowledge and experience

---

[15] Res. 748 (VIII), Nov. 27, 1953.

[16] Res. 747 (VIII), Nov. 27, 1953.

[17] Res. 742 (VIII), Nov. 27, 1953. See U.N. General Assembly, Eighth Session,
Report of the Ad Hoc Committee on Factors . . ., Doc. A/2428 (Aug. 4, 1953).
See also Rao, *loc. cit.*, p. 232.

of the specialized agencies are used to the best advantage."[18] The committee was renewed annually on an *ad hoc* basis until 1949 when it was established for three years. In 1951 its name was changed to Committee on Information from Non-Self-Governing Territories, and in 1952 it was renewed for a further period of three years.

Throughout its existence, the committee has been the subject of political controversy. It was created over the protests of some of the administering powers that the Assembly was exceeding its proper jurisdiction. These powers have since then felt justified in their fear that the anti-colonial states intended to push the committee beyond the realm of discussion into the realm of action. In 1952, the Fourth (Trusteeship) Committee of the Assembly adopted a proposal to extend the committee indefinitely—*i.e.,* to make it permanent. France, the United Kingdom, and Belgium announced they would no longer participate in the committee if this recommendation were approved by the Assembly. The move carried with it the plain implication that the committee was to become a permanent organ of the United Nations with functions relative to non-self-governing territories similar to those of the Trusteeship Council relative to trust territories. This would, of course, amount in effect to placing colonies under trusteeship without trusteeship agreements—a move that would seem, not only to violate the voluntary principle of the trusteeship system but also, as a consequence, to give the United Nations a larger measure of control.

The issue did not come to a crisis, however, as the Assembly adopted a compromise sponsored by the United States for a three-year extension of the committee. The end of this period will coincide with the date for consideration of the problem of review of the Charter, and it may be expected that, if a review conference is held, proposals may well be made for a permanent United Nations organ to supervise the administration of non-self-governing territories other than trust territories. Other proposals have been made of this general nature. In 1952, the Assembly adopted a resolution expressing the hope that administering states, when transmitting information, would furnish annually as complete information as possible on any action taken to bring the reports of the Committee on Information from Non-Self-Governing Territories to the attention of the authorities responsible for the implementation of educa-

[18] Res. 66 (I), Dec. 14, 1946.

tional, economic, and social policy in the territories and on any problems that arise in giving effect to the general views expressed in these reports. The resolution was supported by the United States but opposed by certain other administering powers.

In 1947, the *Ad Hoc* Committee on Information rejected proposals by the Soviet Union and other Members calling for visits by representatives of the United Nations to non-self-governing territories and asserting the right of the United Nations to receive and examine petitions from non-self-governing territories. A resolution of the Assembly in 1954, however, expressed the view that United Nations missions should visit non-self-governing territories in certain circumstances.

In 1947 in the discussion of the report of the *Ad Hoc* Committee in the Fourth Committee of the Assembly, the anti-colonial states, led by the Soviet Union and India, proposed that the transmission of political information be recommended and that the data received be compared only with the metropolitan areas of administering powers, with no use to be made of comparative information from similar geographic zones. This would have led to the curious situation of comparing the Gold Coast to the United Kingdom instead of, say, to French Equatorial Africa. These states also proposed that the special committee be called upon to make such recommendations as it deemed appropriate. Over objections, such as that expressed by the United Kingdom that these proposals would make the special committee a rival of the Trusteeship Council, the proposals were carried by close votes in the Fourth Committee, but they were rejected in the Assembly by substantial majorities.

A further question that has arisen under Article 73(e) is the type of information to be reported. The Charter refers to "statistical and other information of a technical nature relating to economic, social, and educational conditions." The omission of political information is conspicuous; for political information is pointedly included among the types that must be reported in connection with trust territories.

The Assembly has gone so far on a number of occasions, however, as to request administering states to include political information in their reports on non-self-governing territories, although it recognized that they were under no obligation to do so. Some administering states including the United States and Denmark, have complied; others, including the United Kingdom and Belgium, have not. The

United Kingdom has even taken the position that it will not transmit officially to the Secretary-General constitutional changes in the non-self-governing territories under its control even though such information is public property.

On the other hand, it has been argued that such a strict interpretation of Article 73(e) is inconsistent with the emphasis and plain intent of the other provisions of that article. Paragraph (a) of the article commits the administering powers "to ensure, with due respect for the culture of the peoples concerned, their political, economic, social, and educational advancement." And paragraph (b) obligates them "to develop self-government, to take due account of the political aspirations of the peoples, and to assist them in the progressive development of their free political institutions, according to the particular circumstances of each territory and its peoples and their varying stages of advancement."

Some analysts have proposed that "political" be inserted among the kinds of information required by Article 73(e). They have further proposed the deletion of the qualifications that the information be "of a technical nature" and that its transmission be "for information purposes, subject to such limitation as security and constitutional considerations may require."[19] Such an amendment would eliminate the legal dispute over the type of information to be transmitted. Whether it would result in modifying the British position is another question. And, of course, it would not touch on the closely related disputes regarding whether a territory is in fact self-governing and who makes that determination.

Proposals Relating to the International Trusteeship System

The Charter, in Article 77, provides for bringing territories under the trusteeship system by means of trusteeship agreements. As noted earlier, three kinds of territories are included—those held under mandate, those which "may be detached from enemy states as a result of the Second World War," and those "voluntarily placed under the system by states responsible for their administration." In fact, however, the trusteeship system has been applied only to mandated territories of the League of Nations, including the Pacific Islands formerly mandated to Japan for which the United States is now the

[19] Clark and Sohn, *op. cit.*, pp. 107-08.

administering authority, and to Italian Somaliland. The failure to bring other territories under the trusteeship system has been a source of disappointment to states that had hoped the system would be the beginning of the end of colonialism.

Scope of the System

In 1947 the Fourth Committee of the General Assembly adopted a proposal by India expressing the hope that Members of the United Nations would submit trusteeship agreements for some or all of the non-self-governing territories as the trusteeship system provided the best means of enabling the peoples of dependent territories to obtain self-government or independence under the collective guidance and supervision of the United Nations. The resolution also declared it to be "the clear intention" of Chapter XII that such territories should be placed under trusteeship. This recommendation was rejected in the Assembly by a vote of 24 to 24 with 1 abstention.[20] Opponents argued that no such "clear intention" was expressed in the Charter, and there was no proof that trusteeship is, in fact, the "surest and quickest" way to independence. It was pointed out that six countries, with almost 500 million people, had attained, or virtually attained, independence outside the trusteeship system since the Charter was signed.[21] The number of such countries has since increased.

It has been suggested that the Assembly itself might be given the power to place a specific territory under trusteeship. In favor of this proposal, it can be argued that the international community, acting through the United Nations, should have available some remedy in case of outrageous exploitation or misgovernment of a dependent territory. An analogy can be drawn with the power of courts to intervene between parent and child, in extreme cases, and to make the child a ward of the state. On the other hand, it can be argued that lodging such power in the General Assembly would give it the right to intervene in the domestic affairs of a state in violation of Article 2(7) of the Charter. In the light of the extreme positions sometimes taken in the past by the anti-colonial states, there would also seem to be ground for fear that the Assembly might be tempted to exercise such power in an irresponsible manner. Further, the rec-

---

[20] A two-thirds vote was required for passage.
[21] Sayre, *loc. cit.*, p. 274.

ord by no means indicates that a territory necessarily makes greater political progress under the trusteeship system than outside it. In any event, the proposal would certainly encounter strong objections from administering states.

Of the territories held under mandate of the League of Nations, all except South-West Africa have either become independent or have been placed under United Nations trusteeship. In the case of South-West Africa, the Union of South Africa, the mandatory power, has wanted to annex the territory. The Assembly has recommended that it be placed under trusteeship, but has refused to go so far as to declare that the Charter required this course. The International Court of Justice has also ruled that there is no legal requirement for trusteeship, but that in the meantime the mandate continues and that South Africa is accountable to the United Nations to the same extent that it was accountable to the League.[22]

"States Directly Concerned"

Article 79 of the Charter provides that: "The terms of trusteeship for each territory to be placed under the trusteeship system, including any alteration or amendment, shall be agreed upon by the states directly concerned, including the mandatory power in the case of territories held under mandate by a Member of the United Nations, and shall be approved as provided for in Articles 83 and 85." The phrase "states directly concerned" has been highly contentious and has been subject to various interpretations. At the San Francisco Conference, the Soviet Union suggested that efforts be made to define the phrase more precisely, but the suggestion was not followed and the Soviet Union itself proposed an even more ambiguous phrase—"states which were or are concerned."[23]

Further efforts at definition were made at the first session of the General Assembly. A great many definitions, or procedures for determining definitions, were proposed. These ranged all the way from proposals that the administering state should be the only state directly concerned to those that the states directly concerned should include every member of the United Nations. Meanwhile, states preparing to place mandated territories under trusteeship

[22] International Court of Justice, *Advisory Opinions* (1950), pp. 128-219. See also U.N. Department of Public Information, *Yearbook of the United Nations, 1946-47*, pp. 205-08, and Sayre, *loc. cit.*, p. 273.

[23] *UNCIO Documents*, Vol. 10, p. 441.

took practical steps to define the phrase themselves, by the expedient of sending proposed texts of the trusteeship agreements to states they thought were concerned. But there was no particular uniformity in their actions. No definition, either theoretical or practical, seemed generally satisfactory. In the end, over the protests of the Soviet Union that the Charter was being violated, the Assembly adopted a resolution proposed by the United States that approval of the trusteeship agreements was subject to the understanding that no definition had been decided on and that no state had "waived or prejudiced its right hereafter to claim to be such a 'state directly concerned' in relation to approval of subsequent proposed trusteeship agreements and any alteration or amendment of those now approved."[24] The Soviet Union thereupon refused to participate in the election of members of the Trusteeship Council and in the initial work of the Council itself.

The question arose again in the Security Council in connection with the strategic trusteeship agreement proposed by the United States for the Pacific Islands formerly mandated to Japan. Despite the fact that at one time or another seventeen states, besides the United States, were brought into the discussion, Syria protested that the Council "was not giving implementation or the correct execution of Article 79 of the Charter," because it "was paying no attention or no consideration at all to the states directly concerned."[25] The Syrian representative himself did not suggest what other states were or should be concerned, but he did move an adjournment so that the matter might be more fully considered and discussed. The motion was defeated by a vote of 5 to 6.

At least one analyst has concluded that as the Charter now stands there is no possibility, legally, of defining the phrase. He has therefore proposed two alternative amendments to the Charter to deal with the problem, one a short draft and one a long draft. In summary, these amendments provide for the "states directly concerned" to be determined by the General Assembly in the case of nonstrategic trust territories, by the Security Council in the case of strategic

---

[24] See U.N. Doc. A/258 (Dec. 12, 1946), p. 13; Res. 63(I) Dec. 13, 1946. See also Elizabeth H. Armstrong and William I. Cargo, "The Inauguration of the Trusteeship System of the United Nations," Department of State *Bulletin*, Vol. 16 (Mar. 23, 1947), p. 520.

[25] U.N. Doc. S/P.V. 124 (Apr. 2, 1947). See also Robert R. Robbins, "United States Trusteeship for the Territory of the Pacific Islands," U. S. Department of State *Bulletin*, Vol. 16 (May 4, 1947), p. 788.

trust territories, and by both the Assembly and the Council in the case of trust territories embracing both strategic and nonstrategic areas. The long draft further spells out in meticulous detail the exact procedure to be followed in negotiating or amending a trusteeship agreement.[26]

To some students of the problem this might seem unnecessarily complicated. A much simpler and perhaps equally effective remedy for the difficulty would be to strike out the reference to "states directly concerned" in Article 79 so that the article would provide that: "The terms of trusteeship for each territory to be placed under the trusteeship system, including any alteration or amendment, shall be approved as provided for in Articles 83 and 85."

Indeed, it is doubtful whether Article 79 is needed in the Charter at all. Article 83 specifies that the Security Council shall approve agreements for strategic areas, and Article 85 provides that the General Assembly shall approve agreements for other areas. This, in practice, probably provides sufficient safeguards for all states. Obviously, the administering state must give its approval in any case. Other Member states have a chance to make their voices heard in the General Assembly, of which all are members, or in the Security Council under Article 31. In practice, in view of the inability to agree on an interpretation of Article 79, this has been all the protection other states have had in any event, and none has complained that its interests have been infringed. As a practical matter, however, the question is of no immediate importance so long as there appears to be little likelihood, as at present, of additional trusteeship agreements being presented to the General Assembly.

United Nations as the Administering Authority

Article 81 of the Charter provides that the administering authority "may be one or more states or the Organization itself." All trust territories have in fact single administering authorities except Nauru, which is administered by Australia on behalf of itself, the United Kingdom, and New Zealand. An abortive attempt was made to declare Jerusalem a *corpus separatum* under the jurisdiction of the Trusteeship Council, and international trusteeship has also

[26] For the texts see George V. Wolfe, "The States Directly Concerned: Article 79 of the United Nations Charter," *American Journal of International Law*, Vol. 42 (April 1948), pp. 384-86.

been suggested, officially or otherwise, for such diverse territories as Eritrea, Trieste, the Ruhr, Antarctica, and Formosa.

At the first session of the General Assembly, India proposed a recommendation that the administering authority as a rule should be the United Nations itself, but this proposal was not adopted.[27] Although the Charter makes such United Nations trusteeships possible, it provides no means for the Organization to assert its jurisdiction in the absence of agreement on the part of whatever nation may be in actual control of the territory in question—or of whatever nations may be concerned in a dispute over the territory. An amendment strengthening the powers of the Assembly in this area would surely be controversial. Moreover, it might be a disservice to the United Nations to overload it with too many problems or to put too great a premium on inciting controversy as an excuse for resort to the Organization. Such an amendment might take the form of a new article authorizing the Assembly by a two-thirds vote to assert the jurisdiction of the United Nations, in the capacity of trustee, over a territory involved in a dispute that threatened international peace and security.

It is interesting to speculate on what might have occurred if, for example, all of Korea had been placed under United Nations trusteeship at the end of the Second World War and had not been divided administratively between the United States and the Soviet Union. Similarly, if a United Nations trusteeship could have been declared over Indochina at the start of the fighting, the situation might now be far different. To mention these two examples, however, is also to indicate the great practical difficulties in the way of United Nations trusteeship in such cases—difficulties that range from political opposition to problems of staffing and financing. In fact, a number of suggestions were made from various sources for United Nations trusteeships over both Korea and Indochina, but none was adopted because of the opposition of one or more states whose support was essential. This fact is not necessarily a conclusive argument against United Nations trusteeship, however.

Concern over the creation of what might be considered an "undesirable" precedent probably has constituted a deterring factor of considerable importance in this connection. Some states might well argue that if the United Nations could establish an international trusteeship over Indochina, it could also do so over Tunisia or some other

---

[27] See U.N. General Assembly, First Session, Second Part, Fourth Committee *Official Records*, Part I, 15th-16th Meetings (Nov. 5-7, 1946), pp. 69-87.

comparable area. Or it might be feared in some quarters that such action could be used as a precedent for intervention by the Organization in Kenya because of Mau Mau terrorism. These arguments may overlook the fact that the situation in Indochina threatened world peace, while the situations in certain other dependent territories, at least at the moment, do not. Nevertheless, these arguments are convincing to some states that object to giving the United Nations additional authority in this area.

Role of Trust Territories in International Security

Some observers have suggested that strategic trusteeships be limited to those territories for which the United Nations is the administering authority.[28] This suggestion, however, is predicated on rather drastic changes to be made simultaneously in other portions of the Charter, and, therefore, cannot reasonably be considered standing alone. But it should be pointed out that under the present Charter, Article 83 vests all functions of the United Nations relating to strategic areas in the Security Council. Consequently, to make the Organization the sole administering authority of strategic trust territories—without other far-reaching changes in the Charter—would turn those territories over to the Security Council and make their administration subject to the same obstructionist tactics that have handicapped the Security Council in the exercise of its other functions under the Charter.

Furthermore, it should be remembered that there is in fact only one strategic trust territory and that is the one held by the United States in the Pacific. It was largely at the insistence of the American Government, which believed that control of these former Japanese islands was essential for defense of the United States, that provision for strategic trusts was written into the Charter in the first place. Accordingly, the United States would certainly not agree to any change that would give the Soviet Union a share in the control of the islands.

Another kind of problem arises in connection with Article 84, which declares it to be the "duty" of the administering authority to see that trust territories play their parts "in the maintenance of international peace and security." The administering authority is authorized to "make use of volunteer forces, facilities, and assistance

---

[28] See Clark and Sohn, *op. cit.*, pp. 113-14.

from the trust territory in carrying out the obligations towards the Security Council undertaken in this regard by the administering authority, as well as for local defense and the maintenance of law and order within the trust territory."

The first eight trusteeship agreements considered by the General Assembly contained similar provisions allowing the administering authority to maintain bases and armed forces in the trust territories. India and the Soviet Union proposed that this authority should be exercised in accordance with the obligations of the administering power to the Security Council and be subject to approval by the Council. This was the intent, it was argued, of Article 84; otherwise the trusteeship agreements should make provision for strategic areas. It was further argued that the obligations of the administering authority to the Security Council would have to be governed by Article 43 of the Charter.

The administering authorities, joined by the United States, Canada, the Netherlands, and Uruguay, replied that such a view would in effect leave the trust territories defenseless pending completion of the arrangements under Article 43. The Assembly agreed, when it rejected the Soviet resolution by an overwhelming vote.[29] The question may be raised again in connection with review of the Charter, but it probably has lost much of its relevance in view of the establishment of the trusteeship system and the fact that there is little likelihood of any immediate voluntary expansion of that system.

Concern over the effects of United States nuclear weapons tests in the Pacific, however, may lead to proposals for an amendment to the Charter prohibiting such tests in any trust territory, strategic or nonstrategic. The possibility that such an amendment may be proposed was foreshadowed in the recent debate in the Trusteeship Council over the petition of the Marshallese people requesting the United States to desist from further nuclear tests in the Trust Territory of the Pacific Islands under administration of the United States. But an amendment of this character could hardly be considered apart from the broader question of atomic disarmament, a question that far transcends the trusteeship provisions of the Charter.

[29] U.N. General Assembly, First Session, Second Part, Plenary *Official Records*, 62nd Meeting (Dec. 13, 1946), p. 128.

Other Problems

A number of Member states have been interested in the idea of putting a time limit on trusteeships, at the end of which the trust territory would become independent or the trusteeship agreement would be reviewed.

Duration of Trusts

Ecuador proposed at the San Francisco Conference that the General Assembly be authorized, by a vote of two thirds of its members "to declare the independence of the countries which are subject to a colonial system, a system of dependency, protectorate or mandate, and which have reached a status of being able to direct by their own means their internal and external affairs, and to fulfill the duties imposed and exercise the rights implied by the status of full sovereignty."[30] Iraq also complained of omission of any provision for terminating trusteeships. As the Iraqi delegate declared: "A territory under trusteeship has no specific way of applying for independence and being granted that independence. It is at the mercy of the trustee power. Had provision been made for that, the Charter would have been better." And Egypt proposed that "in all trust territories, within its competence, the General Assembly shall have the power to terminate the status of trusteeship, and declare the territory to be fit for full independence, either at the instance of the administering authority, or upon the recommendation of any member of the Assembly."[31]

The question of a time limit on trusteeship agreements was reopened in the General Assembly in 1946. The Soviet Union then proposed an amendment that each agreement should "remain in force for a period of . . . years and thereafter shall be reviewed and modified according to the degree of attainment of the purposes set forth in Article 76 of the Charter." This amendment was adopted by the Fourth Committee by a vote of 20 to 14 with 1 abstention. A Soviet proposal that the period be set at five years was rejected, and later a Chinese-Indian proposal for ten years was agreed to by a vote

---

[30] *UNCIO Documents,* Vol. 3, p. 405.
[31] For Iraqi statement see *ibid.,* Vol. 8, pp. 133-34. For Egyptian statement see *ibid.,* Vol. 10, p. 510.

of 20 to 7 with 8 abstentions.[32] The amendment was omitted from the trusteeship agreements, however, when the administering authorities declared it was not acceptable.

In placing Italian Somaliland under trusteeship, the Assembly did set a specific period of ten years. It has also asked the Trusteeship Council to include in a separate section of its report to the Assembly information on the estimated time required for each trust territory to attain self-government or independence. The administering authorities have declared this to be impractical, if not impossible. As the next best thing, therefore, the Trusteeship Council has directed the Secretary-General to include in his reports such information as he can obtain from existing data that will throw light on the subject.

The action of the Assembly in regard to Somaliland, one of the most backward of the trust territories, has created problems in other territories that are more advanced but do not have a target date for independence.[33] Most trust territories will have been under trusteeship for almost nine years by 1955—and under mandate, of course, for twenty-five years or so before that. The question of putting a specific time limit on trusteeships may therefore very well be reopened at a conference to review the Charter.

If the question is reopened, the idea would probably be supported by strong arguments from those who have been urging that the trust territories move toward independence as rapidly as possible. In particular, it is pointed out that a specific time limit tends to minimize the possibility of unfortunate misunderstandings arising between the administering authorities and the trust territories regarding whether—or when—independence may be granted. It also encourages both parties to accelerate their plans and their programs to the end that the trust territory may be able to conduct its own affairs effectively when the designated time arrives. On the other hand, the idea has certain practical disadvantages stemming from the obvious fact that various territories are in different stages of development. Moreover, as actual and potential progress is not easy to measure, it would be extremely difficult to predict exactly when the people of a trust territory might be ready to stand on their own feet. In most cases, the argument runs, if the principle of a

---

[32] U.N. General Assembly, First Session, Second Part, Fourth Committee, *Official Records*, Part I, 27th Meeting (Dec. 12, 1946), pp. 174-80.

[33] Wieschoff, *loc. cit.*, p. 132.

time limit were to prevail, the tendency would be to make the trust period too short rather than too long inasmuch as the urge for independence ordinarily far outstrips the capacity of trust areas to make practical progress toward self-government.

Participation of Indigenous Inhabitants in United Nations Activities

Certain of the anti-colonial nations, in particular India and Syria, have sought by various means to increase the participation of indigenous inhabitants of non-self-governing and trust territories in the work of the United Nations. This has been carried to the point of providing representation for the people of these territories in the Trusteeship Council and in the Committee on Information from Non-Self-Governing Territories.

A number of administering authorities, including the United States and France, have attached natives of their trust territories to their United Nations delegations, but the administering authorities generally have opposed the more extreme proposals as dual representation.

In 1952, the Trusteeship Council established a committee of El Salvador, France, Iraq, Thailand, the United Kingdom, and the United States "to study the possibility of associating more closely the inhabitants of the trust territories in the work of the Council."[34] And in 1954, a Syrian resolution on this subject was defeated by a tie vote of 6 to 6. The Syrian delegate announced he would bring the matter up again in the Assembly. Subsequently, the Assembly passed a resolution recommending to the Trusteeship Council various steps "to develop further the participation of the indigenous inhabitants in its work" through the media of visiting missions and the right of petition. Among these steps were suggestions that visiting missions actively seek out public opinion on important problems in the trust territories and encourage public discussion in the territories of the annual reports of the administering authorities.[35]

The Committee on Information from Non-Self-Governing Territories has also concerned itself with this problem. In 1952, Brazil, Cuba, Ecuador, Egypt, India, and Pakistan joined in proposing that the committee accept, on the initiative of the administering

[34] Res. 426 (X), Mar. 26, 1952.
[35] Res. 853 (IX), Dec. 14, 1954.

authorities concerned, the participation of representatives of territories with a wide measure of economic, social, and political responsibility. India was even more specific with a suggestion of a form of associate membership on the committee, and expressed the view that there should be four such associate members each session, with territories that had achieved self-government being given priority.[36] Administering powers successfully resisted the latter proposal on the ground that it would create dual representation, but they were unable to block a resolution of the Assembly inviting the administering states to make possible the association of qualified indigenous representatives of non-self-governing territories in the work of the Committee on Information.[37] It seems clear from the debates that most of the anti-colonial powers anticipated a form of representation independent of the delegation of the administering state and this the administering states cannot accept. This is another question that might be raised at a Charter review conference.

United Nations Representation in Trust Territories

In 1953 the Assembly failed to approve by the necessary two-thirds vote a resolution proposed by the Fourth Committee recommending that the Trusteeship Council consider "designating one or more United Nations representatives for the trust territories for an initial period of two years." These representatives, the resolution suggested,

might, *inter alia,*
(a) Act in an observatory and advisory capacity on all matters affecting the operation of the International Trusteeship System;
(b) Perform a liaison function in the relations between the United Nations, the Administering Authorities and the peoples of the Trust Territories;
(c) Offer good offices, when and where required, in matters relating to the Trusteeship System;
(d) Assist in the appropriate dissemination in the Trust Territories of information about the United Nations;
(e) Make periodic visits to each Trust Territory in the area to which he

[36] U.N. General Assembly, Seventh Session, *Official Records*, "Report of the Committee on Information from Non-Self-Governing Territories," Supplement No. 18 (1952), pp. 10-11.
[37] Res. 645 (VII), Dec. 10, 1952.

is assigned, devoting to each such Territory a period of time appropriate to the conditions and problems prevailing therein;

(f) Report annually to the Secretary-General on his observations and his work, with particular reference to the objectives of the International Trusteeship System and the provisions of the Trusteeship Agreements.[38]

The vote in the Assembly on this resolution was not sufficient to meet the two-thirds requirement; it was, however, sufficiently large to suggest that the last has not been heard of the issue, which was raised by Afghanistan, Brazil, Pakistan, and Saudi Arabia. The approval of such a resolution would be a move toward greater international control of trust territories and is interpreted by administering authorities as derogatory of their own authority in the territories.

Both the Assembly and the Trusteeship Council have from time to time expressed their concern over the desirability of increasing the flow of information about the United Nations to the inhabitants of trust territories and of increasing the understanding by those inhabitants of the role of the United Nations in their lives. A relatively simple development of this character, in the view of many people, would be easier to accomplish and much less objectionable than the more far-reaching proposal of the Fourth Committee.

The experience of the United Nations with Chapters XI, XII, and XIII of the Charter has been marked by a split between the traditional colonial powers and the newly independent states. Great progress has been made, however, in extending self-government since the United Nations was organized. But it should not be inferred that all of this progress has been due solely to the Organization. Much of it would have occurred in the absence of the Organization.

Many of the problems that have arisen in the United Nations relating to the powers, functions, and responsibilities of the Organization in regard to dependent peoples might be solved by amendment of the Charter, assuming that agreement could be reached on such amendments. Practically all of these problems, however, are caused by underlying differences of approach as between the colonial and anti-colonial powers. It is doubtful, therefore, whether an attempt to develop new provisions of the Charter

---

[38] "Means Toward Improving the Functioning of the International Trusteeship System," U.N. Doc. A/2608 (Dec. 6, 1953), Annex F.

would resolve these differences. In fact, such an attempt might aggravate them.

Furthermore, even if amendments were somehow agreed to by the required two-thirds majority of the Member states, they might never come into force. It is highly likely that any amendment to increase greatly the authority of the Organization with respect to dependent peoples would be vetoed by either the United Kingdom or France, which—by failing to ratify them—could prevent the amendment from becoming effective. Similarly, any amendment to restrict the authority of the United Nations in this field would undoubtedly be unacceptable to the Soviet Union, which could prevent such an amendment from becoming effective by refusing to ratify it.

Perhaps what is most needed in this field of United Nations activity is not amendment of the Charter but a more reasonable approach on the part of all concerned in a spirit of mutual accommodation.

PART FIVE

PROPOSALS RELATING TO GENERAL ORGANIZATIONAL STRUCTURE AND ADMINISTRATION

CHAPTER X

Membership and Voting in the Security Council

Pʀᴏʙᴀʙʟʏ the most important organizational problem confronting the United Nations is that of the future of the Security Council. The inability of the Council to act in the manner that the framers of the Charter had expected became manifest soon after the Organization came into being and has become increasingly apparent as the years have passed. Not only has the frequent use of the veto by the Soviet Union been a source of the trouble, but also there have been growing doubts among the smaller nations that the Council is as broadly representative as it should be to act for the Organization as a whole with respect to the maintenance of peace.

Questions involving the membership and the voting procedure of the Security Council were vital issues in the formulation of the Dumbarton Oaks Proposals and in the final negotiations leading to the agreement on the Charter at the San Francisco Conference. These questions continue to be issues of great public interest and will so remain so long as the Charter continues to "confer on the Security Council primary responsibility for the maintenance of international peace and security,"[1] and the Member states "agree to accept and carry out the decisions of the Security Council."[2] Because of this delegation of responsibility and power to the Council, proposals to change either its composition or its procedures are bound to awaken keen interest everywhere, especially in the major nations that now enjoy permanent membership and special voting privileges in the Council.

Proposals for Changing Membership

Secretary of State Stettinius, in presenting the Charter to the Senate for its advice and consent to ratification, noted that the five nations given permanent membership on the Security Council were selected because they "possess most of the industrial and military resources of the world. They will have to bear the principal responsi-

[1] Art. 24 (1).
[2] Art. 25.

299

bility for maintaining peace in the foreseeable future. The provisions of membership recognize this inescapable fact."[3]

The composition of the Security Council is firmly embedded in the Charter. Article 23 states that the Council shall consist of eleven members and five of them—China, France, the United Kingdom, the Soviet Union, and the United States—are named as permanent members. The six nonpermanent members are elected by the General Assembly for two-year terms. There is no provision, short of amendment of the Charter, however, for the replacement of permanent members, for the addition of new permanent members, or for changing the size of the Council. In these respects the Charter differs substantially from the Covenant of the League of Nations, which authorized the League Council, "with the approval of the majority of the Assembly" to "name additional Members of the League, whose Representatives shall always be Members of the Council."[4] Hence it was possible, when Germany and the Soviet Union joined the League, in 1926 and 1934, respectively, to give them seats as permanent members without formally amending the Covenant. The Covenant also permitted an increase in the number of nonpermanent members of the Council by the same procedure.

There was considerable opposition at the San Francisco Conference to the rigidity of the composition of the Security Council, on the ground that the "great powers" of the 1940's might not be the same as the "great powers" of the 1960's. But the concept of associating power and responsibility as they existed in 1945, and not as they *might* exist at some projected time in the future, prevailed. In the past ten years, however, there have been a number of changes in the world situation that raise significant questions about the composition of the Security Council. The problem of Communist China seeking representation in the United Nations, the attainment of independence and increasing world stature by India, the growing importance of many Asian countries, the readmission of Western Germany, Japan, and Italy to the society of nations, but not to the United Nations, and the development of regional and other collective defense groupings, all have overtones that might seriously affect the organization of the Council.

Up to the present time, relatively little attention has been given

[3] *Charter of the United Nations,* Hearings before the Senate Committee on Foreign Relations, 79 Cong. 1 sess., p. 211.

[4] Art. 4(2) of the Covenant.

to the problem of reconstituting the Security Council, despite the fact that it has not been one of the most successful operating organs of the United Nations. In the public mind, the weaknesses of the Council have largely been associated with excessive use of the veto by the Soviet Union. But, although there is no assurance that the Council would be more effective, especially in the field of enforcement action, without some modification of the veto power or a relaxation of cold-war tensions, it is conceivable that some change in the composition of the Council might improve its functioning in the pacific settlement of disputes. Furthermore, it is possible to envisage changes in the composition of the Council that might of themselves decrease cold war tensions and thereby encourage more effective action in so far as enforcement measures are concerned.

Aside from certain of the supranational proposals for changes in the organization of the Security Council and other suggestions of a type that would change fundamentally the nature of the United Nations—such as reorganization without the Soviet Union or the withdrawal of the United States—suggestions to reconstitute the Council have been made along the following lines: the permanent members might be changed; the number of permanent members might be increased; the Council as a whole might be increased in size; the Council might be decreased in size; permanent membership as a concept might be abolished; and the Council might be reconstituted to give more direct representation to regional groups of states.

Permanent Membership for India

Despite the fact that the problem of membership on the Security Council has not been given more than passing attention up to the present time, there is accumulating evidence that this question might loom very large in the event of a General Conference for review of the Charter. The matter has apparently been given some study in the Department of State. One high official recently alluded to the theoretical possibility of proposing "changes, including additions, in the membership of the five permanent members of the Security Council."[5]

Reference has also appeared in the press to discussions in the

[5] David W. Wainhouse, Deputy Assistant Secretary of State for International Organization Affairs, "Some Problems of Charter Review," U. S. Department of State *Bulletin*, Vol. 31 (Nov. 15, 1954), p. 740.

executive branch "two or three layers down from the top" relating to some workable method of "cushioning" the possible admission of Communist China to the United Nations. The suggestion has been made that Communist China be admitted to membership in the United Nations but not given a seat on the Security Council. "Neither of the Chinas," according to this idea, "would keep the permanent seat on the Security Council now held by Nationalist China." With the removal of Nationalist China from the Security Council, but with both Nationalist and Communist China being members of the United Nations, "it would then be necessary to name another Asian nation to the vacant seat in order to keep a proper balance. Under the compromise being discussed India would be proposed for the vacancy." In support of this suggestion, it was argued that the seating of India on the Council instead of either Nationalist or Communist China "would contribute to the goal of increasing the stature of Prime Minister Nehru and a middle of the road government in India as the focus of leadership for wavering Asian peoples. The threat is, of course, that Communist China will become such a focus."[6]

This suggestion does not envisage any enlargement of the Council, but rather the substitution of India as a permanent member in lieu of Nationalist China. In view of the fact that an amendment to the Charter would be necessary to bring about such a result, it would be just as feasible from a legal point of view, and perhaps more practical from a political point of view, merely to increase the number of permanent members from five to six.

Trygve Lie has recently referred to suggestions "that the number of Permanent Members be increased to six, with total membership [in the Security Council] set at thirteen," thus involving the election of seven, instead of six, nonpermanent members. "In such event," he suggests, "India's candidacy for Permanent Membership should be seriously considered." He added that "*if* the number of members is increased, Asia should have a priority in the form of a stronger representation than that which it now enjoys."[7] But an amendment to the Charter that would add India as a permanent member of the Council instead of substituting it for Nationalist China would not meet the political problem posed by the controversy over the possible seating of Communist China.

[6] Marquis Childs, "Red Chinese Problem," *St. Louis Post Dispatch* (July 30, 1953).

[7] Trygve Lie, *In the Cause of Peace* (1954), p. 433.

Quite apart from the political issues involved, however, there have been other indications that India might be considered for a permanent seat on the Council. Prime Minister Nehru is on record as having remarked that India is "obviously the fourth country" in the world after the United States, the Soviet Union, and Red China. Although the Government of India has not filed an official request for a permanent seat on the Council, Nehru has made it clear that the position of India is such as to enable his Government to demand that Indian counsel be given more weight in international affairs.[8]

More Adequate Regional Representation

General Romulo, Chairman of the Philippine Delegation to the United Nations, on various occasions has urged the desirability of Asia having more adequate representation on the Security Council. He has called on the United Nations "to revise the understanding or misunderstanding of San Francisco," which reserved no place on the Council for a nonpermanent member from Asia. In this connection, he has proposed that consideration be given to "the abolition of permanent seats in the Security Council."[9] Thus he would seek additional Asian representation not through the formula of adding one member, but by doing away with the principle of permanent membership. British representative Sir Gladwyn Jebb also has suggested that one "far-reaching" reform of the Charter that might meet with acceptance at a conference for review of the Charter might be "some enlargement of the present membership of the Security Council so as to give greater effect to what the Charter calls the principle of 'equitable geographical representation.'"[10]

Consideration cannot be given to the matter of state membership on the Council without enquiring whether the concept of selecting the nonpermanent members with due regard "to equitable geographical distribution"—as the Charter now provides in Article

[8] *New York Times* (Oct. 1, 1954). See also *ibid.* (Sept. 24, 1953), in which Nehru is quoted as stating that "it is going to be less and less feasible in the future for any world organization to leave Asia out of account."

[9] Address of General Carlos P. Romulo, Chairman of the Philippine Delegation to the Ninth Session of the General Assembly. See U.N. General Assembly, Ninth Session, Plenary, *Official Records,* 479th Meeting (Sept. 27, 1954), pp. 82-83.

[10] Sir Gladwyn Jebb, "The British Commonwealth, the United States of America and the United Nations." Speech delivered at Johns Hopkins University, Baltimore, Md., Jan. 13, 1954, Central Office of Information, London, *International Survey,* No. 145, App. 1 (Jan. 28, 1954).

23(1)—might not be replaced by a system of regional representation. It has been suggested that the Council might be reconstituted along regional lines by projecting regional organizations into the universal machinery of the United Nations.[11] One proponent of such a development has noted: "If the Security Council were to consist of representatives from North America, India, China, the Soviet Union, Western Europe, Eastern Europe, Latin America, Africa, the Middle East, and Southeast Asia, it could provide an institution capable of arriving at decisions binding on, and supported by, the peoples of the world."[12]

In actual practice the nonpermanent members are considered as representing—in some respects at least—the principal geographic regions of the world. Thus it is customary to elect one nonpermanent member from the Arab states, one from Western Europe, one from the British Commonwealth, one from Eastern Europe, and two from Latin America. This is far different, however, from the idea of selecting representatives of regional organizations such as the North Atlantic Treaty Organization and the Organization of American States. In the one case members of the Council are states from a geographic area. In the second case, however, the regional organizations might select states to represent the regional organization itself or might simply select a delegation to represent and vote on instructions from the regional organization.

Such proposals to reconstitute the Council along regional lines are far more radical in their organizational implications than suggestions to change the membership of the Council. In some instances they presuppose the creation of federal type institutions in each of these areas, which in turn would be represented in the world organization. In others they suggest in effect a reversion to the approach to a world international organization first put forth during the war by Sir Winston Churchill who believed that any world-wide international organization should be based on regional groupings because only countries directly affected by a dispute could be expected to "apply themselves with sufficient vigor to secure" settle-

<hr/>

[11] Robert D. Hayton, "Thoughts on a Role for the Inter-American Regional Group in the Community of Nations," *Proceedings of the American Society of International Law at its Forty-eighth Annual Meeting, April 22-24, 1954* (1954), p. 64.

[12] R. W. G. Mackay, Comments on "Expanding the United Nations Community," *Annals of the American Academy of Political and Social Science*, Vol. 296 (November 1954), p. 102.

ment of a dispute.[13] This view was rejected in the Declaration of Four Nations on General Security agreed to at Moscow on October 30, 1943, which recognized the necessity of establishing a "general international organization."[14]

The growing importance of regional defense pacts during the postwar years does suggest, however, that a conference for review of the Charter might give renewed consideration to the regional approach to international organization. Methods of giving representation to regional organizations, or developing closer relationships between the United Nations and such regional organizations, short of a complete revamping of the United Nations Charter, might take the form of changing the composition of the Security Council. Proposals of this type would require not only amendments to the Charter but in most cases substantial changes in agreements establishing the regional organizations themselves. It would be hard to envisage such a development without the conclusion, at a minimum, of a series of protocols to these agreements authorizing the regional organizations to elect representatives to the Council.

Flexible Membership

Proposals to change the membership of the Security Council by amendment of the Charter are subject to the criticism that the composition of the Council should not be written inflexibly into the Charter. As one writer observed, who could have said in 1945 that the United States, the United Kingdom, the Soviet Union, France, and China would be the "all-powerful five Great Powers" a decade later.[15] By the same token, if the Charter should be amended to change the composition of the Security Council in 1956, who could say that change would still be a logical one in 1966?

Perhaps consideration could profitably be given to providing for greater flexibility in determining the composition of the Council. One suggestion is that of amending the Charter to provide "some method for redetermining every 10 years who should be permanent members of the Security Council."[16] Such an amendment might fol-

---

[13] *The Memoirs of Cordell Hull,* Vol. 2 (1948), p. 1642.

[14] U.S. Department of State *Bulletin,* Vol. 9 (Nov. 6, 1943), p. 308.

[15] Clark Eichelberger, "The General Assembly," *Annual Review of United Nations Affairs, 1951* (1952), p. 16.

[16] Statement of C. Leeds Bauman, Minneapolis Attorney, *Review of the United Nations Charter,* Hearings before a Subcommittee of the Senate Committee on Foreign Relations, 83 Cong. 2 sess., Pt. 7, pp. 855-56.

low the provision of the Covenant of the League of Nations, noted earlier, that gave the Assembly and the Council of the League a voting formula enabling them to change the composition of the Council without resorting to the laborious amendment procedure.

Political Considerations in Reconstituting the Council

Any alteration relating to the composition of the Security Council, whether involving a change in permanent members, increase in size, abolition of permanent membership, change to regional representation, or a formula for changes in the future by a method less difficult than formal amendment of the Charter could only be brought about by amendment. An amendment on this delicate subject to be effective would have to be acceptable to the present permanent members of the Security Council, including Nationalist China and the Soviet Union.

There is at the very least considerable doubt whether Nationalist China would be willing to approve an amendment changing the composition of the Council along some of the lines suggested above. China could hardly be expected to vote itself out of its permanent seat, although there is the possibility of persuading Nationalist China to accept an increase in the number of permanent members, an increase in the total membership, or some change involving greater regional representation. The day may come, however, when Communist China would have enough votes in the General Assembly so that its representatives, instead of the representatives of Nationalist China, could be seated in that organ. In such circumstances, Nationalist China might find it necessary to accept some kind of compromise arrangement that would go so far as to reconstitute the Council in a manner similar to that suggested above, possibly without either Nationalist or Communist China being represented, at least as permanent members on the Council.

There would surely be some question whether the Soviet Union would be willing to accept any proposal to reconstitute the Security Council. The addition of India as a permanent member might be acceptable to the Soviet Union. Such an admission would set a precedent, however, for the admission of Japan or Western Germany or Italy.

Any suggestions to change the size or composition of the Security

Council would raise complex problems. The framers of the Charter were concerned with the problem of size. On the one hand, they desired to keep the Council as small as possible to enable it to deal effectively and efficiently with its business. The larger the Council, the greater the difficulty of obtaining the necessary action. At the same time, there was constant pressure to increase the size of the Council so that more states might have a chance to be elected to membership. It was necessary at the San Francisco Conference to strike a balance between the various groups of states desiring representation, between the great powers and the lesser powers, and at the same time to keep the Council small enough to be efficient.

If consideration should be given to enlarging the Council, there is the possibility of setting up a third category of members—semi-permanent members—as was the case in the Council of the League of Nations. States not having permanent status might be eligible for re-election and thus expect to serve on a fairly continuous basis. This device would not grant such semi-permanent members the special voting privileges now accorded permanent members but would give them the added importance that would attach to continuous membership on the Council. If the size of the Council were to be increased by the addition of new permanent members, it would increase the opportunity of using the veto. If Germany, Italy, and Japan, for example, were given permanent seats on the Council, it might be necessary to make some changes in the voting formula lest the Council become even less effective than it has been in recent years. On the other hand, if the power of the Council should be reduced to the making of recommendations instead of taking decisions relating to enforcement action, the matter of membership on the Council and voting in that organ would assume lesser importance.

Although there is a possibility that considerable pressure might develop in favor of increasing the size of the Council, it is doubtful that it would be politically practicable to reduce its size. Since the establishment of the United Nations, there has been constant complaint that small states do not have adequate representation on the Council. It is extremely unlikely that they would consent to further reductions in their representation.

In the present state of international tension, any proposals to change the composition of the Council will unavoidably be considered in political terms. Questions would arise regarding how the

newly admitted states would vote, and whether they would be inclined to side with the free world or the Soviet world. So long as
the veto is retained, however, does it really make a great deal of
difference? Or, so long as the General Assembly is gradually replacing the Security Council as the most influential United Nations
organ, does it make much difference how the Council, hampered
as it is by the veto, is constituted? These are questions that must
be kept in mind in considering the practicability of such proposals.
Their practicability cannot be judged outside the context of the
total international situation.

The political implications of changes in the membership of the
Security Council might be very far-reaching. It is difficult to imagine, for example, that there could be much tampering with the composition of the Council without precipitating a bitter power struggle over the question of Chinese Communist representation. Such
a struggle might seriously damage the United Nations. On the other
hand, it is not impossible to imagine a situation in two or three
years in which certain changes in the membership of the Council
might become a *quid pro quo* in negotiating, within the framework
of the United Nations system, a peaceful settlement between the
free world and the Communist-dominated nations.

The likelihood that any of these proposals might be acceptable
depends in large measure on the situation prevailing if and when a
conference for review of the Charter is held. Yet in that very fact
may be found their strength. Former Secretary-General Trygve Lie,
in advancing his suggestion that the number of permanent members might be increased from five to six, indicated some doubt
"whether this is practical policy in the prevailing international
situation."[17] But currently, the international situation seems to be
undergoing something of a change. It is too early to judge whether
this trend will continue. If the comment of President Eisenhower
in December 1954 that there is less danger of war today than at any
time since 1950[18] should prove true, however, it may be that far-
reaching changes of the type suggested might prove feasible in one
or two years. They should not be rejected outright at this time. In
such circumstances and in view of the fact that the assumption of
great power unanimity that underlies much of the authority of the
Security Council has thus far proven in error, serious study might

[17] Lie, *op. cit.*, p. 433.
[18] Transcript of President Eisenhower's Press Conference on Foreign and Home
Affairs, *New York Times* (Dec. 9, 1954).

well be given to the composition of the Council itself as well as to the matter of circumscribing the veto.

Background of the Veto Problem

With very few exceptions, most Americans tend to identify the great power veto as the principal element of weakness in the Charter, and many have urged the United States Government to take steps to modify it, to eliminate it, or to curb its excessive use. There may be some difference of opinion whether the veto is a cause or a result; whether it is bad in itself or whether it is merely symptomatic of the gulf that exists between the Soviet Union and the non-Communist world. But there is almost complete agreement among the American people that the Soviet Union has overstepped the bounds of propriety in resorting to the veto some sixty times in ten years, and that something ought to be done about it. They say that the veto has disrupted the work of the Security Council and greatly weakened the United Nations as a whole, that it has blocked the admission of peace-loving nations and prevented the peaceful settlement of disputes. They claim that it has embittered great power relations, has confused and delayed the process of negotiation, and has compelled Members of the United Nations to seek out alternative methods of coping with problems that the Security Council should have handled with efficiency and dispatch. Finally, they argue that as a result of all these things, it has dealt the cause of the United Nations a blow so far as its prestige is concerned.

As a result of the controversy over the veto both in this country and abroad, a large number of proposals have been advanced either to change the voting procedures in the Security Council by formal amendment of the Charter or to meet the problem in some more indirect fashion. As a preliminary to the analysis of these proposals, it is necessary first to review the origins of Article 27 and the way the veto has worked in practice.[19]

[19] On this problem generally see Leland M. Goodrich and Edvard Hambro, *Charter of the United Nations: Commentary and Documents* (1949), Chap. 5; Dwight E. Lee, "The Genesis of the Veto," *International Organization,* Vol. 1 (February 1947), pp. 33-42; Norman J. Padelford, "The Use of the Veto," *International Organization,* Vol. 2 (June 1948), pp. 227-46; Myres S. McDougal and Richard N. Gardner, "Veto and the Charter: An Interpretation for Survival," *Yale Law Journal,* Vol. 60 (February 1951), pp. 256-92; Subcommittee on the United Nations Charter, Senate Committee on Foreign Relations, *Review of the United Nations Charter: A Collection of Documents,* S. Doc. 87, 83 Cong. 2 sess.

The voting procedure of any international organization is important because it determines the degree of control that the various members exercise over the activities of the organization. Article 27, which lays down the rules for voting in the Security Council, is one of the most important articles in the Charter. It has both a positive and a negative side. In its *positive* sense it means that, when important decisions are taken by the Council, they will have the strength and the influence of the great powers back of them. In its *negative* sense it means that any great power, at its own discretion, can block action on any substantive matters considered by the Council.

At the Dumbarton Oaks Conference, the participating governments were concerned above all with the creation of an international organization capable of maintaining world peace and se-curity.[20] They knew from experience that aggressors act quickly, and that unless those interested in the maintenance of law and order can move with speed and precision, their cause may be lost. Thus the Dumbarton Oaks Proposals carefully avoided one of the glaring weaknesses of the League of Nations—the division of authority between the Assembly and the Council with respect to enforcement action. The proposals recommended that primary responsibility for the maintenance of peace be vested in the Security Council of the new organization, which was to be a small body made up of only eleven members, geared to act speedily and decisively in time of crisis without interference from the General Assembly.

Moreover, the Security Council was to be equipped with the "teeth" necessary to do its job. The Council of the League of Nations could suggest, could advise, could recommend, but in the final analysis each state decided for itself the extent to which it would back up the decisions of the Council with its armed forces. The Security Council, on the other hand, was to be given full authority to make decisions relating to the prevention and suppression of aggression that would be binding on *all* the Members of the Organization. Obviously, in the execution of its security functions the Council would have to rely chiefly on the great states whose collective industrial strength and military might had been so successful

---

(Jan. 7, 1954), pp. 562-81; Subcommittee on the United Nations Charter, Senate Committee on Foreign Relations, *The Problem of the Veto in the United Nations Security Council*, Staff Study No. 1, 83 Cong. 2 sess. (Feb. 19, 1954).

[20] See the volume in this Brookings series, *A History of the United Nations Charter*.

in the struggle against the Axis nations. Given the concentration of power in the world, there seemed to be no other alternative. Thus the teamwork and the unity that had characterized the United Nations war effort could be utilized in maintaining peace. In keeping with their responsibilities, the five powers were awarded a special status in the Security Council in respect to tenure and voting procedure.

In respect to tenure, the Dumbarton Oaks Proposals followed the example of the League of Nations in recommending permanent seats on the Security Council for the five great powers. On the assumption that the maintenance of peace is of concern to *all* states, however, six nonpermanent members were to be elected by the Assembly. Thus the great powers were to be in a minority so far as numbers were concerned.

In respect to voting procedure, the conferees at Dumbarton Oaks could not reach agreement, and the matter was postponed until the Crimea Conference in February 1945. There President Roosevelt submitted a formula that was approved by Marshal Stalin and Prime Minister Churchill and was later accepted by China. This formula, in effect, reinforced the special position of the permanent members by assuring each of them that the new organization could take no important action without its consent. It also guaranteed them that, through their control of the amending process, their special position could not be changed unless they collectively agreed to such change.

The veto was thus the price the United Nations had to pay in order to ensure the participation of the great states and to provide the military power necessary to back up the decisions of the Security Council. Representatives of the permanent members repeatedly told the small and medium-sized states that it was either a Charter with the veto or no Charter at all. "You may go home from San Francisco—if you wish," Senator Connally warned the delegates, "and report that you have defeated the veto. Yes . . . you can say you defeated the veto. . . . But you can also say, 'We *tore up the Charter!*'"[21] Faced with a choice of this kind, the smaller states protested with all the vigor at their command. But in the end they accepted Article 27 by a vote of 30 to 2 with 15 states abstaining.[22] Be-

[21] Tom Connally and Alfred Steinberg, *My Name Is Tom Connally* (1954), p. 283.

[22] The fifteen states that abstained generally opposed the veto provision but withheld their votes to avoid a demonstration of disunity.

fore they did so, however, they took note of the following assurance contained in the joint statement of June 7, 1945, made by the four sponsoring powers interpreting Article 27: "It is not to be assumed that the permanent members, any more than the non-permanent members, would use their 'veto' power willfully to obstruct the operation of the Council."[23]

Origins and Provisions of Article 27

The Yalta voting formula, as it was approved by the San Francisco Conference as Article 27 of the Charter, provides that the Council shall make its decisions on procedural matters "by an affirmative vote of seven members." It also provides that decisions on other matters are to be made by a majority of seven "including the concurring votes of the permanent members; provided that, in decisions under Chapter VI, and under paragraph 3 of Article 52, a party to a dispute shall abstain from voting." There are thus three types of matters on which the Security Council may vote: procedural, quasi-judicial, and political. If the question under consideration is a simple matter of procedure—such as the designation of a chairman or fixing the date and place of a meeting—the vote of *any* seven members is sufficient to determine the position of the Council. In all other cases, however, decisions are made by an affirmative vote of seven members, *including* the five permanent members, except that in connection with the pacific settlement of disputes, parties to the dispute must abstain from voting.[24]

This means that when the Council is performing its "quasi-judicial" function of promoting the peaceful settlement of disputes, no nation, whether large or small, can be a judge in its own case. No party to a dispute is entitled to vote on certain questions such as: whether a matter should be investigated; whether the continuation of a situation or dispute is likely to threaten the peace; whether the parties should be called on to settle the dispute by means of their own choice; whether the Council should recommend terms of settle-

[23] See text of statement in U.N. Information Organizations and U.S. Library of Congress, *Documents of the United Nations Conference on International Organization,* Vol. 11 (1945), pp. 711-14. (Hereinafter cited as *UNCIO Documents.*)
[24] See Francis O. Wilcox, "The Yalta Voting Formula," *American Political Science Review,* Vol. 39 (October 1945), pp. 943-56; see also, "The Rule of Unanimity in the Security Council," *Proceedings of the American Society of International Law* (1946), pp. 51-83.

ment; whether the dispute should be referred to the General Assembly or to a regional agency, and so on. It should be noted, however, that if a permanent member is *not* a party to a dispute, it can
veto questions of this type on any grounds it wishes.

Finally, whenever the Security Council is performing its "political" functions of taking action with respect to the maintenance of
peace and security, a unanimous vote of the five great powers is
necessary. The concurrence of all the permanent members is required, for example, for decisions involving: a determination of the
existence of a threat to the peace or a breach of the peace; the use
of armed force or other enforcement measures; the approval of
agreements for the supply of armed forces for the use of the Security
Council; and recommendations concerning the regulation of armaments. Similarly, unanimity is required in connection with certain
other votes of a political character including the recommendations
of the Security Council with respect to the admission of new Members and the selection of a Secretary-General.

At the San Francisco Conference, the smaller powers vigorously
attacked the unanimity requirement as the negation of the democratic principles on which the United Nations ought to rest.[25] They
charged that it delivered up the world to the domination of what
was in effect a governing body of big powers. They insisted that it
was a gross violation of the sovereign equality of states. And they
argued that it was a permanent invitation to the great powers to
veto at will the peaceful settlement of disputes.

In fact, the provisions of Article 27 reach into every corner of the
Charter. Generally speaking, no important decision can be taken by
the Security Council without the approval of the permanent members. Any great power, if it chooses to do so, can block the admission
of new Members. It can prevent the expulsion of a Member or the
suspension of membership rights. It can hold up the appointment
of the Secretary-General. It can block the accession of a state to
the Statute of the International Court of Justice. More important
still, it can prevent the adoption of an amendment to the Charter
by refusing to ratify it. Thus the veto power is imbedded with what
might seem to be eternal finality in the fundamental framework of
the United Nations.

Proponents of the veto pointed out that Article 27 represented a

---

[25] For a summary of the discussion of this problem at the San Francisco Conference, see *UNCIO Documents*, Vol. 11, pp. 304-63.

significant advance over the provisions of the Covenant of the League of Nations. In the Council of the League, substantive decisions could be taken only by a unanimous vote of *all* its members. The smallest and weakest member—perhaps a state of only a million inhabitants—could block action. Thus the Yalta voting formula does not vest the permanent members of the Security Council with any right that the permanent members of the League Council did not possess under the League. What it does is to remove the veto power from the nonpermanent members of the Council. Moreover, no state—not even a great power—is permitted to vote if it is a party to a dispute before the Council under the peaceful settlement articles of the Charter. No state can be a judge in its own cause. These advances represent substantial forward steps in the slow and painful evolution of international organization.

Soviet Misuse of the Veto

Although most of the framers of the Charter were not naive about the prospects for world peace, it is fair to say that they were hopeful that the great powers would conclude that their basic national interests might best be served by working together in a spirit of harmony and unity within the framework of the United Nations. They had collaborated to win the war. With the responsibility for the maintenance of world order in their hands, they might respond in the same co-operative way to win the peace. The Yalta voting formula, by requiring a certain amount of teamwork before the Security Council could function effectively, might even serve as a kind of cement that would help bind the great powers together.

When the Security Council began to function, this hope rapidly faded as the Soviet Union used the veto from the outset to block action. Beginning on February 16, 1946, when the Soviet Union voted down a United States proposal relating to the withdrawal of foreign troops from Syria and Lebanon, Soviet representatives used the veto sixty times during the next ten years, which openly revealed the growing dissension among the big powers and seriously hampered the work of the Council. Forty-three of these votes were cast during the first four years of the United Nations when the Council was in its formative stages. They thus had a profound impact on the new organization, disrupting its activities at a critical point in its evolution.[26]

[26] See the volume in this Brookings series, *The Organization and Procedures of the United Nations.*

The effect of the veto has been felt in nearly every area of the work of the Security Council, as the following examples of matters vetoed illustrate: on September 20, 1946, a resolution providing for a Security Council Commission to investigate frontier incidents along the Greek border; on October 1, 1946, a recommendation that Italy be admitted to membership in the United Nations; on June 22, 1948, a resolution approving the plan of the United Nations Atomic Energy Commission for atomic control; on October 25, 1948, a resolution relating to the lifting of the Berlin blockade; on October 18, 1949, a resolution proposing a census and verification of armed forces and conventional armaments of Member states; and on October 12, 1950, the re-election of Secretary-General Lie.[27]

Nearly half of the vetoes—some twenty-eight—have been used to prevent admission of new Members to the United Nations. On two occasions a formal veto has been used to reject candidates for the post of Secretary-General. Some twenty-one have been used in connection with disputes and situations before the Council, and four have dealt with problems of armaments control. Apart from the Soviet Union, France is the only other permanent member to have resorted to the veto. On one occasion, June 26, 1946, the French representative voted with the Soviet Union against the majority of the Council on the ruling of its President that a resolution dealing with the Spanish question was procedural and therefore not subject to the veto. Fourteen months later, France vetoed a Soviet proposal providing for the creation of a commission on Indonesia.

This does not mean that the Soviet Union has exercised a monopoly on negative voting. In fact, voting statistics show that during at least the first year of the United Nations, the other great powers in the Council cast more negative votes than the Soviet Union. It does mean, however, that the negative votes of the other great powers have not been vetoes—that is, they have not resulted in blocking action on measures supported by seven other members of the Council.[28]

Statistics, of course, do not tell the whole story, for there is no way of measuring what might be called the "prenatal" effect of the veto. No doubt many constructive ideas never reached the voting stage in the Council because of the impending threat of a Soviet

[27] For the complete list see *ibid.*, and U.S. Library of Congress, Legislative Reference Service, *Report [on the] Use of the Veto in the Security Council Through 1953* (1953). Reprinted in S. Doc. 87, 83 Cong. 2 sess., pp. 577-80.

[28] See Padelford, *loc. cit.*, pp. 231-32. In 165 votes, the Soviet Union voted "no" on 24 occasions, China 27, Great Britain 29, the United States 34.

veto. Moreover, many problems that should have been handled by the Council have had to be met by costly, time-consuming resort to other channels of action.

It has frequently been argued that the Soviet Union, by its obstructionism, has not only violated the Charter but has scrapped the implied promise made at the San Francisco Conference by the permanent members of the Security Council not to use their veto power "wilfully" to obstruct the operation of the Council. Strictly speaking, of course, the Soviet Union—as all other members of the Council—has a right to vote against any proposal that it considers inimical to its national interest. Clearly Article 27, coupled with the principle of state sovereignty, permits disagreement as well as agreement. Nevertheless, in view of the unique role of the great powers in the United Nations, the unanimity requirement places on them a special responsibility to use the veto sparingly and to exert every effort to reconcile divergent views in order to make the Organization work.

Attempts to Deal with the Veto Without Amending the Charter

Formal revision of the Charter is not the only means by which the problem of the veto could be met. Many other methods have been suggested. Some of these, such as the reinterpretation of the Charter or the proposal that the great powers consult together before formal votes are taken, involve agreement among the permanent members to make Article 27 function more smoothly. Still others, such as the strengthening of the General Assembly, or the conclusion of collective defense pacts, are designed to by-pass the veto by the creation of security machinery outside the Security Council. Most of these methods have been explored since 1946 but with only partial success.[29]

Students of the Charter may differ over the basic causes of the veto, but most of them will agree that the Security Council had a discouraging beginning. When the Council convened in January 1946, its supporters hoped that it would not be confronted by any major problems at the outset in order that it might devote its time

---

[29] See the volumes in this Brookings series, *The United Nations and the Maintenance of International Peace and Security;* and *Regional Security and the United Nations.*

to working out more precise and detailed rules of procedure. These hopes were quickly shattered. After a few weeks, the Council was confronted by the difficult Iranian problem. Then in rapid succession came the situations in Greece, Indonesia, and Syria and Lebanon. Seriously impeded by its lack of rules of procedure, the Council was forced to improvise, and in many instances unfortunate precedents were established.

There is little doubt, also, that too much emphasis was placed on formal voting as the Council got under way. At the San Francisco Conference, it was hoped by many of the delegates that great power differences might be reconciled through frequent consultations and that formal "show-downs" would be avoided. In practice, the Council did not function that way. After the Conference, consultations among the five permanent members became the exception rather than the rule. More and more it became customary to insist on record votes—a practice that creates many difficulties in connection with the work of an international diplomatic body. This tended to widen the rifts between the Soviet Union and the Western powers rather than to narrow them. Even more discouraging, however, was the development of increasing bitterness between them caused by events outside the United Nations. This bitterness was exacerbated by the repeated use of the veto by the Soviet Union. As a result of the situation in the Security Council, the veto problem was brought before the General Assembly.

Resolutions of the General Assembly

At the first session of the General Assembly in the fall of 1946, the Assembly, after long and acrimonious debate, adopted a resolution requesting the permanent members "to make every effort, in consulting with one another and with fellow members of the Security Council to ensure that the use of the special voting privilege of its permanent members does not impede the Security Council in reaching decisions promptly." The resolution further recomended to the Council "the early adoption of practices and procedures, consistent with the Charter, to assist in reducing the difficulties in the application of Article 27 and to ensure the prompt and effective exercise by the Security Council of its functions."[30]

This exhortation did not result in any important changes in the

[30] Res. 40(I), Dec. 13, 1946.

practices and procedures of the Council, nor did it bring about any diminution in the use of the veto. By the time the second session of the General Assembly convened, opposition to the veto had increased substantially. Secretary of State Marshall certainly reflected prevailing opinion when he pointed out that the "abuse of the right of unanimity" had prevented the Security Council from fulfilling its true functions, particularly in cases relating to the peaceful settlement of disputes and the admission of new members. In the circumstances, the United States had come to the conclusion that "the only practicable method for improving this situation," was a "liberalization of the voting procedures in the Council."[31] Largely as a result of American leadership, the General Assembly adopted a resolution requesting the Interim Committee to consider the problem of voting and report its conclusions to the third session of the Assembly.[32]

Following the report of its Interim Committee, the General Assembly, on April 14, 1949, approved a third resolution on the veto question by a vote of 43 to 6, with 2 abstentions.[33] The resolution, which summed up the long study of the Interim Committee, included the following recommendations:

1. The Security Council should deem some thirty-five decisions procedural and conduct its business accordingly. These decisions, which were annexed to the resolution, were considered by the Interim Committee to be procedural in accordance with its interpretation of the Charter.

2. The permanent members should seek agreement on the possible kinds of decisions in which they might forbear to exercise their veto right when seven affirmative votes are cast in favor of such decisions. In seeking agreement, the permanent members were to give favorable consideration to the list of twenty-one such questions prepared by the Interim Committee. Included in the list were a number of clearly substantive decisions such as those relating to the admission of new Members, and certain pacific settlement matters.

3. The permanent members, in order to avoid excessive use of the veto, should consult together on important decisions to be taken by the Security Council. Moreover, they were to exercise their veto only when they considered the question of vital importance, taking

---

[31] U.S. Department of State *Bulletin,* Vol. 17 (Sept. 28, 1947), pp. 621-22.
[32] Res. 117(II), Nov. 21, 1947.
[33] Res. 267(III), Apr. 14, 1949.

into account the interests of the United Nations as a whole, and stating on what ground they consider this condition to be present.

4. In concluding agreements conferring functions on the Security Council, Members of the United Nations should be careful to provide voting procedures with respect to the exercise of such functions that would exclude the rule of unanimity of the permanent members to the greatest extent feasible.

This resolution represented the best solution the General Assembly could find for the veto problem in 1949. It was the result of the prevailing opinion that the principle of unanimity was and should remain a fundamental principle of the Charter. It was based on the idea that no formal amendments were necessary; that great power unanimity was more a matter of mutual understanding, self-restraint, and willingness to co-operate.

The United States representative to the United Nations, Ambassador Austin, pointed out that the resolution was a means of "giving life to the unanimity principle and making it work." He said:

> It represents a policy of gradual liberalization of the voting procedures of the Security Council through processes of interpretation and application of the principles of the Charter and through agreement of the members of the Security Council. We rely on processes of discussion, definition, regulation, and practice to move us forward toward our objective and not upon revolutionary change. We recommend restraint and self-discipline to member nations in accordance with the letter and spirit of the Charter as an appropriate means of giving life to the unanimity principle and keeping it within proper bounds.[34]

Broadening the Definition of "Procedural Matters"

Admittedly much could be done to minimize the impact of the veto if the Security Council would broaden the definition of procedural matters. Article 27 provides for different voting procedures for substantive and procedural questions, but it fails to define these two terms. In the wide range of decisions the Council must make, therefore, it is largely up to the Council, working within the framework of the Charter, to determine which of these may or may not be subject to the veto.

At the San Francisco Conference, the four sponsoring powers put forth a relatively narrow interpretation of the word "procedural." In the statement they issued to the Conference on Article 27, they

[34] See U.S. Department of State *Bulletin*, Vol. 20 (April 1949), pp. 512-15.

agreed that a simple procedural vote should govern decisions of the Security Council reached under Articles 28-32 inclusive. This means, said the four powers, that the Council will, by a vote of any seven of its members:

> . . . adopt or alter its rules of procedure; determine the method of selecting its President; organize itself in such a way as to be able to function continuously; select the times and places of its regular and special meetings; establish such bodies or agencies as it may deem necessary for the performance of its functions; invite a member of the Organization not represented on the Council to participate in its discussion when that member's interests are specially affected; and invite any state when it is a party to a dispute being considered by the Council to participate in the discussion relating to that dispute.[35]

The sponsoring powers listed two other notable exceptions to the veto: no single member of the Council could alone prevent the discussion of a situation or dispute brought to the attention of the Council; and parties to such disputes could not be prevented by a veto from being heard. Beyond this point, the sponsoring governments argued, decisions of the Council "may well have major political consequences and even initiate a chain of events which might, in the end, require the Council under its responsibilities to invoke measures of enforcement." For such decisions the unanimity rule should apply.

This was a rough definition. It left uncertain the question regarding what was procedural and what was substantive, and this could be cleared up only by time and experience. It followed that if decisions on whether questions before the Council were procedural or substantive in nature could be considered to be procedural and could be taken by an affirmative vote of any seven members, then gradually the area within which the veto would operate might be diminished. The four-power statement, however, precluded such a decision on the preliminary question. Should such a question arise, the statement provides, "the decision regarding the preliminary question as to whether or not such a matter is procedural must be taken by a vote of seven members of the Security Council, including the concurring votes of the permanent members." The inevitable result has been for the Council to take a narrow rather than a broad view of the limits within which the procedural vote can function.

In actual practice differences of opinion have arisen many times

[35] *UNCIO Documents*, Vol. 11, p. 428.

whether a particular question is substantive or procedural. On several occasions this has led to the so-called "double veto"; with the first veto cast to prevent a question from being considered procedural, and the second veto used to block the measure as a substantive question. Three times the Soviet Union has resorted to the double veto: in 1946, against a resolution to keep the Spanish question, dealing with action to be taken against the Franco regime, on the agenda; in 1947, against a resolution requesting the General Assembly to consider the dispute between Greece on the one hand, and Albania, Yugoslavia, and Bulgaria on the other; and in 1948, on a resolution to establish a committee to hear evidence on the overthrow of the government in Czechoslovakia. In this way, the Soviet Union has added to the list of matters subject to the veto.[36]

The Council has made it clear, however, in at least one case, that the veto cannot be used to transform matters that are recognized as procedural under the Charter or the four-power statement into substantive questions. The issue arose in 1950, when the representative of Nationalist China opposed a resolution inviting the Chinese Communist regime to attend meetings of the Council during its discussion of the Formosan problem. The Nationalist representative insisted that his negative vote be registered as a veto, although other delegates pointed out that the question before the Council was clearly procedural and the veto, therefore, could not apply. A second vote was taken in order to determine whether the Council considered the matter procedural in nature. The only negative vote was cast by Nationalist China. The President of the Council then ruled that the resolution had been deemed procedural, and the Council upheld his ruling.

This incident is worth noting because some students of the Charter believe it serves as a useful precedent in establishing the rule that the great powers cannot resort to the double veto unless supported by a majority of the Council. Obviously, if such an interpretation were accepted, it would bring about a significant reduction in the scope of the veto. It is doubtful, however, whether the facts warrant such an optimistic conclusion. Actually, in this particular case, no real doubt existed; the point at issue was one that

[36] See Subcommittee on the United Nations Charter, Staff Study No. 1, 83 Cong. 2 sess., pp. 18-19. See also the volume in this Brookings series, *The Organization and Procedures of the United Nations*.

had been placed in the procedural category in the four-power statement at the San Francisco Conference, and in the circumstances, it is difficult to see why it was necessary for the Council to take a vote on the matter at all. The incident constitutes, at best, a very weak precedent. Certainly, it does not justify any assumption that the first half of the double veto has been abolished or has even received a serious setback.

Most people who are familiar with the work of the United Nations probably dislike the double veto far more than they dislike the veto itself. But it would seem to be a logical outgrowth of the principle of unanimity. The only way it can be eliminated from the United Nations system is by mutual agreement among those empowered to wield it.[37]

Practice of Abstention

Most of the attempts to liberalize the voting procedures of the Security Council have been blocked by Soviet intransigence. The one significant exception relates to the practice of the Council with respect to the abstention of permanent members from the vote.

A strict interpretation of Article 27 could hold that no substantive action could be taken by the Security Council without the concurring votes of *all five* permanent members. Practice has firmly established the contrary. Curiously enough, it was the Soviet representative in the Council who started the long series of precedents in 1946 when he abstained from voting on a resolution on the Spanish question with the explanation that, although he did not like the resolution, he did not want to prevent its passage by casting a negative vote.[38] Since that time, abstention has become a common practice in the Council and has injected an element of flexibility into the rigid framework of Article 27. Very often members of the Council are dissatisfied with a resolution yet they do not want to oppose the will of the majority. Abstention gives the permanent members a relatively easy way out; they avoid the responsibility for supporting a measure that they dislike, but they permit the Council to take positive action assuming, of course, that sufficient support is forthcoming for the proposal from other mem-

[37] On this problem see Leo A. Gross, "The Double Veto and the Four-Power Statement on Voting in the Security Council," *Harvard Law Review,* Vol. 67 (December 1953), pp. 251-80.

[38] U.N. Security Council, First Year, *Official Records,* 39th Meeting (Apr. 29, 1946), pp. 242-43.

bers. A great many resolutions have been approved by the Council with one or more permanent members abstaining. Thus the number of vetoes has been reduced considerably, and the Council has been able to function much more effectively than would have been possible otherwise.

Although some controversy has arisen over the question, it would appear that the absence of a permanent member from a meeting of the Council has the same legal effect as an abstention. In both the Iranian case in 1946 and again in the Korean case in 1950, the Council approved resolutions at a time when the representative of the Soviet Union was voluntarily absent from the chamber. Some of these resolutions, especially those relating to the aggression against South Korea, were of far-reaching importance. To be sure the Soviet representative has vigorously contended that these latter decisions were not valid because, in the absence of Communist China and the Soviet Union, the Council was illegally constituted. He has even argued, in a curiously inconsistent way, that it is necessary under the Charter to obtain the concurring votes of *all* five permanent members before an important decision can be taken. But the Soviet position was rejected by the Council. The United States pointed out that, in a long line of precedents, members of the Council had accepted the principle that an abstention from the vote by a permanent member does not constitute a veto.[39] Neither the Soviet Union nor any other great power had ever challenged the legality of such decisions. As the voluntary absence of a permanent member is so clearly analogous to abstention, it would seem to have the same legal effect.

Even more important is the obvious fact that if the Soviet view were accepted, it would mean that any one of the great powers, by the simple process of boycotting the meetings, could completely paralyze the work of the Security Council. But Article 28 of the Charter requires the Council to be so organized "as to be able to function continuously." Clearly this requirement could not be met if any of the permanent members could stop the work of the Council merely by remaining away from its meetings.

A point that was made earlier in this study might well be restated here. As the Charter makes no provision for its interpretation, Members of the Organization may interpret any particular

---

[39] "Precedent Contradicts Soviet Allegation of Illegality in U.N. Action," U.S. Department of State *Bulletin,* Vol. 23 (July 10, 1950), pp. 48-50.

article as they see fit. Article 27 was drafted in broad, general terms. Experience thus far would indicate that there is a great deal of elasticity in this portion of the Charter if the Members wish to use it.[40]

The Development of Pacts under Article 51

Concurrently with the attempts to obtain agreement among the permanent members of the Security Council voluntarily to restrict their use of the veto to reasonable proportions, far-reaching steps have been taken to develop the concept of collective defense outlined in Article 51. As the lack of unanimity among the great powers has become more apparent, the determination of Member states to build, through the conclusion of mutual defense pacts, a system of collective security that would not be subject to the crippling effects of the veto has increased.[41] Some people have criticized these pacts on the ground that they are designed to by-pass the United Nations. It would be more accurate to say that they are designed to circumvent the unsatisfactory situation that developed in the United Nations as a result of the veto impasse. As Senator Vandenberg said, they are "inside the Charter and outside the veto."[42]

In fact—and this is a point critics too often forget—Article 51 was inserted in the Charter for the precise purpose of serving as a counterbalance to Article 27. At the San Francisco Conference a good many states were concerned lest their security be jeopardized by the veto. The Latin-American countries were particularly anxious to fit the Inter-American system into the United Nations in such a way as to make sure that regional security efforts could not be thwarted by the veto. They argued that if an Asiatic or European power should attack a Latin-American country, any permanent member of the Security Council could interpose its veto under Article 27 and prevent the Council from taking effective action. In such an event, they raised the question whether the nations of the new world would have to stand by and watch the aggression take place.

---

[40] On the question of abstention see Yuen-Li Liang, "Abstention and Absence of a Permanent Member in Relation to the Voting Procedure in the Security Council," *American Journal of International Law*, Vol. 44 (October 1950), pp. 694-708.

[41] On this problem see above, Chaps. I and VI. See also the volume in this Brookings series, *Regional Security and the United Nations*.

[42] Arthur H. Vandenberg, Jr., ed., *The Private Papers of Senator Vandenberg* (1952), p. 403.

They claimed that they could not accept the Charter unless some provision was made to enable Members of the United Nations to take collective defense measures whenever the Council failed to act because of the veto. In the main, it is the logic of this argument that underlies the provisions of Article 51, and the United States has taken the lead in concluding collective defense arrangements embracing some forty-nine signatories.

This approach to the veto problem is admittedly a piecemeal one, but it is a realistic one, and it is possible that within the next few years most Member states in the free world will be formally linked together in a number of collective defense pacts, under the umbrella of Article 51. It should be emphasized, however, that the collective action provided for under the article need not fall within the terms of a formal agreement. This was pointed out by the United States representative when the Security Council, during its consideration of the Greek question, failed to approve the recommendations of its Commission of Investigation. He said,

> The continued failure . . . of the Security Council to take effective action in this case because of the USSR veto cannot . . . preclude individual or collective action by States willing to act, so long as they act in accordance with the general purposes and principles of the United Nations. This is particularly true when such individual or collective action is in support of a policy or course of action which has the approval of a clear preponderance of the permanent and nonpermanent members of the Security Council.[43]

Few people would argue that collective defense pacts under Article 51 could ever be a satisfactory substitute for a Security Council sparked by genuine great power unity. It should be kept in mind, too, that none of these pacts provide for a "veto-less" system of collective security. But so long as the conflict between the Communist and non-Communist nations remains, they constitute one realistic way of developing security in the free world without encountering the destructive impact of the Soviet veto.

The Thomas-Douglas proposal, which is analyzed in detail elsewhere in this study, is another form of a pact that could be concluded under Article 51.[44] Proponents of the plan argued that there were two principal ways of avoiding the impasse caused by the veto. One was to amend the Charter, which would result in driving out

[43] U.N. Security Council, Second Year, *Official Records*, 180th Meeting (Aug. 12, 1947), p. 1910.
[44] See above, Chap. VI.

those Members that would not agree to the necessary changes. The other was to by-pass the veto rather than to attempt to eliminate it at the risk of ruining the United Nations.[45] The Thomas-Douglas proposal would accomplish the latter purpose by substituting the vote of two thirds of the General Assembly, but including the affirmative votes of three of the great powers, for the vote of the Security Council, which includes the unanimous vote of all five of the great powers. The effect would be to create an outer and an inner ring of Member states. The outer ring would still be subject to the veto but the inner ring would agree to operate under the two-thirds rule in order to repel aggression.

For the United States, this proposal would mean abandoning its right of veto with respect to enforcement measures. Supporters of the proposal insisted, however, that the two-thirds requirement in the General Assembly would adequately protect American national security interests. Even if the Soviet Union signed the agreement, it could not obtain sufficient support in the Assembly for a vote against American national security interests because its maximum strength there rarely exceeds seven or eight votes. Moreover, the requirement that three of the great powers must concur before any action could be taken would enable the United States, France, and Great Britain to vote down any proposal that they jointly opposed. So long as the Western alliance held firm, any Soviet attempt to control the Assembly would be foredoomed to failure.

Given the world situation in 1950, the Department of State believed that the United States could best achieve its objective of building an effective collective security system within the framework of the Charter by supporting the "Uniting for Peace" resolution and by expanding the network of regional and bilateral security pacts. This attitude no doubt reflected the desire of the department not to provoke a violent controversy over the United Nations—either among the Member states, or among the American people. It also stemmed in part from a reluctance to enter into an agreement that would bind the United States to support in every case the decision of two thirds of the General Assembly with respect to enforcement action.

Since the adoption of the "Uniting for Peace" resolution, interest in the Thomas-Douglas proposal appears to have dwindled. If the

---

[45] *Revision of the United Nations Charter,* Hearings before a Subcommittee of the Senate Committee on Foreign Relations, 81 Cong. 2 sess., pp. 43 ff.

resolution should fail to accomplish its purpose, however, something like the Thomas-Douglas plan might once again win considerable public support.

Greater Use of the General Assembly

One possible solution to the veto dilemma, although it may be an inadequate one, lies in the continued transfer of the peace-keeping functions of the Security Council to the General Assembly. Here the trend is unmistakable. Gradually, since 1946, the number of political issues handled by the General Assembly has been increasing, while the activity of the Security Council has declined. In some cases important questions have been dropped from the agenda of the Council and later brought before the Assembly for action. In still other instances, the Council has been deliberately by-passed. Problems that, in normal circumstances, would have been considered and dealt with by the Council have been referred directly to the Assembly in order to avoid an impasse caused by the veto.[46]

The climax of this movement came in 1950 with the approval of the "Uniting for Peace" resolution. In this resolution, as pointed out earlier in this study, the Members of the United Nations attempted to organize the Assembly for effective action in the event of a stalemate in the Council.[47] The Assembly agreed that "if the Security Council, because of lack of unanimity of the permanent members, fails to exercise its primary responsibility for the maintenance of international peace and security in any case where there appears to be a threat to the peace, breach of the peace, or act of aggression, the General Assembly shall consider the matter immediately with a view to making appropriate recommendations to Members for collective measures, including in the case of a breach of the peace or act of aggression the use of armed force when necessary, to maintain or restore international peace and security."[48]

This does not mean that the Security Council was abandoned. Indeed, the Assembly went out of its way to reiterate the primary responsibility of the Council for the maintenance of peace and security. What it does mean is that it is now possible for the United Nations to recommend that Member states take collective action against aggression if the General Assembly approves such action by

[46] See below, Chap. XI.
[47] See above, Chaps. I and VI.
[48] Res. 377 (V), Nov. 3, 1950.

a two-thirds vote. It means that an aggressor may be confronted by the United Nations even if enforcement action is vetoed in the Council.

Even so, the "Uniting for Peace" resolution falls far short of providing an adequate substitute for the Security Council. The Assembly is at best an unwieldy body and is not geared for speedy action. Moreover, it can only recommend the use of collective measures; the nature and extent of those measures will depend on the will of the Member states and their individual determination regarding what they should do in the circumstances. A vote in the Council may be in the form of a binding decision rather than a recommendation, and it carries with it the weight and the power of the five permanent members. In the Assembly, on the other hand, it cannot be certain that the two-thirds majority required for a recommendation for collective security action will include states with sufficient military strength to carry out the recommendation. To vote for a project is one thing; to help carry it out is another matter.

Although the "Uniting for Peace" resolution charts a course for getting around the veto, it is still to be fully implemented. It remains for the General Assembly to take those steps necessary to place itself in a state of readiness so that it can meet future emergencies with vigor and dispatch.

Proposals for Amending the Charter

There is much to be said in favor of the various attempts to alleviate the veto problem by methods that fall short of formal amendment of the Charter. Many people, and many governments, however, feel strongly that the issue should be met by a frontal attack on Article 27.

Historically, of course, there is a very intimate relationship between Article 27 and the possible revision of the Charter. At the San Francisco Conference, it was largely the vigorous opposition of the small states to the veto that led to a liberalization of the amending process. They reluctantly accepted the veto only after the insertion of Article 109 in the Charter and the assurance that there would be an opportunity for them to put forth appropriate amendments at a special conference for review of the Charter if the situation war-

ranted.[49] If such a conference should be held, the veto might well
be the focal point of attention. The fact is, however, that although a
review conference can adopt amendments to Article 27 over the
objection of the Soviet Union, such amendments could not go into
force unless ratified by the Soviet Union. Moreover, a bitter struggle
to limit the veto power conceivably might exacerbate world tensions
even to the point of forcing some Member states to withdraw from
the United Nations. For these reasons, it is imperative that the
United States examine its position with great care and determine
just what changes it might be willing to support.

Modifications in Present Voting Formula

The proposals that have been made range from the complete
elimination of the veto—and these involve a wide variety of voting
formulae—to limitations on its use in certain problem areas. The
pattern of these proposals is generally the same as the one considered at the San Francisco Conference. There, for example,
Ecuador proposed that eight affirmative votes be required for *all*
decisions of the Security Council. Iran suggested nine. Egypt pre-
ferred eight, with the concurring votes of four permanent members
required for important decisions. Cuba recommended a simple
majority vote for procedural questions, with a two-thirds vote (including two thirds of the permanent members) for decisions concerning the maintenance of peace and security. El Salvador proposed an interesting procedure according to which questions not
receiving the unanimous approval of the great powers should be
referred to the General Assembly for final action. Australia upheld
the veto for enforcement action, but contended that the votes of
three great powers should suffice for decisions respecting the peaceful settlement of disputes.[50]

Similar proposals have been advanced in the discussions in the
General Assembly of the veto problem and these may well be
renewed as the time for the General Conference approaches. In
1946, for example, the Philippines proposed that Article 27 be
amended so that substantive decisions of the Security Council be

[49] See the volume in this Brookings series, *A History of the United Nations
Charter*. See also Chap. I, above.
[50] For a summary of the discussion of this problem at the San Francisco Conference see *UNCIO Documents*, Vol. 11, pp. 304-63.

made "by an affirmative vote of seven members, including the concurring votes of at least three permanent members."[51] New Zealand
has put the matter in still another way by suggesting that one
permanent member should be required to obtain the concurrence
of at least one other permanent member in order to exercise the
right of veto.[52] Still other Members have urged the complete abolition of the veto with the Security Council taking its decisions by a
qualified majority vote of from seven to ten members.

There are essentially two types of proposals involved here. The
first is the proposition that the Security Council be permitted to
take its decisions by a majority of six, seven, or eight votes without
reference to the special position of the great powers. The second is
that the veto principle be retained with the proviso that the negative vote of more than one permanent member should be required
to prevent a decision of the Council.

So far as the first proposition is concerned, it is open to the same
objections that were raised at the San Francisco Conference. Although it would be more democratic, and would avoid the objectionable features inherent in the veto, it would place more voting
power in the six nonpermanent members of the Council than their
position in the world entitles them to wield. It is obvious how
ineffective a decision of the Council would be, even though approved by all the nonpermanent members, if five or even four of the
permanent members voted against it.

As for the second proposition, it would be less objectionable than
the first in that it would require a certain amount of support from
the great powers before a decision of the Council could be reached.
But admittedly it offers no permanent protection against the veto.
It might work temporarily. But assuming, for example, that in the
course of time additional permanent members should be seated on
the Security Council, the threat of the veto, even with the negative
votes of two great powers required, might be just as deadening as
it is today.

Proposals like these will confront the United States with hard
reality. Given the present state of world affairs, are the American
people willing to relax the veto on an across-the-board basis and
permit the Security Council to make decisions that vitally affect

---

[51] U.N. General Assembly, First Session, *Letter from the Philippine Republic
to the Secretary-General and Enclosed Draft Resolution Concerning the Method
of Voting in the Security Council*, Doc. A/C.1/34 (Nov. 6, 1946).

[52] U.N. Doc. A/AC.18/38 (Mar. 12, 1948).

American national interests without our express approval? Up to the present time, the United States has not found it necessary to invoke the veto, but it has made it clear that it would not hesitate to use it if the situation demanded. There are three important facts, however, that should not be forgotten: (1) the United States would not have entered the United Nations without the veto; (2) the American people never know when the protection of their vital interests might require its use; and (3) the future political alignments within the United Nations cannot be predicted with certainty.

Even more important, under any of these proposals the United States would be called upon to give up the veto as the legal safeguard of its position in the Security Council. This might not prove serious so long as the United States retains the friendly co-operation of a large majority of the Council members. But the possibility cannot be overlooked that the world situation may change radically in the next ten or twenty years, in which case the United States might find the veto a valuable insurance policy.

Before the American people reach a conclusion with respect to the abolition of the veto they must find the answers to some very difficult questions, including the following: Is the United States willing to permit the Charter to be amended—involving, perhaps, important changes in the nature of its obligations in the United Nations—without its consent? Would the United States be willing to allow the Security Council to order economic or diplomatic sanctions against an aggressor nation without its approval, or to turn over to the Security Council the right to use United States armed forces—even against its wishes—in order to put down aggression in other lands? At the present time, there is no indication that any substantial number of American citizens would endorse abolition of the veto in these respects.

Elimination of Veto in Admission of New Members

Another approach, which has commanded considerable support, would be to restrict the use of the veto to certain well-defined areas and to eliminate it entirely with respect to the admission of new members and the peaceful settlement of disputes. This position was approved by the Senate in 1948 when it adopted the Vandenberg Resolution—which supported the idea of collective defense pacts under the Charter—by an overwhelming vote of 64 to 4. As the Senate Committee on Foreign Relations pointed out in reporting the resolution to the Senate: "It is precisely in these areas that the activities of the Security Council have been hampered so far. The committee believes that if agreement could be reached on these two points, much will have been done to free the Charter from the shackles of the veto."[53] This remains the policy of the United States Government, as is indicated by a recent statement of Secretary of State Dulles:

Today the executive branch of the government is very largely guided by the provisions of the so-called Vandenberg resolution which called for the elimination of the veto particularly with respect to two matters, that is, the admission of new members, and with respect to Chapter VI, dealing with the pacific settlement of international disputes.[54]

In urging the total elimination of the veto on the admission of new Members, two fundamental factors should be kept in mind.[55] The first is that such a step would mean membership for a good many states, such as Italy and Portugal, whose admission the United States has consistently supported, but it might also result in the admission of certain Communist countries whose membership the United States has vigorously opposed. The latter possibility is not immediate unless one of the package membership deals mentioned earlier is entered into. To date, however, the Soviet satellite states have not been able to win a majority vote in the Security Council or the Assembly. The second factor is a more difficult one, for it involves what might seem to some a curious inconsistency in United States policy. Can the United States, in good conscience, vote to eliminate the veto with respect to the admission of new Members, yet insist on its right to use the veto in order to prevent the Chinese Communist regime from representing China in the Security Council? If the veto should apply to questions of representation, should it not also apply to the more fundamental question of admitting new Members?

[53] S. Res. 239, 80 Cong. 2 sess. See Senate Committee on Foreign Relations, *Reaffirming the Policy of the United States to Achieve International Peace and Security Through the United Nations and Indicating Certain Objectives to be Pursued,* S. Rept. 1361, 80 Cong. 2 sess. (May 19, 1948).

[54] *Review of the United Nations Charter,* Senate Hearings, 83 Cong. 2 sess., Pt. 1, p. 18.

[55] The problem of membership is discussed in detail above in Chap. IV.

With respect to the peaceful settlement of disputes, even before the Charter was signed, there was a strong feeling in the United States that it was unwise to set up the principle of great power unanimity in such a way that the veto might be used. One of the prime functions of the Security Council is to encourage Members of the United Nations that have disputes or differences to resolve those differences by peaceful means of their own choice. If, therefore, two states have failed to arrive at a settlement by such means and the case has come before the Council, why should any great power want to stop them?

At the San Francisco Conference, some members of the United States delegation were deeply disturbed over the potential harm that might flow from this particular provision in the Charter. One member of the delegation commented that nothing could be more ridiculous than that a permanent member should be able to veto the peaceful settlement of a dispute in which it is not involved. Senator Vandenberg, for example, thought it was "absurd," but the delegation accepted the Yalta formula as the best arrangement that could be devised in the circumstances.[56] It was on this issue that the smaller countries became most heated in their denunciation of the veto concept. So thorough was their opposition, that an Australian amendment, which would have classified all decisions of the Security Council under Chapter VI of the Charter as decisions on procedural matters, was defeated by the relatively narrow margin of 10 to 20 with 15 states abstaining from the vote.[57] Only a considerable amount of persuasion by the great powers prevented that vote from carrying.

In the opinion of many, the principal argument advanced by the permanent members was not very logical then, and it appears even less logical now. Under the "chain-of-events" theory, the great powers insisted that their unanimity on peaceful settlement matters was essential inasmuch as a decision of the Council ordering an investigation or setting up a commission of inquiry might have major political consequences and might even initiate a series of events that, in the end, might require the Council to resort to enforcement measures. On the other hand, the smaller states argued that if the Council is performing a purely conciliatory function,

[56] Vandenberg, Jr., *op. cit.*, p. 196.
[57] *UNCIO Documents*, Vol. 11, pp. 492-95.

without authority to compel the parties to follow any particular course of action, no single state should be in a position to interfere with this desirable objective by casting its veto.

The history of the past decade would appear to have justified the position of the smaller states. Of the 60 vetoes cast by the Soviet Union through June 1954, at least 23 have related to disputes and situations before the Council. These have dealt with such matters as the Spanish question, the Greek frontier situation, Indonesia, the Berlin blockade, and the more recent Guatemalan crisis.

It is true that in some cases the Council has been able to circumvent the veto and accomplish its purpose in spite of the opposition of a great power. In 1946, for example, when the Soviet Union vetoed a resolution relating to the withdrawal of troops from Syria and Lebanon, Great Britain and France complied with the sentiment of the majority of the Council and withdrew their troops. No one can doubt, however, that the continued application of the veto has hampered greatly the machinery for peaceful settlement contemplated in the Charter.

The Palestine question is a recent case in point. For some four years this issue had been free from the veto—although by no means "settled." During the first half of 1954, however, the situation underwent a significant change when the Soviet Union vetoed two important measures before the Council. As a result there has been, and there will probably continue to be, some hesitation in using the Security Council to further peaceful settlement of the Palestine question.

In practice, the Council has treated questions arising under Articles 28 to 32 of the Charter as procedural in nature, although there has been some disagreement over the creation of subsidiary organs to conduct inquiries and investigations. Similarly, the Council has considered as procedural such matters as the placing of questions on the agenda, the calling of witnesses, the inauguration of fact-finding studies, and the removal of items from the agenda. But relatively little progress can be expected in this direction so long as the Soviet Union insists on a narrow rather than a liberal interpretation of Article 27.

At the San Francisco Conference, the United States delegation reluctantly agreed that the veto could apply to peaceful settlement issues because it believed that such a move would promote unity among the great powers. As this did not prove to be the case, there would seem to be no logical reason a different course should not be adopted. Secretary of State Dulles has stated the case recently, as follows: "There is nothing in Chapter VI which can be compulsory or which seriously touches any nation's sovereignty. It means merely the setting up of procedures for arbitration, good offices, and things of that sort, and it is hard to say really why there should be a veto sought by any country upon those processes."[58]

Elimination of Veto in Enforcement Action

It is one of the characteristics of the proposals for supranational government that they envisage the elimination of the veto. Unrestricted state sovereignty and the veto go hand in hand. It is only natural, therefore, that the proponents of world government should make a determined attack on Article 27. This is true, in a unique way, of the ABC Plan, which has been described earlier in this study.[59] Among other things, the plan calls for the establishment of an effective international police force and the elimination of the veto "in matters specifically concerning aggression and preparation for aggression."[60]

It is not entirely clear whether the proponents of the plan want to do away with the veto entirely, or whether they are primarily concerned with its elimination in connection with enforcement action and the regulation of armament. Senator Mundt of South Dakota has stated that he would have the veto altered "so it would not be operative in the Security Council on matters of aggression, and on matters applying to the revision and restriction and control of weapons of mass destruction."[61] Resolutions introduced into the Congress sponsoring the plan generally reflected this view.[62]

The ABC Plan proposes a reorganized Security Council made up of ten representatives, two each from the United States, the Soviet Union, and the British Commonwealth, one each from France and China, and two representing the small states. Decisions on vetoless matters would be made, under the proposal, by a majority of six out

[58] *Review of the United Nations Charter,* Senate Hearings, 83 Cong. 2 sess., Pt. 1, p. 18.

[59] See above, Chap. III.

[60] Ely Culbertson, "The ABC Plan for World Peace," *Reader's Digest* (June 1948).

[61] *Revision of the United Nations Charter,* Senate Hearings, 81 Cong. 2 sess., p. 183.

[62] See S. Con. Res. 50, 80 Cong. 1 sess.; also S. Con Res. 104, 81 Cong. 2 sess.

of ten. Among other powers, the Security Council would determine the maximum limit of world production of heavy armament of certain specified categories. The plan also provides for the creation of a world peace force in which the international contingent, made up of recruits from the small states, would be under the control of the Council acting without the veto. The national contingents, furnished by the great powers, would operate as reserves if needed.

Proponents of the plan have not clearly explained the rationale underlying their proposed limitation of the veto. They place emphasis on the immediacy of the world crisis and the need to take far-reaching action in order to avert an atomic war. The way to do it, they believe, is to grant to the United Nations sufficient authority to deal effectively with the two critical problems of aggression and the regulation of armaments at the same time avoiding a full-fledged world government.

In awarding the great powers eight of the ten votes in the Security Council, the ABC Plan would seem to magnify unduly the preponderant influence of those powers in the Organization. It can be argued, of course, that such a voting arrangement would more nearly reflect the effective military strength of the Member states; and that two votes without the veto should be worth more to the small states than six votes with the veto. On the other hand, the small states could hardly be expected to be enthusiastic over any proposal that would have the effect of substantially increasing their responsibility for the maintenance of peace and at the same time reducing their voting strength.

Moreover, it is precisely with regard to these two areas of activity of the Council—enforcement action and the regulation of armament —that strong sentiment prevails in the United States for the retention of the veto. The United States Government has indicated a willingness to relinquish the veto with respect to the regulation of armament but only after the establishment by treaty of an effective international system of inspection and control with adequate safeguards. There has not been the slightest hint from official quarters that the United States would even consider giving up its right to veto enforcement action. The official position on this point was made clear—especially in so far as the use of American troops is concerned—when the Senate Committee on Foreign Relations recommended ratification of the Charter to the Senate in 1945. The report stated:

The special position of the United States as one of the five permanent members of the Security Council whose approval is needed for any enforcement action needs to be emphasized once again in this connection. No United States forces can be employed, no enforcement action of any kind against a nation breaking the peace can be taken, without the full concurrence of the United States acting through its delegate on the Security Council.[63]

Changes in Both Representation and Voting

Still another approach to the problem is developed in the Clark-Sohn proposal. It recommends the establishment of an Executive Council of fifteen members to be elected by the General Assembly. Six of these representatives would come from the six largest states—China, India, the Soviet Union, the United States, the United Kingdom, and France—with the members voting as individuals. Decisions taken by the Council would require eleven affirmative votes out of fifteen. The proposal states:

> It is clear that no decision, great or small, should be prevented by the veto of any single nation. . . . On the other hand, it is important that every decision of the Executive Council should be based on so considerable a majority vote that it would presumably represent and be supported by a preponderance of public opinion throughout the world. To this end, the voting provisions should not be so rigid as to prevent the new Council from functioning promptly and effectively in any circumstances, and yet should be such as to insure, so far as possible, that decisions shall never represent a minority of the world's population.[64]

The sponsors of the plan believe this two-fold objective could be achieved by increasing the size of the Council to fifteen and requiring a minimum vote of eleven members. The population of the six largest powers is roughly 1,400,000,000, or about 60 per cent of the total world population. The population of the other seventy-six countries—assuming the organization is universal in scope—is approximately 1,000,000,000, or roughly 40 per cent of the world total. Given these figures, no decision could be reached unless approved by members representing both a majority of the states and a majority of the population of the world. This would be true even in the unusual case of a decision being taken with the four most populous countries voting against the other eleven members of the Council.

[63] Senate Committee on Foreign Relations, *Charter of the United Nations*, S. Ex. Rept. 8, 79 Cong. 1 sess. (July 16, 1945), p. 9.

[64] Grenville Clark and Louis B. Sohn, *Peace Through Disarmament and Charter Revision* (Preliminary Print, 1953), pp. 59-60.

In the context in which it is offered, *i.e.,* a total plan for world government in which members of the Executive Council would be presumed to represent the world community instead of the nation-state, the voting aspects of the proposal would appear to have some merit. Certainly, if the veto were completely abolished, it would seem to some to be a good idea to enlarge the Council so as to make it more representative, and to increase the percentage of the total vote required for decisions.

Given the present world situation, however, the proposal is subject to all the criticisms raised earlier in connection with the elimination of the veto. Moreover, it would seem to place too much emphasis on the population factor and the desirability of the Council taking decisions that would have the support of a majority of the member states. Is it conceivable that such decisions would have any lasting import in the Organization if four of the great powers refused to accept them?

Somewhat related to this type of proposal is the suggestion that some balanced system of weighted representation and voting be adopted for the Security Council. The present arrangement under which each of the eleven members has one vote is unfair, the argument runs, inasmuch as great inequalities exist among the Members with respect to population, production, national wealth, armed strength, and general influence in the world. The small countries—some perhaps with a population of only a few million—are not in a position to give real substance and vitality to the decisions of the Council. The question is raised, therefore, whether it is wise to grant them the same voting power as the permanent members in arriving at important decisions.[65] Should not the permanent members have a larger voting power because of the heavy responsibility they shoulder?

No specific proposals appear to have been advanced to carry out this general suggestion. Meanwhile, however logical it may appear on the surface, there would seem to be at least two fundamental arguments against it. In the first place, the nonpermanent members of the Council are informally regarded in practice as representing various regional groups or blocs of states—such as the Arab League, the Commonwealth countries, or Latin America. Consequently, their votes may carry far more weight and influence than the votes of

[65] See Amry Vandenbosch and Willard N. Hogan, *The United Nations: Background, Organization, Functions, Activities* (1952), pp. 86-90.

individual states. In the second place, at the San Francisco Conference, the small countries bitterly opposed the veto and the privileged position thus bestowed on the five permanent members by the Charter. It is highly unlikely that they would be inclined to make any further concessions that would add to the voting strength of the great powers in the Council. To them, the veto is bad enough; the veto coupled with weighted voting would probably be intolerable. Weighted voting in the General Assembly, where the veto does not exist, is another matter, which is dealt with later in this study.[66]

Limiting the Role of the Security Council

Most of the proposals to amend the Charter that have been examined so far are directed at changing the voting formula in Article 27, either by eliminating the veto or by modifying it in some particular respect. One other remedy, which has been put forth in certain British circles, would drastically alter the fundamental character of the Security Council by stripping it of its present enforcement powers under Chapter VII of the Charter and limiting its authority to that of making recommendations. The most obvious flaw in the Charter, argue the proponents of this point of view, is the veto. But so long as the Security Council is endowed with compulsory powers, it will not be possible to abolish the veto, for no permanent member could subscribe to a Charter that compelled it to submit to the will of a majority on the Council.

The answer to the present dilemma, therefore, it is argued, lies in giving the Council the same limited power granted the Council of the League of Nations; it should possess the authority to "recommend" but not to "command." This would permit the Council to operate under a simple majority rule. As compulsory power is a fiction, so the argument runs, and as it is unrealistic to talk about using coercion against a great state, such a change would not result in any real weakening of United Nations authority. Would not most loyal Members respond to a "recommendation" supported by Great Britain, France, and the United States as promptly as they would respond to a "decision" of the Council?[67]

According to this line of reasoning, Members of the United Nations face two clear alternatives. Either they should allow the Se-

[66] See below, Chap. XI.
[67] See the articles on "United Nations Reform," *New Commonwealth*, Vol. 25 (Mar. 16 and Mar. 30, 1953).

curity Council to fall into disuse, or they should eliminate its powers with respect to enforcement action and then permit it to carry on as the executive agency of the United Nations. If the latter course were followed, resistance to aggression would probably have to be organized either by the recommendatory action of the General Assembly or the Council, or by nations banded together under collective defense pacts like the North Atlantic Treaty.

Admittedly, the United Nations was not created for the purpose of taking enforcement measures against one of the permanent members of the Security Council. It can be argued, therefore, that this proposal merely brings the authority of the Council into harmony with its real power. At the same time, if agreement could be reached to eliminate the veto, the Council would be freed for the performance of its other duties such as those relating to the admission of new Members and the election of the Secretary-General. This proposal would revive the concept underlying the League of Nations, *i.e.,* that sovereign states—particularly the great powers—cannot be compelled to take any action they do not want to take. It would recognize frankly the virtual inability of the United Nations to stop aggression when the vital interests of a great power are involved, and would not place on the Organization responsibilities that it is not equipped to bear.

To some people there may be a certain amount of refreshing realism in such a proposal. Clearly, a Council with recommendatory powers would be far better than no Council at all. And there is little doubt that there is a role in the United Nations Organization for a small, executive organ that can act with greater dispatch than an unwieldy General Assembly.

Possible Courses of Action

There appear to be three separate and distinct courses of action open to the United States with respect to the veto problem. Two of these do not involve revision of the Charter. The third—that of formal amendment to the Charter—raises a whole range of possibilities that should be studied carefully before any General Conference for review of the Charter is convened.

The first course of action is to explore further what can be done to obtain agreement among the great powers to make Article 27 a more effective part of the Charter. If the permanent members of the Security Council would agree to refrain from using the veto except in those cases where their vital interests are directly involved, if they would consult together to iron out their differences, if they would subscribe to a liberal interpretation of the Charter, then much progress could be made. All these methods have been suggested in the United Nations since 1946 with little success.

The second course is to circumvent the veto by avoiding the Security Council. This could be done by organizing the General Assembly for more effective action in the security field and by further developing the free-world network of collective defense pacts. Both these methods have been used with considerable success since 1946.

So far as the third course is concerned—which would necessitate amendment of the Charter—the alternatives available include the following:

1. Eliminate the veto entirely and make all Security Council decisions subject to the affirmative votes of any seven members or even a simple majority.

2. Retain the veto principle but provide that the negative vote of more than one permanent member should be required to prevent a decision of the Security Council.

3. Limit the use of the veto to certain well-defined areas, eliminating it entirely with respect to the admission of new Members and the peaceful settlement of disputes.

4. Do away with the veto with respect to the two vital areas of enforcement action and the regulation of armaments.

5. Adopt some other system of weighted representation and voting for the Council so that voting strength would more nearly correspond to the population and political influence of the various Member states.

6. Change the fundamental character of the Security Council by stripping it of its enforcement powers and limiting its authority to that of making recommendations.

In the report to the President on the results of the San Francisco Conference the importance of great power unity was frequently emphasized. As the report pointed out: "It was taken as axiomatic at Dumbarton Oaks, and continued to be the view of the Sponsoring Powers at San Francisco that the cornerstone of world security is the unity of those nations which formed the core of the grand alliance against the Axis."[68] Today neither the unity nor the world security envisaged exists.

Many people are convinced that the veto is merely a symbol of the fundamental differences that exist among the great powers, that it is a reflection of their disunity instead of its underlying cause. If such analysis of the problem is correct, then no solution of the veto question is adequate unless it helps resolve the friction and tension that embitter the relations among the permanent members.[69]

As one observer states, the key to the use of the veto is the existence or nonexistence of great power antagonism. Given harmonious relations among the great powers, there will be no serious stalling of the peace machinery of the United Nations. But so long as friction and conflict are present, the veto will be resorted to by a great power or group of great powers that might otherwise find themselves outvoted in an important matter of power politics.[70]

The framers of the Charter believed that the main problems that would face the United Nations in the postwar period would arise from the repression of Germany and Japan instead of from increasing rivalry among the victorious nations. Consequently, when the Security Council was confronted by a series of issues that involved the conflicting interests of the great powers themselves, it was cast in quite a different role in which the principle of unanimity could not satisfactorily apply.

As the time approaches for a decision on a General Conference to review the Charter, however, there is every indication that the Soviet Union will continue to oppose any basic revision of Article 27. Both the Soviet Union and its satellite states have consistently argued that any liberalization of the veto would undermine the principle of unanimity on which the United Nations is based and might result in the destruction of the Organization itself. As a Soviet representative stated in 1949:

[68] U.S. Department of State, *Charter of the United Nations: Report to the President on the Results of the San Francisco Conference by the Chairman of the United States Delegation, The Secretary of State,* Publication 2349 (June 26, 1945), p. 68.

[69] See Vandenbosch and Hogan, *op. cit.,* p. 150; Padelford, *loc. cit.,* p. 228; Eugene P. Chase, *The United Nations in Action* (1950), p.183.

[70] Padelford, *loc. cit.,* p. 228.

The delegation of the Soviet Union had already pointed out that the principle of unanimity of the permanent members of the Security Council or "the right to veto," as it was sometimes called, was one of the basic provisions of the Charter and the very cornerstone of the structure of the United Nations.[71]

Since the establishment of the United Nations, this position has been repeated many times. In line with this reasoning, the Soviet Union has vigorously opposed all resolutions in the General Assembly designed to limit the use of the veto. It bitterly denounced the North Atlantic Treaty. It resisted to the end the "Uniting for Peace" resolution. And it has rejected any and all suggestions that the language of Article 27 be formally changed. It can be argued that the Soviet approach is undemocratic and that it is deliberately calculated to destroy the efficiency of the United Nations. In all probability, however, so long as the Soviet Union remains in the United Nations, and so long as it can be outvoted by what it refers to as the "mechanical majority," it will insist on the retention of the veto and the protection it affords.

There remains, of course, the possibility that the Soviet Union might undergo a fundamental change in attitude that would result in easing the tensions between it and the Western powers. To the extent that such a change is based on good faith, it might bring in its wake a partial solution to the veto problem.

There is another possible change in the world situation that the American people cannot afford to ignore. During the first ten years of the history of the United Nations, most of the members of the Security Council have been friendly to the United States. Support by a friendly majority has made it unnecessary for the United States to resort to the veto. The extent to which this favorable situation might be altered by the ebb and flow of world politics should also have a direct bearing on the American decision with respect to the veto problem.

[71] See U.N. General Assembly, Third Session, Plenary, *Official Records,* 192nd Meeting (Apr. 13, 1949), p. 55.

CHAPTER XI

Representation and Voting in the General Assembly[1]

ALTHOUGH public opinion in the United States has been deeply disturbed over the veto and the problem of voting in the Security Council, there has been relatively little interest in the problem of voting in the General Assembly. This remains true in spite of the fact that the prestige and influence of the Security Council have been declining and that of the General Assembly has been rising.[2]

Under the Charter, voting power in the Security Council, where decisions on nonprocedural questions require the concurring votes of the five permanent members, is heavily weighted in favor of the great powers. In the General Assembly, where all Member states have an equal voice, the scales are balanced in favor of the smaller nations. The great powers were willing to accept such an arrangement at the San Francisco Conference because they believed their interests could be adequately protected by their right of veto in the Security Council. At the time, this seemed a reasonable assumption. The Security Council was charged with the primary responsibility for the maintenance of peace, and it was in that organ that the really important decisions of the United Nations were to be taken. The General Assembly, which possesses only the power of recommendation, was destined, they believed, to be an organ of lesser political significance.

[1] The materials in this chapter have been adapted from *Representation and Voting in the United Nations General Assembly,* Staff Study No. 4, written by Francis O. Wilcox for the Subcommittee on the United Nations Charter, Senate Committee on Foreign Relations, 83 Cong. 2 sess. (September 1954).

[2] On this problem generally see the volume in this Brookings series, *The Organization and Procedures of the United Nations.* Also see Leland M. Goodrich and Edvard Hambro, *Charter of the United Nations: Commentary and Documents* (1949), pp. 188-90; Daniel S. Cheever and H. Field Haviland, Jr., *Organizing for Peace: International Organization in World Affairs* (1954), pp. 87 ff.; John Foster Dulles, *War or Peace* (1950), pp. 191 ff.; Allan Hovey, Jr., "Voting Procedure in the General Assembly," *International Organization,* Vol. 4 (August 1950), pp. 412-27; Amry Vandenbosch and Willard N. Hogan, *The United Nations: Background, Organization, Functions, Activities* (1952), pp. 116 ff.; Louis B. Sohn, *Cases and Other Materials on World Law* (1950), pp. 316-47; Elizabeth McIntyre, "Weighted Voting in International Organizations," *International Organization,* Vol. 8, (November 1954), pp. 484-97.

As the tension during the postwar years between the Soviet bloc and the free world has increased, however, the importance of the Security Council, when compared with that of the General Assembly, has declined. The accompanying table shows in a quantitative way, the extent to which the Assembly has displaced the Council as a forum for the handling of international political issues. During the early years of the Organization, as the framers of the Charter intended, the Council functioned as the principal political organ of the United Nations. Since 1948, however, its importance has steadily decreased, and the frequency of its meetings has been greatly reduced.

POLITICAL ISSUES CONSIDERED BY GENERAL ASSEMBLY AND SECURITY COUNCIL,
JAN. 1, 1946 TO JUNE 30, 1953[a]

Period	General Assembly	Security Council
Jan. 1–June 30, 1946	2	8
July 1, 1946–June 30, 1947	6	8
July 1, 1947–June 30, 1948	9	14
July 1, 1948–June 30, 1949	15	10
July 1, 1949–June 30, 1950	13	12
July 1, 1950–June 30, 1951	24	12
July 1, 1951–June 30, 1952	17	9
July 1, 1952–June 30, 1953	18	5
Total	104	78

[a] Table from Hans J. Morgenthau, "The United Nations and the Revision of the Charter," *The Review of Politics,* Vol. 16 (January 1954), p. 4.

Given this shift of power within the structure of the United Nations, the importance of a careful evaluation of the voting procedures in the General Assembly becomes apparent. Thus far, relatively few suggestions for changes in the existing system have been made. In any event, it will be helpful to examine briefly present voting practices in the Assembly and then turn to the proposals that have been advanced for change in this regard.

Present Voting Procedure

In the past, international organizations ordinarily have been based on two fundamental principles: the legal equality of states and the requirement of unanimity in voting. In practice, this has meant that very small nations such as Luxembourg and Iceland have participated in international assemblies on a basis of legal equality with large nations such as the United States, China, and India. "Russia and Geneva have equal rights," declared Chief Justice Marshall in 1825,[3] and this principle of state equality has been applied to international conferences as well as to international commerce.

It has meant, too, that whenever the point has been reached for an international conference to make a decision, any small state, as well as any large one, has been in a position to block resolutions on substantive questions by casting a negative vote. Sometimes small countries have responded to the pressure of other states and have abandoned their opposition; at other times, one or a few states have prevented conferences from arriving at decisions that, but for their opposition, might have been approved.

Provisions of the Charter

At the San Francisco Conference, the framers of the United Nations Charter accepted the first of these principles, that of sovereign equality, but rejected the second, that of unanimity in voting. Article 18, which lays down the procedure for voting in the General Assembly, provides that each member "shall have one vote"; that decisions of the Assembly on important questions "shall be made by a two-thirds majority of the members present and voting"; and that "decisions on other questions . . . shall be made by a majority of the members present and voting."

The fundamental proposition, expressed in Article 2, that the United Nations is based on the sovereign equality of all its Members is reiterated in Article 18. Each Member is given one vote. Theoretically, it would have been possible to devise a system of weighted voting that would accord Member nations a number of votes more commensurate with their relative importance in world affairs. But the practical difficulties involved in building a formula that would take account of the various factors that need to be measured were so great, and traditional concepts of sovereign equality of states so strong, that the matter was not given serious consideration either at Dumbarton Oaks or the San Francisco Conference. The

---

[3] In the case of *The Antelope,* 10 Wheaton 66.

time-honored doctrine of one-state-one-vote became part and parcel of the United Nations system.[4]

The only exception to this principle is found in the privileged position of the Soviet Union. At the San Francisco Conference, in accordance with an arrangement made at the Yalta Conference, Byelorussia and the Ukraine, which are constituent republics of the Soviet Union and do not qualify as "states" in the normally accepted sense of that term, were admitted as Members of the United Nations. They each have one vote, which, combined with that of the Soviet Union, makes a total of three votes for one Member. Actually, this arrangement involves considerably more than two additional votes for the Soviet Union. It is also entitled to two additional delegations. This not only triples its voting power, but its speaking power as well.

With respect to the principle of unanimity, the Charter turns its back on the past. No doubt the experience of the League of Nations was, in large part, responsible for this departure. Article 5 of the League Covenant gave every member of the League a veto by providing that, with certain exceptions, "decisions at any meeting of the Assembly or of the Council shall require the agreement of all the Members of the League represented at the meeting." This requirement by no means paralyzed the League Assembly. It did, however, hamper its activity and on some occasions prevented it from reaching important decisions strongly supported by a majority of the Members.

As indicated above, Article 18 of the Charter provides for votes on two types of questions: the so-called important questions that require a two-thirds majority, and all "other questions" that call for a simple majority. It will be noted that the majority required under the article is a majority of the members "present and voting." Members abstaining from the vote are considered as not voting. Thus by a simple majority the General Assembly may decide that decisions on questions other than those enumerated in Article 18 are of sufficient importance to require a two-thirds vote. It can also modify or abolish these additional categories by a majority of the members present and voting.

The two-thirds majority for the handling of important questions

[4] See the volume in this Brookings series, *A History of the United Nations Charter*.

seems to have worked fairly well in practice. No doubt it has served as a deterrent to hasty and ill-considered action by the Assembly. But it has not prevented action on any measure desired by a large majority of the Member states. During the first six years of the United Nations, there were eighteen instances in which draft resolutions (or portions of resolutions), received a simple majority in the committees of the Assembly but were not adopted because they failed to secure the necessary two-thirds vote in the Assembly itself.

The principal effect of Article 18 is to reject the veto with respect to votes in the General Assembly. This is a move in the direction of more democratic voting procedures in world affairs in that it decreases the *negative* power of individual states to block action. At the same time, it increases the *positive* power of groups or blocs of states that may wish to band together to accomplish their objectives within the United Nations system, in some cases against the wishes of a minority of the Members.

The General Assembly, of course, does not possess international legislative authority. It can study, it can debate, it can recommend, but it cannot legislate. In general, apart from the approval of the budget, it cannot make decisions that are binding on the Members of the United Nations.

Within these limitations, however, the scope of activity of the Assembly is far broader than that of the Security Council. It may discuss and make recommendations on any matter within the scope of the Charter or relating to the functions and powers of any United Nations organ (Article 10). Similarly, it may make recommendations concerning the general principles of co-operation in the maintenance of peace and security, including the problem of disarmament (Article 11). It may promote international co-operation in the economic, social, cultural, educational, and health fields (Article 13). And it may recommend measures for the peaceful adjustment of any situation likely to impair the general welfare or friendly relations among nations (Article 14).

It is true that votes of the General Assembly on these matters are only recommendatory. But there can be little doubt that many resolutions of the Assembly such as those relating to Korea, Palestine, Communist China, and atomic energy have had a tremendous influence on the course of world events. Recommendations with wide support among the Members of the United Nations may be more effective than decisions that are approved in a half-hearted manner and are supposedly binding on Member states.

Effect of One-State-One-Vote Principle

The principle of one-state-one-vote results in obvious inequalities in the General Assembly. Only nine states can boast a population of 40 millions or more. Some twenty-six states have a population of 5 millions or under, including Iceland with 146,000 and Luxembourg with 300,000. Two countries—China and India—contain almost half the total population of Member states.

In the circumstances, it is theoretically possible to obtain a majority of 31 votes, which represents only a little over 5 per cent of the population of the Member states. A vote of the twenty-one smallest countries, representing only about 2.3 per cent of the total population, could prevent the two-thirds majority needed for the approval of "important" resolutions. On the other hand, if a contest should arise between the large and small states, a two-thirds majority could be rolled up by forty of the smallest nations with a population of only about 11 per cent.[5] This is a hypothetical danger that should not be emphasized too much because it probably never will develop in practice in such an extreme form. Member states are unlikely ever to divide on important issues merely because of population differences. Even so, these figures illustrate the lack of balance that exists between population and voting strength; states with a very small minority of the total population of the Member states are in a position to control decisive votes and to frustrate the will of other states with a heavy population majority.

Similar inequalities exist with respect to national wealth, productivity, national territory, military power, and other factors. The Soviet Union, for example, has a total area of 8,700,000 square miles. This is more than 1,000 times the area of El Salvador. An even greater margin of difference exists with respect to the gross national product. According to the best estimates available, some six Member states had a gross national product of less than $200 million in 1952 or 1953. In contrast, the gross national product of the United States is estimated at $363 billion for 1953. The comparable figure for the Soviet Union is $100 billion, for the United Kingdom, $45 billion, and for France, $39 billion.[6]

[5] See Vandenbosch and Hogan, op. cit., p. 116.
[6] Data supplied by the Legislative Reference Service of the Library of Congress.

Practice of Bloc Voting

The situation has been complicated further by the development of what has come to be known as bloc voting in the General Assembly. By pooling or combining their voting strength on particular issues, groups of small states are able to exert an influence far out of proportion to either their population or their political importance.

Although this tendency toward bloc voting has developed considerably since 1945, the line-up in the General Assembly varies a great deal depending on the issue. The five states of the Soviet bloc invariably will be found on the same side. The seven Arab countries often vote as a unit especially with respect to Israeli-Arab problems and resolutions having to do with dependent areas. In most cases, at least two thirds of the twenty Latin-American states will be found in the same camp.[7] On the other hand, there is no predictable solidarity among the countries of Western Europe. The Benelux states (Luxembourg, Belgium, and the Netherlands) vote together on some issues as do the Scandinavian countries. The seven nations in the British Commonwealth frequently do not vote as a unit. Nevertheless, during the past few years, the free world countries have demonstrated a remarkable unity whenever the most vital issues are up for a vote. The 52 to 5 vote on the "Uniting for Peace" resolution in 1950 is a case in point.

An interesting example of what the small states can do when they are effectively organized occurred during the third session of the Assembly when the resolution providing for the use of Spanish as one of the working languages of the Organization was approved by a vote of 32 to 20 with 5 abstentions. In that case, the small states successfully opposed the large ones. The Latin-American and the Arab countries, with a few supporting votes, outvoted the United States, China, three of the British Commonwealth nations, and all of Europe, including the United Kingdom.[8]

Sir Carl Berendsen of New Zealand called attention to this problem in the plenary session of the General Assembly in 1947. He said:

Another . . . source of irresponsibility is the system of bloc voting that has grown up. Let no one tell me that what we have seen even at this session

[7] On this subject generally see Margaret Ball, "Bloc Voting in the General Assembly," *International Organization*, Vol. 5 (February 1951).

[8] Res. 247 (III), Dec. 7, 1948. See also U. N. Doc. A/799 (Dec. 11, 1948).

and on many occasions, of groups of Powers voting as one, is a good system. Some of these blocs are large; indeed, they can become so large as, in effect, to constitute a veto with regard to any question of importance requiring a two-thirds majority. That is not a proper exercise of responsibility.[9]

Thus far, this problem has not proved serious so far as the United States is concerned. As one would expect, bloc voting has produced some evils, as Sir Carl pointed out. But generally, with some few exceptions, the democratic processes in the General Assembly have worked fairly well, and the United States has received the kind of co-operation that has enabled it to achieve its policy objectives in the United Nations, especially in the political field.

But the fact should be kept in mind that the United Nations by no means has reached its outer limits with respect to membership. There are now pending nineteen applications for membership, including fourteen countries approved by the General Assembly as qualified under the Charter. If the Organization continues to expand, and especially if the balance of power should be altered by the admission of a number of small states, a reconsideration of the voting procedures in the Assembly might become a more pressing issue.

Experience with Weighted Voting in Other International Organizations

For a long time, the states of the international community have been groping for a satisfactory voting formula that would prove workable in practice and still be compatible with the principle of state sovereignty.[10] In a number of international organizations, extra voting power has been given to states with colonial possessions. This practice was adopted early in the life of the Universal Postal Union and persists today. Thus for voting purposes, Portuguese colonies in West Africa form a separate country as do the Portuguese colonies in East Africa, Asia, and Oceania.[11] Such an arrangement may have its commendable features in granting some voting power to people

[9] U. N. General Assembly, Second Session, Plenary, *Official Records,* 107th Meeting (Nov. 3, 1947), p. 695.

[10] On this general question see Sohn, *op. cit.,* pp. 316-47.

[11] See Art. 8 of *Convention on Universal Postal Union* (Revision of July 5, 1947). U.S. Department of State, *Treaties and Other International Acts,* Series 1850. In the International Telecommunications Union, the International Wine Office, and the International Office of Chemistry, votes were awarded for colonial possessions.

living in areas that have not yet attained their independence and, in practice, it may work fairly well for postal purposes. However, a formula that gives more votes to Portugal than to India and China together is obviously not a very good index of the relative importance of the Members.

In some cases, also, attempts have been made to relate the financial contributions of Members to their voting power. This was true of the former International Institute of Agriculture established in Rome in 1905. The convention setting up the Institute created five classes of membership with the number of votes allotted to states in each category increasing in arithmetical progression. The contributions of states in the various categories increased in geometric progression. Article 10 of the convention established the various categories as follows:[12]

Groups of Nations	Number of Votes	Units of Assessment
I	5	16
II	4	8
III	3	4
IV	2	2
V	1	1

More successful perhaps are the attempts that have been made to relate voting power to the varying interests of states in a particular problem. The International Sugar Council and the International Wheat Council are cases in point.[13] The International Sugar Agreement of 1953, for example, provides that a total of 2,000 votes are to be apportioned among the Council members, divided equally between the exporting and importing countries. In general, the number of votes assigned to each importing state is related to the average imports of that state. Countries such as Saudi Arabia and Jordan, with relatively small imports, have 15 votes. The largest importing countries, the United Kingdom and the United States, have 245 votes each. The 1,000 votes allocated to the exporting countries are assigned in much the same fashion. Decisions of the Council are taken by a majority of the votes cast by the exporting states and a majority of the votes cast by the importing states.

[12] William M. Malloy, compiler, *Treaties, Conventions, International Acts, Protocols and Agreements Between the United States of America and Other Powers 1776-1909*, S. Doc. 357, 61 Cong. 2 sess., Vol. II (1910), p. 2143.

[13] See *International Sugar Agreement*, Hearings before the Senate Committee on Foreign Relations on S. Ex. B, 83 Cong. 2 sess., pp. 28-29; and *International Wheat Agreement*, Hearings before the Senate Committee on Foreign Relations on S. Ex. H, 83 Cong. 1 sess., pp. 20-24.

Of a somewhat similar character are the complicated voting procedures used by the International Bank for Reconstruction and Development and the International Monetary Fund.[14] In these organizations, the voting power of each member reflects its proportionate share of the total capital to which the members as a whole have subscribed. As of June 30, 1954, for example, Panama had subscribed to less than 0.005 per cent of the capital of the bank and was entitled to 252 votes out of a total of 105,485. The United States, on the other hand, having subscribed to 34.71 per cent of the capital was assigned 32,000 votes, or approximately one third of the total.[15]

Up to the present time, population has been rarely used in international organizations as a factor in determining voting strength. The European Consultative Assembly, which is the deliberative organ of the Council of Europe, appears to be one of the few current exceptions to the rule. Article 26 of the Statute of the Council provides that member states shall be entitled to the number of representatives as follows:[16]

Belgium	6	Netherlands	6
Denmark	4	Norway	4
France	18	Sweden	6
Irish Republic	4	United Kindom	18
Italy	18		——
Luxembourg	3	Total	87

Although voting strength in the Consultative Assembly is based roughly on population, the scale nevertheless remains weighted in favor of the small states. Thus Luxembourg with a population of less than one one-hundredth that of France nevertheless has one sixth the number of votes that France has. Moreover, a two-thirds vote is required for all resolutions approved by the Assembly. This means that even if the three largest states—France, Italy, and the United Kingdom—were to support a proposal, their 54 combined votes would still be short of the total of 58 necessary for approval.

On the whole, it has not been easy to induce states to depart from

[14] U.S. Department of State, *Treaties and Other International Acts,* Series 1501, and 1502.
[15] International Bank for Reconstruction and Development, *Ninth Annual Report to the Board of Governors, 1953-1954,* pp. 52, 67.
[16] *Statute of the Council of Europe,* published by the Council of Europe (May 5, 1949), p. 8. See also the *Statute for the European Community* (Arts. 16-17) that provides for a two-house parliament with representation based, in part, on population.

the principle of one-state-one-vote. It has been done in a relatively few cases where international organizations have been set up to deal with special problems.

Current Proposals Relating to Weighted Voting in the United Nations

There have been two main proposals relating to weighted voting in the United Nations. The first relates to balanced weighted voting and was set forth by John Foster Dulles in 1950 in his book, *War or Peace*. The second was suggested by New Zealand in the First Committee of the General Assembly and relates the voting power of a state to its contribution to the United Nations budget.

Balanced Weighted Voting

Although the suggestions made in the Dulles proposal were general in character, they embrace some interesting possibilities. His proposal is one of the few of its kind that has been advanced by individuals now holding important posts in public life.

Dulles points out that in the Congress there are two ways of voting. In the Senate each state, regardless of size, has two votes. New York with its 15 million people, and Nevada with its 150,000, possess equal voting strength. In the House of Representatives, however, where representation is based on population, New York has 45 votes to Nevada's one. With this example in mind, he commented:

> I would not abolish in the United Nations an Assembly vote which, like that of our Senate, reflects the sovereign equality of all nations and gives them all an equal vote. But there might be introduced, in addition, a system of "weighted" voting so that the result would indicate, roughly, a verdict in terms also of ability to play a part in world affairs. Then it should be provided that decisions on important matters would require a simple majority, rather than two-thirds, under each of the two voting procedures.[17]

He apparently was thinking of other factors in addition to population. The weight of the recommendations of the Assembly, he contends, would be far greater than it is at present if votes reflected "not merely numbers but also ability to contribute to the

[17] Dulles, *op. cit.*, pp. 191-94.

maintenance of international peace and security." This point he stressed again in January 1954, when he said:

If the General Assembly is to assume greater responsibilities, then should there not be some form of weighted voting, so that nations which are themselves unable to assume serious military or financial responsibilities cannot put those responsibilities on other nations? Should there be, in some matters, a combination vote whereby affirmative action requires both a majority of all the members, on the basis of sovereign equality, and also a majority vote, on some weighted basis, which takes into account population, resources, and so forth?[18]

This proposal would not disturb existing machinery—although it would require revision of the Charter. It is designed to fit into the present Organization without any major alterations or adjustments. Its author does not suggest the creation of a second Assembly, nor even the need for additional delegates. He merely proposes that each vote in the Assembly be tallied twice; the first tally would correspond to the present sovereign-state arrangement with each state casting one vote; in the second tally additional votes would be awarded to states depending on their ability—because of population, productive capacity, armed strength, etc.—to contribute to the maintenance of world peace. A simple majority under each of the two procedures would be necessary for the Assembly to reach a decision. The use of these two procedures could have a double effect. It would not take away from the small nations their ability to protect their vital interests in the United Nations. So long as they could command a simple majority of the votes—and the large majority of Member states are relatively small nations—they could prevent decisions that might prove inimical to them. At the same time it would place in the hands of the larger states a potential veto that they could exercise in order to block what they might consider irresponsible action on the part of the smaller countries.

Moreover, if this kind of balanced-weighted voting were introduced, it would equip the General Assembly to assume full responsibility for such organizational matters as the selection of the Secretary-General and the admission of new Members. As things stand now, this responsibility is shared with the Security Council where the negative vote of a permanent member has often blocked action.

Few people would question the logic of bestowing on the major

[18] *Review of the United Nations Charter,* Hearings before a Subcommittee of the Senate Committee on Foreign Relations, 83 Cong. 2 sess., Pt. I, p. 7.

powers added weight in connection with important organizational decisions. But it is certainly not logical to permit any single state, by its use of the veto, to tie the hands of the United Nations with respect to such issues. This dilemma could be resolved if the interests of the great powers were reflected by an appropriate system of weighted voting in the Assembly. In this event, the responsibility of the Council with respect to such matters might well be brought to an end.

As ingenious as the Dulles plan is, it raises certain extremely difficult questions. Would the smaller nations agree to any proposal that would reduce the relative importance of their role in the General Assembly? At the San Francisco Conference, they deeply resented the privileged position given to the great powers in the United Nations. By the same token, would they not now resist any adverse readjustment in the balance of power that was so carefully worked out at the Conference? More important still, what criteria would be considered in computing the voting strength of the different members? Population? Literacy? Territorial possessions? National wealth? National product? Financial contribution to the United Nations? Foreign trade? Military strength? Willingness to contribute to the maintenance of world peace? And if several of these factors should be used, how much importance should be attached to each?

It is here that the crux of the problem of weighted voting is encountered. From a mathematical point of view, it would be far simpler to use a single criterion, such as population, and apportion the votes accordingly. But the differences between the states are so vast that any single factor would result in a false picture of the relative importance of various countries in the world and would concentrate voting power in the hands of a few states in an unrealistic way. If, for example, an attempt were made to award votes directly in proportion to total population, then two Member States, India and China, would be entitled to nearly one half the voting power in the General Assembly, and Burma would have six times as many votes as Norway. If military strength were the standard, considerably more than half the votes would go to the United States and the Soviet Union. On the other hand, if world trade were to be the standard, Great Britain would receive a relatively large number of votes and the Soviet Union would be further down the scale.

The problem of weighted voting must be approached realistically.

Clearly the small countries, which have been used to the principle of legal equality, would not underwrite any system of voting that gives the great powers fifty or one hundred votes to their one. They might, however, agree to a system that would be far less discriminatory from their point of view. The problem then, would seem to be one of agreeing on two or three criteria—such as population, national production, and contribution to the United Nations—and balancing them in such a way as to reflect, on a considerably reduced scale, the relative importance of the various countries in the organization. It might then be possible to set up four or five categories of states, as in the case of the International Institute of Agriculture, with each state receiving from one to five votes, depending on its importance.

Any proposal for weighted voting in the General Assembly should also take into consideration the unique position of the Soviet Union, which, together with its two constituent republics, Byelorussia and the Ukraine, already possesses three votes. The difficulty of removing voting power that has already been granted is apparent. Nevertheless, before any new formula is fixed, it would seem desirable to offset, in so far as possible, the initial advantage given to the Soviet Union.

At present, the chief weakness of the Dulles proposal is at once its greatest strength. If it were spelled out in detail, it might stir up vigorous opposition. So long as it remains couched in general terms, it will probably command the support of a good many people even though it may not serve as a definitive solution to the problem.

Voting Strength and United Nations Contributions

It has been suggested by at least one Member state that voting power should be directly related to the contribution of a state to the United Nations budget. In 1950, the New Zealand delegate to the First Committee of the General Assembly called attention to the "obvious elements of absurdity" that are involved in granting to a small nation the same voting power accorded a country with a population of 200 millions. He said:

Equally there is much unreality in giving to a member without armed forces and one without any desire or willingness to supply armed forces even for common defense the same voting power as to those which do possess armed forces and have from time to time, by the devotion of the lives of their citizens, proved their willingness to undertake those international duties which are correlative to all international rights.

He went on to point up the complexity of the problem, suggesting that "voting must be based on many considerations and not on population alone." He stated: "Perhaps a voting power to each member roughly equal to the proportion which its financial contribution to the funds of the United Nations bears to the total contribution would provide a system of rough justice and efficiency."[19]

Inasmuch as the United Nations is based on the principle of sovereign equality, which implies equal obligations as well as equal rights, there would seem to be some logic in this suggestion. In some organizations with small expenditures, members contribute to the budget on an equal or nearly equal basis. No member of the International Telecommunications Union, for example, pays more than 5 per cent of the budget, and the highest contribution in the Universal Postal Union is approximately 8 per cent.

The United Nations, however, with a much larger budget than any other international organization, constitutes a special case. In 1954, only 16 Member states contributed more than 1 per cent each of the budget. Nine contributed as little as 0.04 per cent each. The five permanent members of the Security Council contributed nearly 70 per cent of the total, with the United States assessed for 33.33 per cent, the Soviet Union roughly 14 per cent, the United Kingdom 10 per cent, France and China approximately 5.5 per cent each.[20] If these figures were translated into proportional voting terms, the United States, with one third of the votes, would be in a position to block any important resolution proposed in the General Assembly, and the five permanent members of the Security Council—assuming they were in agreement to do so—could always command a two-thirds majority in the Assembly. Also the United States, the United Kingdom, and France would have a simple majority of the votes before any voting began.

Such an arrangement would be open to serious objection. It would draw an invidious distinction between rich and poor Members. Even more important, as the United States delegation to the

[19] U.N. General Assembly, Fifth Session, First Committee, *Official Records,* 359th Meeting (Oct. 11, 1950), p. 98.
[20] Tables prepared by U.S. Department of State. See Subcommittee on the United Nations Charter, Senate Committee on Foreign Relations, *Review of the United Nations Charter: A Collection of Documents,* S. Doc. 87, 83 Cong. 2 sess. (Jan. 7, 1954), pp. 719-20.

United Nations has repeatedly pointed out, it would be most unfortunate if any single Member state were to be placed in such a
position that it could exert undue influence over the Organization.
Given the tremendous differences that exist among Members with
respect to their capacity to pay, the contributions scale would seem
to be an even less reliable criterion than population for determining
voting strength.

On the other hand, from the point of view of the United States,
if any reshuffling of voting power is contemplated, financial contribution certainly should not be ignored. It is a well-known fact that
some of the strongest advocates of state equality show much less
enthusiasm for that principle when it comes to the question of
apportioning the expenses of an international organization. The
Latin-American countries, for example, are strong supporters of the
principle of the legal equality of all states. But the United States,
which has only one vote out of twenty-one in the inter-American
system, bears more than half the expenses of the Organization of
American States.

Perhaps the relationship between legal equality and financial
responsibility has not been stressed enough in the United Nations.
It is suggested that if an arrangement could be worked out to give
some additional voting strength to Member states that do their
best to meet their financial responsibilities, it might have at least
one salutary effect; it might encourage some states to increase their
contributions, in order to gain voting power, and thus improve
the budgetary situation of the Organization.

In this connection consideration might also be given to certain
special United Nations programs, such as those dealing with Korean
reconstruction and Palestine refugees, which are financed by voluntary contributions. In such instances, even more than in the
regular United Nations budget, the main burden has fallen on the
United States. Although the figures vary somewhat from year to
year, the United States has contributed over 65 per cent of the
total for the United Nations Children's Fund, some 60 per cent of
the funds for the United Nations technical assistance program, 61
per cent of the Palestine refugee program, and more than 65 per
cent of the funds going to the United Nations Korean Reconstruction Agency.

If it is not possible to work out a general voting formula that
would take into account the contributions of Members to the regular

United Nations budget, it might still be feasible to accord additional voting power of an *ad hoc* nature to states contributing heavily to these special programs. This could be done by devising a weighted voting formula for the Executive Board of the Children's Emergency Fund, for example, which is charged with the general supervision of that particular program. It would seem logical that those governments that make heavy contributions to such programs should be given additional control over the expenditure of the funds.

Proposals for Weighted Voting in a Supranational Organization

In addition to the suggestions outlined above, a number of proposals have been advanced, relating to representation and voting, by groups and individuals who advocate the establishment of some kind of supranational organization. Although these ideas have a limited application to the United Nations as it is presently constituted, it may be worth-while to review them briefly for whatever light they may shed on the problem under consideration.

In the General Assembly, in line with the principle of sovereign equality, each state is represented by five delegates and five alternates, but each delegation has only one vote. The supranational proposals, for the most part, would abandon the principle of state sovereignty by advocating fundamental changes in the size and character of the representation to which each country is entitled. Most of them recommend some form of weighted or proportionate representation, the net effect of which would be a system of weighted voting.

Representation Based on Population

Among the most fully developed of the plans for supranational government is the Clark-Sohn proposal.[21] This proposal calls for the creation of a United Nations peace force and would delegate to the General Assembly certain legislative authority, especially with respect to the enforcement of universal disarmament and the control of atomic energy. Representation in the Assembly, under

[21] See Grenville Clark and Louis B. Sohn, *Peace Through Disarmament and Charter Revision* (Preliminary Print, July 1953).

the proposal would be based solely on population. Each Member of the United Nations would be entitled to one representative for each five million population or major fraction thereof. Small states with a population of more than 100,000 and not more than 2,500,000 would be entitled to one representative, and Members with large populations would be limited to thirty representatives. International entities with a population of 100,000 or less—such as San Marino and Monaco—would be entitled to a delegate with the right to participate in the discussion but without the right to vote. The formula would be adjusted from time to time taking account of world population increases, in order to ensure that the number of representatives should never exceed 400. The net effect of the plan would be to create a General Assembly of 382 representatives and 3 delegates to represent a world population of 2,400 millions.

The sponsors of this proposal specifically reject any system of weighted representation based on economic resources, productive capacity, literacy, trade, national income, or related factors. As pointed out in their study:

> They believe that all such plans, which necessarily give weight to wealth and other economic factors that are largely the result of geography and history, involve an anachronistic discrimination. Such a discrimination would run counter to the inherent equality of all individuals, which in the modern world should not and cannot be denied. They have, therefore, come to the conclusion that the true solution lies in an apportionment based fundamentally on population. It is for reasons of workability only that in the foregoing proposal upper and lower limits have been placed on the representation of any nation.[22]

By limiting to thirty the maximum number of representatives the largest countries might have, and by counting the people of the non-self-governing territories for purposes of representation, the proposal would keep fairly even the voting strength of the great powers. China, the Soviet Union, the United States, and India would be given thirty representatives, the United Kingdom twenty-five, and France nineteen. On the other hand, Germany would be entitled to only fourteen, Italy to nine, Japan to seventeen, and Indonesia and Pakistan to fifteen each. Some forty nations would have only one representative. With such a wide spread in voting power, the more populous Member nations would be given a dominant position in the General Assembly. As a practical matter, it is extremely doubtful, at best, that the smaller countries would

[22] *Ibid.*, p. 21.

be willing to accept any system in which India or China would be allotted almost as many votes as the twenty Latin-American states combined.

In one other important respect, this proposal departs from the principle of state sovereignty. It suggests that representatives to the General Assembly be chosen in national elections or by vote of the national legislatures. This, it is argued, would "stress the desirability that the representatives shall receive their mandate directly from the peoples of the respective nations."[23]

A Bicameral World Legislature

Somewhat similar to the Clark-Sohn proposals are the recommendations of the British parliamentary group for world government. In their Plan "A" they call for the creation of a world legislative body made up of two chambers, the upper chamber consisting of "one representative of each nation state appointed in a manner to be determined by that state."[24] The intention here apparently is to provide for some continuity with the present General Assembly. The group also argues that such an arrangement would "tend to secure the representation of some valuable men and women who were not willing to submit themselves to popular suffrages."[25]

In contrast to the upper house, the lower chamber would consist of representatives of Member states "in numbers proportionate to population." This would reflect in some degree the balance achieved by the Senate and the House of Representatives in the United States Congress. Although the British Parliamentary Group do not spell out their plan in any detail, they evidently contemplate placing an upper limit on the number of representatives from any state. In a note dealing with the lower chamber they point out that "the reason for weighting the representation is to avoid the overwhelming preponderance of the nations with the largest population, and thus make it more attractive to join."[26]

In suggesting a double-vote system based on the sovereign equality of states and some form of weighted representation, the British Parliamentary Group approach somewhat the Dulles proposal. The

[23] *Ibid.*, p. 23.
[24] World Association of Parliamentarians for World Government, *Report of the Second London Parliamentary Conference on World Government* (September 1952), pp. 101-07.
[25] *Ibid.*, p. 105.
[26] *Ibid.*

principal difference would seem to be that the Dulles proposal does not suggest changing the simple unicameral character of, or the method of representation in, the present General Assembly. It would obtain a double vote by mathematical rather than by physical changes.

Federal Union and Atlantic Union

Supporters of Federal Union and some supporters of Atlantic Union have advocated a two-house union legislature comparable, with some variations, to the House and Senate of the United States Congress. As one proponent has stated, the lower house would be "based completely on the population and the other modifying this principle of equal men in favor of equal states."[27] This two-house legislature would exercise the authority granted to it, within the limited geographical area made up of the fifteen democracies first suggested for membership in the Union.

According to the formula for representation presented by this proposal—which was for illustrative purposes only—one representative would be allotted in the lower house for every million inhabitants. On this basis, the United States would have received 129 of the 280 seats, in accordance with the population statistics then available. In the senate, it was proposed that each self-governing nation with less than 25 million inhabitants should be given two senators, with two additional senators for every population increment of 25 millions or major portion thereof up to 100 millions. Under this arrangement the United States would be allotted eight of the forty seats.

Under the proposed plan, the three largest countries (France, 42; Great Britain, 47; the United States, 129) would have 218 out of 280 representatives in the house and 16 out of 40 in the senate. Thus an equitable balance would be achieved, with the small states holding a substantial majority in the senate and the large states commanding a majority in the house. No one member state could possibly control either house, and the voting strength of each member would diminish relatively as other states entered the union.

Inasmuch as the suggested membership of the proposed union has varied somewhat, those who support Federal Union have refrained from developing their formula for representation in

[27] Clarence Streit, *Union Now* (1940), p. 142.

any detail. The exact number and distribution of seats would depend on the list of participating states. Under their proposal, however, representatives in both houses of the union legislature would be elected by popular vote, would vote as individuals, and would be responsible to the people rather than to their national governments. With respect to voting, the Atlantic Union Committee has stated:

> It is likely . . . that the constitution of an Atlantic Union would provide for a two-thirds or even three-fourths vote on questions of particular concern to its constituent peoples. This, together with provision for two houses in the Union's legislature, would afford protection to minority interests. Such protection, which could be carried as far as the people forming the Union believed desirable, would have to satisfy the American people in order to secure their ratification of the Union's constitution.[28]

Voting Power and Regionalism

Still another approach to the problem was developed in 1948 by the Committee to Frame a World Constitution. This committee used the concept of regionalism as a basis for representation in a world assembly. The formula that they devised was designed to accomplish two major objectives: (1) to de-emphasize national boundary lines and minimize the importance of the nation-state; and (2) to develop a method of representation based on population, yet weighted in favor of those countries with the richest experience in democratic government.[29]

Under the proposal of the committee, a federal convention would be convened consisting of delegates chosen by direct election in the member states, one delegate for each million in population or major fraction thereof. This body would then subdivide into nine electoral colleges, corresponding to nine regions of the world, for the purpose of nominating and electing a president and the members of the world council or legislature. The council would be made up of nine members from each region with eighteen elected at large, or a total of ninety-nine. Representatives would vote as individuals rather than as members of instructed delegations.

The nine regions are delineated in the draft constitution roughly as follows: (1) Europa, made up of the continent of Europe and the

---

[28] Atlantic Union Committee, *Twenty Questions on Atlantic Union* (1950), pp. 14-15.

[29] Committee to Frame a World Constitution, *Preliminary Draft of a World Constitution* (1948).

United Kingdom; (2) Atlantis, consisting of the United States of America with the United Kingdom if the latter so decides, and certain kindred communities; (3) Eurasia, including Russia and certain east Baltic or Slavic or south Danubian nations; (4) Afrasia, made up of the Near and Middle East, and the states of North Africa; (5) Africa, south of the Sahara; (6) India and Pakistan; (7) Asia Major, consisting of China, Korea, Japan, and other nations of the north- and mid-Pacific; (8) Austrasia, made up of Indochina and Indonesia, and certain other mid- and south-Pacific countries; and (9) Columbia, made up of the Western Hemisphere south of the United States.[30]

It will be noted that some of these regions would have a greater representation in proportion to population than others. Thus Asia Major (China, Japan, Korea), with about 25 per cent of the population of the world, would receive 11 per cent of the total representation, while Columbia (Latin America) would have the same number of representatives with only about 7 per cent of the population. The three regions of the Western World—Europa, Atlantis, and Columbia—with about a fifth of the population of the world, would be given one third of the representation.

Admittedly, this device of grouping kindred nations or cultures together into regions for representation and voting purposes would have certain theoretical advantages that some of the other proposals would not have. Certainly no single region, and no bloc of two or three regions, could dominate the world assembly or prevent the approval of desirable measures. Moreover, the formula provides a basis for representation other than mere population statistics without undue discrimination against any area of the world.

This is obviously a very complex proposal, which assumes that people and governments are willing to move much further in the direction of world government and regionalism than is probably the case. There is little in the experience of the United Nations to date that would indicate that its Member states are ready to pool their voting power with their neighbors on a purely regional basis. Geographic proximity or contiguity does not necessarily result in compatibility or friendly relations between states. Indeed, many neighboring states, such as India and Pakistan or Japan and Korea, often find themselves at odds and would probably find strong political reasons for refusing to join a regional grouping of this kind.

[30] *Ibid.*, Art. V.

Balanced Representation

Certain groups have also suggested that representation and voting be weighted on the basis of population and other factors. For the most part, they do not explain in any detail the procedure by which this might be accomplished. The United World Federalists, for example, have long favored a system of "balanced representation" in their projected world legislative assembly. In 1949 a spokesman for the organization stated:

> It is unlikely that a system of representation, based solely upon population, with no upper or lower limits, would be more acceptable or desirable, for then India and China, with their vast millions, would receive a voting power out of proportion to their present role in the world.
>
> Again, we do not seek to provide a precise formula, but we suggest that in addition to population other factors might be taken into account, such as economic development and education.[31]

And in 1950, it was suggested that such factors as population, industrial capacity, monetary contribution, and regional formulas ought to be taken into account. Other representatives of United World Federalists have expressed, in general terms, the same point of view.[32]

In their Plan "B," which is designed to remove what they regard as certain imperfections in the United Nations Charter, the British Parliamentary Group for World Government arrived at the same conclusion. Plan "B" recommends that the governments of Member states of the United Nations take action "to improve the representative character of the Assembly, by, for example, introducing the principle of weighted voting possibly by establishing a bicameral Assembly and relating representation in one of the chambers to economic and/or population factors."[33] But the means for implementing the proposal are not indicated in the plan.

Representatives Voting as Individuals

One common feature of the supranational proposals is the proposition that representatives to a world assembly should be popularly

---

[31] *To Seek Development of the United Nations into a World Federation*, Hearings before the House Committee on Foreign Affairs on H. Con. Res. 64, 81 Cong. 1 sess., p. 163.

[32] *Revision of the United Nations Charter*, Hearings before a Subcommittee of the Senate Committee on Foreign Relations, 81 Cong. 2 sess., pp. 523-24, 127.

[33] World Association of Parliamentarians for World Government, *Report of the Second London Parliamentary Conference on World Government*, p. 108.

elected and should cast their votes as individuals. Although such a recommendation might be considered essential in any plan for world government in which state sovereignty is relegated to the background, if it were transplanted to the General Assembly, as suggested in some of these proposals, it would involve a fundamental change in the character of the United Nations.

If some kind of weighted representation should be considered for the General Assembly, it would be especially important to keep the problem of responsibility in mind. At present, delegations to the Assembly are appointed by the governments of the Member states, are responsible to those governments, and ordinarily vote in accordance with instructions received from their governments. The lines of responsibility are clear and direct. Any other arrangement, in existing circumstances, might well result in an unmanageable dispersal of power that would prove embarrassing both to the Member states and to the United Nations.

Advocates of world government generally argue that if their plans were put into operation, elected delegates probably would vote in national blocs in the beginning, but as time went on, this tendency would be overcome. As some of them state it:

> It is true that the Representatives of a particular nation would tend to vote the same way on issues of great importance to that nation. . . . It can, however, be expected that there would develop in the course of time a spirit of representing the interests of the world as a whole rather than those of individual nations; and that the Representatives would more and more tend to vote in accordance with their judgment as to the best interests of all the peoples, as in the case of national parliaments where the interests of the whole nation have become of no less importance than the interests of a particular section or group.[34]

The arguments against such an arrangement in an organization of sovereign states are apparent. The first has to do with the relations between democratic countries and totalitarian systems. Delegates from democratic nations might possibly vote as individuals, but it is inconceivable that the representatives of totalitarian states, whose official acts would be closely supervised by their governments, would ever be in a position to do so. As a result, the democratic countries might be placed at a serious disadvantage, not only because of the divergence of views within their own ranks, but also because of the enforced solidarity that would characterize the voting

[34] Clark and Sohn, *op. cit.,* pp. 47-48.

of all delegates, from whatever states, who might owe allegiance to world communism.

In the second place, the resulting lack of discipline among the delegates attending the meetings of the General Assembly might prove harmful to the United Nations program. What practical benefits, for example, could come from the passage of a particular resolution if it were approved by a majority of uninstructed delegates, only to be repudiated by the Member governments that have the responsibility for putting the recommendations of the Assembly into force?

Finally, with the conduct of diplomacy as complicated as it is, states find it extremely difficult to develop a unified, cohesive foreign policy even in the best of circumstances. It would seem unlikely that most governments and the people they represent would want to abdicate their responsibility for the conduct of foreign relations to persons voting as "individuals" and thus beyond their control in an international organization.

An Illustrative Proposal for Balanced Weighted Voting

In a recent staff study released by the Subcommittee on the United Nations Charter of the Senate Committee on Foreign Relations an illustrative formula for weighted voting was set forth.[35] This formula was based, in part, on the past experience of international organizations and would not constitute a drastic departure from present procedures. The idea was not final in form; rather it was presented as a tentative suggestion in order to stimulate further discussion of an important issue. The formula, which is presented in the accompanying table, reveals, in a concrete way, some of the complexities and difficulties involved in working out a system of weighted voting.

It is suggested in this illustration, in line with the Dulles proposal referred to above, that the vote of each Member state in the General Assembly be counted twice; once on the basis of one vote for each state and the second time on the basis of a weighted formula. A majority of each of the votes would be required for the General

[35] See Subcommittee on the United Nations Charter, Senate Committee on Foreign Relations, *Representation and Voting in the United Nations General Assembly*, Staff Study No. 4, 83 Cong. 2 sess. (September 1954), pp. 19-23.

Assembly to reach a decision. In this weighted voting formula, how-ever, only two criteria are taken into account; the population of a state and its contribution to the United Nations. Each state would be awarded from two to ten votes with the scale running from one to five for each criterion. Votes would be awarded for population in accordance with the following scale: States under one million would receive one vote; one to five millions, two votes; five to twenty millions, three votes; twenty to one hundred millions, four votes; and over one hundred millions, five votes. For United Nations con-tributions, the scale would be: States contributing less than $20,000 to the regular United Nations budget would receive one vote; $20,000 to $100,000, two votes; $100,000 to $500,000, three votes; $500,000 to $2 million, four votes; and all over $2 million, five votes.

Several observations may be made about the possible results of this kind of illustrative weighted voting system.

1. It would increase the relative voting strength of certain Mem-bers—particularly the great nations—but it would not materially alter the balance of power in the General Assembly.

2. The Latin-American and the Arab Member states would lose somewhat, as indeed they would in almost any system of weighted voting that could be devised. Thus the twenty Latin-American states, with a total of 91 out of the 338 votes in the General As-sembly, would command only 27 per cent of the votes instead of the strategic one third they now control. The six Arab states would drop from 10 per cent to roughly 8 per cent.

3. Unless the votes of the Ukraine and Byelorussia were dis-counted somewhat, as suggested earlier in this study, the Soviet bloc would pick up voting strength. The five Soviet-controlled states now command 8 per cent of the votes; under the illustrative schedule they would claim 11 per cent. The so-called neutralist states of India, Indonesia, and Burma would also add slightly to their voting power.

4. Two other groups of states, generally inclined to parallel Ameri-can policy, would either hold their own or would gain voting strength. The members of the North Atlantic Treaty Organization that are in the United Nations would continue to hold roughly one fifth of the votes. The seven British Commonwealth countries would increase their voting power from 11.6 per cent to 15 per cent.

5. If other criteria, such as national income, productivity, and

ILLUSTRATIVE WEIGHTED VOTING FORMULA—UNITED NATIONS GENERAL ASSEMBLY VOTING STRENGTH IN ORDER OF POPULATION, FINANCIAL CONTRIBUTION, AND COMBINED WEIGHTED VOTES[a]

Population Vote

Rank	Country	Population[b] (in thousands)	Vote	Per Cent of Population Vote
1	China	463,493	5	2.87
2	India	367,000	5	
3	United States	156,981	5	
4	U.S.S.R.	151,663	5	
5	United Kingdom	122,537[d]	5	
6	France	91,128[d]	5	
7	Indonesia	78,163	4	
8	Pakistan	75,842	4	
9	Brazil	54,477	4	
10	Ukraine	30,960	4	
11	Mexico	26,922	4	2.30
12	Poland	24,977	4	
13	Egypt	21,425	4	
14	Turkey	20,934	4	
15	Philippines	20,631	4	
16	Iran	19,798	3	
17	Thailand	19,193	3	
18	Burma	18,859	3	
19	Argentina	18,054	3	
20	Yugoslavia	16,729	3	
21	Ethiopia	15,000	3	
22	Canada	14,430	3	
23	Union of South Africa	12,912	3	
24	Czechoslovakia	12,340	3	
25	Afghanistan	12,000	3	1.73
26	Colombia	11,768	3	
27	Netherlands	10,377	3	
28	Peru	8,864	3	
29	Belgium	8,706	3	
30	Australia	8,649	3	
31	Greece	7,761	3	
32	Sweden	7,125	3	
33	Saudi Arabia	7,000	3	
34	Chile	5,932	3	
35	Cuba	5,927	3	
36	Byelorussia	5,568	3	
37	Venezuela	5,280	3	

Contribution Vote

Rank	Country	Contribution[c] (in dollars)	Vote	Per Cent of Contribution Vote
1	United States	13,765,290	5	3.05
2	U.S.S.R.	5,843,950	5	
3	United Kingdom	4,047,400	5	
4	France	2,374,750	5	
5	China	2,321,060	5	
6	India	1,404,200	4	
7	Canada	1,362,900	4	
8	Ukraine	776,440	4	
9	Australia	722,750	4	
10	Poland	714,490	4	2.44
11	Sweden	681,450	4	
12	Brazil	578,200	4	
13	Argentina	578,200	4	
14	Belgium	560,940	4	
15	Netherlands	516,250	4	
16	Czechoslovakia	433,650	3	
17	Denmark	322,140	3	
18	Union of South Africa	322,140	3	
19	Mexico	309,750	3	
20	Pakistan	309,750	3	
21	Turkey	268,450	3	
22	Indonesia	247,800	3	
23	Byelorussia	206,500	3	
24	Norway	206,500	3	
25	New Zealand	198,240	3	1.83
26	Egypt	194,110	3	
27	Philippines	185,850	3	
28	Yugoslavia	181,720	3	
29	Colombia	169,330	3	
30	Venezuela	161,070	3	
31	Cuba	140,420	3	
32	Chile	136,290	3	
33	Iran	115,640	3	
34	Greece	86,730	2	
35	Peru	74,340	2	
36	Thailand	74,340	2	

Combined Vote

Rank	Country	Vote	Per Cent of Combined Vote
1	China	10	2.96
	U.S.S.R.	10	
	United Kingdom	10	
	United States	10	
	France	10	
2	India	9	2.66
3	Brazil	8	2.37
	Poland	8	
	Ukraine	8	
4	Argentina	7	2.07
	Australia	7	
	Belgium	7	
	Canada	7	
	Egypt	7	
	Indonesia	7	
	Mexico	7	
	Netherlands	7	
	Pakistan	7	
	Philippines	7	
	Sweden	7	
	Turkey	7	
5	Byelorussia	6	1.78
	Chile	6	
	Colombia	6	
	Cuba	6	
	Czechoslovakia	6	
	Iran	6	
	Union of South Africa	6	
	Venezuela	6	
	Yugoslavia	6	
	Afghanistan	5	
	Burma	5	
	Denmark	5	
	Ethiopia	5	

Population Vote

Rank	Country	Population[b] (in thousands)	Vote	Per Cent of Population Vote
39	Yemen	4,500	2	
40	Denmark	4,334	2	
41	Syria	3,381	2	
42	Ecuador	3,350	2	
43	Norway	3,327	2	
44	Haiti	3,200	2	
45	Bolivia	3,089	2	
46	Guatemala	2,938	2	
47	Uruguay	2,365	2	1.15
48	Dominican Republic	2,336	2	
49	New Zealand	1,995	2	
50	El Salvador	1,986	2	
51	Liberia	1,648	2	
52	Israel	1,607	2	
53	Honduras	1,513	2	
54	Paraguay	1,464	2	
55	Lebanon	1,320	2	
56	Nicaragua	1,128	2	
57	Costa Rica	850	1	
58	Panama	841	1	.57
59	Luxembourg	301	1	
60	Iceland	148	1	
	Total	2,012,026	175	

Contribution Vote

Rank	Country	Contribution[c] (in dollars)	Vote	Per Cent of Contribution Vote
38	Israel	70,210	2	
39	Burma	53,690	2	
40	Iraq	49,560	2	
41	Ethiopia	41,300	2	
42	Afghanistan	33,040	2	1.22
43	Syria	33,040	2	
44	Saudi Arabia	28,910	2	
45	Guatemala	28,910	2	
46	Bolivia	24,780	2	
47	El Salvador	24,780	2	
48	Luxembourg	24,780	2	
49	Dominican Republic	29,650	2	
50	Lebanon	20,650	2	
51	Panama	20,650	2	
52	Costa Rica	16,520	1	
53	Ecuador	16,520	1	
54	Haiti	16,520	1	
55	Honduras	16,520	1	
56	Iceland	16,520	1	.61
57	Liberia	16,520	1	
58	Paraguay	16,520	1	
59	Nicaragua	16,520	1	
60	Yemen	16,520	1	
	Total	41,300,000	164	

Combined Vote

Rank	Country	Vote	Per Cent of Combined Vote
6	Iraq	5	1.48
	New Zealand	5	
	Norway	5	
	Peru	5	
	Saudi Arabia	5	
	Thailand	5	
7	Bolivia	4	
	Dominican Republic	4	
	El Salvador	4	
	Guatemala	4	1.18
	Israel	4	
	Lebanon	4	
	Syria	4	
	Uruguay	4	
8	Ecuador	3	
	Haiti	3	
	Honduras	3	
	Liberia	3	
	Luxembourg	3	.89
	Nicaragua	3	
	Panama	3	
	Paraguay	3	
	Yemen	3	
9	Costa Rica	2	.59
	Iceland	2	
	Total	339	

[a] From Subcommittee on the United Nations Charter, Senate Committee on Foreign Relations, *Representation and Voting in the United Nations General Assembly*, Staff Study No. 4, 83 Cong. 2 sess. (September 1954), pp. 20–21.
[b] Statistical Office of the United Nations, *Population and Vital Statistics Reports*, Series A, Vol. VI, No. 2 (April 1954).
[c] Subcommittee on the United Nations Charter, Senate Committee on Foreign Relations, *Review of the United Nations Charter: A Collection of Documents*, S. Doc. 87, 83 Cong. 2 sess. (Jan. 7, 1954), pp. 719–20.
[d] Aggregate figure, including non-self-governing territories and dependencies. In this illustrative formula, France, a permanent member of the Security Council is awarded five votes even though its total population falls below the 100 million suggested for the first category of states.

foreign trade, were taken into account, the states of Western Europe and the British Commonwealth countries would improve their relative standings somewhat. The more complicated the formula, however, the more opposition it would be likely to encounter.

6. In this formula the votes were calculated on the basis of the contribution of each Member to the *regular* United Nations budget. Clearly, this is not the most satisfactory criterion. It would be better —although perhaps not very practical—if a schedule could be devised to reflect the ability and the willingness of the United Nations Members to contribute man power, military equipment and supplies, as well as bases and other facilities toward the maintenance of world peace.

Weighted Voting and United States Policy

In spite of the growing importance of voting in the General Assembly, this remains one of the relatively unexplored areas of the Charter. Little research has been done on this problem, and few practical suggestions have been made for improving the present situation. Nor does the experience of international organizations in the past shed much helpful light on the subject. It is apparent that the whole question needs careful analysis before the United States Government can be in a position to consider seriously any specific proposals for changing the present provisions of the Charter.

It is easy, perhaps, for students of the Charter to place too much emphasis on the technical imperfections of the present system of voting. In practice, Article 18 seems to have worked fairly well. Indeed, it can be said that it is one of the articles of the Charter that, on the whole, has been implemented most smoothly. As a result, there has been relatively little pressure in the United Nations for change in this article.

In summarizing the analyses above, however, two points seem inescapable.

In the first place, there are striking inequalities among the sixty Members of the United Nations with respect to population, armed strength, national income, territory, contributions to the Organization, and other factors. The present system of awarding one vote to each state thus confers on the smaller countries a voting strength far out of proportion to their size.

In the second place, if any departure were to be made from the principle of one-state-one-vote, it would have to be a modest one with a relatively low ceiling placed on the voting power of the great nations. For the small states, having been in a favorable voting position for many years, could be expected to put up a vigorous fight to block any proposal that would seriously alter what is in effect their privileged status in the General Assembly, just as the great powers might be expected to oppose any change in their privileged status in the Security Council.

This does not mean that a satisfactory *quid pro quo* could not be arranged. It would appear that the problem of weighted voting is closely related to other possible revisions of the Charter. The small states, in other words, might be persuaded to make concessions in this respect if the Assembly were given sufficient authority to take vigorous and effective action on behalf of world peace.

Voting in the General Assembly is very serious business. Any significant realignment of votes might have an adverse impact on United States policy—either now or at some time in the unpredictable future. The United States should not propose the principle of weighted voting, unless it makes certain, through a careful analysis of the facts, that such a move would be in its national interest. For example, any formula that would result in a substantial decrease in voting power for the twenty Latin-American countries would clearly be open to grave objections. Generally speaking, these nations have been the most consistent supporters of United States policy in the United Nations on questions that most vitally affect American national interests. The position of the United States on this issue must also be conditioned by the probability that a number of states—including the relatively great powers of Germany, Japan, and Italy—may be admitted to the United Nations within the next few years. With a possible increase in membership that may run as high as 35 per cent, voting patterns in the Assembly could undergo drastic changes.

Up to the present time, the United States has been able to retain its position of leadership in the General Assembly through the logic of its argument and the justice of its cause. In a political organization where each state has one vote, it has been able to rally the small countries to the cause of the free world. Theoretically, there may seem to be logical reasons for supporting some system of weighted voting for the General Assembly. From a practical point of view, however, many people believe it might be better to let well enough alone.

CHAPTER XII

Jurisdiction of the International Court of Justice

T HE LATE Senator Robert A. Taft wrote in 1951: "I believe that in the long run the only way to establish peace is to write a law, agreed to by each of the nations, to govern the relations of such nations with each other and to obtain the covenant of all such nations that they will abide by that law and by decisions made thereunder." He commented further that "without any veto power" the nations must also agree that "they will submit their disputes to adjudication and abide by the decision of an impartial tribunal."[1] The conditions to which Senator Taft referred do not exist in the international community today.

There is no international law in the same sense that domestic law exists, and there is no international court that has the far-reaching authority of a national judicial body. The Charter does not give legislative authority to the United Nations, and there are no community forces to compel acceptance of judicial decisions. Neither is there agreement that disputes will be submitted to the International Court of Justice nor assurance, if they are voluntarily submitted, that the decisions of the Court will be enforced. Parties to a dispute need not resort to the International Court unless they choose to do so, either in a particular case or by reason of their having accepted the compulsory jurisdiction of the Court pursuant to Article 36 of the Statute. Nevertheless, if they do refer a dispute to the Court, under Article 94 of the Charter they undertake "to comply with the decision." If the Security Council finds it necessary, it may "decide on measures" to give effect to the judgment but, unless there were a threat to the peace, it is doubtful that the Security Council could take enforcement action.[2]

[1] Robert A. Taft, *A Foreign Policy for Americans* (1951), pp. 39-40. Similarly, Senator Walter F. George wrote in 1955: "The development of rules of law to regulate the conduct of nations in their relations with each other in such a way that war may be avoided is perhaps the most important single task man can perform in his eternal quest for peace." Subcommittee on the United Nations Charter, Senate Committee on Foreign Relations, *The International Court of Justice*, Staff Study No. 8, 84 Cong. 1 sess. (May 1955), p. III.

[2] See Clyde Eagleton, *International Government* (1948), p. 347.

It is clear that international law is on quite a different footing from domestic law. Although states normally obey what is described as "international law," one authority has pointed out, "they do so with a sort of implied gentleman's understanding that it must not be too exigent in its demands upon them. . . . International order can only be placed on a firm foundation if there is assurance that power . . . will be forthcoming to maintain or restore it if a breach occurs."[3]

Law and judicial institutions are an inseparable part of the community in which they operate. Any examination of proposed changes pertaining to the international juridical aspects of the United Nations is thus limited by the fact that the International Court, its jurisdiction, the law that it applies, and the judicial institutions related thereto must stay in step with the fundamental nature of the United Nations. Should the United Nations at some future date become a federation with supranational powers instead of an association of sovereign states, the function of international law and the Court might be quite different than it is at present.

Role of the International Court in the United Nations System

The International Court of Justice is the direct successor to the Permanent Court of International Justice.[4] The Permanent Court, although not an organ of the League of Nations, had a close relationship to it. In fact, the relationship between the two was so close that, prior to the creation of the United Nations, it was suggested by some that the new International Court should be an institution separate from the new United Nations because the old court "has to some extent suffered . . . from its organic connection with the League, which, whether logically or not, resulted in its prestige being dependent to some extent upon the varying fortunes of the League."[5] This view was not, however, generally accepted. As a result, the relationship between the new International Court and the United Nations is even closer than that which existed between

[3] J. L. Brierly, "International Law: Some Conditions of Its Progress," *International Affairs*, Vol. 22 (July 1946), p. 358.

[4] For full history of the work of the Permanent Court and the International Court see annual articles by Manley O. Hudson in *The American Journal of International Law*, beginning Vol. 17 (1923) and each January issue thereafter.

[5] *Cf.* W. Frankel, "The Future of the Permanent Court of International Justice," *The London Quarterly of World Affairs* (January 1945), p. 116.

the Permanent Court and the League. The new Court is "the principal judicial organ of the United Nations" and Members of the United Nations are *ipso facto* parties to the Statute of the Court.

When consideration was given during the Second World War to the type of court that might be associated with the projected postwar international organization, there was general agreement that the Statute of the Permanent Court of International Justice was a suitable basis on which to begin drafting a Statute for the new Court.[6] Indeed, when the United Nations Committee of Jurists, consisting of representatives from forty-four nations, met in Washington in 1945 to prepare a draft statute for the new court, it took the old Statute as the point of departure for its discussions. It posed only four "issues" for the consideration of the San Francisco Conference.

First was the question whether the Court should be viewed as a *new* body, or as the *old* body revised. The Conference decided that the Court should be a new organization, thus simplifying the problem of associating with it the United States and the Soviet Union, which had not been members of the old Permanent Court.

Second was the question whether the Court should have compulsory or optional jurisdiction over legal disputes. Despite the fact that a majority of the delegations favored compulsory jurisdiction, the Conference decided to retain, with minor modifications, the provisions of Article 36 of the old Statute.[7] The United States Government strongly favored the latter course. That article gave the Court jurisdiction over all cases referred to it by the parties and permitted states at any time to accept the compulsory jurisdiction of the Court with respect to legal disputes.

Third was the method of nominating judges. Again in this case, the Conference accepted with minor changes the provisions of the old Statute calling for elections by the Council and the Assembly from lists of persons nominated by the national groups of the states members of the Permanent Court of Arbitration.

Fourth, there was the question of the scope of the authority of the Court to render advisory opinions when so requested by the proposed new international organization. The Charter provides not only that the General Assembly and the Security Council may re-

[6] See the volume in this Brookings series, *A History of the United Nations Charter.*

[7] See U.N. Information Organizations and U. S. Library of Congress, *Documents of the United Nations Conference on International Organization,* Vol. 13 (1945), pp. 390-92. (Hereinafter cited as *UNCIO Documents.*)

quest advisory opinions, but that the Assembly may authorize "other organs of the United Nations and specialized agencies" to request such opinions.[8]

The changes between the old Statute and the new were, in the words of one authority, "comparatively trivial."[9]

Present Jurisdiction
of the Court

The International Court of Justice has two types of jurisdiction. It may consider "all cases which the parties refer to it," but "only states may be parties in cases before the Court."[10] Second, the authorized organs and specialized agencies of the United Nations may request the Court "to give an advisory opinion on any legal question."[11] The jurisdiction of the Court therefore does not extend to individuals. Moreover, its jurisdiction with respect to states that are parties to the Statute is not automatic. It has jurisdiction over disputes between states only if the parties have agreed to refer the dispute to the Court, if there is provision for such jurisdiction in a treaty, or by virtue of both parties to the dispute having accepted the so-called "optional clause."[12]

Thus if a state breaches a rule of international law or an agreement, the state cannot be brought before the Court unless it has in fact consented to the jurisdiction of the Court by one of the methods indicated. Even if the Court acquires jurisdiction, a state found liable for a violation of law cannot be punished. The Court hands down decisions. But in the absence of methods for coercing states to comply with decisions of the Court, the decisions can be ignored even though they may carry considerable moral weight. For various reasons, however, states are reluctant to ignore the decisions of the Court.

[8] Article 96 of the Charter.
[9] Eagleton, *op. cit.*, p. 346.
[10] See Articles 36 and 34 of the Statute.
[11] Article 96 of the Charter.
[12] Article 36(2) of the Statute, the so-called "optional clause," provides in part that "states parties to the present Statute may at any time declare that they recognize as compulsory *ipso facto* and without special agreement, in relation to any other state accepting the same obligation, the jurisdiction of the Court in all legal disputes concerning: a. the interpretation of a treaty; b. any question of international law; c. the existence of any fact which, if established, would constitute a breach of an international obligation; d. the nature or extent of the reparation to be made for the breach of an international obligation."

The authority of the Court to give advisory opinions when requested enables the organs of the United Nations to seek advice on legal matters if they wish to do so. As indicated by the term "advisory opinion," questions that the Court may answer in response to a request from a United Nations organ have no binding effect. The organs requesting the opinion, as well as the states affected by such opinion, may, or may not, accept it as a guide to conduct. In some instances, however, when the Assembly has authorized organs to request advisory opinions, it has specified that such opinions are to be binding.[13]

Criticism of the Court

Whether the International Court of Justice in the ten years since its establishment has fulfilled the high expectations that many held in 1945, is a debatable question. "That the United Nations' International Court of Justice as an advisory organ has been all but abandoned by the U.N. will come as a shock to the American lawyer, legislator and layman," one commentator has declared.[14] "It is . . . unlikely," according to the former Registrar of the Court in commenting on the activity of the Court in disputes between states, "that any important questions between States on different sides of the border line [the Iron Curtain] will in the near future be submitted to the Court. . . ."[15] Others hold a contrary view. Professor Lauterpacht, elected judge of the Court in 1954, for example, believes that the Court has "not only vindicated the expectations attached to its establishment at the end of the Second World War" but "they have exceeded it." The Court "has proved the most successful institution of the United Nations."[16]

Certainly, any individual who may have expected the International Court to become a major factor in the settlement of political disputes of the type that might lead to war must be disappointed. As one observer has stated:

[13] See International Court of Justice, *Yearbook, 1953-54,* p. 43.

[14] See Louis B. Wehle, "The United Nations By-passes the International Court as the Council's Advisor: A Study in Contrived Frustration," *University of Pennsylvania Law Review,* Vol. 98 (February 1950), p. 285.

[15] Edvard Hambro, "The International Court of Justice," *International Affairs,* Vol. 30 (January 1954), p. 39.

[16] Oliver J. Lissitzyn, *The International Court of Justice: Its Role in the Maintenance of International Peace and Security* (1951), foreword by H. Lauterpacht.

The immediate effect of the Court's activity as an organ for the settlement of disputes has not been spectacular. It would be difficult to maintain that any judgment or advisory opinion of the Court had the specific effect of preventing recourse to violence in an international dispute. . . . It would be difficult to deny, on the other hand, that the use of the Court has in some instances contributed to the relaxation of tension between contestants.[17]

The Court, however, has not been able to avoid the impact of the cold war. When a majority of the nations have thought their interests in particular disputes might best be served by supporting resolutions of the General Assembly seeking advisory opinions from the Court, as in the cases relating to the admission of new Members to the United Nations, they have voted for such resolutions. But advisory opinions have not always influenced the actions of those who felt their political interests would be adversely affected by accepting the opinion of the Court.[18]

Criticisms of the International Court of Justice have been of two general types. First are criticisms of the failure of Member states to use the Court in the settlement of their differences. Disputes between Members have been brought before the political organs of the United Nations even though legal aspects of such disputes might have been referred to the Court. The reluctance of Member states to accept the compulsory jurisdiction of the Court is evidence of their desire to be free to decide whether disputes to which they may be parties should be referred to the Court, to the political organs of the United Nations, or dealt with in some other fashion.

The second group of criticisms concerns the failure of United Nations organs to request advisory opinions from the Court in appropriate cases. Once disputes between Member states have been presented to the Security Council or to the General Assembly, those organs have not advised parties to take the legal aspects of their disputes to the Court. Furthermore, once the political organs of the United Nations have been seized of disputes, they have not been inclined to request advisory opinions either on the legal issues of the disputes or on the question of authority of the organs concerned to take jurisdiction and to act. Each of these criticisms has been

---

[17] *Ibid.*, p. 100. Another has commented: "The organs of the United Nations prefer to handle their affairs on a political basis rather than by reference to the Charter or the Court." Clyde Eagleton, "The United States and the United Nations," *New York University Law Review*, Vol. 29 (January 1954), p. 30.

[18] See above, Chap. IV.

recognized by the General Assembly in resolutions passed by that body.

It is probably true that a little law is better than no law, and an International Court with limitations is better than no International Court. As one authority has stated: "A start has been made in the right direction. For the first time in history, adjudication of disputes between states by a standing international tribunal with world-wide functions has become a reality. Further progress must of necessity be slow."[19] International jurisdiction is not likely to grow much faster than court jurisdiction grew in the United States where more than fifty years elapsed before the states of the Union would accept judgments of the Supreme Court on boundary questions and more than eighty years before other questions of importance between states were submitted to the Court.[20]

Although there are many who have expressed disappointment that the International Court has not played a larger role in postwar international relationships, if blame is to be fixed for this situation, it should not rest on the Court. It is governments that have emphasized the political aspects of issues and have tended to ignore their juridical aspects. International legal instruments exist and are available for use if Member states were willing to use them.

Proposals Not Involving Charter Amendment

Proposals to change the powers of the United Nations with respect to judicial settlement range from those that suggest that marked improvement could be made without the necessity of any amendments to the Charter or Statute, to those that maintain that any changes short of the creation of a world federation, with enforceable world law, would be only a delusion. Some believe that great transformations could be wrought if only the attitudes of states were to change. It is not the mechanism that is at fault, they maintain, but the states that operate the mechanism. Others believe that some improvements might be made by amendment of the Statute of the Court to give it broader jurisdiction than it now has.[21] And there

[19] Lissitzyn, *op. cit.*, p. 101.

[20] See Charles Warren, "The Supreme Court and Disputes Between States," *International Conciliation,* No. 366 (January 1941), pp. 20-42.

[21] Article 69 of the Statute provides that amendments are to be effected "by the same procedure as is provided by the Charter" except that the General Assembly on recommendation of the Security Council may adopt necessary provisions

are some who believe a complete rewriting of the Charter is essential to create an organization based not on the supremacy of the sovereign state as presently constituted, but on the supremacy of law, enacted by a supranational legislature, interpreted by a supranational court, and enforced by a supranational executive.

Many critics of the current state of international law believe that it has been developed about as far as it can be in the light of the present status of the international community, but they seek a way to give it somewhat more practical application to that community. The fact that the differences between the Statute of the Permanent Court and the Statute of the International Court are relatively slight lends credence to the proposition that a review now of the Statute of the new Court would not be likely to result in any important changes. One authority in noting that there is little difference, save in name, between the old and the new Court, has written:

> There is no lack of rules, customary or conventional, to be applied by international courts in the determination of cases. We do not urgently need either more or better international courts, or more or better rules of law. But we do need a comprehensive organization in which law will cease to be a detached limb and become an integrated member of an international body politic.[22]

Those who believe that the international community is not likely to undergo substantial change in the near future, either as the result of amendment of the Charter or by reason of a lessening of cold war tensions, tend to propose modifications that might be brought about by voluntary means.

Acceptance of Compulsory Jurisdiction

In the years since the International Court has been in operation, it has had before it in one form or another only sixteen disputes

---

concerning states that are parties to the Statute, but not Members of the United Nations. Presumably, the "procedure" referred to is that of Article 108 of the Charter. The question might be raised, however, whether the Statute will be open for amendment in the event of, and at the time of, a General Conference called pursuant to Article 109 of the Charter, in the absence of specific mention of amending the Statute as being one of the subjects open for consideration at the Conference. Article 70 of the Statute gives the Court power "to propose such amendments to the present Statute as it may deem necessary" and it would seem that the Court might well be giving consideration to what, if any, amendments it may wish to initiate with respect to the Statute.

[22] Brierly, *loc. cit.*, p. 360.

between states. Furthermore, Members have not often accepted the optional clause of the Statute, which gives the Court compulsory jurisdiction in specified categories of disputes as among states that have adhered to the clause. In 1949, in summarizing some thirty-four acceptances of the optional clause, one writer noted that "the compulsory jurisdiction of the Court is diminished in many cases by crippling reservations."[23]

The issue whether the Charter should provide for compulsory jurisdiction or leave it to Member states to opt such jurisdiction if they so wished, was settled at the San Francisco Conference. There, largely as the result of the opposition of the United States and the Soviet Union, compulsory jurisdiction in limited types of cases was not written into the Charter. Although there is still criticism of the decision of the Conference, in recent years even more criticism has been directed at the tendency of states to accept the optional clause, subject to a variety of reservations.[24] The General Assembly in 1947 took note of the lagging pace of acceptance of compulsory jurisdiction and the tendency to accept that jurisdiction, subject to limiting reservations. In a resolution then adopted the Assembly drew the attention of the "States which have not yet accepted the compulsory jurisdiction of the Court in accordance with Article 36, paragraphs 2 and 5, of the Statute, to the desirability of the greatest possible number of States accepting this jurisdiction with as few reservations as possible."[25]

Thirty-six states are now bound by the compulsory jurisdiction article of the Statute.[26] Some thirty Member states, including the Soviet Union, have not filed or renewed declarations accepting the

---

[23] Louis B. Sohn, "The Development of International Law: The Jurisdiction of the International Court of Justice," *American Bar Association Journal*, Vol. 35 (November 1949), pp. 924-25.

[24] The reservations attached by the United States are frequently cited as examples of restrictive-type reservations. One of them excepted from the jurisdiction of the Court "disputes with regard to matters which are essentially within the domestic jurisdiction of the United States of America as determined by the United States of America." S. Res. 196, 79 Cong. 2 sess. See also Francis O. Wilcox, "The United States Accepts Compulsory Jurisdiction," *American Journal of International Law*, Vol. 40 (October 1946), p. 700.

[25] Res. 171(II), Nov. 14, 1947.

[26] For listing of states accepting compulsory jurisdiction, with their reservations, see International Court of Justice *Yearbook* for various years. See also "Preliminary Report of the Committee on Review of the Charter of the United Nations," American Branch of the International Law Association (Apr. 12, 1955) (mimeo.), and the volume in this Brookings series, *The Organization and Procedures of the United Nations*.

compulsory jurisdiction in any form. One student of the Charter suggested in 1949 that the most obvious change that would broaden the scope of the business of the Court "would be acceptance of the Optional Clause—i.e., compulsory jurisdiction by the International Court of Justice in legal disputes—without reservation. . . . No amendment of the Charter would be needed."[27] He proposed that the United States take the lead in dropping its reservations to the optional clause.

Thus there exists a simple way to increase the business of the Court as well as the area of its jurisdiction. Without amendment of the Charter, Member states could agree to submit legal aspects of disputes to the Court. This could be done by agreement on a case-by-case basis, or it could be done by wider acceptance of the optional clause. A substantial trend on the part of parties to the Statute to adhere to the optional clause without restrictive reservations should serve to narrow the areas of political conflict. Often disputes debated before the Security Council or the General Assembly involve some questions of law. But these legal issues are either ignored or subjected to political debate—a situation that is neither good for the state of international law nor conducive to the settlement of disputes. If all disputant states and their supporters were, by reason of unconditional acceptance of compulsory jurisdiction of the Court, precluded from presenting to the political organs of the United Nations legal aspects of their cases, time would be saved, the issues would be narrowed, and more satisfactory settlements might be expected.

The difficulty would still be present, of course, of drawing some kind of satisfactory line between legal disputes and political issues and of determining the political weight to be given to legal issues. In the present state of international law and of international politics, there are few precedents to help in making these crucial decisions. Moreover, it must be recognized that in many disputes it is not legal problems that are at fundamental issue, but it is the facts that are in dispute. As one observer has commented: "It is regrettable that the States have not yet found it possible to accept compulsory jurisdiction, but in the present day political atmosphere it would probably be unwise to force the pace and try to introduce it."[28]

[27] Clyde Eagleton, "Proposals for Strengthening the United Nations," *Foreign Policy Reports*, Vol. 25 (Sept. 15, 1949), pp. 101-02.

[28] Hambro, *loc. cit.*, p. 34.

In the light of recent debate on the Bricker Amendment and the fact that the principal reservation of the United States to the optional clause relates to the right of the United States to determine for itself what matters constitute "domestic jurisdiction," the likelihood of an American move in this direction seems rather remote.

As a matter of fact, if individual states do not wish one by one to accept the optional clause, the organs of the United Nations would seem to have it within their power on their own initiative to broaden the scope of the work of the Court in disputes between states. It has been proposed, for example, that the Council and the Assembly take the initiative and voluntarily "adopt the practice of refusing to consider legal disputes, and of recommending to the parties that such disputes be taken to the Court." Although the Council and the Assembly could only "recommend" such action, and parties could not be compelled to take their disputes to the Court, it is suggested that such a regular procedure "would exercise great influence toward reaching settlement."[29]

There may be some doubt whether this suggestion is realistic. The Council and the Assembly are political organs. As such, they reflect the international mores of which they are a part. They would not be likely to accept such a proposal unless there was strong evidence that the world community insisted that a proper preliminary to political consideration of disputes would be disposition of their legal aspects by the Court. Moreover, if Member states individually are unwilling to accept the optional clause, they could hardly be expected to support resolutions in the Council or the Assembly that would close those organs to those Member states that are unwilling to refer legal aspects of their disputes to the Court.

Greater Use of
Advisory Opinions

Although all the principal organs of the United Nations as well as the specialized agencies are authorized to ask the International Court for advisory opinions on legal questions, the General Assembly is the only organ that has done so. But the Assembly has requested only seven advisory opinions in nine years, and other organs frequently have considered issues with legal aspects but have invariably subordinated legal questions to political considerations. The

[29] Eagleton, "Proposals for Strengthening the United Nations," *loc. cit.*, p. 110.

Assembly in 1947, having in mind that up to that time the Court had been virtually without business of any kind, recommended that:

. . . organs of the United Nations and the specialized agencies should, from time to time, review the difficult and important points of law within the jurisdiction of the International Court of Justice which have arisen in the course of their activities and involve questions of principle which it is desirable to have settled, including points of law relating to the interpretation of the Charter of the United Nations or the constitutions of the specialized agencies, and if duly authorized according to Article 96, paragraph 2, of the Charter, should refer them to the International Court of Justice for an advisory opinion.[30]

This resolution has had relatively little effect, however, on increasing the use of the Court.

There have been many instances during the history of the United Nations and its specialized agencies when questions have been raised regarding the existence of authority of the Charter for specific action. As a special committee of the American Society of International Law has put it, "in many cases the Members concerned almost automatically challenge the competence of the United Nations in order to delay action or to channel the discussion away from the merits of the case. There are in consequence several hundreds of cases in which the competence of the Organization has been challenged."[31] This situation was invited by the drafters of the Charter, who indicated that each organ was to interpret its competence for itself.[32]

In the event a question is raised regarding the competence of some organ of the United Nations to take action, the only device now available to decide the question of competence, aside from the action of the organ itself, is for the organ to request an advisory opinion from the International Court. There is no doctrine of judicial review by which acts of United Nations organs may be measured against the Charter. There is no appeal from a decision of an organ that it has competence to act in a specific case.

It has been said that "The Charter's glaring deficiency in neglecting to provide for a single authoritative organ of interpretation has made each United Nations Organ almost a law unto itself."[33] Yet if

[30] Res. 171(II), Nov. 14, 1947.
[31] "Report of Special Committee on Reference to the International Court of Justice of Questions of United Nations Competence," *Proceedings of the American Society of International Law* (1950), p. 257.
[32] See *UNCIO Documents*, Vol. 13, pp. 709-10.
[33] Philip E. Jacob, "The Legality of the United Nations Action," *University of Pittsburgh Law Review*, Vol. 13 (Fall 1951), p. 38.

there were a provision in the Charter by which the jurisdiction of organs of the United Nations might be challenged and decisions by such organs confirmed or overruled by the Court, Member states might find themselves bound by interpretations with which they did not agree. Indeed, it was noted at the San Francisco Conference that "in cases where it is desired to establish an authoritative interpretation as a precedent for the future, it may be necessary to embody the interpretation in an amendment to the Charter."[34]

The problem of obtaining authoritative interpretations of the Charter and other instruments setting up international agencies has given rise to certain suggestions. One proposal, as has been noted, was put forth by the Assembly itself, which has been concerned that organs have not made enough use of their authority to seek advisory opinions with respect to "points of law relating to the interpretation of the Charter."[35] Without amendment of the Charter, it would be possible for the Security Council and the Assembly, as well as other organs of the United Nations and the specialized agencies, voluntarily to accept the decisions of the Court on interpretation of the Charter. Although it is true that the opinions would be only "advisory" and could thus be accepted or rejected, what is needed in the opinion of many people is willingness on the part of the organs and of the Member states to be guided by such opinions.

Another proposal that goes further than voluntary extension of the practice of seeking advisory opinions has been suggested by a Committee of the American Branch of the International Law Association. It has proposed that:

> . . . either by a special Charter amendment or as part of a larger revision, jurisdiction . . . be conferred on the International Court of Justice to deal with disputes concerning the jurisdiction of United Nations organs and the constitutional validity of their decisions. *Alternatively,* regulations . . . be adopted by all the principal organs of the United Nations providing for an automatic request for an advisory opinion of the Court whenever one of these organs should disagree with a Member State or States on the question of its competence to deal with a particular question or on the validity of a decision made or to be made by it.[36]

This alternative suggestion envisages that the automatic request for an advisory opinion would be made conditional on acceptance by the states concerned as well as by the organ of the decisiveness of the

---

[34] *UNCIO Documents,* Vol. 13, pp. 709-10.

[35] Res. 171(II), Nov. 14, 1947.

[36] American Branch of the International Law Association, "Preliminary Report," p. 23.

opinion in the particular dispute. In order to avoid "frivolous complaints" regarding jurisdiction, the challenge would need the endorsement of a limited number of states.

Former Secretary-General Lie has made a somewhat similar suggestion to deal with instances when action of the Security Council
or General Assembly is branded as "illegal." He has raised the question:

> . . . whether or not it might be possible to agree on an arrangement
> whereby both the majority and the minority [in the Council or the
> Assembly], as well as the Secretary-General, receives the right to request
> an advisory opinion from a special organ—in instances where a decision
> passed by a legal majority is still branded illegal. The judicial body might
> be a panel of the International Court of Justice, or it might be a body
> set up for the purpose—preferably not elective, but constituted jointly, for
> example by the President of the International Court of Justice and the
> Secretary-General.[37]

Acceptance of proposals along these lines would serve to give
some semblance of legal validity, or invalidity, to actions of United
Nations organs. Perhaps as a consequence, wider public support
might be enlisted for those United Nations actions that might be
supported by opinions of the Court. Certainly a Member state that
questioned the jurisdiction of an organ only to find that the Court
decided in favor of the jurisdiction of that organ would be in a
most difficult position if it then refused to accept that decision as
binding. On the other hand, it could not be assumed that the Court
would always sustain jurisdictional claims of organs. Furthermore, if
one of the results of acceptance of these suggestions were to bring
more questions of interpretation of the Charter before the Court, a
valuable body of interpretations would be accumulated over the
years.

The fundamental question raised by these proposals is whether
they circumvent the principle that a state must consent before it can
be bound to accept as final a decision of the International Court.
Neither the suggestion of former Secretary-General Lie nor the alternative proposal of the Committee of the International Law Association would go so far as to compel a Member state to accept an interpretation of the Court of the jurisdiction of any United Nations
organ. If Lie's suggestion were not couched in terms of requesting
an "advisory opinion," however, or if the proposal of the Committee of the International Law Association were not made conditional

---

[37] Trygve Lie, *In the Cause of Peace* (1954), p. 433.

on the Members agreeing in advance to accept the judgment of the Court, it would be necessary to analyze them in terms of their impact on national sovereignty. Thus, for example, if the Assembly, over the objections of the United States, were to adopt a resolution allegedly invading the domestic jurisdiction of the United States, and if the Court were to sustain the action of the Assembly, the question would arise regarding what action might be taken to compel the United States to accept the resolution as a "constitutional" exercise of authority by the Assembly. Even more pointed questions might be raised if there were objections to the use of the veto in cases before the Security Council.

The difficulty with these suggestions, even though they do not go so far as to make advisory opinions regarding interpretation of the Charter binding, is that they tend to substitute legal judgments for political judgments in a world community that does not always accept law as the basis for action.

Voluntary Referral of
Claims Cases

Consideration will be given later to proposals to permit individuals and international organizations, as well as states, to be parties in contentious cases before the International Court. Such changes would involve amendment of the Charter. It has been suggested, however, that short of amendment, the states themselves could make greater use of the Court in nationalization cases (e.g., claims against states that have nationalized private property of foreign nationals) by agreeing among themselves to refer these cases to it. At the present time, when a claimant is the national of a state other than the state against which the nationalization claim runs, his only relief is through political and diplomatic channels. Voluntary agreement on the part of the states concerned, however, could establish a method by which the state of the claimant national could espouse the claim on his behalf before the International Court, thus circumventing, in effect, the requirement that only states could appear as parties.[38] One difficulty with this suggestion is that the states that

[38] For discussion of this possibility see E. A. S. Brooks, "Subsidiary Judicial Authorities of the United Nations Organization to Hear and Decide Claims by Individuals and Corporations Against States," *The International Law Quarterly,* Vol. 3 (October 1950), pp. 523-29; see also A. Lyman, "Suggestions for the Enlargement of the Jurisdiction of the World Court to Include Private Litigation," *Journal of the Bar Association of the District of Columbia,* Vol. 13 (August 1946).

have nationalized private property may not be willing to have their action judged by an international tribunal. Nationalization cases often have political overtones that make it difficult for the nationalizing state to submit to third party judgments without a most careful definition of the terms and procedures to be followed.

The suggestion that the International Court be given jurisdiction in claims cases presented by the governments on behalf of their nationals is not new. In 1943, a committee of the American Bar Association recommended the establishment of a system of interrelated permanent courts, with ultimate appeal to the World Court, to have obligatory jurisdiction over claims of governments made on behalf of their nationals. As recently as July 1954, one legal authority drew attention to this earlier suggestion of the Bar Association. He emphasized the need for a system of judicial chambers to handle claims cases with ultimate appeal to the International Court. He pointed out that although there are clauses in the Charter providing that the Court is the principal judicial organ and is authorized to sit in chambers, there have in fact been no subsidiary bodies created and the Court has sat only as a full Court. Reading these clauses together, this authority argued that claims cases might well be handled without amendment of the Charter. He suggested that effect has not been given these provisions "because of concern for the Senate's reaction." In a summary of the arguments in support of handling claims cases through a system of international courts, he wrote:

It is clear that a long-felt need exists; that a thorough-going system for settling existing claims in an orderly fashion would assist in avoiding irritations of the "Cold War"; would build up a great wealth of international law precedents; would avoid the disadvantages attendant upon the miscellany of *ad hoc* tribunals which are now used sporadically; would clear up foreign office claims dockets; might result in a wider interest in, and understanding of, the United Nations . . .; and last, but by no means least, would do much-needed justice to American business with interests abroad. . . .[39]

The principal difficulty with all of these proposals for changes in the existing system is that there is no evidence of a will on the part of states to make more adequate use of the legal machinery that is now available. It has been pointed out earlier in this study that the

---

[39] Willard B. Cowles, "Review of the United Nations Charter and Adjudication of International Claims," *American Journal of International Law*, Vol. 48 (July 1954), pp. 463-64.

Charter has potentialities for growth that have not been utilized. A Deputy Under Secretary of State in testifying before a congressional committee in 1950 remarked: "There is no question but that the Charter can carry much more traffic if its members desire to have it do so."[40] That observation is equally applicable to the Statute of the International Court of Justice.

Proposals Requiring Charter Amendment

Unless the Charter or the Statute is amended, there are limits to the type of jurisdiction and the type of case the International Court could consider. Although there would seem to be nothing to prevent Member states from agreeing outside the Charter to submit any type of dispute to the Court, whether of a legal nature or otherwise, and to accept as binding decisions in such cases, there remains the problem of enforcement in the event a Member failed to abide by its agreement. There is also the possibility that organs of the United Nations might agree outside the framework of the Charter to abide by advisory opinions of the Court. As advisory opinions can only be sought on "legal questions," however, the Court might refuse to accept jurisdiction if advisory opinions were sought on political issues unless the Charter and the Statute were amended to give the Court this additional jurisdiction.

It has also been noted that the jurisdiction of the Court with respect to the parties who may appear before it in contentious cases or with respect to the rendering of advisory opinions, is limited. Only United Nations organs or agencies may seek advisory opinions. Only states may be parties in contentious cases. Individuals and international organizations may not appear as parties before the Court.[41]

Extending Jurisdiction of Court
in Political Matters

After publication of the Dumbarton Oaks Proposals, the Netherlands Government suggested "the appointment of an independent

---

[40] *Revision of the United Nations Charter,* Hearings before a Subcommittee of the Senate Committee on Foreign Relations, 81 Cong. 2 sess., p. 385.

[41] Proposals to permit individuals to be parties before the Court will be discussed later. Note might be taken here, however, of the suggestion that one of the weaknesses "in the jurisdiction of the Court is that international organizations cannot be parties before it—not even the United Nations. . . ." See Hambro, *loc. cit.,* p. 34. In the United States, of course, both the states and the national government may be parties before the Supreme Court.

body of eminent men . . . who should be readily available to pronounce upon decisions of the Security Council whenever an appeal to that effect [is] addressed to them, either by the Council or by a party to the case in question. This body . . . [would] pronounce upon the matter solely from the point of view of whether the Council's decision was in keeping with moral principles."[42] The New Commonwealth Society in England, which gave its approval to the Netherlands proposal, suggested the addition of an article to the Charter as follows:

All disputes coming before either the Security Council or the General Assembly of a nature likely to endanger the maintenance of international peace and security shall, other reasonable means of peaceful settlement having been tried and failed, be referred . . . to an International Tribunal in Equity, such reference to be by an affirmative vote of any seven members of the Security Council or a two-thirds majority vote of the General Assembly. The decision of the Tribunal shall be binding upon parties to the dispute. Article 94, paragraph 2 applies to the decision of the Tribunal.[43]

A proposal along similar lines was submitted by Belgium to the San Francisco Conference. It suggested that any state that felt its "essential rights" were infringed by a recommendation or decision of the Security Council should be permitted to carry the question to the International Court for an advisory opinion. If the Court found that such "essential" rights had been disregarded by the Council, the Council would be bound "either to reconsider the question or to refer the dispute to the Assembly for decision."[44]

These suggestions are essentially techniques to involve the Court in political aspects of cases. They propose to transfer disputes from political organs or from a political atmosphere to a judicial environment regardless whether there may be questions of law involved in them. But it has been pointed out that: "It is to be doubted whether

[42] For discussion see S. (m), "An Equity Tribunal in the Context of Present Policy," *The New Commonwealth for Justice and Security,* Vol. 9 (September 1949), p. 213.

[43] The effect of the reference to Article 94 is to give to the Security Council the problem of "deciding upon measures to be taken to give effect to the judgment in the event one of the parties should not accept the decision as binding." *Ibid.,* p. 214.

[44] *UNCIO Documents,* Vol. 12, pp. 48-49. See also Hans Kelsen, *The Law of the United Nations* (1951), pp. 446-47n., and suggestion by Schuyler W. Jackson, "International Legislation: Discussion of Methods for Its Improvement," *American Bar Association Journal,* Vol. 43 (March 1948), pp. 206-09, in which he proposes that "if a dispute has not been settled . . . under the preceding provisions of Chapter VI, then the Security Council should be bound to direct that such dispute be placed before the International Court of Justice for settlement."

much would be gained in the formative stage of world organization by placing the action of an already weak Security Council under the control of an even weaker Court. A clash between the Council and the Court might be fatal to both."[45] Moreover, so long as the function of the Court in proposals of this type is to be only advisory in nature, refusal of the organs and the Member states concerned to accept the advice given might impair the authority of the Court in other types of cases.

If the Court should be given authority to make binding decisions in political disputes referred to it, the question must be raised regarding how the judgments could be enforced. It has been suggested that such proposals are not practical unless there is force available to put the collective will of the international community behind the judgment of the Court. There is serious doubt, however, that states today would be willing to delegate that much authority to the international community.[46]

A second question to be raised in connection with granting the Court authority to make binding decisions in disputes that the political organs of the United Nations have not been able to settle, relates to the method by which the Court would reach its decisions in cases in which there might be no applicable law or precedent. Is it enough simply to give such authority to a body of eminent men? If it is argued that in such cases the International Court would be bound by "principles of justice," a further question is whether there are principles of justice equally acceptable to such diversified cultures as those of China, the Soviet Union, and the Western world. The New Commonwealth Society, commenting on the practicability of its proposal, pointed out:

> In view of present Russian recalcitrance alone, the mere formulation of such a radical proposal is sufficient to show how impossibly utopian is any hope of its realisation. Apart from the question of whether nations would be prepared for any such unprecedented surrender of their sovereignty in questions which they would certainly consider as coming within the scope of their "domestic jurisdiction" or national honour, any change of this type would require consent of the permanent members of the Council and this would be impossible to obtain.[47]

---

[45] Lissitzyn, *op. cit.,* p. 96. For more detail see Report by a Committee of Austrian Lawyers, "The Equity Tribunal," *New Commonwealth,* Vol. 8 (November 1944), pp. 305-06.

[46] For discussion see P. C. Jessup, "The Subjects of a Modern Law of Nations," *Michigan Law Review,* Vol. 45 (February 1947), p. 406.

[47] S. (m), "An Equity Tribunal in the Context of Present Policy," *loc. cit.,* p. 214.

Granting International Organizations
Access to the Court

Neither the Charter nor the Statute of the Court makes provision for the United Nations or any international organization to have access to the International Court or to be parties to disputes considered by the Court, despite the fact that such organizations are recognized as having legal personality.[48] Yet situations can be envisaged in which international organizations may have disputes between themselves, in which states may want to take legal action against an international organization, and in which organizations may wish to bring legal proceedings against states.

A committee of the American Branch of the International Law Association has tentatively suggested that the restrictions in Article 34 of the Charter be abolished so as to permit the United Nations as well as other international organizations to have "access to the Court equal to that enjoyed by States." The committee stated that: "There may even be no objection to authorizing the General Assembly to grant [regional organizations] . . . the right to become parties in cases before the Court."[49] This proposal distinguishes, however, between access to the Court and the actual bringing of a case before it. So far as bringing a case before the Court is concerned, such action would

> . . . still depend on the consent of the parties to such cases, expressed either *ad hoc* in a special agreement accepting the jurisdiction of the Court for a particular dispute, or in advance in an agreement accepting the jurisdiction of the Court with respect to certain categories of disputes with international organizations.[50]

It is suggested nevertheless that the optional clause could be opened for acceptance by international organizations with the result that it might then be possible to create:

[48] See for example Article XV, Constitution of the Food and Agriculture Organization, which provides: "The Organization shall have the capacity of a legal person to perform any legal act appropriate to its purpose. . . ." Signed at Quebec, Oct. 16, 1945, U. S. Department of State, *Treaties and Other International Acts*, Series 1554. See also Advisory Opinion of International Court of Justice relative to reparation for injuries suffered in service of United Nations, International Court of Justice, *Reports of Judgments, Advisory Opinions and Orders* (1949), pp. 174, 178-79, 187.

[49] American Branch of the International Law Association, "Preliminary Report," p. 7.

[50] *Ibid.*, p. 8.

. . . compulsory jurisdiction in relations between those organizations which accept the Optional Clause and the States which have also taken that step. Alternatively, a special protocol may be opened for signature, similar in content to the Optional Clause, through which international organizations and States may accept the jurisdiction of the Court in legal disputes between them.[51]

There is little doubt that adoption of this proposal, which would require amendment of the Charter and the Statute, would broaden the theoretical jurisdiction of the Court. It might be questioned, however, whether there is a demonstrable need for international organizations generally to have access in their own right to the Court. Many of them now have a limited type of access. If disputes develop between individual states and particular international organizations, most, but not all, organizations may request advisory opinions on legal questions. Furthermore, even in situations in which a particular international organization has not sought an advisory opinion, it may under Article 66 of the Statute appear if it is able to furnish information on the question at issue.

Those aspects of these suggestions that go further than simply giving international organizations "access" to the Court and seek to put them on an equal footing with sovereign states respecting disputes as among the organizations and in acceptance of the optional clause, raise the question whether sovereign states are yet ready to confer such aspects of statehood on any international organization. It may well be doubted that states would be willing to take such action at the present time.

Empowering Court to Settle Disputes
Between Individuals and States

It was noted earlier that suggestions have been made that in limited types of cases, states might agree to espouse before the International Court the claims of individuals against other states, with the consent of the latter, thus avoiding the limitation of Article 34 of the Statute that only states may be parties before the Court. One suggestion is to amend Article 34 so that it would provide that:

The Court shall have jurisdiction:
(1) in disputes between States;
(2) in disputes between States and private and public bodies or private

[51] *Ibid.*

individuals in cases in which States have consented, in advance by special agreement, to appear as defendants before the Court.[52]

This proposal is described as "a significant departure in the substantive and procedural law" that could "take place without affecting the vital interest of States," but which could not be affected without amendment of the Charter. It is argued that this change would free the International Court of "the shackles" of the present wording of Article 34, making it possible for states to agree to "appear as defendants at the instance of private individuals or corporations of foreign nationality in all cases in which, under international law, their State would possess the right to espouse their claim."[53]

This proposal raises profound questions, the detailed discussion of which go beyond the scope of this study. Although the language of the proposed amendments makes it clear that a state could become a defendant only with its consent, it must be remembered that even in the domestic law of many states, including the United States, the situations in which an individual can bring an action against his government are closely limited as a result of the carryover from English law of the concept that the king can do no wrong.

A variation on the suggestion that individuals be allowed to appear before the Court as plaintiffs in limited types of cases and a proposal that goes one step further, is that "international judicial authorities or courts should be established and given jurisdiction to deal with disputes between individuals of different nationalities."[54] Here the difficulties are even greater than those that would flow from the suggestion noted above because the problem of delimiting the type of case that could be taken to the Court would be tremendous. In the United States, for example, citizenship is no bar to a court action, and, therefore, an American citizen could sue an alien resident or traveler in United States courts. Thus this proposal in its broadest aspects, might involve transferring to international jurisdiction automobile accident cases in which the parties might happen to be of different nationalities. Some authorities conclude, however, that the proposal is premature because of the undeveloped state of international law, which would first need to be codified.[55]

[52] H. Lauterpacht, "The Subjects of the Law of Nations," *The Law Quarterly Review*, Vol. 63 (October 1947), p. 458.

[53] *Ibid.*, pp. 458-59.

[54] See Brooks, *loc. cit.*, pp. 523-29.

[55] *Ibid.*, p. 527.

Even the simplest proposal to permit individuals to become parties before the International Court must be considered in the light of its effect as a first step. This is illustrated by the proposal considered above for the amendment of Article 34. In advancing this proposal, it was noted that it would not affect "any vital interest of States," but it was also noted that

> . . . any developments along the lines suggested may *pave the way* for a change even more far reaching. That change would consist in conceding a right of appeal before the highest international authority to the State's own nationals against any violations of their rights under international law. A truly revolutionary change of that nature would presuppose one even more radical and fundamental—the previous acknowledgment of rights enjoyed by the State's own subjects as originating in international law. . . . The recognition by the international society of fundamental human rights and freedoms is not a chimera. It is, in essence, part of existing law as expressed in the Charter of the United Nations.[56]

This is a doctrine that would give many Americans pause. Certainly in the light of the Fujii case, it would not be acceptable to the Supreme Court of California, which found that the human rights provisions of the Charter do not have a domestic legal effect within the United States.[57]

If the premise is accepted that an individual, regardless of his relationship to his own state is nevertheless a subject of international law that may impose obligations on him and give him rights, no particular difficulties are encountered so long as the law is applied to him through the instrumentalities of his own state. Indeed, Article I of the Constitution of the United States confers on the Congress power to "define and punish . . . offenses against the law of nations," and it has generally been accepted that international law is binding on the United States and individuals under its jurisdiction. Difficulty arises, however, when international law is to be applied to a state or to citizens of that state by some authority external to the state itself because such application implies the existence of power to coerce the sovereign state.

Establishment of an International Criminal Court

It has been recognized for many years that individuals are capable of committing crimes against the law of nations. Individuals who engage in piracy or violate international conventions on the slave

---

[56] Italics supplied. Lauterpacht, *loc. cit.,* p. 459.
[57] See *Fujii* v. *State of California,* 242 Pacific (2d) 617.

trade, narcotics, or traffic in women and children, for example, are engaging in criminal acts against the law of nations. There has been no agreement, however, that violations of international law by individuals should be subject to punishment by international courts.

The literature of international law is replete, however, with suggestions to create an international court with jurisdiction over individuals charged with crimes against the law of nations.[58] Recent discussions about the creation of an international criminal court culminated in the report made in 1953 by the United Nations Committee on International Criminal Jurisdiction. This organ was created by a resolution of the General Assembly of December 1952.[59] During twenty-three meetings held in the summer of 1953, the committee pursuant to the resolution, explored "the implications and consequences of establishing an international criminal court and . . . the various methods by which this might be done."[60] It studied the relationship of such a court to the United Nations and proposed a series of amendments to a draft statute for an international criminal court that had been prepared by a similar committee in 1951.

After careful consideration and discussion of ideas submitted to the committee, it reached the conclusion that it did "not wish to give its proposals any appearance of finality" because *there was no evidence that States wished to establish a court, or that, even if it were established, States would be willing to give it the measure of consent and cooperation which was vital to its functioning.*"[61] Moreover, there was a strong feeling among some of the members of the committee that the substantive law to be applied by such a court has not "sufficiently matured to make the creation of an international criminal jurisdiction practicable."[62]

Recent proposals to establish an international court with criminal jurisdiction have arisen because of the provisions on criminal jurisdiction in the Genocide Convention, the convention establishing the European Coal and Steel Community, and draft proposals con-

[58] For full discussion of this problem see U.N. General Assembly, Third Session, *Historical Survey of the Question of International Criminal Jurisdiction: A Memorandum Submitted by the Secretary General to the International Law Commission*, Doc. A/CN.4/7/Rev. 1 (1949); U.N. General Assembly, Seventh Session, *Official Records*, Supplement No. 11 (1952); U.N. General Assembly, Ninth Session, *Official Records*, Supplement No. 12 (1954).

[59] Res. 687(VII), Dec. 5, 1952.

[60] *Ibid.*

[61] Italics supplied. U.N. General Assembly, Ninth Session, *Official Records*, Supplement No. 12 (1954), p. 22.

[62] *Ibid.*

cerning the international control of atomic energy. Documents such as the Universal Declaration of Human Rights and the experience of the *ad hoc* international tribunals established at Nuremberg and Tokyo to try war criminals have also contributed to the idea.

Examination of these experiences has led some lawyers and laymen to the conclusion that the scope of individual responsibility to the international community is increasing. Thus in the case of the charter establishing the Nuremberg Tribunal, Article 6 listed three categories of crimes subject to the jurisdiction of the Tribunal that involved *individual* responsibility, *i.e.,* crimes against peace, crimes against humanity, and war crimes.[63] The Genocide Convention provides in Article IV that "Persons committing genocide . . . shall be punished, whether they are constitutionally responsible rulers, public officials or private *individuals.*"[64] And an unofficial draft treaty on atomic energy appearing in the *Bulletin of the Atomic Scientists* contains this interesting suggestion:

35. Any of the United Nations permanently represented in the Security Council may indict any *individual* before the United Nations Criminal Court for violation [of the prohibitions contained in the proposed Convention].

36. An *individual* so indicted shall be surrendered to the custody of the United Nations Criminal Court. . . .[65]

These are submitted as examples of a trend to hold the individual, as distinguished from the state, accountable to the rules of international law, whether that law owes its origin to treaty or to custom and precedent. Even though the trend may be in this direction, there is still a strong feeling in many quarters that the duties

[63] See U.N. General Assembly, Third Session, *The Charter and Judgment of the Nuremberg Tribunal: Memorandum Submitted by the Secretary-General to the International Law Commission,* Doc. A/CN.4/5 (1949).

[64] Italics supplied. See Art. IV, Res. 260(III), Dec. 9, 1948.

[65] Italics supplied. "Draft Treaty," *Bulletin of the Atomic Scientists,* Vol. 1 (1946), pp. 11-13. Reference to the Geneva Convention of 1937 would now presumably be replaced by reference to the draft convention submitted by the United Nations Committee on International Criminal Jurisdiction. See testimony of Professor John S. Toll, representing the Federation of American Scientists, in Hearings before the Subcommittee on the United Nations Charter, Senate Committee on Foreign Relations, *Review of the United Nations Charter,* 84 Cong. 1 sess., Pt. 12, pp. 1778-83. See also in this connection the suggestion of the late Senator Brien McMahon to the Senate on Jan. 27, 1947, to the effect that the atomic control commission should report control violation to the International Court and not, as proposed in the United States plan, to the Security Council. *Congressional Record,* Vol. 93, Pt. 1, 80 Cong. 1 sess., pp. 610-13, at p. 613.

imposed by international law are not yet so clearly defined as to warrant granting criminal jurisdiction to an international court. One of the prerequisites of domestic American law, for example, is that a criminal statute so vague as to leave the standard of guilt to the "variant views of the different courts and juries which may be called upon to enforce it" cannot be justified under the terms of the Sixth Amendment, which requires that the accused has the right to be "informed of the nature and the cause of the accusation."[66]

Such problems as these are discussed in the report of the United Nations Committee on International Criminal Jurisdiction. On the matter of international criminal jurisdiction and the present state of international law, even those who favored the establishment of a court recognized the "rather primitive stage of inter-State relations." The views of those who felt that an international criminal court was a desirable future development, though not practical at present, were represented in the report as follows:

An international criminal court presupposed an international community with the power necessary to operate the court, and such power did not exist. A surrender of some present State sovereignty would be the condition for the establishment of the court, and such surrender was highly unlikely. Therefore, the court would be powerless, and its establishment would be an empty gesture. It would be improper to establish the court before international criminal law had been defined in generally adopted conventions. . . .[67]

In order to understand the nature of an international criminal court, it may be well to examine briefly the revised draft statute for such a court that was studied by the United Nations Committee on International Criminal Jurisdiction. Under the draft statute, the court would consist of fifteen judges, elected, regardless of their nationality, by representatives of states from among persons of high moral character. Trial would be by the judges and not by a jury. The jurisdiction of the court would not be presumed, but must be specifically conferred by a state either by convention, by special agreement, or by unilateral declaration. Jurisdiction of the court would be over "natural persons, whether they are constitutionally responsible rulers, public officials or private individuals," but

---

[66] *United States* v. *Cohen Grocery Co.*, 264 Fed. 218, 220 (1920), affirmed 255 U. S. 8 (1921).

[67] U.N. General Assembly, Ninth Session, *Official Records*, Supplement No. 12, p. 4.

such jurisdiction could not be asserted unless it had been specifically conferred by the state of which the accused was a national and the state where the crime was allegedly committed.

In order for a case to be brought before the court, a state would need to institute the proceedings. An agent of the state would then present sufficient evidence to a committing chamber of five judges, acting as a kind of grand jury, which would then certify to that fact before an indictment could be filed with the court. The case would then be presented to the court by a prosecuting attorney appointed by the complainant state.

The decision of the court would be by a majority vote of the judges participating in the trial except that in cases involving imposition of the death penalty or life imprisonment in which there may be an equal division of votes, the presiding judge should have the deciding vote. The purpose of the court would be to "try natural persons accused of crimes generally recognized under international law." The law to be applied would be "international law, including international criminal law, and where appropriate, national law."[68]

Analysis of the draft statute indicates that the principle of national sovereignty is immediately involved. As soon as the formulation of a law is envisaged that operates directly on an individual, and a court to interpret, apply, and enforce that law, the relationships between the individual and the state to which he owes his allegiance are changed in a very significant way. This means that in some respects the individual would have obligations that are outside or beyond the state of which he is a national and that the international community might invade state sovereignty and act directly against the individual. As noted above, the United Nations committee reported that some members felt that "a surrender of some present State sovereignty would be the condition for the establishment of the court, and such surrender was highly unlikely."[69]

Establishment of an International Court of Human Rights

Although the proposal to create an international criminal court is based on the theory that individuals are subjects of international law and may be punished for its violation, it must also be noted that in the case of the Genocide Convention the "persons" who may

[68] For revised draft statute see *ibid.*, Annex, pp. 23-26.
[69] *Ibid.*, p. 4.

commit genocide include "constitutionally responsible rulers" and "public officials."[70] Proposals to create an International Court of Human Rights are based on the theory that individuals have rights as well as duties under international law and that individuals may need procedures to protect themselves from infringement by states of human rights and fundamental freedoms that the United Nations is obligated to promote.[71]

An interesting proposal has recently been made for a "United Nations writ of habeas corpus and an international court of human rights." This proposal would recognize that the Charter grants individuals the right to petition the organization for "redress of denials of human rights and fundamental freedoms." It suggests that the United Nations "enact its equivalent of the Habeas Corpus Act. . . . Such a resolution would require that an appropriate judicial organ issue, as a matter of right, an order [to a State] to show cause why the writ should not issue where it appears that the detention is without cause or for causes which would shock the conscience of mankind."[72]

This United Nations writ would issue to a state holding a person in detention in violation of the fundamental human rights guaranteed by the Charter. The state to which the writ would be addressed would be expected to answer it. If cause for the detention could not be shown in such answer, "the State would be required to deliver the petitioner to the custody of the United Nations, either actively or constructively, within or without its territory, depending on the necessities of the case."[73] Once the individual has been surrendered to the United Nations, he would be "entitled to a hearing for the determination of his rights." The General Assembly under Article 7(2) could create such "subsidiary organs as may be found necessary . . ." and pursuant thereto, it is proposed that the Assembly establish an International Court of Human Rights.[74]

The crucial question, as this proposal recognizes, is whether the international writ of habeas corpus and the determination of the court would be obeyed. It apparently does not expect such writs to be obeyed by the Soviet dominated states. The role to be played by such a writ "would be to give hope to the enslaved and protection

---

[70] Art. IV, Res. 260(III), Dec. 9, 1948.
[71] See above, Chap. IX.
[72] Luis Kutner, "A Proposal for a United Nations Writ of Habeas Corpus and an International Court of Human Rights," *Tulane Law Review,* Vol. 28 (June 1954), p. 417.
[73] *Ibid.,* p. 435.
[74] *Ibid.,* p. 439.

to the free. In countries where the craving for human dignity is mute and imaginations of men are still, the writ, if wisely and courageously applied, could become an inspiring symbol of the determination of the free world to protect the ancient culture and religious traditions embodied in the ideals of freedom and democracy."[75]

There have been other proposals for the creation of an International Court of Human Rights.[76] As noted above, these proposals, like those concerning the establishment of an International Criminal Court, are based on the assumption that individuals, as well as states, are subjects of international law. If this concept is carried very far and the individual, regardless of his citizenship, has legal rights and obligations stemming not from the state of which he is a citizen, but from treaties or international law, a significant step would be taken in the direction of world citizenship. It is hard to envisage such a situation without recognizing the existence of some type of supranational government. If there is no supranational governmental force able to give the individual rights and enforce obligations on him, then his so-called international rights and duties in many cases would be worth little.

In determining the practicability of proposals to create new international courts or to expand the jurisdiction of the present International Court of Justice, what counts most is not what states *should* do, but what they *will* do. Certainly, any attempt to create an international court with jurisdiction over individuals has implications so broad as to call for fundamental changes in the United Nations system. Such changes would require amendment of the Charter. It is doubtful whether Members of the United Nations are yet prepared to surrender to an international court substantial control over their nationals.

A comparison between the Covenant of the League of Nations and the Charter of the United Nations reveals many substantial differences. That is not true with respect to the Statute of the old Permanent Court of International Justice and the Statute of the new International Court of Justice. The fact that the Statute of the Permanent Court drafted in 1919 stood the test of time and was accepted with only slight changes as the basis of the Statute for the

---

[75] *Ibid.*, p. 440.
[76] See U.N. Economic and Social Council, Commission on Human Rights, Second Session, *Australia: Draft Proposals for an International Court of Human Rights,* Doc. E/CN.4/AC.1/27 (May 10, 1948).

new International Court indicates that the status of the Court in the international community of the twentieth century is reasonably well fixed. Nevertheless, a number of important criticisms have been made relating to the jurisdiction and operation of the International Court since the Second World War. These criticisms arise not from the actions of the Court itself, its conduct, or the conduct of the judges, but rather from the general attitudes of states toward the Court; attitudes that in turn are traceable at least in part to the tensions in the postwar world.

Criticisms of the Court and suggestions for its improvement, however, are peripheral to the main problem—the problem of getting sovereign states to subject themselves to a rule of law. Law cannot exist outside of the society of which it is a part. To the extent that there exists a world community that accepts the same basic premises of right and wrong, of freedom and slavery, and that has somewhat the same concepts of wealth and poverty, and of religion, there is a possibility of formulating an international law in some respects similar to that which is experienced in the domestic sphere. But even granted the possibility that a body of laws might receive general acceptance in a cohesive international community, which does not exist today, there still remains the problem of interpreting such law—a task primarily for the courts—and the problem of getting states to accept interpretation of the law—a requirement that might in some instances go so far as to involve the creation of an international police force.

In short, it must be recognized that any substantial changes in the Statute of the International Court of Justice would need to be related to the political realities of the day. The future of the International Court would seem to be inexorably linked to the future of the United Nations as a whole.

CHAPTER XIII

Functions, Organization, and Status of the Secretariat

THE Secretary-General of the United Nations has two principal areas of operation: one is administrative and the other is political. The relevant provisions of the Charter are so broadly worded, however, that the Secretary-General himself can decide whether he will be primarily a "Secretary" supervising administrative forces as they service the United Nations, or primarily a "General" concerned with political and strategic problems and decisions. Whether the Secretary-General and the Secretariat concentrate primarily on administrative functions, political functions, or manage effectively to combine both is dependent on the personality and character of the Secretary-General as well as on the year-to-year guidance given him by the General Assembly, the Security Council, the Economic and Social Council, and the Trusteeship Council.

Authority of the Secretary-General

The Secretary-General's administrative role is set forth in Article 97, which states that "he shall be the chief administrative officer of the Organization." Article 98 provides that he shall act in his capacity as Secretary-General at all meetings of the Assembly, the Security Council, the Economic and Social Council, and the Trusteeship Council "and shall perform such other functions as are entrusted to him by these organs."

The political role of the Secretary-General is derived principally from Article 99, which authorizes him to "bring to the attention of the Security Council any matter which in his opinion may threaten the maintenance of international peace and security." As chief officer of the Secretariat, he also derives considerable political influence from the fact that Article 7 establishes the Secretariat as one of the "principal organs of the United Nations." Additional authority of the kind that can be developed into political influence by a strong Secretary-General is found in the requirement in Article 98 that he must make an annual report to the Assembly on the work of the Organization, and in Article 100, which provides that the Secretary-General and staff are not to "seek or receive instructions from any government or from any other authority external to the Organization."

Although the Charter gives the Secretary-General of the United Nations a stronger basis for exercising political influence than the Covenant gave the Secretary-General of the League of Nations, the question whether he should be a general manager or a leader with political influence was, according to one study, "not without ambiguity."[1] Thus although suggestions were considered at the San Francisco Conference to require that the Secretary-General of the United Nations should bring peace and security matters to the attention of the Security Council, and the General Assembly as well, the final provisions made for his authority in this respect are permissive rather than mandatory, and are applied only to the Security Council and not to the General Assembly. Nevertheless, this authority was described by the Preparatory Commission of the United Nations as "a quite special right which goes beyond any power previously accorded to the head of an international organization."[2] The Secretary-General of the League had no such authority.

Despite some ambiguity in the language of the Charter with respect to the nature of the duties of the Secretary-General, the view has been expressed that:

> There was wisdom in their conclusion to entrust the solution to the process of growth and experiment. But at the same time the general direction of the desired evolution was clearly indicated: the Secretary-General of the United Nations is intended to be a more powerful official than was the Secretary-General of the League.[3]

The first Secretary-General, Trygve Lie, took immediate steps to develop the political powers of the office. As one analyst has noted, Lie "apparently believed that his time and energy should be devoted to political negotiations in the interests of world peace, and that the administrative aspects of his role should be delegated to assistants."[4] Lie himself has reported that when he took office he

[1] Carnegie Endowment for International Peace, *The United Nations Secretariat* (1950), p. 11.

[2] *Report of the Preparatory Commission of the United Nations*, Doc. PC/20 (1945), pp. 86-87.

[3] Carnegie Endowment for International Peace, *The United Nations Secretariat*, p. 11.

[4] Waldo Chamberlin, "Strengthening the Secretariat: Analysis and Proposition," *Annals of the American Academy of Political and Social Science*, Vol. 296 (November 1954), p. 131.

"was determined that the Secretary-General should be a force for peace." He recognized, however, that the influence he might exert was "a moral power, not a physical one, ... The Secretary-General, it was said, should be more the general than the secretary—but where were his divisions?"[5]

It does not follow from the fact that the Secretary-General was to have both administrative and political functions that they might not be blended. Nevertheless, by the time Lie's term ended, and he was succeeded by Dag Hammarskjold, there was criticism to the effect that the Secretariat had "lacked effective leadership for seven years" with a consequent deterioration of employee morale.[6] There are some indications that the second Secretary-General may be less aggressive in asserting the political powers of the office and more concerned with its administrative and managerial problems. His recent report on plans to reorganize the Secretariat, which was approved by the ninth session of the General Assembly, emphasized his great interest in administrative matters. It suggested that he expected to delegate "political responsibility within specific fields" to his under-secretaries.[7] Nevertheless, the action of the General Assembly in the fall of 1954 in giving Hammarskjold responsibility for acting on behalf of the Organization in its efforts to obtain the release of American flyers held by the Chinese Communists indicates the important nature of the political influence vested in the office of the Secretary-General.

Secretary-General Hammarskjold views his role not as "what has been called 'a third line' in the international debate"; neither is it "for him to initiate 'compromises' that might encroach upon areas that should be exclusively within the sphere of responsibility of the respective national governments." Rather, the Secretariat should form "a most complete and objective picture of the aims, motives and differences of the Member Nations" and beyond that the Secretary-General "should express with full frankness to the government concerned . . . the conclusions at which he arrives on issues before the Organization," such conclusions being "completely detached from any national interest or policy and based solely on

---

[5] Trygve Lie, *In the Cause of Peace* (1954), p. 42.

[6] Chamberlin, *loc. cit.*, p. 133.

[7] U.N. General Assembly, Ninth Session, *Report of the Secretary-General on the Organization of the Secretariat*, Doc. A/2731 (Sept. 21, 1954), p. 5.

the principles and ideals to which the governments have adhered as Members."[8]

The question whether the political or the administrative function is to receive the greater emphasis in the future might be a matter for consideration at a General Conference to review the Charter. Existing provisions of the Charter, however, are so flexible that substantial changes in emphasis could take place without amendment. It is possible that some of the suggestions made at the San Francisco Conference might be revived and serve to give firmer guidance regarding the role to be played by the Secretary-General. Thus Article 99 might be amended to *require* the Secretary-General to bring matters that in his opinion threaten the maintenance of international peace and security to the attention of the Council. Or further, in view of the increased importance of the General Assembly, the Secretary-General might be authorized, or directed, by amendment of the Charter to bring such matters to the attention of the General Assembly or the Security Council.[9]

Although the Secretary-General, consistent with the practices of the other organs, might interpret his authority to bring peace and security matters to the attention of the Council, to extend to simple disputes not likely to threaten peace—a judgment that could be reversed only by his removal—consideration might be given to broadening the authority of Article 99 to cover issues arising out of the peaceful settlement of disputes. It is to be expected, however, that suggestions to increase the political authority of the Secretary-General would be resisted by Members that would feel such authority might be in derogation of their sovereignty and their right to decide when international situations in which they may be involved should be brought to international attention.

There is also the possibility of reviving the suggestion, first put forth by the sponsoring governments at the San Francisco Conference as an amendment to the Dumbarton Oaks Proposals, that there should be four or five deputy secretaries-general to be chosen in the same manner as the Secretary-General. The suggestion was rejected for a variety of reasons, among which were the view that

[8] Address by Secretary-General Hammarskjold before the American Association for the United Nations, Sept. 14, 1953, U.N. Department of Public Information, Press Release SG/336 (Sept. 14, 1953), p. 7.

[9] Leland M. Goodrich and Edvard Hambro, *Charter of the United Nations: Commentary and Documents* (1949), p. 502.

the existence of such positions would be in derogation of the political authority of the Secretary-General and the opinion that such positions would be subject to political control. A renewal of this proposal would seem unlikely in the light of the practice that has developed of apportioning the topmost posts in the Secretariat among nationals of the five permanent members of the Security Council and also in view of the fact that the General Assembly itself can at any time bring influence to bear on the Secretary-General, requiring him to revise the organization of the Secretariat in accordance with the wishes of the Assembly.

Organization of the Secretariat

There is no provision in the Charter that gives definitive guidance on how the Secretariat is to be organized. The result is that the general organizational pattern of the Secretariat is determined by the General Assembly, and the details are developed by the Secretary-General within the prescribed budgetary limits. The decision was made during the first part of the first session of the Assembly that the Secretary-General should set up the Secretariat so that it could perform effectively the functions and services required. The Secretary-General was instructed, however, to divide his operations into eight principal units, established on a functional basis as distinct from being created to serve the principal organs of the United Nations.[10]

Although the general framework of organization can be changed at any time on the initiative of the General Assembly, in recent years the Assembly has shown a disposition to be guided by the recommendations of the Secretary-General as they relate to organizational matters.[11] Secretary-General Lie did not undertake any substantial changes in the organization during his tenure of office. Shortly after Secretary-General Hammarskjold took office, however, he proposed certain fundamental changes in the Secretariat.[12] The eighth session of the Assembly recommended that the Secretary-

[10] See the volume in this Brookings series, *The Organization and Procedures of the United Nations.*

[11] For background see U.N. Department of Public Information, Research Section, *The Secretariat of the United Nations* Doc. ST/DPI/SER.A/69 (May 13, 1952); also see U.N. Doc. A/2554 (Nov. 12, 1953); U.N. Doc. A/2731 (Sept. 21, 1954); and U.N. Doc. A/2745 (Oct. 7, 1954).

[12] U.N. Doc. A/2554 (Nov. 12, 1953).

General proceed along the lines of the reorganization he had suggested, and at its ninth session "approved generally the measures" he had adopted.[13] The effect of this action by the Assembly was to approve some important modifications in the upper echelon of the Secretariat.

The Secretary-General's plan brought into his immediate office the former Department of Legal Affairs, the Office of Personnel, and the Office of the Controller. In addition, two under-secretaries without operating responsibilities for specific departments were transferred to his immediate office. Another important aspect of the reorganization was the consolidation of the separate Department of Economic Affairs and Department of Social Affairs into one unified Department of Economic and Social Affairs.[14] The former offices of assistant secretaries-general have been abolished and their places taken by officers with the title of under-secretary. Except for the two under-secretaries in the office of the Secretary-General, however, the other under-secretaries will have responsibility for the operation of particular departments.

The process of reorganization is continuing. As has been noted, the Secretary-General contemplates that the new organization will enable him to make certain delegations of "political responsibility within specific fields." At the same time, "all officials of the top echelon . . . will have the responsibility for the performance of activities within their respective fields and, in principle, the delegation from the Secretary-General of administrative responsibility will be complete."[15] The Secretary-General also has suggested that the reorganization will result in some financial savings. In presenting his proposed changes to the Fifth Committee at the ninth session of the General Assembly, he emphasized that his plan would (1) reduce the number of high ranking officials reporting directly to him from twenty to sixteen, (2) create more clear-cut lines of authority than have existed in the system, and (3) give the new top-level positions the same status with each other—a matter that is largely concerned with diplomatic privileges and immunities.[16]

The changes in the organization of the Secretariat brought about by approval of these proposals will be the most complete that has taken place since the Organization was established. It is yet too

[13] Res. 886(IX), Dec. 17, 1954.
[14] For description of the plan see U.N. Doc. A/2731 (Sept. 21, 1954).
[15] Ibid.
[16] Ibid.

early to determine whether the new organization will prove more effective than the one that has served the United Nations since its inception. But the changes made illustrate the flexibility that now exists within the Charter relative to the operations of the Secretariat.

Status of the International Civil Servant

Every member of the staff of the United Nations undertakes, on appointment, "to exercise in all loyalty, discretion and conscience the function" entrusted to him "as an international civil servant of the United Nations." In the discharge of this function he is "not to seek or accept instructions . . . from any government or other authority external to the Organization."[17] Except for reference to "loyalty," the substance of this oath is set forth in Article 100 of the Charter.

The relationship of this oath to the obligations that an international civil servant has toward his own state poses one of the most difficult problems raised by the creation of the United Nations and the establishment of a permanent civil service. Commentators on the Charter have noted cases in which an employee of the United Nations might be required in connection with United Nations enforcement functions, to engage in the formulation of plans for military action against the state of which he is a national—activities that might be "deemed treasonable" under the laws of his country.[18] In such an eventuality Article 100 (2) would seem to apply because Member states have undertaken "to respect the exclusively international character of the responsibilities of the Secretary-General and the staff and not to seek to influence them in the discharge of their responsibilities."

The extent to which Article 100 writes into the Charter a new concept of international loyalty may be debatable. In any event the concept, which did not exist at the time the Covenant of the League of Nations was drafted, developed over a period of years.[19] The limits of this "international loyalty" have not been finally defined despite the affirmation of some that the cardinal principle is "that the members of the staff owe loyalty exclusively to the Organiza-

---

[17] U.N. Secretariat, *Secretary-General's Bulletin*, Regulation 1.9, Doc. ST/AFS/SGB/94 (Dec. 1, 1952).

[18] Goodrich and Hambro, *op. cit.*, p. 505.

[19] F. R. Scott, "The World's Civil Service," *International Conciliation*, No. 496 (January 1954), p. 286.

tion."[20] Certainly, the unprecedented development since the Second World War of international organizations serviced by international civil servants has injected new and strange elements into the relationship between states and their nationals that are employed by international organizations. National obligations of such employees with respect to military service, payment of taxes, and exemption from civil and criminal jurisdiction have raised problems for both them and Member states as well.[21]

Although the establishment of the United Nations has not altered the general relationship between the Member states and their nationals or imposed obligations directly on the citizens or subjects of the Member states, it does seem to have altered to some extent the relationship between Member states and those of their nationals who accept employment with the United Nations and its subsidiary agencies. No less than 5,000 individuals find themselves in this situation. It is beyond the scope of this study to examine this new relationship in any detail. Some major problems have developed, however, that raise difficult questions about the employee relationships outlined in the Charter. Similar problems have arisen regarding employee relationships in some of the specialized agencies.

Article 101 gives the Secretary-General authority to appoint the staff of the Secretariat. In carrying out this function, he is to give due regard to the selection of a staff on as broad a geographical basis as possible, but his paramount obligation is to recruit officials of high competence and integrity. There is no provision for Member states to nominate individuals to be employed by the Secretary-General. The first Secretary-General has stated, however, that it was his "custom in connection with filling of the highest posts in the Secretariat . . . to secure nominations from the governments."[22] There would seem to be no special problem in connection with this practice if the Member governments make a sufficient number of nominations to enable the Secretary-General to exercise a relatively free choice regarding persons to be selected for a particular position.

The question has arisen, however, whether the Secretary-General might recruit, or continue to employ, individuals about whom there might be some doubt regarding their loyalty to their governments.

[20] Goodrich and Hambro, *op. cit.*, p. 505.
[21] For discussion of some of the problems see Martin Hill, *Immunities and Privileges of International Officials* (1947).
[22] Lie, *op. cit.*, p. 46.

The issue first arose in connection with the continued employment by the United Nations of Czechoslovak nationals after the Communist coup in Czechoslovakia. The matter later became of concern to the United States as the result of hearings in October 1952, by the Internal Security Subcommittee of the Senate Committee on the Judiciary during which some seventeen United Nations staff members of United States nationality pleaded the protection of the Fifth Amendment of the United States Constitution as a basis for refusing to answer questions. Subsequently, a federal grand jury returned a "presentment" that charged there was "infiltration into the United Nations of an overwhelmingly large number of disloyal United States citizens."[23] No individuals were indicted as a result of this general finding, but Secretary-General Lie on December 5, 1952, terminated the employment of those permanent staff members of United States nationality who had refused to answer questions before the grand jury on the ground of possible self-incrimination. It was Lie's view that United Nations employees who pleaded the Fifth Amendment in such circumstances "ought to go" because they "had not conducted themselves as international civil servants should."[24] An issue was posed, however, whether the Charter should be changed to compel the Secretary-General "to accept the standards of 'loyalty' or 'subversion' used by any one Member State" and thereby have his authority to employ staff members restricted.[25]

Eleven Americans whose employment was terminated by the Secretary-General were subsequently awarded damages by the United Nations Administrative Tribunal. The question of the authority of the Tribunal was taken to the International Court for an advisory opinion, and the Court advised that the decisions of the Tribunal were final and that the Assembly could not refuse to pay the awards. The United States, having failed in its efforts in the General Assembly and in the Court to prevent payment of the awards, was instrumental during the ninth session of the Assembly in obtaining approval of a resolution providing for payment of the awards from the staff assessment fund rather than from funds made directly

[23] For discussion see *ibid.*, pp. 386-405.

[24] *Ibid.*, p. 397. See also U.N. Doc. A/2364 (Jan. 30, 1953), p. 26.

[25] W. Friedmann, Comments on "Strengthening the Secretariat," *Annals of the American Academy of Political and Social Science*, Vol. 296 (November 1954), p. 135.

available to the Organization by Member states.[26] Thus the resolution of the Assembly complied with the resolution of the Congress
to the effect that "no part of the funds . . . appropriated by the
Congress for the United Nations shall be used for the payment of
such awards."[27]

A bill approved by the United States Senate in 1954 but not
passed by the House of Representatives would make it a crime for
any United States citizen to "accept any office or employment in or
under the United Nations or any organ or agency thereof" unless
he "has received . . . the security clearance required."[28] Such legislation, desirable as it might be from the standpoint of the United States,
would also have the effect of limiting the freedom of the Secretary-
General in employing members of the Secretariat, and of raising the
question whether nationals of other Member states could be employed by the Secretary-General unless approved by the governments of such states. Executive Order No. 10422 of January 9, 1953,
as amended by Executive Order 10459 of June 2, 1954, has much the
same effect but does not carry a criminal penalty. Under this order
an International Organizations Employees Loyalty Board conducts
hearings on the loyalty of present or potential United States employees of international organizations and results of the investigations "are then evaluated against a standard of loyalty to the
Government of the United States."[29] Final decision on the employment or termination of employment is left to the heads of the
international organizations, but in view of the report of the Commission of International Jurists to the effect that the Secretary-
General can and should discharge staff employees who engage in
subversive activities against their countries,[30] it seems clear that
current practice gives those Member states that insist what amounts
to a veto on the employment of certain of their citizens by the

[26] Res. 888 (IX), Dec. 17, 1954.

[27] H. Con. Res. 262, 83 Cong. 2 sess. (Aug. 20, 1954). Also see Extension of
Remarks of Hon. Harold Ostertag, *Congressional Record* (daily ed., Mar. 16,
1955), pp. A-1787-88.

[28] See Senate Committee on the Judiciary, *Report to Accompany S. 3, on
Preventing Citizens of United States of Questionable Loyalty to United States
Government from Accepting any Office or Employment in or under United
Nations*, S. Rept. 223, 83 Cong. 1 sess. (May 4, 1953).

[29] U. S. Department of State *Bulletin*, Vol. 31 (July 5, 1954), pp. 21-22.

[30] United Nations, "Opinion of Commission of Jurists to the Secretary-General"
(Nov. 29, 1952), Mimeo.

Secretary-General. Whether it is a violation of Article 100 to tell the Secretary-General "whom not to employ," as suggested by one commentator, that is the practice today.[31] It may well give rise to proposals for amendments to the Charter in the event a General Conference to review the Charter is held.

Although Article 100 of the Charter does not mention "loyalty," there has been no clear resolution of the issue of the relationship between an international civil servant and his employer as distinguished from that which he owes to his state. That the "loyalty" issue is not dead is indicated by the fact that it was revived again in October 1954 after it presumably had subsided as a result of the Secretary-General's permitting the United States to investigate its citizens employed by the United Nations. A report on standards of conduct within the international civil service stated that in any conflict between national and international loyalties, the conduct of the international civil servant must "clearly reflect" his obligation to the international organization. It continued by suggesting that such loyalty might be made easier by the understanding that "legitimate national interests" could only be served by the promotion of world peace and prosperity, and the "successful progress of the international organizations toward these objectives."[32] Ambassador Lodge denounced this "perfectly preposterous concept" and stated that it was "perfectly ridiculous" because "no American who works for an international organization puts himself above the law of the United States. . . . There's no allegiance at all to the United Nations . . . it has none of the attributes of government."[33] Hammarskjold issued a clarifying statement to the effect that the interpretation given the report of the advisory committee was unfortunate as it was merely a "paraphrase" of Article 100. In his words: "Loyalty to the U.N., in the sense in which I understand the board to have used the phrase, does not bring a staff member in conflict with the duties of a good citizen of a member nation, which has pledged itself to observe the terms of the Charter."[34]

As a result of United States concern over the possibility that some

[31] Scott, loc. cit., p. 288.

[32] See U.N. International Civil Service Advisory Board, Report on Standards of Conduct in the International Civil Service, Doc. Coord./Civil Service/5 (1954), pp. 3-5, 11-14.

[33] Copyrighted interview. U. S. News & World Report (Nov. 26, 1954), p. 98.

[34] New York Herald Tribune (Oct. 12, 1954).

of its nationals employed by the United Nations might now or in the future become engaged in subversive activities, the concept of international officials responsible only to the United Nations, which found expression in Article 100, is in a much more questionable status now than it was at the time of the adoption of the Charter.

Proposals for Strengthening the Secretariat

Secretary-General Lie was criticized by some on the ground that he devoted too much attention to the political potentialities of his job and not enough attention to its administrative aspects; that had he directed as much of his ability to administrative pursuits as to political, the Secretariat might today be even a more potent force in the international community than it is. Certainly the Secretariat can do a great deal to encourage international amity, promote the peaceful settlement of disputes, co-ordinate the work of the specialized agencies, and in many other ways promote the objectives of the United Nations. The mere existence of a well-organized Secretariat, with continuity of office, that is pledged to serve the international community injects a new and forceful element into international relations.

Within the broad definitions in the Charter of the authority and functions of the Secretary-General, there are many ways in which the Secretariat can exert great influence. Existing rules of procedure of the principal organs of the United Nations, for example, permit the Secretary-General to include items on their provisional agendas, and this gives him an opportunity to affect the deliberations of those bodies. In addition, resolutions calling for reports from the Secretary-General on a variety of subjects enable him to sway the thinking on many important issues merely by reason of the fact that such reports give him a chance to put ideas before the various organs in an official way. Even without amendments of the Charter, there are a number of ways the influence of the Secretariat can be expanded or curtailed.

One of the obvious methods of increasing the influence of the Secretariat would be for the organs to increase the scope of the functions they ask the Secretary-General to undertake for them. Article 98 states that the Secretary-General "shall perform such other functions as are entrusted to him" by the Assembly, the

Security Council, the Economic and Social Council, and the Trusteeship Council. This provision constitutes authority for a broad delegation of functions. There would, of course, be limitations on the type of "functions" that might be entrusted to the Secretary-General. There seems little doubt, however, that by this device there is a possibility for increasing the stature and influence of the Secretariat if Member states so wish. Secretary-General Hammarskjold has indicated, even so, that there is a "limit on the volume of the tasks that can be handled effectively," by the Secretariat, "irrespective of the additional funds, personnel and facilities that might be placed at their disposal." He notes that this "forces the responsible organs to make a choice between urgent and less urgent projects."[35]

Despite the ambiguity of the authority of the Secretary-General with respect to co-ordination of activities and operations of the specialized agencies, his position at the center of the United Nations system gives him a unique opportunity to promote co-ordination. A recent study has observed that "nothing short of heroic measures are required to bring genuine coordination to a system in which separatism, jurisdictionalism, and jealously guarded autonomy are prevalent characteristics."[36] It noted further that the Secretary-General could assume a leadership around which forces dissatisfied with the lack of co-ordination might rally. Secretary-General Hammarskjold is aware of this problem. In his annual report for 1954, he pointed out that only by means of further developing "co-operation among the various specialized agencies within the United Nations family" could the "full effect of a joint and concerted effort of all the agencies be realized."[37]

Various devices are available to the Secretary-General to assist him in bringing together many of the activities of international organizations. The agreements between the United Nations and the Specialized Agencies contemplated by Article 63, activities in connection with the examination of their budgets, the work of the Administrative Committee on Co-ordination, and preparation of annual reports on the work of the organs of the United Nations,

[35] U.N. General Assembly, Ninth Session, *Official Records,* Supplement No. 1, (1954), p. xv.
[36] Carnegie Endowment for International Peace, *The United Nations Secretariat,* p. 33.
[37] U.N. General Assembly, Ninth Session, *Official Records,* Supplement No. 1, p. xiv. See also Chap. VIII above.

all give the Secretary-General techniques by which he can focus attention on, and encourage action with respect to, the problem of co-ordination.[38]

One suggestion that has been made to help the Secretary-General obtain information that might be valuable in discharging his functions under Article 99 of the Charter is that "consideration might well be given to the creation of an intelligence service." It was suggested that if Lie had "been permitted to have an adequate intelligence service of his own, it might have been able to warn him of the impending aggression [in Korea] in time for him to have prevented the attack by calling to the attention of the Security Council the preparations that were being made for the attack."[39] Such a service would be attached to the Secretary-General's immediate office.

Without a more complete description of the nature of the proposed intelligence service, it is difficult to analyze it adequately. One commentator, however, has termed it "indeed undesirable," pointing out that the suggestion is morally against the Charter, which contemplates open diplomacy; could never be as effective as the intelligence services of Member states; would clash with similar services of Members; would be tremendously expensive; and, in the hands of an unscrupulous Secretary-General, might be "used for dangerous purposes."[40]

In the light of earlier comments respecting the problem of international loyalty, it seems highly doubtful whether any proposal to give the Secretary-General a staff whose functions could be even remotely associated with the prevailing concept of "intelligence" functions would prove acceptable to Member states. Furthermore, the idea that any organ of the United Nations might legitimately carry on an intelligence activity seems based on the conception that the United Nations has supranational elements that it does not possess. Should the time come when such matters as atomic energy and armaments are under effective international control, a proposal that the Secretary-General be given certain types of intelligence func-

[38] For a description of the co-ordinative use of these devices, see Carnegie Endowment for International Peace, *The United Nations Secretariat*, pp. 31-40.

[39] Chamberlin, *loc. cit.*, pp. 132-33.

[40] Awni Khalidy, Comments on "Strengthening the Secretariat," *Annals of the American Academy of Political and Social Science*, Vol. 296 (November 1954), p. 136.

tions might be acceptable to Members, but probably would not be approved before that time.

In considering suggestions to change the role of the Secretariat, care must be taken to avoid thinking of the organ as comparable to the executive branch of the United States Government. Even though the Secretary-General may be referred to as the "chief executive," he is, according to one study, "the executive, not of a government, but of a federation of sovereign governments. In comparison with the President of the United States . . . the Secretary-General . . . has a muted role." Nevertheless, "the office has great, even in a sense unprecedented, potentialities for executive leadership."[41]

These potentialities for influence in international relations exist in the present Charter. The duties of the Secretary-General are outlined in such general terms that the nature of the office can be determined to a large extent by the personality of the incumbent and the degree of guidance given him by the United Nations organs. No substantial suggestions have been made on possible changes in the nature and duties of the position of the Secretary-General. Plenty of room has been found within the Charter for growth in the direction of asserting the political potentialities of the office. Ample room has also been found for developing the administrative aspects of the office.

It has been suggested that the absence of confining detail in the Charter permits the flexible evolution of the powers of the Secretary-General in response to the developing needs of the Organization. There would appear to be little evidence that there is any urgent need for substantial redefinition of the powers of the Secretary-General either in the direction of expansion or curtailment.

[41] Carnegie Endowment for International Peace, *The United Nations Secretariat*, p. 20.

CHAPTER XIV

Budgetary and Financial Problems[1]

I T IS OFTEN said that the veto is the greatest single problem the United Nations faces. But money is the lifeblood of any organization. And the financial problems the United Nations has encountered—although less spectacular—have proven almost as difficult and, in some ways, even more complex than the veto.

Despite its importance, however, the financial side of the United Nations has received relatively little attention from the American public or from authors and critics. For the most part, the criticisms that have emerged are general in character. Some people complain that the United Nations is spending too much; others insist that it is not spending enough. In the Congress there is some fear that the Organization may be taking on too many activities—particularly in the relief and refugee fields where large and continuing expenditures may be involved. There are also recurring criticisms that the United States is still contributing too large a portion of the total United Nations budget and that some of the other Members have not assumed their fair share of expenses. Finally, there are some complaints that there is a certain amount of waste, mainly through overlapping and duplication of effort within the United Nations system.

How have the financial provisions of the Charter worked out in practice? Where have funds for the United Nations come from and how have they been spent? What are the main problems that have arisen in financing the various activities of the United Nations? What suggestions have been made for changing the present arrangements? Such questions should be of interest to the Government and the people of the United States who, from the very beginning, have been by far the largest financial contributors to the United Nations.

[1] The materials in this chapter have been adapted from *Budgetary and Financial Problems of the United Nations,* Staff Study No. 6, written by Francis O. Wilcox for the Subcommittee on the United Nations Charter, Senate Committee on Foreign Relations, 83 Cong. 2 sess.

Provisions of the Charter

The main provisions of the Charter dealing with financial matters are found in Articles 17, 18, and 19.[2] Article 17 provides that:

1. The General Assembly shall consider and approve the budget of the Organization.

2. The expenses of the Organization shall be borne by the Members as apportioned by the General Assembly.

3. The General Assembly shall consider and approve any financial and budgetary arrangements with specialized agencies referred to in Article 57 and shall examine the administrative budgets of such specialized agencies with a view to making recommendations to the agencies concerned.

Several important points should be noted in connection with this article. In the first place, the purse strings of the United Nations are placed squarely in the hands of the General Assembly. Authority to approve the budget puts the Assembly in a very strategic position, for it carries with it the power of co-ordinating and controlling the various activities of the United Nations. This follows the precedent established by the League of Nations and is based on the principle that all Members of the Organization should have a voice in the allocation and expenditure of funds.

In the second place, Article 17 bestows on the General Assembly far-reaching authority to apportion the expenses of the Organization among the Members. At the same time, it places on the Members an international legal obligation to meet these expenses in the manner agreed upon by the Assembly. No set of principles is provided for the apportionment of expenses. The only limitation is that found in Article 18, which provides that budgetary decisions must be approved by a two-thirds vote of the Assembly. Flexibility is thus the keynote. As the United States delegation to the San Francisco Conference pointed out:

At the Conference there was some discussion of the desirability of specifying in detail the budgetary procedures and methods of apportioning expenses, but all such suggestions were in the end rejected on the ground

---

[2] On this subject generally see Leland M. Goodrich and Edvard Hambro, *Charter of the United Nations: Commentary and Documents* (1949), pp. 183-91, 324-50; Amry Vandenbosch and Willard N. Hogan, *The United Nations: Background, Organization, Functions, Activities* (1952), Chaps. 8, 10; Eugene P. Chase, *The United Nations in Action* (1950), Chaps. 7, 13; Senate Committee on Expenditures in the Executive Departments, *United States Relations with International Organizations*, S. Rept. 90, 82 Cong. 1 sess.; and Carnegie Endowment for International Peace, *The Budget of the United Nations* (September 1947).

that the Charter should be held as much as possible to the description of fundamental powers and functions, and that the General Assembly could safely be left to take care of details through its own subsequent regulations.[3]

In the third place, Article 17 underlines the autonomous character of the various specialized agencies within the United Nations system. Instead of a single, co-ordinated budget, a policy of financial independence has prevailed. Ten autonomous agencies have developed with ten separate and independent budgets. Under the provisions of Article 17, and in practice, the General Assembly has its foot in the door of the specialized agencies, but that is about all.[4]

One other provision of the Charter should be mentioned. Article 19 imposes a penalty on Members that fail to make their financial contributions to the Organization. Any Member whose arrears equals the amount of the contributions due from it for the two preceding years loses its vote in the Assembly. The Assembly may, however, lift the penalty if it is satisfied that the failure to pay stems from conditions beyond the control of the Member. Although the specific conditions are not stipulated in the Charter, presumably they would include severe economic depressions or great natural disasters such as earthquakes and floods.

Current Budgetary Practices

It is often pointed out by supporters of the United Nations that the cost of maintaining the Organization is quite small. The annual contribution of the United States to the administrative budget of the Organization is only about 8 to 10 cents per capita or, to put it in still another way, less than half of what is spent for the sanitation of New York City. It is also less than the amount spent by the United States on a single destroyer.

It is true that the normal contribution of the United States represents only a very small fraction of the total national budget. It should be kept in mind, however, that there are various budgets and funds within the United Nations system, and it is not always easy to distinguish between them. The accompanying table gives

[3] U. S. Department of State, *Charter of the United Nations: Report to the President on the Results of the San Francisco Conference by the Chairman of the United States Delegation, The Secretary of State,* Publication 2349 (June 26, 1945), p. 57.
[4] See above, Chap. VIII.

UNITED NATIONS AND THE SPECIALIZED AGENCIES AND SPECIAL PROGRAMS, EXPENDITURES, 1946–53[a]

Organization	1946	1947	1948	1949	1950	1951	1952	1953	Total
A. The United Nations......	$19,330,287	$27,290,241	$38,387,531	$42,575,368	$43,746,264	$48,628,383	$50,270,153	$49,292,552	$319,520,779
B. The specialized agencies:									
ILO...........	2,711,212	3,720,661	4,147,704	5,034,154	5,266,854	5,834,589	6,389,539	6,509,775	39,614,488
FAO...........	376,535	5,172,987	4,174,000	4,654,519	4,504,052	4,581,456	4,830,334	5,064,399	33,358,882
UNESCO.......	1,052,374	6,212,825	6,696,799	7,780,000	7,162,794	7,989,102	8,726,107	7,972,937	53,592,938
ICAO.........	719,254	1,690,044	2,284,865	2,344,880	2,946,080	3,020,779	3,191,748	3,150,032	19,347,682
UPU..........	132,095	168,608	866,510	297,388	301,837	354,100	416,978	435,413	2,972,929
WHO..........	116,333	1,718,860	4,442,874	4,776,608	6,108,299	6,259,247	7,938,850	8,112,605	39,473,676
ITU..........	b	b	807,289	2,994,252	1,639,039	1,382,194	1,591,875	1,455,733	9,960,982
WMO..........	—	—	—	—	—	185,755	179,259	271,911	636,925
Subtotal..........	5,107,803	18,683,985	23,510,041	27,881,801	27,930,155	29,607,222	33,264,690	32,972,865	198,958,502
C. Special programs financed by voluntary contributions:									
UNTA.........	—	—	—	—	—	6,642,376	22,305,988	22,662,016	51,610,380
UNRWA[c].....	—	—	—	39,115,975	19,220,237	42,130,595	26,778,934	29,192,012	156,437,753
UNICEF.......	—	815,240	31,453,980	46,664,735	35,932,593	22,571,234	13,526,630	12,506,630	163,471,042
UNKRA........	—	—	—	—	496,835	4,132,705	52,964,159	28,695,324	86,289,023
UNREF........	—	—	—	—	—	—	—	847,908	847,908
IRO..........	—	75,675,840	132,167,476	119,401,807	85,446,702	1,376,391	1,515,136	1,603,731	412,691,915
ICAO, joint support....	—	—	—	2,017,942[d]	906,356	—	—	—	7,419,556
Subtotal..........	—	76,491,080	163,621,456	207,200,549	142,002,723	76,853,301	117,090,847	95,507,621	878,767,577
Total.........	24,438,090	122,465,306	225,510,028	277,657,718	213,679,142	155,088,906	200,625,690	177,772,978	1,397,246,858

[a] Subcommittee on the United Nations Charter, Senate Committee on Foreign Relations, *Budgetary and Financial Problems of the United Nations*, Staff Study No. 6, 83 Cong. 2 sess., p. 4.

[b] Prior to 1948, the International Telecommunication Union was made up of separate bureaus with varying membership. It was established in its present form by the Atlantic City convention of 1947.

[c] Includes expenses of predecessor agency, United Nations Relief for Palestine Refugees in 1949 and 1950.

[d] Covers 1947–49 on some projects.

The abbreviations used above stand for the following: ILO—International Labour Organisation; FAO—Food and Agriculture Organization; UNESCO—United Nations Educational, Scientific and Cultural Organization; ICAO—International Civil Aviation Organization; UPU—Universal Postal Union; WHO—World Health Organization; ITU—International Telecommunication Union; WMO—World Meteorological Organization; UNTA—United Nations Expanded Program of Technical Assistance; UNRWA—United Nations Relief and Works Agency for Palestine Refugees in the Near East; UNICEF—United Nations International Children's Fund; UNKRA—United Nations Korean Reconstruction Agency; UNREF—United Nations High Commissioner for Refugee Emergency Fund; IRO—International Refugee Organization.

the expenditures of the United Nations system in the three major categories.

In the first place there is the regular budget of the United Nations Organization—sometimes referred to as the administrative budget— which covers expenditures for headquarters maintenance, field missions, salaries, travel and transportation, equipment and supplies, printing, and other overhead expenses. This regular budget is financed by the sixty Members of the United Nations who make contributions on a scale determined by the General Assembly under Article 17. The budget for 1954 was approximately $48 million of which $41.3 million was assessed against the Members. Of this amount the United States contributed 33.33 per cent, or roughly $13.7 million.

Quite apart from the regular budget are the budgets of the ten specialized agencies, each with a financial system of its own. In fiscal year 1953, the United States contributed varying amounts to eight of the agencies aggregating approximately $10 million. The International Bank for Reconstruction and Development and the International Monetary Fund finance their own operations from earnings and do not receive annual contributions from their members.

Even more important from a financial standpoint is a third category—the so-called voluntary programs—which are financed by voluntary contributions of Member states. As these programs are of an operational nature and involve the expenditure of unusually large sums for nonadministrative purposes, they are not included in the regular budget. The United States has ordinarily contributed from 50 to 70 per cent of the funds available to four of the voluntary programs—the United Nations Expanded Program for Technical Assistance, the United Nations Children's Fund, the United Nations Korean Reconstruction Agency, and the United Nations Relief and Works Agency for Palestine Refugees in the Near East. In the fiscal year 1953 these contributions totaled roughly $71.5 million.[5]

Finally, note should be taken of the kind of extraordinary expenditures incurred in the Korean conflict. Although estimates vary considerably, it is probable that more than $5 billion was spent by the United States each year in carrying out this enforcement action.

[5] In July 1955, the Congress also authorized appropriations for a United States contribution to a fifth voluntary program, the United Nations Refugee Emergency Fund.

The contributions of Member states—whether in the form of man power, equipment, clothing, transportation, food, or troop maintenance generally—were not budgeted through the United Nations.

The accompanying table shows United States contributions in the three major categories discussed above.

Apportionment of Expenses:
The Regular Budget

In accordance with a resolution of the General Assembly approved in 1946, the expenses of the United Nations Organization are apportioned broadly according to capacity to pay. In calculating the relative capacity of Members to contribute, the Committee on Contributions is under instructions from the Assembly to take into account available estimates of national incomes together with the following principal factors: (1) the temporary dislocation of national economies arising out of the war; (2) comparative income per head of population; and (3) the ability of members to obtain foreign currency (dollars).[6]

There is one other important limiting factor approved by the Assembly in 1946; that is, that no Member should be required to contribute more than one third of the regular budget.[7] In 1946 the Committee on Contributions recommended that the United States, based on its ability to pay, should contribute 49.89 per cent of the total. The United States protested this apportionment on the ground that the United Nations is an Organization of sovereign equals and that it would be unwise for any one Member to bear a preponderance of the administrative costs. Such a situation was viewed as conducive to making the Organization too dependent on a single Member, and opened the way for the Member in question possibly to exert an undue influence in the management of the Organization.[8] The United States finally agreed to a temporary assessment of 39.89 per cent. This figure was reduced to 39.79 per cent in 1949, and a

[6] The Committee on Contributions is a special committee of ten members elected by the General Assembly and serving as individuals. The committee is charged, among other things, with the responsibility of determining the capacity of states to pay and recommending to the General Assembly the apportionment of expenses among the Members. Res. 14(I), Feb. 13, 1946.

[7] See "Scale of Contributions to the Budget of the United Nations for the Financial Years 1946 and 1947 and to the Working Capital Fund," Res. 69(I), Dec. 14, 1946.

[8] "Statement by Ernest A. Gross (United States) . . . on the Question of a Ceiling on Contributions to the United Nations Budget, September 30, 1948," U. S. Department of State Press Release No. 13 (Sept. 30, 1948).

Organization	1949 United States Contribution	1949 United States Percentage of Total Assessment	1950 United States Contribution	1950 United States Percentage of Total Assessment	1951 United States Contribution	1951 United States Percentage of Total Assessment	1952 United States Contribution	1952 United States Percentage of Total Assessment	1953 United States Contribution	1953 United States Percentage of Total Assessment
A. The United Nations	$13,841,032	39.89	$16,601,021	39.89	$13,576,243	39.79	$16,394,244	38.92	$15,440,860	36.90
B. The specialized agencies:[b]										
ILO	1,091,739[c]	19.13	848,058	18.35	1,269,868	22.00	1,466,412	25.00	1,538,991	25.00
FAO	1,250,000	25.00	1,250,000	27.10	1,420,800	27.10	1,355,000	30.00	1,673,750	30.00
UNESCO	3,601,424[c]	41.88	2,887,173	38.47	2,814,381	37.82	2,785,400	35.00	2,855,609	33.33
ICAO	498,004	18.69	463,979	18.47	453,319	24.08	698,610	24.97	807,273	27.00
UPU	8,781	4.43	12,056	4.34	12,341	4.38	13,867	4.31	18,520	4.63
WHO	1,860,884	38.77	1,918,220	38.54	3,070,931[c]	36.00	2,481,159	35.00	2,866,667	33.33
ITU	58,393	7.76	146,311	8.04	457,376	12.00	109,264	7.83	113,150	7.98
WMO	—	—	—	—	—	—	24,855[c]	12.67	36,253	12.67
Subtotal	8,369,225	—	7,525,797	—	9,499,016	—	8,934,567	—	9,910,213	—
C. Special programs financed by voluntary contributions:										
UNTA	—	—	—	—	12,007,500	—	11,400,000	—	8,171,333	—
UNRWA[d]	8,000,000	—	10,000,000	—	25,450,000	—	50,000,000	—	16,000,000	—
UNICEF	25,491,692	—	15,356,361	—	7,106,114	—	10,000,000	—	6,666,667	—
UNKRA	—	—	—	—	—	—	—	—	40,750,000	—
UNREF[e]	—	—	—	—	—	—	—	—	—	—
IRO	70,643,728	—	70,447,729	—	25,000,000	—	676,312	—	653,814	—
ICAO, joint support	1,103,366	—	547,939	—	650,000	—				
Subtotal	105,238,786	—	96,352,029	—	70,213,614	—	72,076,312	—	72,241,814	—
Total	127,449,043	—	120,478,847	—	93,288,873	—	97,405,123	—	97,592,887	—

[a] Subcommittee on the United Nations Charter, Senate Committee on Foreign Relations, *Budgetary and Financial Problems of the United Nations*, Staff Study No. 6, 83 Cong. 2 sess., p. 6.

[b] This list does not include the International Bank for Reconstruction and Development or the International Monetary Fund, which are financed by capital subscriptions from member governments and income from operations rather than by annual contributions.

[c] Amounts include advances to the working capital fund, which stand to the credit of the United States.

[d] Includes expenses of predecessor agency in 1949 and 1950.

[e] No contributions made from appropriated funds prior to fiscal year 1955.

The abbreviations used above stand for the following: ILO—International Labour Organisation; FAO—Food and Agriculture Organization; UNESCO—United Nations Educational, Scientific, and Cultural Organization; ICAO—International Civil Aviation Organization; UPU—Universal Postal Union; WHO—World Health Organization; ITU—International Telecommunication Union; WMO—World Meteorological Organization; UNTA—United Nations Expanded Program of Technical Assistance; UNRWA—United Nations Relief and Works Agency for Palestine Refugees in the Near East; UNICEF—United Nations Children's Fund; UNKRA—United Nations Korean Reconstruction Agency; UNREF—United Nations High Commissioner for Refugees Emergency Fund; IRO—International Refugee Organization.

year later cut still further to 38.92 per cent. Subsequent to that time additional annual reductions took place until 1954 when the one-third ceiling finally went into effect.

One of the principal difficulties confronting the Committee on Contributions in determining the capacity of Members to pay has resulted from the lack of adequate statistics. Complete and accurate data on production, national incomes, and related matters often do not exist, and when they do exist, they are subject to different interpretations. The states in the Soviet orbit in particular have been inclined either to withhold their economic statistics or to twist them to suit their own purposes.

Another complicating factor has been the serious dollar shortage suffered by many Members since the war. Inasmuch as its headquarters is located in New York, most expenditures of the Organization must be made in dollars. This imposes a hardship on some Members over and above their actual financial capacity to pay. In order to alleviate this situation, the Secretary-General has been authorized to accept as large a proportion of payments as possible from Members in currencies other than dollars. During 1953 some 28.55 per cent of the contributions to the regular budget was made in other currencies—mainly in Swiss francs.

The determination of the relationship between the capacity of Members to pay and their per-capita incomes has posed still another problem. In 1946 the General Assembly resolved that in normal times the per-capita contribution of Members should not exceed the per-capita contribution of the Member bearing the highest assessment. In effect, this meant that countries such as Canada and Sweden, with relatively small populations and high incomes, should not contribute more per capita than the United States. This principle has not proved entirely practicable, however, especially since the United States contribution has been reduced to 33.33 per cent. A comparable reduction for other high-income countries could only mean that a greater financial burden would fall on the poorer nations. The per-capita contribution of the United States to the 1954 regular budget was 8.6 cents; the contribution of Canada amounted to 9.2 cents; of New Zealand, 9.7 cents; and of Sweden, 9.5 cents. Iceland topped the list with 11 cents per capita.

The Budget Process

The United Nations budget probably is given as careful a scrutiny as any budget of a similar size anywhere in the world. Representatives from Member states in the General Assembly often spend days debating relatively modest sums that would be considered by some national legislatures in a matter of hours or even minutes. Rarely have so many important people spent so much time on such a relatively small budget.

In general, the United Nations budget procedure is comparable to that used by the Federal Government of the United States. When budget estimates for a particular fiscal year have been carefully worked out in the Secretariat, they are submitted to the Secretary-General for his approval. They are then sent to the Advisory Committee on Administrative and Budgetary Questions of the Assembly, where they are studied in minute detail. This committee normally spends four or five months reviewing the various programs, hearing witnesses and preparing its recommendations for the use of the Assembly.

The final stage comes when the Assembly convenes in September. At that time the Fifth Committee of the Assembly gives the budget close scrutiny, normally devoting most of its session covering ten or eleven weeks to examining the estimates and debating financial and administrative matters generally. Both the Secretary-General, or his representative, and the chairman of the Advisory Committee, participate actively in the meetings of the Fifth Committee. The final result, which is usually a bundle of compromises somewhere between the recommendations of the Advisory Committee and the Secretary-General, is submitted to the General Assembly for its approval.

A study of the regular budget figures since 1946 reveals some interesting facts. While the United States contribution has been reduced from 39.89 per cent to 33.33 per cent, the Soviet assessment has been increased by about the same amount, from 7.73 per cent in 1946 to 14.15 per cent in 1954. The five great powers take care of more than two-thirds of the budget, with the United States contributing almost as much as the Soviet Union, the United Kingdom, France, and China combined. During the fiscal year 1954 some forty-four states contributed less than 1 per cent and fifteen states contributed less than $25,000 each.

Although the United Nations has encountered much the same difficulty that the League of Nations did in collecting contributions from Member states, up to the present time the situation has not become serious. A number of Members lag behind in their payments but always manage to complete their contributions before the expiration of the two-year period provided by the Charter. At the end of 1952, for example, some twenty-seven Members were in arrears. Yet two years later all the contributions for 1952 had been collected, and no state was sufficiently in arrears to justify the penalty set forth in Article 19.

The Republic of China, of course, faces the most difficult problem. At present its resources are limited to the island of Formosa with a population of something less than 10 millions. Nevertheless, it continues to pay the fifth largest assessment in the United Nations calculated on the productive capacity of continental China with its huge population of more than 450 millions. At the end of 1952 China was still in arrears $4,823,680—which at that time was more than half the total amount still owed the United Nations by all the Members combined.

Because some Members customarily do not make their contributions until late in the fiscal year, the United Nations draws heavily on its working capital fund to meet current obligations. This revolving fund, which was established in 1946 for the purpose of financing the first year of the Organization, is now maintained at a level slightly in excess of $21 million, and is also available to meet emergency expenses.

Review of Expenditures

It is not the purpose here to present in any detail the expenditures of the United Nations. Moreover, although the regular budget figures are broken down in several ways, no over-all tabulation of expenditures for the United Nations system as a whole is available. It may be worth-while, however, to call attention to several rather significant trends.

If the expenditures for the regular United Nations budget and the budgets of the specialized agencies are any indication, it would appear that the period of rapid expansion is over. The regular budget began at $19.3 million in 1946, when the Organization was getting under way, rose rapidly to a high of $50.3 million in 1952, and dropped to $47.8 million in 1954. The budget approved for 1955 is $46.5 million. The figures are somewhat comparable for the specialized agencies although the termination of the International Refugee Organization in 1952 marked a very considerable reduction for the group as a whole. For the rest of the specialized agencies the trend continued slightly upward in 1954 and 1955.

This leveling-off period is probably due to two main factors. The first is the persistent efforts on behalf of economy that the United States and other Member states have put forth in the Advisory Committee and in the Fifth Committee of the General Assembly. The second is the legislative ceilings that the Congress has placed on the contribution of the United States to several of the specialized agencies. To be sure, the Congress did not intend, through the imposition of these legislative ceilings, to freeze for all time the amounts that the United States Government might find it in the national interest to provide for the support of these organizations. Nevertheless, the fact that the United States contributions to the Food and Agriculture Organization, the International Labour Organisation, and the World Health Organization are now limited by law to a fixed sum each year may have a deterring effect on expansionist tendencies in these and other agencies.

Although there is little room for optimism at the present time, it may be possible to look forward to a reduction, within the next few years, in the size of the voluntary programs. Most of these programs are of a relief character arising out of the war or stemming from United Nations activities in Korea and Palestine. The United Nations Children's Fund, which was launched in 1948, and the Expanded Technical Assistance Program, which began its activities in 1950, are long-range programs and probably will be a charge on the United Nations budget for a good many years. On the other hand, the Relief and Works Agency for Palestine Refugees and the Korean Reconstruction Agency, which will both require large annual outlays during the next few years, are agencies with temporary mandates. They can be terminated, as in the case of the International Refugee Organization, when their tasks are completed. Unless, therefore, some other large-scale United Nations activity is launched, such as an economic development program, total expenditures under the Organization conceivably could be reduced considerably within a relatively short time.

Proposals for Changes

In order to examine the proposals that have been made for change in methods of financing, six general problems have been selected for consideration. It is believed that a consideration of them will bring out the main issues confronting the United Nations in the financial field and the principal suggestions that have been made for change.

Limiting the Authority of the
General Assembly

The first general problem area relates to the financial authority of the General Assembly and the suggestion that the Charter be amended so as to take away from the Assembly the power to determine the budget of the United Nations and to apportion its expenses among the Members.

From time to time since the ratification of the Charter, members of the United States Congress have expressed surprise that the Charter bestows on the Assembly the broad financial authority found in Article 17. Does this mean, some have inquired, that the United States is obligated to pay into the United Nations treasury whatever amount the Assembly determines to be our share of the expenses? Suppose it should decided to authorize large sums for the economic development of the underdeveloped areas? Does Article 17 mean that the United States would be bound to contribute 50 or 60 per cent of such amounts if the Assembly so voted?

From the point of view of the international legal obligations of the United States, the answer to such questions is an affirmative one. Under Article 17, the General Assembly apportions the regular budgetary expenses of the Organization by a two-thirds vote, and the resulting assessments constitute binding obligations on the Member states. Practically, however, it is very doubtful that the Assembly would resort to this authority and impose on the United States Government huge financial responsibilities that it is unwilling to assume.

In any event, such questions reflect a legitimate desire to protect the national interests of the United States by keeping the United Nations what it was designed to be in the first instance—an organization of sovereign states. They also reflect a determination not to leave the United States, by far the wealthiest Member of the United Nations, vulnerable to unreasonable financial demands from poor and underdeveloped countries.

At the San Francisco Conference, there was relatively little debate on this point. It is significant, however, that the Conference approved a revision of the Dumbarton Oaks Proposals relating to expenditures that had the effect of imposing a direct obligation on the Members to bear the expenses as apportioned by the Assembly. "In approving the text," according to the *rapporteur's* report, "the committee took into account the view of the Advisory Committee of Jurists that this obligation should be clearly stated in the Charter."[9]

In practice, there has been little indication of discrimination by the General Assembly against the United States. To the contrary, the success of efforts made by the United States to obtain a steady reduction in its assessment over the years would seem to reflect a fairly general desire on the part of the other Member states to be equitable in their approach to such matters.

This is not to say that the method of apportioning expenses used by the Assembly has worked perfectly. Every year when the Committee on Contributions makes its recommendations, there is a certain amount of dissatisfaction expressed by Member states whose contributions have been raised. This has been especially true of the Soviet Union whose assessment has nearly doubled in ten years. But by and large the Members have accepted the apportionment of the Assembly with good grace. Inasmuch as the regular budget now seems to be fairly well stabilized, it appears that there should be no serious trouble on this point in the immediate future.

Those who object to the present procedure would probably be hard pressed to suggest anything better. Obviously, if each Member, mindful of national budget pressures and domestic politics, were allowed to determine the amount it could conveniently contribute every year, the United Nations would be plunged into fiscal anarchy. Confronted thus by a situation in which it would have no sure source of funds, the Organization would be subject to the financial whims of sixty different states each convinced of the justice of its cause in seeking to reduce its own contribution to the lowest possible level.

Suppose, however, the General Assembly should attempt to step beyond the proper bounds of its competence under Article 17. This is not likely to happen inasmuch as Member states are restrained from approving large programs because of their own budget limitations. But if it should, and if the United States should find itself unable to obtain the support of the twenty states necessary to block action, at least two courses would be open to it. In the first place, the Congress could withhold the funds. The effect of that action would be that the United States would lose its vote in the Assembly after two years. In the second place, as a last resort, the United

[9] U.N. Information Organizations and U. S. Library of Congress, *Documents of the United Nations Conference on International Organizations,* Vol. 8 (1945), p. 495.

States might even consider withdrawing from the Organization.

Actually, of course, there is an automatic, although somewhat imprecise, limit on assessments by the Assembly against the United States through increases in the over-all budget. This limit operates through the fact that, if the United Nations budget were doubled, for example, it would be more difficult for some of the small Member states to meet even a portion of the increase than for the United States to double its contribution.

On the whole, Article 17 seems to have worked fairly well in practice. There appears to be little sentiment for change in the Charter, either in the authority of the Assembly to apportion expenses, or in modifying the requirement of a two-thirds vote for decisions on important questions.

Placing a Ceiling on the Budget

The second general problem relates to the desirability of placing a fiscal ceiling on the budget of the United Nations so that annual expenditures might be kept within reasonable limits agreed upon in advance. This idea is somewhat comparable to the ceiling the United States Congress has set by statute for the Federal debt.

It is obviously desirable that the annual expenditures of the United Nations and of the specialized agencies should be kept at a level that will permit the Organization to perform its proper functions in an effective manner. Equally important, of course, is the corollary that the budget should never be allowed to reach a point that might compel Members to withdraw from the United Nations because of their unwillingness or inability to pay their fair share of expenses. As Senator Vandenberg stated in 1946:

> I should consider it fatal to our aspirations if the United Nations should permit its aspirations to so far outrun its resources that any peace-loving nation would ever find it financially impossible to maintain its membership . . . or that it should ever lose its vote because of unavoidable arrears. This must never become a so-called "rich man's club," it must always remain the "town meeting of the world."[10]

During the first five or six years of the United Nations, Members were confronted with ever-increasing expenditures at a time when many of them could ill afford to pay. As noted above, expenditures

[10] Arthur H. Vandenberg, Jr. (ed.), *The Private Papers of Senator Vandenberg*, (1952), p. 239.

under the regular budget grew from a modest initial outlay of $19.3 million in 1946 to a high of $50.3 million in 1952. At the same time, the establishment of the specialized agencies, together with heavy expenditures for certain voluntary activities such as the Children's Fund and the Palestine refugee program, began to take their toll. These growing contributions, together with the expenses involved in establishing permanent missions at United Nations headquarters and attending meetings all over the world, began to give many Member governments serious concern. The problem was complicated by the fact that a large proportion of their new obligations was payable in dollars. In 1950, the report of the Fifth Committee of the General Assembly warned that "if costs continued to increase, there would be a grave danger that essential activities might be seriously limited by lagging contributions."[11]

These factors have given rise to repeated suggestions from Member states that a ceiling be imposed on the regular budget of the United Nations and that expenditures for the year be kept within the stipulated amount. This could be done either by having the Assembly approve a simple resolution or by the approval of a formal amendment to the Charter. In the former case, the stipulated amount—$35 million is the figure most often suggested—could be revised upward or downward in accordance with the will of the Assembly; in the latter case, the figure could not be changed without going through the difficult process of amending the Charter each time the ceiling was revised.

There are sound arguments in favor of stabilizing the level of the regular expenditures of the United Nations at or near the present level. As the Australian delegate pointed out earlier, it would be helpful for planning purposes if the Member states could know for some years in advance approximately what their commitments would be with respect to United Nations activities.[12] Even more important is the legitimate fear shared by many people that, if the Organization moves too far and too fast in the direction of taking on new activities and new responsibilities, it would subject the United Nations to undue stresses and strains and jeopardize the entire program. If a reasonable limit is not imposed on expansion, it is argued, worthwhile programs might suffer, and serious damage might be done to an already overburdened staff.

[11] U.N. Doc. A/1734 (Dec. 14, 1950), p. 5.
[12] *Ibid.*, p. 7.

A good many Member states, however, have vigorously opposed the budget ceiling as being neither practicable nor desirable. Although they favor economy in expenditures, they insist that the Organization should have the financial means at its disposal at all times so that it can discharge effectively its essential functions. Some are especially anxious not to hamper activities in the field of social and economic advancement. Still others point out that the special responsibilities of the United Nations in the political field, and the uncertainties of the future, constitute a sufficient justification for not limiting requests that might come from the General Assembly in this respect.

The most persuasive argument, however, is the fact that through economy measures inaugurated during the past few years, the regular budget has stopped in its upward climb. Following a high of $50.3 million in 1952, expenditures dropped to $49.3 million in 1953 and $47.8 million in 1954. The budget approved for 1955 is an even lower $46.5 million. As a result, by October 1954—with the exception of the states in the Soviet orbit, which favor the elimination from the budget of certain activities that they deem to be "incompatible" with the principles and provisions of the Charter— the pressure to establish a budget ceiling was gradually subsiding.

One final point should be made in this connection. The regular United Nations budget comprises a relatively small portion—in 1952 it was less than 20 per cent—of the funds spent in the United Nations system. The real danger, therefore, does not come from that source. If the United Nations should encounter financial distress, it will not be because of the regular budget; it will be because of the heavy burdens undertaken by the Members in connection with the voluntary programs.

Establishing One Budget for All United Nations Programs

A third general problem relates to the proposal that the present distinction between the regular United Nations budget and the budgets for voluntary programs be eliminated and one over-all budget be established for United Nations activities.

By far the largest portion of the United Nations budget is that for voluntary programs such as the United Nations Expanded Program for Technical Assistance (UNTA), and the programs of the United Nations Korean Reconstruction Agency (UNKRA), the United

Nations Relief and Works Agency for Palestine Refugees in the Near East (UNRWA), the United Nations Children's Fund (UNICEF), and the United Nations Refugee Emergency Fund (UNREF). As might be expected, this particular type of financing has given rise to various kinds of criticisms. In the first place, the distinction between the regular budget and the voluntary programs is not necessarily a logical one; it developed primarily because voluntary contributions offered the only practical basis on which the Organization could secure funds and support for certain programs. Moreover, a certain amount of criticism has been leveled at both the extent and the use of these various funds. No doubt there has been some duplication and overlapping of effort as well as excessive expenditures for administrative purposes.

The main criticism in the United States, however, arises from the fact that a number of the Members of the United Nations are reluctant to contribute a greater share of the expenses. Indeed, one of the current problems the Organization faces is the possibility that some of the voluntary programs, such as UNKRA and UNRWA, are in danger of collapsing because of a shortage of funds.

A few statistics may serve to highlight this point. As of September 1954, only fourteen of the sixty Member states had pledged contributions to each of the four voluntary programs for the current year.[13] Although fifty-eight Members pledged assistance to the technical assistance program, only twenty-one were listed as supporting UNRWA, and thirty as promising aid to UNKRA. Some thirty-three members pledged assistance to UNICEF.

The response to UNKRA has been especially disappointing. In spite of an authorized target figure of $266 million, which the General Assembly in 1953 approved by an overwhelming majority, payments from governments had totaled only $112 million by September 1954. Because of lack of support, UNKRA was forced to cut back its authorized 1953-54 program from $130 million to $85 million, and even then less than half the funds required for the reduced program had been collected by September 1954. Moreover, 95 per cent of the assistance received by the agency has come from four governments.

These results occurred despite the persistent efforts of the Negotiating Committee for Extra-Budgetary Funds of the General As-

[13] See U.N. General Assembly, Ninth Session, *Report of the Negotiating Committee on Extra-Budgetary Funds*, Doc. A/2730 (Sept. 20, 1954).

sembly to stimulate contributions. In 1953, the committee invited representatives of all the Member states to a special meeting at which the Secretary-General and other top officials discussed the financial requirements of the voluntary programs and encouraged pledges to them. Throughout the year the committee continued its efforts in a variety of ways including letters addressed to Member states, and other diplomatic approaches to them.

The reasons for this lack of enthusiasm for certain United Nations programs are not difficult to find. In some cases the cause may be the chronic shortage of dollars that has hampered the Organization since its inception. In other cases, it may be the unfamiliarity of people in various parts of the world with the work of the United Nations. When important gaps in popular understanding exist even in the United States, where the headquarters is located, it is easy to understand how such gaps might be multiplied in faraway countries such as Liberia, Peru, Burma, and Yemen. It should also be kept in mind that the UNICEF and technical assistance programs have virtually a universal appeal carrying with them tangible and immediate benefits for a great many countries, whereas both UNKRA and UNRWA have mainly a local or regional impact and, as such, reflect tangible returns for relatively few states.

Moreover, the United Nations, like most human institutions, has to face up to political realities. Many of the underdeveloped countries, for understandable reasons, question the idea of making contributions to large-scale programs involving relief operations in some distant part of the world, when they need to exert every effort to raise the standard of living within their own borders. Even so, there is a disturbing tendency among many Member states, some of which are in fairly sound financial condition, to discuss, to vote, and not to contribute. One of the compelling needs of the United Nations today is the development among the Members of a deeper sense of individual and collective responsibility for the successful completion of multi-lateral programs launched by the Organization.

One possible answer to the present dilemma would be to take these programs off the present voluntary basis, provide for them in the regular United Nations budget, and assess the Members for their fair share of the programs. If this could be done, it would not only guarantee participation in important United Nations activities by the total membership, but it would also do away with certain weaknesses that have beset the voluntary programs from the outset. At the present time, for example, funds for the technical assistance program are pledged on a year-to-year basis with pledges subject to parliamentary approval in many different states. With financial resources so uncertain, it is extremely difficult for the agencies of the United Nations concerned to plan their programs with any degree of efficiency. Moreover, it becomes almost impossible to launch long-term projects or to enter into long-term commitments with staff members or consultants. These are formidable handicaps for any enterprise of this kind to overcome. If the program were incorporated into the regular United Nations budget, it would put technical assistance funds on a more stable plane and would enable the agencies concerned to carry out their projects on a continuing basis instead of in the disjointed, haphazard manner in which they are sometimes forced to operate.

There are, however, at least three significant advantages to the present voluntary arrangement:

1. Each Member may contribute what it wishes each year in accordance with its interest in the various programs and its ability to pay.

2. Inasmuch as the voluntary programs are financed separately, the regular budget is not increased to a level where it would be beyond the capacity of the Members to support over a period of years.

3. So far as the United States is concerned, the Congress has indicated its willingness to contribute more than one third of the budgets of some of the voluntary programs if they are not on a continuing obligatory basis.

Budget figures are inescapably harsh. If all United Nations expenses—excluding the specialized agencies—were incorporated into a single over-all budget, the result would be a total annual budget of something less than $200 million for 1955. This would mean a figure of approximately four times the present regular budget. It is obvious that if the contributions of each Member were increased by that amount, it would put a serious strain on the financial position of a number of states. Some Members might well give serious consideration to withdrawing from the Organization. From a practical point of view, therefore, it is doubtful that the objective referred to above could be achieved unless one of two things were to happen: either it would be necessary to reduce drastically the amounts spent for the voluntary programs; or the United States would have to raise its contribution to the regular budget far in excess of its present level of 33.33 per cent.

If it is not yet possible to do away with voluntary financing, consideration could still be given to the possibility of moving in that general direction. Would it not be possible, for example, to increase the regular budget to $100 million and then make sizable contributions from that budget to each of the voluntary programs? This would mean that every Member, through doubling its contribution to the regular budget, would be assuming at least a limited share of the financial responsibility for each program. States with more ample means would still be called on to make relatively large amounts available on a voluntary basis. As the voluntary programs are reduced in scope, a larger proportion of their total costs could be charged against the regular budget.

In fact, the technical assistance program has already reached a point where, with relatively minor adjustments, it could be absorbed into the regular budget, although the participation of states not Members of the Organization would present a problem. As of 1954, only two Member states were not contributing. Moreover, with the three major exceptions noted below, the Members contribute to technical assistance in about the same ratio as they are assessed for the regular budget. The United States contributes some 55 per cent as contrasted with its regular contribution of 33.33; China contributes 0.06 per cent as against its regular budget assessment of 5.62 per cent; and the Soviet Union, which is assessed 14.15 per cent for 1954, agreed to contribute 3.95 per cent of the technical assistance fund. It appears, therefore, that the bulk of the deficiency the United States is making up by contributing in excess of 33.33 per cent can be attributed to the Soviet Union and China.

If the United States should decide to urge the consolidation of the voluntary programs with the regular budget, however, it should consider carefully the effect of such a move on the control of the programs in question. So long as they are kept on a voluntary basis, the United States, as the largest contributor, is in a position to exercise greater influence than would be the case if the voluntary programs were covered into the regular budget.

Use of Private Sources of Income

From time to time, the suggestion has been made that the United Nations should put forth greater efforts to obtain funds from private sources. In 1951, for example, the Senate Committee on Expenditures in the Executive Departments declared:

Independent sources of income must be found for the United Nations and the specialized agencies in order to relieve Member governments of their present heavy financial burdens. These sources might be developed by the performance of services for private business and educational concerns, or by obtaining private grants in support of some portions of their work.[14]

Thus far, the United Nations has derived only an insignificant fraction of its annual budget from nongovernmental sources. An unusual exception occurred in 1947-48 when the Children's Fund collected some $12 million in a special world-wide appeal for voluntary contributions. The success of this drive resulted from the unique humanitarian appeal that this particular program had at the end of the war when children in many countries were suffering because of the severe shortage of food and medical supplies. Although the Fund has encouraged various campaigns for contributions in individual countries since that time, it is significant that it has not been found possible to repeat the successful 1947-48 experiment. From 1947 to 1953, the Fund received from private sources (including organized campaigns) a total of $13,655,000—with only $144,000 collected in 1952, and $828,000 in 1953. This represents about 7 per cent of its total income during these years.

The experience of the Children's Fund seems to have demonstrated quite conclusively that organized campaigns, although helpful in isolated instances, do not offer a real solution to the difficult problem of financing international agencies over a long period of time. Moreover, as a general principle, it would seem unwise for the United Nations to seek funds through regular governmental channels and then supplement those funds by soliciting private contributions within the Member states. If many such appeals were made, the prestige of the United Nations could eventually suffer.

[14] S. Rept. 90, 82 Cong. 1 sess., pp. 69-70.

Nor can the private foundations and other nongovernmental agencies be expected to assume a sizable proportion of the burden. They carry on a number of helpful activities in many countries that tie in closely with programs of the United Nations—especially in the fields of health and agriculture—but the funds expended are not a part of the United Nations budget. They have extended the Organization a few small grants, the most notable of which is the $3.1 million given to the United Nations High Commissioner for Refugees by the Ford Foundation in 1952. This was for the purpose of undertaking a pilot project working toward a permanent solution to the so-called "hard-core" refugee problem.

The private foundations have not been inclined to make grants to the United Nations for several reasons. In the first place, they do not want to make it possible, through their grants, for United Nations agencies to launch projects that the Member states themselves have not actively approved or supported. Perhaps even more important, they do not want to become involved in contributing to large-scale programs of a relief character that could easily drain off their resources for years to come. As a result of these factors, together with the desire not to move into areas that are more properly the responsibility of the international community, the few grants they have made have been relatively small and for very special purposes.

So far as the regular budget is concerned, efforts to augment the income derived from Member contributions have certainly not been successful. The two most promising sources are the guided tours of the United Nations headquarters, which will return an estimated $400,000 for 1954, and the sale of United Nations postage stamps, which will net about the same figure. Somewhat less is derived from rentals and the sale of United Nations publications. Unless new fund-raising activities are launched, however, such sources probably cannot be counted on to return more than 2 or 3 per cent of the annual budget figure.

Meanwhile, a number of proposals—generally without supporting analysis—have been advanced with the thought of uncovering some yet untapped source of revenue for the United Nations. There is, for example, the suggestion that Member governments might agree to impose a small fee on certain types of international commerce or on tourists going from one country to another, for the benefit of the United Nations. There is also the suggestion that those nongovernmental agencies that have a particular interest in certain aspects of the activity of the United Nations might be willing to supplement the contributions of the Members. Finally, it has been suggested that profits accruing from the International Bank, international development corporations, international canals and airways, and other internationally controlled monopolies administered for the benefit of the international community, might also be used in this way.[15]

Some of these plans would probably call for a formal amendment of the Charter. Others could be brought into effect by agreement among the Member states. In any event, it can be assumed that any proposal that would have the effect of putting the United Nations into competition with private-business concerns, or of granting to the United Nations even a limited taxing power, would raise a great protest and would meet with strong opposition.

Authorizing the United
Nations to Levy Taxes

A good many proponents of world government believe that the only satisfactory way to cure the financial ills of the United Nations is to give it the power to levy and collect taxes within the Member states. A variety of proposals supporting this view has been set forth by individuals and organizations. The most detailed of these is found in the Clark-Sohn proposal wherein it is suggested that the General Assembly should have power "to lay and collect an income and other taxes which, taken together, shall in no event exceed in any year 2 per cent of the estimated world gross product for that year."[16]

The proponents believe this amount would be necessary for the United Nations to carry out the expanded program of activities they recommend in the economic and collective security fields. The revenues would come from income taxes collected from taxpayers in the upper brackets, from excise taxes on such items as motor vehicles, gasoline, liquor, and tobacco, or from export and import duties. A United Nations Revenue Officer would be stationed in each Member state to receive directly the taxes of those individuals called on to pay.

Most of the other supranational proposals are more general in

[15] C. W. Jenks, "Some Legal Aspects of Financing International Institutions," *Grotius Society Transactions*, Vol. 28 (1943), p. 93.

[16] Grenville Clark and Louis B. Sohn, *Peace Through Disarmament and Charter Revision* (Preliminary Print, July 1953), p. 25 ff. See also above, Chap. VIII.

character and somewhat less ambitious in scope. The United World Federalists, for example, suggested in 1949 that the kind of world organization they have in mind "should have authority to raise dependable revenue under a carefully defined and limited but direct taxing power independent of national taxation."[17] Two other world federalist groups, the World Movement for World Federal Government, and the World Association of Parliamentarians for World Government, have expressed much the same view. In a joint meeting held in Copenhagen, in 1953, they recommended that the world assembly should be given the power to raise revenue for United Nations purposes. "The maximum percentage of estimated world income to be collected for United Nations purposes," declared the conference, "must be defined in the Charter, and should be levied proportionately to the national income of each member state."[18] The Committee to Frame a World Constitution, as well as the Federal Union group would also bestow on a central world or regional legislative body the right to levy taxes.

The advocates of world government argue their case vigorously. Their main contentions, however, can be reduced to one essential principle—reliability of revenue. They question whether the United Nations or any other world organization can do its job effectively, if it does not have a reliable source of income from year to year. This point of view was summed up at the Copenhagen Conference as follows:

A new tax collector can hardly expect to be greeted with loud and pro-longed cheers; but unless the U.N. has its own taxing power, it cannot act independently of national governments, and can therefore have no real authority. The United Nations at present relies on contributions from the nations, which are liable to withhold the money if they dislike what U.N. is doing; in fact, certain countries have already withdrawn their help from the specialized agencies. Taxation of individuals is just a special example of the enforcement of law on individuals described above; it is likewise necessary because people who fail to pay taxes can be brought to book, while nations cannot.[19]

[17] This policy, adopted in 1949, was modified in 1950 by the elimination of the words "independent of national taxation." In 1954 the United World Federalists General Assembly deleted all reference to direct taxing power. See *Platform*, United World Federalists, Inc., Adopted June 18-20, 1954, Eighth General Assembly, Washington, D.C.

[18] John Pinder, *U.N. Reform: Proposals for Charter Amendment* (September 1953), p. 23.

[19] *Ibid.*, p. 12.

The question of the financial independence of the United Nations goes to the heart of the issue. Supporters of the concept of state sovereignty insist that sovereign nations cannot afford to supply the United Nations with an independent source of income precisely because they want to be in a position to hold back contributions in the event they disapprove of what the Organization is doing. For Member states to lose control of the purse strings of the United Nations would be tantamount to losing control, to a considerable degree, of its programs.

There is also vigorous opposition to the idea of taxation by the United Nations on the ground that it would invade, in a dangerous way, an area that has been traditionally reserved to the exclusive jurisdiction of the sovereign Member states. Even groups such as the World Association of Parliamentarians for World Government are restrained by that argument. At their London Conference in 1952 the group pointed out that they were "attracted" by the idea that the United Nations should be allowed to levy taxes on individual citizens. "We finally decided to recommend against it," they added. "The incidence of taxation is peculiarly a matter of domestic consideration."[20]

Apart from the fact that such far-reaching proposals would require, in so far as the United States is concerned, amendments to both the Charter of the United Nations and the United States Constitution, many difficult questions remain to be answered. For example: Would not a direct tax on individuals cause resentment among the people and lose public support for the United Nations? Would the American people, already complaining about extensive foreign-aid programs, agree to large increases in United Nations expenditures? Could agreement be reached on the kind of taxes that would be fair and equitable in view of the various conditions that exist in different states? Who would be responsible for the collection of such taxes? What machinery would be set up for the enforcement of tax laws against individual citizens? These may not be insuperable problems, but given the present state of world affairs, they are difficult enough to make unlikely the adoption of any United Nations tax system in the near future.

[20] World Association of Parliamentarians for World Government, *Report of the Second London Parliamentary Conference on World Government* (September 1952), p. 115.

Equalizing the Contributions
of Permanent Members

There are two other types of proposals that have been advanced with respect to the financial and budgetary activities of the United Nations. The first involves the possibility that the General Assembly might be given more authority to co-ordinate the work of the specialized agencies especially through approval of their budgets and programs. The second involves the feasibility of introducing some form of weighted voting so that the voting strength of Member states could be brought more into line with their financial contributions to the United Nations. As both these ideas have been dealt with in detail earlier in this study, it will suffice merely to call attention to them here.[21]

Irrespective whether the idea of weighted voting meets with general approval, however, there is one other related proposal in the financial field that would seem to merit consideration. It is the suggestion that every Member holding a permanent seat on the Security Council—with the high privileges flowing from that position—should be required to make an annual contribution to the United Nations equivalent to the amount assessed against any one of them.

The inequality in the financial assessments as between the great powers on the one hand, and the smaller states on the other, is understandable, it is argued, for there is a considerable difference in the status and prestige of the two groups within the United Nations. No such difference, however, exists among the five permanent members of the Security Council. They are on a basis of equality with each other. They share the same privileged status, the same permanent membership rights, the same veto power. Why, therefore, should they not be required to contribute an equal amount to the budget of the Organization?

In the early days of the United Nations, it could be argued that certain Member states, devastated by war, should be assessed somewhat less than they might be expected to pay in more normal times. But the devastation of war has been largely repaired and most of the great powers, with the exception of Nationalist China, are in fairly sound economic condition. It is true, of course, that the capacity to pay of the five permanent members of the Council,

[21] See above, Chaps. VIII and XI.

based on such factors as their national incomes or their gross national products, varies considerably. But the amount involved is a relatively small one when compared to the annual outlay of these Members for defense purposes. It may seem logical to some, therefore, to move in the direction of equalizing the financial responsibilities of the great powers at least so far as the regular United Nations budget is concerned.

From a purely financial point of view, there would not seem to be any insuperable obstacles in the way of such a change, nor would any amendment of the Charter be necessary. In 1954, the five permanent members of the Council were assessed a total of $28.1 million, with China and France assessed $2.3 million each, Great Britain $4.0 million, the Soviet Union $5.8 million, and the United States $13.7 million. If this amount were divided equally among the five powers, it would mean that each one would have been called upon to contribute some $5.6 million. Although this is not a large amount, it would more than double the contributions of France and China, and would certainly work some hardship on the latter Government for reasons already explained.

It should be kept in mind, too, that it has not been easy to obtain reductions in the annual contribution of the United States to its present level. Opposition to this proposal might, therefore, be expected not only from those countries that would have to make up the sizable reduction given the United States, but also from Members that might be reluctant to depart from the capacity-to-pay principle, which has formed the basis for United Nations assessments up to the present time. In all probability the idea would meet with wider acceptance if a decision should be reached in the future to add other permanent members—such as Germany, Italy, Japan and India—to the Security Council.[22]

Contribution of Members to Enforcement Action

The United Nations action to stem aggression in Korea put the problem of contributions in a somewhat different perspective. The total amount spent on various United Nations activities prior to June 25, 1950, appeared insignificant when compared to the vast resources in both man power and materiel, that were poured into

[22] On this point see above, Chap. X.

the Korean conflict. Inasmuch as the greatest share of the burden
fell on the United States, this raised in a very pointed way the
question of what might be done under the Charter to encourage
each of the Member states to assume a larger share of the responsibility of any future enforcement action. Admittedly, this is not
a budgetary problem in the strict sense of the term. It is considered
here, however, because it has a very direct bearing on the financing
of the United Nations and particularly on the question of financial
contributions.

Problem of Contributions
in the Korean Conflict

During the three years of hostilities in Korea, only fifteen nations,
in addition to the Republic of Korea and the United States, contributed armed forces. As against the 45,000 men furnished by the
fifteen nations, the United States contributed over 450,000 and
actually rotated more than one million men through Korea. The
United States also furnished a considerable portion of the equipment and supplies required for the total effort.

There are various reasons advanced—including the limited number of ground forces available and the total defense requirements
of the free world—to explain why Member states did not respond
more effectively to the call for action in Korea. Some nations had
already committed certain of their forces to those areas that were
considered of vital importance to the free world. Still others were
ready to send troops to Korea if the United Nations had been willing
to guarantee their territorial integrity while their armed forces
were fighting overseas. Even so, some forty-six Members gave their
economic support, forty-three governments contributed at different
stages to the Korean relief program, and some forty countries
pledged co-operation in the United Nations embargo against the
shipment of strategic materials to Communist China. A few countries
contributed naval vessels or dry-cargo ships. Others sent field hos-
pital units and medical supplies. Some contributed fighter squadrons and air-transport facilities, while others made available sea
and air bases. Nevertheless, as Senator Knowland of California has
pointed out, "both in the Congress and in the country there is a
very real concern that the burdens ought to be more evenly spread,
in the event of future necessity for collective security action. If

nations are to benefit by the system of collective security, they should be prepared to assume their full obligations."[23]

Way of Meeting the Problem

In view of the duration of hostilities in Korea and the large number of casualties involved, doubt has frequently been expressed that many Members of the United Nations would be inclined to regard any similar venture in the future with any real enthusiasm. Nevertheless, two recent developments indicate that, if another enforcement action should become necessary, it might be possible for the United Nations to approach, with somewhat greater success, a larger number of states for contributions in armed forces and in other types of military assistance.

In the first place, President Eisenhower has outlined a new policy that may have some appeal to states that are willing to make troops available but are unable to furnish them with the necessary logistic support. In March 1954, Ambassador Lodge testified before the Senate Committee on Foreign Relations that if the United States Government, during the Korean crisis "had not required states having valuable manpower to reimburse us in dollars for the supplies which we provided them, we might well have had perhaps as much as three divisions more."[24] Some nations, he pointed out, were unable to participate in the Korean enterprise because they did not have the mechanized equipment, the transportation facilities, or the dollars necessary to put their troops on a battlefront so far away from home. These factors tended to reduce considerably the man power contribution of various Members.

Presumably, the United States does not intend to let this happen again for want of logistic support. Ambassador Lodge said:

The President's policy is that, while in principle each nation involved in a United Nations effort to repel an aggression should equip and supply its own troops to the extent that it is able, the overriding consideration should be the maximum contribution of effective manpower. When any such nation is willing to contribute effective manpower but not able to provide for logistic support, the Department of Defense should furnish to such nation military equipment, supplies, and services; without requirement of payment to the extent that the Department of State, in consultation

[23] *Review of the United Nations Charter,* Hearings before a Subcommittee of the Senate Committee on Foreign Relations, 83 Cong. 2 sess., Pt. 1, p. 14.
[24] *Ibid.,* p. 40.

with the Departments of Treasury and Defense, may determine such nation cannot reasonably be expected to pay.[25]

In the second place, as has been noted earlier in this study, the Collective Measures Committee of the United Nations has under-taken a comprehensive study of the techniques for organizing and co-ordinating the contributions of armed forces and other types of assistance that Members might make to any future collective action against an aggressor.[26] In the event the United Nations is called upon to take enforcement action, the committee has pointed out in one of its reports that "a primary objective shall be to secure the maximum contribution of effective military forces."[27] At the same time, it emphasized the fact that the contributions of states "may be military, political, economic or financial; direct or ancil-lary." The committee then analyzed in some detail the various types of assistance that might be given and, in accordance with the terms of the "Uniting for Peace" resolution, called upon Members to ear-mark certain units of their armed forces for possible use of the United Nations.

Obviously, no catalogue of collective measures, no matter how detailed, can guarantee an effective response when an aggressor appears. But in Korea, the United Nations started without any previous experience with collective enforcement measures. Now, at least, with the analysis of the Collective Measures Committee avail-able, Member states should have an increasing awareness of their responsibilities toward collective security and a much better notion of the types of assistance they can render.

Another important point should be noted. As originally drafted, the Charter envisaged a system in which Member nations, in accord-ance with special agreements provided for in Article 43, would be obligated to make armed forces, assistance, and facilities available to the Security Council for enforcement purposes. So long as Ar-ticle 43 remains a dead letter, any such contributions must be made on a purely voluntary basis. This means that, if the United Nations should be confronted by another situation requiring enforcement action, some Member governments would probably find other more urgent uses for their armed forces.

Theoretically, there are several ways in which this problem could

[25] *Ibid.*
[26] See above, Chap. VI.
[27] See U.N. Doc. A/2713 (Aug. 30, 1954).

be met. Further attempts might be made to conclude the agreements that Article 43 contemplates between the Member states and the Security Council. The fruitless efforts of the Military Staff Committee during the past decade, however, would indicate that there is not much hope in that direction. Similarly, any attempt formally to amend the Charter so as to bestow on the General Assembly compulsory powers comparable to those outlined in the Charter for the Security Council would appear to be foredoomed to failure.

Another alternative method for ensuring a wider distribution of the man power burden in the event of future enforcement action is found in the proposal for a general collective defense pact under Article 51. The signatories to such a convention would pledge themselves to support enforcement measures against any nation deemed to be an aggressor by a vote of the General Assembly. Moreover, they would agree in advance to make available to the Security Council or to the General Assembly on call, certain designated military, naval, and air components for enforcement purposes. In this way, the United Nations would know precisely what it could count on from its Members in the way of military assistance to keep the peace.[28]

So long as the man power and other contributions to United Nations enforcement action remain on a voluntary basis, this problem will constitute one of the major issues of the United Nations. Regardless how the issue is resolved, one thing is certain—the people of the United States might be expected to be more willing to contribute generously to the regular United Nations budget and its various special programs if the other Members could be counted on to contribute a greater share of man power, money, and materiel for enforcement purposes.

From the day of its creation, the United Nations has been confronted by a fiscal dilemma. It was recognized, on the one hand, that a relatively small budget might prove inadequate to meet the many demands placed on the Organization. On the other hand, a very large budget would tend to make it impossible for many Members to meet their financial obligations and participate in the work of the Organization. The problem may be stated in another way. The expenditures of the United Nations must remain within such reasonable limits that the cost of membership is financially tolerable

[28] See above, Chap. VI.

for the poorest as well as the wealthiest Member. This means that the United Nations must not be overburdened with functions and projects it is not prepared to carry out. At the same time, if important tasks need to be performed and the Organization ought to assume the responsibility for them, proper ways and means should be found to make effective action possible.

In spite of the devastation brought by the war, the shortage of dollars, and the wide variation in the national incomes of its sixty Member states, the United Nations has met its financial problems reasonably well. Its regular budget has decreased steadily for several years. No urgent and important task legitimately within the scope of action of the United Nations has been left undone because of a lack of funds. And no Member has been forced to withdraw because it could not pay its contribution.

But as a result of the experience of the past ten years, a number of suggestions have emerged relating to the financing of the United Nations. These proposals range all the way from the idea that the General Assembly should be shorn of its power to apportion the expenses of the Organization among its Members, to the suggestion that the United Nations be given limited authority to levy and collect taxes in order to supplement its income. In some cases, these proposals would necessitate formal amendment of the Charter. In most instances, however, the objectives contemplated could be achieved by informal agreement among the Member states.

Some of these proposals, if adopted, might help the United Nations to function more smoothly. What is needed, however, more than anything else in the financial realm is a recognition on the part of all Members of their responsibility in the job to be done. No agreements, formal or informal, can take the place of a determination on the part of individual states to carry their full share of the burden. This spirit of co-operation cannot be engendered overnight. It involves, among other things, a long educational process by which the people and the governments of many countries become better acquainted with the work of the United Nations.

There is one potential source of income that should not be ignored. At the present time, some nineteen applications for membership—including such countries as Italy, Japan, Austria, Portugal, Ireland, and Finland—are pending before the United Nations. If the fourteen countries judged by the General Assembly to be qualified for membership were admitted, together with Western

Germany, contributions to the regular United Nations budget could be increased by nearly 15 per cent with very little corresponding increase in operating expenses.

It would seem, therefore, for financial reasons at least, that every effort should be made to break the current impasse on membership. In the opinion of many people the admission of these states would add greatly to the effectiveness of the United Nations in dealing with the political problems of the world. Their contributions to the budget would be just as helpful in strengthening the financial posture of the organization.

One final observation seems inescapable. The regular and voluntary financial burdens that the United Nations imposes are small when compared with the cost of war; they represent only a minor fraction of the national budgets of the Member states. When measured against the probable cost of fighting an atomic war, the normal financial burdens of the United Nations are infinitesimal.

PART SIX

CONCLUSION

CHAPTER XV

The Problem of Achieving Change

IN 1945, fifty-one nations took the position that their national interests would be promoted by participation in the United Nations. Not one of those nations has reconsidered its action and withdrawn. Indeed, nine additional states have been admitted to the Organization, and there have been another twenty-one applicants for admission.[1]

National interest will undoubtedly be used by Member states in the years ahead as a standard to determine first, whether to support the calling of a General Conference to review the Charter, and second, whether to support or oppose any alterations in the United Nations system. But this standard changes with the times. When the President of the United States remarked in late 1954 that there is "no longer any alternative to peace" and in June 1955 that "there is no alternative" to being "loyal to the spirit of the United Nations and dedicated to the principles of its Charter," his statements were undoubtedly influenced by changes in the total international situation that have taken place since the war.[2] What may have been a guiding interpretation of the national interest in 1945 might not be acceptable in 1955.

The Changed World of 1955

Ten years is a relatively short span of time in history. In the decade 1945-55 weapons of mass destruction have been forged that

---

[1] In this connection, Walter Lippmann has recently written: "That the United Nations have come through the past 10 years, and that membership is now prized in every nation is—if one stands off and looks at it—extraordinary. These have been 10 dangerous years. . . . It is astounding, therefore, that the universal society of the United Nations survives, and that it is, if anything, more deeply rooted, more tenaciously adhered to, than it was ten years ago." *New York Herald Tribune* (June 14, 1955).

[2] Statement of President Eisenhower, Oct. 19, 1954, on occasion of honor awards ceremony. U. S. Department of State *Bulletin*, Vol. 31 (Nov. 1, 1954), p. 636. Also, Address by President Eisenhower at Opening Session of Tenth Anniversary Meeting of the United Nations, San Francisco, June 20, 1955. *Ibid.*, Vol. 33 (July 4, 1955), p. 4.

threaten the continued existence of mankind; many colonies and dependent areas have become independent and influential in world affairs; Germany, Japan, and Italy, defeated in war, have regained much of their former economic strength and may again become important military factors; the three big powers, the United States and the United Kingdom on the one hand, and the Soviet Union on the other, that stood together to win the war, have been split by a deep-rooted ideological conflict; the danger to freedom inherent in fascism has been replaced by the danger inherent in international communism; potential breaches of the peace that existed in 1945 are insignificant when compared with the threat that the cold war may erupt into a hot war.

The political complexion of the world has changed so drastically in these years that a careful reappraisal of international relationships is required. Inasmuch as the United Nations Charter is the only instrument dealing with these world-wide relationships, it is essential that there be a thorough and careful examination of the Organization to determine its role in the new setting.

Earlier in this volume, certain fundamental assumptions that underlay the drafting of the Charter were noted. These included the assumption of continued co-operation among the five major powers, and the likelihood of the early conclusion of the peace treaties. But if a conference to review the Charter is to be held in the near future, it will be necessary to proceed on the basis of different assumptions that might include at least the following: (1) that, for a substantial period in the future, there may be continued tensions between the free and the Communist world; (2) that there exists the possibility that these tensions might lead to war; and (3) that atomic and hydrogen weapons, if used in war, might be expected to place in jeopardy the very survival of mankind.

Whether assumptions of this kind would justify seeking changes in the United Nations system is one of the questions that must be considered frankly. Certainly they are so radically different from those that underlay the Charter in 1945 that any thoroughgoing attempt in 1957 or 1958 to draft a new Charter might be expected to result in an instrument quite different from the existing one.

The question whether the Charter should be redrafted or amended, however, cannot be approached solely on the basis of whether the new assumptions might logically require a new instrument. There are other factors to be considered. For example, even though there might be a consensus that a particular change in the United Nations system is desirable, there might be serious problems with respect to the timing of such changes and the methods of achieving them. The fact that a change might be desirable, perhaps even for a majority of the Member states, does not mean that to seek it would be practicable.

Scope of Proposed Changes

There are few who blame the United Nations for the postwar deterioration in international relations and for existing tensions. On the other hand, there are many who believe that the United Nations could be a more effective instrument than it has been for reducing tension, or at least for preventing tensions from increasing to the point where peace might be threatened. It is this belief that has inspired many of the proposed changes in the United Nations system that have been examined earlier in this study. Not all of those who propose changes, however, seek to strengthen the United Nations. In some quarters, there is a fear that the Organization has too much authority and that, as a consequence, proposals for change should move in the direction of limiting the scope of its activities. In other quarters, there is a widespread belief that the United Nations as presently constituted is not responsible for existing tensions and that it could not now be reorganized to help mitigate those tensions. It is argued therefore, that for the time being at least, there should be no substantial changes in the United Nations system.

An examination of the proposals reviewed in this study indicates that they can be grouped, for the most part, into four broad categories. First are the numerous suggestions that more power and authority be given to the United Nations by such changes as abolishing the veto, establishing an international police force, and, in general, by moving toward the creation of some kind of supranational organization. Second are proposals that would not substantially alter the nature of the system but would seek to improve its operations by giving life to articles of the Charter that have lain dormant, developing mechanisms for the maintenance of peace outside the Charter but related thereto, and, in general, overhauling some parts of the existing machinery of the United Nations. Third are the plans calling for reducing the authority of the United Nations by limiting its activities in the field of enforcement action or in economic, social, and humanitarian matters. Finally, there are the far-reaching suggestions to alter radically the nature of the present Organization, not by moving in the direction of supranationality, but rather by changing the composition of the United Nations through the expulsion of certain states or the withdrawal of others.

Up to this point, attention has been focused primarily on the analysis of various proposals for change. Relatively little attention has been given to the nature or strength of public or governmental support for these changes. It is true, however, that suggestions envisaging a sharp break with the present system, either by moving rapidly toward world government or by substantially reducing the authority of the United Nations, do not seem to command wide governmental or public support at this time. Indeed, relatively few of the specific proposals for change considered in this study can be said to have widespread support.

If there are to be changes made in the United Nations system, however, there must come a time when general proposals should be particularized and when particular proposals must be able to command public support in terms of actual votes in the General Assembly.

Methods of Changing the United Nations System

Changes in the United Nations system may come about in a variety of ways other than by amending the Charter. As noted earlier, the Charter has been profoundly influenced during the past ten years by interpretation, custom and usage, the failure on the part of Member states to implement certain articles, the passage of organic-type resolutions by the General Assembly, the conclusion of various treaties or agreements including regional defense pacts, and by the changed conditions in the international situation.

Many of the suggestions considered in this study might be brought into effect without amending the Charter. The permanent members of the Security Council, for example, could agree not to exercise their undeniable right under the Charter to use the veto in such matters as the admission of new Members and in the peaceful settlement of disputes. Furthermore, the Article 51 pact proposal, whereby states would agree in advance to take joint action against an aggressor if the Assembly were to approve such action, would bring about a substantial change in the United Nations system without following the formal amending procedure. This is not to say that modifications of this type would not need to be approved by individual states in accordance with their domestic constitutional processes. It seems reasonably clear, however, that they could be brought about by agreements that would not involve amendment of the Charter but would in fact have the effect of reshaping the United Nations system in very significant ways.

Those who make the point that the Charter of 1945 has been amplified by custom and usage and who suggest that the United Nations system may still be modified in important respects by methods other than formal amendment do not go unchallenged. Senator Bricker, for example, has stated that: "A number of world-government enthusiasts advance the reactionary theory that the United Nations Charter should be amended, if necessary, by interpretation rather than by formal amendment." This proposition, he suggests, "is based on the wholly false premise that the United Nations Charter is a world constitution. The United Nations Charter is [instead] a treaty" and hence a contract rather than a constitutional document.[3]

The logic of this argument would seem to lead to the conclusion that if the United Nations Charter is viewed as a "constitution" that creates a "government," it may be interpreted, gradually changed by custom, and subject to a process of growth similar to that which has taken place with respect to the constitutions of most sovereign states. But if the Charter is viewed as a "treaty" or a "contract," it is not a flexible instrument and is not subject to informal change in any fundamental sense.

There is danger that such words as "constitution," "contract," and "world government," may cloud the real issues. The concern here is with whether suggested changes, if considered desirable, may be attained only by the process of amending the Charter or whether it is reasonable to believe that they may be attained in some other way.

By way of illustration, one of the proposals for change examined earlier in this volume was that activities of the United Nations in the economic and social fields should be reduced in scope.[4] Another proposal was that the domestic jurisdiction clause should be con-

---

[3] *Congressional Record*, Vol. 100, Pt. 10, 83 Cong. 2 sess., p. 13459.
[4] See above, Chap. VIII.

strued more strictly so that the United Nations would be less active in areas viewed in some quarters as being within the domestic jurisdiction of Member states. In these cases, it would be possible to draft amendments to the Charter that would have the desired effect. It would also be possible, however, without amendment, to obtain similar results by reducing the funds available for economic and social purposes, by action of the Assembly restricting the functions of the Commission on Human Rights and other related commissions, or by general insistence on the part of Members of the United Nations that the domestic jurisdiction clause be placed under more careful surveillance. These changes could be brought about, in other words, by interpretation and practice. They would not be of the type that would be submitted to Member states individually for approval as amendments of the Charter.

It is virtually impossible, of course, to draft any written instrument, whether it be called a treaty, a contract, or a constitution, that does not have some element of flexibility about it.[5] A document such as the United Nations Charter is unavoidably more flexible in nature than many other written instruments. It defines in broad terms relations between sixty nations with wide variations in their cultures and traditions. In addition, it declares that the "Chinese, French, Russian, English, and Spanish texts are equally authentic" (Article 111), but fails to give the International Court of Justice any binding powers to interpret its provisions. The result is that the Charter is often what a majority of the Member states in any organ say it is, and what they say it is in 1955 may be different from what they might have said it was in 1945.

So far as the permanent members are concerned, however, interpretation of the Charter is, in the final analysis, a matter of individual national concern. The General Assembly can only recommend. The Security Council can take decisions to act, but no important decision can be taken over a veto of one of the five major powers. Thus a nation such as the United States can refuse to accept interpretations with which it does not agree. But continued opposition by a great power to interpretations favored by a majority may create antagonism in the international community and develop an

---

[5] Justice Holmes in connection with a case involving interpretation of the word "income" as used in the United States Constitution and as used in a statute wrote: "A word is not a crystal, transparent and unchanged, it is the skin of a living thought and may vary greatly in color and content according to the circumstances and the time in which it is used." *Towne* v. *Eisner,* 245 U.S. 418 (1918), p. 425.

adverse world opinion. This is the chief deterrent to ignoring such interpretations. The Soviet Union, for example, which has earned the reputation of being a "strict constructionist" in its attitude toward the Charter, has argued against the "constitutionality" of many resolutions including those creating the Interim Committee, the Commission for the Unification and Rehabilitation of Korea, and the Collective Measures Committee.

If the United Nations is to develop without amendments to the Charter, it is necessary to strike a balance somewhere between the extreme positions of loose and strict construction. The idea that the Charter is an instrument so flexible that, if an amendment is not feasible, the same result may be obtained by interpretation or by the passage of a special resolution, may be dangerous not only for individual Member states but for the Organization itself. A Member state that supports a questionable broad construction on one occasion might find the precedent thus set to be against its interests on another occasion. A General Assembly that might by narrow voting margins seek to expand unduly the area of its recommendatory power would probably find its recommendations ignored and its influence weakened in a relatively short period of time.

Even within the area of balance between two extremes of loose and strict construction, there is considerable room for gradual growth and development. But this must be an evolutionary process accepted by the great majority of Members. It is essential in considering the practicability of proposals that the techniques of change not endanger the proposals themselves.

It is to be expected that, in the event a review conference is held, public attention will be focused primarily on changes that may be brought about by amendment of the Charter. It must be borne in mind, however, that other techniques of change, some intentional, such as the process of interpretation or the conclusion of collateral treaties, and others unintentional, such as those that are attributable to growth and changed international conditions, have been used in the past and may be used in the future to alter the United Nations system.

The Issue of a Review Conference

There appear to be at least three schools of thought in the United States with respect to the desirability of convening a conference to review the Charter. One group believes that such a conference might be helpful in strengthening the United Nations and that the United States ought to throw its weight behind the movement to convene it. Another group, including some staunch supporters of the United Nations, is vigorously opposed to Charter review on the ground that it would prove detrimental to the United Nations and to American foreign policy generally. A third group believes it would be prudent to await a final decision on the matter at least until the tenth session of the General Assembly or until some later date.

The Case for Review of the Charter

The most persuasive argument in favor of a conference for review of the Charter is the obvious fact that far-reaching changes have taken place in the world since the San Francisco Conference, that the Charter has become outmoded in some respects because of these changes, and that it must now be brought up-to-date in order to conform to the realities of the new world in which it has to function. By far the most significant of these changes, and the one to which proponents of review constantly refer, is the development of atomic and hydrogen weapons. The development of these weapons in effect, has meant that an organization that was geared to prevent a total war with conventional weapons almost overnight was confronted by the possibility of an absolute war with nuclear weapons. Secretary John Foster Dulles points out, that the Charter "was obsolete before it actually came into force,"[6] and Philippine representative Romulo has argued the case before the General Assembly as follows:

The United Nations was not built to the scale of the atomic age in which we now live. Another way of putting this idea is to say that, in the short space of nine years, the Charter of the United Nations has become dangerously obsolete to the degree that under its existing provisions the Organization is powerless to act effectively to forestall universal catastrophe.[7]

It is not necessary to elaborate on this argument here except to point out that the development of nuclear weapons has had, in fact, a two-fold impact on the United Nations. First, it has placed in the hands of a potential aggressor such a tremendous concentration of power that it drastically alters any conception of aggression that

[6] "U. S. Constitution and U.N. Charter: An Appraisal," Address by Secretary Dulles, Aug. 26, 1953, U. S. Department of State *Bulletin*, Vol. 29 (Sept. 7, 1953), p. 310.

[7] U.N. General Assembly, Ninth Session, Plenary, *Official Records*, 479th Meeting (Sept. 27, 1954), p. 82.

might have evolved in a period when conventional weapons alone were available. And second, it has injected into traditional patterns of thought about the Organization and the use of collective security machinery so many new and difficult problems that principles once agreed upon now seem to need complete re-evaluation.

Some proponents of review insist that if the members of the various delegations to the San Francisco Conference had visualized the changes that were about to take place in the world, a different kind of Charter might have emerged. If they had been aware of the tremendous destructive power of atomic energy, it is argued, they might have taken quite a different approach to those portions of the Charter dealing with enforcement action and the regulation of atomic energy. Similarly if they had realized that the wartime coalition of great powers was soon to disintegrate, they probably would have reconsidered the provisions of Article 27 dealing with the veto.

This argument may be disputed. It may be contended that even if the delegations at the San Francisco Conference had known of these impending changes, the Charter would not have been drafted in substantially different form. The fact remains, however, as has been noted above, that a number of the basic assumptions on which the United Nations was built no longer exist. Until proper changes are made in the Charter, therefore, the Organization cannot be expected to function with maximum effectiveness.

A second argument often put forth is that it is a matter of simple good faith for the United States Government to support the convening of a General Conference. At the San Francisco Conference, a number of important provisions of the Charter were adopted over the vigorous opposition of many of the smaller states. These states accepted the Charter on the assumption that the Members would have an opportunity to review their handiwork after a ten-year trial period. At that time, the United States delegation made clear its intention to support the convening of such a conference at the end of ten years. As a matter of honor and good faith the United States Government should now redeem that pledge.

There is some indication that the smaller states may use this argument with telling effect. As Peruvian delegate Belaunde reminded the General Assembly in 1953, the small states "pressed for and obtained the promise in Article 109, that the Charter would be revised. Hence, this article is not only a statutory provision but also the fulfilment of an honourable promise which enables us to work for the revision of the Charter."[8]

This argument takes on added importance when it is recalled that the third paragraph of Article 109, which provides for a review conference after ten years, is what might be called a "one-shot" proposition. In 1955, a review can be ordered by a simple majority vote of the General Assembly. After 1955, however, this special proviso of the Charter becomes a dead letter unless some device to prolong a decision in 1955 is developed. Thereafter, no conference for review of the Charter can be convened unless it is approved by a two-thirds vote of the General Assembly.

In the third place, some proponents contend, the United Nations has demonstrated its inability to discharge effectively its prime responsibility—the maintenance of international peace and security. Now that the weaknesses of the Charter have been revealed, it is imperative that a conference be convened in order to revitalize the United Nations and to give it the authority it needs to deal speedily and decisively with those who violate the peace. This is the supreme challenge of our time, and the United Nations ought to be equipped to meet it.

There is, of course, a wide divergence of view among the proponents regarding just what steps are necessary to take care of the present inadequacies of the United Nations. But whether they propose curbing the extensive use of the veto, creating an international police force to keep the peace, or developing some form of world government with the authority to formulate rules of law binding on the Member states, they believe that the time has come to draft a new formula and that a conference for review of the Charter is the logical place to do the drafting.

The Greek delegation expressed the view of some others, during the eighth session of the General Assembly, when it pointed out that

> . . . the United Nations was conceived by its founders as a living reality, as a continuing process destined to attain its high purposes by a constant adaptation and adjustment to changing circumstances. This necessary flexibility cannot be achieved unless the constitutional statute governing our Organization undergoes such periodic revision as its trials and its errors dictate in order better to fit into the patterns of the every-day life of the international community.[9]

[8] U.N. General Assembly, Eight Session, Plenary, *Official Records*, 439th Meeting (Sept. 21, 1953), p. 70.
[9] *Ibid.*, p. 67.

Three other arguments, which are developed in more detail below, may be noted at this point: (1) a conference for review of the Charter would provide an excellent opportunity to evaluate the accomplishments of the United Nations and to restore public confidence in the Organization; (2) a conference could be very helpful in making numerous drafting changes in the Charter necessary to bring that document up to date; and (3) such a conference should be called because it would reveal the opposition of the Communist states to the basic principles of the Charter and be of significant propaganda value to the free world.

The Case Against Review of the Charter

Some opponents of review of the Charter contend that a review conference held in 1956 or 1957 would be foredoomed to failure because of the Soviet veto. They believe, moreover, that such a conference would have serious negative results in widening the gulf between the Communist states and the free world and in laying bare grave policy differences among the free nations. Instead of resolving the differences resulting from the cold war, it would aggravate them.

"Heated debate and acrimonious haggling over controversial amendments," says Benjamin V. Cohen, former Counsellor of the Department of State, "not only may increase tensions between the free world and the Soviet Union, but may accentuate differences among the free nations and within the free nations. . . . A general conference may prove to be a divisive and not a uniting force."[10]

That the conference would be torn with controversy is taken for granted on the basis of the experience of the United Nations up to the present time. The discussion of any important amendments—such as those relating to disarmament, membership, domestic jurisdiction, or the veto—would inevitably result in a full dress debate with the usual bitter charges and counter charges. The situation in this respect could be much worse than it was in 1945 when the negotiating countries were emerging from the war. On the other hand, if these central problems are not discussed in considerable detail, no real good could possibly come from a conference.

The controversy over human rights and domestic jurisdiction is

[10] "The United Nations: A Vital Interest of the United States," U.N. Day Address by Benjamin V. Cohen before the Washington Ethical Society, Oct. 24, 1954 (Mimeo.).

a very pertinent case in point. Any attempt to redefine the competence of the United Nations in this area, in all probability, would lead to endless arguments over Tunisia, Morocco, the Indians in South Africa and other specific issues that have been the source of a great deal of friction in the United Nations. Meanwhile, the Soviet Union could be expected to exploit the differences between the colonial and anti-colonial powers thus encouraging a feeling of distrust and suspicion among the free nations.

More than that, a review conference might serve as a serious divisive force within the United States. So far there is little indication that American public opinion is solidly back of any amendment to the Charter the United States Government might propose or that a two-thirds vote in the Senate could be obtained even if agreement were reached in the conference. In any event, it is argued, it would greatly damage the prestige of the United States if the debate on the Bricker Amendment, the treaty power, and human rights were transferred from the Senate to the forum of the United Nations.

In the second place, opponents of a conference contend, the Charter is not the obsolete document many people seem to assume. It is not rigid or inflexible but is a living, growing instrument that has demonstrated in many ways its capacity to meet new and changed conditions.

Moreover, those who urge the improvement of the Charter through the formal amending process will do well to keep in mind the history of that instrument. It was drafted during the war. If it had not been practically completed before hostilities ceased, the great powers would have encountered much more difficulty in reaching agreement on many issues, and it is possible that there would have been no Charter at all. Certainly, the Charter that finally emerged from the San Francisco Conference is a more workable document than the Member states could have framed at any time since the Conference. Given present world conditions, there is little reason to suppose that a better Charter could be approved now either with or without a review conference.

Opponents of review of the Charter also point out that structural changes in the Charter or the United Nations system cannot resolve the basic differences that divide the world today. What is needed is not more law and more international machinery, but more compliance with the law and more co-operation with the Organization that is already in existence. They contend that new procedures, new organizational patterns, or new commitments will not save mankind from another great war. These are not the real issues in the cold war; they are false issues that should not be permitted to mislead the American public. Actually, the dangers and the tensions that exist today are in no way due to structural defects in the United Nations Charter. These dangers and tensions stem from the conflicting policies of sovereign states, and they would exist regardless of technical or organizational imperfections in the Charter. Only when a more viable political climate prevails in the world can it be expected that agreement can be reached on those structural changes in the United Nations that will enable the Organization to fulfill its main function of maintaining world peace.

Former Ambassador Ernest A. Gross stated the problem as follows: "We do not face a band of cattle rustlers. Something close to one-quarter of the human race, led by despots, defies the Charter. This is not to say that they will always stay that way; but it does say that a mere reformulation of the obligation will not change the nature either of the revolt or of the threat."[11]

In the fourth place, opponents of Charter review argue that it is wrong to assume that the great powers made any commitment at San Francisco to convene a review conference. Article 109 promises nothing except that the question will be placed on the agenda of the General Assembly at the time of its tenth regular session. Moreover, the smaller countries that insisted on the inclusion of Article 109 in the Charter did so largely because of their concern over the veto and the concentration of authority in the Security Council. In view of the gradual shift in power that has taken place from the Security Council to the General Assembly, where the small states wield more influence and the veto does not apply, the main justification they had for insisting on a conference no longer exists. For these reasons, it is argued, a conference is not only unnecessary, it is undesirable. There would be very little to gain; there would be much to lose. Certainly a disservice could be done to the cause of peace if controversy over amendments to the Charter were allowed to hold up progress that the United Nations could continue to make under its present Charter.

Several officials of the United States Government have repeatedly pointed out that they are aware of these dangers and pitfalls that

[11] Ernest A. Gross, "Revising the Charter. Is It Possible? Is It Wise?" *Foreign Affairs,* Vol. 32 (January 1954), p. 213.

are inherent in Charter review. They realize also that a review conference might generate false hopes and might encourage attempts to redraft the Charter that could weaken and endanger the United Nations. They are determined, however, "not to lose the good that is, in the search for something better."[12] Secretary of State Dulles summarized his position on this point as follows:

> There are some risks in calling the conference. I find very few things that can be done in this world which amount to anything without accepting some risk. It is a question of balancing the possible disadvantages against the advantages, and I believe the advantages of a review conference exceed the possible disadvantages.[13]

Alternatives Before the United Nations

The desirability of convening a conference for review of the Charter would depend in large measure on the objectives that such a conference might be designed to achieve. When Member states cast their votes in the autumn of 1955 for or against a conference, they may have quite different purposes in mind. It might be helpful, therefore, to examine briefly the proper scope of review and to outline the various alternatives before the United Nations. There are a number of alternatives, and they might not be mutually exclusive. States favoring a review conference might have in mind one or more of five possible objectives:

1. To obtain agreement on certain technical drafting changes in the Charter.

2. To draft an entirely new Charter creating a different organization.

3. To amend the Charter with respect to basic issues such as the veto and the admission of new Members.

4. To utilize the conference for propaganda purposes.

5. To evaluate the work of the United Nations and determine what if any changes can be made without amending the Charter.[14]

Redrafting the Charter

Some have suggested that a conference for review of the Charter might confine its activities to technical redrafting in order to clear

---

[12] *Review of the United Nations Charter,* Hearings before a Subcommittee of the Senate Committee on Foreign Relations, 83 Cong. 2 sess., Pt. 1, p. 6.

[13] *Ibid.,* p. 11.

[14] On this point see Gross, *loc. cit.*

up ambiguities in language and to bring the Charter up-to-date. Former Ambassador Gross has characterized this as a "punctuation" conference.

This conceivably could serve a very worthy purpose. The Charter is by no means a perfect document from the point of view of drafting, and, in some cases, the distance between what the instrument provides and what the Organization actually does is great indeed. It has been estimated there are presently twenty-four articles of the Charter that, in whole or in part, have been modified, left dormant or become obsolete.[15] It might be worthwhile, therefore, to clear away some of these unused provisions and then proceed to make those technical changes in the language of the Charter that are necessary if the document is to be kept abreast of changing world conditions.

On the other hand, it may be questioned whether the technical imperfections of the Charter have a great deal to do with the success or failure of the United Nations. Would a mere redrafting of the Charter give new stature and authority to the Organization? Could the Charter be opened up for technical changes without the conference becoming involved in interminable discussions over basic issues? Just where is the line between form and substance? And how important is it to codify or rewrite the Charter at this particular stage in the history of the United Nations?

There is considerable doubt in the minds of some people, that a review conference called for such a limited purpose would be worth the effort and the expense involved. The risks might be all out of proportion to the possible gains. This is especially true when it is recalled that revisions of a noncontroversial nature that are considered desirable by the Member states can be brought to the attention of the General Assembly at any time, and the Charter could be amended without the formality of a conference.

A New Charter

At the other extreme, there is the suggestion advanced in some quarters that the review conference, once convened, might draft an entirely new Charter providing for the establishment of some other organization of sovereign states or even a world government.

[15] See Jacob Robinson, "The General Review Conference," *International Organization*, Vol. 8 (August 1954), pp. 316-30. A number of examples are set forth in Chap. I above.

Proponents of this point of view recall the bold decision taken by the Constitutional Convention of 1787. When the framers of the Constitution went to Philadelphia, their mandate was to revise the Articles of Confederation. They soon agreed, however, that the critical situation confronting the thirteen colonies called for vigorous and far-reaching action. So they disregarded their instructions, scrapped the Articles of Confederation and drafted an entirely new constitution. By the same token, it is argued, the review conference could put aside the Charter and draw up a completely new instrument if the world situation warrants such action in 1956 or 1957.

Presumably, this could be done. The language of Article 109 clearly contemplates that the conference is to be held "for the purpose of reviewing the present Charter." There is no legal limitation in the Charter, however, that would prevent the delegates from subjecting that document to a complete revision or from agreeing on amendments that would change fundamentally the basic nature of the United Nations. Theoretically, the Charter could be amended out of existence if the Member states so agreed.

This is not, however, the point of view of the United States Government. The Secretary of State and his subordinates on several occasions have emphasized that the United States would expect the conference for review of the Charter to function within the framework of the existing Charter. This approach to the problem was well stated by David W. Wainhouse, Deputy Assistant Secretary of State for International Organization Affairs. He said there are those who will want "some sort of super-state," as well as those who

. . . would like to see the United States withdraw from the United Nations. Still others would like to see the U.S.S.R. and its satellites expelled and the United Nations turned into a closely-knit military alliance. While . . . these advocates are entitled to express their opinion, we have already found it helpful to think in terms of excluding such proposals from the proper scope of Charter review. We believe that the purpose of such review is to strengthen the existing organization, not to destroy it or completely change its character.[16]

Amendment of the Charter on Important Issues

A somewhat different approach is envisaged in the third alternative, that of seeking amendments to the Charter with respect to

[16] "Some Problems of Charter Review," U. S. Department of State *Bulletin,* Vol. 31 (Nov. 15, 1954), p. 739.

such vital issues as membership, the veto, and domestic jurisdiction. It has been suggested that this type of meeting could develop into a "showdown" conference, "in which [the United States] would propose major changes which must be accepted 'or else.' " It is contended that such an approach would appeal to "some who advocate 'kicking the Russians out' . . . precisely because it would precipitate a break-up in the organization."[17]

Clearly the last thing that most friends and allies of the United States in the free world and the so-called neutral states want is such a major showdown with the Soviet Union. And the supporters of the United Nations in the United States are extremely anxious to avoid any step that might result in impairing the authority and prestige of the Organization.

It is by no means clear, however, that a sincere attempt to amend the Charter would necessarily result in this kind of showdown with the Soviet Union. In this connection the time factor may be of considerable significance. A review conference could not be convened before 1956 at the earliest and, in view of the presidential election in the United States in that year, it might be unwise to schedule it before 1957. With the world situation in constant flux, it is extremely difficult to foresee the exact nature or posture of free world relations with the Soviet Union by that time. If the Geneva conference of 1955 is any indication, it is not inconceivable that tensions will have been relaxed enough to justify some hope for progress.

Moreover, there is little likelihood that the Soviet Union would approach a review conference in a "showdown" mood. Presumably, the Soviet Union believes that its membership in the United Nations is in its national interest, and it is highly unlikely that it would permit itself to be maneuvered into a position in which it would be compelled to withdraw from the Organization. It would be far simpler, from the Soviet point of view, merely to vote in the conference against any amendment it opposes, and then later, by withholding ratification, to prevent it from coming into force.

Even if all amendments were ultimately rejected, some advantages might accrue to the free world as a result of the debate and vote process. Certainly those changes in the Charter receiving large majority votes, even if they did not come into force, would still carry "great moral weight" and be considered as "an important con-

---

[17] Gross, loc. cit., p. 205.

tribution to the interpretation and application of the Charter."[18]

Even so the risks involved in a conference of this kind are very real, and it would be unwise to ignore them. Some exceedingly difficult questions need to be answered. To what extent is the United Nations responsible for the fundamental differences between the Communist states and the free world, and to what extent might changes in the Charter dissolve these differences? What are the prospects that constructive proposals could come out of such a conference? Would the American people be united on basic policy questions that might arise? Would the conference split the free world or might it be expected to achieve a modicum of unity on a variety of difficult issues? And if the conference should fail, how serious would be the impact of failure on the United Nations?

Before a Charter review conference is called, there must be careful consideration of the chances of failure, and the consequences that would flow therefrom, as well as the chances of success. Once the conference is held, a new set of conditions would exist in the world. The problem, therefore, is to determine whether those conditions might be detrimental to the interests of the United States or of the United Nations as a whole or whether they might further the cause of world peace.

A Propaganda Conference

Some of those who despair of real progress through amending the Charter still believe the free world might gain extensive propaganda advantages from a review conference. They picture the unfolding of events at the conference somewhat as follows. One by one various proposals to strengthen the United Nations would be examined. One by one they would be put to the vote only to be opposed by the Soviet Union and its satellite states. The net result would be to reveal to the entire world the un-co-operative nature of Soviet policy and to demonstrate, beyond any shadow of doubt, the complete unwillingness of the Soviet Union to yield ground on issues the free world considers important. With the Soviet Union on the "wrong" side of every question, the democratic countries might expect to win a resounding propaganda victory.

The soundness of this line of reasoning has been questioned. If the main purpose of the conference is to seek a propaganda advan-

[18] Robinson, loc. cit., p. 320.

tage in the cold war, then the fundamental purposes of the United Nations are likely to be trampled in the process. What should be a by-product of the conference would become an end in itself, with the dangerous result that the public might get a completely distorted view of the United Nations and its shortcomings. This would tend to undermine American confidence in the United Nations and American support for international co-operation generally.

Moreover, it cannot be assumed that the issues at the conference would always be clear-cut. Would a full dress debate on the veto, for example, redound to the advantage of the United States in view of its unwillingness to give up the veto with respect to the use of its armed forces, and in view of the reluctance of France and Great Britain to surrender their veto on questions affecting their colonial interests? Would a discussion of the membership problem actually be helpful to the cause of the free world given the continued vigorous opposition of the United States to the seating of Communist China as a member of the Security Council? And what about a consideration of such complex matters as domestic jurisdiction, colonialism, and economic development where free world unity is ominously lacking? Might not that do more harm than good? Obviously, the United States would not emerge, in every case, as the victor.

It may also be questioned whether the Soviet Union would necessarily come to such a conference with an altogether negative position. It is conceivable that the Soviet delegation might present a set of proposals that they could maneuver, with the aid of certain Asian-African states, in such a way as to put the United States and the other free nations on the defensive rather than the offensive. This possibility should not be overlooked.

Review of the Charter

Finally, a word should be added about the fifth alternative—that of reviewing the progress of the United Nations during its first ten years, searching for its weak spots, and determining where improvements might be made without resort to amendment of the Charter. This could result in two important advantages: first, in restoring faith and confidence in the United Nations by creating a better understanding of its role in world affairs; and second, in strengthening the United Nations system within the present framework of the Charter so as to make possible more effective operations in the years to come.

In this connection, it is significant that Administration leaders have generally used the expression "review of the Charter," and have carefully refrained from referring to "Charter revision" or to a "Charter revision conference." The United States Government, in other words, does not start with the assumption that the Charter must be amended in any particular way, or indeed, that it be amended at all. This being the case, the concept of "review" as against actual "revision" takes on added importance.

An official of the Department of State has argued the case for review of the Charter as follows:

> As a minimum a review of the Charter and constitutional procedures and practices should bring greater understanding to our people and to the peoples of the world as to how essential the United Nations is to the peace, security and well-being of Americans and the rest of the free world. It should bring about an understanding of the extent to which the potentialities of the Charter are being realized. It can help measurably to refurbish the faith we have in the present Charter without raising false hopes and expectations.[19]

Having said that, some people will still question whether a "stock-taking" conference of this character would produce satisfactory results. An appraisal of the United Nations record—a review in the strict sense—might prove a relatively barren task unless the deliberations were guided with considerable skill. From the beginning such a conference would be faced with a vexatious dilemma. If, on the one hand, delegates were precluded from discussing formal amendments of the Charter, they would be confronted by the ever-present danger of becoming involved in sterile debates about unimportant details that have no real bearing on the success of the United Nations. On the other hand, if the debate were unlimited, they would run the risk of consuming a great deal of time in a rather futile discussion of controversial issues about which little or nothing could be done.

A Compromise Proposal

Some who are in favor of the general idea of Charter review but

[19] David W. Wainhouse, "The United States and Charter Review," U. S. Department of State *Bulletin,* Vol. 30 (Apr. 26, 1954), p. 645.

who have reservations, given the present unsettled state of world affairs, about the advisability of calling a review conference have advanced a compromise proposal that the General Assembly will no doubt consider when the issue comes before it in the autumn of 1955.[20] The proposal would, in effect, keep alive the concept of review but would postpone any final decision on the matter this year by the simple device of creating a special committee of the General Assembly that would be charged with the responsibility of studying the various issues involved and making its recommendations at some later time on the date and place of the conference. After its preliminary inquiry, if the committee should decide that conditions were unfavorable to convening a conference, it might recommend against it or it might recommend a delay of indefinite duration. Such a committee could be kept in existence over a period of several years if necessary in order to give the matter its continuing attention.

If there should be a division of opinion in the General Assembly over the Charter review issue, this type of proposal would have the advantage of releasing the Assembly from the necessity of making a final decision in 1955. Moreover, if a conference should be held, the timing and the methods chosen for approaching the problem of review may determine the success or failure of the venture. Careful study of the problem by a continuing committee, not handicapped by having to do its work in public, would tend to reduce the risks involved and provide greater assurance that the objectives of such a conference could be attained.

Many strong advocates of review, particularly those who insist that the United Nations push ahead with all possible speed, are inclined to oppose this type of proposal on the ground that it is merely another device to postpone indefinitely the review conference. What is needed now, it is argued, is not more delay and more time for study, but concrete action of a positive character. This can be brought about only by setting a date for the conference; for then and then only will the governments and the peoples of the Members

---

[20] See, for example, the testimony of Mrs. Franklin D. Roosevelt, Joseph E. Johnson, and Clark Eichelberger, before a Subcommittee of the Senate Committee on Foreign Relations, *Review of the United Nations Charter*, Senate Hearings, 84 Cong. 1 sess., Pt. 12, pp. 1803, 1920, 1699. See also Clark Eichelberger, *U.N.: The First Ten Years* (1955), pp. 95-96.

of the United Nations feel compelled to move forward and arrive at those decisions necessary to avert another world catastrophe.

It is clear that when the national interest of the United States is expressed on calling a review conference and on possible changes in the Charter, this will have greater international significance than similar expressions on the part of many Member states. This is true not only because of the power of the United States, but because it was by far the most influential government in the creation of the United Nations. The Senate vote of 89 to 2 approving American participation in the Organization is evidence of the broad American support that then existed for it.

In the past decade, it has been the United States that has sparked many of the significant developments in the United Nations system. The creation of the Little Assembly, the "Uniting for Peace" resolution, the United Nations action against aggression in Korea, suggestions for the control of atomic weapons and for the development of peaceful uses of atomic energy, the creation of regional defense pacts within the purview of the Charter—are only a few of the developments that were initiated by the United States. They indicate the tremendous influence the United States has had on the Organization.

The attitude of the United States Government toward the United Nations reflects the interest of the American people. During the months that lie ahead, the interest of the people reflected in their public discussion of review of the Charter will point the general direction they want to take. Whatever role the Government plays it must be acceptable to the American people. It follows that what individual Americans think and do about the United Nations is of very great importance.

In the final analysis, of course, the success of the United Nations is dependent, in a very large degree, on the kind of public support the Organization receives in the various Member states. By the same token, the success or failure of any movement for revision of the Charter will depend on the force of public opinion and its impact on the foreign offices of the world.

As this study indicates there is no dearth of ideas on possible methods of advancing the national interest and the cause of world peace through changes in the United Nations system. Although there may be a tendency to reject some suggestions as impractical or visionary, it is well to remember that what is impractical today may become practical tomorrow. And the existence of ideas that may not be attainable forthwith may encourage the taking of the day-to-day steps that are essential to solid progress. If the American people approach the problem of Charter review in this frame of mind, the United States may have another challenging opportunity to help the Members of the United Nations build for a better tomorrow.

APPENDIXES

APPENDIX A

Charter of the United Nations[1]

WE THE PEOPLES OF THE UNITED NATIONS
DETERMINED

to save succeeding generations from the scourge of war, which twice in our life-time has brought untold sorrow to mankind, and

to reaffirm faith in fundamental human rights, in the dignity and worth of the human person, in the equal rights of men and women and of nations large and small, and

to establish conditions under which justice and respect for the obligations arising from treaties and other sources of international law can be maintained, and

to promote social progress and better standards of life in larger freedom,

AND FOR THESE ENDS

to practice tolerance and live together in peace with one another as good neighbors, and

to unite our strength to maintain international peace and security, and

to ensure, by the acceptance of principles and the institution of methods, that armed force shall not be used, save in the common interest, and

to employ international machinery for the promotion of the economic and social advancement of all peoples,

HAVE RESOLVED TO COMBINE OUR EFFORTS
TO ACCOMPLISH THESE AIMS.

Accordingly, our respective Governments, through representatives assembled in the city of San Francisco, who have exhibited their full powers found to be in good and due form, have agreed to the present Charter of the United Nations and do hereby establish an international organization to be known as the United Nations.

[1] Source: Photographic reproduction of the text given in *Charter of the United Nations and Statute of the International Court of Justice,* U. S. Department of State Publication 2368 (1945), pp. 1-20, which is a facsimile of the Charter agreed to at the San Francisco Conference.

CHAPTER I

PURPOSES AND PRINCIPLES

Article 1

The Purposes of the United Nations are:

1. To maintain international peace and security, and to that end: to take effective collective measures for the prevention and removal of threats to the peace, and for the suppression of acts of aggression or other breaches of the peace, and to bring about by peaceful means, and in conformity with the principles of justice and international law, adjustment or settlement of international disputes or situations which might lead to a breach of the peace;

2. To develop friendly relations among nations based on respect for the principle of equal rights and self-determination of peoples, and to take other appropriate measures to strengthen universal peace;

3. To achieve international cooperation in solving international problems of an economic, social, cultural, or humanitarian character, and in promoting and encouraging respect for human rights and for fundamental freedoms for all without distinction as to race, sex, language, or religion; and

4. To be a center for harmonizing the actions of nations in the attainment of these common ends.

Article 2

The Organization and its Members, in pursuit of the Purposes stated in Article 1, shall act in accordance with the following Principles.

1. The Organization is based on the principle of the sovereign equality of all its Members.

2. All Members, in order to ensure to all of them the rights and benefits resulting from membership, shall fulfil in good faith the obligations assumed by them in accordance with the present Charter.

3. All Members shall settle their international disputes by peaceful means in such a manner that international peace and security, and justice, are not endangered.

4. All Members shall refrain in their international relations from the threat or use of force against the territorial integrity or political independence of any state, or in any other manner inconsistent with the Purposes of the United Nations.

5. All Members shall give the United Nations every assistance in any action it takes in accordance with the present Charter, and shall refrain from giving assistance to any state against which the United Nations is taking preventive or enforcement action.

6. The Organization shall ensure that states which are not Members of the United Nations act in accordance with these Principles so far as may be necessary for the maintenance of international peace and security.

7. Nothing contained in the present Charter shall authorize the United Nations to intervene in matters which are essentially within the domestic jurisdiction of any state or shall require the Members to submit such matters to settlement under the present Charter; but this principle shall not prejudice the application of enforcement measures under Chapter VII.

CHAPTER II

MEMBERSHIP

Article 3

The original Members of the United Nations shall be the states which, having participated in the United Nations Conference on International Organization at San Francisco, or having previously signed the Declaration by United Nations of January 1, 1942, sign the present Charter and ratify it in accordance with Article 110.

Article 4

1. Membership in the United Nations is open to all other peace-loving states which accept the obligations contained in the present Charter and, in the judgment of the Organization, are able and willing to carry out these obligations.

2. The admission of any such state to membership in the United Nations will be effected by a decision of the General Assembly upon the recommendation of the Security Council.

Article 5

A Member of the United Nations against which preventive or enforcement action has been taken by the Security Council may be suspended from the exercise of the rights and privileges of membership by the General Assembly upon the recommendation of the Security Council. The exercise of these rights and privileges may be restored by the Security Council.

Article 6

A Member of the United Nations which has persistently violated the Principles contained in the present Charter may be expelled from the Organization by the General Assembly upon the recommendation of the Security Council.

CHAPTER III
ORGANS

Article 7

1. There are established as the principal organs of the United Nations: a General Assembly, a Security Council, an Economic and Social Council, a Trusteeship Council, an International Court of Justice, and a Secretariat.

2. Such subsidiary organs as may be found necessary may be established in accordance with the present Charter.

Article 8

The United Nations shall place no restrictions on the eligibility of men and women to participate in any capacity and under conditions of equality in its principal and subsidiary organs.

CHAPTER IV
THE GENERAL ASSEMBLY

Composition
Article 9

1. The General Assembly shall consist of all the Members of the United Nations.

2. Each Member shall have not more than five representatives in the General Assembly.

Functions and Powers
Article 10

The General Assembly may discuss any questions or any matters within the scope of the present Charter or relating to the powers and functions of any organs provided for in the present Charter, and, except as provided in Article 12, may make recommendations to the Members of the United Nations or to the Security Council or to both on any such questions or matters.

Article 11

1. The General Assembly may consider the general principles of cooperation in the maintenance of international peace and security, including the principles governing disarmament and the regulation of armaments, and may make recommendations with regard to such principles to the Members or to the Security Council or to both.

2. The General Assembly may discuss any questions relating to the maintenance of international peace and security brought before it by any Member of the United Nations, or by the Security Council, or by a state which is not a

Member of the United Nations in accordance with Article 35, paragraph 2, and, except as provided in Article 12, may make recommendations with regard to any such questions to the state or states concerned or to the Security Council or to both. Any such question on which action is necessary shall be referred to the Security Council by the General Assembly either before or after discussion.

3. The General Assembly may call the attention of the Security Council to situations which are likely to endanger international peace and security.

4. The powers of the General Assembly set forth in this Article shall not limit the general scope of Article 10.

Article 12

1. While the Security Council is exercising in respect of any dispute or situation the functions assigned to it in the present Charter, the General Assembly shall not make any recommendation with regard to that dispute or situation unless the Security Council so requests.

2. The Secretary-General, with the consent of the Security Council, shall notify the General Assembly at each session of any matters relative to the maintenance of international peace and security which are being dealt with by the Security Council and shall similarly notify the General Assembly, or the Members of the United Nations if the General Assembly is not in session, immediately the Security Council ceases to deal with such matters.

Article 13

1. The General Assembly shall initiate studies and make recommendations for the purpose of:
a. promoting international cooperation in the political field and encouraging the progressive development of international law and its codification;

b. promoting international cooperation in the economic, social, cultural, educational, and health fields, and assisting in the realization of human rights and fundamental freedoms for all without distinction as to race, sex, language, or religion.

2. The further responsibilities, functions, and powers of the General Assembly with respect to matters mentioned in paragraph 1(b) above are set forth in Chapters IX and X.

Article 14

Subject to the provisions of Article 12, the General Assembly may recommend measures for the peaceful adjustment of any situation, regardless of origin, which it deems likely to impair the general welfare or friendly relations among nations, including situations resulting from a violation of the provisions of the present Charter setting forth the Purposes and Principles of the United Nations.

Article 15

1. The General Assembly shall receive and consider annual and special reports from the Security Council; these reports shall include an account of the measures that the Security Council has decided upon or taken to maintain international peace and security.

2. The General Assembly shall receive and consider reports from the other organs of the United Nations.

Article 16

The General Assembly shall perform such functions with respect to the international trusteeship system as are assigned to it under Chapters XII and XIII, including the approval of the trusteeship agreements for areas not designated as strategic.

Article 17

1. The General Assembly shall consider and approve the budget of the Organization.

2. The expenses of the Organization shall be borne by the Members as apportioned by the General Assembly.

3. The General Assembly shall consider and approve any financial and budgetary arrangements with specialized agencies referred to in Article 57 and shall examine the administrative budgets of such specialized agencies with a view to making recommendations to the agencies concerned.

Voting

Article 18

1. Each member of the General Assembly shall have one vote.

2. Decisions of the General Assembly on important questions shall be made by a two-thirds majority of the members present and voting. These questions shall include: recommendations with respect to the maintenance of international peace and security, the election of the non-permanent members of the Security Council, the election of the members of the Economic and Social Council, the election of members of the Trusteeship Council in accordance with paragraph 1(c) of Article 86, the admission of new Members to the United Nations, the suspension of the rights and privileges of membership, the expulsion of Members, questions relating to the operation of the trusteeship system, and budgetary questions.

3. Decisions on other questions, including the determination of additional categories of questions to be decided by a two-thirds majority, shall be made by a majority of the members present and voting.

Article 19

A Member of the United Nations which is in arrears in the payment of its financial contributions to the Organization shall have no vote in the General Assembly if the amount of its arrears equals or exceeds the amount of the contributions

due from it for the preceding two full years. The General Assembly may, nevertheless, permit such a Member to vote if it is satisfied that the failure to pay is due to conditions beyond the control of the Member.

Procedure

Article 20

The General Assembly shall meet in regular annual sessions and in such special sessions as occasion may require. Special sessions shall be convoked by the Secretary-General at the request of the Security Council or of a majority of the Members of the United Nations.

Article 21

The General Assembly shall adopt its own rules of procedure. It shall elect its President for each session.

Article 22

The General Assembly may establish such subsidiary organs as it deems necessary for the performance of its functions.

CHAPTER V

THE SECURITY COUNCIL

Composition

Article 23

1. The Security Council shall consist of eleven Members of the United Nations. The Republic of China, France, the Union of Soviet Socialist Republics, the United Kingdom of Great Britain and Northern Ireland, and the United States of America shall be permanent members of the Security Council. The General Assembly shall elect six other Members of the United Nations to be non-permanent members of the Security Council, due regard being specially paid, in the first instance to the contribution of Members of the

United Nations to the maintenance of international peace and security and to the other purposes of the Organization, and also to equitable geographical distribution.

2. The non-permanent members of the Security Council shall be elected for a term of two years. In the first election of the non-permanent members, however, three shall be chosen for a term of one year. A retiring member shall not be eligible for immediate re-election.

3. Each member of the Security Council shall have one representative.

Functions and Powers
Article 24

1. In order to ensure prompt and effective action by the United Nations, its Members confer on the Security Council primary responsibility for the maintenance of international peace and security, and agree that in carrying out its duties under this responsibility the Security Council acts on their behalf.

2. In discharging these duties the Security Council shall act in accordance with the Purposes and Principles of the United Nations. The specific powers granted to the Security Council for the discharge of these duties are laid down in Chapters VI, VII, VIII, and XII.

3. The Security Council shall submit annual and, when necessary, special reports to the General Assembly for its consideration.

Article 25

The Members of the United Nations agree to accept and carry out the decisions of the Security Council in accordance with the present Charter.

Article 26

In order to promote the establishment and maintenance of international peace and security with the least diversion for armaments of the world's human and economic resources, the Se-

curity Council shall be responsible for formulating, with the assistance of the Military Staff Committee referred to in Article 47, plans to be submitted to the Members of the United Nations for the establishment of a system for the regulation of armaments.

Voting
Article 27

1. Each member of the Security Council shall have one vote.

2. Decisions of the Security Council on procedural matters shall be made by an affirmative vote of seven members.

3. Decisions of the Security Council on all other matters shall be made by an affirmative vote of seven members including the concurring votes of the permanent members; provided that, in decisions under Chapter VI, and under paragraph 3 of Article 52, a party to a dispute shall abstain from voting.

Procedure
Article 28

1. The Security Council shall be so organized as to be able to function continuously. Each member of the Security Council shall for this purpose be represented at all times at the seat of the Organization.

2. The Security Council shall hold periodic meetings at which each of its members may, if it so desires, be represented by a member of the government or by some other specially designated representative.

3. The Security Council may hold meetings at such places other than the seat of the Organization as in its judgment will best facilitate its work.

Article 29

The Security Council may establish such subsidiary organs as it deems necessary for the performance of its functions.

Article 30

The Security Council shall adopt its own rules of procedure, including the method of selecting its President.

Article 31

Any Member of the United Nations which is not a member of the Security Council may participate, without vote, in the discussion of any question brought before the Security Council whenever the latter considers that the interests of that Member are specially affected.

Article 32

Any Member of the United Nations which is not a member of the Security Council or any state which is not a Member of the United Nations, if it is a party to a dispute under consideration by the Security Council, shall be invited to participate, without vote, in the discussion relating to the dispute. The Security Council shall lay down such conditions as it deems just for the participation of a state which is not a Member of the United Nations.

CHAPTER VI

PACIFIC SETTLEMENT OF DISPUTES

Article 33

1. The parties to any dispute, the continuance of which is likely to endanger the maintenance of international peace and security, shall, first of all, seek a solution by negotiation, enquiry, mediation, conciliation, arbitration, judicial settlement, resort to regional agencies or arrangements, or other peaceful means of their own choice.

2. The Security Council shall, when it deems necessary, call upon the parties to settle their dispute by such means.

Article 34

The Security Council may investigate any dispute, or any situation which might lead to international friction or give rise to a dispute, in order to determine whether the continuance of the dispute or situation is likely to endanger the maintenance of international peace and security.

Article 35

1. Any Member of the United Nations may bring any dispute, or any situation of the nature referred to in Article 34, to the attention of the Security Council or of the General Assembly.

2. A state which is not a Member of the United Nations may bring to the attention of the Security Council or of the General Assembly any dispute to which it is a party if it accepts in advance, for the purposes of the dispute, the obligations of pacific settlement provided in the present Charter.

3. The proceedings of the General Assembly in respect of matters brought to its attention under this Article will be subject to the provisions of Articles 11 and 12.

Article 36

1. The Security Council may, at any stage of a dispute of the nature referred to in Article 33 or of a situation of like nature, recommend appropriate procedures or methods of adjustment.

2. The Security Council should take into consideration any procedures for the settlement of the dispute which have already been adopted by the parties.

3. In making recommendations under this Article the Security Council should also take into consideration that legal disputes should as a general rule be referred by the parties to the International Court of Justice in accordance with the provisions of the Statute of the Court.

Article 37

1. Should the parties to a dispute of the nature referred to in Article 33 fail to settle it by the means indicated in that Article, they shall refer it to the Security Council.

2. If the Security Council deems that the continuance of the dispute is in fact likely to endanger the maintenance of international peace and security, it shall decide whether to take action under Article 36 or to recommend such terms of settlement as it may consider appropriate.

Article 38

Without prejudice to the provisions of Articles 33 to 37, the Security Council may, if all the parties to any dispute so request, make recommendations to the parties with a view to a pacific settlement of the dispute.

CHAPTER VII

ACTION WITH RESPECT TO THREATS TO THE PEACE, BREACHES OF THE PEACE, AND ACTS OF AGGRESSION

Article 39

The Security Council shall determine the existence of any threat to the peace, breach of the peace, or act of aggression and shall make recommendations, or decide what measures shall be taken in accordance with Articles 41 and 42, to maintain or restore international peace and security.

Article 40

In order to prevent an aggravation of the situation, the Security Council may, before making the recommendations or deciding upon the measures provided for in Article 39, call upon the parties concerned to comply with such provisional measures as it deems necessary or desirable. Such provisional measures shall be without prejudice to the rights, claims, or position of the parties concerned. The Security Council shall duly take account of failure to comply with such provisional measures.

Article 41

The Security Council may decide what measures not involving the use of armed force are to be employed to give effect to its decisions, and it may call upon the Members of the United Nations to apply such measures. These may include complete or partial interruption of economic relations and of rail, sea, air, postal, telegraphic, radio, and other means of communication, and the severance of diplomatic relations.

Article 42

Should the Security Council consider that measures provided for in Article 41 would be inadequate or have proved to be inadequate, it may take such action by air, sea, or land forces as may be necessary to maintain or restore international peace and security. Such action may include demonstrations, blockade, and other operations by air, sea, or land forces of Members of the United Nations.

Article 43

1. All Members of the United Nations, in order to contribute to the maintenance of international peace and security, undertake to make available to the Security Council, on its call and in accordance with a special agreement or agreements, armed forces, assistance, and facilities, including rights of passage, necessary for the purpose of maintaining international peace and security.

2. Such agreement or agreements shall govern the numbers and types of forces, their degree of readiness and general location, and the nature of the facilities and assistance to be provided.

3. The agreement or agreements shall be negotiated as soon as possible on the initiative of the Security Council. They shall be concluded between the Security Council and Members or between the Security Council and groups of Members and shall be subject to ratification by the signatory states in accordance with their respective constitutional processes.

Article 44

When the Security Council has decided to use force it shall, before calling upon a Member not represented on it to provide armed forces in fulfillment of the obligations assumed under Article 43, invite that Member, if the Member so desires, to participate in the decisions of the Security Council concerning the employment of contingents of that Member's armed forces.

Article 45

In order to enable the United Nations to take urgent military measures, Members shall hold immediately available national air-force contingents for combined international enforcement action. The strength and degree of readiness of these contingents and plans for their combined action shall be determined, within the limits laid down in the special agreement or agreements referred to in Article 43, by the Security Council with the assistance of the Military Staff Committee.

Article 46

Plans for the application of armed force shall be made by the Security Council with the assistance of the Military Staff Committee.

Article 47

1. There shall be established a Military Staff Committee to advise and assist the Security Council on all questions relating to the Security Council's military requirements for the maintenance of international peace and security, the employment and command of forces placed at its disposal, the regulation of armaments, and possible disarmament.

2. The Military Staff Committee shall consist of the Chiefs of Staff of the permanent members of the Security Council or their representatives. Any Member of the United Nations not permanently represented on the Committee shall be invited by the Committee to be associated with it when the efficient discharge of the Committee's responsibilities requires the participation of that Member in its work.

3. The Military Staff Committee shall be responsible under the Security Council for the strategic direction of any armed forces placed at the disposal of the Security Council. Questions relating to the command of such forces shall be worked out subsequently.

4. The Military Staff Committee, with the authorization of the Security Council and after consultation with appropriate regional agencies, may establish regional subcommittees.

Article 48

1. The action required to carry out the decisions of the Security Council for the maintenance of international peace and security shall be taken by all the Members of the United Nations or by some of them, as the Security Council may determine.

2. Such decisions shall be carried out by the Members of the United Nations directly and through their action in the appropriate international agencies of which they are members.

Article 49

The Members of the United Nations shall join in affording mutual assistance in carrying out the measures decided upon by the Security Council.

Article 50

If preventive or enforcement measures against any state are taken by the Security Council, any other state, whether a Member of the United Nations or not, which finds itself confronted with special economic problems arising from the carrying out of those measures shall have the right to consult the Security Council with regard to a solution of those problems.

Article 51

Nothing in the present Charter shall impair the inherent right of individual or collective self-defense if an armed attack occurs against a Member of the United Nations, until the Security Council has taken the measures necessary to maintain international peace and security. Measures taken by Members in the exercise of this right of self-defense shall be immediately reported to the Security Council and shall not in any way affect the authority and responsibility of the Security Council under the present Charter to take at any time such action as it deems necessary in order to maintain or restore international peace and security.

CHAPTER VIII
REGIONAL ARRANGEMENTS
Article 52

1. Nothing in the present Charter precludes the existence of regional arrangements or agencies for dealing with such matters relating to the maintenance of international peace and security as are appropriate for regional action, provided that such arrangements or agencies and their activities are consistent with the Purposes and Principles of the United Nations.

2. The Members of the United Nations entering into such arrangements or constituting such agencies shall make every effort to achieve pacific settlement of local disputes through such regional arrangements or by such regional agencies before referring them to the Security Council.

3. The Security Council shall encourage the development of pacific settlement of local disputes through such regional arrangements or by such regional agencies either on the initiative of the states concerned or by reference from the Security Council.

4. This Article in no way impairs the application of Articles 34 and 35.

Article 53

1. The Security Council shall, where appropriate, utilize such regional arrangements or agencies for enforcement action under its authority. But no enforcement action shall be taken under regional arrangements or by regional agencies without the authorization of the Security Council, with the exception of measures against any enemy state, as defined in paragraph 2 of this Article, provided for pursuant to Article 107 or in regional arrangements directed against renewal of aggressive policy on the part of any such state, until such time as the Organization may, on request of the Governments concerned, be charged with the responsibility for preventing further aggression by such a state.

2. The term enemy state as used in paragraph 1 of this Article applies to any state which during the Second World War has been an enemy of any signatory of the present Charter.

Article 54

The Security Council shall at all times be kept fully informed of activities undertaken or in contemplation under regional arrangements or by regional agencies for the maintenance of international peace and security.

CHAPTER IX
INTERNATIONAL ECONOMIC AND SOCIAL COOPERATION
Article 55

With a view to the creation of conditions of stability and well-being which are necessary for peaceful and friendly relations among nations based on respect for the principle of equal rights and self-determination of peoples, the United Nations shall promote:

    a. higher standards of living, full employment, and conditions of economic and social progress and development;

    b. solutions of international economic, social, health, and related problems; and international cultural and educational cooperation; and

c. universal respect for, and observance of, human rights and fundamental freedoms for all without distinction as to race, sex, language, or religion.

Article 56

All Members pledge themselves to take joint and separate action in cooperation with the Organization for the achievement of the purposes set forth in Article 55.

Article 57

1. The various specialized agencies, established by intergovernmental agreement and having wide international responsibilities, as defined in their basic instruments, in economic, social, cultural, educational, health, and related fields, shall be brought into relationship with the United Nations in accordance with the provisions of Article 63.

2. Such agencies thus brought into relationship with the United Nations are hereinafter referred to as specialized agencies.

Article 58

The Organization shall make recommendations for the coordination of the policies and activities of the specialized agencies.

Article 59

The Organization shall, where appropriate, initiate negotiations among the states concerned for the creation of any new specialized agencies required for the accomplishment of the purposes set forth in Article 55.

Article 60

Responsibility for the discharge of the functions of the Organization set forth in this Chapter shall be vested in the General Assembly and, under the authority of the General Assembly, in the Economic and Social Council, which shall have for this purpose the powers set forth in Chapter X.

CHAPTER X

THE ECONOMIC AND SOCIAL COUNCIL

Composition

Article 61

1. The Economic and Social Council shall consist of eighteen Members of the United Nations elected by the General Assembly.

2. Subject to the provisions of paragraph 3, six members of the Economic and Social Council shall be elected each year for a term of three years. A retiring member shall be eligible for immediate re-election.

3. At the first election, eighteen members of the Economic and Social Council shall be chosen. The term of office of six members so chosen shall expire at the end of one year, and of six other members at the end of two years, in accordance with arrangements made by the General Assembly.

4. Each member of the Economic and Social Council shall have one representative.

Functions and Powers

Article 62

1. The Economic and Social Council may make or initiate studies and reports with respect to international economic, social, cultural, educational, health, and related matters and may make recommendations with respect to any such matters to the General Assembly, to the Members of the United Nations, and to the specialized agencies concerned.

2. It may make recommendations for the purpose of promoting respect for, and observance of, human rights and fundamental freedoms for all.

3. It may prepare draft conventions for submission to the General Assembly, with respect to matters falling within its competence.

4. It may call, in accordance with the rules prescribed by the United Nations, international conferences on matters falling within its competence.

Article 63

1. The Economic and Social Council may enter into agreements with any of the agencies referred to in Article 57, defining the terms on which the agency concerned shall be brought into relationship with the United Nations. Such agreements shall be subject to approval by the General Assembly.

2. It may coordinate the activities of the specialized agencies through consultation with and recommendations to such agencies and through recommendations to the General Assembly and to the Members of the United Nations.

Article 64

1. The Economic and Social Council may take appropriate steps to obtain regular reports from the specialized agencies. It may make arrangements with the Members of the United Nations and with the specialized agencies to obtain reports on the steps taken to give effect to its own recommendations and to recommendations on matters falling within its competence made by the General Assembly.

2. It may communicate its observations on these reports to the General Assembly.

Article 65

The Economic and Social Council may furnish information to the Security Council and shall assist the Security Council upon its request.

Article 66

1. The Economic and Social Council shall perform such functions as fall within its competence in connection with the carrying out of the recommendations of the General Assembly.

2. It may, with the approval of the General

Assembly, perform services at the request Members of the United Nations and at the requ of specialized agencies.

3. It shall perform such other functions as specified elsewhere in the present Charter or may be assigned to it by the General Assemb

Voting

Article 67

1. Each member of the Economic and Soc Council shall have one vote.

2. Decisions of the Economic and Social Cou cil shall be made by a majority of the memb present and voting.

Procedure

Article 68

The Economic and Social Council shall set commissions in economic and social fields and the promotion of human rights, and such oth commissions as may be required for the perfor ance of its functions.

Article 69

The Economic and Social Council shall inv any Member of the United Nations to participa without vote, in its deliberations on any matt of particular concern to that Member.

Article 70

The Economic and Social Council may ma arrangements for representatives of the speci ized agencies to participate, without vote, in deliberations and in those of the commissio established by it, and for its representatives participate in the deliberations of the specializ agencies.

Article 71

The Economic and Social Council may ma suitable arrangements for consultation with nc governmental organizations which are concern with matters within its competence. Such arrang

nts may be made with international organiza-
ns and, where appropriate, with national or-
izations after consultation with the Member
the United Nations concerned.

Article 72

1. The Economic and Social Council shall
pt its own rules of procedure, including the
thod of selecting its President.

2. The Economic and Social Council shall meet
required in accordance with its rules, which
ll include provision for the convening of meet-
s on the request of a majority of its members.

CHAPTER XI

DECLARATION REGARDING
NON-SELF-GOVERNING TERRITORIES

Article 73

Members of the United Nations which have or
ume responsibilities for the administration of
ritories whose peoples have not yet attained
ull measure of self-government recognize the
nciple that the interests of the inhabitants of
se territories are paramount, and accept as a
red trust the obligation to promote to the ut-
st, within the system of international peace and
urity established by the present Charter, the
ll-being of the inhabitants of these territories,
, to this end:

a. to ensure, with due respect for the culture of the peoples concerned, their political,
economic, social, and educational advancement, their just treatment, and their protection
against abuses;

b. to develop self-government, to take due
account of the political aspirations of the
peoples, and to assist them in the progressive
development of their free political institutions,
according to the particular circumstances of
each territory and its peoples and their varying
stages of advancement;

c. to further international peace and security;

d. to promote constructive measures of development, to encourage research, and to co-
operate with one another and, when and where
appropriate, with specialized international bodies with a view to the practical achievement of
the social, economic, and scientific purposes
set forth in this Article; and

e. to transmit regularly to the Secretary-
General for information purposes, subject to
such limitation as security and constitutional
considerations may require, statistical and other
information of a technical nature relating to
economic, social, and educational conditions in
the territories for which they are respectively
responsible other than those territories to which
Chapters XII and XIII apply.

Article 74

Members of the United Nations also agree that
their policy in respect of the territories to which
this Chapter applies, no less than in respect of their
metropolitan areas, must be based on the general
principle of good-neighborliness, due account being taken of the interests and well-being of the rest
of the world, in social, economic, and commercial
matters.

CHAPTER XII

INTERNATIONAL TRUSTEESHIP SYSTEM

Article 75

The United Nations shall establish under its
authority an international trusteeship system for
the administration and supervision of such territories as may be placed thereunder by subsequent
individual agreements. These territories are
hereinafter referred to as trust territories.

Article 76

The basic objectives of the trusteeship system,

in accordance with the Purposes of the United Nations laid down in Article 1 of the present Charter, shall be:

  a. to further international peace and security;

  b. to promote the political, economic, social, and educational advancement of the inhabitants of the trust territories, and their progressive development towards self-government or independence as may be appropriate to the particular circumstances of each territory and its peoples and the freely expressed wishes of the peoples concerned, and as may be provided by the terms of each trusteeship agreement;

  c. to encourage respect for human rights and for fundamental freedoms for all without distinction as to race, sex, language, or religion, and to encourage recognition of the interdependence of the peoples of the world; and

  d. to ensure equal treatment in social, economic, and commercial matters for all Members of the United Nations and their nationals, and also equal treatment for the latter in the administration of justice, without prejudice to the attainment of the foregoing objectives and subject to the provisions of Article 80.

Article 77

1. The trusteeship system shall apply to such territories in the following categories as may be placed thereunder by means of trusteeship agreements:

  a. territories now held under mandate;

  b. territories which may be detached from enemy states as a result of the Second World War; and

  c. territories voluntarily placed under the system by states responsible for their administration.

2. It will be a matter for subsequent agreement as to which territories in the foregoing categories

will be brought under the trusteeship system ar upon what terms.

Article 78

The trusteeship system shall not apply to ter tories which have become Members of the Unite Nations, relationship among which shall be base on respect for the principle of sovereign equalit

Article 79

The terms of trusteeship for each territory be placed under the trusteeship system, includir any alteration or amendment, shall be agreed upc by the states directly concerned, including th mandatory power in the case of territories hel under mandate by a Member of the United N tions, and shall be approved as provided for Articles 83 and 85.

Article 80

1. Except as may be agreed upon in individu trusteeship agreements, made under Articles 7 79, and 81, placing each territory under the tru teeship system, and until such agreements hav been concluded, nothing in this Chapter shall k construed in or of itself to alter in any mann the rights whatsoever of any states or any peopl or the terms of existing international instrumen to which Members of the United Nations may r spectively be parties.

2. Paragraph 1 of this Article shall not be i terpreted as giving grounds for delay or postpon ment of the negotiation and conclusion of agre ments for placing mandated and other territori under the trusteeship system as provided for Article 77.

Article 81

The trusteeship agreement shall in each ca include the terms under which the trust territo will be administered and designate the authori which will exercise the administration of the tru territory. Such authority, hereinafter called th administering authority, may be one or more states or the Organization itself.

Article 82

There may be designated, in any trusteeship agreement, a strategic area or areas which may include part or all of the trust territory to which the agreement applies, without prejudice to any special agreement or agreements made under Article 43.

Article 83

1. All functions of the United Nations relating to strategic areas, including the approval of the terms of the trusteeship agreements and of their alteration or amendment, shall be exercised by the Security Council.

2. The basic objectives set forth in Article 76 shall be applicable to the people of each strategic area.

3. The Security Council shall, subject to the provisions of the trusteeship agreements and without prejudice to security considerations, avail itself of the assistance of the Trusteeship Council to perform those functions of the United Nations under the trusteeship system relating to political, economic, social, and educational matters in the strategic areas.

Article 84

It shall be the duty of the administering authority to ensure that the trust territory shall play its part in the maintenance of international peace and security. To this end the administering authority may make use of volunteer forces, facilities, and assistance from the trust territory in carrying out the obligations towards the Security Council undertaken in this regard by the administering authority, as well as for local defense and the maintenance of law and order within the trust territory.

Article 85

1. The functions of the United Nations with regard to trusteeship agreements for all areas not designated as strategic, including the approval of the terms of the trusteeship agreements and of their alteration or amendment, shall be exercised by the General Assembly.

2. The Trusteeship Council, operating under the authority of the General Assembly, shall assist the General Assembly in carrying out these functions.

CHAPTER XIII
THE TRUSTEESHIP COUNCIL

Composition

Article 86

1. The Trusteeship Council shall consist of the following Members of the United Nations:

    a. those Members administering trust territories;

    b. such of those Members mentioned by name in Article 23 as are not administering trust territories; and

    c. as many other Members elected for three-year terms by the General Assembly as may be necessary to ensure that the total number of members of the Trusteeship Council is equally divided between those Members of the United Nations which administer trust territories and those which do not.

2. Each member of the Trusteeship Council shall designate one specially qualified person to represent it therein.

Functions and Powers

Article 87

The General Assembly and, under its authority, the Trusteeship Council, in carrying out their functions, may:

    a. consider reports submitted by the administering authority;

b. accept petitions and examine them in consultation with the administering authority;

c. provide for periodic visits to the respective trust territories at times agreed upon with the administering authority; and

d. take these and other actions in conformity with the terms of the trusteeship agreements.

Article 88

The Trusteeship Council shall formulate a questionnaire on the political, economic, social, and educational advancement of the inhabitants of each trust territory, and the administering authority for each trust territory within the competence of the General Assembly shall make an annual report to the General Assembly upon the basis of such questionnaire.

Voting

Article 89

1. Each member of the Trusteeship Council shall have one vote.

2. Decisions of the Trusteeship Council shall be made by a majority of the members present and voting.

Procedure

Article 90

1. The Trusteeship Council shall adopt its own rules of procedure, including the method of selecting its President.

2. The Trusteeship Council shall meet as required in accordance with its rules, which shall include provision for the convening of meetings on the request of a majority of its members.

Article 91

The Trusteeship Council shall, when appropriate, avail itself of the assistance of the Economic and Social Council and of the specialized agencies in regard to matters with which they are respectively concerned.

CHAPTER XIV
THE INTERNATIONAL COURT OF JUSTICE

Article 92

The International Court of Justice shall be the principal judicial organ of the United Nations. It shall function in accordance with the annexed Statute, which is based upon the Statute of the Permanent Court of International Justice and forms an integral part of the present Charter.

Article 93

1. All Members of the United Nations are *ipso facto* parties to the Statute of the International Court of Justice.

2. A state which is not a Member of the United Nations may become a party to the Statute of the International Court of Justice on conditions to be determined in each case by the General Assembly upon the recommendation of the Security Council.

Article 94

1. Each Member of the United Nations undertakes to comply with the decision of the International Court of Justice in any case to which it is a party.

2. If any party to a case fails to perform the obligations incumbent upon it under a judgment rendered by the Court, the other party may have recourse to the Security Council, which may, if it deems necessary, make recommendations or decide upon measures to be taken to give effect to the judgment.

Article 95

Nothing in the present Charter shall prevent Members of the United Nations from entrusting the solution of their differences to other tribunals by virtue of agreements already in existence or which may be concluded in the future.

Article 96

1. The General Assembly or the Security Council may request the International Court of Justice to give an advisory opinion on any legal question.

2. Other organs of the United Nations and specialized agencies, which may at any time be so authorized by the General Assembly, may also request advisory opinions of the Court on legal questions arising within the scope of their activities.

CHAPTER XV

THE SECRETARIAT

Article 97

The Secretariat shall comprise a Secretary-General and such staff as the Organization may require. The Secretary-General shall be appointed by the General Assembly upon the recommendation of the Security Council. He shall be the chief administrative officer of the Organization.

Article 98

The Secretary-General shall act in that capacity in all meetings of the General Assembly, of the Security Council, of the Economic and Social Council, and of the Trusteeship Council, and shall perform such other functions as are entrusted to him by these organs. The Secretary-General shall make an annual report to the General Assembly on the work of the Organization.

Article 99

The Secretary-General may bring to the attention of the Security Council any matter which in his opinion may threaten the maintenance of international peace and security.

Article 100

1. In the performance of their duties the Secretary-General and the staff shall not seek or receive instructions from any government or from any other authority external to the Organization. They shall refrain from any action which might reflect on their position as international officials responsible only to the Organization.

2. Each Member of the United Nations undertakes to respect the exclusively international character of the responsibilities of the Secretary-General and the staff and not to seek to influence them in the discharge of their responsibilities.

Article 101

1. The staff shall be appointed by the Secretary-General under regulations established by the General Assembly.

2. Appropriate staffs shall be permanently assigned to the Economic and Social Council, the Trusteeship Council, and, as required, to other organs of the United Nations. These staffs shall form a part of the Secretariat.

3. The paramount consideration in the employment of the staff and in the determination of the conditions of service shall be the necessity of securing the highest standards of efficiency, competence, and integrity. Due regard shall be paid to the importance of recruiting the staff on as wide a geographical basis as possible.

CHAPTER XVI

MISCELLANEOUS PROVISIONS

Article 102

1. Every treaty and every international agreement entered into by any Member of the United Nations after the present Charter comes into force shall as soon as possible be registered with the Secretariat and published by it.

2. No party to any such treaty or international agreement which has not been registered in accordance with the provisions of paragraph 1 of

this Article may invoke that treaty or agreement before any organ of the United Nations.

Article 103

In the event of a conflict between the obligations of the Members of the United Nations under the present Charter and their obligations under any other international agreement, their obligations under the present Charter shall prevail.

Article 104

The Organization shall enjoy in the territory of each of its Members such legal capacity as may be necessary for the exercise of its functions and the fulfillment of its purposes.

Article 105

1. The Organization shall enjoy in the territory of each of its Members such privileges and immunities as are necessary for the fulfillment of its purposes.

2. Representatives of the Members of the United Nations and officials of the Organization shall similarly enjoy such privileges and immunities as are necessary for the independent exercise of their functions in connection with the Organization.

3. The General Assembly may make recommendations with a view to determining the details of the application of paragraphs 1 and 2 of this Article or may propose conventions to the Members of the United Nations for this purpose.

CHAPTER XVII
TRANSITIONAL SECURITY ARRANGEMENTS

Article 106

Pending the coming into force of such special agreements referred to in Article 43 as in the opinion of the Security Council enable it to begin

the exercise of its responsibilities under Article 42, the parties to the Four-Nation Declaration, signed at Moscow, October 30, 1943, and France, shall, in accordance with the provisions of paragraph 5 of that Declaration, consult with one another and as occasion requires with other Members of the United Nations with a view to such joint action on behalf of the Organization as may be necessary for the purpose of maintaining international peace and security.

Article 107

Nothing in the present Charter shall invalidate or preclude action, in relation to any state which during the Second World War has been an enemy of any signatory to the present Charter, taken or authorized as a result of that war by the Governments having responsibility for such action.

CHAPTER XVIII
AMENDMENTS

Article 108

Amendments to the present Charter shall come into force for all Members of the United Nations when they have been adopted by a vote of two thirds of the members of the General Assembly and ratified in accordance with their respective constitutional processes by two thirds of the Members of the United Nations, including all the permanent members of the Security Council.

Article 109

1. A General Conference of the Members of the United Nations for the purpose of reviewing the present Charter may be held at a date and place to be fixed by a two-thirds vote of the members of the General Assembly and by a vote of any seven members of the Security Council. Each Member of the United Nations shall have one vote in the conference.

2. Any alteration of the present Charter recommended by a two-thirds vote of the conference shall take effect when ratified in accordance with their respective constitutional processes by two thirds of the Members of the United Nations including all the permanent members of the Security Council.

3. If such a conference has not been held before the tenth annual session of the General Assembly following the coming into force of the present Charter, the proposal to call such a conference shall be placed on the agenda of that session of the General Assembly, and the conference shall be held if so decided by a majority vote of the members of the General Assembly and by a vote of any seven members of the Security Council.

CHAPTER XIX

RATIFICATION AND SIGNATURE

Article 110

1. The present Charter shall be ratified by the signatory states in accordance with their respective constitutional processes.

2. The ratifications shall be deposited with the Government of the United States of America, which shall notify all the signatory states of each deposit as well as the Secretary-General of the Organization when he has been appointed.

3. The present Charter shall come into force upon the deposit of ratifications by the Republic of China, France, the Union of Soviet Socialist Republics, the United Kingdom of Great Britain and Northern Ireland, and the United States of America, and by a majority of the other signatory states. A protocol of the ratifications deposited shall thereupon be drawn up by the Government of the United States of America which shall communicate copies thereof to all the signatory states.

4. The states signatory to the present Charter which ratify it after it has come into force will become original Members of the United Nations on the date of the deposit of their respective ratifications.

Article 111

The present Charter, of which the Chinese, French, Russian, English, and Spanish texts are equally authentic, shall remain deposited in the archives of the Government of the United States of America. Duly certified copies thereof shall be transmitted by that Government to the Governments of the other signatory states.

IN FAITH WHEREOF the representatives of the Governments of the United Nations have signed the present Charter.

DONE at the city of San Francisco the twenty-sixth day of June, one thousand nine hundred and forty-five.

Statute of the International Court of Justice [1]

Article 1

THE INTERNATIONAL COURT OF JUSTICE established by the Charter of the United Nations as the principal judicial organ of the United Nations shall be constituted and shall function in accordance with the provisions of the present Statute.

CHAPTER I
ORGANIZATION OF THE COURT

Article 2

The Court shall be composed of a body of independent judges, elected regardless of their nationality from among persons of high moral character, who possess the qualifications required in their respective countries for appointment to the highest judicial offices, or are jurisconsults of recognized competence in international law.

Article 3

1. The Court shall consist of fifteen members, no two of whom may be nationals of the same state.

2. A person who for the purposes of membership in the Court could be regarded as a national of more than one state shall be deemed to be a national of the one in which he ordinarily exercises civil and political rights.

Article 4

1. The members of the Court shall be elected by the General Assembly and by the Security Council from a list of persons nominated by the national groups in the Permanent Court of Arbitration, in accordance with the following provisions.

2. In the case of Members of the United Nations not represented in the Permanent Court of Arbitration, candidates shall be nominated by national groups appointed for this purpose by their governments under the same conditions as those prescribed for members of the Permanent Court of Arbitration by Article 44 of the Convention of The Hague of 1907 for the pacific settlement of international disputes.

3. The conditions under which a state which is a party to the present Statute but is not a Member of the United Nations may participate in electing the members of the Court shall, in the absence of a special agreement, be laid down by the General Assembly upon recommendation of the Security Council.

Article 5

1. At least three months before the date of the election, the Secretary-General of the United Nations shall address a written request to the members of the Permanent Court of Arbitration belonging to the states which are parties to the present Statute, and to the members of the national groups appointed under Article 4, paragraph 2, inviting them to undertake, within a given time, by national groups, the nomination of persons in a position to accept the duties of a member of the Court.

2. No group may nominate more than four persons, not more than two of whom shall be of their own nationality. In no case may the number of candidates nominated by a group be more than double the number of seats to be filled.

Article 6

Before making these nominations, each national group is recommended to consult its highest court of justice, its legal faculties and schools of law, and its national academies and national sections of international academies devoted to the study of law.

Article 7

1. The Secretary-General shall prepare a list

[1] Source: Photographic reproduction of the text given in *Charter of the United Nations and Statute of the International Court of Justice,* U. S. Department of State Publication 2368 (1945), pp. 21-30, which is a facsimile of the Statute agreed to at the San Francisco Conference.

in alphabetical order of all the persons thus nominated. Save as provided in Article 12, paragraph 2, these shall be the only persons eligible.

2. The Secretary-General shall submit this list to the General Assembly and to the Security Council.

Article 8

The General Assembly and the Security Council shall proceed independently of one another to elect the members of the Court.

Article 9

At every election, the electors shall bear in mind not only that the persons to be elected should individually possess the qualifications required, but also that in the body as a whole the representation of the main forms of civilization and of the principal legal systems of the world should be assured.

Article 10

1. Those candidates who obtain an absolute majority of votes in the General Assembly and in the Security Council shall be considered as elected.

2. Any vote of the Security Council, whether for the election of judges or for the appointment of members of the conference envisaged in Article 12, shall be taken without any distinction between permanent and non-permanent members of the Security Council.

3. In the event of more than one national of the same state obtaining an absolute majority of the votes both of the General Assembly and of the Security Council, the eldest of these only shall be considered as elected.

Article 11

If, after the first meeting held for the purpose of the election, one or more seats remain to be filled, a second and, if necessary, a third meeting shall take place.

Article 12

1. If, after the third meeting, one or more seats still remain unfilled, a joint conference consisting of six members, three appointed by the General Assembly and three by the Security Council, may be formed at any time at the request of either the General Assembly or the Security Council, for the purpose of choosing by the vote of an absolute majority one name for each seat still vacant, to submit to the General Assembly and the Security Council for their respective acceptance.

2. If the joint conference is unanimously agreed upon any person who fulfils the required conditions, he may be included in its list, even though he was not included in the list of nominations referred to in Article 7.

3. If the joint conference is satisfied that it will not be successful in procuring an election, those members of the Court who have already been elected shall, within a period to be fixed by the Security Council, proceed to fill the vacant seats by selection from among those candidates who have obtained votes either in the General Assembly or in the Security Council.

4. In the event of an equality of votes among the judges, the eldest judge shall have a casting vote.

Article 13

1. The members of the Court shall be elected for nine years and may be re-elected; provided, however, that of the judges elected at the first election, the terms of five judges shall expire at the end of three years and the terms of five more judges shall expire at the end of six years.

2. The judges whose terms are to expire at the end of the above-mentioned initial periods of three and six years shall be chosen by lot to be drawn by the Secretary-General immediately after the first election has been completed.

3. The members of the Court shall continue to

discharge their duties until their places have been filled. Though replaced, they shall finish any cases which they may have begun.

4. In the case of the resignation of a member of the Court, the resignation shall be addressed to the President of the Court for transmission to the Secretary-General. This last notification makes the place vacant.

Article 14

Vacancies shall be filled by the same method as that laid down for the first election, subject to the following provision: the Secretary-General shall, within one month of the occurrence of the vacancy, proceed to issue the invitations provided for in Article 5, and the date of the election shall be fixed by the Security Council.

Article 15

A member of the Court elected to replace a member whose term of office has not expired shall hold office for the remainder of his predecessor's term.

Article 16

1. No member of the Court may exercise any political or administrative function, or engage in any other occupation of a professional nature.

2. Any doubt on this point shall be settled by the decision of the Court.

Article 17

1. No member of the Court may act as agent, counsel, or advocate in any case.

2. No member may participate in the decision of any case in which he has previously taken part as agent, counsel, or advocate for one of the parties, or as a member of a national or international court, or of a commission of enquiry, or in any other capacity.

3. Any doubt on this point shall be settled by the decision of the Court.

Article 18

1. No member of the Court can be dismissed unless, in the unanimous opinion of the other members, he has ceased to fulfil the required conditions.

2. Formal notification thereof shall be made to the Secretary-General by the Registrar.

3. This notification makes the place vacant.

Article 19

The members of the Court, when engaged on the business of the Court, shall enjoy diplomatic privileges and immunities.

Article 20

Every member of the Court shall, before taking up his duties, make a solemn declaration in open court that he will exercise his powers impartially and conscientiously.

Article 21

1. The Court shall elect its President and Vice-President for three years; they may be re-elected.

2. The Court shall appoint its Registrar and may provide for the appointment of such other officers as may be necessary.

Article 22

1. The seat of the Court shall be established at The Hague. This, however, shall not prevent the Court from sitting and exercising its functions elsewhere whenever the Court considers it desirable.

2. The President and the Registrar shall reside at the seat of the Court.

Article 23

1. The Court shall remain permanently in session, except during the judicial vacations, the dates and duration of which shall be fixed by the Court.

2. Members of the Court are entitled to peri-

ic leave, the dates and duration of which shall
fixed by the Court, having in mind the distance
tween The Hague and the home of each judge.

3. Members of the Court shall be bound, un-
ss they are on leave or prevented from attending
illness or other serious reasons duly explained
the President, to hold themselves permanently
the disposal of the Court.

Article 24

1. If, for some special reason, a member of the
urt considers that he should not take part in the
cision of a particular case, he shall so inform the
esident.

2. If the President considers that for some spe-
l reason one of the members of the Court should
t sit in a particular case, he shall give him notice
cordingly.

3. If in any such case the member of the Court
d the President disagree, the matter shall be
ttled by the decision of the Court.

Article 25

1. The full Court shall sit except when it is ex-
essly provided otherwise in the present Statute.

2. Subject to the condition that the number of
lges available to constitute the Court is not
ereby reduced below eleven, the Rules of the
urt may provide for allowing one or more judges,
cording to circumstances and in rotation, to be
spensed from sitting.

3. A quorum of nine judges shall suffice to con-
tute the Court.

Article 26

1. The Court may from time to time form one
more chambers, composed of three or more
lges as the Court may determine, for dealing
th particular categories of cases; for example,
or cases and cases relating to transit and com-
nications.

2. The Court may at any time form a chamber
for dealing with a particular case. The number of
judges to constitute such a chamber shall be determined by the Court with the approval of the
parties.

3. Cases shall be heard and determined by the
chambers provided for in this Article if the parties
so request.

Article 27

A judgment given by any of the chambers provided for in Articles 26 and 29 shall be considered
as rendered by the Court.

Article 28

The chambers provided for in Articles 26 and
29 may, with the consent of the parties, sit and exercise their functions elsewhere than at The Hague.

Article 29

With a view to the speedy despatch of business,
the Court shall form annually a chamber composed of five judges which, at the request of the
parties, may hear and determine cases by summary
procedure. In addition, two judges shall be selected for the purpose of replacing judges who find
it impossible to sit.

Article 30

1. The Court shall frame rules for carrying out
its functions. In particular, it shall lay down rules
of procedure.

2. The Rules of the Court may provide for as-
sessors to sit with the Court or with any of its
chambers, without the right to vote.

Article 31

1. Judges of the nationality of each of the
parties shall retain their right to sit in the case
before the Court.

2. If the Court includes upon the Bench a judge
of the nationality of one of the parties, any other
party may choose a person to sit as judge. Such
person shall be chosen preferably from among

those persons who have been nominated as candidates as provided in Articles 4 and 5.

3. If the Court includes upon the Bench no judge of the nationality of the parties, each of these parties may proceed to choose a judge as provided in paragraph 2 of this Article.

4. The provisions of this Article shall apply to the case of Articles 26 and 29. In such cases, the President shall request one or, if necessary, two of the members of the Court forming the chamber to give place to the members of the Court of the nationality of the parties concerned, and, failing such, or if they are unable to be present, to the judges specially chosen by the parties.

5. Should there be several parties in the same interest, they shall, for the purpose of the preceding provisions, be reckoned as one party only. Any doubt upon this point shall be settled by the decision of the Court.

6. Judges chosen as laid down in paragraphs 2, 3, and 4 of this Article shall fulfil the conditions required by Articles 2, 17 (paragraph 2), 20, and 24 of the present Statute. They shall take part in the decision on terms of complete equality with their colleagues.

Article 32

1. Each member of the Court shall receive an annual salary.

2. The President shall receive a special annual allowance.

3. The Vice-President shall receive a special allowance for every day on which he acts as President.

4. The judges chosen under Article 31, other than members of the Court, shall receive compensation for each day on which they exercise their functions.

5. These salaries, allowances, and compensation shall be fixed by the General Assembly. They may not be decreased during the term of office.

6. The salary of the Registrar shall be fixed by

the General Assembly on the proposal of the Cou

7. Regulations made by the General Assem shall fix the conditions under which retirem pensions may be given to members of the Co and to the Registrar, and the conditions un which members of the Court and the Regis shall have their traveling expenses refunded.

8. The above salaries, allowances, and co pensation shall be free of all taxation.

Article 33

The expenses of the Court shall be borne by United Nations in such a manner as shall be cided by the General Assembly.

CHAPTER II

COMPETENCE OF THE COURT

Article 34

1. Only states may be parties in cases bef the Court.

2. The Court, subject to and in conformity w its Rules, may request of public international ganizations information relevant to cases befor and shall receive such information presented such organizations on their own initiative.

3. Whenever the construction of the const ent instrument of a public international org zation or of an international convention adop thereunder is in question in a case before the Co the Registrar shall so notify the public inte tional organization concerned and shall comm cate to it copies of all the written proceedings.

Article 35

1. The Court shall be open to the states par to the present Statute.

2. The conditions under which the Court s be open to other states shall, subject to the spe provisions contained in treaties in force, be

wn by the Security Council, but in no case shall
ch conditions place the parties in a position of
equality before the Court.

3. When a state which is not a Member of the
ited Nations is a party to a case, the Court shall
the amount which that party is to contribute
vards the expenses of the Court. This provision
all not apply if such state is bearing a share of
e expenses of the Court.

Article 36

1. The jurisdiction of the Court comprises all
ses which the parties refer to it and all matters
ecially provided for in the Charter of the United
tions or in treaties and conventions in force.

2. The states parties to the present Statute may
any time declare that they recognize as compul-
y *ipso facto* and without special agreement, in
ation to any other state accepting the same obli-
tion, the jurisdiction of the Court in all legal
putes concerning:

    a. the interpretation of a treaty;

    b. any question of international law;

    c. the existence of any fact which, if estab-
lished, would constitute a breach of an international obligation;

    d. the nature or extent of the reparation to
be made for the breach of an international obligation.

3. The declarations referred to above may be
de unconditionally or on condition of reci-
ocity on the part of several or certain states, or
a certain time.

4. Such declarations shall be deposited with
Secretary-General of the United Nations, who
all transmit copies thereof to the parties to the
tute and to the Registrar of the Court.

5. Declarations made under Article 36 of the
tute of the Permanent Court of International
stice and which are still in force shall be deemed,
etween the parties to the present Statute, to be
eptances of the compulsory jurisdiction of the

International Court of Justice for the period which
they still have to run and in accordance with their
terms.

6. In the event of a dispute as to whether the
Court has jurisdiction, the matter shall be settled
by the decision of the Court.

Article 37

Whenever a treaty or convention in force provides for reference of a matter to a tribunal to have
been instituted by the League of Nations, or to the
Permanent Court of International Justice, the
matter shall, as between the parties to the present
Statute, be referred to the International Court of
Justice.

Article 38

1. The Court, whose function is to decide in
accordance with international law such disputes
as are submitted to it, shall apply:

    a. international conventions, whether gen-
eral or particular, establishing rules expressly
recognized by the contesting states;

    b. international custom, as evidence of a
general practice accepted as law;

    c. the general principles of law recognized
by civilized nations;

    d. subject to the provisions of Article 59,
judicial decisions and the teachings of the most
highly qualified publicists of the various nations, as subsidiary means for the determination
of rules of law.

2. This provision shall not prejudice the power
of the Court to decide a case *ex aequo et bono*, if
the parties agree thereto.

CHAPTER III
PROCEDURE

Article 39

1. The official languages of the Court shall be
French and English. If the parties agree that the

case shall be conducted in French, the judgment shall be delivered in French. If the parties agree that the case shall be conducted in English, the judgment shall be delivered in English.

2. In the absence of an agreement as to which language shall be employed, each party may, in the pleadings, use the language which it prefers; the decision of the Court shall be given in French and English. In this case the Court shall at the same time determine which of the two texts shall be considered as authoritative.

3. The Court shall, at the request of any party, authorize a language other than French or English to be used by that party.

Article 40

1. Cases are brought before the Court, as the case may be, either by the notification of the special agreement or by a written application addressed to the Registrar. In either case the subject of the dispute and the parties shall be indicated.

2. The Registrar shall forthwith communicate the application to all concerned.

3. He shall also notify the Members of the United Nations through the Secretary-General, and also any other states entitled to appear before the Court.

Article 41

1. The Court shall have the power to indicate, if it considers that circumstances so require, any provisional measures which ought to be taken to preserve the respective rights of either party.

2. Pending the final decision, notice of the measures suggested shall forthwith be given to the parties and to the Security Council.

Article 42

1. The parties shall be represented by agents.

2. They may have the assistance of counsel or advocates before the Court.

3. The agents, counsel, and advocates of par-

ties before the Court shall enjoy the privilege and immunities necessary to the independent exercise of their duties.

Article 43

1. The procedure shall consist of two parts written and oral.

2. The written proceedings shall consist of the communication to the Court and to the parties of memorials, counter-memorials and, if necessary, replies; also all papers and documents in support.

3. These communications shall be made through the Registrar, in the order and within the time fixed by the Court.

4. A certified copy of every document produced by one party shall be communicated to the other party.

5. The oral proceedings shall consist of the hearing by the Court of witnesses, experts, agents counsel, and advocates.

Article 44

1. For the service of all notices upon persons other than the agents, counsel, and advocates, the Court shall apply direct to the government of the state upon whose territory the notice has to be served.

2. The same provision shall apply whenever steps are to be taken to procure evidence on the spot.

Article 45

The hearing shall be under the control of the President or, if he is unable to preside, of the Vice President; if neither is able to preside, the senior judge present shall preside.

Article 46

The hearing in Court shall be public, unless the Court shall decide otherwise, or unless the parties demand that the public be not admitted.

Article 47

1. Minutes shall be made at each hearing and signed by the Registrar and the President.

2. These minutes alone shall be authentic.

Article 48

The Court shall make orders for the conduct of the case, shall decide the form and time in which each party must conclude its arguments, and make all arrangements connected with the taking of evidence.

Article 49

The Court may, even before the hearing begins, call upon the agents to produce any document or to supply any explanations. Formal note shall be taken of any refusal.

Article 50

The Court may, at any time, entrust any individual, body, bureau, commission, or other organization that it may select, with the task of carrying out an enquiry or giving an expert opinion.

Article 51

During the hearing any relevant questions are to be put to the witnesses and experts under the conditions laid down by the Court in the rules of procedure referred to in Article 30.

Article 52

After the Court has received the proofs and evidence within the time specified for the purpose, it may refuse to accept any further oral or written evidence that one party may desire to present unless the other side consents.

Article 53

1. Whenever one of the parties does not appear before the Court, or fails to defend its case, the other party may call upon the Court to decide in favor of its claim.

2. The Court must, before doing so, satisfy itself, not only that it has jurisdiction in accordance with Articles 36 and 37, but also that the claim is well founded in fact and law.

Article 54

1. When, subject to the control of the Court, the agents, counsel, and advocates have completed their presentation of the case, the President shall declare the hearing closed.

2. The Court shall withdraw to consider the judgment.

3. The deliberations of the Court shall take place in private and remain secret.

Article 55

1. All questions shall be decided by a majority of the judges present.

2. In the event of an equality of votes, the President or the judge who acts in his place shall have a casting vote.

Article 56

1. The judgment shall state the reasons on which it is based.

2. It shall contain the names of the judges who have taken part in the decision.

Article 57

If the judgment does not represent in whole or in part the unanimous opinion of the judges, any judge shall be entitled to deliver a separate opinion.

Article 58

The judgment shall be signed by the President and by the Registrar. It shall be read in open court, due notice having been given to the agents.

Article 59

The decision of the Court has no binding force except between the parties and in respect of that particular case.

Article 60

The judgment is final and without appeal. In the event of dispute as to the meaning or scope of the judgment, the Court shall construe it upon the request of any party.

Article 61

1. An application for revision of a judgment may be made only when it is based upon the discovery of some fact of such a nature as to be a decisive factor, which fact was, when the judgment was given, unknown to the Court and also to the party claiming revision, always provided that such ignorance was not due to negligence.

2. The proceedings for revision shall be opened by a judgment of the Court expressly recording the existence of the new fact, recognizing that it has such a character as to lay the case open to revision, and declaring the application admissible on this ground.

3. The Court may require previous compliance with the terms of the judgment before it admits proceedings in revision.

4. The application for revision must be made at latest within six months of the discovery of the new fact.

5. No application for revision may be made after the lapse of ten years from the date of the judgment.

Article 62

1. Should a state consider that it has an interest of a legal nature which may be affected by the decision in the case, it may submit a request to the Court to be permitted to intervene.

2. It shall be for the Court to decide upon this request.

Article 63

1. Whenever the construction of a convention to which states other than those concerned in the case are parties is in question, the Registrar shall notify all such states forthwith.

2. Every state so notified has the right to intervene in the proceedings; but if it uses this right, the construction given by the judgment will be equally binding upon it.

Article 64

Unless otherwise decided by the Court, each party shall bear its own costs.

CHAPTER IV
ADVISORY OPINIONS

Article 65

1. The Court may give an advisory opinion on any legal question at the request of whatever body may be authorized by or in accordance with the Charter of the United Nations to make such a request.

2. Questions upon which the advisory opinion of the Court is asked shall be laid before the Court by means of a written request containing an exact statement of the question upon which an opinion is required, and accompanied by all documents likely to throw light upon the question.

Article 66

1. The Registrar shall forthwith give notice of the request for an advisory opinion to all states entitled to appear before the Court.

2. The Registrar shall also, by means of a special and direct communication, notify any state entitled to appear before the Court or international organization considered by the Court, or, should it not be sitting, by the President, as likely to be able to furnish information on the question, that the Court will be prepared to receive, within a time limit to be fixed by the President, written statements, or to hear, at a public sitting to be held for the purpose, oral statements relating to the question.

3. Should any such state entitled to appear before the Court have failed to receive the special communication referred to in paragraph 2 of this Article, such state may express a desire to submit a written statement or to be heard; and the Court will decide.

4. States and organizations having presented written or oral statements or both shall be permitted to comment on the statements made by other states or organizations in the form, to the extent, and within the time limits which the Court, or, should it not be sitting, the President, shall decide in each particular case. Accordingly, the Registrar shall in due time communicate any such written statements to states and organizations having submitted similar statements.

Article 67

The Court shall deliver its advisory opinions in open court, notice having been given to the Secretary-General and to the representatives of Members of the United Nations, of other states and of international organizations immediately concerned.

Article 68

In the exercise of its advisory functions the Court shall further be guided by the provisions of the present Statute which apply in contentious cases to the extent to which it recognizes them to be applicable.

CHAPTER V
AMENDMENT

Article 69

Amendments to the present Statute shall be effected by the same procedure as is provided by the Charter of the United Nations for amendments to that Charter, subject however to any provisions which the General Assembly upon recommendation of the Security Council may adopt concerning the participation of states which are parties to the present Statute but are not Members of the United Nations.

Article 70

The Court shall have power to propose such amendments to the present Statute as it may deem necessary, through written communications to the Secretary-General, for consideration in conformity with the provisions of Article 69.

APPENDIX C

Membership of the United Nations[1]

ORIGINAL MEMBER STATES

Argentina
Australia
Belgium
Bolivia
Brazil
Byelorussian Soviet Socialist Republic
Canada
Chile
China
Colombia
Costa Rica
Cuba
Czechoslovakia
Denmark
Dominican Republic
Ecuador
Egypt
El Salvador
Ethiopia
France
Greece
Guatemala
Haiti
Honduras
India
Iran
Iraq
Lebanon
Liberia
Luxembourg
Mexico
Netherlands
New Zealand
Nicaragua
Norway
Panama
Paraguay
Peru
Philippines
Poland
Saudi Arabia
Syria
Turkey
Ukrainian Soviet Socialist Republic
Union of South Africa
Union of Soviet Socialist Republics
United Kingdom of Great Britain and
    Northern Ireland
United States of America
Uruguay
Venezuela
Yugoslavia

STATES SUBSEQUENTLY ADMITTED TO MEMBERSHIP[2]

Afghanistan (November 9, 1946)
Burma (April 19, 1948)
Iceland (November 9, 1946)
Indonesia (September 28, 1950)
Israel (May 11, 1949)
Pakistan (December 30, 1947)
Sweden (November 9, 1946)
Thailand (December 15, 1946)
Yemen (December 30, 1947)

STATES PARTIES TO ONLY THE STATUTE OF THE INTERNATIONAL COURT OF JUSTICE[3]

Japan (April 2, 1954)
Liechtenstein (March 29, 1950)
San Marino (February 18, 1954)
Switzerland (July 28, 1948)

[1] As of December 31, 1954.
[2] Dates given are those on which the General Assembly approved the admission of the state to membership.
[3] All Member states are *ipso facto* parties to the Statute, but states that are not Members of the United Nations can become parties to the Statute in accordance with the provisions of Article 93(2) of the Charter. Dates given are those on which the state deposited with the Secretary-General its instrument of accession to the Statute.

INDEX

Index

ABC plan for world government, sponsored by Citizens Committee for U.N. Reform: amendment of U.N. Charter to eliminate veto, limit armaments, and create U.N. police force, proposals, 70, 335-37; armed forces of United States, use of, question of national sovereignty, 70, 72; implications of plan, 72-73; international force as deterrent to aggression, 69-70, 71, 72, 73, 335; Soviet Union, proposal of ultimatum to, 71, 72; summary of plan, 70-71; United Nations, impact on, 72; world-wide pact under *Art. 51*, proposal, 70

Administrative and Budgetary Questions of the General Assembly, Advisory Committee on, 21, 244, 427, 429

Administrative Committee on Co-ordination, 245

Admission of New Members, Committee on, 21

Afghanistan, views on U.N. representation in trust territories, 295

Agencies under United Nations. *See* Organs, subsidiary.

Aggression (*see also* Enforcement measures; Korea): Committee on the Question of Defining, creation of, 21; efforts to define, 162-64

Aggressor, if member of universal organization, question of advance plans to halt, 56, 90, 118, 121

Albania, membership rejection and U. S. attitude, 82, 99

American Assembly, opinion on Charter review, 35

American Association for the United Nations: automatic membership of every state, proposal, 87-88; regional associations, disadvantages of, 149

American Bar Association, Jurisdiction by World Court in claims cases, proposal, 389

American Society of International Law, on competence of United Nations being challenged by Members, 385

Antarctica, proposals respecting: disputed areas to be given to United Nations as source of income, 63-64; international trusteeship, 287-88

Anti-colonial powers, attitude toward non-self-governing territories and trusteeship system, 267, 270, 271, 275, 281, 293, 294, 295, 466

Anti-Communist alliance, proposal for change of United Nations to, 3, 118

Arab-Asian states: Charter review, attitude toward conference for, 46; non-self-governing territories, attitude, 270, 276; Tunisia and Morocco, Arab demands for consideration of situation by Assembly, 278; voting as unit, 350

Argentina:
conference to review Charter, attitude, 36, 39
membership in United Nations: plan to expedite admissions, 99; proposal that General Assembly interpret provisions of Charter dealing with own powers, 97

Armaments, Commission for Conventional, establishment (1947) by Security Council, and union (1952) with Atomic Energy Commission in Disarmament Commission, 20, 184-85, 202

Armaments, conventional, regulation and reduction (*see also* Atomic energy; Disarmament Commission): charter provisions, 181-82; elimination of veto with respect to enforcement action and armament, discussion, 335-37, 341; French proposal to collect information, 202-04; record of United Nations disappointing, 218-19; Soviet proposal for one-third reduction, 200-02

Armstrong, Hamilton Fish, opinion on regional pacts, 150

Article 51, regional security and collective defense pacts, building collective security under, 2, 18-19, 145-56, 324-27

Article 51, world-wide pact proposed

outvoting great powers, 350-51; veto, **attitude, 24, 35, 311-12**

Smith, Senator H. Alexander, objection to seating of Communist China, 112-13

South Africa, Union of: South West Africa, relations, 285; treatment of Indians in, question of domestic jurisdiction, 129

South East Asia Collective Defense Treaty, relation to Charter, 18-19, 147, 151

South West Africa, advisory opinion of International Court of Justice on status of, 285

Sovereignty: Article *51* pact, effect on, 160, 161; **atomic-energy control,** limited surrender of, 191; Charter provisions respecting sovereign equality of states, 53, 54-55, 61, 346-47; human rights, question of conflict with domestic jurisdiction, 254, 260-63, 396, 400, 401; legal equality of states, a basis of international organizations, 345-46; limitations of, as accepted by France, Italy, Netherlands, and West Germany, regarding transfer of powers on certain conditions to an international organization, 61*n;* Member states obligated to accept ratified amendment, even if they voted against it, 25; taxes, question if Members would share with United Nations the power of levying, 229-30; unanimity of great powers on Council, a violation of sovereign equality, claim of small powers, 313; U. S. position against supranationality, 55, 60-61, 158; U. S. sovereignty, infringement, claim, by *Arts. 55* and *56,* 234-35; world governments, authority superior to any state, proposals, 57-58, 61-69, 79-80, 178, 230-33

Soviet bloc (*see also* Communist nations *and* Soviet Union): conference to review Charter, opposition, 40, 45; human rights, opposition to U. S. proposals in field of, 234; Interim Committee, legality challenged, 22; voting as unit, 350, 369

Soviet Union (*see also* Communist nations *and* Soviet bloc):

abstention from voting, initiation of practice, 322-23

alliances, system and character of, 147-48, 152

amendments to Charter and changes in United Nations, objections, 22, 33

armaments, proposal for one-third reduction, 200-02

Article *51* pact, attitude, 148, 161

atomic weapons, convention prohibiting, proposal, 187-90

conference to review Charter, opposition, 45-46

Disarmament Commission, proposals on disclosure and reduction of forces, attitude, 205-06, 208-09

expulsion from United Nations, impossibility, 104, 105-08

human rights, objections to U. S. proposal for world-wide study of 233-34

Interim Committee, and other U. N. agencies, challenge to legality, 22, 126, 461

Korea, absence of representative from Council at time of aggression against, 13, 117, 141

military man power, refusal to reduce, 188, 210

non-self-governing peoples question of applicability of Charter provisions, 277, 296

package deals in admission of members, attitude, 98

reorganization of United Nations without Soviet Union, views of Gen. Mark W. Clark, Secretary Dulles, Herbert Hoover, and others, 105-08

role of trust territories in international security matters, to be subject to Security Council, proposal by India and, 289-90

Trusteeship Council, question of usefulness on, 272

veto, use of: against admission of states, 82, 85, 95, 98, 114, 315; in other matters, 1-2, 121, 254, 299, 301, 309, 314-16, 317, 324, 342-43

votes in United Nations, 91, 347

withdrawal of United States from United Nations, proposal: effect